"I TURNED, AS I USUALLY DO, TO MY 'REAL ESTATE BIBLE.'"

Tom Kelly,
Syndicated Columnist and
Talk Show Host

"No single volume of real estate material has done more to bring clarity of meaning and understanding of subject matter than Alan Tonnon's 'The Complete Guide to Washington Real Estate Practices.' No wonder practitioners across the state have retitled it 'The ARGUMENT SETTLER.'"

Evangeline E. Anderson
Real Estate Commissioner
and Past President
Seattle King County
Association of Realtors

"Practicing real estate with out a copy of Washington Real Estate Practices makes about as much sense as fishing without bait."
Jim Stacey

Author of "**Seattle Homes"** and instructor

"This book will be of help to all persons involved in the real estate industry as well as to the property owner."

Bo Cooper
Real Estate Instructor
Pierce College

"WHAT'S MORE...CONCENTRATION ON THIS STATE MAKES THE BOOK STAND OUR IN THE MORASS OF GENERALIZED REAL ESTATE PUBLICATIONS."

Seattle P-I on the
first edition

THE COMPLETE GUIDE TO WASHINGTON REAL ESTATE PRACTICES

By ALAN N. TONNON, J.D.

First Edition
1st Printing 1977
2nd Printing 1978
3rd Printing 1979 with Supplement
4th Printing 1980 with Supplement

Second Edition -- Complete Revision
1st Printing 1981

Third Edition -- Complete Revision
1st Printing 1988
2nd Printing 1990

Fourth Edition -- Complete Revision
1st Printing 1998

Address all correspondence to:
Washington Professional Publications
P.O. Box 1147
Bellevue, Washington 98009
(425) 451-0130
(425) 643-7087 Fax

This publication is designed to provide accurate and authoritative information in regard to the subject matter covered. It is sold with the understanding that the publisher is not engaged in rendering legal, accounting or other professional service. If legal advice or other expert assistance is required, the services of a competent professional person should be sought.

From a Declaration of Principles jointly adopted by a Committee of the American Bar Association and a Committee of Publishers and Associations.

Library of Congress Catalog Card Number 765 8651
ISBN #0-9614167-1-8

to
JOAN, my wife,
who made many
things possible
- including this book

FOURTH EDITION
ACKNOWLEDGMENTS

Many people have given me ideas and suggestions for this fourth revision of the Guide. Not all the suggestions have been utilized, but a "Thank You" to all.

A special thanks to Jim Stacey who volunteered to act as editor of the various drafts in preparing the Fourth Edition. His suggestions made it a better book.

A special thanks for John W. Reilly, Attorney-at-law, Honolulu, for his continuous sharing of material, ideas and concepts.

Many thanks to Dick Justham for his computer magic in the final formatting of the book.

Thank you to the Community College Teachers, University Professors, and Real Estate Instructors and real estate practitioners who have shared their experiences with the Guide and their suggestions.

Many thanks to my wife, Joan (my publisher) without whom this book and the various three revisions would not have been possible.

Last, but not least, I wish to thank you and the other people who made the first three editions of the Guide, the best selling real estate book in Washington State. The Guide was written for the people of Washington involved in real estate: students, attorneys, real estate licensees, escrow, title insurance and financing people; and the consumers of real estate: buyers and sellers, tenants and landlords, homeowners and investors. Your helpful suggestions have helped the Guide grow from 1,360 terms and practices in the first edition, to 1,840 in the second edition, to over 2,150 in the third edition and now over 2,475 in the fourth edition.

While the author recognizes the contributions of many people, he is solely responsible for any mistakes that appear. He solicits comments, criticisms or suggestions that you may have for future revisions.

ALAN TONNON
Bellevue, Washington

HOW TO USE THIS BOOK

General textbooks on real estate law and practice provide adequate background information, but always leaves one uncertain of what is the **law and practice in Washington**. Specific treatise on subjects such as tax, condominiums, appraisal, law, and the like, are excellent source material but requires one to maintain an extensive and expensive real estate library. What I wanted was a comprehensive, single-volume, ready reference, instant answer book to the many questions on real estate posed to me as an attorney, teacher, speaker and practicing real estate broker. *The Complete Guide to Washington Real Estate Practice* is my attempt to meet this need for a functional real estate reference book -- one that is **specifically geared to Washington**.

The book is a glossary of over 2,475 of the most frequently encountered real estate terms and practices. The last sections of the book contains an extensive list of real estate abbreviations, the Realtor's Code of Ethics, the Real Estate Brokerage Relationships Act.

The Guide has been accepted as a required or recommended book in many real estate educational courses in the State; therefore the Guide has been revised, expanded and updated to take into account the continuous, complex and important developments on both a national and state level.

At the end of some of the definitions there is a reference to Washington State Law by RCW section number. RCW stands for the Revised Code of Washington, which are the statutes of the State. Another reference is to WAC. WAC stands for the Washington Administration Code, which are the Rules and Regulations adopted by the various departments or commissions of the State of Washington. The author believes all citations are current as of January 1, 1998. It is therefore recommended that the reader verify the applicable law for any changes in these statutes since the date of publication. However, the reader is cautioned that the legal requirements stated in the book can and will change due to legislative action (both State and Federal laws) by Federal and State court decisions and the adoption or termination of Rules and Regulations by Administrative Agencies (both Federal and State).

Definitions that appeared in the first three editions have been revised, and in many cases expanded, in order to provide the most current and precise answers possible. Under each work is a basic definition, in many cases, practical examples and cross-references to aid the reader in understanding related items.

A work of caution, competent legal and/or accounting counsel should be sought to thoroughly analyze and explain the legal and tax ramifications of a particular real estate transaction.

Take a few minutes and get to know the book -- see all of the different kinds of information it has to offer -- so that when you use it, you will use it to its fullest advantage. You should find it a useful tool for understanding and participating in the many aspects of real estate in Washington. The book is intended to be a stand alone reference work; however it will be of great aid as a reference in your study of real estate.

AAA TENANT - A "triple A" tenant is a well-known business tenant with an exceptionally high credit rating, or one whose national or local name will lend prestige to a shopping center or office project. (*See* ANCHOR TENANT.)

ABANDONMENT - The voluntary surrender or relinquishment of possession of real property with the intention of terminating one's possession or interest, but without giving or vesting this interest in any other person. Mere non-use is not sufficient; there must be some overt act to indicate that the owner will not reclaim the property. For example, the owner of an easement footpath across a neighboring property might demonstrate his/her intent to abandon the easement by erecting a fence between the two properties. Each case of possible abandonment must be evaluated on its own facts to determine that the property or property right has indeed been legally abandoned.

A tenant vacating leased property with the intent of no longer performing under the terms of the lease is a case of abandonment. The landlord then gains full possession and control of the abandoned property, but the lessee may remain liable for rent until the lease expires. If the landlord accepts the abandonment — that is, agrees to terminate the tenancy — it is recognized as a surrender, and the tenant is no longer obligated to pay future rents under the terms of the lease. (*See* SURRENDER.)

The Washington Landlord Tenant Act was amended in 1973 to permit a landlord to dispose of personal property abandoned by a tenant provided there had been abandonment of the tenancy and an accompanying default in the payment of rent. Once it has been determined that a tenant has abandoned the premises, the landlord may immediately enter and take possession of any property of the tenant. The landlord must store the property in a reasonably secure place and shall make a reasonable effort to provide the tenant with the location of the stored property so that the tenant may, with reasonable diligence, recover it uninjured. The notice should include the fact it will be sold 45 days from the date of the notice and the proceeds applied against money due the landlord for rent, storage and transportation cost. Any excess must be held for one year, after which it becomes the property of the landlord. Similar legislation has been challenged in other states as an unconstitutional taking of property without due process of law. (*See* LANDLORD TENANT ACT.) *Reference:* RCW 59.18.310.

In Washington, a claimant may abandon a homestead by filing a declaration of abandonment in the public record. Merely leaving such premises will not officially constitute an abandonment of a person's homestead rights. (*See* EQUITY OF REDEMPTION, HOMESTEAD.)

There is also an income tax consequence of an abandonment. The taxpayer-owner who abandons real estate may be able to treat the abandonment as a "sale" for which the taxpayer received no payment (other than relief from any mortgages or liens.) In this case, the taxpayer may claim a loss to the extent of the adjusted basis in the property.

The operator of a self storage facility has an automatic lien against property stored at the facility if the tenant fails to pay rent. If the operator decides to sell the property to satisfy the rental charge, the tenant must be notified in writing that the property will be sold if the rental charge is not paid. The operator must sell the property in a commercially reasonable manner. Any proceeds not claimed by the tenant within six months must be turned over to the State as abandoned property.
Reference: RCW 19.150

In 1994, The Washington State Uniform Building Code (UBC) was amended to provide that oil tanks abandoned for more than one year shall be removed from the ground unless the local fire chief determines that the removal of the tank is not necessary. (*See* OIL TANKS.)
Reference: RCW 19.27

ABATEMENT - A reduction or decrease in amount, degree, intensity or worth, such as in rent. For example, in a lease, the tenant may be entitled to an abatement of rent during the time the premises are made uninhabitable by fire, flood or other acts of God.

The Washington Landlord Tenant Act provides for an abatement of rent if the landlord fails to maintain the premises as required under the law. If the tenant is current in the payment of rent, and if, after sending written notice to the landlord informing him/her of the defective conditions, the landlord fails to remedy the defective conditions within the specified time period for particular defects provided for in the law, the tenant has four (4) alternative methods of abatement:

1. Give written notice that the tenant is terminating the tenancy with reasons for the termination and the date it will occur. The tenant is entitled to a prorata (proportionate) refund of any prepaid, unused rent. Depending on the condition the tenant left the unit, the tenant may be entitled to a refund of all or part of any damage deposit.
Reference: RCW 59.18.090.

2. Submit to the landlord a good faith estimate by the tenant of the cost to perform the repairs necessary to correct the defective condition if the repair is to be done by licensed or registered persons. If no licensing or registration requirement applies to the type of work to be performed, the cost if the repair is to be done by responsible persons capable of performing such repairs may be given to the landlord with the complaint describing the defects. If the landlord fails to commence the repairs within a reasonable time, the tenant may contract with the lowest bidder to do the repairs, pay for the repairs and deduct that amount from the rent up to one month's rent. This method may be used as often as necessary; however, all repairs made within one year cannot total more than two month's rent.
Reference: RCW 59.18.100.

3. The tenant may repair the defective condition and deduct the cost of repairs from the rent provided the cost does not exceed one-half month's rent. All repairs must be done in a competent manner and conform to all applicable codes.
Reference: RCW 59.18.090

4. The tenant may ask a court or arbitrator to:

(a) Determine the diminution in rental value of the premises due to the defective condition and to render judgment against the landlord for the rent paid in excess of such rental value.

(b) Order the landlord to make the necessary repairs or authorize the tenant to do so.

(c) Terminate the rental agreement and provide the tenant reasonable time to locate a different unit. (*See* LANDLORD TENANT ACT.)
Reference: RCW 59.18.110 and .120

When a defect is discovered in a seller's title and the seller refuses to correct this defect before closing, the buyer can seek specific performance of the contract with an abatement from the purchase price because of the defect. For example, Mr. Lee entered into a contract to purchase Mr. Morris' $100,000 house. At the time of closing, a title search reveals that Mr. Morris had not paid $5,000 in property taxes. Mr. Morris refuses to pay the taxes, and also changes his mind about selling the property to Mr. Lee. Mr. Lee could deposit $95,000 into court and force a sale of the property in an action for specific performance. Mr. Lee would then pay the county the $5,000 in unpaid taxes and obtain clear title to the property.

If a property owner is maintaining a nuisance on his/her property, such as a plant emitting harmful fumes, an abutting owner may bring an action to abate the nuisance, that is, seek a reduction of the degree or intensity of pollution.

A house, condominium, or apartment unit where illegal drugs are sold may be declared a moral nuisance by a city or a county prosecutor and may be closed (sealed) through abatement proceedings for up to one year.
Reference: RCW 7.43 and 7.48A.

ABLE - A term referring to the financial ability of a purchaser as in the phrase, "ready, willing, and able buyer," used to determine if a broker is entitled to a commission. "Able" refers to financial capability. It does not mean the buyer must have all the cash for the purchase; it means the buyer must be able to qualify for and arrange the necessary financing within the time specified in the purchase agreement. Sometimes, the buyer must first sell his/her existing property before being "able" to purchase another property. (*See* CONTINGENCY, PROCURING CAUSE.)

ABSENTEE OWNER - A property owner who does not reside on the property. Usually, an absentee owner will rely on a property manager to successfully manage the investment.

The Securities and Exchange Commission (SEC) has closely scrutinized the sale of resort condominium units to investors (e.g. Ocean Shores). Of particular interest to the SEC are cases in which the developer or his/her agents have stressed the economic and investment benefits of absentee ownership, and have offered property management as a part of the purchase transaction. In certain cases, the SEC requires that the developer register the condominium security with the SEC prior to selling any of the units. (*See* REAL PROPERTY SECURITIES REGISTRATION.)

There have been many recent changes in federal tax laws dealing with the ownership of depreciable real property where the owner is absent most of the year but vacations there part of the year. These changes are aimed at lessening the tax depreciation advantages of such absentee ownership. In this area, tax advice from experienced counsel should be sought. (*See* REAL ESTATE SECURITIES, TIME SHARING, VACATION HOME.)

Under the Washington Landlord Tenant Act, if the landlord does not reside in the State of Washington, he/she must designate a person who resides in the county where the premises are located who is authorized to act as his/her agent for purposes of service of notices and process. If no such person is designated, then the person to whom the rental payments are made shall be considered the agent of the landlord for purposes of service of notices and process. (*See* LANDLORD TENANT ACT.)
Reference: RCW 59.18.060.

ABSOLUTE - Describes something that is unrestricted and without conditions or limitations, as in a fee simple absolute estate or an absolute conveyance.

ABSOLUTE FEE SIMPLE TITLE - The best title to real property; it conveys the highest bundle of rights. (*See* FEE SIMPLE.)

ABSORBER - A coated panel in a solar heat collector that absorbs the solar radiation which is then transmitted through the cover plate by absorber fluid passages and converted to heat energy.

ABSORPTION BED - A shallow trench that contains a distribution pipe to pass effluence from the septic tank so that it is absorbed into the soil.

ABSORPTION RATE - An estimate or forecast of the rate at which a particular type of space - such as new office space, new housing, new condominium units and the like - will be sold or occupied each year within a specific market area. A prediction of this rate is often involved in a feasibility study or an appraisal in connection with a request for financing. (*See* FEASIBILITY STUDY.)

ABSTRACT OF JUDGMENT - A document that must be filed in a county where the judgment debtor has real estate in order to effectuate a judgment lien on the real estate. (*See* GENERAL LIEN, JUDGMENT LIEN ATTACHMENT, LIS PENDENS.)

ABSTRACT OF TITLE - A concise, summarized history of the title to a specific parcel of real property, together with a statement of all liens and encumbrances affecting the property. It shows the title passing from owner to owner. The abstractor (the person who prepares the abstract of title) searches the records in the office of the Auditor and records of Courts of the county where the property is situated, Federal Court records and other official sources. He/she then summarizes the various instruments affecting the property and arranges them in chronological order of recording, starting with the original grant of title. The abstract also includes a list showing which public records the abstractor has searched, and which records he/she has not searched, in preparing his/her report.

The abstract of title does not guarantee or assure the validity of the title of the property. It merely discloses those items about the property which are of public record, and thus does not reveal such things as encroachments, forgeries and the like. The abstractor, therefore, is liable only for damages caused by his/her negligence in searching the stated public records.

An abstract of title is required when application is made to the office of the Auditor of the county where the property is situated for registration of land under the Torrens System. Other than that, the abstract is rarely used in Washington because it is time consuming and costly to prepare, and it is difficult for the ordinary person to comprehend without an attorney's assistance. In practice, title insurance is used in all real estate transactions in Washington. (*See* TITLE INSURANCE, TORRENS SYSTEM.)
Reference: RCW 65.08, RCW 65.12, RCW 48.29.

ABSTRACTION - The allocation of the value of the property between land and improvements. An appraisal method whereby the appraiser estimates the land value of any improved property by deducting, or abstracting, the value of any site improvements from the overall sale price of the property. The amount remaining is the estimated sale price, or indicated value of the land. Also called the allocation or extraction method.

ABUTTING OWNER - An owner of land which borders on or shares a common boundary with any contiguous property. The major problems between abutting owners occur in connection with encroachments, party walls, light and air easement and lateral support. (*See* ACCESS, LATERAL AND SUBJACENT SUPPORT.)

ACCELERATED COST RECOVERY SYSTEM (ACRS) - The 1986 Tax Reform Act eliminated accelerated depreciation (called "cost recovery" since 1981) on investment real estate. The 1986 Act established a new Modified Accelerated Cost Recovery System (MACRS) for all investment real estate that is used in trade or business or held for the production of income acquired after 1986.

Investment property acquired prior to 1981 used the Asset Depreciation Range (ADR) life system and real property acquired between 1981 and 1986 used ACRS. If a transaction involves a property which used either or both of the depreciation systems, use the service of an accountant to determine the adjusted cost basis. (*See* MODIFIED ACCELERATED COST RECOVERY SYSTEM (MACRS).)

For property previously placed in service, the original period and method of depreciation or cost recovery will remain in effect for as long as the property is kept in service by the same owner for an eligible use. Thus, some taxpayers will have depreciation calculated for: (1) property placed in service before 1981 (ADR), (2) property placed in service between 1981 and 1986 (ACRS) and (3) property placed in service after 1986 (MACRS).

ACCELERATION CLAUSE - A clause in a promissory note, real estate contract, mortgage or deed of trust which gives the lender (also called the mortgagee, beneficiary) the right to call all sums due and payable in advance of the fixed payment date upon the occurrence of a specified event, such as a sale, default in a payment or some other term or condition, assignment or further encumbrance of the property. Usually the payee has the option to accelerate the note upon default of payment of any installment when due, provided he or she gives adequate notice and specifies a time within which the defaulting party can cure the default. In addition to nonpayment, the payee may also accelerate for other breaches of provisions in the contract such as failure to pay taxes and assessments, or failure to keep the property insured or in repair.

The provision for acceleration must be expressly set forth in the mortgage, deed of trust, the promissory note, or real estate contract document; otherwise, the right does not exist. There should be a consistency between the acceleration provision stated in the promissory note and that stated in the mortgage or deed of trust. Without this clause, the seller would have to sue the buyer as each installment payment becomes due and unpaid. (*See* ALIEN-

ATION CLAUSE, DEED OF TRUST, DUE ON SALE CLAUSE, MORTGAGE, PREPAYMENT PRIVILEGE.)

An acceleration clause is also called a **due on sale** clause or **alienation** clause when it provides for acceleration upon the sale of the property.

ACCEPTANCE - The expression of the intention of the person receiving an offer (offeree, usually the seller) to be bound by the exact terms of the offer. The acceptance must be communicated to the one making the offer (offeror, usually the buyer). An acceptance must be *unequivocal* and *unconditional.* Any qualified acceptance which adds new conditions is an implied rejection of the offer. This implied rejection, called a *counteroffer*, has the legal effect of reversing the position of the original parties. The original offeror is now the new offeree and may accept or reject the counteroffer. If the offer pertains to real property, the acceptance must be in writing. (*See* STATUTE OF FRAUDS.)

The individual (usually the buyer) making the offer has the right to revoke his/her offer any time prior to receiving notice of the seller's acceptance. This is true even if the buyer has stated that he/she will keep the offer open for a certain time, so it is important for the broker to communicate such acceptance to the buyer or offeror as soon as possible. Communication is particularly significant because a buyer might effectively revoke his/her offer to purchase at a time after the seller has accepted the offer, but before such acceptance has been effectively communicated to the buyer.

Also, the acceptance must be made within the time limit stated in the offer. If no time limit is stated, then the acceptance is valid if made within a reasonable time of the offer. A late acceptance is, at most, a counteroffer.

If the offer prescribes a specific method of acceptance, then the acceptance is not effective unless that method is used. For example, if the buyer requests the seller to accept his/her offer by fax, then that method must be used. If the offer does not specify any method of acceptance, then any reasonable and customary method may be used. Thus the acceptance of a mailed offer may be accomplished by use of the mail and it becomes an effective and binding contract when deposited in the mail. Where the acceptance is communicated in an unusual manner (such as placing it in an ad in the newspaper), then the contract is not effective until and unless the acceptance is received by the buyer within a reasonable time (what constitutes a reasonable time depends on the facts of each particular case and custom within the community). To avoid confusion that might be caused by the communication rule, some offers specify that the acceptance is not effective unless a signed copy is received by the offeror or broker within a certain time.

An owner who has listed property with a broker is under no obligation to accept an offer from a buyer at the listing price. The listing is an employment agreement, not an offer to sell. It therefore creates no power of acceptance in the buyer. The owner may, however, owe a real estate commission to the broker.

Voluntary and unconditional acceptance of a deed by the buyer/grantee is essential to a valid delivery of the deed. If the grantee does not want title to the property, he/she need not take it. Acceptance is often inferred from certain acts of the grantee, such as taking possession, recording the deed, paying the sales price, or obtaining a mortgage on the property. The courts will usually presume acceptance when the grantee is benefited by the transaction, but a court would probably not presume acceptance when Mr. Coffey grants his $100,000 house heavily encumbered with $150,000 in debt and full of building code violations to Mr. Larson who dies without ever being aware the property was deeded to him. If, however, the property was free and clear of debt and code violations, the court would probably presume acceptance by the unaware decedent and the property would thus pass to his estate, provided there was a valid delivery. (*See* DELIVERY, LISTING, OFFER AND ACCEPTANCE.)

Once an offer is expressly or implicitly rejected, it is extinguished, and the offeree may no longer make a valid acceptance unless the offeror revives the original offer. (*See* COUNTEROFFER.)

ACCESS - The physical way by which property is approached, or a method of entrance into or upon a property. A general or specific right of ingress and egress to a particular property. A property owner has the right to have access to and from his/her property to a public street or highway abutting thereon, including the right to the flow of light and air from the street to the property. (*See* EASEMENT.)

Under the Landlord Tenant Act, the tenant shall not unreasonably withhold his/her consent to the landlord to enter the dwelling unit in order to inspect the premises, make necessary or agreed repairs, decorations, alterations, or improvements; supply services as agreed; or show the dwelling unit to prospective purchasers, mortgagees or tenants. However, the landlord shall not abuse the right of access nor use it to harass the tenant. Except in cases of emergency or where impracticable to do so, the landlord shall give the tenant at least two days notice of his/her intent to enter and shall enter only during reasonable hours; however, only one day's notice is necessary to show the unit to prospective or actual purchasers or tenants. As long as the request is not unreasonable, the tenant cannot refuse access to the landlord. The landlord will be liable for any damages he/she causes by an entry made without the consent of the tenant, except for non-negligent damages caused under emergency circumstances, such as if the tenant left the bathtub water running. The landlord may enter the unit without consent in case of emergency or abandonment. (*See* LANDLORD TENANT ACT.)
Reference: RCW 59.18.150.

ACCESSIBILITY - The relative ease of entry upon a site and the location to different transportation facilities. This is an important factor in evaluating the suitability of a site for a particular use.

ACCESSION - The acquisition by an owner of title to additions or improvements attaching to his/her property as the result of the annexation of fixtures, or the result of alluvial deposits along the banks of streams by accretion. For example, if Mr. Brown builds a fence on his neighbor's property without an agreement permitting Mr. Brown to remove it, ownership of the fence accedes to the neighbor, unless the neighbor requires that it be removed. (*See* ALLUVION.)

ACCESSORY BUILDING - A building located on a lot and used for a purpose other than that of the principal building on the same lot. For example, a garage, pump house or storage shed would be considered an accessory building if erected on the same parcel of land as the property's main building.

ACCOMMODATION PARTY - A party who, without receiving any consideration, signs a negotiable instrument (such as a promissory note) as maker, acceptor or endorser to accommodate another party and enhance the creditworthiness of the paper by lending his/her name as further security. For example, a brother who co-signs a bank note with his sister so that she can borrow money to buy a house would be an accommodation party to the lending contract. (*See* GUARANTOR.)

ACCORD AND SATISFACTION - The settlement of an obligation. An accord is an agreement by a creditor to accept something different from or less than what the creditor feels he/she is entitled. When the creditor accepts the consideration offered by the debtor for the accord, the acceptance constitutes a "satisfaction," and the obligation of the debtor is extinguished. For these rules to apply, it is essential that the obligation be in dispute (that is, an unliquidated debt). For example, Dan Mark owes Gary Johnson $100, but Mr. Johnson accepts $75 as full satisfaction of the debt. The prior agreement is not extinguished until the accord is fully performed (when the $75 is paid and accepted). (*See* NOVATION.)

ACCOUNT PAYABLE - A liability (debt) representing an amount owed to a creditor, usually arising from purchase of merchandise or materials and supplies; not necessarily due or past due.

ACCOUNT RECEIVABLE - A claim against a debtor usually arising from sales or services rendered; not necessarily due or past due, the opposite of an account payable.

ACCOUNTING - The fiduciary duty of an agent to maintain and preserve the property and money of the principal. The agent must keep accurate records of funds and documents. (*See* AGENCY.)

ACCOUNTING PERIOD - The time period for which operation statements, such as the income and expense statements and balance sheets are prepared. The time period should be clearly indicated on the financial statements.

ACCOUNTING PRINCIPLES - The principles that explain current accounting concepts and practices and guide in the selection among alternative methods for reporting transactions. Generally accepted accounting principles are divided into three levels: pervasive principles, broad operating principles, and detailed principles. The three types of principles determine the operation of the financial accounting process. All three levels of principles are conventional. They have developed on the basis of experience, reason and custom; they become generally accepted by agreement (often tacit agreement) and are not formally derived from a set of postulates.

ACCREDITED BUYERS REPRESENTATIVE (ABR) - The ABR designation showing specialization in representing buyers is awarded by the Real Estate Buyer's Agent Council (REBAC) of the National Association of Realtors® to those Realtors® who have completed a two day course, successfully completed a written examination and demonstrated practical experience in the field of buyer representation.

ACCREDITED LAND CONSULTANT (ALC) - A professional designation conferred by the Realtors Land Institute (RLI).

ACCREDITED MANAGEMENT ORGANIZATION (AMO) - A professional designation conferred upon management organizations meeting the standards set by the Institute of Real Estate Management (IREM).

ACCREDITED RESIDENT MANAGER (ARM) - A professional designation conferred by the Institute of Real Estate Management (IREM).

ACCRETION - The gradual and imperceptible addition to land by alluvial deposits of soil through natural causes, such as shoreline movement caused by streams or rivers. There are some areas of Puget Sound where the gradual effects of tide and waves have added much land. This added land becomes the property of the riparian or littoral owner. Conversely, the owner can lose title to his/her land that is gradually washed away through erosion (avulsion). (*See* ALLUVION, AVULSION, RIPARIAN.)

ACCRUAL METHOD - An accounting method of reporting income in which expenses incurred and income earned for a given period are reported, although such expenses and income may not yet have actually been paid or received. The accrual method is considered to be the most accurate method. It is the right to receive, not the actual receipt, which determines the inclusion of the amount in gross income. Similarly, expenses are deducted when the taxpayer's liability becomes fixed and definite, not when he/she actually pays the expense. The accrual method is generally not available for use by individuals.

The other popular accounting method is the cash basis method in which income is only reported upon receipt and expenses are reported only when they are actually paid. (*See* CASH METHOD.)

ACCRUED - That which has accumulated over a period of time such as accrued depreciation, accrued interest or accrued expenses. Accrued expenses are expenses which are incurred but not yet payable, such as interest on a note or taxes on real property. In a closing statement, accrued expenses are credited to the purchaser, since he or she will be paying these expenses for the benefit of the seller.

ACCRUED DEPRECIATION - A bookkeeping account that shows the total amount of depreciation taken on an asset since it was acquired; also called accumulated depreciation. For appraisal purposes, it is often called diminished utility, which is the difference between the cost to replace the property (as of appraisal date) and the property's current appraised value as judged by its "observed condition." (*See* BOOK VALUE, DEPRECIATION (APPRAISAL).)

ACKNOWLEDGMENT - A formal declaration made before a duly authorized officer, usually a notary public, by a person who has signed a document. It is designed to prevent forged and fraudulently induced documents from taking effect. The officer witnesses and confirms the signature as being the voluntary act and genuine signature of the person signing it, who is personally known to the officer or whose identity is proved by adequate identification. The officer will be liable for damages caused by his/her negligent failure to identify adequately the person signing, as where forgery occurs.

Conveyances of real property by Indians must be acknowledged before a judge of a court of record (e.g., Supreme Court or Superior Court.)

A document will not be accepted for recording unless it is acknowledged. A foreign acknowledgment (one taken outside of Washington) is valid if it is valid where made. The signature of the foreign officer is sufficient evidence that the acknowledgment is taken in accordance with the laws of the place where made and of the authority of the officer to take the acknowledgment, thus entitling the acknowledged document to be recorded. While Washington Statutes allow instruments transferring property in Washington to be acknowledged before any properly authorized officer in another state, the instruments may not be recorded until there is proof that the officer taking the acknowledgment was authorized to do so.

If there is any material crossed out, erased, or changed in the document, the officer must initial these changes if so approved by the parties, otherwise the document will not be acceptable for recordation. Due to modern methods of reproducing documents, some attorneys recommend using blue ink so everyone knows which document is the original and which is the copy. (*See* AFFIDAVIT, APOSTILLE, ATTESTATION, NOTARY PUBLIC, RECORDING.)

The typical acknowledgment for an individual's signature in Washington is:

STATE OF ____________________ }
County of _______________________ } ss

On this__day of________, A.D. 19_, before me, the undersigned, a Notary Public in and for the State of______, duly commissioned and sworn personally appeared ___________to me known to be the individual__described in and who executed the foregoing instrument, and acknowledged to me that ___ signed and sealed the said instrument as _____ free and voluntary act and deed for the uses and purposes therein mentioned.

WITNESS my hand and official seal hereto affixed the day and year in this certificate above written.

Print Name
Notary Public in and for the State of
residing at ______________________________
My commission expires:____________________

References: RCW 64.04, 64.08, 64.20 and 73.20

ACQUISITION - The process by which property ownership is achieved. The methods by which title to real property is transferred may be classified as: (1) voluntary conveyance (*deed),* (2) transfer by *devise* (dying with a will) or *descent* (dying without a will), (3) transfer by *adverse possession,* (4) transfer by *accession,* and (5) transfer by *public action* or by *operation of law.* (*See* DEED.)

ACQUISITION APPRAISAL - The appraisal for market value of a property to be acquired for a public use by governmental condemnation or negotiation. The purpose of the appraisal is to set the amount of just compensation to be offered the property owner. (*See* CONDEMNATION.)

ACQUISITION COST - The amount of money or other valuable consideration expended to obtain title to property, which includes, in addition to the purchase price, such items as closing costs, appraisal fees, mortgage origination fees, finance charges and title insurance. (*See* BASIS.)

ACRE - A measure of land equal to 43,560 square feet; 4,840 square yards; 4.047 square meters; 160 square rods; or 0.4 hectare. A square mile contains 640 acres (256 hectares). (*See* MEASUREMENT TABLES.)

ACRE FOOT - A volume of water, sand, or minerals, equal to an area of one acre with a depth of one foot (43,560 cubic feet); used in measuring irrigation water. If a liquid, it equals 325,850 gallons.

ACREAGE ZONING - Zoning intended to reduce residential density by requiring large building lots. Also called large-lot zoning. (*See* DENSITY, ZONING.)

ACT OF GOD - An act of nature not created by or capable of human control, such as a tidal wave, flood, volcanic eruption or earthquake. Many contracts include a "force majeure" clause which temporarily or permanently relieves the parties of performance of a contract where an Act of God has destroyed or damaged the subject matter or prevented performance. (*See* FORCE MAJEURE.)

ACTION PRICE - A price lower than the asking or listed price that will generate serious negotiations toward a sale.

ACTION TO QUIET TITLE - A court action to establish ownership of real property. The *action* results in removing any cloud on the title. Normally a lender will not commit to a mortgage or deed of trust on a parcel of real property with a cloud on the title. If the complainant is successful in the court action, the title is made quiet or clean. (*See* QUIET TITLE.)

ACTUAL DAMAGES - Those damages that a court of law will recognize as a direct result of a wrong, as opposed to special or punitive damages imposed by courts as a deterrent and as a punishment.

ACTUAL NOTICE - Express information or fact; that which is known; actual knowledge. Constructive notice, on the other hand, is knowledge that is implied by law; that which the law charges one with knowing. Thus, for example, a person having either actual or constructive notice of the prior rights of a third party to a property normally takes the property subject to that third party's rights. One cannot claim the benefits of the recording law if he/she takes title to property with actual notice of a previously executed but unrecorded instrument. There is also a third type of notice called inquiry notice, where circumstances, appearances, or rumors are such that one has a duty to inquire further into a certain state of affairs that might establish ownership of property in a person other than the one claiming such ownership. (*See* CONSTRUCTIVE NOTICE, INQUIRY NOTICE, RECORDING.)

ACTUARY - A person, usually associated with an insurance company or savings and loan association, skilled in calculating the value of life interests and annuities. (*See* LIFE ESTATE.)

ADA - -*See* AMERICANS WITH DISABILITIES ACT.

ADD-BACK - The practice of deferring the payment of a portion of interest due and adding this amount to the balloon payment due at the end of the loan. (*See* NEGATIVE AMORTIZATION.)

Also refers to the practice of "adding back" certain allowable tax deductions on the tax returns of self employed individuals to assist in qualifying for a loan.

ADD-ON INTEREST - A method of computing interest whereby interest is charged on the entire principal amount for the specified term, regardless of any periodic repayments of principal that are made. The end result is an effective interest charge that is almost double the stated rate. The borrower is paying interest on the full principal sum for the entire loan period (and not on the declining balance), even though the principal is being reduced each month. (*See* ANNUAL PERCENTAGE RATE, BLOCK INTEREST, INTEREST.)

ADDENDUM - An additional agreement or list attached to and made part of a document. There often is insufficient space to write all the details of the transaction on the Purchase and Sale Agreement form, so the parties will attach one or more addendums or supplements to the document. The addendum should be incorporated by reference in the contract and should be dated and signed or initialed by all the parties. (*See* RIDER.)

ADDITION - Any construction which increases a building's size or significantly adds to it. For example, constructing a second floor on top of a one level structure would be an addition.

ADDITIONAL CHARGE MORTGAGE - A mortgage-type instrument used to secure an additional advance of money from the holder of the mortgage to the mortgagor subsequent to the original loan transaction. (*See* FUTURE ADVANCES.)

ADDITIONAL DEPOSIT - The additional earnest money given by the buyer to the seller under an earnest money agreement (Purchase and Sale Agreement). The additional deposit is usually given between the time of the initial deposit and the opening of escrow. Many brokers believe it is a good business practice to get an additional deposit that will bring the total deposit up to five to ten per cent of the purchase price if they were only able to obtain a small initial deposit. Otherwise, there may not be enough money to pay some of the costs incurred in escrow (title policy, commission, escrow fees, attorney fees, etc.) in the event the buyer defaults. For example, Jamie Johnson might deposit $1,000 with her offer to purchase Jodie Coffey's $90,000 condominium unit and agree to pay an additional deposit of $4,000 within five working days after seller's acceptance. In the event the buyer breaches the contract, the seller can elect to keep all deposit money, including the additional deposit, as her liquidated damages.

Care must be exercised to see that the language of the Purchase and Sale Agreement provides that the initial earnest money deposit and any additional deposit will serve as liquidated damages. (*See* DEPOSIT, LIQUIDATED DAMAGES.)

ADDITIONAL SPACE OPTION - A right within a lease giving a tenant the option to expand the tenant's leased space during the lease term as required and on terms specified in the lease.

ADHESION CONTRACT - A contract which is very one-sided, favoring the party who drafted the document. In fact, an adhesion contract can be so one-sided that doubt arises as to it being a voluntary and uncoerced agreement because it implies a serious inequality of bargaining power. Courts will not enforce provisions in adhesion contracts which are unfair and oppressive to the party who did not prepare the contract. Contracts with a lot of fine print, such as franchise agreements, mortgages and leases, are sometimes challenged as adhesion contracts on the basis that the nondrafting party did not have a chance to bargain on the various provisions of the agreement. Also called a "take it or leave it" contract. (*See* BOILER PLATE, UNCONSCIONABILITY.)

An insurance contract (property, title, life) is sometimes challenged as being an adhesion contract. Courts have held that any ambiguity is to be construed in favor of the insured and any exclusion from coverage must be clearly and conspicuously stated. Courts will also apply the doctrine of unconscionability. (*See* BOILER PLATE, UNCONSCIONABILITY.)

ADJOIN - Connect or join. If two pieces of property touch each other, they *adjoin* or *abut* each other. (*See* ABUTTING OWNER.)

ADJUSTABLE RATE LOAN - *See* ADJUSTABLE RATE MORTGAGE (ARM).

ADJUSTABLE RATE MORTGAGE (ARM) - A broad term for all real estate loans, mortgages or deeds of trust with an interest rate that can change and is not fixed for the term of the loan. They are also referred to as a Flexible Rate Mortgage or Variable Rate Mortgage. In Washington all these terms are normally used even though the security document is a deed of trust. An ARM has a lower start interest rate than a fixed rate loan due to the fact the interest rate can go up during the term of the loan to a rate substantially higher than a normal fixed rate loan, thereby lowering the risk factor to the lender over the life of the loan. The note rate changes at specific intervals (e.g., first of each month, every six month or annual) with the note rate for the next interval of the loan being adjusted up or down in the same ratio as the increase in the specific index; for example, is indexed to a national index such as a six-month treasury index. Usually there is a "cap" in the loan which provides that a note rate cannot increase over a specific amount; for example, 1% in a single interval of time. Sometimes, there is a lifetime rate increase cap, also referred to as a ceiling. (*See* BASING INDEX.)

ADJUSTABLE RATE MORTGAGE (ARM)

The adjustable rate loan has created its own glossary of terms, such as:

Conditional Extensions - A fixed rate loan with a single automatic rate change at the end of five years (called a 5/25 loan) or seven years (called a 7/23 loan) in accord with a pre-set formula in the promissory note. Most of these hybrids are extended conditionally providing that the owner still occupies the home, has made payments on time and has no liens against it. A few lenders offer unconditional thirty year loans with the single adjust after five or seven years. Others offer true balloon loans with no commitment to refinance at the end of the call period.

Current Index - The current value of a recognized index as calculated and published nationally or regionally. The current index value changes periodically and is used in calculating the new note rate as of each rate adjustment date.

Fully Indexed Rate - The index value at the time of application plus the gross margin stated in the note.

Gross Margin - An amount, expressed as percentage points, stated in the note which is added to the current index value on the rate adjustment date to establish the new note rate.

Life of Loan Cap - A ceiling the note rate cannot exceed over the life of the loan, usually five or six additional percentage points.

Note Rate - This rate determines the amount of interest charged on an annual basis to the borrower. The note rate is also called the "accrual rate", "contract rate" or "coupon rate".

Payment Adjustment Date - The date the borrower's monthly principal and interest payment may change.

Payment Cap - Limits the amount of increase in the borrower's monthly principal and interest at the payment adjustment date, if the principal and interest increase called for by the interest rate increase exceeds the payment cap percentage. This limitation is often at the borrower's option and may result in negative amortization.

Payment Rate - The rate at which the borrower repays the loan. This rate reflects buy-down or payment caps.

Periodic Interest Rate Cap - Limits the increase or decrease in the note rate at each rate adjustment, thereby limiting the borrower's payment increase or decrease at the time of adjustment.

Rate Adjustment Date - The date the borrower's note rate may change.

Subsidy Buy-down - Funds provided usually by the builder or the seller to temporarily reduce the borrowers' monthly principal and interest payment as an inducement to purchase.

ADJUSTED BASIS - The original basis of a property reduced by certain expenses and increased by certain improvement costs. The original basis determined at the time of acquisition is reduced by the amount of depreciation, amortization or depletion allowances taken by the taxpayer, and by the amount of any uncompensated losses suffered by the taxpayer with respect to the property. It is then increased by the cost of capital improvements. The amount of gain or loss recognized by the taxpayer upon sale of the property is determined by subtracting the adjusted basis on the date of sale from the adjusted sales price. (*See* BASIS, DEPRECIATION [TAX], GAIN.)

ADJUSTED SALES PRICE - In an appraisal, the estimated sales price of a comparable property after additions and/or subtractions have been made to the actual sales price of the comparable for improvements and deficiencies when compared to the subject property being appraised. In theory, the adjusted sales price is what a comparable property would sell for if it were exactly equal in terms of all of its features to the subject property. (*See* APPRAISAL.)

ADJUSTMENTS - In real estate appraisal, the increases or decreases to the sales price of a comparable property to arrive at an indicated value for the property being appraised. Adjustments may be made for several reasons. The first adjustment is for seller concessions and the second is for time of sale if there has been a change in market conditions since the comparable sale. Adjustments are then made for location and dissimilarities in the physical characteristics between the subject and the comparable property, and the indicated value is increased or decreased for each difference or dissimilarity. (*See* COMPARABLES, DIRECT SALES COMPARISON APPROACH, MARKET-DATA APPROACH.)

In real estate closings, adjustments refer to the credits and debits of a closing (settlement) statement such as real property tax, insurance, and rent prorations.

ADMINISTRATIVE RULES AND REGULATIONS - Regulations issued by an administrative agency that have the force and effect of law. The State's Real Estate Commission often adopts rules and regulations to complement the licensing law. The Rules and Regulations are part of the Washington Administrative Code. (*See* LICENSE LAW, REAL ESTATE COMMISSION.)
Reference: WAC 308-124, WAC 308-124A, WAC 308-124H

ADMINISTRATOR - A person appointed by the court to settle the estate of a person who has died intestate, that is, without leaving a will. (*See* EXECUTOR.)

ADMISSION TO PRACTICE RULE (APR 12) - Other then one of the principals or an attorney, no individual may select, prepare, and complete legal documents incident to the closing of a real estate and personal property transaction unless certified as provided by Admission to Practice Rule by the Washington Supreme Court. An individual admitted under Rule 12 is called a Limited Practice Officer (LPO). Admission to Practice Rule 12 was adopted by the Washington Supreme Court after ruling that the selection and completion of legal documents by any one other than an attorney constituted the unauthorized practice of law. Legal documents include deed, promissory notes, guarantees, deeds of trust, reconveyances, mortgages, satisfactions, security agreement, releases, Uniform Commercial Code, documents, assignments, contracts, real estate excise tax, affidavits, and bills of sale. The unauthorized practice of law is a misdemeanor offense. (*See* ESCROW AGENT.)

AD VALOREM - Latin for "according to valuation," usually referring to a type of tax or assessment. Washington's General Sales Tax is an ad valorem tax, which is calculated as a percentage of the value of everything that changes hands, such as retail sales of foods, clothing, goods and the like. The State Excise Tax is also an ad valorem tax which is paid by the seller based on the actual consideration of the transfer. Real property tax is an ad valorem tax based on the assessed valuation of the property. The key to the ad valorem system of taxation is that each property shall bear a tax burden which is proportionate to its value. (*See* EXCISE TAX ON REAL ESTATE SALES.)

ADVANCE - The giving of consideration before it is due. Money is advanced by one party, such as a mortgagee or vendor, to cover carrying charges (like taxes and insurance) on the property which were not properly paid by the other party in default. Such amounts paid are credited to the account of the advancing party. For example, a second mortgagee might advance delinquent first mortgage payments of the borrower in order to prevent a foreclosure of the secured property.

Also refers to additional funds disbursed under an open-end mortgage or to advances made by a construction lender to a developer-borrower. (*See* DRAW.)

ADVANCE FEE - A practice of some lenders to ask for a non-refundable fee to cover future services to be rendered. This practice was rarely seen in Washington until recent years. A small but growing number of commercial-investment orientated brokers are starting to use the concept in conjunction with an acquisition or employment contract.

Advance fees for the arranging of financing has resulted in consumer abuses in Washington. Under the Mortgage Brokers Law adopted in Washington in 1987, prior to the payment of an advance fee, a mortgage broker must make a detailed written disclosure to the borrower. A mortgage broker must place any advance fee into a trust account and is prohibited from actually receiving any fee until the borrower actually obtains a loan. In some cases, the law permits a mortgage broker to receive a fee not to exceed $300 plus certain costs if the borrower fails to close on the loan. (*See* MORTGAGE BROKER PRACTICES ACT.)
Reference: RCW 19.146

ADVERSE FINANCIAL CHANGE CONDITION - A condition in a loan commitment entitling the lender to cancel the commitment if the borrower's financial circumstances prior to the closing of the transaction suffers a materially adverse change, e.g., loss of job.

ADVERSE POSSESSION - The acquiring of title to real property owned by someone other than the true owner by means of open, notorious, and continuous possession for a statutory period of time, seven or ten years in Washington. The burden to prove title is on the possessor.

To claim adverse possession under the **under (7) year** statutory period, a possessor must show that he/she has been in possession under **a claim of right or color of title** (such as a defectively executed deed); that he or she was in actual, open and notorious possession of the premises so as to constitute reasonable notice to the record owner; that possession was both exclusive and hostile to the title of the owner (that is, without the owner's permission and evidencing an intention to maintain the claim of ownership against all who may contest it); that possession was uninterrupted and continuous for at least the prescriptive period stipulated by state law; and that he/she paid all taxes legally assessed on the property during the period of adverse possession.
Reference: RCW 7.28

Contrary to popular belief, it is possible to acquire title through adverse possession without "color of title" (a defective title). Washington statutes provide that, without "color of title," the length of time which the adverse possession must continue is ten years.

Successive occupation of the premises by persons who are successors in interest (e.g., by relationship of contract or descent) can be added together or "tacked on" for the purpose of the seven years continuous use requirement. For example, a father adversely occupied a certain parcel of land for five years and upon his death his son succeeded to his interest; the son can "tack on" to his father's five year's prior possession.

To remember the required elements, remember the word "POACH", i.e., possession which is open, actual, continuous and hostile.

Originally the main purpose of the Washington adverse possession statute was to insure the fullest and most productive use of privately owned land. Title to real property owned by the state or federal government, including property such as streets and parks dedicated to the public, cannot be obtained by adverse possession. Also, adverse possession does not run against certain owners under a disability, such as minors or mental incompetents. However, such an owner must commence an action to recover his/her land within three years after the disability ceases to exist or lose the land. One who claims title to property by adverse possession does not have marketable title until he/she obtains and records a judicial decree quieting the title or a quit claim deed from the record title holder. However, the adverse possessor need not take an affirmative legal action to gain title; the burden to bring legal action rests on the person claiming title (the true owner) and must be brought within the statutory period of time (seven or ten years) from the time the adverse possessor (or that person's ancestor, devisor or assignor) took possession or title can be lost.

Co-tenants normally cannot claim adverse possession against each other without an actual and clear ejectment of one co-tenant by another.

In modern times adverse possession usually involves boundary disputes between adjoining property owners. (*See* ADVERSE USE, COLOR OF TITLE, OPEN AND NOTORIOUS, POSSESSION, QUIET TITLE ACTION, PRESCRIPTION, TRESPASS.)

ADVERSE USE - The prescriptive acquisition of the right to a limited use of the land of another, such as a pathway easement across another's property. In order to acquire an easement by adverse use, the claimant must generally satisfy the same requirements as those for adverse possession with the exception of exclusive use, including the prescriptive 10 year time period. While most easements cannot be lost by mere nonuse an easement created by an adverse user can be terminated by nonuse for the prescriptive period of adverse possession. (*See* ADVERSE POSSESSION, PRESCRIPTIVE EASEMENT.)

ADVERTISING - The public promotion of one's products and services. In real estate, advertising is governed by various rules and regulations established by federal, state, local and private authorities.

A broker MUST use in his/her advertisement the full name of the licensed broker or company as it appears on the real estate license issued by the Real Estate Program of the Department of Licensing. Salesperson or associate broker cannot advertise in their name alone. The State's license laws prohibit the use of *blind ads*; that is, advertisements placed by a real estate licensee on behalf of the seller or buyer which do not include the name of the licensed real estate broker.

Real Estate Licensee Selling Own Property: The Real Estate Program of the Department of Licensing requires a real estate licensee selling his/her own property to indicate to the public in all advertisements that the owner is licensed. Some brokerage firms now require that the licensee list his/her property with the firm and submit the listing promptly to the MLS if the firm is a member since the employing broker is responsible for all of the professional actions of each of his/her licensees. Other brokerage firms while not requiring the property to be listed require the owner to inform the broker that the property will be advertised. (*See* LICENSING LAW.)
Reference: RCW 18.85

Truth-in-Lending: Federal Truth-in-Lending laws require certain types of disclosure information if the advertisement includes specific financing terms or credit terms. (*See* TRUTH-IN-LENDING ACT.)

HUD Guidelines: In 1995 the U. S. Department of Housing Urban Development (HUD) provided guidelines and acceptability of some everyday terms that have been included in media advertising which found to be in violation of certain laws of discrimination. Advertising runs into trouble when its language or image creates the perception that one type of buyer is preferred over another on the basis of race, color, familial, religion, handicap, national origin or sex. HUD has published and made available "How to Write a Non-Discriminatory Ad." The National Association of Realtors® has stated that the golden rule to follow when preparing an ad is to focus all descriptions on the property and none on the potential buyer.

Recreational Subdivisions: By Washington statute, advertising relating to subdivision sales (second home sites or recreational developments) must not contain any false or misleading statements. No part of any material contained in the Property Report may be used for advertising purposes unless the report is used in its entirety. (*See* WASHINGTON LAND SALES DEVELOPMENT ACT.)
Reference: RCW 58.19

No advertisement may promise investment value when such value cannot be proven.

AESTHETIC VALUE - The value attributable to beauty created by improvements and natural surroundings. A densely wooded lot can add aesthetic value to the property.

AFFIANT - A person who swears to or affirms the truth of a statement in an affidavit. (*See* AFFIDAVIT.)

AFFIDAVIT - A sworn statement reduced to writing and made under oath before a Notary Public or other official authorized by law to administer an oath. The affiant (person making the oath) must swear before the Notary that the facts contained in the affidavit are true and correct.

An affidavit has many uses. For example, affidavits are used to give sworn statements at hearings and in applications for professional licenses. The following is an example of a simple affidavit format.

STATE OF WASHINGTON }
 } ss
COUNTY OF KING }

____________________ being duly sworn, deposes and says that he/she is the
____of
(Office Held)

____,
(Name of Company)

the applicant named in the foregoing application, and that the statements made in the application are true and correct to the best of (his)(her) knowledge and belief.
Subscribed and sworn to before me this_______ day of _________________, 19____

Print Name
Notary Public in and for the State of Washington,
residing at
My commission expires:

(*See* ACKNOWLEDGMENT, NOTARY PUBLIC.)

AFFIRMATION - A declaration as to the truth of a statement. An affirmation is used in lieu of an oath, especially where the affiant objects to taking an oath for personal or religious reasons.

AFFIRMATIVE COVERAGE - A provision in an insurance policy by which the insurance company affirmatively insures against a loss due to a specific risk generally not covered by the standard insurance policy being purchased. For example, insurance against loss due to violation of a restrictive covenant or for earthquake damage, often called an endorsement.

AFFIRMATIVE MARKETING PROGRAM - A program designed to inform all buyers in the minority community of homes for sale without discrimination and to provide Realtors® with procedures and educational materials to assist in compliance with the law. An active affirmative marketing program is currently being conducted by many Realtor boards in conjunction with the federal Department of Housing and Urban Development (HUD). After a local Realtor board adopts the affirmative action program, the board is then responsible to HUD for compliance.

HUD also requires developers to submit affirmative fair housing marketing plans prior to HUD granting any feasibility or refund reservations. These plans are intended to encourage the integration of minority groups into housing. In addition, HUD has published specific advertising guidelines, some of which prohibit the selective use of advertising with a discriminatory effect.

AFFORDABLE HOUSING - Housing for individuals or families whose incomes are a certain percentage of or below the median for the area as determined by HUD and adjusted for family size. Affordable housing projects are usually developed in conjunction with governmental assistance and/or as a condition of a development agreement with the appropriate government authority.

The intent of affordable housing projects is to recognize the acute shortage of housing and to provide housing for persons otherwise unable to afford it. An affordable housing unit may be subject to certain conditions, restrictions and requirements in respect of resale and occupancy requirements.

AFFORDABILITY INDEX - A standard established by the National Association of Realtors® to gauge the ability of consumers to afford to buy a home, which has become widely used by the media. NAR issues a monthly press release which states the current index number. On the index, 100 means that a family earning the national median income has exactly enough money to qualify for a mortgage on a median-priced home with a 20% down payment.

AFIDA - *See* AGRICULTURAL FOREIGN INVESTMENT DISCLOSURE ACT.

A-FRAME CONSTRUCTION - A type of residential construction in which the exterior design of the building resembles the letter A, usually found in recreation-oriented developments.

AFTER-ACQUIRED - Something which was acquired after a certain event takes place.

An after-acquired title is acquired by a grantor of property **after** the grantor has attempted to convey good title. Upon the grantor's obtaining good title, it will automatically pass by operation of law to his/her grantee. For example, Smith conveys his farm to Jones on January 1, 1974. Smith did not have valid title on January 1 because he held title to the property under a forged deed. On March 5, 1974 Smith received good title under a properly executed deed. Jones automatically acquired good title on March 5.
Reference: RCW 64.04.070

Note that an after-acquired title will not pass automatically to a grantee under a quitclaim deed unless the instrument includes such a provision, otherwise it will transfer only the grantor's current interest in the land if any.

Fixtures which are bought, paid for and installed by the property owner-mortgagor are subject to the lien of the mortgage. In addition, many mortgages provide that all fixtures found on the property **after** the mortgage has been made are subject to the mortgage.

The Uniform Commercial Code (UCC) has established guidelines to settle conflicting claims between mortgagees and chattel security claimants involving prior rights to after-acquired property, such as appliances bought on time and installed on the mortgaged premises. Under the UCC a debtor can grant a superior security interest in such after-acquired property to a chattel mortgagee. (*See* FIXTURE.)

AFTER TAX INCOME - An accounting term meaning the amount left after deducting income tax liability from taxable income. The cash flow from an investment after deducting applicable taxes.

AGE - (1) As applied to a structure, the effective age is the years of age indicated by the condition and utility of the structure, as opposed to the actual or chronological age. (2)

The Federal Equal Credit Opportunity Act prohibits discriminatory lending practices based on considerations of old age. (*See* AGE-LIFE DEPRECIATION.)

AGE-LIFE DEPRECIATION - An appraisal method of computing depreciation based on the condition of a property and its economic life. The estimated effective age (based on condition) is added to the estimated remaining economic life of the property.

The effective age is then divided by the sum of the two to indicate the total percent of depreciation. As an example, a house has an effective age of ten years and a remaining economic life of forty; the depreciation is twenty percent (ten divided by fifty). (*See* DEPRECIATION [APPRAISAL]).

AGENCY - A relationship created when one person, the **principal**, delegates to another, the **agent**, the right to act on his/her behalf in business transactions and to exercise some degree of discretion while so acting. There is a vast body of law, both common and statutory, controlling the rights and duties of principal and agent. In addition to this general law of agency, which is applicable to all business transactions, state licensing laws also directly affect the agency relationship between real estate licensees, their clients and the public. Although agency law is separate from contract law, the two frequently come together in interpreting relationships between real estate agents and their principals.

Note that the payment of consideration need not be involved in an agency relationship. One may gratuitously undertake to act as an agent and will be held to the standards of agency upon assumption of those duties.

An agency may be a **general agency**, as when a principal gives a broker a general power of attorney to purchase or dispose of a parcel of real property on behalf of the principal, or it may be a **special agency**, such as the standard listing contract wherein the broker is only employed to find a ready, willing, and able buyer and is not authorized to sell the property nor to bind his/her principal to any contract for the sale of the property.

A client and broker can create a principal/agent relationship with the consequential duties and responsibilities arising from this status, even though the broker does not have a written contract and thus, usually cannot collect a commission if the principal is unwilling to pay a commission. In other words, the creation of the agency relationship may be implied from the acts of the parties and does not depend on the existence of a written contract. A licensee often represents the buyer in a transaction without having any written agreement. Once the agency relationship is created, certain rights and obligations attach to it and the licensee is liable for any breaches of the required duties.

Before the adoption of the Real Estate Brokerage Relationships Act, which became law on January 1, 1997, almost all of the duties owned to a principal by a broker, associate broker or salesperson were derived from the common law of agency. The new Act substantially redefines the relationship between real estate licensees and between real estate licensees and their customers. The Act was adopted in response to the transformation which has occurred since 1980 in the real estate brokerage business. In 1980 with the exception of a few real estate licensees, the normal relationship was that the listing agent placed the seller's property into the marketplace, usually via a multiple listing service (MLS) and other licensees/member of the MLS would become subagents of the listing broker and try to sell it. Almost every licensee represented the seller. Almost no one represented the buyer. However, in many cases, the buyer though she/he **was being represented** by the selling licensee. The early 1980s saw the slow growth of buyer's agency wherein the buyer was being represented. The later half of the 1980s saw a battle in the real estate brokerage industry over growing buyer's brokerage.

In 1986 the issue was recognized by the State Real Estate Commission when it adopted a Rule and Regulation which became effective April 1, 1987. The Rule and Regulation required a selling agent to provide the principals (buyers and sellers) involved in a real estate sales transaction oral and/or written disclosure as to whom the agent was representing in the transaction. The Rule and Regulation was rescinded by the Commission after the adopting of the Real Estate Brokerage Relationships Act.

The Real Estate Brokerage Relationships Act requires all licensees to provide a pamphlet on the Law of Real Estate Agency in the form prescribed in Section 13 of the Act. (*See* APPENDIX C, REAL ESTATE BROKERAGE RELATIONSHIP ACT.)

The real estate licensee is generally subject to three distinct areas of liability for breach of fiduciary or statutory duties to his/her principal: (1) the principal can bring civil action against the licensee-agent for money damages, (2) demand a refund of any real estate commission paid by the principal to the agent, and (3) the state licensing authority can bring disciplinary proceedings for violation of its regulations.

Under common law principles, the agent owes the principal personal performance, loyalty, obedience, disclosure of material facts (such as a proposed new school, highway relocation, or new zoning ordinance that would tend to increase the property value over the agreed upon listing price), to take reasonable care not to exceed the authority granted to him/her or to misrepresent material facts to the principal or to third parties, to keep proper accounts of all moneys, and to place the principal's interests above those of the persons dealing with the principal.

Under the new statutory structure of Agency there are: (1) specific duties of a licensee in general; (2) duties of a licensee as a seller's agent; (3) duties of a licensee as a buyer's agent; and (4) duties of a licensee as a dual agent.
Reference: RCW 18.86

Without the principal's authorization, an agent cannot disclose to a third party confidential information or information that hurts his/her principal's bargaining position, such as the fact that the seller is forced to sell due to loss of job, or a pending divorce or poor health, or that the seller will actually accept less than the listing price.

Confidential information learned during the course of the agency cannot be used at a later date against the principal, even after the transaction is closed. This includes financial information used in negotiations involving subsequently listed properties.

While agents are required by law to provide their principals with all material and pertinent facts; race, creed, color, religion and sex are not material facts and cannot be disclosed even at the principal's request.

The State license laws require additional duties of the agent in a principal/agent relationship. For instance, an agent must disclose in writing any interest the agent may have in the property, such as when one of his/her salespeople or a relative or related corporation offers to purchase the listed property. For example, an agent must disclose that his/her sister was submitting an offer using her married name. An agent may not act for both the seller and the buyer without their written consent nor may the agent commingle the principal's money or other property with his/her own. A broker may not advertise property without the specific authorization of the owner. A broker must present all written offers to his/her principal.
Reference: RCW 18.85

In dealing with third persons, for whom he/she is not an agent, an agent must be fair and honest, and exercise care and diligence because he/she is liable for knowingly making material misrepresentations or doing negligent acts. The principal also may be liable to the third person for all acts the agent performs within the scope of his/her employment.

An agency may be terminated between a principal and an agent at any time, except if the agency is coupled with an interest. However, if the agency is terminated prior to the stated expiration date in a listing, there could be a claim for money damages (a real estate commission). An agency is terminated by the death or incapacity of either party (notice of death is not necessary), destruction or condemnation of the property, expiration of the terms of the agency, mutual agreement, renunciation by the agent or revocation by the principal, bankruptcy of the principal (since the title of the property is transferred to a receiver), or completion of the agency. (*See* AGENCY COUPLED WITH AN INTEREST, DUAL AGENCY, EQUAL DIGNITIES RULE, GENERAL AGENT, IMPUTED INTEREST, LISTING, POWER OF ATTORNEY, RESPONDEAT SUPERIOR, SCOPE OF AUTHORITY, SPECIAL AGENT, TERMINATION OF LISTING, UNDISCLOSED AGENCY.)

A real estate broker is not prohibited by license law or agency law from representing both parties, provided that the dual agency is disclosed to the parties.

Real Estate Licensing Laws prohibits a real estate licensee from charging or accepting compensation from more than one party in a transaction without first making full disclosure of all the facts to all the parties interested in the transaction. (*See* AGENCY DISCLOSURE.)

AGENCY BY ESTOPPEL - An agency created when the principal intentionally or negligently causes a third party to believe that another is the principal's agent and the third party relies on that representation. Also called ostensible agency. In theory, the principal who caused such reliance is stopped from denying the existence of an agency relationship.

AGENCY BY RATIFICATION - An agency created "after the fact" by a principal, expressly or impliedly, affirming the conduct of the party claiming to act as his/her agent. There must be proof that the principal was aware of the act or acts and either accepted the benefits or elected to be bound by the agent's conduct. Agency by ratification could occur when one spouse signs a contract concerning community property and the other spouse does not sign but acts in a manner so a third party could be led to believe the unsigning spouse agrees with the action of the signing spouse.

AGENCY COUPLED WITH AN INTEREST - An agency relationship in which the agent is given an interest in the subject of the agency (the property). Such an agency cannot be revoked by the principal nor is it terminated upon the death of the principal. For example, a broker may supply the financing for a condominium and/or development provided the developer agrees to give the broker the exclusive listing to sell the finished condominium units or lots. The developer would not be able to revoke the listing after the broker had provided the financing.

AGENCY DISCLOSURE - Good real estate practice requires that a listing agent and a selling agent provide to their respective principals in a real estate transaction with oral and/or written disclosure of whom the agent represents in the transaction.

This notice is now handled in part by a required pamphlet which under the provisions of the Real Estate Brokerage Relations Act, any real estate licensee must deliver to individual(s) that the licensee may work with on a real estate transaction. The real estate licensee still must clearly inform the individual as to whose agent he/she is.

Good real estate practice dictates disclosure should be confirmed in a separate paragraph titled "Agency Disclosure" in the Purchase and Sale Agreement, which should contain the following information:

"AGENCY DISCLOSURE: At the signing of this agreement the selling agent (insert name of selling licensee and the company name as licensed) represented . . . .(insert seller, buyer, or both seller and buyer.)

The listing agent (insert name of listing licensee and company name as licensed) represented . . . . (insert seller, or both seller and buyer).

Each party signing this document confirms that prior oral and/or written disclosure of agency was provided to him/her in this transaction."

The licensee's conduct in the real estate transaction shall be in conformity with the agency disclosure made. The payment of compensation or the obligation to pay compensation to a licensee is not necessarily determinative of a particular agency relationship. (*See* AGENCY, LICENSING LAW, REAL ESTATE BROKERAGE RELATIONS ACT.)
Reference: RCW 18.85; RCW 18.86

AGENT - Agent means a real estate licensee who has entered into an agency relationship with a buyer or seller. One who is authorized to represent and to act on behalf of another person (called the principal). Unlike an employee who merely works for a principal, an agent works in the place of a principal. A real estate licensee is the agent of the client, which may be either the seller or buyer, to whom he/she owes statutory and fiduciary obligations. "Buyer's Agent" means a licensee who has entered into an agency relationship with only the buyer in a real estate transaction. "Seller's Agent" means a licensee who has entered into an agency relationship with only the seller. (See AGENCY, DUAL AGENCY, FIDUCIARY, REAL ESTATE BROKERAGE RELATIONSHIP ACT.)

The main difference between an agent and an employee is that the agent may bind his/her principal by contract, if within the scope of authority of the agent, whereas an employee may not, unless given express authorization. Note: a minor cannot appoint an agent to execute his/her contracts, but an adult may designate a minor to act as his/her agent. (*See* POWER OF ATTORNEY.)

AGGRIEVED - Having suffered loss or injury from infringement or denial of rights; injured. The term also refers to an injured person who has lost some personal or property rights or has had an obligation or burden imposed on him/her.

AGREED BOUNDARIES - A doctrine affecting rights of ownership to boundaries. Where there is uncertainty as to the location of the true boundary line between adjoining parcels of land, the landowners can mutually agree and establish a boundary line. If the parties act in conformity with the agreed boundary, then the doctrine of agreed boundaries holds that line to be the legal boundary line between the properties.

AGREEMENT OF SALE - A written contract between buyer and seller covering the sale of specific real property. Some of the names for this contract in Washington are purchase agreement, purchase and sale agreement or earnest money agreement. (*See* CONTRACT, REAL ESTATE PURCHASE AND SALE AGREEMENT.)

AGRICULTURAL FOREIGN INVESTMENT DISCLOSURE ACT - The Agricultural Foreign Investment Act of 1978 requires reporting of all direct and indirect acquisitions and holdings of agricultural land (including timber land) by a foreign person. Acquisitions must be reported within 90 days after the acquisition. The penalty for failure to file is a fine of up to 25% of the value of the land. The report is to be filed on Form ASCS-153 with the office of the Agricultural Stabilization and Conservation Service of the U.S. Department of Agriculture in the county where the land is located.

"Agricultural land" basically includes any land which is currently used, or was used within the past five years, for agricultural, forestry or timber production purposes. The Act does not apply to land of one acre or less or from which agricultural, forestry or timber products yield less than $1,000 in annual gross sales. (*See* ALIEN, FOREIGN INVESTMENT IN REAL PROPERTY TAX ACT OF 1980.)

AGRICULTURAL LIEN - A statutory lien advanced to a farmer to secure money or supplies for raising a crop. The lien attaches only to the crop, not to the land. Also called a crop lien.
Reference: RCW 60.11

AIDS (Acquired Immune Deficiency Syndrome) - In 1986, the Washington State Human Rights Commission issued staff policy guidelines addressing AIDS and real estate transactions. Under the guidelines, Acquired Immune Deficiency Syndrome (AIDS) and related medical conditions are considered disabilities under the Washington State Law Against Discrimination.

The Washington State Human Rights Commission has stated that questions or inquires about AIDS, or any of its related conditions are improper questions by any prospective landlord, tenant, home buyer or seller.

The guidelines specifically prohibit an agent for a landlord, home seller or lessor to engage in conjecture or in any way disclose whether a former tenant, owner or resident was perceived to have had or was know to have had AIDS or any AIDS-related condition.

The guidelines also provide that it is an unfair practice for an appraiser of a financial institution to lower the value of real property because a person with AIDS, or who is perceived to have AIDS, resides in the property or is a neighbor to the property.

It is unfair practice for an owner, manager or other agent to require any tenant who is known to have or perceived to have AIDS or a related condition, to meet different standards of tenancy or to deny the same terms, conditions or privileges as granted to a non-disabled tenant.

Property owners and landlords must be especially careful to ensure that any tenant who has or is perceived to have AIDS or AIDS-related conditions, be free from harassment because of his/her status.

AIDS is not a relevant factor of discussion or disclosure during a real estate transaction. Even with authorization, the Washington guidelines appear to bar the disclosure. (*See* DISCRIMINATION, LICENSING LAWS.)
Reference: RCW 18.85 and RCW 49.60.

AIREA - *See* AMERICAN INSTITUTE OF REAL ESTATE APPRAISERS.

AIR PARK - A tract of land that adjoins or is part of an airport and is improved with commercial, industrial and office space.

AIRPORT ZONING - Regulations that aim to reduce potential hazards to aircraft (including electronic interference) by governing land uses, building height and natural growth in the areas surrounding an airport.

AIR RIGHTS - The rights to the use of the open space or vertical plane above a property. Ownership of land includes the right to all air above the property. Until the advent of the airplane, this right was unlimited. Now the courts permit reasonable interference with one's air rights, such as use of aircraft, so long as the owner's right to use and occupy the land is not lessened. Thus, low-flying aircraft might be unreasonably trespassing and their owners would be liable for any damages. Governments and airport authorities often purchase air rights adjacent to an airport, called an aviation easement, to provide glide patterns for air traffic.

Air rights may be sold or leased and buildings constructed thereon, such as was done with the Pan Am Building above Grand Central Station in New York City. Until recently, none of the major metropolitan areas in the State of Washington has experienced sufficient scarcity of developable lands to justify extensive use of air rights as has occurred in New York City, Chicago or Honolulu. The major examples of the utilization of air rights in Washington are Freeway Park and the State's Convention Center over I-5 in downtown Seattle.

The air itself is not real property; however, airspace is real property when described in three dimensions with reference to a specific parcel of land.

A Maryland case has decided that where there are separate owners of the land and the air rights, the air rights may be separately assessed for tax purposes.

ALIEN - A person born outside the jurisdiction of the United States who has not been naturalized under the Constitution and laws of this country. Aliens are allowed to acquire or hold an interest in land in Washington. They have complete rights as to any interests in land and any conveyance. (*See* AGRICULTURAL FOREIGN INVESTMENT DISCLOSURE ACT, FOREIGN INVESTMENT IN REAL PROPERTY TAX ACT OF 1980.)

ALIENATION - The act of transferring ownership, title, or an interest or estate in real property from one person to another. Property is usually sold or conveyed by voluntary alienation, as with a deed or assignment of lease. Involuntary alienation takes place when property is sold against the owner's will as in a foreclosure sale or tax sale. (*See* ACQUISITION, RESTRAINT ON INTUITION.)

ALIENATION CLAUSE - A clause in a promissory note, mortgage, deed of trust or real estate contract which provides that the balance of the secured debt becomes immediately due and payable at the option of the lender upon the alienation of the property by the borrower. Alienation is usually broadly defined to include any transfer of ownership, title, or an interest or estate in real property, including a sale by way of real estate contract or an Assignment of Purchaser's Contract and Deed. Also called a due on sale clause. (*See* ACCELERATION CLAUSE, DUE ON SALE CLAUSE.)

ALLEGATION - A statement by a party to a legal action of what he/she expects to prove. A declaration made as if under oath but prior to proof, such as an assertion made in a pleading or summons.

ALLIGATOR - Slang for a real estate investment that devours large amounts of cash and produces excess losses.

ALL-INCLUSIVE DEED OF TRUST - A security device which is a purchase money deed of trust subordinate to, but which still includes, the encumbrance or encumbrances to which it is subordinated. Similar to a wrap around mortgage with the obvious exception that a deed of trust rather than a mortgage is used. (*See* WRAP AROUND MORTGAGE.)

ALLODIAL SYSTEM - The free and full ownership by individuals of rights in land, which is the basis of real property law in the United States. By contrast, under the feudal system ownership of the land was vested in the king or sovereign. The king then allotted select land to his noblemen, chiefs and others. Such allotments were on a revocable basis and only represented the right to administer or use the land.

ALLOTMENT - The funds allocated for the purchase of mortgages within a specified time by a permanent investor with whom a mortgage loan originator has a relationship but not a specific contract in the form of a commitment. The allotment may state the investor's requirements as to processing, loan terms, and/or underwriting standards. (*See* SECONDARY MORTGAGE MARKET.)

ALL-RISKS POLICY - A property insurance policy that covers all perils, except those specifically excluded in writing.

ALLUVION - That actual increase of soil on a shore or bank of a river, added by the process of accretion. Also called alluvium, it is the fine material, such as sand or mud, carried by water and deposited on land. The words alluvion and accretion are sometimes mistakenly used as synonyms. (*See* ACCRETION.)

ALTA EXTENDED TITLE INSURANCE - An extended coverage policy that insures the insurer (often the lender) against title defects not normally covered in the standard title insurance policy, such as unrecorded documents and rights of parties in possession. There is a one-time premium charge for the policy. The use of ALTA extended policy is standard practice with lenders who normally are unable to inspect the insured premises to discover off-record defects such as easements, encroachments or rights of parties in possession. There are few exceptions to an ALTA extended policy and the burden is on the title company to make a physical inspection of the premises to discover any unrecorded matters. (*See* TITLE INSURANCE.)

ALTERNATIVE DISPUTE RESOLUTION PROCESS - A mediation program sponsored by the Washington Association of Realtors® via local (county) Associations of Realtors® for disputes between Realtors® and their clients and customers.

Mediation is a voluntary process which people in a dispute can use to reach an agreement and thereby resolve the dispute. With the help of an impartial mediator they work towards a mutually agreeable solution. The mediator is not a judge - rather an expert in a process that focuses on the issues of conflict and helps defuse the emotions involved.

Mediation can be an effective, inexpensive alternative to litigation. If the parties fail to reach agreement - they can still arbitrate or litigate the issues.

The Realtor® Mediation Program is administered by a separate non-profit entity which performs mediation services for other groups in addition to WAR. Its mediators are trained and certified professionals who understand real estate issues and meet the criteria set by the National Association of Realtors®.

ALTERNATIVE MORTGAGE INSTRUMENT - A type of mortgage that differs from the standard fixed mortgage in either the amount of principal, the interest, repayment terms or the periodic payments. Some examples are the variable rate mortgage, graduated payment mortgage, renegotiable rate mortgage, the adjustable rate loan, the pledged account mortgage, the reverse annuity mortgage and the shared appreciation mortgage.

AMBIENT AIR - Any unconfined portion of the atmosphere; the outside air. Federal clean air laws set ambient air standards.

AMENITIES - Features, both tangible and intangible, which enhance and add to the desirability of real estate. In condominiums, for example, common amenities include a swimming pool, a fireplace, a good view, beach access and the like.

AMERICAN INSTITUTE OF REAL ESTATE APPRAISERS (AIREA) - A professional organization formerly affiliated with the National Association of Realtorsâ. AIREA promotes professional practice and ethics in the real estate appraisal industry and identifies experienced, competent, ethical appraisers by awarding the MAI (Member, Appraisal Institute) and RM (Residential Member) designations. In 1991, AIREA was merged with the Society of Real Estate Appraisers into the Appraisal Institute. The only designations awarded now are the MAI and SRA (Senior Residential Appraiser). (*See* APPRAISAL INSTITUTE.)

AMERICAN LAND DEVELOPMENT ASSOCIATION (ALDA) - A national trade association for the real estate development industry, especially those involved in recreation and second home development.

AMERICAN LAND TITLE ASSOCIATION (ALTA) - An association founded in 1907, representing more than 2,100 title abstractors, title insurance companies, title insurance agents and associate members. Since the role and responsibility of the title industry, and of its ALTA members, is to guarantee the safe, efficient transfer of real property, the ALTA membership functions cooperatively and effectively to provide protection for consumers and lenders alike. Members of the association use standardized title insurance forms developed by ALTA to provide uniformity within the industry.

AMERICAN PLANNING ASSOCIATION (APA) - A professional trade association comprised of both publicly and privately employed planners. APA was formed by the merger of the American Institute of Planners and the American Society of Planning Officials.

AMERICAN REAL ESTATE AND URBAN ECONOMICS ASSOCIATION (AREUEA) - The principal professional organization of real estate education, AREUEA consists of both educators and professional practitioners. The association publishes a journal of articles dealing with land use, urban economics and related topics.

AMERICAN SOCIETY OF APPRAISERS (ASA) - An appraisal organization consisting of persons involved in the appraisal of both real and personal property. The society sponsors the designation ASA and FASA (Fellow).

AMERICAN SOCIETY OF CONSULTING PLANNERS - A professional society whose membership is limited to private planning firms. The society offers various services to its members and serves as a representative for consulting planners.

AMERICAN SOCIETY OF FARM MANAGERS AND RURAL APPRAISER - The oldest professional association of appraisers, it confers the designation ARA (Accredited Rural Appraiser).

AMERICAN SOCIETY OF HOME INSPECTORS, INC. (ASHI) - A professional trade organization whose membership specializes in the physical inspection of homes. ASHI publishes numerous pamphlets and proceedings, conducts seminars and provides a Standards of Practice.

AMERICAN SOCIETY OF INDUSTRIAL SECURITY - A professional association of industrial security personnel that provides training, leading to the designation of Certified Protection Professional (CPP).

AMERICAN SOCIETY OF REAL ESTATE COUNSELORS (ASREC) - A professional organization, affiliated with the National Association of Realtors®, comprised of individuals with proven success in real estate counseling who serve clients on a fee basis. The society offers it members exclusive use of the professional designation CRE (Counselor of Real Estate).

AMERICAN STANDARD - A standard used for the measurement of office space that can be occupied by the tenant for furnishings and employees. The standard is accepted by the American National Standards Institute.

AMERICANS WITH DISABILITIES ACT (ADA) - -A federal law designed to eliminate discrimination against individuals with disabilities by mandating equal access to jobs, public accommodations, government services, public transportation and telecommunications.

ADA prohibits discrimination on account of a disability in the full and equal enjoyment of goods and services provided by a place of "public accommodation," including hotels, shopping centers and professional offices and applies to private entities that own, lease or operate virtually all commercial facilities. Exempted are private clubs and religious organizations.

Employers of a minimum number of employees must make reasonable accommodations to the job or work environment so as to enable a qualified person with a disability to perform the functions of that employment position. Examples include schedule modifications, special equipment, reserved accessible parking spaces and access to rest rooms.

Specific requirements include removal of architectural and communication barriers, if such removal is "readily achievable" in existing privately owned places of public accommodation. Recognizing the need for guidelines, the U.S. Department of Justice has established priorities for making changes. The first priority is the "get-to the-door" standard; this includes installing ramps, widening entrances and providing accessible parking spaces. The second priority is provision of access to all areas where goods and services are made available to the public - adjusting display racks or using raised or Braille signage are two such examples. The third priority is accessibility to restroom facilities. The final priority is free access to all remaining areas.

The Internal Revenue Code was amended to enable eligible small businesses to receive a tax credit for certain costs of compliance with ADA. A deduction of up to $15,000 per year is allowed for expenses associated with the removal of Code-qualified barriers for any entity, regardless of the entity's size.

Legal remedies include private civil action to obtain corrective action in providing auxiliary aids or facility alteration. ADA encourages the use of alternative dispute resolution including settlement, mediation and arbitration. Courts may assess a civil penalty against an entity found to be in noncompliance with the act. Fines are assessed in an amount not exceeding $50,000 for a first violation and in an amount not exceeding $100,000 for any subsequent violation.

Real estate brokers, salespersons and appraisers need to evaluate the possible application of ADA to their practice. In particular, brokers and salespersons should alert their commercial real estate and investor clients to the existence of ADA, to the need to have leases reviewed by knowledgeable counsel, and to the advisability of having offices inspected by a knowledgeable architect. Because of the potential liability to fee appraisers under ADA, real estate appraisers may need to insert a limiting condition in their appraisal reports. (*See* DISABILITY.)

AMICUS CURIAE - Literally, "friend of the court." Persons who are not parties to a lawsuit but who are interested in the outcome may be permitted to file legal briefs with the court.

AMORTIZATION - The gradual repayment or retiring of a debt by means of systematic payments of principal and interest over a set period, so that at the end of the period there is a zero balance. The principal is thus directly reduced or amortized over the life of the loan (hence the term "direct reduction loan").

The amortized mortgage came into vogue as a result of the many realty foreclosures during the depression of the 1930's. Prior to that time, most mortgages were payable at interest only for five years with the entire principal due at maturity. Savings and loan associations were the leaders in introducing amortized loans on residences. The standards set by the Federal Housing Administration were also influential in switching to the long-term amortized loan.

Most post 1980 mortgages are fully amortized (e.g. self-liquidating) and are paid in equal monthly installments, which include interest and amortization of principal. The interest is set at a predetermined percentage rate and is charged only on the unpaid balance. As the payments are made, the amount allocated to interest decreases and that applied to reduction of principal increases. For example, Mr. Hawkins has obtained a new mortgage in the amount of $40,000, amortized over a period of 25 years at an interest rate of 9%. Based on amortization table figures, the monthly payment on this mortgage is $335.68, and if Mr. Hawkins continues to make this monthly payment for twenty-five years, at the end of that period the mortgage will have been repaid in full, including interest. At the beginning of the loan period, the monthly payment will go primarily to the payment of interest, plus a small amount to principal. In the case of the $40,000 loan, the first monthly payment will include $300 of interest, and $35.68 of principal. As the principal amount is reduced, the interest is calculated on an increasingly lower amount, and the monthly payment toward interest decreases while the payment toward principal increases. By the time the loan balance has been reduced to $20,000, the interest payment will be only $150, while the principal payment will have increased to $185.69. It may come as a surprise that at the end of 25 years, Mr. Hawkins will have paid in a total of $100,704 to pay back his original $40,000 loan.

An **extended-term amortized** loan, or **balloon** mortgage, is often used in real estate contracts and in commercial and industrial real estate loans with very stable and secure tenants. The amortized payments are based on a payment schedule that is longer than the actual term of the loan. (*See* ADJUSTABLE RATE MORTGAGE.)

AMORTIZATION SCHEDULE - A table showing the amounts of principal and interest due at regular intervals and the unpaid balance of the loan after each payment is made.

Example of Amortization Table:
9% Table — Monthly Amortized Payments

Term in Years	**5**	**10**	**15**	**20**	**25**	**30**	**35**
Amount							
39,000	809.67	494.08	395.59	350.91	307.30	313.81	305.76
40,000	830.43	506.75	405.73	359.91	335.68	321.86	131.60
41,000	851.19	519.42	415.88	368.91	344.08	329.90	321.44

(*See* AMORTIZATION, ANNUAL, CONSTANT.)

ANCESTOR - A person from who one lineally descends (such as a father or grandmother) and from whom land is lawfully inherited. Under Washington State discrimination laws, it is unlawful to discriminate on the grounds of a person's ancestry. Under the Federal Fair Housing law, it is unlawful to discriminate on the basis of a person's national origin. (*See* DESCENT)

ANCHOR BOLT - A bolt that secures the sill of the house (the lowest horizontal member of the house frame) to the foundation wall.

ANCHOR TENANT - Major department or chain stores which are strategically located in shopping centers so as to give maximum exposure to smaller satellite stores, also referred to as a magnet store or traffic generator. In the usual strip shopping center, two anchor stores, such as a supermarket and a super-drugstore, are located at opposite ends of a mall with smaller stores in between. This helps to generate maximum sales volumes in the entire shopping center; of importance to the lessor since most lease rents are based on a percentage of gross sales. (*See* PERCENTAGE LEASE, SHOPPING CENTER.)

In recent years the Federal Trade Commission has sought to limit the powers of the anchor tenant in controlling the selection of satellite tenants and their merchandise.

ANGLE - A measure of rotation about a point, generally used in surveys to show the relationship of one line to another. Angles are usually measured in a clockwise direction and, in the United States, are normally measured in degrees — 360 degrees to a full circle or one full rotation back to the point of beginning. Each degree is broken down into 60 minutes and each minute into 60 seconds. For example, the direction of a line may be written as North 42° 20¢ 15² easterly. This line would be located using north as the line of reference and measuring an angle easterly which is 40 degrees, 20 minutes, and 15 seconds clockwise from north.

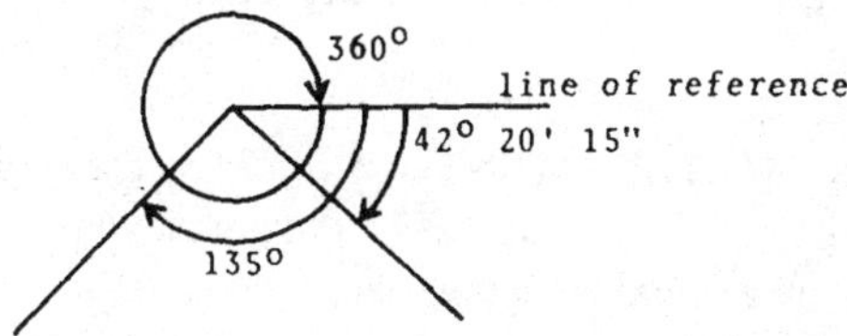

Reference lines can be north or south and angles can be east or west of the reference line. (*See* AZIMUTH, DEGREE.)

ANNEXATION - An addition to property by the act of joining or uniting one thing to another, as in attaching personal property to real property, thus creating a fixture. For example, a sink becomes a fixture when it is annexed to the plumbing outlet.

ANNUAL CONSTANT - *See* CONSTANT.

ANNUAL DEBT SERVICE - The amount of money on an annual basis required for payment of interest and principal on all security interests on the real property (e.g., mortgages, deeds of trust and real estate contracts), also called debt service coverage.

Many real estate lenders are more concerned with the ratio between net operating income and annual debt service than they are with the loan to value ratio. (*See* AMORTIZATION SCHEDULE, CONSTANT.)

ANNUAL EXCLUSION FOR GIFT TAX - The Economic Recovery Act of 1981 increased the annual gift tax exclusion from $3,000 to $10,000 per donee per year. Thus, a mother could make six $10,000 gifts to six different children in one year (a total of

$60,000), no part of which would be subject to the gift tax. She could repeat the process every year. Her husband could give an additional $10,000 to each of the same donees each per year.

It is possible to make a gift of a fractional interest in real property which does not exceed $10,000 and thereby avoid paying gift tax. (*See* GIFT TAX.)

ANNUAL LOAN CONSTANT - A ratio of the annual debt payment on a loan to the original amount borrowed. The loan constant is also referred to as a *mortgage constant.* (*See* CONSTANT.)

ANNUAL MEETING - A yearly meeting of shareholders of a corporation or members of an association held for the purpose of permitting them to vote on the election of directors and various other matters of corporate or association business. Shareholders who cannot be physically present may vote via proxy.

A condominium association usually has an annual meeting in addition to special meetings throughout the year.

ANNUAL MORTGAGOR STATEMENT - A report by the lender or servicing agent to the mortgagee (borrower) detailing what taxes and interest were paid during the year, and how much principal balance remains on the loan.

ANNUAL PERCENTAGE RATE (APR) - The actual yearly cost of credit stated to the nearest one-eighth of one percent. Any lender subject to the federal *Truth-in-Lending Act* must fully disclose the APR to the borrower. There are tables available from any Federal Reserve bank which may be used to facilitate computing the annual percentage rate. It is permissible to use the abbreviation "APR" when referring to the rate. Use of the annual percentage rate permits a standard expression of credit costs, which facilitates easy comparison of lenders. The APR is usually different from the contract or nominal interest rate of interest and includes the impact on the effective interest rate by discounts points and other finance charges. (*See* TRUTH-IN-LENDING LAWS.)

ANNUAL REPORT - A statement of the financial status and progress of a corporation during its previous fiscal year. It is usually presented to the corporate stockholders prior to the annual stockholders' meeting.

A report which the Secretary of State requires every corporation to file annually with the Office in Olympia showing a current list of officers, directors and the name of the registered agent.

ANNUITY - An annuity transaction is an agreement between an individual (annuitant) who transfers property to another person (obligor) in exchange for the obligor's unconditional promise to pay a designated sum of money at fixed intervals for a specified length of time.

Real property is sometimes traded or exchanged for a private annuity. Private annuity (like between father and son) means the obligor is not in the business of writing annuity contracts. The buyer pays for the property by guaranteeing a monthly income to the seller for the seller's remaining life. The payments are determined by reference to standard annuity tables. Properly structured, a private annuity transaction involving the transfer of appreciated realty to another member of the annuitant's family can produce savings in estate tax, income tax and gift tax.

The proper use of annuity tables, such as the Inwood Table, will provide a factor to be multiplied by the desired yearly income to estimate the present worth of an investment (what amount the investor should pay to acquire the property).

ANTENUPTIAL AGREEMENT - A contract entered into between a man and woman (each person should have his/her own legal counsel) in contemplation of marriage to settle the property rights of both. In Washington, under certain circumstances, the parties to a marriage can provide that their separate property will not become community property by way of an antenuptial agreement. (*See* COMMUNITY PROPERTY.)

ANTICIPATORY BREACH - An anticipatory breach or repudiation of a contract occurs when either party prior to the performance of an obligation or payment of money, declares by words or acts an intention not to perform. At that time, the other party, not being in default, is entitled to enforce the contract in court without first having to offer or tender performance. (*See* TENDER.)

ANTI-FRAUD PROVISION - The provisions in both the federal and state securities laws which make it unlawful for any person, in connection with the offer, sale, or purchase of any security, to directly or indirectly employ any device, scheme or artifice to defraud, to make any untrue statement of a material fact; or to omit to state a material fact necessary in order to make the statements made, in the light of the circumstances under which they are made, not misleading; or to engage in any act, practice, or course of business which operates or would operate as a fraud or deceit upon any person. The federal anti-fraud provisions are covered under Rule 10B-5 of the Securities Exchange Act of 1934, and come into play when there is the requisite minimal contact with interstate commerce in the offer of the security, such as where the United States mail is used. The Washington anti-fraud provisions are found in RCW 21.20, and are similar to the federal provisions. It is important to note that even though the offer of a security may be exempt from the registration requirement under the private offering exemption, the intrastate offering exemption or the Regulation A exemption, the offer is still subject to the anti-fraud provisions. In the event a purchaser of a security is injured by any violation of the anti-fraud provision, he/she can sue for rescission of the contract and recover the amount paid for the security plus interest from the date he/she purchased the security. (*See* INTRASTATE EXEMPTION, PRIVATE OFFERING, REGULATION A, RESCISSION, RULE 10B-5.)

ANTITRUST LAWS - State and federal laws designed to maintain and preserve business competition. The Sherman Anti-trust Act (1890) is the principal federal statute covering competition which is defined by most courts as "that economic condition in which prices are determined by market forces without interference from private concerns and there is reasonable freedom of entry into most businesses." Section I of that Act provides "every contract, combination in the form of trust or otherwise, or conspiracy, in restraint of trade or commerce among the several States, or with foreign nations, is declared to be illegal." For example, price fixing, certain boycotts, certain restraints placed on franchisees by franchisors. The State of Washington has adopted legislation similar to the Federal Act.

At times, certain real estate brokerage activities have come under scrutiny of the Federal Government by the Federal Trade Commission, such as the setting of general commission rates or the exclusion of brokers from membership in local boards/associations or in multiple listing services due to unreasonable membership requirements. As a result of these cases, local real estate associations no longer directly or indirectly influence commission rates or commission splits between cooperating brokers. At least one case indicates clients should be specifically informed that commission rates are negotiable between client and broker.

APARTMENT BUILDING - A building having separate units for permanent tenants who rent or lease them. Common facilities, such as lights, heat, elevator, and garbage disposal services, are provided and common entrance and hallways are maintained by the owner of the apartment house.

APOSTILLE - A certificate issued by an authority appointed for such purpose by a foreign nation which takes the place of diplomatic or consular acknowledgment of a document pursuant to the Hague "Convention Abolishing the Requirement for the Legalization for Foreign Public Documents." (*See* ACKNOWLEDGMENT.)

APPEAL - The legal process of taking a case decision to a higher court seeking a review, reversal and/or retrial of the case. The party making the appeal is called the appellant; the other side is the appellee.

APPOINTMENTS - Furnishings, fixtures, or equipment found in a home, office, or other building. Items which may either enhance or detract from the intrinsic value of the property.

APPORTIONMENT - (1) The division or partition of property into proportionate parts as where tenants in common seek partition of the property. (2) The division into proportionate (though not necessarily equal parts) of the real estate carrying charges and transaction costs between buyer and seller at the closing of a sale. (*See* CARRYING CHARGES, CLOSING, CLOSING COSTS, PRORATE.)

APPRAISAL - The process of formulating, supporting and communicating an opinion of value. An appraisal is usually required when real property is sold, financed, condemned, taxed, insured, or partitioned. Note that an appraisal is an estimate, not a determination, of value. The appraiser does not determine value; parties to the transaction establish value.

An appraisal may be in the form of a lengthy written report, a completed form, a simple letter, or even an oral report.

The three major approaches to estimating market value are:

1. **Market Data Approach**: A comparative analysis of recent sales prices of similar properties, after making necessary adjustment for any differences in the properties. This approach, also called the Direct Sales Comparison or Comparative Market Analysis approach, is used most frequently by real estate brokers in evaluating residences.

2. **Cost Approach**: An estimated value based on the cost of reproduction or replacement value of the improvements, less depreciation, plus the value of the land (land value being usually determined by the market data approach). The cost approach is used primarily to determine the value of service type properties such as churches, post offices and the like.

3. **Income Approach**: An estimated value based on the capitalization of net operating income from a property at an acceptable market rate. Often referred to as the income capitalization approach. It is concerned with the present worth of future benefits of the property, and is used mostly in connection with income producing properties such as apartment buildings.

In most appraisals, the appraiser reconciles (correlates) the information derived from using all three approaches (where applicable) and considers the purpose of the appraisal, the type of property, and the adequacy of the compiled data to determine the relative weight to be given to each approach in reaching his/her conclusion of value. Moreover, these three different appraisal methods serve as checks on each other when all are used for the same property. The cost of the appraisal is usually incurred by the person seeking the appraisal for his/her use.

When an independent appraisal is required, most lending institutions require the services of an appraiser who is an active, designated member of a professional appraisal association, such as a member of the Appraisal Institute, the American Society of Appraisers, the National Association of Master Appraisers or the National Association of Independent Fee Appraisers. (*See* ADJUSTED SALES PRICE, APPRAISAL FOUNDATION, APPRAISAL REPORT, ARM'S LENGTH TRANSACTION, COMPARABLE, CONCESSIONS, CONDEMNATION, CONFORMITY, CONTRIBUTION, COST APPROACH, INCOME APPROACH, MARKET DATA APPROACH.)

APPRAISAL FOUNDATION - In 1987, eight of the nation's major appraisal associations signed articles of incorporation which created a self-regulating organization for the purpose of developing appraisal standards and appraiser qualifications.

APPRAISAL INSTITUTE - An organization that began January 1, 1991. The Appraisal Institute is the result of a merger of the former American Institute of Real Estate Appraisers (AIREA) and the Society of Real Estate Appraisers. The surviving designations are the MAI, Member of the Appraisal Institute and SRA, Senior Residential Appraiser.

APPRAISAL PROCESS - A systematic step-by-step analysis used by a real estate appraiser to accurately reach an opinion of value. While each appraisal assignment varies according to the purpose of the appraisal and the approach(es) used, a well-done estimate of value will follow some standardized procedure. (*See* APPRAISAL, APPRAISAL REPORT, MARKET VALUE, VALUE.)

APPRAISAL REPORT - The appraisal report prepared in accordance with the Uniform Standards of Appraisal Practice contains the definition of value to be applied, the estimate and effective date of the valuation, the appraiser's signature and certifications and limiting conditions, description of the property and rights being appraised, general and specific data, and sufficient justification to support the value estimate, consideration of each of the three approaches; and the reconciliation. It is common for the report to include such supporting documentation as maps, floor plans and photos. (*See* APPRAISAL, APPRAISER.)

APPRAISER - One who estimates the value of real property (land and/or building). One who possesses the necessary qualifications, ability, education and experience to conduct the appraisal of real or personal property. Unlike other individuals involved in a real estate transaction, the appraiser's fee is not based upon the value of the subject property. An appraiser may be employed to determine value for many reasons: sale price, insurance coverage, loan value, development costs and many other purposes. (*See* APPRAISAL.)

Appraisers may be independent contractors or employed by the government lending institutions, or trust companies. Some of the professional designations an appraiser might possess are MAI and SRA. (*See* APPRAISAL INSTITUTE.)

In 1993, Washington adopted the Certified Real Estate Appraiser Act which states that only individuals who meet and maintain minimum standard of competence and conduct may provide certified or licensed appraisal services to the public in Washington. (*See* CERTIFIED REAL ESTATE APPRAISER.)
Reference: RCW 18.140, WAC 308-125.

APPRECIATION - A temporary or permanent increase in the worth or value of property due to economic or related causes; the opposite of depreciation.

APPROACHES TO VALUE - -The various acceptable methods used by appraisers in deriving an estimate of value. There are three traditional approaches to value: (1) cost approach, (2) sales comparison approach, and (3) income approach.

APPROPRIATION - The act of selecting, devoting, or setting apart land for a particular public use or purpose, such as a public park or school; also called dedication. (*See* EMINENT DOMAIN.)

APPURTENANCE - That which belongs to something, but not immemorially; all those rights, privileges and improvements which belong to and pass with the transfer of the property but which are not necessarily a part of the actual property. Appurtenances to real property pass with the real property to which they are appurtenant unless a contrary intention is manifested. A deed normally describes the property granted and then states, "together with all appurtenances." Typical appurtenances are rights-of-way, easements, water rights and any property improvements. The appurtenant may affect other land; for example, an access easement over adjoining land.

APPURTENANT - Belonging to; adjunct; appended or annexed to. For example, the garage is appurtenant to the house; or the common interest in the common elements of a condominium is appurtenant to each apartment. Appurtenant items pass with the land when the property is transferred. (*See* LIMITED COMMON AREA.)

APR - *See* ANNUAL PERCENTAGE RATE.

APR 12 - *See* ADMISSION TO PRACTICE RULE.

ARBITRAGE - The spread or difference between interest rates; common term when considering an all-inclusive or wraparound mortgage financing. For example, Hoyt John sells his parcel to Kimberly Bliss for $10,000 by way of a purchase money mortgage at 9%. Kimberly Bliss then sells the parcel to Kathy Baima under a wraparound mortgage at 9 1/2%. Kimberly Bliss uses the monthly payments to pay her debt to Mr. John and the 0.5% arbitrage is income to Kimberly Bliss. (*See* WRAPAROUND MORTGAGE.)

ARBITRATION - The nonjudicial submission of a controversy to selected third parties for their determination in the manner provided by agreement or by law. Disputes between the listing broker and cooperating broker are often settled by arbitration with both parties agreeing to comply with the final decision of the arbitrator. Members of a multiple listing service often (in some cases must) submit to arbitration all controversies concerning other members, rather than litigate such controversies.

Many disputes involving construction are settled according to detailed rules established by the American Arbitration Association. The prime feature of a binding arbitration is that it is fast and final, which can be good or bad depending on whether you win or lose!

Many lease documents specify a fixed rental for a certain period with subsequent rent renegotiations based on appraisal value. If the parties cannot agree upon the appraisal value, the matter is resolved by a form of arbitration. Normally, the lessor and the lessee each select an appraiser, and those two appraisers agree upon a third appraiser to help them determine the final appraised value.

A less rigid form of settlement is that of combining mediation with arbitration. Under this new approach, an independent third party first attempts to get the parties in dispute to compromise and settle the controversy themselves. In the event that such attempts at conciliation fail, however, the third party is empowered by the parties to make the final decision as in a straight arbitration proceeding.

The Washington Association of Realtors® has established an alternative Dispute Resolution Process which is a voluntary mediation program. (*See* ALTERNATIVE DISPUTE RESOLUTION PROCESS.)

ARCADE - A series of arches on the same plane, either open or closed. A walkway or passageway with an arched roof, frequently with shops along one or both sides. A passageway open on the street side, usually colonnaded. A colonnaded sidewalk.

ARCHITECTURAL DRAWINGS - Data prepared or assembled by an architect that form part of a proposal or part of contract documents. The data may include such things as plot plans, floor plans, elevations, or sections, but usually not mechanical, electrical, structural plans or other specialized data furnished by consultants to the architect. (*See* WORKING DRAWINGS.)

ARCHITECTURE - (1) The science and art of structural design. (2) The style in which a building is designed and built.

AREA - A description of the space enclosed within the boundaries of a parcel of land. Two major assumptions are used in attributing an area to a parcel of land: (1) the area is computed as if the surface were level, and (2) the parcel is assumed to be at sea level. Thus, in a 20% sloping parcel at Sequim, Washington (elevation 209 feet), the land surface in a ten acre parcel actually contains more square feet than the ten acres called for in the legal description. These assumptions are necessary in order to obtain consistent descriptions of land.

The area of a house includes the outside walls to the main flat surface of the exterior brick or wood siding. The total living area often includes stairways, porches, utility rooms, common walls, servants' quarters and garage apartments that are separate units.

ASSOCIATION OF REAL ESTATE LICENSING LAW OFFICIALS (ARELLO) - ARELLO serves as a national clearing house of information and statistical data for its members who consist of both real estate commissioners and real estate administrators. Its members come from all 50 states, 3 Canadian provinces, Guam, Puerto Rico, and the Virgin Islands. A joint committee of ARELLO and the National Association of Realtors drafted several Model License Laws since the early '60s and '70s. Many of the recommendations have been adopted by the State of Washington and many other states.

ARM - An adjustable rate mortgage or deed of trust (*See* ADJUSTABLE RATE LOAN.)

ARM'S LENGTH TRANSACTION - A transaction in which the parties are dealing from equal bargaining positions. Parties are said to deal "at arm's length" when each stands upon the strict letter of his/her rights and conducts the business in a formal manner without trusting the other's fairness or integrity and without being subject to the other's control or dominant influence (as is sometimes the case in transactions between related parties). The absence of an arm's length transaction may give rise to tax consequences when there is a transfer of property at less than fair market value. Whether there existed an arm's length transaction is also relevant to the "willing-buyer, willing-seller" concept in the estimation of market value. The lack of an arm's length transaction will be reflected when it is used as a comparative sale. (*See* APPRAISAL.)

ARRANGER OF CREDIT - Under the federal Truth-in-Lending Law, a person who regularly arranges for the extension of consumer credit by another person if a finance charge will be imposed, if there are to be more than four installments, and if the person extending the credit is not a creditor. The term does not include a real estate broker who arranges seller financing of a dwelling or real property.

ARREARS - The state of being delinquent in paying a debt. Also, in many cases, mortgage interest and real estate taxes are paid in arrears; that is, at or after the end of the period or year for which they are due or levied; the opposite of in advance.

ARTICLES OF INCORPORATION - A formal document which spells out the purposes, powers, capitalization and basic rules of operation for a corporation. It must contain the corporate name (must not be misleading or deceptive), duration (perpetual), a lawful purpose for existing, number of authorized shares and par value (if any), description of classes of stock (if more than one), statement that corporation will not commence business until at least $500 has been paid in for shares, limitation on shareholders preemptive rights (if any), registered office and registered agent, number, names, addresses of initial directors (to serve until first annual meeting), and name(s) and address(es) of incorporator(s).
Reference: RCW 23B.02.020

The corporate name must include as the last word thereof the word "Limited", "Incorporated", "Corporation", or "Company", or the abbreviation "Ltd.", "Inc.", "Corp.", or "Co.". (*See* CORPORATION.)
Reference: RCW 23B.04.010

AS-BUILT DRAWINGS - Architectural drawings showing the precise method of construction and the location for the installation of equipment and utility lines. As-built drawings are usually prepared by an architect with the cooperation of the general contractor to the project.

"AS IS" - Words in a contract intended to signify that no guarantees whatsoever are given regarding the subject property and that it is being purchased exactly as it is found. It is intended to be a disclaimer of warranties or representations. Washington courts favor consumers and tends to prevent sellers from using "as is" wording in a contract to shield themselves from the possible fraud of their not disclosing material defects in the property.

While an "as is" clause may give some protection to the seller from unknown defects, the clause is inoperative when the seller actively conceals or misrepresents the condition of the property. In Washington the broker (agent) for the seller and the seller have the affirmative duty to inform the buyer of any defect.

Sellers can protect themselves by being quite specific in the contract about, for example, recurring plumbing problems, cracked foundation, leaky roof, a den built without a building permit, all in "as is" condition. If, for example, the roof defect was not obvious and the buyer did not know of this material defect but the seller did know, then a general "as is" clause is probably worthless.

In appraisals, "as is" is an indication that the value estimate is made with the property in its current condition, which may not be the highest and best use, or may not include needed repairs.

Since January 1, 1995, almost all sellers of residential property must disclose the condition of the property in writing by completing and giving a prospective buyer a State mandated disclosure form. This disclosure must be provided whether the property is sold using the services of a real estate licensee or when sold directly by the seller to the buyer. (*See* CAVEAT EMPTOR, REAL PROPERTY TRANSFER DISCLOSURE STATEMENT.)
Reference: RCW 64.06

Additionally, it is now standard practice for the buyer of a residence to employ the services of a professional inspection service to perform a detailed inspection of the improvements on the property prior to buying the property. (*See* PHYSICAL AND STRUCTURAL INSPECTION.)

ASBESTOS - A highly fire-resistant material manufactured from naturally occurring minerals and not easily destroyed or degraded by natural processes. Asbestos has been used in a wide variety of household products such as ceilings, wall and pipe coverings, floor tiles, roofing and siding materials. The Environmental Protection Agency reports that, according to studies of workers exposed to asbestos, the fiber has been found to cause lung and stomach cancer. Real estate salespeople must reveal to the prospective buyer the known presence of asbestos on the property. (*See* HAZARDOUS SUBSTANCE OR WASTE.)

ASH DUMP - A container under a fireplace where ashes are temporarily deposited. Ashes can be removed later through a cleanout door.

ASKING PRICE - The listed price of a parcel of real estate; the price at which it is offered to the public by the seller or broker. An asking price differs from a firm price in that it implies some degree of flexibility in negotiation. For this reason, some sellers object to their listing brokers using the phrase "asking price" in their advertisements of the seller's property.

ASSEMBLAGE - The combining of two or more adjoining lots into one large tract. This is usually done to increase the value of the individual lots because a larger building capable of producing a larger net return may be erected on the larger parcel. The resulting added value is called **plottage**.

A developer may make use of option contracts to tie up the right to purchase the desired adjacent parcels. Care must also be taken through exact surveys to avoid the creation of gaps or strips between the acquired parcels through faulty legal descriptions.

ASSESSED VALUATION - The value that the taxing authority (County Assessor) places upon real or personal property for the purpose of taxation. This calculation may not correspond to the market valuation.

In Washington, the County Assessor is authorized to use as a tax basis one hundred percent of the "true and fair value" (market value). The final tax bill is established by multiplying the assessed value times the various tax rates set by various taxing authorities. The final tax bill is determined in October prior to the tax year. In Washington the tax year is on a calendar basis, January 1st through December 31st. The final tax bill becomes a lien against the property on January 1st. A person may pay his/her tax bill after February 15th. If the tax bill is more than $50, a person has the option of paying in two installments, if the first installment is paid by April 30th. If the first half of the property tax is not paid by April 30th, the privilege of paying in two installments no longer exists. Failure to pay the first installment by April 30th makes the entire tax bill due and payable May 1st.

Washington tax law makes special provisions for certain properties being assessed differently. For example, land may be dedicated to **timber use** and assessed at its value in such use; or land may be classified **open space** and assessed at its value in such use. (*See* OPEN SPACE TAXATION LAW, PROPERTY TAXES, REAL ESTATE TAX STATEMENT, TAX RATE.)

ASSESSMENT - (1) The allocation of the proportionate individual share of a common expense, as where the owners of condominium units are assessed for their proportionate share of maintenance expenses for the building. Individual condominium owners are subject to special assessments benefiting the project as a whole and not funded through regular maintenance charges. (*See* CONDOMINIUM ASSOCIATION.)

(2) An official valuation of real property for tax purposes based on appraisals by local government officials; synonymous with assessed value. Sales prices of comparable land are used to estimate land values while building values are based on an amount representing the improvement's replacement cost, less depreciation.

(3) A specific tax imposed for a definite purpose, such as curbs or sewer line in a neighborhood which benefits the land assessed. (*See* SPECIAL ASSESSMENT.)

(4) An official determination of the just compensation to be paid a property owner for the taking of the property for a public purpose (condemnation).

(5) An additional capital contribution of corporate shareholders or members of a partnership or association to cover a capital expenditure.

ASSESSMENT ROLLS - Public records of the assessed values of all lands and buildings within a specific area (a county). Thus, an owner can compare his/her assessed valuation with that of similar properties and appeal if the owner feels the property was overassessed.

ASSESSOR - A public official who appraises property for tax purposes. He/she determines only the assessed value, not the tax rate. (*See* COUNTY ASSESSOR.)

ASSET - Something of value owned by a person; a useful item of property. Assets are either financial, as cash or bonds; tangible or intangible; or physical, as real or personal property. Accountants analyze financial balance sheets made up of assets and liabilities to determine the net worth, which is the difference between the two.

ASSIGNMENT - The transfer of the right, title and interest in property by an individual (the assignor) to another individual (the assignee). In real estate there are assignments of Purchase and Sale Agreements, deeds of trust, mortgages, real estate contracts, leases, etc.

Most contracts consist of rights and duties. Unless personal, duties can normally be delegated or assigned. For example, a listing contract **creating an agency relationship** is personal in nature and the listing broker cannot assign the contract to another broker without the principal's consent. The duty to pay rent is not personal and normally can be assigned unless the rental agreement or lease restricts it.

In any assignment, the assignee becomes **primarily** liable and the assignor remains **secondarily** liable as surety, unless there is a **novation** (substitution of liability) agreement relieving the assignor from liability. The assignee acquires the same title, right and interest in the particular contract which his/her assignor has, but no better title. It is often said that an assignee stands in the shoes of his/her assignor, taking his/her rights and remedies subject to any defenses which the obligator has against the assignor.

An attempted assignment of a mortgage or deed of trust without the promissory note transfers nothing to the assignee; but the assignment of the note without the mortgage or deed of trust gives the assignee the right to the security.

Many real estate contracts in Washington provide that the buyer shall not assign the real estate contract without the prior written approval of the seller. Where the seller wants an anti-assignment clause, the prudent buyer shall require in the Purchase and Sale Agreement that the real estate contract contains language to the effect that the seller's consent shall not be unreasonably withheld. Such a provision means the seller cannot act arbitrarily. An arbitrary act or decision is one that is arrived at through the exercise of will or by caprice, one supported by mere option or discretion and not by a fair or substantial reason. (*See* ESTOPPEL, NOVATION, OPTION, SUBLEASE.)

ASSIGNMENT OF LEASE - The transfer of all title, right, and interest that a lessee possesses in certain real property. The document used to convey a leasehold is called an assignment of lease rather than a deed.

The assignee of a lease is liable on the basis of his/her holding the land, legally known as **privity of estate**. The assignor is liable on the basis of **privity of contract** with the landlord.

If a lease has an assignment clause requiring the consent of the landlord, the landlord may not unreasonably or arbitrarily withhold his/her consent. An assignment of a lease in violation of an anti-assignment restriction is not void, but is voidable at the lessor's discretion. Such an assignment is good between assignor and assignee. The issue that it is invalid on the basis of a lack of lessor's approval can be raised only by the lessor.

A lender may condition the loan for the leased premises on obtaining assignment of leases as collateral security. The assignment may even permit the lessor to collect the rental payments. (*See* ASSIGNMENT.)

ASSIGNMENT OF RENTS - An agreement between a property owner and a mortgagee by which the mortgagee receives, as security, the right to collect rents from the mortgagor's tenants, although the mortgagor continues to have the sole obligation to the tenants under the lease.

ASSOCIATE BROKER - A real estate license classification describing a person who has qualified as a real estate broker but who works for and is supervised by another broker. (*See* LICENSING LAW.)

ASSOCIATE OF ARTS DEGREE IN REAL ESTATE - A two year degree program developed by the Washington State Community College System.

The Degree is designed to provide in-depth instruction in the body of knowledge, attitudes and skills necessary to prepare a student for a career in the real estate industry. Additional courses will prepare the student to assume a management position within the industry. This curriculum is divided into two groups, required courses and elective courses. The required courses are fundamental and essential for a basic, workable knowledge of real estate and management.

If you are interested in the Associate of Arts Degree Program or the real estate courses available in a community college, you should contact the business office of your local community college for details. (*See* CERTIFICATE IN REAL ESTATE.)

ASSOCIATED GENERAL CONTRACTORS OF AMERICA (AGCA) - AGCA serves as a leading representative for the construction industry. Four classifications of construction contractors are represented: buildings, heavy industrial, municipal utility construction and highway.

ASSOCIATION - A group of people gathered together for a business purpose which is treated as a corporation under tax law. The danger of a poorly drafted partnership or limited partnership agreement is that the Internal Revenue Service may attempt to treat the partnership as an association (e.g., corporation) for tax purposes. The IRS uses the following test: If the organization has more corporate than non-corporate characteristics, it will be taxable as an association, with the resulting unfavorable double tax features. The four corporate characteristics used in this test are: (1) continuity of life, (2) centralization of management, (3) limited liability, and (4) transferability of interest. (*See* ARTICLES OF INCORPORATION, CONDOMINIUM ASSOCIATION, UNINCORPORATED ASSOCIATIONS, WASHINGTON ASSOCIATION OF REALTORS.)

ASSOCIATION OF UNIT OWNERS - All of the unit owners of a condominium acting as a group, in accordance with the Declaration and By Laws, for the administration of the project. The association of unit owners must be incorporated. (*See* CONDOMINIUM ASSOCIATION, WASHINGTON STATE HOMEOWNERS ASSOCIATION ACT.)

ASSUMED BUSINESS NAME - Every person(s) who carries on, conducts, or transacts business in Washington under any trade name shall register that trade name with the Department of Licensing. The registration requirements includes sole proprietorship or gen-

eral partnerships; foreign or domestic limited partnership; and foreign or domestic corporation. An individual or corporation may not use any name, not even his/her or its own, which is a distinctive feature of a trade name already in use by another if such use tends to confuse in the public's mind the business of such person with that of the other and the prior user may be entitled to relief regardless of actual fraud or intent to deceit by subsequent appropriator. (*See* FICTITIOUS NAME.)
Reference: RCW 18.85.170, RCW 19.80.010, RCW 23B04.010, RCW 25.10, RCW 25.15.

ASSUMPTION FEE - A service charge levied by a lender to a buyer who takes title to property by assuming an existing mortgage. The charge can be a fixed amount, for example, $250.00 or a percentage of the outstanding balance, for example, one percent. The fee is paid to the lender at the time of the closing of the purchase.

ASSUMPTION OF MORTGAGE - The act of acquiring title to property which has an existing mortgage or deed of trust on it, and agreeing to be personally liable for the terms and conditions of the mortgage, including payments. In effect, the buyer (grantee) becomes the principal guarantor on the mortgage note and is primarily liable for the amount of any deficiency judgment resulting from a default and foreclosure on the property. The original mortgagor (grantor) is still liable as surety on the note if the grantee defaults. The personal liability of the purchaser to pay the mortgage debt is usually created by an assumption clause placed in the deed (or assignment of lease if a leasehold mortgage is involved). Normally a deed need only be signed by the grantor, but where there is an assumption clause, both buyer and seller sign the deed so that the buyer becomes personally bound to the assumption.

Since there is little reason for a lender to relieve the original seller from liability on the assumed note, most lenders prefer to have both the buyer and seller remain liable on the note. In certain cases, however, the lender will relieve the seller from continuing liability; this is accomplished by way of a novation (substitution of liability). If a lender does allow an assumption, the lender charges an assumption fee. Neither VA nor FHA assumptions require the prior approval of the lender or government. The courts have sustained the right of the lender to require payments of an assumption fee and loan interest modification as consideration for its waiver of the acceleration clause. (*See* ACCELERATION CLAUSE, ASSUMPTION FEE, DUE ON SALE CLAUSE, NOVATION, SUBJECT TO MORTGAGE OR DEED OF TRUST, SUBROGATION.)

AT-RISK RULES - Special rules set up by the Internal Revenue Service to restrict leverage opportunity by limiting the taxpayer's deductible losses to the amount he or she has "at risk." A taxpayer is generally considered "at risk" to the extent of cash contributed and amounts borrowed for which he or she is liable for payment from personal assets.

Prior to the 1986 Tax Reform Act, the at-risk rules generally did not apply to real estate activities. The Act extends the at-risk rules to real estate investment losses incurred on property placed in service after December 31, 1986, subject to certain exceptions. The most important exception provides that nonrecourse debt secured by real estate used in the activity is treated as an amount at-risk, so long as the loan is made by a party who is regularly and actively engaged in real estate lending. This is true even if the loan is made by a related party, provided that the terms of the loan are commercially reasonable and substantially the same as could be obtained from an unrelated lender. Except in unusual circumstances, seller-financing of real property of any type will generally not be considered at risk.

After a taxpayer's cumulative total deductions in connection with a property exceed the amount for which the taxpayer is at-risk, the taxpayer can take no further deductions on the property until the amount for which the taxpayer is at-risk is increased. Losses which are disallowed for a taxable year under the at-risk rule are carried forward indefinitely and are allowed as deductions in a succeeding tax year to the extent that the taxpayer increases the amount at-risk in the activity giving rise to the losses.

ATRIUM - Usually the main area of a structure with a ceiling of a translucent material that allows sunlight into the interior quarters.

ATTACHED HOUSING - Residential units that are physically attached but intended and designed for occupancy as individual housing units. The units may be in the form of a duplex, triplex or fourplex as well as row houses which may extend for a complete city block. In contrast, most residential units are in the form of single family *detached* units.

ATTACHMENT - The legal process of seizing the real or personal property of a defendant in a lawsuit, by levy or judicial order, and holding it in the custody of the court as security for satisfaction of the judgment. The lien is thus created by operation of law, not by private agreement. The plaintiff may recover such property in any action upon a contract, express or implied. Real property is attached by recording a copy of the **writ of attachment** (in Washington commonly called a Lis Pendens) in the County Auditor's Office (County Recorder). The attachment thus creates a lien against the property before entry of a judgment so that the plaintiff is assured there will be property left to satisfy the judgment. The lien can be enforced by issuance of execution after a judgment for the plaintiff. An attachment may arise from an action for payment of money upon an unsecured contract. The property may not be sold or encumbered free of the attachment without satisfaction or release of the attachment, or the posting of a cash bond equal to plaintiff's claim plus costs. An attachment is not available where a party brings an action to effect payment of a secured debt (mortgage or deed of trust). (*See* LIS PENDENS.)

ATTESTATION - The act of witnessing another's signing of an instrument, performed by a subscribing witness.

ATTIC - Accessible space located between the top of a ceiling and the underside of a roof. Inaccessible spaces are considered structural cavities.

ATTORNEY-IN-FACT - A competent person who is authorized by another person to act in his/her place. In real estate transactions an attorney-in-fact must be so authorized by way of a written and notarized instrument called a power of attorney, which must be recorded at the Office of the County Auditor (County Recorder) in the County where the real property is located prior to the recordation of the documents signed. An attorney-in-fact has a fiduciary relationship with his/her principal. His/her only qualification is that he/she be a competent and non-interested party. The attorney-in-fact need not be an attorney at law, although people may give a power of attorney to their lawyers.

An attorney-in-fact may have a general or specific power; however, even one with general powers may not act in any way contrary to the principal's interests (for instance, selling the principal's property for inadequate consideration) or act in his/her own interests (for example, conveying the principal's land to himself/herself). The listing broker should think carefully about the possible conflict of interest problems before accepting a power of attorney from the client. If a broker decides to use a power of attorney for his/her principal, it should only occur after the broker's attorney has prepared written instructions detailing exactly the terms and conditions the broker is authorized to act upon.

An attorney-in-fact appointed by a minor is not competent to convey title to real property owned by the minor. (*See* POWER OF ATTORNEY.)

ATTORNEY'S FEES - Moneys an attorney charges for his/her legal services. In Washington unless provided for by statute or in a contract, attorney's fees usually cannot be recovered by an aggrieved party in a lawsuit or binding arbitration. It is therefore important to insert a clause in all contracts (especially promissory notes) to the effect that, in the event of litigation arising from the contract, the prevailing party shall be entitled to reimbursement of all attorney's fees and costs.

ATTORNMENT - The act of a tenant formally agreeing to become the tenant of a successor landlord, as in attorning to a mortgagee who has foreclosed upon the leased premises. Attornment establishes a new tenancy, with the mortgagee being the landlord, and acts as a defense against the defaulting mortgagor's claim for rent.

In a long-term lease situation, an attornment agreement is typically entered into by a sublessee with a fee owner of the land and a mortgagee holding a mortgage on the fee or on the master leasehold estate. The sublessee seeks to protect his/her estate from destruction by reason of the premature termination of the master leasehold or from loss by reason of the foreclosure of the mortgage when the sublessor defaults. The attornment agreement provides that, in the event of termination or foreclosure, the sublease shall continue, just as if the owner or the mortgagee were the lessor in a lease with the sublessee for a term equal to the unexpired term of the sublease, and upon the same terms and provisions. (*See* NONDISTURBANCE.)

ATTRACTIVE NUISANCE - A doctrine of tort law stating that a person who maintains on his/her property a condition which is dangerous and inviting to children (because of their inability to detect the peril) owes a duty to exercise reasonable care to protect children from the danger. Thus an owner who maintains a large unfenced swimming pool, a discarded refrigerator or an unmarked drainage pit may be liable for injuries caused to trespassing children. Building construction sites should be adequately secured to prevent inquisitive children from being injured.

AUCTION - A form of selling land or personal property whereby verbal offers are taken and the property is sold to the highest bidder. Washington State requires auctioneers selling real estate to have an auctioneer's license and a real estate license. Real estate auctions are generally used in tax sales, and with hard-to-sell properties. If the auction is "without reserve," the auctioneer cannot withdraw goods or bid on them personally or through an agent.

In the secondary mortgage market, the Federal National Mortgage Association uses a unique auction-type purchasing procedure termed a Free Market System Auction.

AUTHORIZATION TO SELL - Listing contract whereby an agent is employed by a seller to procure a buyer for the property. (*See* AGENCY, LISTING.)

AUTRE VIE - French for "another life" and used to describe a life estate measured by the life of someone other than the life tenant, as in a life estate "to Alex during the life of Don."

AVULSION - A loss of land due to a sudden or violent action of nature resulting in the washing away of the land. A riparian owner generally does not lose title to the land lost by avulsion, e.g., the boundary lines stay the same no matter how much soil is lost. This differs from erosion where the land is gradually and imperceptibly washed away and the riparian owner loses title to the land washed away and as a result the boundary lines change. (See ACCRETION.)

AXIAL GROWTH - City growth that occurs outward along main transportation routes. This pattern is usually star shaped.

B

BACK-END FEES - Fees or commissions earned by a syndicator, usually the managing general partner, when a property owned by the syndication is sold. These fees are normally subordinate to the investors receiving their original investment back plus a guaranteed or preferred return on their investment.

BACKFILL - The earth or selected material such as aggregate used to fill in around foundation walls after they are completed or to fill other excavated voids or to compact soil.

BACK-TO-BACK LEASE - An agreement made by a landlord as a concession to a prospective tenant, in which the landlord agrees to take over the tenant's existing lease in return for the tenant's agreement to lease space in the landlord's commercial building, office building, or industrial park. (*See* CONCESSIONS.)

BACKUP OFFER - An offer to buy submitted to a seller with the understanding that the seller has already accepted a prior offer. Sometimes the seller accepts the backup offer contingent on the failure of the sales transaction on the part of the first purchaser within a specified period of time. The seller must be careful how he/she proceeds, however, when the time for performance under the first contract has expired. Rather than just immediately treat the contract as terminated and arrange to convey the property to the backup buyer, the seller should make sure that he/she has fully performed, or made a full and adequate tender of such performance, to the first purchaser. Otherwise, the seller may find that he/she is contractually bound to convey the same property to two different buyers. The best practice is to obtain a release from the first purchaser. (*See* RESCISSION, TENDER.)

A real estate agent should be cautious about encouraging his/her client to breach any existing contract and accept a better second offer since the agent might be sued by the first buyer for the tort of intentional interference with a contract.

It is recommended that the principals to the first transaction execute a formal rescission agreement terminating the first transaction before the seller proceeds with the second or backup offer.

BAILMENT - The delivery of personal property from the bailer (owner) to the bailee with the agreement, express or implied, that the property shall be returned or properly accounted for when the special purpose is accomplished, such as leaving a car with a parking attendant. (*See* PLEDGE, SELF STORAGE.)

BALANCE SHEET - An itemized financial statement setting forth personal or corporate assets, liabilities and net worth (difference between the assets and liabilities) as of a specified date. Most lending institutions require a self-employed applicant for real estate financing to submit a balance sheet, usually on a form attached to the loan application.

BALCONY - An unroofed platform enclosed by a railing or parapet, which projects from the wall of a building for the private use of tenants, or for exterior access to the upper floors. When a balcony is roofed, enclosed and has operating windows, it is considered part of the room it serves. (*See* LANAI.)

BALLOON PAYMENT - A payment under an installment note or obligation which is substantially larger than the normal (usually monthly) installment payments, and which often repays the debt in full; the remaining balance which is due at the maturity of a note or obligation. Both fixed and adjustable rate mortgages can have a "call" provision which means that the lender can require a balloon payment or a refinance at the end of a specified number of years. (*See* ADJUSTABLE RATE MORTGAGE (ARM).)

For example, Mr. Shannon sells his condominium unit for $50,000, with a down payment of $10,000, and a balance of $40,000 by way of a real estate contract at 10% interest, payable at $353.60 per month (amortized on a 30-year schedule), with the balance due in full at the end of five years. If the buyer makes the full five years of payments, at the end of that time he will have paid-off only $1764 of principal, leaving a balance of $38,236 to be paid in the final balloon payment. If the buyer elects to payoff the real estate contract in a shorter period of time, the balloon payment will be correspondingly higher. The amount of the balloon payment can be easily determined by use of a loan progress chart. This chart can also be used to determine what portion of a fully amortized loan remains to be paid at any given moment in time. The final balloon payment is sometimes called a "bullet."

A note or obligation which provides for a lump sum payment at the end of the term is sometimes called a partially amortized loan.

When the Federal Truth-in-Lending provisions apply, the amount of a balloon payment must be clearly stated in the contract.

A real estate loan with a balloon payment as the final payment is sometimes referred to as a balloon mortgage.

BAND OF INVESTMENT - An appraisal technique used in evaluating income property to determine the appropriate **cap rate** to apply to the subject property; the sum of the mortgage and equity position of the buyer. The band of investment for a particular property is derived from a synthesis of mortgage and equity rates which market data reveal to be applicable to comparable properties. The appropriate **cap rate** is the sum of the mortgage requirement rate (a constant representing the interest on and recapture of the mortgage component of the total value of the property) and the equity rate (the anticipated cash flow to the equity investment, as indicated by comparable sales). Thus, each portion of a property's interest or ownership is multiplied by the rate of return required to attract money into that type of ownership position.

For example, assume an investor wishes to purchase an apartment house in Tacoma. As his/her representative, you have investigated recent sales of similar types of apartment complexes. You have also found that financing is available for two-thirds of the purchase price, at 9 1/4% interest, for a term of 25 years. The mortgage requirement rate (constant) is 10.18%. The remaining one-third of the purchasing price will be paid by the investor in cash and he/she wants a return on his/her invested money of 11%. The overall cap rate is derived as follows:

	Percent of Value	**Rate**	**Product**
Mortgage	66.67	.1018	6.79
Equity	33.33	.11	3.67
Cap Rate (weighted average)			10.46

(*See* CAP RATE, CONSTANT, INTERNAL RATE OF RETURN.)

BANK INSURANCE FUND (BIF) - The fund operated through the Federal Deposit Insurance Corporation (FDCI) which insures deposits of commercial and savings banks and manages the assets and liabilities of insolvent banks. (*See* FEDERAL DEPOSIT INSURANCE CORPORATION.)

BANK PARTITIONS - Floor-fastened partitions of approximately five to six feet in height.

BANKRUPTCY - A condition of financial insolvency in which a person's liabilities exceed assets and the person is unable to pay current debts. Bankruptcy may be voluntary, as when the debtor petitions the court of his/her own accord, or it may be involuntary, as when three or more creditors force payment of a debt of $1,000 or more, which the debtor cannot pay.

When a person enters into federal bankruptcy proceedings, all assets become vested in a court appointed trustee or receiver who liquidates these assets to pay claims held against the debtor by his/her general creditors. Bankruptcy discharges the debtor from further liability on all debts then owed, except for such exempted debts as tax claims, alimony and support payments, liability for malicious injury and fraud, and debts not listed/scheduled as debt of the debtor.

Once declaring bankruptcy, a person cannot file again for another seven years. Generally, a bankrupt person must wait at least two years before becoming eligible for a new loan from an institutional lender. The fact that a person went bankrupt will usually be reported by most credit agencies for a period of ten years.

A creditor of the bankrupt, whose claim is secured by a mortgage on real property, is normally entitled to the proceeds of the mortgaged property prior to any distribution of the bankrupt's assets to general creditors. As a general rule, the discharge in bankruptcy affects a debtor's personal obligations but it does not destroy voluntary liens against the debtor's property. Fraudulent conveyances, however, are void, and transfer of the insolvent debtor's property to a creditor within prescribed periods (such as 90 days) of filing the bankruptcy petition may be voided by the trustee in bankruptcy, since it enables a preferred creditor to get a greater percentage of the debt over other creditors. One of the fundamental policies of bankruptcy is to insure equality of distribution among creditors.

The bankruptcy of either party to a real estate agency agreement (listing) terminates the agency because title to the property passes to the trustee in bankruptcy.

A broker representing the debtor in the sale of property in a bankruptcy case should note these three points: (1) the broker must be a disinterested person; (2) court approval for the employment of a broker is required; and (3) once the sale is completed, the Bankruptcy Court must approve the commission, not to exceed a reasonable amount.

Many commercial leases and some real estate security agreements (mortgages and deeds of trust) contain default clauses. The leases provide that if the tenant files for bankruptcy, the landlord may terminate the lease. The security agreements provide that the lender may accelerate the debt and foreclosure on the loan if the borrower files for bankruptcy. Under the Federal Bankruptcy Act, however, forfeiture and termination clauses conditioned on insolvency or bankruptcy are now unenforceable and are a nullity.

The bankruptcy of a mortgagor or a grantor to a deed of trust note will affect foreclosure proceedings if the bankruptcy is initiated before the foreclosure proceedings have begun. In such cases, the title to the property passes to the trustee in bankruptcy, and the referee (usually the judge) of the bankruptcy court must authorize the commencement of foreclosure proceedings. The filing of the petition in bankruptcy acts as an automatic stay of the foreclosure. The stay restrains the enforcement of all judgments and all judicial and voluntary liens, as well as all acts to create liens, to collect or enforce claims, or to recover property until the case is discharged or the stay is vacated. The party foreclosing must obtain a release from stay to proceed with the foreclosure. Note that the trustee can seek to void the mortgage on any proper ground such as a lack of consideration.

There are several other types of bankruptcy actions designed to reorganize and save a debtor's business operation. These actions have the debtor's "rehabilitation" as their prime goal. Under the former federal Chapter X proceedings, available to corporations only, the reorganization may be either voluntary or involuntary. It does not affect secured debts, that is, those that are secured by liens (mortgage/deed of trust loans, real estate taxes), although it does suspend any pending foreclosure proceedings. A court-appointed referee is responsible for setting up the reorganization of the operation. The debtor is allowed to retain possession of the property while arranging a plan for payment. Although such proceedings deal only with unsecured property, the court can order a suspension of all actions by a lender and thus prevent foreclosure. There is no trustee, but a receiver will be appointed by the court if the debtor is not permitted to remain in possession.

BARGAIN AND SALE DEED - A deed which recites a consideration and conveys all of the grantor's interest in the property to the grantee. A bargain and sale deed usually does not include warranties as to the title of the property conveyed; however, the grantor asserts by implication that he/she has possession of, a claim to, or interest in, the property conveyed. Trustees, fiduciaries, executors and officers of the court often convey the real property under their control by way of a bargain and sale deed, sometimes with a covenant against the grantor's acts. (*See* COVENANT, QUITCLAIM DEED, SPECIAL WARRANTY DEED, WARRANTY DEED.)

BARGAIN SALE - A sale of property for less than its fair market value. The IRS may treat such a sale as a part gift and part sale transaction. (*See* GIFT TAX.)

BASE LINE AND MERIDIAN - An imaginary set of lines running at right angles, used by surveyors to locate and describe land under the Rectangular Survey Method of property description used in most states, including Washington.

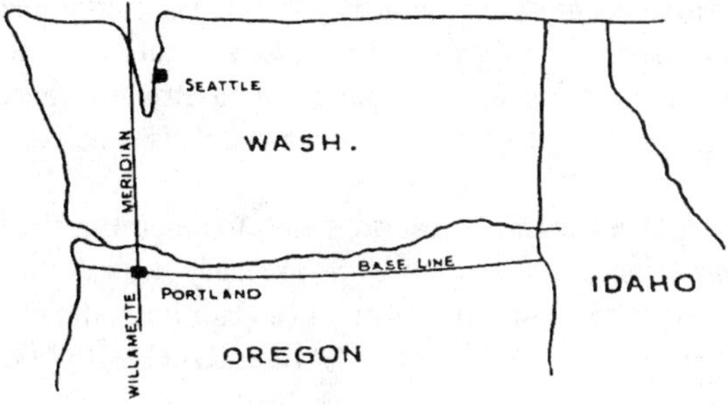

The base line is a line of latitude chosen as a principle line of reference in a government survey which runs east and west. The base line used for the State of Washington runs approximately through Portland. Latitude lines are referred to simply as base lines.

Meridians are imaginary north-south lines which intersect base lines to form a starting point for the measurement of land. The meridian used in Washington is the Willamette Meridian. (*See* DESCRIPTION, LEGAL DESCRIPTION, METES AND BOUNDS.)

BASE PERIOD - A time interval or starting point used for calculating certain business and economic data, frequently found in escalation clauses. The determination of the base year has great significance in commercial leases where it is used to establish the cutoff year preceding rent escalation. The parties usually arrive at a complex formula for determining the base index, from which stems future rent increases to match increases in operating expenses, utilities, services, and property taxes.

For example, if 1996 is used in a lease as the base year, it would be given an index of 100; if costs increased four percent in 1997 in relation to 1996 costs, then the 1997 index would be 104 and lease rents would be raised if so specified in the lease document.

BASE RENT - The minimum rental stipulated under a percentage lease. The first year is called the base year. The second and each succeeding year is called a comparison year. (*See* BASE PERIOD, PERCENTAGE LEASE.)

BASE SHOE - Molding used at the junction of the baseboard and the floor; also called a carpet strip or toe molding.

BASE TOP MOLDING - A thin strip placed on top of the baseboard and parallel to the wall to cover gaps between the wall and the baseboard and give the molding a finished appearance.

BASEBOARD - A board running around the bottom of the wall perpendicular to the floor. A baseboard covers any gap between the floor and the wall, protects the wall from scuffs, and provides a decorative accent.

BASEMENT - A space of full story height below the first floor wholly or partly below the exterior grade, which is not used primarily for living accommodations. Space, partly below grade, which is used primarily for living accommodations or commercial use is not defined by FHA as basement space. The space is a basement if there is six feet or more from the bottom of the joints to the flooring, otherwise, it is considered to be crawl space.

BASING INDEX - A measure of interest rates used to determine the interest rate charged on *adjustable rate mortgages.* Six-month U. S. Treasury Bill rates are one example of an index used to determine the rate on such mortgages. Normally the basing index is beyond the direct control of the lender. (*See* ADJUSTABLE RATE MORTGAGE.)

BASIS - The dollar value which the Internal Revenue Service attributes to an asset for purposes of determining annual depreciation and gain or loss on the sale of the asset. The determination of basis is of fundamental importance in tax aspects of real estate investments. All property has a basis. If property was acquired by purchase, the owner's basis is the cost of the property including all acquisition costs plus the cost of any capital expenditures for improvements to the property during the ownership period, minus any depreciation actually taken or allowable. The basis is also reduced by any untaxed gain "carried over" to the new property in cases where the new property is acquired through a like-kind tax exchange or an involuntary conversion. This new basis is called the property's **adjusted basis**.

If property was acquired by gift, the basis is the donor's basis at the time of the gift plus the gift tax paid by the donor (if any), plus the value of any capital expenditures for improvements made to the property by the donee, reduced by any depreciation allowable or actually taken by the donee. In certain cases in which the transaction is part gift and part sale, the maximum basis is the fair market value of the property on the date of the transfer plus any capital expenditures by the new owner for improvements to the property, minus any depreciation allowable or actually taken by the new owner.

If the property was acquired by inheritance, the heir (or heirs) will have as the basis for determining gain "a stepped-up basis" on the property, that is, the fair market value of the property as of the date of death, plus any capital expenditures made by the heir subsequent to the inheritance, minus any depreciation taken or allowable by the heir.

If the property was acquired in a totally or partially tax-deferred exchange, the basis of the new property received in the exchange is determined by reference to the basis of the old property exchanged. Frequently, however, tax-deferred exchanges become partially taxable because of the receipt of cash or other unlike property in addition to the property of a like kind. If cash or other property is received, the gain on the exchange is taxable to the extent of such cash or other property. Thus, when a gain is partly recognized, the basis of the property received will be the basis of the property exchanged, reduced by other property or cash received and increased by the amount of taxable gain.
Reference: IRC Sec. 1031

Another important consideration is the allocation of basis. If the taxpayer purchases depreciable real estate, he/she must allocate the basis between the land, which is not depreciable, and the improvements, which are depreciable. A taxpayer often uses the same allocation as that determined by the county tax assessor. The taxpayer must also allocate his/her basis between the building and the fixtures and furniture in the building for separate calculation of depreciation, gain or loss.

In the development of a large tract of land, the developer should consider allocating the purchase price among different portions of the tract according to their relative values for the purpose of determining his/her tax basis in each portion. The determination of the cost of portions of land on the basis of the fair market value of each portion has been approved by the Tax Court, as has been the allocation of cost according to front footage, release prices, tentative sales prices, and assessed valuation.

Due to the importance of basis, the various adjustments to it, and the tax consequences arising from the various adjustments, real estate investors should seek competent advice on a real estate investment — a tax accountant, an "enrolled agent", a tax attorney, or a good, experienced commercial-investment broker. (*See* ACCELERATED COST RECOVERY SYSTEM, (ACRS), DEPRECIABLE REAL PROPERTY, MODIFIED ACCELERATED COST RECOVERY SYSTEM (MACRS), RECAPTURE OF DEPRECIATION, STEPPED-UP BASIS.)

BASIS POINT - A unit of measurement. One one-hundredth of one percent. Used to describe the amount of change in the market price of bonds and many debt instruments, including mortgages and deed of trusts. For example, 50 basis points is the difference between a 9 percent and a 9 1/2 percent loan.

BATTEN - Narrow strips of wood or metal used to cover joints either on the interior or the exterior as in "board and batten"; may be used for decorative effect.

BAY - An unfinished area or space between a row of columns and the bearing wall, typically found in industrial and warehouse facilities. Usually, the smallest area into which a building floor can be partitioned.

BAY WINDOW - A window which forms a bay in a room, projects outward from the wall, and is either supported by its own foundation or is cantilevered.

BEACH - Land on the margin of the sea, lake or river. Land lying between the lines of high water and low water; land over which, if a tidal stream or body of water is involved, the tide ebbs and flows.

In Washington when a person talks of a beach, it is necessary to distinguish whether or not the beach joins a body of water over which the tide ebbs and flows (it then should be referred to as tide land) or enjoins a body of water which is not subject to tidal action (it then should be referred to as shore land).

The State of Washington asserted its right to the beds and shore of all navigable bodies of water in the State Constitution of November 11, 1889.

Most tide or shore lands in the State of Washington are in private ownership. It has only been since 1971 that the State has been prohibited from selling any more of its tide or shore land to other than public entities. However, it is still possible to lease either tide or shore lands for a period not to exceed 55 years.

In reality there are very few public beach areas in the State of Washington. The majority of the public beach area that does exist is along the Pacific Ocean.
Reference: RCW 79.01.

In many cases boaters, tourists, and vacationers are committing a technical trespass when they step on the beach or walk in the water in front of somebody's property. (*See* SHORELINE, TIDE LANDS.)

BEAM - A structural member which transversely supports a load.

BEARING WALL - A main or supporting wall referred to as a load-bearing wall, usually supporting a roof above. In a condominium, all bearing walls are common elements. Non-bearing walls, such as certain partitions, are owned by the apartment owner.

BED-AND-BREAKFAST - Usually a portion of a single-family home that is rented on an overnight or short-term basis. Typically in a resort area. In addition to lodging, breakfast is sometimes provided in the owner/operator's home. Local ordinances should be checked to see if such use is permitted.

BEDROCK - The solid rock underlying soils and other surface formations.

BEDROOM COMMUNITY - A section of the community that serves as a residential area for an adjoining or nearby metropolitan area.

BEFORE AND AFTER METHOD - An appraisal method employed in determining just compensation of land which has been partially taken by condemnation. The value of the remaining property is the difference between its value before the partial taking and after. For example, assume a 100 acre parcel is worth $2.00 per square foot before the state condemns the front 50 acres. After the condemnation, the rear 50 acres is valued at $.50 a square foot. Under the before and after method, the amount of compensation due for the remaining property in the condemnation award is the difference between the value of the whole property before the taking and the value of the remainder after the taking — or $1.50 per square foot. Thus the condemnee is entitled to $2.00 per square foot for the 50 acres taken and $1.50 per square foot on the 50 acres remaining. (*See* CONDEMNATION, JUST COMPENSATION, SEVERANCE DAMAGES.)

The before-and-after method is also used in modernization cases; that is, an appraiser may take the value of property before and after remodeling to determine if the value increased more than the modernization costs.

BENCH MARK - A permanent reference mark (PRM) affixed to a permanent object, such as an iron post or brass marker embedded in a sidewalk, used to establish elevations and altitudes above sea level over a surveyed area.

The elevations are based on the official datum and each bench mark has its own recognized official elevation. Thus, a surveyor can start at any bench mark to set his/her elevation measurements. Where there is no datum for an area, surveyors use the base elevations set by the U.S. Geological Survey. (*See* DATUM, GEODETIC SURVEY SYSTEM, MONUMENT.)

BENEFICIARY - (1) One in whose favor a trust operates, or in whose behalf the income from a trust estate or trust deed is drawn. (2) One who receives funds from a life insurance policy. (3) One who lends money on real property and takes back a note and deed of trust as security for the debt as evidenced by a promissory note. (*See* DEED OF TRUST.)

BENEFIT OF BARGAIN RULE - A rule of damages in which a buyer who has been defrauded can recover the difference between the actual value of the property and the value of the property as represented to him/her, as opposed to merely recovering out-of-pocket loss. (*See* DAMAGES.)

BEQUEATH - To leave personal property to another by will as a bequest. Bequest is the noun form. To leave real property by will is to "devise." (*See* DEVISE, LEGACY.)

BETTERMENT - An improvement to real property, such as a sidewalk or road, that substantially increases the property's value; it is a capital expenditure as compared to repairs or replacements. The measure of value is not in the improvement's actual cost, but rather in the enhanced value added to the property. (*See* SPECIAL BENEFIT.)

BIANNUAL - Occurring twice a year; semiannual. For example, real property tax payments may be due biannually, in April and October. (*See* ASSESSMENT, PROPERTY TAXES.)

BID - 1. To offer to purchase for a specific price a parcel of real property at an auction or a judicial sale as in the foreclosure of a mortgage or at a trustee's sale under the power of sale in a deed of trust. (*See* AUCTION.)

A mortgagee under a mortgage and the beneficiary under a deed of trust usually place a bid for the balance of the debt due plus the costs of the foreclosure. (*See* DEED OF TRUST, MORTGAGE.)

2. Formal procedure of submission, by a list of contract bidders, of sealed proposals to perform certain work at a cost specified in the proposal, usually within a set period of time. Intended to ensure the client and contractors with an objective and competitive method of fulfilling job requirements at the lowest cost.

BIENNIAL - Occurring every two years.

BILATERAL CONTRACT - A contract in which each party promises to perform an act in exchange for the other party's promise to perform.

In Washington the standard Purchase and Sale Agreement form is an example of a bilateral contract in which the buyer and seller exchange reciprocal promises to buy and sell the property. If one party refuses to honor his/her promise and the other party is ready to perform his/her part of the agreement, the non-performing party is said to be in default. Neither party is liable to the other until there is first a performance or tender of performance by the non-defaulting party. Thus, where the buyer refuses to pay the purchase price, the seller usually must tender the deed into escrow to show that he/she is ready to perform his/her part of the bargain. In some cases, tender is not necessary.

The listing forms used in Washington are about equally divided between unilateral contracts (a promise for an act) and bilateral contracts (a promise for a promise). Regardless of the form of the contract, Washington's Supreme Court has declared that a listing contract is a bilateral contract under which the broker agrees to use his/her best efforts to locate a ready, willing and able purchaser for the property and the seller promises to pay the broker a commission if the broker produces such a buyer or when the property is sold. Once signed by the broker and seller, the listing contract becomes binding on both.

In a unilateral contract, one party must actually perform (and not just promise to perform) for the contract to be binding. For example, in an option, the optionor (seller) promises to keep a specific offer to sell open for a specific time in exchange for the performance of an act by the optionee (buyer), e.g., the actual payment (not just the promise to pay) of the option money. When the option is exercised, a bilateral contract to buy and sell is created according to the terms set forth in the option. It is recommended that a fully completed Purchase and Sale Agreement with all necessary addendums be signed by all parties and attached to the option. The Purchase and Sale Agreement/exhibit will address many of the details commonly left out of an option. (*See* BUYING YOUR HOME, OPTION, REAL ESTATE PURCHASE AND SALE AGREEMENT, TENDER, UNILATERAL CONTRACT.)

BI-LEVEL HOUSE - A house built on two levels with the entrance being in between both levels. The entryway has a landing with stairs leading to the upper level and another set of stairs leading down to the lower level.

BILL OF SALE - A written agreement by which one person sells, assigns or transfers his/her right to, or interest in, personal property to another. The transfer of the personal property can be effected by mention in the deed or, as is more common, by a separate bill of sale document. A bill of sale may be with or without warranties covering defects or unpaid liens of the property.

A bill of sale is sometimes used by the seller of real estate to evidence the transfer of personal property, such as when the owner of a store sells the building and includes the store equipment and trade fixtures. A bill of sale would be used when the purchaser is an investor and for tax reasons (faster depreciation write-off allowed for personal property) he/she wants a separate accounting for the personal property involved to establish a basis for purposes of depreciation. The broker in a transaction involving personal property should see that there is an accurate inventory taken of the items included in the bill of sale. (*See* BASIS.)

BINDER 1. An expression used in some states to refer to the earnest money or deposit made by a potential purchaser when he/she makes an offer on a piece of real estate. Not commonly used in the State of Washington. (*See* EARNEST MONEY.)

2. A written instrument giving immediate insurance coverage until a regular insurance policy can be issued, usually obtained pending the closing of a real estate transaction.

BIRD DOG - A salesperson whose sole job is to "flush out" new listings. Upon obtaining a lead, the bird dog salesperson turns everything over to his/her broker or to another salesperson better experienced to handle the transaction. (*See* ADMINISTRATIVE ASSISTANT.)

In some states it refers to any person capable of furnishing leads, such as postal carrier, mover, barber or even a newspaper boy. The bird dog usually expects to be paid a finder's fee. In Washington, a bird dog must have an active real estate license to be paid a finder's fee. (*See* LICENSE LAW.)
Reference: RCW 18.85

BI-WEEKLY PAYMENT LOAN - A loan that calls for 26 half-month payments a year, rather than the normal 12 monthly payments a year. Sometimes referred to as a "Canadian Loan" where its use is common. It results in an earlier loan retirement date and therefore, less total interest costs than with a typical fully amortized loan with regular monthly payments.

Many borrowers are reluctant to take out a bi-weekly loan due to the larger total payment required over the year. To obtain the same results there are three other alternatives; for example, take out a standard thirty (30) year loan requiring the normal monthly payment, then arrange with an escrow company to collect your bi-weekly payments and make your normal payments. Some people question the additional expense of the escrow services; however, it does provide the borrower the flexibility of going back to monthly payments. The second alternative is to send in an extra amount against principal every month which over the year would equal an additional monthly payment. A third alternative is in the same month each year to send in two normal payments with one designated "apply solely to principal."

BLACKTOP - Asphalt paving used in streets and driveways.

BLANKET MORTGAGE - A mortgage which is secured by several properties or a number of lots. (*See* ALL-INCLUSIVE DEED OF TRUST.)

A blanket mortgage is often used to finance proposed subdivisions or development projects. The developer normally seeks to have a "partial release" clause inserted in the mortgage or deed of trust so that he/she can obtain a release from the blanket mortgage/deed of trust for each lot, according to a specified release schedule. For example, assume a developer obtains a $500,000 mortgage to cover the development of 50 lots. He/she might be required to pay off $12,500 of principal in order to get each lot released from under the blanket mortgage. Occasionally, the federal government will secure a blanket lien against all properties owned by a person who has defaulted on his/her income taxes.

A blanket mortgage may also be used when one desires to buy a house plus an adjacent vacant lot and finances the purchase with a single mortgage that covers both properties. (*See* PARTIAL RELEASE.)

The same thing may be done with a deed of trust, which is referred to as an all-inclusive deed of trust. (*See* PARTIAL RELEASE.)

Since 1992 it is unlawful for a developer to make a sale of lots or parcels within a development which is subject to a blanket encumbrance which does not contain within it terms or by supplementary agreement, a provision which shall unconditionally provide that the purchaser of a lot or parcel encumbered thereby can obtain the legal title, or other interest contracted for, free and clear of the lien of such blanket encumbrance upon compliance with the terms and conditions of the purchase agreement, unless the developer shall elect and comply with one of the following alternative conditions.

1. The developer shall deposit earnest moneys and all subsequent payments on the obligation in a neutral escrow depository, or real estate trust account regulated under RCW 18.85.310, until such time as all payments on the obligation have been made and clear title is delivered, or any of the following occurs:

    a. A proper release is obtained from such blanket encumbrance;
    b. Either the developer or the purchaser defaults under the sales contract

and there is a forfeiture of the interest of the purchaser or there is a determination as to the disposition of such moneys, as the case may be; or

c. The developer orders a return of such moneys to such purchaser.

2. The title to the development is held in trust under an agreement of trust until the proper release of such blanket encumbrance is obtained.

3. The purchaser shall receive title insurance from a licensed title insurance company against such blanket encumbrance.

Reference: RCW 58.19.180

Under the Washington Condominium Act, a developer cannot sell an individual condominium unit which is subject to blanket encumbrances.
Reference: RCW 64.34

BLENDED RATE - The interest rate of a refinanced loan that is higher than the existing rate of the old loan but lower than the current market rates; it is often used in a wraparound mortgage situation. (*See* WRAPAROUND MORTGAGE.)

BLIGHTED AREA - A declining area, usually in the inner city, in which real property values are seriously affected by detrimental influences, such as encroaching inharmonious property uses or rapidly depreciating buildings with no immediate prospect of improvement. (*See* URBAN RENEWAL.)

BLIND AD - An advertisement that does not include the name and address of the person placing the ad; an ad that lists only a phone number or post office box address. Licensed brokers are prohibited by state license laws from using blind ads. (*See* ADVERTISING.)

BLIND POOL - A securities offering of interest in unspecified and yet to be determined properties. Also called a nonspecified property offering. In a blind pool, an investor usually places his/her money in reliance on the general partner's ability to locate and put together suitable investments. Some states, such as New York, prohibits "blind pool" offerings, i.e., they only permit the offering of securities in existing, selected properties or specific properties proposed for development. Washington permits blind pool offerings which meet certain requirements. (*See* REAL ESTATE SECURITIES.)

BLOCK - *See* LOT, BLOCK, AND SUBDIVISION.

BLOCKBUSTING - An illegal and discriminatory practice whereby one person induces another to enter into a real estate transaction from which the first person may benefit financially, by representing that a change in the neighborhood with respect to race, sex, religion, color or ancestry of the occupants may occur which may result in the lowering of property values or an increase in the crime rate. Such a practice violates both state and federal anti-discrimination laws. Also, called "Panic-Peddling" in some publications. (*See* PANIC PEDDLING.)

The term blockbusting includes subtle as well as obvious forms of racial inducements, so that a representation may be unlawful even if race is not explicitly mentioned. For example, the uninvited solicitations of real estate listings in a racially transitional neighborhood are prohibited representations if it can be shown: (1) the solicitations are made for profit, e.g., to earn a real estate commission, (2) intended to induce the sale of a dwelling, and (3) that the solicitations would convey to a reasonable person, under the circumstances, the idea that members of a particular race are or may be entering the neighborhood. (*See* DISCRIMINATION, FEDERAL FAIR HOUSING LAW.)
Reference: RCW 49.60.223, The 1968 Fair Housing Law - H.R. 25.60, Title 8, WAC 308-124F-020(f)

BLUEBOOK - A real estate reference book containing amortization and balloon payment tables which are extremely useful to the residential salesman. The bluebook is updated each November, and is a valuable source of information published by Professional Publishing Corporation, San Rafael, California.

BLUEPRINT - A working plan used on a construction job by trades people; an architectural drafting or drawing which is transferred to chemically treated paper by exposure to strong light causing the paper to turn blue, thus reproducing the drawing in white.

BLUE SKY LAWS - State securities laws designed to protect the public from fraudulent practices in the promotion and sale of securities, e.g., through limited partnerships, syndications or bonds. Blue Sky laws require that securities be registered with the State Securities Administrator and that the issuer disclose (usually in a prospectus) all pertinent facts about the investment to prospective purchasers.
Reference: RCW 21.20

BOARD - Usually refers to the local organization of the Washington Association of Realtors® and the National Association of Realtors®, e.g., Asotin County Board of Realtors®. There are 33 local board of Realtors® in the State of Washington. Since 1989, most local board have replaced the term board with association. (*See* LOCAL ASSOCIATION or BOARD OF REALTORS®, NATIONAL ASSOCIATION OF REALTORS®, WASHINGTON ASSOCIATION OF REALTORS®.)

May also refer to the Board of Directors of a Homeowners Association or Corporation.

BOARD FOOT - A measure of lumber one foot square by one inch thick; 144 cubic inches = 1' x 1' x 1".

BOARD OF DIRECTORS - The governing body of a corporation which is elected periodically by shareholders and is authorized to carry on the business affairs of the company. There must be at least one director of a corporation, he/she does not have to be a resident of the State of Washington. Unless required in the bylaws, the directors need not be shareholders of the corporation.
Reference: RCW23B.08.020

A director who acts as a broker in negotiating the sale or purchase of corporate property cannot accept a commission for his/her services without express authorization from the board of directors to act as a broker and receive a commission.

A condominium association is administered by a board of directors. Among other duties, the board is charged by law with the duty to see that adequate insurance is obtained if so required by the bylaws, and failure to do so would subject individual directors to personal liability.
Reference: RCW 64.34

Washington has not experienced the incidents of abuses of control of condominium associations' boards of directors by developers as have occurred in some other states. (*See* ARTICLES OF INCORPORATION, ASSOCIATION, CONDOMINIUM ASSOCIATION, CORPORATION.)

BOARD OF EQUALIZATION - A county reviewing Board with the power to adjust certain inequities in tax assessments. Equalization is the adjustment of the assessed valuation of real property in a particular taxing district to achieve a parity with the level of assessment of other property in the districts. (*See* PROPERTY TAX.)

In each county there is "a Board of equalization of the assessment of the property of the county." The Board meets commencing on the first Monday in July each year, primarily to hear taxpayers appeals from assessments determined by the County Assessor. Under the Department of Revenue rules, a taxpayer wishing to protest an assessment must file the protest with the county board by July 15 of each assessment year or, if later, within 30 days after receiving an assessment or change of value notice. In some counties, property tax advisors assist taxpayers in completing the forms and developing the valuation information necessary to present their cases most effectively. The Board also reviews claims for real or personal property tax exemptions, other than the exemption claims administered by the Department of Revenue.

Hearings before the Board are informal. The taxpayer states his/her case first and the assessor or a deputy presents reasons for upholding the assessment. The Boards do not ordinarily announce reasons for their decisions, which may uphold the assessor or reduce the assessment. The Board has no jurisdiction to reduce taxes as such. Where necessary, a board of equalization may be reconvened by the Department of Revenue, even years after the assessment has been made, to correct valuation errors. (*See* BOARD OF TAX

APPEAL.)
Reference: RCW 84.48, WAC 458-14-056, WAC 458-15-120.

BOARD OF TAX APPEAL - A real property owner or a County Assessor dissatisfied with the decision of the County Board of Equalization may appeal to the State Board of Tax Appeal by filing a Notice of Appeal with the County Auditor's office within 30 days after the local Board's decision.

Hearings before the Board of Tax Appeal are informal unless the appellant elects a formal hearing. For the property owner appealing an adverse decision by the County Board, the election of a formal hearing at the State level has one disadvantage: As a result of making such an election, the property owner gives the County Assessor the right to appeal to the Courts if the County Assessor is unhappy with the results. However, the property owner also has a same right of appeal.

A difficult appeal on property tax values is conducted by a Hearing Examiner. The Board issues a written decision usually within 60 to 90 days after the conclusion of the hearing.

If the decision of the Board of Tax Appeals is adverse to the County, the property owner may file a suit for refund of taxes in Superior Court. The refund statue requires that the taxpayer has paid the tax "under written protest, setting forth all of the grounds upon which such tax is claimed to be unlawful or excessive." The refund law suit must be commenced not later than June 30th of the year following the year in which the taxes became payable. (*See* BOARD OF EQUALIZATION.)
Reference: RCW 84.08, WAC 455-08, RCW 84.68

BOILER PLATE - The standard, fixed language in a contract such as is found in most mortgages, deeds of trust, purchase and sale agreements, and leases. Where such language is too one-sided, the contract might be challenged as an adhesion contract. When a preprinted form contract or lease is used, any uncertain or ambiguous terms will be construed against the party who furnished the form. (*See* ADHESION CONTRACT.)

BOILER ROOM - A questionable promotional technique whereby multiple "cold pitch" phone calls are made by land sales companies to the public to create leads for the sale of real estate, usually vacant land or property located in another area or state. These telephone solicitors are required to have real estate licenses. (*See* LICENSE LAWS.)
Reference: RCW 18.85

BOMA - *See* BUILDING OWNERS AND MANAGERS ASSOCIATION INTERNATIONAL.

BONA FIDE - Real, actual, in good faith. A bona fide purchaser (BFP) is one who acquires property in good faith and for a valuable consideration without knowledge, actual or constructive, of the prior rights or equities of third persons. Bona fide purchasers

are protected under the recording statutes against the rights of third parties with a prior unrecorded interest in the same property unless the third party is in possession, which would have provided the bona fide purchaser actual notice. (*See* CONSTRUCTIVE NOTICE, GOOD FAITH, RECORDING.)
Reference: RCW 65.08 and 65.12.195

BOND - An interest-bearing certificate issued by a government as a means of financing real estate projects and community improvements such as schools and parks. General obligation bonds are designated to be repaid out of property taxes. A debt instrument; an obligation to pay; a security issued by a corporation by means of which the corporation borrows money. Such a bond may be secured (mortgage) or unsecured (debenture). (*See* DEBENTURE, PERFORMANCE BOND, PROMISSORY NOTE.)

BONUS CLAUSE - A prepayment clause in an installment contract, deed of trust, mortgage, or note providing for a special payment to be made to the lender in the event of full or partial payment before the scheduled due date. (*See* PREPAYMENT.)

BOOK VALUE - The amount at which an asset is carried on personal, partnership or corporate financial books. Book value is computed as the cost or acquisition price, less depreciation, plus improvements and additions. It is the adjusted basis of an asset, and usually differs from appraised or market value. Book value serves as the basis of computing profits or losses derived from a sale. The book value of a property can be determined at any given time by adding the depreciated value of the improvement to the allocated value of the land. (*See* BASIS.)

BOOT - In a tax deferred exchange, boot is the receipt of an asset other than "like for like" property used to make up the difference in value or equity between exchanged properties. Boot may be in the form of cash, notes, gems, the market value of an asset such as a mortgage, land contract, personal property, good will, a service, or a patent offered in an exchange. The taxable gain in an exchange is recognized immediately to the extent of boot, while other gain from the exchange may be deferred until subsequent transfer.

Where liabilities (mortgages, deeds of trust, etc.) are assumed by both parties to an exchange of property, the amount of the liabilities are netted to determine a net boot. A net liability assumed by one party to the exchange is boot to the other party. This is true whether the party to whom the property is transferred assumes the liability or merely takes the property subject to the liability. (*See* BASIS, DEFERRED OR DELAYED EXCHANGE, EXCHANGE.)

BOUNDARIES - The perimeters or limits of a parcel of land as fixed by legal description which, in Washington, is by one of three methods: government survey, recorded plats or by metes and bounds description.

Boundary disputes are controversies between adjoining owners as to the proper location of the dividing line between the properties. Some abutting owners enter into a boundary agreement in which they stipulate that a certain dividing line, such as a fence, serves as the true boundary of the properties. Such an agreement must be in writing to be enforceable by either party.

To lessen the risk of boundary problems, particularly in a purchase of undeveloped land, the prudent buyer often requires the seller to stake or survey the property. (*See* AGREED BOUNDARIES.)

BRACING - Framing lumber nailed at an angle in order to provide rigidity.

BRACKETING - A selection process used by an appraiser of comparable sales that are higher or lower in value, larger or smaller in square footage or superior or inferior in quality than the subject property being appraised. By the use of comparables, the appraiser is able to position the value estimation of the subject property within a value range.

BRANCH MANAGER - An associate broker who is designated by the principal broker of a real estate brokerage office and licensed with the Real Estate Program of the Department of Licensing as the person directly in charge of and responsible to said principal broker for the real estate operations conducted at a branch office. (*See* BRANCH OFFICE.)
Reference: RCW 18.85.190 and WAC 308-124-021

BRANCH OFFICE - Any secondary place of business apart from the principal or main office from which real estate business, including telephone transactions, is conducted.

Each branch office must have a branch manager, who is responsible for the operations of the branch.

The branch office must be located at a definite place of business which is zoned commercial, and must be more than a post office box, telephone, telephone answering service or car.

So long as a salesman is employed by a broker and works out of a duly established office of the brokerage firm, it is permissible for him/her to make business calls from his/her home and maybe allocate some of his/her expenses for tax purposes. (*See* BRANCH MANAGER, SITE OFFICE.)
Reference: RCW 18.85.190 and WAC 308-124-021

BREACH OF CONTRACT - Violation of any of the terms or conditions of a contract without legal excuse; default, nonperformance, such as failure to make a payment when due. The nonbreaching party to the contract normally has three possible alternative remedies: (1) rescission of the contract; (2) action for money damages; or (3) an action for specific performance. (*See* ANTICIPATORY BREACH, ELECTION OF REMEDIES, RESCISSION, SPECIFIC PERFORMANCE.)

BREAK-EVEN POINT - In residential or commercial property, the figure at which occupancy income is equal to all required expenses and debt service. It is the point at which gross income is equal to fixed costs plus all variable costs incurred in developing that income. Use of the break-even analysis is important to the calculation of the profitability of a building. In new larger commercial projects, the standby financing commitments usually require that the project be leased up to its break-even point before a permanent lender will fund a takeout mortgage.

BRIDGE LOAN/BRIDGE FINANCING - 1. Short-term loan to cover the period between the termination of one loan, such as the interim construction loan, and the beginning of another loan, such as a permanent takeout loan; or the loan between the acquisition of a property and its improvement or development to make it qualify for a permanent loan. It is sometimes used to provide the funds for the costs incurred in the conversion of an apartment house into a condominium. (*See* GAP FINANCING, SWING LOAN.)

2. A residential financing arrangement in which the buyer of a new home borrows money and gives a second mortgage on the buyer's unsold home to fund the acquisition of a new home. This loan is useful where the seller of the new home will not accept an offer "subject to the sale of the buyer's home" or where the buyer needs to raise the down payment by a certain date or else lose the opportunity to purchase the new home.

BRIDGING - Small wood or metal pieces placed diagonally between the floor joists. Bridgings disburse weight on the floor over adjacent joists, thus increasing the floor's load capacity. (*See* FLOOR LOAD.)

BRITISH THERMAL UNIT (BTU) - A unit of measure of heat, used in rating the capacity of air conditioning and heating equipment. A BTU represents the amount of heat required to raise the temperature of one pound of water one degree Fahrenheit at approximately 39.2°F.

BROKER - One who acts as an intermediary between parties to a transaction. A real estate broker is a properly licensed party (individual, or a corporation, partnership, limited liability company or limited liability partnership) who, for a valuable consideration or promise of consideration, serves as a special agent to others to facilitate the sale or lease of real property. A broker who acts as an intermediary for a fee must be licensed by the Real Estate Program of the Department of Licensing. (*See* LICENSING LAW.) The type of brokerage actions requiring a license is the purchase, sale, exchange, rental or negotiation therefor, of real estate or interests including leases and/or options therein, and for business opportunities or interest therein, belonging to others, or sale of any interest therein. If a person holds himself/herself out to the public as being a broker, a license is necessary, even if no services are rendered.

A real estate broker is an independent businessperson who sets the office policies. A broker hires employees and salespeople, determines their compensation, and supervises their activities. The broker is free to accept and establish or reject agency relationships with principals. (*See* REAL ESTATE BROKERAGE RELATIONSHIPS ACT.)

Brokers represent their principals and accept the fiduciary responsibility of exercising care, skill, and integrity in carrying out their instructions. Generally, a broker's duties are confined to advertising property and to finding a person ready, willing, and able to deal on the terms stipulated by and acceptable to the principal. However, legal restrictions are now imposed on brokers by legislative action, and in recent years, federal, state, and local fair housing laws have been passed which place new social obligations on them. Brokers cannot legally refuse, due to race, religion, sex, or national origin, to show, sell, rent, or otherwise negotiate regarding property listed with them. All offers must be submitted by the agent to the principal. (*See* DISCRIMINATION.)

The Real Estate Brokerage Relationship Act which became effective January 1, 1997, specifically authorized what is variously known as "assigned", "split", "limited" or "designated" agency. This is the relationship by which two licensees affiliated with the same broker can represent different parties in a transaction while the broker is authorized to act as a dual agent. This appointment of the broker as the dual agent allows each of the individual licensees to be the full representative of their individual principal, be it the seller or the buyer. (See AGENCY, REAL ESTATE BROKERAGE RELATIONSHIPS ACT.)
Reference: RCW 18.86

To qualify as a broker, a person must have been active full-time for two years as a Washington licensed real estate salesperson, within five years of applying for the Broker's Examination, complete one hundred twenty hours of approved real estate education (must include one course in brokerage management, one course in real estate law, one course in business management and one elective course.), take and pass a State broker's written examination, possess the necessary good character and reputation, pay the appropriate fees and obtain his/her license. All courses must have been approved by the Washington State Real Estate Commission. A person who has a broker's license and is employed by another broker, usually as a salesperson, is called an **associate broker**.

An individual who is actively licensed and in good standing as a broker in another state, or was so licensed within the previous six months, and who meets the other requirements to be a broker in the State of Washington may sit for the Washington State Broker's Examination.

In common usage, many people use the term broker to refer to a real estate company which employs licensed salespeople or associate brokers to represent the office.

A broker is permitted by law to hire others to assist the brokerage in representing its clients. While the broker can be a corporation or a partnership, limited liability company or limited liability partnership, its salespeople must be individuals. Some brokers continue to actively sell, some are sales managers, and others are primarily administrative brokers doing little or no listing and selling.

A licensed broker in Washington cannot recover a commission from his/her principal unless the employment agreement is in writing and the amount of the commission is provided for in the written agreement.. (*See* EXAMINATION, REAL ESTATE LICENSING, INDEPENDENT CONTRACTOR, LICENSING LAW, SALESMAN.)
Reference: RCW 18.85, WAC 308-124

BROKER ASSOCIATE - *See* ASSOCIATE BROKER

BROKERAGE - That aspect of the real estate business which is concerned with bringing together the parties and completing a real estate transaction. Brokerage involves exchanges, options, rentals, trade-ins and management of property, as well as sales.

In most cases, a real estate salesperson will find a ready, willing and able buyer to purchase a property, either on the terms specified by the seller in the listing contract or on new terms acceptable to the seller. For the service, the seller normally pays a commission based on a percentage of the gross sales price. In Washington a buyer may enter into a Buyer's Broker Agreement with a real estate agent and pay a real estate commission on the successful acquisition of the parcel of property or the consummation of a lease or the execution of an option. Any commission is paid directly to the broker (or real estate company) who then divides the commission with the listing or selling salesperson according to a prearranged schedule contained in a contract between the broker and the salesperson. (*See* COMMISSION.)

BROKERAGE COMMISSION - The rate of compensation a broker receives for performing his/her employment contract (a listing or a Buyer's Broker Agreement), or the commission received by a cooperating broker who procures a ready, willing and able buyer for another broker's listing, as through the multiple listing services.

There are no longer any established brokerage commission schedules in Washington. In fact, any attempt by a group of real estate licensees to fix brokerage rates would be a violation of antitrust laws. Custom and usage normally prescribe the acceptable commission rates for the various transactions. In larger transactions, commission rates are determined by negotiation between principal and broker, often on a graduated basis, such as seven percent of the first $100,000 and four percent of the balance. In order for the broker to recover a commission or fee, there must be a written contract for the payment of same. (*See* ANTITRUST LAWS, COMMISSION, MULTIPLE LISTING (MLS).)

BROKER ASSOCIATE - *See* ASSOCIATE BROKER

BROKER-DEALER - One licensed to buy and sell securities. The National Association of Securities Dealers issues a broker-dealer license for general securities or a Direct Participation Program license limited to real estate securities. (*See* REAL PROPERTY SECURITIES REGISTRATION.)

BTU - *See* BRITISH THERMAL UNIT.

BUDGET - A balance sheet or statement of estimated receipts and expenditures. Property managers must be well skilled in the preparation of an accurate budget for operating apartment complexes, office buildings or condominium projects.

Budgets take many different forms. The cash operating budget details the positive and negative cash flows of a property from month to month. It usually does not contain depreciation, bad debt losses, and other noncash items. The capital improvements budget outlines a fiscal program for making capital repairs, replacements, or additions to a property over a stated period of time. A budget is no more reliable than the person who prepares it.

BUDGET MORTGAGE - A mortgage with payments set up to cover more than interest and principal reductions. In addition to monthly amortized principal and interest payments, the monthly payments may include an amount equal to one-twelfth of the year's property taxes, a pro rata share of the fire insurance, and any other payments which, if not paid, could result in a foreclosure on the property. The all-inclusive payment facilitates the payment by the purchaser of such expenses, and protects the mortgagee in the event the purchaser cannot make these payments when they become due in one large lump sum payment. The use of the budget mortgage is especially common in residential mortgages, especially in VA and FHA loans; however, the term is rarely used in Washington.

BUFFER ZONE - A strip of land separating one parcel from another. Sometimes a developer of a large residential subdivision will leave certain land undeveloped as a buffer (often referred to as a green belt) between adjoining land which might be incompatibly zoned, such as an industrial park.

BUILDER'S RISK INSURANCE - Fire, liability and extended coverage insurance written to cover the special risks of a building under construction. Coverage increases automatically as the building progresses and terminates at completion. Such a policy should be replaced by permanent insurance when the building is ready for occupancy.

BUILDING CODES - Rules set up by local, state or municipal governments to regulate building and construction standards. Building codes are designed to provide minimum standards to safeguard the health, safety and welfare of the public by regulating and controlling the design, construction, quality, use and occupancy, location and maintenance of all buildings and structures. The establishment of building codes is a valid exercise of the state's police power and is thus a valid restriction on an owner's use of his/her property. The codes are divided into specialized areas such as plumbing code, electrical code, fire code, etc., and are enforced by way of issuance of building permits, certificates of occupancy and inspections. Fines can be imposed on violators. In Washington, the establishment and enforcement of building codes is the responsibility of the City Council for an incorporated city and the County Council for all others. (*See* BUILDING PERMIT.)

BUILDING HEIGHT - - The total height of a building measured from the ground floor to the top of the outer surface of the roof. Usually, local zoning ordinances regulate the maximum height of a building, sometimes restricting or reducing heights based on the proximity of a structure to setback lines.

BUILDING LIEN - - A claim or lien on a property for unpaid work performed or materials provided. (See MECHANIC'S LIEN.)

BUILDING LINE - A setback line, a line beyond which one may not build any improvements on a parcel of real estate, e.g., with five feet of the sides or thirty feet from the front or twenty feet from the back. Building line restrictions may be created by designating them on a recorded subdivision plat, by inserting a restriction in the deed, or by local ordinance. The main purposes for establishing building lines are to insure a degree of uniformity in the appearance of buildings and to create a right to unobstructed light, air and view. If building line restrictions are contained in more than one of the above, the most restrictive will prevail.

BUILDING OWNERS AND MANAGERS ASSOCIATION (BOMA) - A national organization of over 4,000 professionals in the high-rise/office building industry, with over 80 local BOMA associations.

The Building Owners and Managers Institute (BOMI) is the related educational institute which provides professional training in all aspects of building management and operations via individual-study courses, which lead to professional certification as a Real Property Administrator (RPA). The seven required courses are Engineering and Building Structures, Real Property Maintenance, Risk Management and Insurance, Accounting and Financial Concepts, Law, Finance, and Management Concepts.

BUILDING PAPER - Fiber-reinforced, waterproof paper treated with bitumen, a natural asphalt from coal, petroleum, or with some other water-resistant compound. Building paper is placed between siding and wall sheathing, around door and window frames, and in other areas to insulate the house and keep out moisture.

BUILDING PERMIT - A written permission granted by a City or County Building Department and required prior to beginning the construction of a new building or other improvement (including fences, fence walls, retaining walls and swimming pools) or the demolition or substantial repair of existing structures or the installation of factory-built housing. The proposed construction must conform to local zoning and the published Uniform Building Code and must be inspected and approved upon completion. If an improvement was made without a proper permit, of if it fails to conform to applicable building codes, the Building Department can order its removal. (*See* BUILDING CODES.)

Any owner contemplating an addition and/or change to his/her property should first check with the appropriate county or municipal building department to avoid any violations. The existence of building code violations may render a seller's title unmarketable. Failure to disclose such violations would appear to constitute a material misrepresentation, entitling the buyer to rescind the transaction and obtain the return of his/her money. (*See* CERTIFICATE OF OCCUPANCY, ZONING.)

BUILDING RESIDUAL TECHNIQUE - An appraisal term for a method of determining the contribution of an improvement to the present value of the entire property, normally used in appraising income property.

When the value of land is known, the appraiser deducts from the net income the amount of net income which must be attributed to the land to justify its value produced by the property. For example, if the land value is $10,000 and the going rate of interest is ten percent then the land itself must return ten percent of its value or $1,000.00 per year, if it is to justify its purchase price. The balance or residue of the net income represents that part attributable to or earned by the building, which is then capitalized in order to arrive at the indicated value of the building. Land value is added to arrive at the value of the property as a whole. (*See* INCOME APPROACH, RESIDUAL PROCESS.)

BUILDING RESTRICTIONS - Limitations on the size or types of improvements established by zoning codes or by private restrictions inserted in a deed or ground lease. Violations of building restrictions may render the title unmarketable. (*See* MARKETABLE TITLE, RESTRICTIONS.)

BUILDING STANDARDS - The specific elements of construction which the owner/developer chooses to use throughout a building. The building standard offered an office tenant, for example, would relate to the type of partitions, doors, ceiling tile, light fixtures, carpet, draperies, and the like.

BUILD-TO-SUIT - An understanding or contract in which a developer/lessor agrees to develop a property or finish certain space to the specifications of a lessee in return for a lease commitment on the part of the prospective tenant. The cost of work done, or a portion thereof, is usually amortized in the form of additional rental payments. Possession is given upon completion.

BUILT-INS - Certain stationary equipment, such as some kitchen appliances, bookcases, cabinets, and furniture, permanently affixed to real property and understood to be included when the property is sold. A built-in may also refer to a garage that is under the same roof as the main building it serves. (*See* FIXTURE.)

BUILT-UP METHOD - An appraisal term meaning a method of determining the discount, or interest rate used in selection of the appropriate capitalization rate. The four basic components of the discount rate are the safe rate, burden of management, non-liquidity, and risk for the specific type of property being appraised. Sometimes referred to as the summation method of rate selection. (*See* CAP RATE, DISCOUNT RATE.)

BUMPER - A device of wood, rubber, or other material used around a loading dock to cushion the impact of delivery trucks.

BUNDLE OF RIGHTS - An ownership concept describing all the legal rights that attach to the ownership of real property, including the right to sell, lease, encumber, use, enjoy, exclude, and will. These rights also include the rights of use, occupancy, cultivation, exploration, the right to license, devise, dedicate, give away, share, mortgage, and trade or exchange. When purchasing real estate, one actually buys the rights previously held by the seller (except those which are reserved or limited in the sale). These rights are called beneficial interests associated with real property interests.

BUNGALOW - A small, one or one-and-one-half-story house.

BURDEN OF PROOF - The obligation to prove the truth or falsity of a fact, either in a trial or an administrative hearing.

BUREAU OF LAND MANAGEMENT (BLM) - A bureau in the U.S. Department of Interior with responsibility to manage and administer federal lands not included under the National Forest or National Park Systems.

BUS DUCT - Electrical conductors which group together multiple circuits used to provide service along a given line in an industrial plant.

BUSINESS AND OCCUPATION (B&O) TAX - A state tax on receipts from sales and other business activities in Washington, which is levied on the person receiving income for the privilege of doing business in Washington. The Business and Occupation Tax applies to all gross receipts derived from sales or services in a trade or business. "Business" is very broadly defined: it covers interest income received in connection with a business, such as interest on real estate contracts, gross rental receipts, brokerage income, and includes all activities engaged in for economic benefit, but not casual sales. A casual sale is a sale of an asset which is not normal in conducting the business, e.g., a real estate brokerage company sells it's used office photo copier.

Anyone subject to the Business and Occupation Tax is required to register with and receive a tax number from the Department of Revenue which collects the tax. Each businessman is required to assess and report his/her own tax according to instructions. The measure of the tax (the value on which it is based), and the rate of the tax (the percentage of the value collected as a tax), vary from one kind of business to another. Schedules of rates for different businesses are available from the Tax Commission. Real estate brokers should be aware of the regulations on their own business and for clients engaged in renting or leasing real property.

Many cities and municipalities in Washington levy Business and Occupation Tax on business activities conducted within their environment. An individual wishing to engage in business activities should contact the local municipal government to determine whether or not it must be paid.
Reference: RCW 82.04.

BUSINESS BROKERAGE - *See* BUSINESS OPPORTUNITIES.

BUSINESS DAY - A day of the week, except Saturdays, Sundays, and holidays; a normal working day. Because of accepted custom and practice, business day is preferable to the use of banking day or working day A possible dispute can arise if a contract fails to state whether the notice be business days or calendar days, although the usual interpretation is that it is calendar days unless specified otherwise. (*See* DATE, HOLIDAYS.)

Some laws require action within so many business days while other laws make reference to calendar days, e.g., under the license law a real estate broker must deposit all funds received for clients the first business day occurring after the receipt of the funds. The Landlord Tenant Act provides that a landlord must give a tenant thirty (30) days written notice when he/she changes any of the rules contained in a rental agreement, assuming it is a provision which the landlord has the right to change during the term of the lease. (*See* HOLIDAYS, LANDLORD TENANT ACT.)

BUSINESS INTERRUPTION INSURANCE - Insurance that covers losses incurred as a result of being unable to conduct business during the repair of the business quarters following a fire or other insured hazards.

BUSINESS LIFE INSURANCE - Life insurance purchased by a business enterprise on the life of a member of the firm. It is often bought by partnerships to protect the surviving partners against loss caused by the death of a partner, or by a corporation to reimburse it for loss caused by the death of a key employee. The insurance proceeds can be designated to fund business activities, hire replacement talent or purchase the decease's interest from his/her estate or a combination of the preceding. It is often referred to as **key man insurance**.

BUSINESS OPPORTUNITIES - Any type of business which is for sale; also called business chance brokerage, or simply business brokerage. These terms are being replaced by the term **business brokerage**, which is probably more accurate. The sale or lease of the business and goodwill of an existing business, enterprise, or opportunity. It includes a sale of all or substantially all of the assets or stock of a corporation, or assets of a partnership or sole proprietorship.

Since 1951, the Real Estate License Law in the State of Washington has included within its coverage the sales of business and business opportunities. The law defines business opportunity as "business, business opportunity and good will of an existing business or any one or combination thereof." Therefore, a real estate salesman's or real estate broker's license entitles its holder to engage in the sale of business opportunities, whether or not real estate is included in the transaction. (*See* GOING CONCERN VALUE, GOODWILL.)

The small number of real estate licensees who have specialized in business brokerage are engaged in the sales of such enterprises as drug stores, grocery stores, service stations, taverns, hotels, motels, hardware stores and the like. Generally, a broker may not be aware of many of the special problems involved in selling a business; therefore, the advice of an experienced business counselor or attorney may be appropriate. (*See* LICENSING LAW.) Only a salesperson experienced in business brokerage should draft a Purchase and Sale Agreement when selling a business due to the fact that there are many provisions in such an agreement which do not normally appear in a Purchase and Sale Agreement. (*See* REAL ESTATE PURCHASE AND SALE AGREEMENT.)
Reference: RCW 18.85

BUSINESS PARK - A development or subdivision designed for office-warehouse or similar use. Also known as an office park, it is an outgrowth of industrial parks.

BUY DOWN LOAN - A financing technique whereby the seller, or perhaps the builder or the buyer of a property, usually a single family residence, pays a lump sum of money at closing or over a period of time to the lender of the permanent financing on the property and thereby reduces the interest rate on the loan for a period of time, usually one to three years. At the end of the pre-set period, the interest rate will increase to the current market interest rate or a pre-set interest rate.

BUYER'S BROKER - A term used to describe a real estate licensee who represents a buyer or a tenant in an agency relationship in a real estate transaction. The Real Estate Brokerage Relationships Act which became effective January 1, 1997, states there is a presumption that the licensee who works with a buyer or tenant represents the buyer or tenant as the Buyer's Agent. The statute provides that unless additional duties are agreed to in writing by the parties that the licensee only owes limited duties specified in the law. A buyer should carefully review the provisions of the Act so he/she understands the limitation on the services to be rendered. (*See* AGENCY, DUAL AGENT, REAL ESTATE BROKERAGE RELATIONSHIPS ACT.)
Reference: RCW 18.86

BUYERS MARKET - An economic situation in which the supply of properties available for sale exceeds the demand. As a result, sellers are often forced to lower their prices and sometimes assist in the financing (with purchase-money mortgages) in order to attract buyers. A decline in prices resulting from an oversupply. (*See* SOFT MARKET.)

BUY-SELL AGREEMENT - 1. An agreement among partners or shareholders to the effect that one party will sell and the other party will buy the other's business interest at a stated price upon the occurrence of a stated event. This form of buy-sell agreement is popularly used in closely held corporations and partnerships to cover the possibility of death or disability of a key participant, or a personal disagreement. Life insurance is commonly used to assure that funds will be available to effect the buy out in case of death. (*See* BUSINESS LIFE INSURANCE.)

2. An agreement entered into by an interim and a permanent lender for the sale and assignment of a mortgage to the permanent lender when a building has been completed. Often the mortgagor is a party to this agreement on the theory that the mortgagor would have a contractual right to insist that the permanent lender buy the mortgage.

BUYING YOUR HOME — A brochure published by HUD, which lenders and mortgage brokers are required by federal law, the Real Estate Procedure Act (RESPA), to give to all prospective borrowers who are seeking a real estate, a HUD publication entitled "Buying your Home."

If you have the time, it is recommended you get a copy of the booklet prior to starting to look for a house and read it with great care, several times. It will help you to understand the home buying process.

The main features of the booklet are:

I. Introduction

II. Buying and Financing a Home

- A. Role of the Real Estate Agent
- B. Selection of an Attorney
- C. Terms of the Agreement of Sale
    - Sales Price
    - Title
    - Mortgage Clause
    - Pests
    - Home Inspection
    - Lead-Based Paint Hazards in Housing Built Before 1978
    - Other Environmental Concerns
    - Sharing of Expenses
    - Settlement Agent/Escrow Agent
    - Settlement Costs
- D. Shopping for a Loan
    - Mortgage Brokers

- Government Programs
- CLOs (Computer Loan Origination System)
- Types of Loans
- Interest Rate, "Points" & other Fees
- Lender-Required Settlement Costs
- Comparing Loan Costs
- Lock-ins
- Tax and Insurance Payments
- Transfer of Your Loan
- Mortgage Insurance
- Flood Hazard Areas

E. Selecting a Settlement Agent

F. Securing Title Services
- Owner's Policy
- Choice of Title Insurer
- Review of Initial Title Report
- Coverage & Cost Savings
- Survey

G. RESPA Disclosure
- Good Faith Estimate of Settlement Costs
- Servicing Disclosure Statement
- Affiliated Business Arrangements
- HUD-1 Settlement Statement
- Escrow Account Operation & Disclosures

H. Processing Your Loan Application
- No Discrimination
- Prompt Action/Notification of Action Taken
- Statement of Reasons for Denial
- Obtaining your Credit Report
- Obtaining Your Appraisal

I. RESPA Protection Against Illegal Referral Fees
- Prohibited Fees
- Permitted Payments
- Penalties

J. Your Right to File Complaints
- Private Law Suits
- Government Agencies
- Servicing Errors

III. Your Settlements Costs

A. Specific Settlement Costs
- Sales/Broker's Commission
- Items Payable in Connection with Loan
- Items Required by Lender to be Paid in Advance

- Escrow Account deposits
- Title Charges
- Government Recording and Transfer Charges
- Additional Settlement Charges
- Total Settlement Charges
- Paid Outside of Closing ("POC")

B. Calculating the Amount you Need at Settlement

C. Adjustments to Costs Shared by Buyer and Seller

BYLAWS - Regulations, rules, or laws adopted by an association or corporation for its management and operation.

As it relates to condominiums, the regulations, rules, or laws adopted by a condominium owners' association or corporation for the condominium's management and operation. In the event of a conflict between the provisions of the Declaration and the bylaws, the declaration prevails except to the extent the Declaration is inconsistent with the Condominium Act. (*See* CONDOMINIUM.)
Reference: RCW 64.34.208

RCW 64.32 details the procedure for adoption of Bylaws and Amendments for a condominium association. Such bylaws normally set forth the manner of selection of the board of directors of the association of owners to which every owner automatically becomes a member. They also state the association's duties, obligations and the requirements for calling meetings which govern the activities of the project.
Reference: RCW 64.32

These self-imposed rules are a form of private law. While a corporate resolution applies to a single act of the corporation, a bylaw is a continuing rule to be applied on all future occasions. Condominium bylaws are initially established by the developer and then are subject to change when the owner's association takes over. The bylaws may be amended, usually by a vote of 60 to 75 percent of the owners. (*See* CORPORATE RESOLUTION.)

CAI — *See* Community Association Institute.

CALL — A reference to a course, distance or monument when a boundary is being run or described in the surveying or platting of a parcel of land. (*See* SURVEY.)

CALL PROVISION — A provision in a mortgage or deed of trust, giving the mortgagee or beneficiary the right to accelerate payment of the debt in full on a certain date or on the happening of a specified condition or conditions. (*See* DUE ON SALE CLAUSE, ACCELERATION CLAUSE.)

CAMPING CLUBS — In 1988, the camping club act was significantly modified to provide greater protection to purchasers of memberships in camping clubs.

The application to the Department of Licensing to sell camping resort contracts must include information assuring the Department that all required governmental permits have been obtained. The application must also include an affidavit of the operator's rights to withdraw, replace, or change the camping resort properties.

After March 21, 1988, any new campground, or campground on which underlying financial obligations are refinanced, must contain protections for purchasers of contracts. The protections must include a non-disturbance agreement. For campgrounds in existence prior to the effective date of the act, the operator must provide financial or other assurances that the campground will remain in operation.

The operator of a camping resort must provide a membership list, when requested, to a purchaser of a camping resort contract.

Prior to offering any promotional prizes or gifts in conjunction with an offering of camping resort contracts, the person making the offering must provide security with the department that the prizes or gifts will be fulfilled.
Reference: RCW 19.105

An individual licensed under the licensing law as a real estate salesperson is exempt from the Act.
Reference: RCW 19.105.345

An entity which is registered under the Washington State Timeshare Act is exempt from the Act.
Reference: RCW 64.36.290

CANCELLATION CLAUSE — A clause that may be included in a commercial or industrial lease granting the lessor or the lessee, the right to terminate the lease term upon the happening of certain stated events or occurrences by the payment from one party to the other of definite amounts of money as consideration. Such consideration usually tends to cover expenses or damages of the party whose rights are being canceled, such as unamortized costs of special improvements, brokerage fees, and possible loss of rental before the property is rerented.

If the tenant cancels, the consideration fee paid to the landlord, plus any unamortized cost of improvements, is a deductible income tax expense in the year of cancellation.

If the landlord cancels, the cancellation fee paid to the tenant is a capital expenditure of the landlord which is amortized over the remaining term of the canceled lease. The cancellation payment to the tenant is akin to a sale and, if the lease is of land which is nondepreciable property, it is a capital asset and the tenant is to report the cancellation fee as a taxable gain in the year of receipt. (*See* LEASE.)

Also, a provision in a residential lease whereby the landlord can cancel the lease upon the sale of the fee simple property; otherwise, the new owner would have to take title subject to the lease.

Prior to accepting a "backup offer," the seller should insert a clause to the effect that acceptance is subject to written cancellation of the prior accepted contract. (*See* BACKUP OFFER.)

CANTILEVER — A projecting beam or overhanging portion of a structure supported at one end only.

CAP — A ceiling or limit on the adjustments made in the payments, interest rate, or balance of an adjustable mortgage loan. (*See* ADJUSTABLE RATE MORTGAGE.)

CAP RATE — *See* CAPITALIZATION RATE.

CAPABLE — Qualified or fit to undertake something. As used in real estate finance, the term is used by lenders in reference to the three "C's" of credit: capacity, capable and competent.

CAPACITY OF PARTIES — The legal ability of a person or organization to enter into a valid contract. A person entering into a contract will fall into one of the following categories:

1. **Full Capacity to Contract** — The unlimited ability of a person to enter a contract which is legally binding upon himself. Most adults (18 years of age) including those who are illiterate, have full capacity to contract and are said to be competent parties. (*See* CONTRACT.)

2. **Limited Capacity to Contract** — The ability of a person to enter into a contract which is legally binding upon himself **only** under certain circumstances. Minors have limited ability to contract, meaning that the contract of a minor is valid only if the minor does not disaffirm such contract during his/her minority or shortly after reaching majority. Contracts made by minors to obtain such necessities as food, clothing and shelter; however, are not voidable by the minor, and will be enforced against him/her. (*See* MINOR.)

3. **No Capacity to Contract** — The lack of ability, under any circumstances, to enter into a valid contract, such as persons who have been adjudicated insane, or officers of a corporation who are not authorized to execute a contract in behalf of the corporation (referred to as **ultra vires**). (*See* CORPORATE RESOLUTION.)

CAPITAL — The money and/or property comprising the wealth owned or used by a person or business enterprise; the accumulated wealth of a person or business.

CAPITAL ASSETS — All property **except** that which is held by a taxpayer primarily for sale to customers in the ordinary course of his/her trade or business. Capital assets include such property as the taxpayer's personal residence, land held for investment, stocks, securities, and machinery and equipment used in business.

CAPITAL EXPENDITURE — The cost of a capital improvement. An improvement which has been made to extend the useful life of a property, or to add to the value of the property, such as a new roof, paved driveway or extensive remodeling or landscaping. In depreciable property, a capital expenditure must be amortized over the remaining useful life of the property or portion of the property to which the improvement belongs; that is, the expense is not currently tax deductible as are repairs which are a recurring type of expenditures. (*See* BASIS, CAPITAL IMPROVEMENT, REPAIRS.)

CAPITAL GAIN — The taxable profit derived from the sale or exchange of a capital asset. The capital gain is the difference between the sales price and the basis of the property. (*See* BASIS.)

Under the Taxpayer Relief Act of 1997 after May 6, 1997, the capital gain rate is 20% for taxpayers whose regular top bracket is 28%, 31%, 36% or 39.6%. The capital gain rate is

10% for taxpayers in the 15% bracket. These rates apply to sales after July 28, 1997, if the property was held more than 18 months.

The holding period starts the day after the date of acquisition, which is the earlier of: (1) the date title passes to you; and (2) the date you take possession and you assume the burdens and privileges of ownership. In disputes involving the starting and closing dates of a holding period, you may refer to Washington State law that applies to your sale or purchase agreement. State law determines when title to property passes.

If you convert a residence to rental property and later sell the house, the holding period includes the time you held the house for personal purposes.

The capital gain rules apply in 1998 and later years, with one further change scheduled for assets purchased after December 31, 2000. If property purchased after 2000 is held for more than five years, the capital gain tax rate will be further reduced to 18%, 8% for those in the 15% bracket.

The law did not change the deductibility of capital losses (*See* CAPITAL LOSSES.)

CAPITAL IMPROVEMENT — Any structure erected as a permanent improvement to real property; any improvement which is made to extend the useful life of a property, or to add to the value of the property. Major repairs, such as the replacement of a roof, are considered to be capital improvements. (*See* BETTERMENT, CAPITAL EXPENDITURE.)

CAPITAL LOSS — A loss derived from the sale of a capital asset. Capital losses are fully deductible against capital gains and if losses exceed gain, the taxpayer may deduct the excess from up to $3,000 of other income. Net losses over $3,000 are carried over to future years. The $3,000 limit is reduced to $1,500 for married persons filing separately. The remainder carries forward to future tax years. (*See* BASIS.)

CAPITALIZATION — A mathematical process for converting net income into an indication of value, commonly used in the income approach to value; the net income of the property is divided by an appropriate (capitalization) rate of return to give the indicated value. (*See* APPRAISAL.)

CAPITALIZATION RATE — The percentage selected for use in the income approach to valuation of improved property. Often called a cap rate. The cap rate is designed to reflect the recapture of the original investment over the economic life of the improvement to give the investor an acceptable rate of return (yield) on his/her original investment and to provide for the return on borrowed capital. In other words, if the property includes a depreciating building, the cap rate provides for the return of invested capital in the building by the end of the economic life (the recapture rate which allows for the building's future depreciation) and the return on the investment in the land and the building.

The selection of an appropriate cap rate is influenced by the conditions under which the particular investment is being operated, as well as the availability of funds, prevailing interest rates, risk, and so on. If the property earns $100,000 per year and the cap rate is 9 percent, then, in determining what the property is worth to the investor, the investor would compute it as follows: $100,000 ÷ .09 = $1,111,111. Only an experienced appraiser can select the appropriate cap rate — a mere 1 percent difference in the suggested capitalization rate could make a 12 1/2 percent difference in the value estimate.

The capitalization rate measures the risk involved in an investment. Thus, the higher the risk (a restaurant) the higher the cap rate; the lower the risk (a post office) the lower the cap rate. (*See* APPRAISAL, BAND OF INVESTMENT, INCOME APPROACH, INTERNAL RATE OF RETURN.)

CAPITALIZE — 1. To provide cash, to fund..

2. An accounting procedure whereby a company records an expenditure as a capital asset on its books, instead of charging it to expenses for the year. This is normally done with capital expenditures, such as the cost of a new roof. (*See* CAPITAL EXPENDITURE, CAPITAL IMPROVEMENT.)

CAPITALIZED-INCOME APPROACH — *See* INCOME APPROACH.

CARPORT — A roofed space having at least one side open to the weather. A carport is often made by extending the house roof to one side, and is primarily designed or used for motor vehicles. This term is usually related to small one- and two-family dwellings. In multifamily properties, a garage may have one or more sides open to the weather and is usually referred to as "covered parking.".

CARRY-BACK FINANCING — Usually refers to the seller taking back a promissory note for part of the purchase price secured by a junior mortgage or deed of trust (a second or third mortgage), wraparound mortgage or all-inclusive deed of trust. May also refer to a seller selling on a real estate contract.

CARRYING CHARGES — 1. Costs incurred in owning property up to the time the development of the property is completed. Normal carrying charges include a developer's costs for payments of property taxes and interest on the land acquisition and construction loans during the time the property is under development. Also called "front money".

Investors and developers are usually concerned with whether they can capitalize certain carrying charges. For instance, if a developer has a proposed development pending and has little or no income to absorb tax deductions, he/she will want to capitalize his/her carrying charges. The rule is that the developer can capitalize annual taxes, mortgage interest and other true carrying charges if the property is unimproved or unproductive.

The election to capitalize is made annually when preparing a tax return. After the project is completed, the developer must deduct the expenses.

2. The regular costs of maintaining a property, such as taxes, insurance, water charges, accrued interest, and the like. These costs are apportioned between buyer and seller at the closing of a real estate transaction. (*See* CLOSING.)

CARRYOVER CLAUSE — *See* EXTENDER CLAUSE.

CASE LAW — *See* COMMON LAW.

CASH — Currency and coins, negotiable checks, and balances in bank accounts.

CASH FLOW — The spendable income from an investment after deducting from gross income all operating and fixed expenses, including principal and interest. The amount of cash derived over a certain measured period of time from operation of income-producing property after debt services and operating expenses, but before depreciation and income taxes. "Net after tax" cash flow includes an allowance for income tax attributable to the income.

Cash flow is different from "net profit". To arrive at net profit, the owner will make a deduction for depreciation but will not deduct for loan principal amortization.

Two benefits of investing in improved, income-producing real property are the tax shelter provided during ownership and the anticipated appreciation in the property value which may be realized upon its sale. Thus, an investment can turn out to be profitable even if there is a monthly negative cash flow. (*See* INTERNAL RATE OF RETURN, NEGATIVE CASH FLOW.)

A cash flow statement is a yearly financial report showing the bottom-line return after taxes. The property manager is often responsible for preparing a cash-flow analysis so that the property owner can evaluate the return on the property investment.

CASH METHOD — An accounting method of reporting income in the taxable year in which the income is actually or constructively received and reporting expenses when actually paid out. Income is constructively received when it is credited, set apart, or otherwise made available to the taxpayer without substantial limitations or restrictions so that he/she could have received it on request. The cash method is sometimes called the cash receipts and disbursements method. It is the opposite of the accrual method. (*See* ACCRUAL METHOD, CONSTRUCTIVE RECEIPT.)

In a commercial rental/lease arrangement wherein the total rental payments for the term of the lease exceed $250,000 and the lessor is on a cash-basis and the lessee is on an accrual method of accounting, the parties to the lease have a Section 467 rental agreement and must take into consideration the special IRS regulations.

Additionally, prepayment of rent must be deducted over the period for which it is paid without regard of the accounting method used by the lessee. A cash basis tax payment cannot deduct prepaid interest in the year in which it is paid.

CASH-OUT — In a listing, cash-out refers to the fact that the seller desires to receive the complete sales price for his/her equity in cash, rather than accept less by taking back a purchase money mortgage or deed of trust.

It could mean "cash to mortgage" where the buyer pays the seller's equity in cash and assumes or takes subject to the existing mortgage. (*See* DUE ON SALE CLAUSE.)

CASHIER'S CHECK — A bill of exchange drawn by a bank upon itself as drawer and payable upon presentation to the bank, like a promissory note executed by the bank. A cashier's check is preferred over an ordinary personal check and is usually required of the purchaser of property by the escrow agent at closing. (See CERTIFIED CHECK, COLLECTED FUNDS.)

A cashier's check is, however, still subject to a stop payment order of the maker. The certified check is only subject to a stop payment order if the maker obtains the bank certification, not in the case where the payee has the maker's check certified in the maker's bank.

CASING — A frame, as of a window or door.

CATWALK — A narrow footing on a bridge or along a girder of a large building. A catwalk may also be a walkway strung from one girder to another or placed over uncovered attic joists.

CAULKING — A flexible putty substance used to fill gaps at fixed joints on a building in order to reduce the passage of air and moisture; as in making watertight building windows.

CAUSE OF ACTION — Facts or circumstances that give rise to a right to file a lawsuit.

CAVEAT EMPTOR — Latin for "let the buyer beware". A buyer should inspect the goods or realty prior to purchase, because he/she buys "as is" and at his/her own risk.

The modern judicial trend is to soften the effect of this ancient doctrine. Today, in Washington, the seller has an affirmative duty to disclose any and all factors known to the seller which might influence the buyer's decision to purchase. The exposure to liability of builders and contractors who previously hid behind the caveat emptor doctrine has also been greatly expanded, especially in the sale of new homes and condominiums. The doctrine still applies to judicial sales.

In Washington in the late 1980s, many multiple listing services adopted a property condition report form patterned after those adopted in a number of states and in particular California. Since the form was given the number 17, one of the many forms made available by a Multiple Listing Service to its members, it became known as Form 17.

The Washington Legislative in 1994 adopted a required form entitled "Residential Real Property Transfer - Seller's Disclosure" which is a five page long fill in the blanks form which the real estate industry refers to as "Real Property Transfer Disclosure Statement" and is still referred to as Form 17. The Seller of residential real property (one to four units) is required to deliver this form, completed to the best of the sellers' knowledge, within five days after all parties to a Purchase and Sale Agreement have signed it. (*See* REAL PROPERTY TRANSFER DISCLOSURE STATEMENT.)
Reference: RCW 64.06

The doctrine of caveat emptor with respect to residential leases has been substantially altered in recent years. In the past, a landlord would lease the premises "as is" with no obligation to make the premises habitable or to make repairs. In Washington, the doctrine has been replaced by an implied warranty of habitability in residential leases, whereby the landlord has an obligation to make the premises fit before the tenant moves in and to continue to keep them fit during the lease. (*See* IMPLIED WARRANTY OF HABITABILITY, LANDLORD TENANT ACT.)
Reference: RCW 59.18.

CC&Rs — Covenants, conditions, and restrictions, which are private restrictions on the use of real property; often simply called restrictions. (*See* DECLARATION OF RESTRICTION.)

CEASE AND DESIST ORDER — An order from a governmental authority directing a person violating the law to refrain from doing a certain act. RCW 18.85 authorizes the Director of Licenses to obtain a cease and desist order against violators of the Real Estate License Law.

CENTRAL BUSINESS DISTRICT (CBD) — A city's downtown area in which is concentrated the main business, governmental, recreational, professional, and service activities of the community.

CERTIFICATE IN REAL ESTATE — A certificate indicating proficiency on the part of the recipient on having completed a required 210 hours course of study in real estate.

The Certificate was developed in the early 1970s by the Washington Real Estate Educational Foundation and the Washington State Real Estate Commission. The Certificate is issued by the Real Estate Program of the Department of Licensing if the recipient satisfies the requirements with none community college courses and by the Real Estate Program and the participating Community College or Vocational-Technical School if the recipient satisfies the requirements in a community college(s).

The curriculum is divided into two groups: required courses, which are Principles of Real Estate, Real Estate Finance, Real Estate Sales Practice and Real Estate Appraisal; and two elective courses, which may be selected in the areas of Real Estate Advanced Sales Practices, Real Estate Law, Real Estate Office Administration, Real Estate Property Management, Real Estate Advanced Appraisal and Real Estate Professional Practices. If you are interested in the community college courses in real estate, contact the business office of your local community college almost all of them offer all the Certificate's required courses. Washington has one of the most comprehensive real estate programs in the United States. (*See* ASSOCIATE OF ARTS DEGREE IN REAL ESTATE.)

CERTIFICATE OF CLAIM — A contingent promise to reimburse an FHA-insured mortgagee for certain costs incurred during foreclosure of an insured mortgage, provided that the proceeds from the sale of the property are enough to cover the costs.

CERTIFICATE OF COMPLETION — A document generally issued by an architect or engineer after inspection of a property that the construction has been completed in compliance with plans and specifications. Final payment under the construction contract is then due and payable when the Certificate of Completion is given. (*See* CERTIFICATE OF OCCUPANCY, HOLDBACK.)

CERTIFICATE OF ELIGIBILITY — A certificate issued by a Veteran Administration regional office to a veteran who qualifies for a VA loan.

The Veteran Housing Act of 1974 permits the administrator to restore a veteran's entitlement to loan guarantee benefits after the property has been disposed of and (1) the prior loan has been paid in full, or (2) the administrator is released from liability under the guaranty, or (3) any loss the administrator has suffered has been repaid in full. It is no longer required that the property have been disposed of for a compelling reason.

The Act also authorizes the administrator to restore a veteran-seller's entitlement and release the veteran from liability to the VA when an immediate veteran-transferee has agreed to assume the outstanding balance on the loan and consented to the use of his/her entitlement to the same extent that the entitlement of the veteran-transferor had been used originally. The veteran-transferee and the property must otherwise meet the requirements of the law. **NOTE**: Reinstatement of eligibility is never automatic, and therefore must always be applied for, preferably at the time of the sale.

Many veteran-sellers presume that they are eligible for a new VA loan after selling their property by way of a loan assumption. On a loan assumption sale, the broker should point out that for the seller to have complete VA entitlement restored, the buyer must be a veteran and must agree to substitute his/her entitlement for the seller's. (*See* VETERANS ADMINISTRATION (V.A.) LOAN.)

CERTIFICATE OF INSURANCE — A certificate in which an insurance company verifies that a particular policy insuring certain parties is in effect for given amounts and coverage. This certificate is often issued when a commercial lease requires that the lessee maintain certain specified insurance coverage. (*See* PRIVATE MORTGAGE INSURANCE.)

CERTIFICATE OF NO DEFENSE — A legal instrument executed by a mortgagor under a mortgage or a grantor under a deed of trust, setting forth the exact unpaid balance of a loan, the current rate of interest, and the date to which interest has been paid. It further states that the borrower has no defenses or offsets against the lender at the time of the execution of the certificate. Once the borrower has executed a certificate of no defense, he/she is thereafter estopped from claiming that he/she did not owe the amount stated in the certificate.

Usually called an **Estoppel Certificate** in Washington, a certificate of no defense is most frequently used when the lender is selling the mortgage/deed of trust to a third party, and the purchaser wants to be assured of the amount and terms of the loan, and that the borrower acknowledges the full amount of the debt. Most loan documents contain a clause obligating the borrower to execute a certificate of no defense upon written request from the lender.

In a landlord-tenant situation, a certificate of no defense is a statement by the tenant setting forth the amount of rent payable and the term of the lease, and acknowledging that the tenant claims no defenses or offsets against the landlord. A certificate of no defense is sometimes required where the landlord is selling the property, or is assigning the lease. This is also called an "offset statement". (*See* REDUCTION CERTIFICATE.)

CERTIFICATE OF OCCUPANCY (CO) — A certificate issued by a city or county building department showing that a building is ready and fit for occupancy, and that there are no building code violations.

Some condominium developers insert language into the sales contract to the effect that upon notification that the units are ready for occupancy, the buyer must accept the unit despite any construction defects which may exist, although acceptance will not prevent the buyer from obtaining redress for such defects. Once the building has been certified for occupancy, the developer can then close the individual sales, transfer the title to the buyers, and, most important, start the takeout financing, so that he/she can pay off his/her construction loan and discontinue his/her high interest payments.

CERTIFICATE OF REASONABLE VALUE (CRV) — A certificate issued by the Veterans Administration setting forth a property's current market value estimate, based upon a VA approved appraisal. The CRV places the ceiling on the amount of the VA loan for a particular property. If the purchase price exceeds the CRV, then the veteran must pay for this excess in cash, since secondary financing is restricted under VA regulations. In practice, the CRV never exceeds the sales price. (*See* VA MORTGAGE.)

CERTIFIED APPRAISER — Under the provisions of FIRREA, an appraiser who has been certified by the appropriate state agent to value real property in the state. The appraiser needs to meet minimum education and examination requirements. Since 1991, only certified appraisers can appraise certain types of real property that involve loans in connection with a federal agency. (*See* FINANCIAL INSTITUTIONS REFORM, RECOVERY, AND ENFORCEMENT ACT (FIRREA).)

CERTIFIED CHECK — A check which the bank guarantees to be good, and against which a stop payment is ineffective if the payee obtains the certification.

Payment by certified check immediately discharges the buyer's duty of performance under a contract. Payment by personal check, however, constitutes conditional performance and does not discharge the buyer's obligation until the check clears (that is, is paid by the depositor's bank).

Certified checks are normally required by escrow companies from purchasers who use out-of-state banks — a reason many brokers have their clients set up a local checking account and transfer funds for the closing of a purchase. Escrow companies now require all parties to make their closing payment by way of a certified check or wired funds before escrow will record the conveyance documents. Some brokers require prospective out-of-state buyers to use a certified check for an earnest money deposit. (*See* CASHIER'S CHECK, COLLECTED FUNDS.)

CERTIFIED COPY — A copy of a document (such as a deed, marriage or birth certificate) signed by the person having possession of the original and declaring it to be a true copy.

CERTIFIED PROPERTY MANAGER (C.P.M.) — A professional real property manager who has qualified by the successful completion of the specified educational courses and written demonstration reports for the C.P.M. designation granted by the Institute of Real Estate Management of the National Association of Realtors®. Presently it is the highest designation a real property manager may earn.

CERTIFY — To testify in writing; to confirm; to guarantee in writing, as in a certified check, to endorse, as with a proper seal.

CERTIORARI — A review by a higher court of a case or proceeding conducted by an inferior court, officer, board, or tribunal to certify the record of such proceeding. A means of obtaining a judicial review.

CESSPOOL — An underground porous pit used to catch and temporarily contain sewage and other liquid refuse, where it decomposes and is absorbed into the soil. (*See* EFFLUENCE.)

CHAIN — 1. An engineer's chain is a series of 100 wire links each of which is one foot in length.

2. A surveyor's chain is a series of wire links each of which is 7.92 inches long. The total length of the chain is four rods, or 66 feet. Ten square chains of land are equal to one acre. It is a method of measurement used in the United States Public Land Surveys.

CHAIN OF TITLE — The recorded history of matters which affect the title to a specific parcel of real property, such as ownership, encumbrances and liens, usually beginning with the original recorded source of the title. It shows the successive changes of ownership, each one linked to the next so that a "chain" is formed.

Ownership of a particular property frequently passes through many hands after the original grant. If there is any broken link in a property's chain of title, then the current "owner" would not have valid title to the property. For example, if there was a forged deed somewhere in the chain, then no subsequent grantee would have acquired legal title to the property.

A Title Insurance company searches and notes the chain of title (also called **running the chain of title**) in its examination of the records of conveyances of the county auditor. Prior to the early 1980s, each title company developed their own Tract Books which contain all pertinent information relative to land conveyances in the county. These Tract Books were based on legal descriptions. Now title companies have computerized their records. The title company traces the title from the original grant, which is usually a letter of patent from the United States or the State of Washington, up to the present ownership. Note: The abstractor, who is usually an attorney in many other states, has been replaced in Washington by title insurance companies.

To be within the unbroken chain of title, the instrument must be capable of being discovered or traced through linking conveyances from the present owner through successive owners to a common grantor. If this cannot be done, it is said that there is a "gap" in the chain. In such cases, there is a cloud on the title and it is usually necessary to establish ownership by a court action called **a suit to quiet title**.

All documents recorded in the chain of title give constructive notice to everyone of the document and its contents. However, if the document is not recorded in the chain of title so that even a diligent search will not reveal its presence, then there is no constructive notice given of the existence of the unrecorded document. A deed not properly recorded is said to be a "wild deed," and is not valid as against a subsequent recorded deed to a good faith purchaser.

Other chain of title problems arise where a person acquires title using one name, and then conveys the property under another name. In such cases, the grantor should indicate the name by which he/she acquired title, for example, "Sally Hines, who acquired title as Sally From." A person searching the title could then check the Grantee Index for the name Sally From. Because of the importance of the chain of title, it is necessary that the parties' names be consistent and be spelled properly. (*See* ABSTRACT OF TITLE, TRINITROGLYCERIN INDEX, RECORDING, TITLE INSURANCE, TITLE SEARCH, WILD DEED.)
Reference: RCW 65.08.

CHAIN STORE — Any one of a number of retail stores under common ownership, under a central management, selling standard merchandise, and operating under a uniform policy. A major chain store is often an anchor tenant in a shopping center. (*See* ANCHOR TENANT.)

CHALET — A housing construction style originating in the Swiss Alps, found mainly in mountainous regions, especially ski resort areas. Its design features large, overhanging eaves that offer protection from heavy winter snowfall. An A-frame.

CHANGE — An appraisal principle recognizing that economic and social forces are constantly at work. The appraiser must view real property and its environment as in transition, taking note of trends that may affect the property in the future.

CHANGE OF NAME — Any person can change his/her name simply by using another name, so long as the name change was not done to defraud. Because of the difficulties of identification, most people changing their names prefer to go through a legal process to effect the change officially. This process is a relatively minor one, an individual applies to the Superior Court of the county in which he/she resides and by petition sets forth the reasons for the requested change; and the Superior Court judge, in his/her discretion, orders a change of name which may be used in place of the former.

A corporation can change its name by amendment to its articles of incorporation.

Whenever any person or corporation undergoes a change of name, care should be taken to reflect such change on any documents which have been recorded under the previous name. For example, a recorded document should be amended to read, "Cathy Jones, being the same person who acquired title as Cathleen J. Arbuckle." (*See* CHAIN OF TITLE, LEGAL NAME, NAME, CHANGE OF.)
Reference: RCW 4.24.130.

CHANGE ORDER — An order to a contractor from the owner, architect or engineer on a construction project, authorizing changes or modifications to the original work as shown in the contract drawings, plans or specifications. A standard AIA form is normally used. A change order usually changes the original contract price.

Condominium developers usually require purchasers of apartment units under construction to submit change orders and pay for special changes to the original apartment package, such as custom carpeting or appliances.

CHATTEL — An item of tangible personal property. The word "chattel" evolved from the word "cattle," one of man's early important possessions. **Chattels real** are annexed to real estate, whereas **chattels personal** are movable. A lease is an example of a chattel real. Chattels are transferred by means of a bill of sale. The Uniform Commercial Code (UCC) regulates the transfer of chattels and the use of chattels as security for debts. (*See* FINANCING STATEMENT.)

CHATTEL MORTGAGE — A mortgage secured by personal property. Under the Uniform Commercial Code, which was adopted in Washington in 1967, the chattel mortgage has been replaced by the security agreement. (*See* CHATTEL, SECURITY AGREEMENT.) *Reference:* RCW 62A.9.

CHECK — (1) A negotiable instrument signed by a maker or drawer authorizing a bank to pay money to the payee or bearer. (2) A government survey designation for a twenty-four square mile unit bounded by two guide meridians and two correction lines. Each check is divided into sixteen townships, each six miles square.

CHECK KITING — Writing a check against funds which are not on deposit on the date the check is written.

CHIMNEY — A stack of brick or other masonry extending above the surface of the roof that carries the smoke to the outside. The smoke is carried inside the chimney through the flue.

CHIMNEY CAP — Ornamental stone or concrete edging around the top of the chimney stack which helps protect the masonry from the elements and improves the draught in the chimney.

CHIMNEY FLASHING — A strip of material, usually metal, placed over the junction of the chimney and the roof to make the joint water tight. Flashings are used wherever the slope of the roof is broken up by a vertical structure.

CHIMNEY POT — A fire clay or terra cotta pipe projecting from the top of the chimney stack. The chimney pot is decorative and also increases the draught of the chimney.

CIPS — Certified International Property Specialist. A real estate designation awarded by the International Real Estate Federation (FIABCI). The designation is earned by completing required educational courses, having experience in international real estate transactions and participating in FIABCI meetings. (*See* FIABCI.)

CIRCLE — A roadway having a circular form with only one access point to the adjoining street.

CISTERN — An artificial reservoir or tank, often underground, for the storing of rain water collected from a roof.

CIVIL RIGHTS ACTS OF 1866 and 1968 — *See* FEDERAL FAIR HOUSING.

CLAIM OF RIGHT — Refers to the occupancy of property by one having no legal right to title but, nevertheless, claiming such a right. It is an adverse possessor's claim to a fee simple title, either under some apparent color of title or by mere naked claim. For example, assume a father gives his daughter the family farm and she works the farm for 25 years until the father dies. No deed was ever prepared as is required under the Statute of Frauds. Most courts would hold that while an oral grant itself is invalid; however, when accompanied by an actual entry and possession for the statutory period of time, it will ripen into title by adverse possession because of her claim of right. (*See* ADVERSE POSSESSION.)

CLAPBOARD — Siding of narrow boards thicker at one edge, used as exterior finish for frame houses.

CLAYTON ANTITRUST ACT — Federal statute that specifically prohibits price discrimination, exclusive dealing arrangements, certain corporate acquisition of stock and interlocking directorates. (*See* ANTITRUST.)

CLEANOUT DOOR — An exterior door located at the base of the chimney for convenient removal of the ashes that were put through the ash dump.

CLEAR SPAN — The condition within a building wherein a given floor area is free of posts, support columns, or shear walls.

CLEAR TITLE — Title to property that is free from liens, defects or other encumbrances, except those which the buyer has agreed to accept, such as a mortgage or deed of trust to be assumed and the like; established title; title without clouds. (*See* CLOUD ON TITLE, MARKETABLE TITLE.)

CLEARANCE LETTER — A letter from a licensed termite inspection company disclosing the results of a property inspection. Sometimes, FHA, VA and some conventional lenders require a clearance letter prior to approving a loan. (*See* TERMITE INSPECTION.)

CLEARANCE POINT — As it relates to industrial properties, in the case of one rail track separating and diverging from another, that point at which a 13-foot spread is reached between the centers of the two tracks.

CLEARING TITLE — The process of examining all recorded and unrecorded instruments affecting a particular property, and taking any necessary action to remove or otherwise cure the title of any defects or clouds in order that the title may become a good, marketable title. (*See* MARKETABLE TITLE, QUIET TITLE ACTION.)

CLIC (COMMERCIAL LEASEHOLD INSURANCE CORPORATION) — A corporation that provides leasehold insurance for commercial and industrial properties, lease payments, and leasehold improvement loans. CLIC is a wholly owned subsidiary of Mortgage Guarantee Insurance Corporation.

CLIENT — The person who employs an agent to perform a service for a fee. Prior to the late 1980s in real estate brokerage, typically the client was the seller and the buyer usually was the **prospect or customer**. Now, usually one agent represents the seller/client and all other real estate licensees represent the buyers when they look at real estate. (*See* AGENCY, AGENT, BUYER'S BROKER, REAL ESTATE BROKERAGE RELATIONSHIPS ACT.)

CLIENT TRUST ACCOUNT — An account set up by a broker to keep client's moneys segregated from his/her general funds. The Rules and Regulations of the Washington Real Estate Commission require each broker to deposit funds which are not to be immediately released to escrow into a trust fund account with a bank or recognized depository within one business day after receipt. The broker is to be the trustee of the client trust account, and all funds deposited in the account must be available for withdrawal on demand. A single client trust account can serve all of the broker's clients, provided that detailed records are maintained and made subject to inspection by the Real Estate Program. Often a real estate company that engages in property management, in addition to sales activity, will set up a separate client's trust account for the property management.

As a result of 1988 legislation, the real estate license law was amended to clarify that a broker shall maintain a pooled interest-bearing escrow account for deposit of client funds, which are nominal, with the exception of property management trust accounts. A nominal deposit is defined as a deposition of **not more than five thousand dollars**. (*See* HOUSING TRUST FUND ACCOUNT.)
Reference: RCW 18.85.310

A rule adopted by the Real Estate Commission recognizes the right of the principals in a transaction to direct the broker to deposit any amount over $5,000 into an interest bearing

account, and to disburse interest as agreed. That separate account must not commingle the funds of any other principals, and the instructions must be in writing.
Reference: RCW 18.85, WAC 308-124E.

One of the main reasons for requiring a broker to maintain a client trust account separate from his/her general account is to protect these moneys from possibly being "frozen" during legal actions against the broker, such as creditor attachments, or probate of a deceased broker's estate. Also, since the account is custodial in nature, the Federal Deposit Insurance Corporation will personally insure each client's funds up to $100,000. The FDIC only insures each account if the account is specifically designated as custodial and the name and interest of each owner in the deposit is disclosed on the depositor's records. Furthermore, by placing these funds in a separate account, brokers are less likely to confuse the trust funds with their personal or business funds and inadvertently use these funds which belong to others for personal or business purposes. (*See* COMMINGLING, REAL ESTATE AUDITOR.)

CLO - COMPUTERIZED LOAN ORIGINATION SYSTEM - An electronic system that furnishes subscribers with the latest data on available loan programs at a variety of lending institutions. A CLO may offer buyer pre-qualifications or mortgage information services. Some CLO systems can process loan applications, underwrite loans and make commitments of funds. MIDANET and LASER are Freddie Mac's and Fannie Mae's automated loan delivery and accounting vehicles respectively.

The use of CLOs raises the problem of referral fees paid to real estate agents using this development in technology. Some lenders have offered CLO systems to real estate agents and will pay them a fee for using the system and referring loans to the lender. HUD believes consumers are interested in the services provided by these systems; namely, access to the interest rates and loan terms of multiple lenders. A real estate agent who offer CLOs must offer the products of multiple lenders. Additionally, the real estate agent is required to disclose to the homebuyer that the agent will receive a fee for the CLO service and further that there are other lenders, not on the system, that may offer more favorable terms.

CLOSE CORPORATION — *See* CORPORATION.

CLOSED-END MORTGAGE — A mortgage that prohibits the mortgagor from using the property as security for further loans; contains a "no further encumbrance" provision.

CLOSED PERIOD — A period in the term of a mortgage or deed of trust that prevents a prepayment. This period can be described as a lock-in period. Lenders of large commercial loans used the lock-in period to insure the investor (owner of the mortgage) an undisturbed flow of cash for a period of time. Life insurance or pension funds who make large commercial loans favor a commercial loan with a closed period so they need not worry about an unexpected amount of cash returned from an investment.

CLOSING — The consummation of a real estate transaction, when the seller delivers title to the buyer in exchange for the purchase price. In Washington standard **Purchase and Sale Agreement** forms, often referred to as Earnest Money Agreement (E/M), closing usually does not occur until the documents are recorded; however, under general rules of real estate law, transfer of title takes place upon delivery of the deed to the grantee.

In real estate practice, there are several informal meanings given to the word **closing** in Washington real estate practice. For example, **closing a sale** is often used to describe the process of getting the buyer and seller to agree to and sign the purchase and sale agreement. The **legal closing** (defined above) refers to the date that title and money are exchanged and **financial closing** refers to the actual disbursements of moneys, as directed in the closing or settlement statements. When a person says, "I'm going to the closing this afternoon," he/she normally refers to the act of going to the lender's office or escrow company to sign the final documents, such as the deed or assignment of lease.

The salesperson usually estimates the date of closing when drawing up the E/M. Forty-five days is a normal period when conventional financing has to be arranged, this gives the buyer enough time to obtain a title report, arrange financing with an appraisal and prepare to move; and to permit the seller to have the conveyance documents prepared, clear any problems with the title, and prepare to move. If government insured financing is required (FHA or VA) sixty to ninety days at a minimum should be provided. If the E/M calls for a real estate contract, the processing time may be shorter. An extension of time for closing may be granted by mutual agreement of the buyer and seller.

The details of closing are typically carried out according to local trade and custom. The procedures usually are not controlled by statute, although certain aspects of the closing are regulated by laws such as the federal Real Estate Settlement Procedures Act (RESPA). Closing may be handled through licensed escrow companies, lenders, banks, attorneys, brokers, or the parties themselves.

Prorations of expenses which are to be shared between the buyer and seller — usually for such operating items as real property taxes, ground lease rent and the like — are normally computed as of the closing date unless a different date (such as the date of occupancy) is specifically stated in the E/M. The term **closing date** in this instance refers to the legal closing date, the date on which documents transferring title from seller to buyer are recorded. (*See* CLOSING COSTS, ESCROW.)

Internal Revenue Service rules require settlement agents to report details of the closing on sales or exchanges of residences with four or fewer unit to the IRS on Form 1099-B.

CLOSING COSTS — Expenses of a sale or refinancing of a loan which must be paid in addition to the purchase price (in the case of the buyer's expenses), or be deducted from the proceeds of the sale (in the case of the seller's expenses). Some closing costs result from legal requirements, others are a matter of local custom and practice. Typical expenses which might be incurred by seller and buyer in an ordinary transaction (but not limited to):

Normal Buyer's Costs	FHA	VA	Conv	Contract	Assumption
Appraisal Fee	X	X	X		
Inspection Fee	X	X	X	X	X
Loan or Assumption Fee	X	X	X	X	X
Credit Report + Photos	X	X	X		
Tax Registration		X	X		
Recording Fee	X	X	X	X	X
Tax Prorations	X	X	X	X	X
Reserve Set-Up	X	X	X		X
Title Insurance	X	X	X	X	
Escrow Fee *	X		X	X	X
Interest Proration	X	X	X	X	X
Mortgage Insurance	X		X		
Fire Insurance	X	X	X	X	X
Flood Insurance	X	X	X		

* Shared (50/50)

Normal Seller's Costs	FHA	VA	Conv	Contract	Assumption
R.E. Sales Commission	X	X	X	X	X
Excise Tax	X	X	X	X	X
Loan Discount (Points)	X	X			
Tax Registration	X				
Recording Fee	X	X	X	X	X
Prepayment Penalty			X		
Title Insurance	X	X	X	X	X
Esrow Fee *	X	Full	X	X	X
Tax Proration	X	X	X	X	X
Encumbrances	X	X	X		
Possible					
Sanitation Inspection	X	X			
Termite Inspection	X	X			

In addition to the above closing costs, which are fixed at a specified amount regardless of the closing date, there are variable expenses — items such as real property taxes, prepaid insurance premiums, interest on assumed obligations and the like — which must be prorated between the seller and the buyer. Because these expenses are directly related to property ownership, they are normally prorated as of the date that title to the property passes, thus making the seller responsible for expenses for the period that he/she owned the property, and the buyer responsible for expenses accruing from the date he/she takes title.

On VA and FHA loans, some typical buyer's costs are: an origination fee, appraisal fee, a termite inspection report (FHA only), tax prorations, recording deed and mortgage, a credit report, a hazard insurance premium, insurance and tax impounds, a title insurance policy, and interest on new-loan funding. Typical seller's costs on FHA and VA loans are: points, commissions, excise tax, attorney's fees to draft the deed, termite work and a VA inspection fee, and a disclosure statement fee on new loans.

A purchaser under new VA financing is not allowed to pay any escrow fees, so all escrow fees will be the sole responsibility of the seller. The FHA limits the amount that a buyer under new FHA financing may pay for escrow fees; therefore, under FHA financing a seller may have to pay more than one-half of escrow fees.

Under the provisions of the federal RESPA law, the lender is required to give the borrower a copy of a government booklet on closing costs entitled "Settlement Costs and You". The lender must also provide a good-faith estimate of closing costs likely to be incurred in financing the property. If both the booklet and estimate are not provided at the time of loan application, they must be mailed within three business days.

CLOSING STATEMENT — A detailed cash accounting of a real estate transaction prepared by an escrow officer or other person designated to process the mechanics of the sale, showing all cash that was received, all charges and credits which were made, and all cash that was paid out in the transaction; also called a settlement statement or a HUD-1. Separate closing statements are prepared for the buyer, showing his/her credits and charges (debits) and the balance due from him/her at closing; the seller, showing his/her credits and charges (debits) and the proceeds he/she will receive at closing; and the escrow officer, showing a detailed accounting of all moneys received and disbursed in the transaction. It is a record of accounts rather than a legal document.

CLOSURE — Refers to the process in a metes and bounds description of returning to the point of beginning. Unless the described parcel is thus "closed", there is no valid legal description.

CLOUD ON TITLE — Any document, claim, unreleased lien, or encumbrance which may impair or injure the title to a property or make the title doubtful because of its apparent or possible validity. Clouds on title are usually revealed by a title search, and may be removed from the public record by a quitclaim deed or a quiet title proceeding initiated by the property owner. While the "cloud" remains, the owner is usually prevented from conveying a marketable title except when it is only a minor nuisance item. Typical clouds on title are: (1) a recorded real estate contract which has not been removed from the record but under which the buyer has defaulted; (2) a recorded option which was not exercised, but which still appears on the record; (3) a recorded mortgage or deed of trust, paid in full, but with no satisfaction of mortgage or full reconveyance recorded; (4) property sold without one spouse's signature; (5) an heir of a prior owner with a questionable claim to the property; (6) the situation in which one of many heirs has forgotten to sign a deed; (7) a lis pendens (pending litigation) having been dropped but not removed from the record; or (8) a lessee in default having an option to purchase, which probably will not be enforceable if he/she breached the lease; or (9) a prior conveyance with an incomplete legal description. (*See* QUIET TITLE ACTION.)

CLUSTER DEVELOPMENT — The grouping of housing units on less-than-normal-size homesites, with remaining land used as common areas. For example, rather than build ten units per acre on a ten acre site, a developer might cluster twenty units per acre and prepare five acres as a common area with facilities for recreation. (*See* PLANNED UNIT DEVELOPMENT.)

CLUSTER ZONING — A zoning provision whereby a specific residential or unit density is prescribed for an entire area. The developer is free to concentrate or disperse the density within the area in accordance with flexible site - planning criteria. This differs from traditional zoning ordinances that allocate zoning on a lot-by-lot basis, prescribing the same maximum density for all single-structure lots within the zoning district. (*See* PLANNED UNIT DEVELOPMENT, ZERO LOT LINE.)

COASTAL ZONE MANAGEMENT ACT — A federal law passed in 1972 recognizing the national interest in the effective planning, management, beneficial use, protection, and development of the salt water and Great Lakes coastal zones. The act calls for states to plan and develop management programs for the land and water resources of their coastal zones.

CODE OF ETHICS — A system of standards of ethical conduct. Because of the nature of the relationship between the broker and client, a high standard of ethics is needed to ensure that the real estate licensee acts in the best interests of both their principal and third parties.

Members of the National Association of Realtors® subscribe to a very strict code of ethics. In fact, many state real estate commissions have incorporated key sections of the code into their rules and regulations governing the conduct of licensees. The National Association of Realtors® has published a booklet called "Interpretation of the Code of Ethics," applying the code to practical situations. There are also approved "Standards of Practice" which interpret some of the Articles of the Code of Ethics. These Standards of Practice may be cited as additional support for alleged Ethics. These Standards of Practice may be cited as additional support for alleged violations of the Code. (*See* APPENDIX B.)

Many of the Code provisions are incorporated into either the Washington State Real Estate License Law or the Rules and Regulations of the Real Estate Commission.
Reference: RCW 18.85 and WAC 308-124

CODICIL — A supplement or addition to a will which normally does not revoke the entire will. A codicil must be executed with the same formalities as a will, and be witnessed by two disinterested persons. (*See* WILL.)

COINSURANCE — A common provision in building insurance policies under which the insured agrees to maintain insurance on his/her property in an amount equal to at least 80 percent of the replacement cost. If the property is not insured to that amount and there is a loss, the insurance company will make the insured share in the loss on a pro rata basis. For example, if the building is insured for only 60 percent of its value and there is a $10,000 loss, the insurance company will pay only $7,500 (60%/80% x $10,000). Thus, it is important for the property owner to review his/her insurance policy from time to time to keep within the 80 percent minimum, as property values are steadily increasing. In addition, the insured can pay for inflation guard coverage. In any event, liability under any insurance policy is limited to the face amount of the policy. One reason for the 80 percent rule is that, generally, no more than 80 percent of a building's value is destroyed by fire; a certain part of the structure will usually be available for salvage.

Generally, coinsurance requirements are included in commercial and industrial hazard policies, and a similar type of coinsurance coverage is found in homeowners' policies. (*See* INSURANCE.)

COLD CALLING — 1. Obtaining listings by door-to-door solicitation of homeowners or by telephone calls to property owners.. Real estate salespeople usually employ these methods when seeking listings in a specific area or when looking for homes of a certain type or with certain features. (*See* FARM AREA.)

2. An unsolicited inquiry to a real estate office from a prospective buyer or seller. Cold calls are usually referred to the salesperson sitting floor duty at the time of the call. (*See* FLOOR DUTY.)

COLD CANVAS — *See* COLD CALL.

COLLAR BEAM — A horizontal beam connecting the rafter at the lower end. The collar beam adds rigidity and helps to divert weight on the roof from the exterior walls.

COLLATERAL — Something of value given or pledged as security for a debt or obligation by a borrower that will be given up if the loan is not repaid. The collateral for a real estate loan is the property itself, which has been hypothecated. If you use anything as collateral without giving up possession, you hypothecate it; if you give up possession, you pledge it. (*See* DEED OF TRUST, MORTGAGE.)

COLLATERAL HEIRS — Heirs descending from the same common ancestor but not from one another. Collateral heirs are not in a direct line of descent they may be sisters, uncles, or cousins, but not a son or daughter, who are lineal descendants.

COLLATERALIZED MORTGAGE — A collateralized mortgage loan is a loan secured by collateral **in addition** to real estate, as with a pledged savings account. Collateralization is taking an existing mortgage and using it as security or collateral for a loan (without having to discount it.)

COLLECTED FUNDS — In 1988 the Washington State Escrow Act was amended to provide that escrow agents could not close a transaction until there were actually funds in the escrow agent's trust account to close the transaction. The law provided that depositing of certain instruments into a trust account would be treated as collected funds.

In part the statute provided: An escrow agent shall not make disbursements on any escrow account without first receiving deposits directly relating to the account in any amounts at least equal to the disbursements. The deposits shall be in one of the following forms:

1. Cash;

2. Interbank electronic transfers such that the funds are unconditionally received by the escrow agent or the agent's depository;

3. Checks, negotiable orders of withdrawal, money orders, cashier's checks, and certified checks that are payable in Washington State and drawn on financial institutions located in Washington State;

4. Checks, negotiable orders of withdrawal, money orders; or

5. Any depository check, including any cashier's check, certified check, or teller's check, which is governed by the provisions of the Federal Expedited Fund Avail ability Act. (*See* CASHIER'S CHECK, CERTIFIED CHECK, ESCROW.)

Reference: RCW 18.44

COLLECTION ACCOUNT — An account established to collect periodic payments on a debt or obligation, to disburse the moneys received as requested by the payee, and to make an accounting to both parties. For example, often a contract requires the buyer to make his/her payments into a collection account at a bank or escrow company which, in turn, pays the real property taxes, lease rent, maintenance fees, mortgage or deed of trust payments, and insurance payments. The collection fees are typically split equally, though the seller is in a better bargaining position to try to persuade the buyer to pay the entire fee since the collection account is generally considered to be for the buyers protection (to insure that the seller makes timely payments). Collection fees are relatively slight, usually in the range of $15.00 per month plus an initial set up fee.

COLLUSION — Two or more parties agree to perform an illegal act. A seller agreeing to reimburse a buyer for the prepaid items on a conventional loan, without having informed the lender, is guilty of committing collusion with the buyer and of entering into a dual contract.

A dual contract can be either written or oral. A dual contract involving a government insured loan is illegal and subject to penalties as described by Section 1010 of U.S.C. Title 18 that provides for a maximum of a $5,000 fine or imprisonment for a maximum of 2 years or both.

The sales contract given the lender must be the only agreement between the parties involved. Charges on the settlement statement that conflict with the agreements in the contract are red flags for existence of a dual contract.

COLOR OF TITLE — A condition which has the appearance of good title, but which in fact is not valid title, as where title is founded on some written document which on its face appears valid and effective, but which is actually invalid.

Example: Mr. Burgess conveys a 10-acre farm to Mr. Sheron by way of a deed. Mr. Sheron enters into possession unaware that Mr. Burgess held his title under a forged deed. Thus, Sheron does not have valid title to the property. By occupying the premises for seven years and paying the annual property taxes, Sheron can acquire legal title to the entire 10-acre parcel by means of adverse possession under color of title, even though he physically occupied only part of the ten acres. This is because the adverse claimant under color of title need only possess a portion of the premises described in the ineffective conveyance to acquire title to the whole parcel. If there were no deed involved and Sheron just adversely occupied part of the 10-acres, after ten years, he would acquire title only to the acreage he actually occupied (or fenced, or cultivated). In addition, a claimant not under color of title has a stronger burden of proof on each of the required elements for adverse possession. (*See* ADVERSE POSSESSION.)
Reference: RCW 4.16 and RCW 7.28.

COMBED (STRIATED) PLYWOOD — Common building material in modern homes, particularly for interior finish. The exposed surface is combed in parallel grooves.

COMMENCEMENT OF WORK — The noticeable beginning of an improvement on real estate. This exact time has significance relative to the effective date of a mechanic's lien (and thus the priority against other liens such as mortgages), as well as protecting a builder against changes in the zoning rules. (*See* MECHANIC'S LIEN, ZONING ESTOPPEL.)

COMMERCIAL ACRE — A term referring to that portion of an acre of newly subdivided land remaining after dedication for streets, sidewalks, and so on.

COMMERCIAL BROKERS ASSOCIATION (CBA) — A broker-owned, non-profit multiple listing service for commercial real estate in the State of Washington. CBA's database includes nine property types: retail, office, industrial, land, multi-family, mobile home parks, farms and ranches, hotels and motels and business opportunities. Listings can be accessed by members via an on-line computer system or by a listing catalog published monthly.

COMMERCIAL INVESTMENT REAL ESTATE INSTITUTE (CIREI) — A professional association of real estate practitioners, including specialists in commercial property marketing and investment analysis, as well as experts in banking, development, law, syndications and consulting. The institute awards the designation CCIM (Certified Commercial Investment Member). CIREI is affiliated with the National Association of Realtors®.

COMMERCIAL LEASEHOLD INSURANCE — Insurance to cover the payment of rent in the event the insured (tenant) cannot pay it. Sometimes required by a commercial lender in a shopping center development as a prerequisite to issuing a leasehold mortgage. (*See* CLIC.)

COMMERCIAL LOAN — A loan on property that produces income.

COMMERCIAL PROPERTY — A classification of real estate which includes income-producing property such as office buildings, gasoline stations, restaurants, shopping centers, hotels and motels, parking lots, and stores. Commercial property usually must be zoned for business purposes.

COMMINGLING — To mingle or mix; for example, to deposit client funds in the broker's personal or general account. A licensee found guilty of commingling funds will generally have his/her license suspended or revoked by the Real Estate Program of the Department of Licensing.

It is an act of commingling for a broker to fail to deposit trust funds into escrow or a client trust account at a bank or recognized depository by the next business day following their receipt. It does not constitute commingling for the broker to hold an uncashed check until acceptance of an offer, when directed to do so by the buyer (offeror); however, before the seller accepts the offer, the broker must specifically disclose the fact that the check is being held in an uncashed form. Similarly, it is not commingling to hold an uncashed check after acceptance of an offer, when directed to do so by the seller (offeree).

As a matter of policy, not cashing checks until an offer is accepted may prevent problems for the broker. Often a buyer submits an offer with a personal check as an earnest money deposit. If the broker deposits the check in his/her client's trust account and the offer is rejected, then the broker is in a position of having to refund the earnest money deposit before the broker knows whether the buyer's check has cleared. If the broker delays in returning the earnest money deposit, he/she will irritate the buyer and ruin a business relationship. Yet, if he/she returns the deposit and the check bounces, he/she is out the money.

A more serious offense than commingling is "conversion", which is the actual misappropriation and use of the client's moneys. (*See* CLIENT TRUST ACCOUNT, CONVERSION.)
Reference: RCW 18.85 and WAC 308-124E.

COMMISSION — The compensation paid to a real estate broker (usually by the seller) for services rendered in connection with the sale, lease or exchange of real property. In order to collect a commission, the broker must be duly licensed in Washington and have a written commission agreement with the party paying the commission. The commission is normally stated as a percentage of the gross sale price, and the exact rate is subject to negotiation (because fixed rates would be in restraint of trade and in violation of antitrust laws). Leasing commissions may be based on graduated percentages over the entire lease term. In most areas in Washington, commission rates are established by custom.

Often a broker will share the commission with another broker who has cooperated in the transaction. In order to share a commission with a salesperson associated with another broker, a broker must process the money through the salesperson's employing broker, except in the case of deferred commissions earned under a prior broker.

Because of the popularity of the Multiple Listing Service in Washington, the listing broker often will share the commission with another salesperson from another real estate company who is responsible for introducing the purchaser into the transaction. When splitting the commission, a broker must process the money through the salesperson's employing broker.

Once the seller accepts the offer from a ready, willing, and able buyer, the seller is technically liable for the full commission to the broker regardless of whether or not the buyer completes the purchase. There is a growing tendency in courts today, however, to prevent a broker from seeking a full commission from the seller in a case where the broker knew or should have known that the buyer was not financially able to complete the purchase. If the offer is made subject to a contingency, the broker cannot collect a commission until the condition is satisfied.

A commission is usually paid on the gross sales price.

A broker who has produced a ready, willing and able buyer on the listing terms is still entitled to his/her commission if the transaction is not consummated for any of the following reasons:

1. The owner changes his/her mind and refuses to sell;

2. The owner's wife who has signed the listing agreement refuses to sign the con tract or deed;

3. There are defects in the owner's title which are not corrected;

4. The owner commits fraud with respect to the transaction;

5. The owner is unable to deliver possession within a reasonable time;

6. The owner insists on terms not in the listing, such as a right to restrict the use of the property; or

7. The owner and buyer agree to cancel the signed contract to purchase.

A controversial situation arises in the use of the standard Purchase and Sale Agreement (E/M) in Washington which contains a clause to the effect that if the seller retains the buyer's deposit as liquidated damages, the broker then agrees to accept one-half of that amount as his/her commission (not to exceed the full commission due). This clause varies from the listing agreement, which provides that the broker would receive a specified percentage of the sales price if he/she obtained a ready, willing and able buyer. It therefore appears that the broker has given the seller the option of whether to sue the buyer for damages, or to retain the deposit money (initial and additional deposits). If the seller decides to retain the deposit the broker may not sue the seller for the full commission, but would have to be satisfied with one-half of the retained deposit. Except where the seller is acting in bad faith, this result is ethically correct, since the broker should not be able to force the seller to enter prolonged litigation, perhaps tying up the property for many months, while he/she seeks his/her full commission. Thus the broker has a personal reason to obtain as high a deposit as is practicable.

Once the commission has been received by the broker, it is then divided, according to a prearranged formula, between the brokerage and salespersons involved in the transaction. Virtually all brokerages retain a portion of the commission — often as much as forty to fifty percent — to pay overhead costs, salaries and profits. Since commission splits vary considerably from company to company, it is necessary that the salesperson have a clear understanding (preferably in writing) with the employing broker as to how he/she is to be paid, when, and what percentage of the gross commission earned.

An innovation in commissions is the 100 percent plan, whereby certain salespeople who achieve a minimum sales level pay monthly service charges to their brokers (to cover the costs of office space, telephones, and supervision) and receive 100 percent of the commissions from the sales which they negotiate.

It is illegal for a license broker to pay a commission to an attorney who does not have a real estate license, and it is illegal for an attorney who is not appropriately licensed to

accept any part of a real estate commission. However, an attorney may be compensated for the value of legal services actually rendered.
Reference: RCW 18.85

The courts have held that a real estate broker or salesperson buying property through his/her own brokerage firm for personal use must still be taxed on the commission he/she would have received for the sale, even though it is reflected as a discount (or a "contra") against the purchase price. Commission income, whether it is received by an employee or independent contractor, is considered "personal service" or "earned" income. (*See* COMPENSATION, DEFERRED COMMISSION, FINDER'S FEE, PROCURING CAUSE.)

Despite the fact that payment of the commission does not necessarily determine agency, a prudent broker/salesperson should discuss and document whom they represent and who is paying for their services. A clear disclosure can dispel any notion that the broker must have represented the person who eventually paid the broker's commission. (*See* AGENCY, LISTING, REAL ESTATE BROKERAGE RELATIONSHIPS ACT.)

COMMISSIONER — (1) A member of the Washington Real Estate Commission. (2) A person appointed by a court of equity in a partition proceeding to advise the court as to the best method of partitioning the property. (*See* PARTITION, REAL ESTATE COMMISSION.)

COMMISSIONER'S ADJUSTED FAIR MARKET VALUE (CAFMV) — A system adopted by HUD in dealing with pre-foreclosure actions. When the local HUD office receives the appraisal, it will calculate a foreclosure bid price by deducting from the appraised value the estimated costs for holding and reselling the property that HUD would incur if it acquired the property. Requirements are thus set for the way originating lenders must bid at foreclosure sales.

The bid must include notification of the anticipated sale date, the name of the fee appraiser and the bid price that a lender must offer to retain the option to convey title to HUD. If a lender bids an amount more than the CAFMV, the right to convey the property to HUD is forfeited.

COMMITMENT — A pledge or promise to do a certain act, such as the promise of a lending institution to loan a certain amount of money at a specified rate of interest to a qualified buyer provided that the loan is obtained on or before a certain date. Unlike a contract of sale, a commitment cannot be specifically performed; however, an aggrieved party may seek money damages upon refusal to loan on the commitment.

A conventional loan commitment may be either firm or conditional. The borrower may apply directly to the lender or use the services of a mortgage broker, usually on a standard form application. The lender then analyzes the applicant's purposes and financial resources and, if they are acceptable, writes the borrower a commitment letter. This commitment letter is, in effect, a detailed offer to loan money according to very specific terms. If the borrower accepts the commitment and satisfies all conditions the lender may have made, such as providing satisfactory appraisal and credit reports, the lending institution prepares the proper mortgage documentation. When the mortgage papers have been executed and the title approved, the lending institution will release the mortgage proceeds to be applied for the purposes for which the loan was made, such as a purchase or refinancing.

With FHA loans, a conditional commitment is an agreement to loan a definite amount of money on a particular property subject to the approval of a presently unknown borrower whose credit and eligibility will have to be checked. A firm FHA commitment is an agreement to insure a loan in a certain amount on a specific property to a designated borrower. A conditional loan commitment fee is usually refunded from the closing costs when the loan is actually made. FHA conditional commitments are good for six months and may be renewed for another six months upon payment of an additional fee.

In large projects, developers often have to pay for or "purchase" a commitment for permanent takeout financing. (*See* BUY DOWN LOAN, STANDBY FEE.)

Commitment also refers to an agreement by a title insurance company to issue a policy in favor of a proposed insured upon acquisition of a specific property. Unlike a binder, however, it is not a contract for temporary insurance. The commitment is for a short period of time and identifies the type of policy to be issued, the estate or interest of the insured, vesting of title, legal description of the property being covered, and any exceptions to coverage. (*See* TITLE INSURANCE.)

COMMITMENT FEE — A deposit or a reservation fee paid for future use of money. Normally the deposit or reservation is placed at the time the commitment is rendered. For a loan to a borrower, the commitment fee may be refunded upon the closing of the loan. A commitment letter should be issued upon receipt of the fee. The commitment letter is a written agreement outlining a future commitment by a lender to reserve funds for a borrower subject to term and conditions.

COMMON AREA CHARGES — Fees charged to tenants by the owner for expenses incurred in the maintenance and upkeep of areas used by all the tenants. Such charges are very common in the leasing of commercial space in Washington. (*See* LEASE, TRIPLE NET LEASE.)

COMMON AREAS — Land or improvements designated for the use and benefit of all residents, property owners and tenants. In a condominium development, common areas frequently include such amenities as corridor or hall areas, elevators, parks, playgrounds, and "green belts." In a shopping center, the common areas are parking lots, malls, and traffic lanes. (*See* CLUSTER DEVELOPMENT, CONDOMINIUM).

COMMON ELEMENTS — Parts of the property which are necessary or convenient to the existence, maintenance and safety of the condominium, or are normally in common use by all of the condominium residents. All condominium owners have an undivided ownership interest in the common elements. Maintenance of the common elements is paid for by the condominium association, and each owner must pay a monthly maintenance assessment, prorated according to his/her individual common interest. Typical examples of common elements are all structural portions of the buildings, including plumbing and electrical pipes and conduits as well as all bearing walls, roof and foundation. (*See* COMMON AREA, COMMON EXPENSE, COMMON INTEREST, CONDOMINIUM, LIMITED COMMON ELEMENTS.)

COMMON EXPENSE — The operating expenses of the condominium property, together with all other sums designated as common expenses by or pursuant to RCW 64.32 (Horizontal Property Regimes Act) or RCW 64.34.6 (Condominium Act) or the Condominium Declaration or the Bylaws of the Owners' Association. (*See* CONDOMINIUM.)

COMMON INTEREST — The percentage of undivided ownership in the common elements belonging to each condominium apartment, as established in the condominium declaration. The applicable percentage is usually computed as a ratio of the square footage of a particular apartment to the total square footage of the building, or as the ratio of the apartment's purchase price to the total sales price of all of the apartment units. The ratio is expressed as a percentage, such as 1.47% or .0147. The percentage of common interest determines an owner's interest in the common elements, the amount an owner will be assessed for maintenance and operation of the common properties, the real estate tax levied against an individual unit, and the number of votes an owner has in the condominium association. (*See* CONDOMINIUM.)
Reference: RCW 64.32.

COMMON LAW — A system of law, or a body of legal rules, derived from decisions of judges based upon accepted customs and traditions and developed in England, is known as the common law because it is believed that these rules were generally recognized and were in full force throughout England. This manner of jurisprudence originated in England and was later incorporated into this country's legal system, either by statute or custom. Common law is now the basis of the laws in every state of the Union except Louisiana, which bases its laws upon the early laws of France. Statutes have been enacted to supplement and supersede the common law in many fields; the common law, however, still governs where there is no statute dealing with a specific subject. A great deal of the common law as it pertains to real estate has been modified by both judicial and legislative action in Washington. However, some real estate law has not been changed and appears to be rather archaic and unsuited to modern business practices and conditions. When considering a real estate principle, it is best to remember the often quoted statement of Justice Wendell Holmes: "Upon this point a page of history is worth a volume of logic." (*See* CASE LAW, EQUITY.)

COMMON PROFITS — (1) In a condominium, the balance of all income, rents, profits and revenues from the common elements remaining after the deduction of the common expenses of a condominium. (2) The profits derived from the operations of a partnership or corporation.

COMMON WALL — A wall separating two living units. In a condominium, most developers declare the common walls to be common elements, and thus traditional party wall rules would not apply. (*See* PARTY WALLS.)

COMMUNITY ASSOCIATION — An association of property owners in either a condominium or residential development which oversees the maintenance and upkeep of common areas and attempts to maintain property values in the area. Such associations are normally incorporated and are governed by a board of directors elected by the property owners. The board is responsible for seeing that deed restrictions and subdivision regulations are not violated as well as overseeing the upkeep of common spaces such as sidewalks and open space.

COMMUNITY ASSOCIATIONS INSTITUTE (CAI) — The CAI is an independent, not-for-profit research and educational organization formed in 1973 to develop and distribute the most advanced and effective guidance for the creation, financing, operation, and maintenance of the common facilities and services in condominiums, townhouse projects, planned unit developments, and open-space communities.

COMMUNITY PROPERTY — A system of property ownership based on the theory that all property acquired during marriage by the industry and labor of either spouse (or both spouses) together with the produce and increase thereof, belong beneficially to both, and they should share equally in property acquired by them through their joint efforts during the marriage.

The community property system of ownership was borrowed from the jurisprudence of France and Spain by a number of western states including Washington. The system was unknown under English common law.

In those states which maintain a community property system, there are two classifications of property — separate property and community property. Separate property is property that either the husband or wife owned prior to the time of marriage, or which was acquired during marriage by inheritance, will or gift. Separate property is entirely free from all interest or claim on the part of the other spouse. However, if funds from the marital community have been used to effectuate improvements to real estate, the resulting increase in the value of the property is presumed to be community property and the marital community has a lien against the real estate to secure reimbursement for the increased value.

All other real property situated in Washington is community property and all personal property, wherever situated, is community property.

Washington State law requires that both a husband and wife join in any listing, encumbrance, sale or purchase contract pertaining to community real property. However, despite the statute, courts have held that a marital community is bound by the act of one spouse where their is "sufficient" evidence of authorization, ratification, or estoppel by the non-signing spouse. If the nonparticipating spouse has knowledge of the transaction and is silent, the courts have held that the community is bound by the acts of a single spouse.

Therefore, the signatures of both spouses should appear on any agreement or contract involving community residential real property.
Reference: RCW 26.16.

Either husband or wife may transfer their separate property and the other spouse need not sign the deed. However, as a matter of practice, title insurance companies and others prefer the signature of both spouses to eliminate any question as to whether the property is actually separate property or community property. In keeping with this both cautious and wise practice, the real estate salesperson who wishes to prevent any occurrence which might later create unnecessary disappointment will recognize the need for obtaining, among other things, the signature of both parties on an instrument of conveyance, or on any other instrument that might affect the title to real property. In the event that a grantor is a bachelor, spinster, widow or widower, it is wise to include, after the party's name, the above appropriate description in order to communicate immediately to anyone seeing the instrument that there was no community property interest in the grantor.

Neither dower, courtesy, nor survivorship rights exist in a community property state. Upon the death of one spouse in case of intestacy the decedent's net share of the community property passes to the surviving spouse. In Washington, a spouse can devise and bequeath only his/her half of the community property of the marriage. (*See* SEPARATE PROPERTY.)
Reference: RCW 26.16, RCW 11.02 and RCW 11.04.

COMMUNITY REINVESTMENT ACT — A provision of the Housing and Community Development Act of 1977 intended to prevent the practice of redlining and disinvestment by lenders in central city areas. To comply with the act, lenders must prepare Community Reinvestment Statements. These statements contain up to four basic elements:

1. The lender delineates a "community" in which its lending activities take place. The lender may use political boundaries, designate an "effective lending terri tory" in which a "substantial portion" of its loans are made, or any other "reason ably delineated local area." Care must be taken that such designations do not unreasonable exclude territory occupied by persons of low or moderate income.

2. The lender must make available a listing of the types of credit it offers in each community.

3. Appropriate notice and information regarding lending activity by territory must be given or made available for public inspection. The specific language of the notice is dictated by the government.

4. The lender has the option to disclose affirmative programs designed to meet the credit needs of the community.

COMMUNITY SHOPPING CENTER — A shopping center of approximately 150,000 square feet and 20 to 70 retail spaces, classified between the smaller neighborhood center and the larger regional center and supported by more than 5,000 families. (*See* SHOPPING CENTER.)

COMPACTION — Matted down or compressed extra soil which may be added to a lot to fill in the low areas or raise the level of the parcel.

COMPARABLES — Recently sold or leased properties which are similar to a particular property being evaluated and which are used to indicate a reasonable fair market value for the subject property. A comparable property need not be identical with the subject property in physical characteristics or location, but the terms of the sale and the market conditions should be similar, or relatively easy to adjust for comparison. In addition to adjustments for time and conditions of sale, adjustments are necessary for differences in location and all features which are recognized by the market as having value. In general terms, the more recent the sale and the fewer the dissimilarities, the better the comparable. The comparables must also fit the definition of value to be applied. As an example, comparable sales which are not arm's length transactions would not fit the definition of market value, but may be liquidation value. The appraiser must carefully select only those comparables which actually fit the definition of value being used. The multiple listing service records are an excellent place to start looking for comparables. However, in an active real estate market, a comparable reference over three months old may be outdated. (*See* APPRAISAL, DIRECT SALES COMPARISON APPROACH.)

COMPARATIVE UNIT METHOD — A method used to determine the reproduction cost in which all components of the building are added together on a unit basis, such as cost per square foot. Some components would be framing, exterior finish, and floor and roof construction. (*See* REPRODUCTION COST.)

COMPARISON METHOD — Also called competitive market analysis. (*See* DIRECT SALES COMPARISON APPROACH, MARKET-DATA APPROACH.)

COMPASS POINTS — The 32 positions marked on a compass to indicate directions, usually used when recording a metes and bounds or other legal description.

COMPENSATING BALANCE — When a bank lends funds to an investor, it may require that the investor keeps a deposit in his/her checking account equal to some percentage of the loan (e.g., 5, 10, 15 percent). The amount required to be left on deposit is the compensating balance. Such amounts effectively increase the interest rate. Usually applied to commercial loans but not to residential loans.

COMPENSATION — Payment for services in the real estate field is generally in the form of commissions based on a percentage of the amount involved in a particular transaction. In commercial-investment transactions, a small but growing number of real estate practitioners are adopting a flat fee policy. It has the advantage of the seller knowing exactly what the commission will be. In some cases the purchaser is paying an agent to represent him/her. It has the advantage that the real estate practitioner will negotiate the lowest possible purchase price due to the fact the buyer is paying the fee and the amount of compensation is not influenced by the purchase price; also, the agent will be able to talk to owners who would not normally talk to a real estate broker once it becomes clear that the seller will pay no commission. (*See* COMMISSION, CONSIDERATION.)

COMPETENT PARTY — A party to a contract who possesses the legal capacity to enter into a binding contract. (*See* CAPACITY OF PARTIES, CONTRACT.)

COMPETITIVE MARKET ANALYSIS — *See* DIRECT SALES COMPARISON APPROACH.

COMPLAINANT — A person who makes a complaint or instigates legal action against another (the respondent).

COMPLETION BOND — A surety bond posted by a landowner or developer to guarantee that a proposed development will be completed according to specifications, free and clear of all mechanics' liens. A completion bond is distinct and separate from a **performance bond**, which is given to an owner by a party to a contract (normally the contractor or subcontractor) to assure that party's performance of the contract provided he/she is paid. With a completion bond the parties may have no underlying contract to perform. Most county subdivision ordinances require the subdivider to post a cash completion bond as a condition to the county's granting approval of a proposed subdivision. Some lenders require an owner to provide a completion bond in addition to a performance bond from the contractor, thus assuring the lender that the development (which is the security for the loan) will be completed whether or not the owner pays the contractor. The bond is drawn in the amount of the total construction cost and is exercised only if the builder can't complete the building. If this happens, the lender can use the bond proceeds to complete and then sell the building to recover the interim loan funds. (*See* PAYMENT BOND, PERFORMANCE BOND, SURETY.)

COMPLIANCE INSPECTION — (1) Inspection of a structure to ensure that all building codes and specifications have been complied with. (2) Inspection of a construction site or structure by either a lending institution (for a conventional mortgage loan) or a government representative (for a FHA or VA loan) to ensure that it complies with all relevant requirements before a mortgage or deed of trust is made or before advances are made under a construction loan. (*See* INSPECTION.)

COMPONENT BUILDING — A prefabricated structure. Completed sections of walls, floors, beams, trusses, roofs, and other housing parts are delivered to a construction site where they are assembled into one housing unit.

COMPOUND INTEREST — Interest computed on the principal sum **plus** accrued interest. At the beginning of the new interest period, all interest is added to the principal, forming a new principal figure on which interest is then calculated. This process repeats itself each interest period — interest may be compounded daily, monthly, semiannually, or annually. Thus, on a $1,000 savings account at 5 percent interest compounded annually, for the first year the amount of interest is $50. In the second year, the new principal balance is $1,050, thus making the second-year interest $52.50. Sometimes referred to as "the magic of compound interest."

COMPS — *See* COMPARABLES

COMPUTERIZED LOAN ORIGINATION SYSTEM (CLO) — A computer network that furnishes subscribers with the latest data on available loan programs at a variety of lending institutions. A CLO may offer buyer pre-qualification or deed of trust/mortgage information services. Some CLO systems can process loan applications, underwrite loans and make commitments of funds.

A number of major lenders have systems that allows agents across the country to initiate mortgage loan applications in their own offices. A loan origination may be undertaken by real estate brokers, insurance agents, lawyers and others who may earn a loan origination fee. HUD has approved the procedure as being in compliance with RESPA so long as (1) full disclosure is made of the fee, (2) multiple lenders are displayed on the computer screen to give the borrower some bases for comparison and (3) the fee is charged as a dollar amount rather than a percentage of the loan.

CONCENTRIC CIRCLE THEORY — An economic theory of city growth which states that, if there are no barriers, cities tend to expand in concentric circles from their point of origin. The model city consists of five zones: the central business district, a zone of transition, a zone of independent working people's homes, a region of better residences, and, last, a group of commuter zones.

CONCESSIONS — 1. Depending on rental market conditions, discounts are sometimes given by landlords to prospective tenants to induce them to sign a lease. Concessions are sometimes encountered in commercial leases, where the lessor may give a number of months' rent free, or provide an allowance to the tenant for renovating or customizing the demised space. A prudent purchaser of a commercial or income-producing property will check all existing leases to see if there are any lease concessions which would reduce the amount of rent receivable (such as one month's free rent per year for the term of the lease). If so, the value of these concessions should be computed to reduce the amount of contract rent specified. An estoppel certificate should also be obtained from tenants. Concessions are negotiable points in a lease that are resolved in favor of the prospective tenant. Another example in leasing a new office building would be the owner's assumption of the lessee's remaining obligation under the lessee's existing lease in another building.

2. A lease of a portion of the premises to conduct a business for a particular purpose such as a refreshment stand at a recreational center.

3. A franchise right granted by a governmental agency to conduct a business.

4. In appraising, unusual terms given by a seller which may warrant the buyer paying a higher contract price for a property than would be the case if the seller did not give the special terms.

CONCILIATION AGREEMENT — A settlement or compromise agreement. Under Washington Discrimination Law, the Washington State Human Rights Commission shall endeavor to obtain a conciliation agreement with the respondent charged with a discriminatory practice. The agreement requires the respondent to do affirmative acts such as selling or renting to the complainant, or to refrain in the future from committing discriminatory acts. (*See* WASHINGTON STATE LAW AGAINST DISCRIMINATION.)
Reference: RCW 49.60.

CONCRETE BASEMENT FLOOR — Generally constructed of concrete reinforced with steel bars within the concrete. The basement floor, along with the foundation walls and the piers provide the support for the structure. Concrete is used because it is moisture proof and inexpensive.

CONCURRENT LEASE — A lease that overlaps the term of an existing shorter-term lease in which the new lessee takes subject to the rights of the first lessee. In effect, the new lessee takes control of the property in the place of the lessor and is entitled to the rents until the first lease expires, at which time the new lessee will be entitled to exclusive possession. The concurrent lease may cover all or part of the same premises as the earlier lease.

CONCURRENT OWNERSHIP — A term referring to ownership by two or more persons at the same time such as joint tenants, tenants in common, or community property. (*See* COMMUNITY PROPERTY, JOINT TENANCY, TENANCY IN COMMON.)

CONDEMNATION — A judicial or administrative proceeding to exercise the power of eminent domain; that is, the power of the government to take private property for public use. The agency taking the property is the condemnor and the person whose property is being taken, either partially or entirely, is the condemnee. In the taking of private property for public use, a fee simple estate or any lesser right, such as an easement, may be acquired. A common example of condemnation is the loss of an owner's access to a street entrance when the county builds a highway.

The right of eminent domain is limited by the Fifth Amendment to the U.S. Constitution, which states: "No person shall be deprived of life, liberty, or property without due process of law; nor shall private property be taken for public use without just compensation." Private property may be taken without the consent of the owner, whose only possible judicial complaints may be that the land was not taken for a sufficient public use or, as is more frequently the case, that just compensation was not paid. The modern trend of the courts is to define the term "public use" broadly to include not only public facilities such as streets, railroads, schools, and parks, but also property which would provide intangible public benefits, such as scenic easements.

The actual appraised value of the property at the date of the summons is generally the measure of valuation used to determine the amount of "just compensation". However, there is usually disagreement as to the appropriate appraised value, and this becomes the basis for most condemnation lawsuits.

Certain items are not considered in determining the value of the condemned property, such as loss of good will, relocation expenses, inconvenience, and the value of improvements added to the property after the date of the summons. This exclusion is especially harmful to operating businesses whose real estate value is much lower than the value of the business as an ongoing concern. After a property has been condemned, all preexisting liens and encumbrances are extinguished and their claims must be asserted against the condemnation award. Typically, the condemnee will be paid the condemnation award within two years after final judgment is rendered. If listed property is condemned, the listing broker typically is not entitled to a commission since the broker did not negotiate the sale.

Under a lease, tenants may be entitled to their share of the condemnation award to compensate them for the loss of their leasehold estates. To avoid this, many lessors insert a condemnation clause into the lease which provides that the lease will be canceled upon condemnation with all proceeds going to the lessor.

Condemnation also refers to the decision by the appropriate public agency that a property is no longer fit and must therefore be closed or destroyed.

When property is condemned, or sold under a threat of condemnation, the owner may defer any profit realized by treating the disposition as an involuntary conversion. He/she must replace the converted property within three taxable years following the end of the tax year in which the conversion occurs. Any excess of the condemnation proceeds over the cost of the new property is then taxable. (*See* ACQUISITION APPRAISAL, BEFORE-AND-AFTER METHOD, EMINENT DOMAIN, INVOLUNTARY CONVERSION, JUST COMPENSATION, POLICE POWER, SEVERANCE DAMAGES, SPECIAL BENEFIT.)

CONDITIONAL SALES CONTRACT — A contract in which the seller retains title to the item sold, but the item is given to the purchaser so long as he/she is not in default on any of the conditions of the contract; sometimes called an **executory contract**. Under this kind of contract, the seller has a security interest in the property and the buyer has an **equitable interest**. Usually, personal property (such as an air conditioner or an appliance) is the subject of a conditional sales contract. When real property is the subject of the contract, the contract is called a real estate contract. Upon the buyer's full performance of the conditions of the conditional sales contract, the seller must transfer legal title to the buyer. The conditional sales contract creating a security interest in a fixture or in an article that will become a fixture has been replaced under the Uniform Commercial Code by an instrument known as a security agreement. (*See* REAL ESTATE CONTRACT, SECURITY AGREEMENT, UNIFORM COMMERCIAL CODE.)

CONDITIONAL USE ZONING — A special land use tentatively approved by a zoning ordinance, which ordinarily requires compliance with stated standards. Such zoning might permit the use of a hospital in a residential zone, but limit the types of functions the hospital can perform. Also called special use zoning.

CONDITIONS — *See* COVENANTS AND CONDITIONS.

CONDO — A common reference to a condominium unit or development, refers to either a particular unit or building. (*See* CONDOMINIUM OWNERSHIP.)

CONDOMINIUM — *See* CONDOMINIUM OWNERSHIP.

CONDOMINIUM ACT — Washington State has two different statutes which apply to condominiums.

The "Horizontal Property Regimes Act" the first statute to enable the creation of a condominium was adopted in 1963 and applies to all condominiums created between 1963 and July 1, 1990. The "Condominium Act" applies to all condominiums created after July 1, 1990.

Reference: RCW 64.32 - Horizontal Property Regimes Act
RCW 64.34 - Condominium Act.

Even though the new Condominium Act only applies to condominiums created after July 1, 1990, a number of its provisions applies to condominiums created before that date for

events occurring after July 1, 1990: separate titles and taxations, application of local ordinances, regulations and building codes; condemnation; construction and validity of declaration and bylaws; description of units, powers of unit owners' association; board of directors and officers; voting and proxies; tort and contract liability; notification on sale of unit; common expenses and assessments; lien for assessments; association records; resale of units; effect of violation on rights of action; attorneys' fees; and definitions, to the extent needed to construe the other applicable sections.
Reference: RCW 64.34.010

Two essential sets of documents create a condominium: (1) the condominium declaration, with its accompanying survey map and plans; and (2) the articles of incorporation and bylaws of the unit owners' association.

The condominium declaration is referred to as a "master deed" in some states. In many ways it cam be compared to a declaration of restrictive covenants and a subdivision plat. Unlike a plat, however, it need not be approved by any governmental entity.

Among the major changes in the 1990 legislation were consumer protection provisions including the requirements that a developer of a new condominium prepare and give to all prospective purchasers a Public Offering Statement which is similar to a full disclosure statement which in part summarizes the over structure of the proposed condominium and provides background information on the developer. In a resale of a condominium unit, the seller must provide a Resale Certificate which in summary form provides financial data on the condition of the condominium association and the attachments provide the basis documentation which created the condominium. (*See* CONDOMINIUM CONVERSION, CONDOMINIUM MAP, CONDOMINIUM OWNERS ASSOCIATION, CONDOMINIUM OWNERSHIP, HORIZONTAL PROPERTY REGIMES ACT, PUBLIC OFFERING STATEMENT, REPLACEMENT RESERVES, RESALE CERTIFICATE, RESCISSION.)

CONDOMINIUM CONVERSION — *See* CONVERSION.

CONDOMINIUM MAP — The detailed site plan containing the layout, location, unit numbers, and dimensions of the condominium units, which is filed for record at the same time as the condominium declaration. The condominium map is generally certified by an architect, land surveyor, or engineer. Also called the condominium plan. (*See* SURVEY MAP.)

CONDOMINIUM OWNERS' ASSOCIATION — An association of the owners of condominium units. It is often in an unincorporated association form, and its main purpose is to control, regulate, and maintain the common elements in the condominium. The voting power of each owner in an association is usually measured by his/her percentage of undivided interest in the condominium. Through the bylaws, the board of directors of a condominium owners' association is authorized to regulate and administer the affairs of the condominium, especially in regard to the maintenance and repair of the common elements. The association has the authority to assess and collect sufficient money to maintain the common areas and to assure the financial stability of the condominium. When a unit owner is in default on his/her monthly charges or special assessments, the association may place a lien against the individual apartment, which can be foreclosed to satisfy the debt.

Under the IRS Code, a condominium owners' association can elect to be treated as a tax-exempt organization. If such an election is made, the association will not be taxed on membership dues, fees, and assessments received from members of the association who own residential units, but it must meet certain income and expenditure tests.

Under the law, membership dues and assessments will not be treated as taxable income, provided that at least 60 percent of the association's gross income comes from membership dues, fees, or assessments; that at least 90 percent of its expenditures are used to acquire, manage, maintain, or improve association properties; and that substantially all of the units or lots owned by members are used as residences (although they need not be owner-occupied).

The association is still taxed as a corporation on investment income and income from a trade or business (for example, rental income or fees from third parties for use of the association's facilities). (*See* ASSOCIATION, CONDOMINIUM OWNERSHIP, HORIZONTAL PROPERTY REGIMES ACT.)

CONDOMINIUM OWNERSHIP — An estate in real property consisting of an individual interest in an apartment or commercial unit and an undivided common interest in the common areas in the condo project such as the land, parking areas, elevators, stairways, recreational facilities and so on. Each condominium unit is a statutory entity that may be mortgaged, taxed, sold, or otherwise transferred in ownership, separately and independently of all other units in the structure. Units are separately assessed and taxed based on the combined value of the individual living unit and the proportionate ownership of the common areas. The unit also can be separately foreclosed upon in case of default on the mortgage note or other lienable payments. In effect, the condominium permits ownership of a specific horizontal layer of airspace as opposed to the traditional view of vertical property ownership from the center of the earth to the sky. Typically, the unit, the percentage of common interest, and the limited common elements are appurtenant to each other and cannot be sold or transferred separately.

Condominium ownership is popular in many urban and resort areas due to the general scarcity of desirable and usable land and the advantages of fee ownership and apartment living. In addition to residential condominiums, many office and professional buildings, industrial plants, medical clinics, recreational developments, and combined apartment and office buildings are using the condominium form of ownership. Each condominium owner has exclusive ownership of his/her individual unit but must, nevertheless, comply with the requirements of the declaration, bylaws, and house rules set up for the protection and comfort of all the condominium owners.

The concept was introduced into this country after considerable and enthusiastic use in Puerto Rico. Interest in the condominium concept and in the passage of enabling statutes was stimulated in part by the U.S. Housing Act of 1961, wherein Congress extended FHA insurance so as to include condominium projects. The first condominium legislation was passed in Washington in 1963, the Washington Horizontal Property Regimes Act, usually referred to as the Condominium Act.

The National Association of Home Builders estimates there will be nearly 200,000 condominium units constructed annually in the 1980s. By the year 2000, it is estimated that more than 50 percent of all new housing starts will be condominiums.

For a condominium to exist under Washington law, the developer must execute and record with the County Auditor a Declaration, survey map and a set of plans. All three (3) instruments must be recorded simultaneously and must be cross referenced to each other by recording information.

Condominium units tend to sell at prices below those of single family homes. However, the life-cycle costs of a condominium (mortgage, utilities, maintenance, and condominium fees) may be equal to or in some cases greater than other forms of housing.

Although all types of consumers own condominiums, couples of 45 - 64 years of age, whose children have left home, and the elderly are the dominant buyers.

The greatest problem consumers have with condominiums is their inability, as an association of property owners, to operate and maintain their commonly owned properties. The failure of these associations to properly maintain the common properties, the study concluded, directly affect the value of each consumer's unit. Many smaller condo projects cannot afford professional management which impacts value. (*See* CONVERSION, CO-OPERATIVE, DECLARATION, HORIZONTAL PROPERTY REGIMES ACT, INSURANCE, INTERSTATE LAND SALES, SURVEY MAP.)
Reference: RCW 64.32.

CONDUIT — A metal pipe in which electrical wiring is installed.

CONFIRMATION OF SALE — A court approval of the sale of property by an executor, administrator, guardian, conservator or commissioner in a foreclosure sale. In most cases, the amount of the broker's commission must also be approved by the court. (*See* PROBATE.)

CONFORMING LOAN — A provision made in accordance with the standardized underwriting criteria of the major secondary market agencies, Fannie Mae and Freddie Mac, and which therefore can be sold to those agencies. By contrast, a loan that does not meet the Fannie Mae/Freddie Mac standards is called a noncomforming loan.

CONFORMITY — An appraisal principle of value based on the concept that the more a property or its components are in harmony with the surrounding properties or components, the greater the contributory value.

CONNECTION LINE — A line used in surveying land that connects a surveyor's monument with a permanent reference mark. (*See* SURVEY.)

CONSEQUENTIAL DAMAGES — 1. A money award made by a court to compensate an injured party for all losses resulting from a breach of contract, which losses a reasonable person could have foreseen at the time the contract was made.

2. That damage arising from the acts of public bodies or adjacent owners to a given parcel of land that impairs the value of that parcel without actually condemning its use in whole or in part. For example, in an inverse condemnation proceeding, consequential damages might be awarded when land is used for a public sewage treatment plant and private land located downwind of the plant suffers a loss in value due to noxious odors.

CONSERVATION — A practice, both by state government and private landowners, of protecting and preserving the natural and scenic resources attendant to lands within the State of Washington, so as to insure the highest long-term benefits for all residents. (*See* ENVIRONMENTAL PROTECTION AGENCY.)

CONSERVATOR — A guardian, protector, preserver, or receiver appointed by the court to administer the person and property of another (usually an adult incapable of managing for himself) and to insure that the property will be properly managed. A conservator does not need a real estate license to sell the protected real estate though the sale does require court approval.

CONSIDERATION — An act or the promise thereof, which is offered by one party to induce another to enter into a contract; that which is given in exchange for something from another. It could also include the promise to refrain from doing a certain think, like filing a justifiable lawsuit (the forbearance of a right). Consideration distinguishes a contract from a gift. Consideration is usually something of value, such as the purchase price of money, though it may be personal services or exchanged property. It is the price bargained for and paid for a promise, and it may be a return promise. Thus, the mere promise to pay money is sufficient consideration, and an earnest money deposit is not necessary for purposes of creating a binding contract.

Even though the sales price is stated in the Purchase and Sale Agreement and earnest money is actually received, the actual consideration which supports the contract is the mutual exchange of promises by buyer and seller to legally obligate themselves to do something they were not before legally required to do; that is, the seller agrees to sell for a certain price and the buyer agrees to pay that price to buy the described property.

As a general rule:

1. There should be a recital of consideration in a deed, as presumptive evidence that something of value was given for the realty. While most contracts must be supported by a valuable consideration, a good consideration (love and affection) is sufficient to support a gift deed between relatives. Except where a fiduciary executes a deed, the actual consideration need not be stated but may be proved by any other legal evidence. In practice, the price paid for property can be calculated by checking to find the excise tax paid. *Reference:* RCW 28.45.

2. A real estate licensee may have his/her license suspended if he/she is a party to naming a false consideration, but not if it is obviously a nominal consideration. (*See* DUAL CONTRACT.)

3. An option must be supported by actual consideration.

4. In a lease, the periodic payment of rent over the rental term is the consideration for the use and occupancy of the premises. However, suppose there is a signed lease for one year at a rent of $400 per month and, after four months, the landlord decides to raise the rent to $500 per month. The tenant promises to pay the increase, but fails to do so, so the landlord brings an action to evict. The tenant will probably win the case, unless the landlord gave additional consideration to support the tenant's promise to pay the increased rent.

5. Courts will not usually inquire into the adequacy of consideration to support a contract. A court will, however, deny an action for specific performance if the parties were not in an equal bargaining position and if the party bringing the action has not paid a fair and sufficient consideration. For example, if the fair market value of the property in question is $200,000 and a buyer (who did not disclose that he/she was a licensed broker) seeks specific performance of a purchase contract in which the purchase price agreed upon is $100,000, a court will probably deny the action.

The question of adequacy of consideration also arises in cases involving an alleged fraudulent conveyance. That is, where a conveyance is made by a seller who is or will thereby be rendered insolvent and who is bankrupt within 90 days of the conveyance, the trustee in bankruptcy will be able to void the conveyance as fraudulent if the price is inadequate. In certain cases, inadequacy of consideration is asserted as evidence of undue influence or evidence that the buyer was not a "bona fide purchaser" for value under the recording law. Also, property transferred without adequate consideration within three years of the grantor's death will be included in the decedent's estate and will be subject to federal estate tax as a gift made in contemplation of death. (*See* COMMISSION, COMPENSATION, DEPOSIT, VALUABLE CONSIDERATION.)

CONSOLIDATE — To unite, combine or incorporate by reference; such as, (1) to combine two mortgages on one property to a single loan; (2) to combine two or more parcels of land (the reverse of the subdivision process); (3) to join a land sales registration with an earlier registration, especially where the property is developed and sold in succeeding phases or increments. Consolidated registration of subdivided land is permitted under both state and federal (HUD) regulations.

CONSTANT — 1. A percentage which, when applied directly to the face value of a debt, develops the annual amount of money necessary to pay a specified net rate of interest on the reducing balance, and to liquidate the debt in a specified time period; a method for determining rate and term on an **annual basis**.

2. The annual payment required per dollar of mortgage money, including both interest and amortized principal. The mortgage constant varies with each change in interest rate and each change in the amortization term, as illustrated in the follow table:

ANNUAL CONSTANT TABLE

Interest Rate	20 Years	25 Years	30 Years
8.00	10.04	9.27	8.81
8.50	10.42	9.67	9.23
9.00	10.80	10.08	9.66
9.50	11.19	10.49	10.10
10.00	11.59	10.91	10.54
10.50	11.99	11.34	10.98
11.00	12.39	11.77	11.43
11.50	12.80	12.20	11.89
12.00	13.22	12.64	12.35

(*See* AMORTIZATION.)

CONSTRUCTION ALLOWANCE — Money or other financial inducement to a lessee that is provided by the lessor to cover the cost, in whole or in part, of preparing a structure for a lessee's occupancy. This could cover costs for partitions, wiring, lighting, standard carpet, and so on. In Washington, it is usually called tenant improvements (TIs).

CONSTRUCTION LOAN — A short-term or **interim** loan to cover the construction costs of a building or development project, with loan proceeds advanced periodically in the form of installment payments as the work progresses. It is a form of "installment payout". In this manner, the outstanding loan balance is matched to the value of the collateral as it grows. Interest on the borrowed money is not normally charged until the incremental construction draws are advanced. When interest is charged on the entire amount even before it is advanced, it is called "Dutch interest". Upon completion of the project, one or more long term, permanent loans, such as those end loans taken out by the buyers of individual condo units, will "takeout" (pay off) the construction loan. (*See* INTERIM FINANCING, SUBORDINATION AGREEMENT, TAKEOUT FINANCING.)

CONSTRUCTIVE — A fiction created by the law, as in **constructive eviction** or **constructive notice**. (*See* RECORDING.)

CONSTRUCTIVE EVICTION — Conduct by the landlord which so materially disturb or impair the tenant's enjoyment of the leased premises that a tenant is effectively forced to move out and terminate the lease without liability for any further rent. This concept is a product of modern property law, which tends to place more emphasis than in the past on the quality of possession or habitability under the lease terms. Constructive eviction might occur when a landlord cuts off the electricity and heating, makes extensive alterations to the premises, or attempts to lease the property to others. The Washington Landlord Tenant Act provides that the tenant must notify the landlord in writing of any condition which deprives the tenant of a substantial part of the benefit and enjoyment of his/her bargain under the rental agreement. If the landlord does not remedy the situation within the time period provided for the type of deficiency, the tenant has several alternative procedures or options. One of them is to move out and terminate the rental agreement. There can be no constructive eviction without the vacating of the premises within a reasonable time of the landlord's act. (*See* ABATEMENT, EVICTION, LANDLORD TENANT ACT.)
Reference: RCW 59.18.

Another example would be if the landlord of a high-rise apartment building failed to provide elevator service. The tenant's duty to pay rent is not terminated if the tenant remains in possession. The tenant can sue to recover possession or bring an action for damages based on the breach of the covenant for quiet enjoyment.

CONSTRUCTIVE FRAUD — Breach of a legal or equitable duty which the law declares fraudulent because of its tendency to deceive others, without any showing of dishonesty or intent to deceive. Under common law, a broker may be charged with constructive fraud for failing to disclose a known material fact when the broker had a duty to speak; for example, a listing broker failed to disclose a **known** major foundation problem not readily observable upon an ordinary inspection.

CONSTRUCTIVE NOTICE — Notice of certain facts which are implied by law to be known by a person because he/she could have discovered the fact by reasonable diligence or by inquiry into public records; a legal presumption that a person is responsible for knowing these facts.

The proper recording of a document in the Office of the County Auditor is constructive notice to all the world of the existence of the document and its contents. Possession of property imparts constructive notice to everyone of the rights of the party in possession. Since constructive notice is a legal presumption, it is often referred to as Legal Notice, as compared to actual notice which is either express or direct knowledge acquired in the course of a transaction. (*See* ACTUAL NOTICE, CHAIN OF TITLE, INQUIRY NOTICE, RECORDING.)
Reference: RCW 65.08.

CONSTRUCTIVE RECEIPT — A theory in tax law that the unrestricted right to receive money is the same as the actual receipt of that money. For example; payment in full on a promissory note is due and is tendered on December 31st and the holder of the note asks that payment be made on January 1st in another tax year, once payment is tendered or available the income is deemed to have been realized for tax purposes.. Thus, if a person has the right and ability to receive payment, which includes profit or income, that profit will be taxed when the **right** to receive it **arises**, regardless of when the payment is actually accepted. (*See* CASH METHOD.)

CONSULTANT — One who gives advice on a specific matter, such as a financial or real estate advisor. (*See* LICENSING LAW.)

CONSUMER CREDIT PROTECTION ACT - *See* TRUTH IN LENDING ACT.

CONSUMER CREDIT REPORT ACT (FAIR CREDIT REPORT ACT) - Federal law that protects consumers from abuse by parties preparing and using credit reports. If additional information on a borrower is given to a financial institution then a lender must provide the applicant with direct access to the information. The applicant has the right to ask that any information not verified or that is obsolete be deleted from the file. The purpose of the act is to insure that the consumer reporting agencies undertake their responsibilities with fairness, impartiality and respect for the consumer's right to privacy. (*See* CREDIT REPORT, FAIR CREDIT REPORTING ACT.)

CONSUMERS' PRICE INDEX (CPI) — A statistic index issued monthly by the U.S. Department of Labor which is used by business as a comparative measure of the cost of goods and service on a month to month basis, year to year basis or against a base period. The base index set by the government for 1967 is 100. In 1987, the CPI was 333.1. There are two different CPI index categories published. There is the CPI for all urban consumers ("CPI-U") and the CPI for urban wage earners and clerical workers ("CPI-W").

The CPI is used in some leases (office, industrial, retail or ground) to be the measure (percentage) of increase at preset intervals (e.g., the base rent of $14,000 per month will be increased at the end of the thirty-sixth month for the next thirty-six months by the CPI for the City of Seattle). Sometimes there is a cap (top level) set on the increase; for example, not to exceed 6% per year. (*See* BASE PERIOD, COST OF LIVING INDEX.)

CONSUMMATE — To bring to completion. In Washington a sale of real property pursuant to an earnest money agreement is consummated upon the closing of the transaction, usually evidenced by the delivery of the deed and funds and the recording of the conveyance documents. (*See* CLOSING.)

CONTIGUOUS — In close proximity; adjoining or abutting; near any point of contact.

Contiguous property owners must to a reasonable degree yield their desired privacy to the general welfare which is contributed to by the operation of legitimate business such as an airport operating near residences. Thus, reasonable inconvenience may be suffered by owners contiguous to commercial enterprises.

Sometimes a seller under a real estate contract which provides for partial release of various parcels will require in the contract that each partial release be contiguous to a parcel previously released; in that case, the buyer may want to specifically define the word contiguous to mean lots or parcels on opposite sides of the same street, alley, easement or right of way. Often, a partial release clause in a mortgage or deed of trust may require that a partial release will be given only on a parcel which is contiguous to a parcel previously released. The term "contiguous" should be precisely defined so the release clause will not be challenged on grounds of uncertainty and vagueness.

CONTINGENCY — A provision placed in a contract which requires the completion of a certain act or the happening of a particular event before a contract is binding. Often a buyer will submit an offer to purchase contingent upon his/her obtaining financing or rezoning. In such a case, the seller should be sure the contingency is specifically detailed and unambiguous, and that there is a definite cutoff date, otherwise the buyer could tie up the seller's property indefinitely as he/she attempts to get financing or rezoning. However, the buyer must exercise due diligence; there is an implied promise to make a "good faith" effort to bring about the condition precedent. Failure to do so may be material breach of the contract.

A party may waive any contingency clause which was inserted for his/her benefit. For example, the buyer could force the seller to sell the property even though the buyer was not able to obtain the zoning for which he/she originally made a contingency in the Purchase and Sale Agreement. A buyer must exercise great care to see that all contingencies that he/she provided for are met or verified. There is a possible danger if the buyer goes ahead and allows the transaction to close prior to the satisfaction of a contingency or the verification of a contingency, that a court may say that by allowing the transaction to close the buyer either agreed that the contingency had been met or that the buyer had waived the contingency and cannot rely on it.

Contingency clauses must be drafted precisely because they frequently become the focal point of a dispute. Consider the following questions when drafting a contingency: what is the condition: for whose benefit is it: can it be waived and by whom; when must it be met; is there a right to extend; and what are the rights and obligations of buyer and seller if the condition is not met despite good faith efforts.

If a contingency is worded to loosely, such as contingent on "my deciding whether it is a good deal or not," then the entire contract is considered "illusory" and unenforceable by either party due to lack of "mutuality of obligation." If the sale is contingent on a "satisfactory" inspection or attorney's review of lease, the courts will try to impose standards of good faith and reasonability so a party cannot back out just because of a change in that party's plans.

A contingent sale must be distinguished from an option. In an option, the optionee has absolute discretion whether or not to exercise the option. In a contingency, the buyer must buy upon the occurrence or nonoccurrence of a specified event, such as loan qualification.

If the buyer inserts a contingency in the offer, the seller may want to counteroffer. For example, if the offer is contingent upon the sale of buyer's home, the seller might add a clause to the effect that "if seller receives another offer (or decides to withdraw the property from sale), buyer will have 72 hours to remove or waive the contingency, otherwise the contract is canceled."

The financing contingency is not only the most frequently used contingency; it is also the most controversial. Even a well-written contingency statement can cause problems. For instance, assume that a financing contingency stated that the offer was contingent upon buyer obtaining a first mortgage loan commitment for $67,500 with interest not to exceed 12 percent per annum and for a term of not less than 30 years, and monthly payments for principal and interest not to exceed $680 plus 1/12 the estimated annual real property taxes and 1/12 the annual insurance premium. Buyers agreed to use good faith and due diligence in obtaining such loan. Buyers qualified for the loan but refused to take the loan because the lender added an interest rate escalation clause. While a court might allow some deviation in the financing commitment, the inclusion of an escalation clause is a material deviation of the terms of the offer to purchase and thus the buyer would not be in breach of the contract for refusing to complete the purchase; the buyer is entitled to a return of the deposit money. However, a buyer who did qualify for financing on the terms stated in an offer but who later gets divorced or otherwise changes circumstances so as to not be qualified at the time of closing may have difficulty defending a lawsuit for enforcement of the purchase contract. Sometimes a cautious seller might add a clause to the effect that "the execution of any loan documents by the buyer shall be deemed to be an acceptance of such loan and a waiver of this contingency." (*See* REAL ESTATE PURCHASE AND SALE AGREEMENT, SPECIAL CONDITIONS.)

CONTINUATION — An **update** of a title search. In the typical transaction, the title company will issue a preliminary title report soon after escrow is opened. At the closing date, the title company will continue the search down to the time of recording the final documents, by checking their Tract Books and Name Index (extracts from the public records) to be sure no intervening rights in the property have arisen. The final title report will then show title in the buyer/grantee. (*See* TITLE INSURANCE, TITLE SEARCH.)

CONTINUING EDUCATION — A requirement that a real estate licensee complete a specified number of educational offerings as a prerequisite to license renewal or reinstatement. (*See* LICENSING LAW.)

CONTINUOUS OPERATION CLAUSE — A shopping center lease provision requiring that key tenants keep their stores in operation and open during specified hours during their lease terms. This clause is for the benefit of not only the landlord but other shopping center tenants as well.

CONTOUR MAP — A topographic map showing the shape of an area of land by means of a series of lines which connect points of equal elevation at set intervals.

CONTRACT — A legally enforceable agreement between competent parties who agree to perform or refrain from performing certain acts for a consideration. In essence, a contract is an enforceable promise.

In real estate, there are many different types of contracts, including listings, contracts of sale, options, mortgages, assignments, leases, deeds, escrow agreements, and loan commitments, among others. Each of these contracts must meet the following minimum requirements:

Competent Parties: There must be at least two bona fide parties to any contract. (Thus, John Sharp cannot agree to deed property to himself. He could, however, convey property to himself and Bob Smith as tenants in common.) Both parties must possess at least limited capacity to contract. Thus, minors cannot deed property they own since they lack the capacity to convey property. Such deed is voidable by the minor. A minor does possess, however, the limited capacity to enter into a valid contract to purchase property from an adult; such a contract would be enforceable by the minor against the adult, but would be voidable by the minor if the minor chose not to complete the purchase during his/her minority. A fiduciary and a corporation must have the proper authority to enter into a contract. When a party to a contract dies, his/her or heirs and assigns may be bound to the contract. (*See* CAPACITY OF PARTIES, DEED, MINOR.)

Writing: All real estate contracts, except those for leases of one year or less, must be in writing to be enforceable. All essential terms of the contract must be complete and certain so that the entire agreement is set forth in the writing and nothing material is left to be agreed upon in the future. Until the contract is signed; everything is negotiable. Once the contract is signed, nothing is negotiable and new consideration is needed to modify the terms of the contract. (*See* STATUTE OF FRAUDS.)

Description: The property must be accurately described so that the parties can identify the subject matter of the contract. The State of Washington has one of the strictest standards in the United States as far as the inclusion of a complete legal description on every document pertaining to real property. Even a Purchase and Sale Agreement must contain a legal description of the property. Failure to include the full legal description in any instrument or document pertaining to real property will raise serious questions as to its enforceability. (*See* LEGAL DESCRIPTION.)

Meeting of the Minds: There must be a valid offer and an unqualified acceptance of that offer, so that the seller understands the terms of the buyer's offer and the buyer understands the method of purchase of the identified property. The parties must agree on all essential terms and not leave anything to subsequent agreement(s); otherwise, all you have are preliminary negotiations and not a binding contract.

Consideration: The contract must be supported by consideration, that is, both parties must be required to do something they were not previously obligated to do. Most contracts require a **valuable consideration** such as a promise to pay money. A gift deed, however, is valid if it merely recites a good, rather than valuable, consideration such as for "love and affection" between relatives. (*See* CONSIDERATION, OPTIONS.)

Legal Purpose: To be enforceable, a contract must contemplate a legitimate purpose. Thus, a contract to lease a building for an illegal gambling casino would not be enforceable, nor would a listing contract to pay a commission to an unlicensed person.

Signature: All parties to be bound by the contract must sign. In the usual real estate transaction, both buyer and seller sign the Purchase and Sale Agreement.

If there is an ambiguity in a contract, the courts will construe the contract most strongly against the party preparing it. For example, since the broker prepares the listing contract, it is construed very strictly against the broker. Thus, if there were any doubt whether the listing was an exclusive agency or an exclusive right-to-sell, the courts would construe it to be an exclusive agency. (*See* LISTING.)

It is not necessary that there be one formal document representing the contract of the parties, though it is often preferable in order to eliminate any disputes as to whether a contract was formed. Sometimes the essentials of a contract, e.g., the offer and the acceptance, arise from separate correspondence between the parties so one formal contract is never actually signed.

Some contracts are discharged upon the death of one of the parties to the contract. However, contracts pertaining to real estate are normally binding on the heirs and assigns of the deceased.

The essential element in every contract is that both parties clearly understand what the writing states as their agreement. Poorly drafted documents, especially those containing extensive legal language, are subject to various interpretations and often lead to litigation. In most instances, the parties would be best advised to engage the services of an experienced real estate attorney to draft a contract accurately reflecting the true intentions of the parties. A broker who attempts to draft legal contracts may be guilty of the unauthorized practice of law. (*See* CONTRACT OF SALE, DEED, LEASE, PRACTICE OF LAW.) *Reference*: RCW 18.85, RCW 19.36 and RCW 64.04.

CONTRACT DOCUMENTS — In terms of real estate development, the agreement between two parties together with all supporting elements which assist in defining, amending, or modifying the agreement and its attendant conditions (drawings, specifications, change orders, addenda). The term is used in standard form documents used by the American Institute of Architects (AIA), such as those between the owner, architect, and general contractor.

CONTRACT OF SALE — A contract for the purchase of real property, commonly called a Purchase and Sale Agreement or an Earnest Money Agreement in which the buyer agrees to purchase for a certain price and the seller agrees to convey title by way of a deed or an assignment of lease (for leasehold property). In addition to binding the parties to the purchase and sale of the property during the period of time required to close the transaction, the contract frequently serves as the initial directions to the escrow company to process the mechanics of the transaction. Thus, it is most important that the parties agree in the contract on all of the pertinent closing details, such as who pays the various expenses of the sale, who bears the risk of loss, the date of occupancy, the proration date, and the like. In essence, the contract of sale is an executory contract to convey, serving as the vehicle to get to the deed, which finally conveys title. Once the contract is signed, the remainder of the transaction is primarily mechanical.

To be enforceable, the contract of sale must be in writing, be signed by the parties to be bound, contain the buyer's and seller's names, contain a full legal description of the property, state the sales price and have a legitimate purpose. If the seller is married, the other spouse must sign the contract so she/he will be bound to release her/his community property interest when the deed is delivered.

Purchase and Sale Agreements are rarely recorded, unless the parties anticipate a particularly long period of time to close the transaction. Normal closing takes approximately thirty to ninety days from the date the contract is signed. A real estate contract should, however, be recorded to protect the buyer, because it is often a period of years before the buyer pays off the contract and obtains legal title to the property.

The standard Purchase and Sale Agreement in Washington usually provides that in the event that the buyer should default and not purchase the property, the seller can elect one of the following remedies: (1) keep the deposit as liquidated damages; (2) sue the buyer for money damages; (3) tender a deed to escrow and sue the buyer to complete the purchase under the terms of the agreement. This last remedy of specific performance is only possible in the instance that money damages cannot adequately compensate the seller for his/her loss. Many Purchase and Sale Agreements contain a provision (if selected) that if the buyer defaults, the seller retains the earnest money deposit (up to five percent) and waivers the other two options. If the seller defaults, the buyer can rescind the agreement and obtain the return of his/her deposit money, or sue the seller for specific performance to have the court compel the seller to sell the property on the agreed terms.

In Washington many brokers use the standard form Purchase and Sale Agreement copyrighted by the Northwest Multiple Listing Services or the Washington Association of Realtors® as the contract of sale. If a broker does not charge a separate fee for completing this form, he/she can assist his/her client in filling it out and advise him/her on inserting appropriate special conditions. As long as this service is rendered incidental to representing his/her client in the purchase or sale of the property, it is not the unauthorized practice of law. However, a real estate licensee cannot prepare any document relating to a real estate transaction if the licensee is not involved in the transaction. (*See* CONTRACT, PURCHASE AND SALE AGREEMENT, REAL ESTATE CONTRACT, SPECIFIC PERFORMANCE.)

CONTRACT PRICE — A tax term used in computation of gain realized from an installment sale. The contract price represents a property's selling price, minus any mortgages assumed or taken subject to by the buyer, plus the excess (if any) of any such liens collected in addition to the seller's adjusted basis at the time of sale. In essence the contract price is the seller's equity in the property. (*See* INSTALLMENT SALE.)

One of the advantages of a real estate contract for the seller is that it permits the "contract price" to be the same as the selling price and thus defer taxes much better than if the buyer assumed or took subject to the mortgage. As an example, taxpayer sells property for $100,000, basis of $70,000 and the gain is $30,000; the down payment is $20,000 with an assumption of an existing $60,000 first mortgage and a purchase money second mortgage of $20,000. Although the selling price is $100,000, the contract price is only $40,000. Thus, of the total amount the seller is to receive ($40,000), the gain ($30,000) represents 75 percent. Therefore 75 percent of the down payment and of each principal payment on the purchase money mortgage is gain, and only the remaining 25 percent is considered return of basis. (*See* REAL ESTATE CONTRACT.)

Alternatively, if the property is sold on a real estate contact, the entire $100,000 selling price would also be the contract price, Therefore, only 30 percent of the down payment would be gain. The remaining gain consists of 30 percent of principal payments received under the contract for deed, which would be taxable only as those principal payments are received (*See* INSTALLMENT SALE.)

CONTRACT RENT — The rental income as stipulated by the parties in a lease. Appraisers often contrast this with economic rent, which is the amount of rent that could be obtained if the property were vacant and available on the open market.

CONTRACTOR — 1. One who contracts or covenants, either with a public body or private parties, to construct works or erect buildings at a certain price. A contractor is ordinarily understood to be the person who undertakes to supply labor and materials for specific improvements under a contract with an owner or principal. A **general contractor** is a contractor whose business operations require the use of more than two unrelated building trades or crafts whose work the contractor superintends or does in whole or in part; the term "general contractor" does not include an individual who does all work personally without employees or other "specialty contractors".

In Washington it is unlawful to submit any bid or do any work as a contractor until such person has registered with the Contractor's Registration, Dept. of Labor and Industry. Prior to an individual, partnership or corporation being issued a certificate of registration, there must be filed with the Department a surety bond. A contractor is precluded from bringing suit unless he/she was registered at the time that he/she agreed to do the work. The courts have often permitted such suits notwithstanding a lack of registration if the contractor has "substantially complied" with the registration requirements. "Substantial compliance" is defined, at a minimum, certain information on file with the Department of Licensing, a current bond or other security and insurance.
Reference: RCW 18.27

A private homeowner should require that the contractor provide a contract which contains at a minimum, the following elements, the date the work will commence and the date the work will be completed, a detailed list of the labor to be performed, a detail list of all material and supplies, who pays for them, who will obtain and pay for all required permits, the amount of the holdback until the contractor is finished and it can be inspected by the homeowners and the homeowner receives copies of all permits and all receipts for all expenditures.

2. If contract provides that the employer retains no control over details of work, but leaves to the other party the determination of the manner of doing it, without subjecting him/her to the control of the employer, the party undertaking the work is a contractor and not an employee. (*See* INDEPENDENT CONTRACTOR.)
Reference: RCW 18.27.

CONTRACTOR'S OVERHEAD — All of a contractor's direct costs other than the costs of labor and materials. Examples of contractor's overhead include job supervision costs, worker's compensation and contractor's insurance.

CONTRIBUTION — An appraisal principle in which the worth of an improvement is what it adds to the entire property's market value, regardless of the actual cost of the improvement. A remodeled basement may not contribute its entire cost to the value of the property, whereas a new bedroom usually will increase a house's value by more than its installation cost.

CONTRIBUTION, RIGHT OF — Cotenants who pay more than their pro rata share of necessary expenses to preserve the property may require a contribution from all other cotenants. These expenses include real property taxes, special assessments, and necessary repairs (but not unique improvements). *(See* TENANCY IN COMMON.)

CONVENIENCE STORE — A retail store that sells items (foods, liquors, sundries) usually bought in a non-selective and impulsive fashion at the most convenient place available.

CONVENTIONAL LOAN — A loan made with real estate as security and not involving government participation in the form of insuring (FHA) or guaranteeing (VA) the loan. The mortgagee can be an institutional lender or a private party. The loan is conventional in the sense that the lender looks solely to the credit of the borrower and the security of the property to assure payment of the debt. Conventional loans include those loans insured by private mortgage insurance companies. Since the lender is not subject to the more stringent government regulations of the FHA and VA, conventional loans are frequently more flexible with respect to terms and interest rates, although they do reflect a higher interest rate and larger down payment requirements due to the higher risk involved. Nonconventional loan interest rates (FHA, VA, FmHA) are fixed by statute. Conventional loans are subject to institutional regulation, which may be statutory (federal, state) or self-created.

CONVERSION — 1. The process of transforming an income producing property, such as a rental apartment building, into a condominium. In essence, the building is often renovated, the existing leases are allowed to lapse and the project is registered with the Office of the County Auditor as a condominium. The process requires considerable expertise in each stage: cost and market analysis, purchase, initial remodeling, appraisal, interim and long-term financing, tenant relocation and the final stage of sales.

In 1978, the City of Seattle adopted an ordinance regulating the conversion of residential rental units to condominiums or cooperatives. The stated reasons for the ordinance was to provide protection for tenants and purchasers in converted buildings and to mitigate the adverse effects of conversion displacement.

The ordinance gives tenants the right to have early notice the apartment complex will be converted, a 120 days notice as to the date the tenant's unit would be offered for sale, a 60-day period of first refusal to purchase the unit occupied and thereafter a 60-day period to purchase any other unit not purchased; however, the tenant has a 15-day period to rescind an offer after acceptance. During the 120 day period, the tenant may be evicted only for "good cause" as provided in the Landlord Tenant Act. A tenant may move on receiving notice of a conversion and receive $350.00 relocation assistance from the landlord.

The ordinance gives consumer protection by providing the units must comply with appropriate housing codes and there must be a full disclosure of the conditions of the units and an itemization of what repairs will be made. (*See* CONDOMINIUM OWNERSHIP, CONDOMINIUM ASSOCIATION, HORIZONTAL PROPERTY REGIMES ACT, PUBLIC OFFERING STATEMENT.)
Reference: RCW 64.32.

2. The appropriation of property belonging to another. The conversion may be illegal, as where a broker misappropriates funds of his/her client; or it may be legal, as where the government condemns property under the right of eminent domain. (*See* COMMINGLING, INVOLUNTARY CONVERSION.)

CONVERTIBLE ARM —A adjustable rate mortgage or deed of trust that gives the borrower the option of converting to a fixed interest rate at certain times during the first five years or seven years of the loan term. (*See* ADJUSTABLE RATE LOAN.)

CONVEYANCE — The transfer of title to real property by means of a written instrument such as a deed or an assignment of lease.

CONVEYANCE TAX — A county tax imposed on the transfer or conveyance of realty or any interest therein by means of deed, lease, real estate contract or Purchaser's Assignment of Contract and Deed. Generally exempt from the tax are mortgages and deeds of trusts, correction deeds, fulfillment deeds if the tax was paid when the underlying contract was recorded, transfers between husband and wife or parent and child. When the transaction is exempt, the document must be accompanied by a supplemental statement to the excise tax affidavit setting forth the grounds for exemption. (*See* EXCISE TAX ON REAL ESTATE SALES, RECORDING.)
Reference: RCW 28.45.

CO-OBLIGOR — One sharing in an obligation with another, such as a co-signor of a promissory note.

COOLING-OFF PERIOD — A kind of grace period provided by law or by contract in which a party to a contract can legally back out of a contract; a right of rescission. Under the Federal Truth-in-Lending law there is a specified three day cooling-off period in security transactions involving a borrower's personal residence. The Federal Interstate Land Sales Act has a cooling-off period of seven calendar days. Contrary to some popular belief, however, there is no automatic right to rescind a real estate purchase contract unless so specified by statute or by contract. (*See* PUBLIC OFFERING STATEMENT, REAL PROPERTY DISCLOSURE TRANSFER STATEMENT, RESALE CERTIFICATE, RESCISSION.)

COOPERATING BROKER — A broker who assists another broker in the sale of real property. Usually, the cooperating broker is the (selling) broker who found the buyer who offers to buy a piece of property which is listed with another (listing) broker. The cooperating broker has no contractual relationship with the seller and therefore must look solely to the listing broker for his/her commission, often split on a 50/50 basis. Co-brokerage occurs so frequent in Washington through the various Multiple Listing Services that some of the MLS have printed Purchase and Sale Agreements that have special sections in the acceptance portion for the cooperating broker to sign and to have the listing broker agree to a commission split. Example of various commission splits would be two-thirds to the selling office and one-third to the listing office, or a fifty-fifty split. (*See* SUBAGENT.)

The Realtor®'s Code of Ethics provides that a Realtor® cooperating with a listing broker should not invite the cooperation of a third broker without the consent of the listing broker. Also, the Realtor® should cooperate with other brokers on property listed by him/her exclusively whenever it is in the interest of the client, sharing commissions on an agreed basis. Negotiations concerning property listed exclusively with one broker should be carried on with the listing broker, not with the owner, except with the consent of the listing broker. (*See* AGENCY, PURCHASE AND SALE AGREEMENT, REAL ESTATE BROKERAGE RELATIONSHIPS ACT.)

COOPERATIVE — Cooperative ownership of an apartment unit means that the apartment owner has purchased shares in a corporation (or partnership or trust) which holds title to the entire apartment building. The cooperative owner is, in essence, a shareholder in a corporation whose principal asset is a building. In return for his/her stock in the corporation, the owner receives a proprietary lease entitling him/her to occupancy of a specific unit in the building. He/she thus occupies but does not own his/her unit. He/she must pay his/her prorata share of the corporation's expenses, which include loan charges, real estate taxes, maintenance, payroll, and the like. The owner can deduct for tax purposes his/her share of the taxes and interest charges.

"Co-ops", as they are often called, are more popular in the Eastern United States than in Washington, where condominium ownership is by far the most popular mode of ownership. Because it is more difficult to obtain financing for a coop, a coop unit generally sells for less than a comparable condominium unit.

Some basic differences between a coop and a condominium are:

1. In a co-op, the corporation owns the building and the apartment dweller owns a proprietary lease and a corresponding number of shares in the corporation. In a condominium, each unit is individually owned. Voting power in a co-op is usually one vote per unit, whereas, in a condo, an owner's voting power is relative to the size or value of the owner's unit (the percentage of common interest).

2. In a co-op, the corporation takes out a single loan on the entire building. In a condominium, there is no loan on the building; rather there are individual loans on those units not fully paid for in cash. Thus financing is often easier for a condominium unit purchaser.

3. Since a condominium owner actually owns his/her unit, he/she is less restricted in the use of his/her apartment than in a co-op tenant under a proprietary lease.

4. Upon resale, the condominium owner may sell to virtually any buyer who can pay the price; whereas the co-op tenant may have to obtain the Board of Directors' approval of the proposed purchaser. Some boards may not want rock musicians, movie-stars or even ex-Presidents. Of course, the Board cannot discriminate on the basis of race, sex, color, religion, ancestry or marital status.

5. Only "individuals" may deduct real estate taxes and mortgage interest attributable to ownership of a co-op, and a corporation is not an individual. Corporations, however, can deduct taxes and interest on condominium units they own. Because of this tax aspect, the promoter of a condominium is therefore in a much better position to sell units to national corporations and other business enterprises for the housing of their executives or use by customers.

6. Since the condominium owner obtains his/her own financing and is responsible for his/her individual property tax assessment, he/she is not responsible for any default on another owner's loan or property taxes. In a co-op, when an owner (tenant-shareholder) defaults on his/her loan or tax payments, the other shareholders must cure the default or risk having the entire project sold for taxes or foreclosed under the blanket loan. This contingent liability is one of the major drawback of co-op ownership.

7. Neither the co-op nor the condominium appear to offer any important income tax advantages over the other if owned by an individual.

8. The owner of a condominium has an interest in real property while a stockholder in a cooperative owns personalty. The condominium unit would be inheritable as realty while the co-op would pass as personalty. Also, as realty, a unit in a condominium would qualify as a homestead where a co-op would not.

9. For a cooperative corporation to qualify to pass through deduction that represents a tenant shareholder's share of real estate taxes and interest, at least 80 percent of the cooperative's gross income must have been derived from individual tenant shareholders. Each of the tenant shareholders must be entitled to occupy a house or apartment in a building owned or leased by the corporation.

The 80 percent rule has been difficult to meet when there is a high vacancy rate or when there are foreclosures. To make it easier to meet the 80 percent requirement, the definition of a tenant shareholder will include the original conveyor for 3 years after acquiring stock and banks whether the stock was acquired by purchase or foreclosure.

When preparing a Purchase and Sale Agreement involving a coop an example of the way a property could be described is:

Ten shares of stock in Muir Apartments, Inc. entitling owner to proprietary use of Apartment 67 and parking stall #3, and co-use of "common elements". (*See* DESCENT.)

CO-OWNERSHIP — *See* COTENANCY

CORE SPACE — *See* RENTABLE AREA, USABLE AREA.

CORNER STAKES — Used by a surveyor in running a survey by metes and bounds. Such stakes are needed to fix the survey on the ground and are set at every change of direction.

CORNICE — A horizontal projection or molding at the top of the exterior walls under the eaves. The cornice is decorative and aids in water drainage. Any molded projection at the top of an interior or exterior wall, in the enclosure at the roof eaves, or at the rake of the roof.

CORPORATE RESOLUTION — A summary of a specific action taken by the Board of Directors of a corporation. The Corporate Secretary normally records the resolution in the minute book of the corporation.

Lenders often request a certificate of resolution to verify that the corporate board has authorized the borrowing of money or the opening of an account. This is called a borrowing resolution and usually has a format similar to the following:

"Upon motion duly made, seconded and unanimously passed, the following resolution was adopted on the 5th day of January 1998. RESOLVED that the Corporation hereby authorizes the borrowing of $25,000 from the Bank of Camas, Washington."

When a corporation is selling real property, a prudent broker should request a resolution from the Board of Directors authorizing the listing of property, the payment of a commission, the sale and designating an authorized officer to sign the various instruments. If the corporation is selling most of its assets, a resolution of two-thirds of the shareholders is also required. (*See* CORPORATION.)
Reference: RCW 23A.

CORPORATION — An artificial person or legal entity, created under state law, consisting of an association of individuals, but regarded in law as having an existence and personality separate and distinct from such individuals. The main characteristics of a corporation are: (1) perpetual existence, that is, the corporation exists indefinitely and only ceases to exist when and if it is properly dissolved through legal proceedings; (2) centralized management in the board of directors; (3) liability of a shareholder limited to the amount of his/her investment; and (4) free transferability of shares.

A corporation has independent capacity to contract and to hold title to real property consistent with the powers given it in its articles of incorporation. Contracts which the corporation was not empowered to enter into (e.g., **ultra vires** or beyond its powers) may not be valid. It is therefore important to ascertain (1) whether the corporation is empowered to enter into the contract, and (2) whether the person signing on behalf of the corporation is authorized to sign. This information is verified by requesting a copy of the certificate of resolution of the Board of Directors authorizing the contract and the person signing it on behalf of the corporation. Normally Board approval is sufficient to authorize a sale of corporate property, but where the sale constitutes most of the corporate assets, shareholder approval (two-thirds) must first be obtained.

Where a new corporation is buying real property, it is important to verify that the articles have been filed and the corporation has in fact been legally formed, otherwise the deed is invalid for lack of a grantee.

A corporation (except a S corporation) is taxed at special corporate income tax rates, and the stockholders must pay an added tax on dividends or other profits received from the corporation.

A closely held corporation is one owned by a relatively few people, all or most of whom are directly involved in the conduct of the business, with very little stock held by outside investors.

Corporations are subject to regulation in the state where they were incorporated and in the states where they do business.

A Washington corporation may be organized by having at least one incorporator sign, acknowledge and file the articles of association (e.g., articles of incorporation) and an initial list of director(s). These are filed together with the appropriate filing fee, at the Office of the Secretary of State in Olympia. The incorporation date is the date of filing the acceptable articles.

The same procedure must be followed by persons desiring to organize a corporate real estate brokerage firm. The Real Estate Program of the Department of Licensing will issue a broker's license to a designated officer of a corporation provided it is a corporation in good standing and has an office or employee with a current broker's license who will directly manage the real estate brokerage business. (*See* LICENSING.)

The full power of a corporation is exercised through the Board of Directors. The Board elects officers to run the routine operations of the business. (*See* ASSOCIATION, CORPORATE RESOLUTION, DOUBLE TAXATION, FOREIGN CORPORATION, S CORPORATION.)
Reference: RCW 23A.

CORPOREAL PROPERTY — Tangible real or personal property, such as buildings, fixtures, and fences. Also referred to as Corporeal Hereditament. A hereditament is property, real, personal or mixed, which under the law may be inherited; may descend, in the absence of a will, to the heirs of a decedent, lineal or collateral. The only real corporeal hereditament is land and what the law considers a part of it. Incorporeal property includes intangibles, such as rents, easements and good will.

CORRECTION DEED — A deed used to correct a prior erroneous deed, as when the grantor's name has been misspelled or when some minor mistake of fact exists. It is also used to correct or change an inaccurate description of a parcel. It usually is a quitclaim deed, also called a deed of confirmation or a reformation deed. Though exempt from excise tax, the correction deed is subject to the appropriate recording fee. A grantor can be forced to execute a correction deed if he/she gave a covenant of further assurance in the original deed. (*See* QUITCLAIM DEED.)

CORRECTION LINES — Provisions in the government survey method made to compensate for the curvature of the earth's surface. Every fourth township line (at 24 mile intervals) is used as a correction line on which the intervals between the north and south range lines are measured and corrected to a full six miles. (*See* GOVERNMENT SURVEY METHOD.)

CORRESPONDENT — A lender whose normal practice is to sell all loans originated to a particular investor or a group of investors. Another similar meaning is an approved FHA lender that is not a fully licensed FHA mortgagee. The net worth requirements and conditions of becoming a FHA approved correspondent are much less stringent as compared to a licensed FHA mortgagee.

CORRIDOR — A passageway or hallway which provides a common way of travel to an exit. A dead end corridor is one which provides only one direction of travel to an exit.

CO-SIGNOR — A person who signs on a promissory note with another person and, thus, becomes legally liable for repayment of the debt.

COST APPROACH — An approach to the evaluation of property based on its reproduction cost or replacement cost. Because most people will not pay more for a property than it would cost to acquire a similar site and erect a similar structure on it, the current reproduction cost of the building plus the value of the land tends to set the upper limit of a property's value. Also called the **Summation Approach**. The primary steps in the cost approach are to (a) estimate the land value; (b) estimate the reproduction cost of the building new; (c) deduct all accrued depreciation from the reproduction cost; and (d) add the estimated land value to the depreciated reproduction cost. If accrued depreciation exceeds 25%, the effectiveness of this approach is severely diminished and an alternative approach (direct sales comparison or income approach) should be selected, if possible.

To estimate land value, the appraiser uses comparable sales of land (in its vacant state). To determine replacement cost, the comparative cost method is used, based on current market costs to construct buildings which are similar in design, type, size and quality of construction. From this reproduction cost is deducted accrued depreciation due to physical deterioration, functional obsolescence and external obsolescence. Finally, the estimated land value is added to the depreciated reproduction cost of the building.

The cost approach is most helpful in the appraisal of special purpose buildings such as schools, churches or post offices. Such properties are difficult to appraise using other methods because there are not many comparable sales and there usually is no income produced by the properties. This method is only appropriate if the property is being used for its highest and best use. (*See* APPRAISAL, COMPARABLES, REPRODUCTION COST.)

COST-OF-LIVING INDEX — An index number indicating the relative change in the cost of living between a selected period of time (using a factor of 100) and another period of time. Escalator clauses in commercial leases often refer to an increase in maintenance expenses to match the increase in the cost of living or an increase in the U.S. Department of Labor's Consumer Price Index. (*See* BASE PERIOD, CONSUMER PRICE INDEX (CPI).)

COST PLUS CONTRACT — A construction agreement in which the owner will pay the cost of all labor and materials plus a certain additional amount based on a set percentage representing profit and contractor's overhead. This is the opposite of a fixed-price contract.

COTENANCY — A form of concurrent property ownership in which two or more persons own an undivided interest in the same property. The law creates a relationship of trust and confidence between cotenants to preclude their acting against the interests of each other. One cotenant is entitled to contributions from his/her cotenants for reasonable sums of money necessarily expended to preserve the property.

There are several forms of co-ownership, each one having unique legal characteristics. The forms of co-ownership recognized in Washington are tenancy in common, joint tenancy, community property, condominium and cooperative, and partnership property. Each of these forms of co-ownership is discussed separately.

Where cotenants sever their joint interests, each takes his/her estate subject to all obvious and permanent benefits and burdens which at the time of the severance may have been appurtenant to or laid upon it for the benefit of the entire estate. Thus a cotenant might have an implied easement to cross over the other partitioned parcel to use a well that was common to all before the partition. (*See* COMMUNITY PROPERTY, CONTRIBUTION, GRANTEE, JOINT TENANCY, PARTNERSHIP, TENANCY IN COMMON, UNDIVIDED INTEREST.)

COUNSELING — A specialty within the real estate industry which involves providing competent, independent advice, professional guidance, and sound judgment on a variety of real estate problems. A counselor attempts to provide the client with direction in choosing from among alternative courses of action. By meeting certain rigid standards, an individual can qualify for the professional designation, C.R.E. (Counselor, Real Estate) conferred by the American Society of Real Estate Counselors.

COUNSELOR OF REAL ESTATE (CRE) — A professional designation given by the American Society of Real Estate Counselors.

COUNTEROFFER — A new offer made in response to an offer received from an offeror. The counteroffer has the effect of rejecting the original offer, which cannot thereafter be accepted unless revived by the offeror's repeating it.

Usually the buyer submits his/her offer to buy on the standard form Purchase and Sale Agreement for the seller's acceptance. If the seller makes any change to the offer, it constitutes a counteroffer and terminates the original offer. Thus if the seller changes the suggested closing date from 10:00 a.m. November 10, 1988, to 11:00 a.m. November 10, 1988, initials the change and signs the Purchase and Sale Agreement, he/she has made a counteroffer. The roles of the parties are thus reversed and the counteroffer itself can be accepted or rejected like an original offer. While it rejects the offer, it still has significance. It now becomes an offer to sell real estate with the seller incorporating most of the terms of the original offer. The purchaser, of course, has no obligation to accept the counteroffer and if he/she ignores it or rejects it then no contract can result.

A common practice has been for the seller to make a change to the buyer's offer initial and date the change and transmit it to the buyer for his/her acceptance. If the buyer then wanted to make a change to the altered Agreement, he/she would, in effect, be making a counter-counteroffer. It is poor practice to submit to escrow a Purchase and Sale Agreement that has many initialed changes, since it is difficult to determine when in point of time there actually exists a valid contract. Many brokers will have the parties execute a counteroffer on a special counteroffer form.

Because it is important to be able to determine the chronology of events, each change should be time dated. Also, the broker must give a copy of the changes to the signing party at the time such changes are made, not afterward.

COUNTERPART — A duplicate or copy of a document. Sometimes used in preparing conveyance documents when there are multiple parties and inadequate time to send a single document to parties located throughout the country for signatures. In such a case, a copy of the document can be sent to each signing party and then all the executed copies can be recorded as one document. Normally counterparts will be treated as a single document although not created simultaneously.

COUNTY — A county in Washington is a local subdivision of the State created by the sovereign power of the State to serve as a branch of the general administration of the State. A county derives such powers as it possesses from the State's general laws and may exercise only such functions of local government and perform only such duties as are imposed on it by the State Legislation. A county is the main governmental unit with which a person must deal with in real estate matters. Real estate records are maintained by the County Auditor for the county; valuation is set by the County Assessor; and lawsuits concerning real estate are handled in County Courts (Superior). (*See* COUNTY ASSESSOR, COUNTY AUDITOR, COURTS.)

COUNTY ASSESSOR — The County Assessor is a county official who by State law completely lists and values all real estate in the county for the purpose of taxation.

The County Assessor may appoint assistants or deputies who are qualified to assist him/her in valuing real property for purposes of taxation. (*See* PROPERTY TAXES.)
Reference: RCW 36.21.

COUNTY AUDITOR — A county official who by State law is responsible for maintaining the majority of records necessary for the proper functioning of County and State Government. This official is sometimes referred to as the County Recorder. In other states, he/she is also called the registrar.

The County Auditor is charged with the responsibilities of: (1) The recording of all deeds and other instruments in writing which by law are or may be filed for public record in the county; (2) Shall examine and settle the accounts of all persons indebted to the County, certify the amount to the County Treasurer, and give to the person paying a discharge upon presentation and filing of the treasurer's receipt thereof; (3) Shall make out and transmit to the State Auditor a complete statement of the State Fund Account as it pertains to real estate; the amount of taxes assessed in the County for the preceding year for state, county, road, bridge, school, and other purposes; and the amount of taxes collected for each assessment.
Reference: RCW 36.22.010.

COURT — (1) A short street, not a main thoroughfare. (2) An open area enclosed on two or more sides by walls or buildings. (3) An official session for the administration of justice — a court of law.

All actions for the recovery of possession of, quieting title to, or for the enforcement of liens upon, real estate must be brought in the County in which situated.

Unless local action is commenced in the County in which the real estate is located, the Court will not have jurisdiction (power) to determine the issues involved.
Reference: RCW 2.08.210.

All actions shall be commenced in the County in which the subject is situated for the recovery of, for the possession of, for the partition of, for the foreclosure of a mortgage on, or for injuries to, real property; and for the right to possession or title to any specific article of personal property.
Reference: RCW 4.12.010.

The federal court system consists of the United States Supreme Court, which is the highest court in the land; courts of appeals and circuit courts — the intermediate courts; and district courts — the lower courts.

State court systems vary, but their fundamental concepts are basically the same as the Federal system. In Washington, there is a high court, called the Supreme court; intermediate courts, called Appellate courts; and lower courts, called Superior courts, District courts or Small Claims court.

COURTESY TO BROKERS — The practice of sharing commissions with cooperating brokers. For example, in the sale of a large subdivision project, the real estate broker representing the developer works for the seller. If a prospective buyer is represented by another broker, the selling broker may extend courtesy to the buyer's broker, and share a part of the commission with him/her. It is not uncommon for a developer to control his/her own brokerage company and elect not to extend courtesy to brokers unless he/she experiences marketing difficulties in selling the project. (*See* COOPERATING BROKER.)

In a "For Sale by Owner" situation, it is common to have the owner agree to a buyer's broker courtesy fee.

COVENANT — A written agreement or promise of two or more parties in which a party or parties pledges to perform or not to perform specified acts on a property, or which specifies certain uses or non-uses of the property. Covenants are found in such real estate documents as leases, mortgages, deeds of trust, real estate contracts, and deeds. Breach of a covenant gives rise to a claim for damages.

Covenants found in general warranty deeds are promises made by the grantor, binding himself and his/her heirs and assigns, warranting that the title is of a certain character and that if the title should be found to be not of that character, the grantor or his/her heirs will compensate the grantee for any loss suffered. Some typical covenants found in deeds are:

1. **Covenant Against Grantors Acts**. This covenant is used in most bargain and sale deeds in which the grantor is a fiduciary, such as an executor, trustee, or guardian. In effect, the covenant states that the grantor has not done or suffered anything to encumber the property, but that he/she makes no warranties concerning the title prior to his/her taking title. This covenant does not **run with the land**. It does not benefit future grantees.

2. **Covenant of Seisin**. The grantor guarantees that at the time of the conveyance he/she owns and is in possession of the property and has the good right to sell it. This covenant relates to the time of transfer and is broken, if at all, at the time of delivery of the deed. The covenant is not broken if there is a lien on the land, but it is broken if the title is in a third person or if the grantor has not the extent of the estate he/she purports to convey. For instance, the Covenant of Seisin is breached where the grantor warrants he/she is seized of a fee simple estate, yet only possesses a life estate.

3. **Covenant Against Encumbrances**. This covenant warrants that the property is clear of any and all encumbrances not specifically excepted in the deed. Therefore, it is important to state all encumbrances as exceptions in the deed. Otherwise, if any encumbrance exists against the property, the grantee can recover his/her expense in paying off the encumbrance, such as paying off the unpaid taxes. Like the Covenant of Seisin, this covenant limits any recovery to the price paid and is broken, if at all, at the time of delivery of the deed. It covers all encumbrances, including those that are known and those unknown to both grantor and grantee. A covenant against encumbrances is not breached, however, where there are open and visible physical encumbrances, such as an easement for power lines or an irrigation ditch.

4. **Covenant of Quiet Enjoyment**. The grantor warrants that the grantee, his/her heirs and assigns, will have the right to the property free of interference from the acts or claims of third parties. The innocent grantees are thus protected from title disputes arising between the grantor and a former claimant. The Covenant of Quiet Enjoyment is breached only by an eviction, actual or constructive, by reason of a title superior to that of the grantor.

5. **Covenant of Warranty of Title**. This covenant assures the grantee that the grantor will bear the expense of defending the grantee's title if any one person asserts a rightful claim to the property. If the covenant is broken due to some third person having a better title, then the grantee may sue for his/her damages up to the value of the property at the time of sale. It usually reads "That the grantor will forever warrant the title to said premises."

6. **Covenant of Further Assurance**. This covenant obligates the grantor to perform any acts necessary to perfect the title in the grantee. It is used to force a grantor to execute a correction deed where there has been some error in the original deed. It is breached when the grantor refuses to pay the proper expenses and charges for obtaining the necessary

documents, such as failure to record a satisfaction of mortgage where required or failure to obtain a quitclaim deed releasing an interest. This covenant is usually enforced in an action for specific performance rather than in a suit for damages. Also called the Covenant of Further Assistance. (*See* DEED, SPECIAL WARRANT DEED, WARRANTY DEED.)

COVENANT NOT TO COMPETE — Agreement given by a seller of a business not to compete against the purchaser in an agreed area for a specified time. (E.g., the seller of the Omak Jewelry Store, agrees not to engage in a similar business for the next five years within ten miles of the business being sold.) This protects the purchaser of the business from the seller opening a competing business and taking all his/her old customers with him/her. It also allows the purchaser to amortize and write-off whatever he/she pays for the covenant over the life of the covenant. Also a similar agreement by employees in an employment contract.

Such covenants are not favored by the courts and are closely scrutinized for possible violation of antitrust laws and as unreasonable restrains on doing business or employment.

COVENANT OF SEIZIN — A clause in a mortgage which warrants that the mortgagor (borrower) has title to the property and the authority to pledge it as collateral.

COVENANTS AND CONDITIONS — Covenants, when contained in a contract, are unconditional promises the breach of which would entitle a person to damages. Conditions, on the other hand, are contingencies, qualifications, or occurrences upon which an estate or property right would be gained or lost. Covenants are indicated by words such as promise, undertake, agree; conditions are indicated by words such as if, when, unless, and provided. Because they are limitations only and do not create obligations, failure of the condition to occur will not entitle either party to damages against the other party. Conditions may be either precedent or subsequent. A **condition precedent** is one which must happen or be performed before a right or estate is gained; a **condition subsequent** is one which, upon its occurrence or happening, will cause a right to be lost or an estate to be terminated.

For example, a lease may contain covenants to repair, pay taxes and assessments, pay rent, and so on. If the tenant breaches a covenant, the landlord may sue the tenant for damages. If the lease contains a certain condition and the tenant breaches the condition, then his/her leasehold interest will be forfeited. Thus, a commercial lease often contains a condition in a defeasance clause that the tenant will forfeit his/her lease upon the tenant's being declared bankrupt or upon illegal use of the premises.

At times, promises may be both conditions and covenants. For example, the concurrent conditions found in contracts for sale are also covenants. The delivery of the deed by the seller and the payment of the purchase price by the buyer are concurrent conditions. Also, they are covenants. Thus, the buyer could sue the defaulting seller for damages once the buyer tendered his/her performance (placed his/her purchase money into escrow). (*See* COVENANT, RESTRICTION.)

COVENANTS, CONDITIONS AND RESTRICTIONS (CC&Rs) — *See* RESTRICTIONS.

COVENANTS RUNNING WITH THE LAND — Covenants which become part of the property and benefit or bind successive owners of the property. In order for the burden of a covenant to run with the land, the covenant must have been created in writing by a promise between a grantor and grantee of the property, it must "touch and concern" the land, it must have been the intention of the original parties that the covenant would run with the land, and subsequent grantees must have notice of the existence of the covenant. An example of a restrictive covenant is an agreement not to build a pig pen on a property. (*See* RESTRICTIVE COVENANT.)

CRAM DOWN — A provision in the federal Bankruptcy Act that permits a settlement of a bankruptcy in certain situations even without the consent of all classes of creditors.

The act requires that the mortgagee's lien be kept on the bankrupt's real property. If the debtor prepares to sell property free of the mortgage, the mortgagee is permitted to bid in at the sale the full amount of the debt. (*See* BANKRUPTCY.)

CRAWL SPACE — 1. The space between the first floor and the ground surface, often found in houses with no basement.

2. The space between the ceiling of the top floor and the roof, often taking the place of an attic.

CREATIVE FINANCING — A generic term used to describe a wide variety of new and innovative financing techniques used to market a property. As interest rates on residential loans climbed to new highs in the late 70's and early 80's, lenders, developers, builders, real estate brokers, buyers and sellers came up with new financing methods to enable the residential real estate market to function. These new and not so new methods if they were different than the traditional 30-year fixed interest F.H.A., V.A. or conventional loan came to be referred to as **creative financing**. (*See* ADJUSTABLE RATE LOAN, ADJUSTABLE RATE MORTGAGE (ARM), BUY DOWN LOAN, EQUITY AIDE/HOME PARTNERS, EQUITY SHARING LOAN, EXTENDED MORTGAGE TERM, FLEXIBLE LOAN INSURANCE PROGRAM (FLIP), GRADUATED-PAYMENT ADJUSTABLE-RATE MORTGAGE, GRADUATED-PAYMENT MORTGAGE, MORTGAGE SUBSIDIES, RENEGOTIABLE-RATE MORTGAGE, REVERSE ANNUITY, SHARED APPRECIATION LOAN, VARIABLE-RATE MORTGAGE, WRAP AROUND MORTGAGE.)

CREDIT — 1. In accounting, the ability of a person to borrow money.

2. Obligations which are due or are to become due.

3. In closing statements, that which is due and payable to either the buyer or seller the opposite of a charge or debit. The credit appears in the right-hand column of the accounting statement.

CREDIT APPLICATION — A written form completed by the borrower at the time a person makes application for a loan. The information given as well as the verification of that and other pertinent facts are used by the lender as part of the loan decision.

CREDIT LOAN — A loan issued strictly upon the financial strength of a borrower without great regard for collateral.

CREDIT RATING — A rating given a person or company to establish credit worthiness based upon present financial condition, experience and past credit history.

CREDIT REPORT — A report detailing the credit history of a person or business, used to determine credit worthiness. The financial status of commercial or industrial tenants can be checked by consulting a Dun and Bradstreet reference book, a local credit report agency, or a local Chamber of Commerce or Better Business Bureau. (*See* CREDIT RATING.)

CREDITOR — The person to whom a debtor owes a debt or obligation.

CROSS-DEFAULTING CLAUSE — A clause in a junior loan instrument which stipulates that a default in a senior loan also triggers a default in the junior loan.

Provision in a lease with option to purchase whereby a default in the lease is a default in the option and terminates both agreements.

CUL DE SAC — A street which is open at one end only and which usually has a circular turnaround; a blind alley. The use of cul de sacs is becoming more popular in residential subdivisions in place of the traditional grid pattern with numerous intersections. (*See* PLANNED UNIT DEVELOPMENT.)

CULVERT — Underground ditch that carries drainage water such as under a highway.

CURABLE DEPRECIATION — Depreciation that can be corrected at a reasonable and economically feasible cost. (*See* FUNCTIONAL DEPRECIATION.)

CURB APPEAL — The impression gained, whether good or bad, of a property when it is first seen, usually from the street while driving by.

CURTILAGE — The enclosed space of grounds and buildings surrounding a dwelling such as the lawn, lanai, patio.

CUSHION — An amount of money computed into a contractor's bid for a project to protect the contractor against possible unforeseen occurrences such as delays in governmental approvals, poor weather, and bidding mistakes.

CUSTODY — (1) The care and keeping of something. (2) Responsibility for a property, as when a mortgagee turns foreclosed property over to the VA (if it was a VA loan). This specialized VA term may or may not include the right of possession of the property.

CUSTOM BUILD HOME — A dwelling unit containing unique features and amenities in contrast to a tract house which has little, if any, uniqueness. Custom built homes are normally built under contract between the builder and the owner.

CUSTOMER TRUST FUND — An impound account maintained for the purpose of setting up a reserve to pay certain periodic obligations such as real property taxes, insurance premiums, lease rent, and maintenance fees, sometimes called an escrow account. Many lenders require the borrower to maintain a customer trust fund as an assurance that the carrying charges will be paid on time. (*See* BUDGET MORTGAGE, IMPOUND ACCOUNT.)

D

DAMAGES — The compensation recoverable in a lawsuit or arbitration hearing by a person who has sustained an injury, either to his/her person or property, through the act or default of another. There is a complex area of law directly concerned with determining the appropriate measure (amount) of damages for specific types of injuries. In cases of fraud, many courts use the "benefit of bargain" rule, awarding as damages the cash difference between the actual value of the property and the value of the property as fraudulently represented to the buyer. In some cases, the courts apply the "out-of-pocket" rule, awarding as damages the difference, if any, between the actual value of that which the plaintiff (the person seeking damages) paid (the consideration) and the actual value of that which he/she received, and any amounts expended in reliance upon the fraudulent party.

Often the seller in a Purchase and Sale Agreement retains the buyer's deposit money as his/her damages when the defaulting buyer decides not to perform the contract to purchase the property. Sometimes the parties agree at the time of signing their contract that a defaulting party will pay a certain amount to liquidate or settle any damages. Damages recoverable by an owner for a lessee's breach of contract to lease would be the excess (if any) of the agreed or contract rent, over and above the rental price the owner would be forced to accept in a pressure situation. The burden of proving damages is always on the plaintiff. (*See* BENEFIT-OF-BARGAIN RULE, CONSEQUENTIAL DAMAGES, LIQUIDATED DAMAGES.)

DAMPER — An adjustable valve at the top of a fireplace which regulates the flow of heated gases into the chimney.

DAMPPROOFING OR WEATHERPROOFING — A horizontal layer of plastic, lead, asphalt, or other water resistant materials placed between the interior and exterior walls to exclude moisture.

DATE — Usually the exact day a legal document is signed. Certain documents such as deeds or long-term leases often contain several dates evidencing different events, such as the day the parties signed the document, the day the document was acknowledged, and/or the day it was recorded.

Though a date is not essential for the validity of most real estate contracts, it has considerable evidentiary value for purposes of (1) proving a deed was delivered on the date specified, (2) determining priority between conflicting deeds, (3) establishing time limits for performance (such as "seller has 48 hours to accept from the date of this offer"), and (4) proving whether or not the statute of limitations has run. (*See* TIME IS OF THE ESSENCE.)

Where the parties to a purchase agreement intend the closing to take place on a certain date (with no extensions of time), they should specify the date and expressly declare that "time is of the essence.''

To avoid confusion, it is best to be quite specific about dates, for instance, stating that "the seller pays up to and including March 28." A period running "to" a certain date does not include that date unless the words "to and including" are used.

Rather than say to 12:00 a.m. and have doubt whether it is midnight or noon, use 11:30 a.m. or 11:30 p.m. Rather than say a 90-day period, put a specific termination date so you avoid arguments whether it is calendar days or 30-day months and whether first and last days are counted.

DATUM — A level surface to which heights are referred. The datum may be an assumed point such as a monument or may be tidal in nature (e.g., mean sea level). The standard datum for most agencies within the state is mean sea level, and it is to this surface that most bench marks are referred. However, notable exceptions include the U.S. Army Corps of Engineers which uses "mean low-low water" as its datum in the area around the Puget Sound. (*See* BENCH MARK.)

DAYS ON THE MARKET — The time period between listing a property and either selling or removing it from the market.

D.B.A. — Abbreviation for "doing business as.". A real estate corporation may use a "dba" under the broker's name without reflecting the incorporation in the dba, e.g., Kwon Lee, Inc., could do business as Kwon Lee Realty. (*See* LICENSING LAW.)

DEALER — An IRS designation for an individual who regularly buys and sells real property. A person is classified as a dealer if, at the time of the sale, he/she held the property "primarily" for sale to customers in the ordinary course of business. Courts have interpreted "primarily" to mean principally or of first importance.

Some real estate investors who actively manage their properties might consider switching from investor to dealer status to avoid the passive income limitation on loss deductions. Under the 1986 Tax Reform Act, if an investor does not "materially participate" in the investment, then losses can be used only to offset income from other passive investments.

Passive losses cannot be used to offset earned income, interest or dividends. Investors avoid dealer status because dealers are not eligible for favorable long-term capital gains tax rates. Real estate dealers cannot use tax-deferred exchanges to defer gain on the disposition of property under a Section 1031 exchange.

DEBENTURE — A type of note or bond given as evidence of debt. Unlike a mortgage or deed of trust promissory note, a debenture is not secured by a specific property. Usually, the issuer executes an indenture or agreement with a trustee such as a bank. The indenture states the amount, interest rate, maturity, and special features of the bond issue, such as its call ability or convertibility. To avoid restriction of future borrowing power, many issuers use subordinated debentures. Sinking fund debentures require a certain amount to be escrowed annually so there will be funds available for redemption.

The Federal National Mortgage Association issues debentures to finance the acquisition of mortgages in the secondary mortgage market. If there is a default on an FHA loan, the government will give interest-bearing debentures to the mortgagee after title is transferred to the FHA. (*See* FEDERAL HOUSING ADMINISTRATION.)

DEBIT — A charge on an accounting statement or balance sheet (appearing in the LEFT-HAND column); the opposite of a credit. Used in bookkeeping and in preparing the closing statement in a real estate transaction.

DEBT COVERAGE RATIO — The relationship between the annual net operating income (N.O.I.) of a property and the annual debt service of the loan on the property. Lenders and investors calculate the ratio to assist them in determining the likelihood of the property generating enough income to pay the loan payments. From the lender's viewpoint, the higher the ratio, the better.

DEBT EQUITY RATIO — The relationship between the total loan amount owed to the lender(s) and the invested capital of the owner(s). In real estate investments this ratio, also known as the leverage ratio, can be very high due largely in part to the loan security of real estate, thus real estate investments are often highly leveraged. Owner-occupied residential real estate typically has a high debt equity ratio, particularly homes recently purchased. A $100,000 home purchased with $20,000 cash and a $80,000 mortgage would have a debt-equity ratio of 4:1 ($80,000/$20,000). (*See* LEVERAGE, LOAN-TO-VALUE-RATIO.)

DEBT SERVICE — The amount of money needed to meet the periodic payments of principal and interest on a mortgage or debt which is being amortized. The periodic payments are typically constant, equal amounts, a portion of which pays off accrued interest with the remainder reducing principal. (*See* AMORTIZATION.)

DEBTOR — One who owes money; the borrower, a maker of a note.

DECEDENT — A deceased person, especially one who has died lately.

DECK — An open porch, often on the roof of a ground floor porch or wing. A paved or hard surface area contiguous to a swimming pool is also called a deck.

DECLARATION OF CONDOMINIUM — The legal document which the developer of a condominium must record with the Office of the County Auditor in order to legally create a condominium under the Washington Condominium Act. The declaration must contain: a precise description of the land, whether leased or fee; description of the materials used to construct the building; common elements and limited common elements; use of the building or buildings and apartments, including restrictive uses; and other detailed legal requirements, such as service of process and provision for amendment of the declaration. The declaration must be recorded, together with a true copy of the bylaws governing the operation of the property, and a Survey Map of the surface of the land and a Set of Plans of the building(s) and apartments.

The declaration must be recorded after "all structural components and mechanical systems" of all buildings containing or compromising any units thereby created are substantially completed. (*See* CONDOMINIUM, CONDOMINIUM ASSOCIATION, HORIZONTAL PROPERTY REGIMES ACT, WASHINGTON CONDOMINIUM ACT.)
Reference: RCW 64.32, RCW 64.34

DECLARATION OF HOMESTEAD — *See* HOMESTEAD.

DECLARATION OF RESTRICTIONS — A statement of all the covenants, conditions, and restrictions (CC&Rs) that affect a parcel of land. A subdivider may note the restrictions on the map or plan when he/she records the subdivision plat. If the restrictions are numerous, the subdivider will draw up a separate document listing all the restrictions and then record this declaration. The restrictions usually aim at a general plan of development and require all lot owners to comply with certain building standards. For example, the CC&Rs may require lot owners to construct homes over a certain size or to obtain prior design approval from a designated architectural control committee. Once recorded, these restrictions in the declaration run with the land and bind all future lot owners. Any owner can enforce the restrictions against any other owner who violates any of the restrictions. A Declaration of Restrictions can be terminated by lapse of a specified time or by agreement of all benefited parties. (*See* RESTRICTION.)

The following are typical provisions of a Declaration of Restrictions:

"Each building or other structure shall be constructed, erected, and maintained in strict accordance with the approved plans and specifications."

"No building shall be located on any lot nearer than 35 feet to the street lot line, nearer than 30 feet to the rear lot line, or nearer than 10 feet to the side lot lines."

"No building or structure shall be more than 25 feet in height as measured from the highest natural grade at any point on the perimeter of the foundation of the structure to the highest point of the roof."

"No animals, livestock, or poultry of any kind shall be raised, bred, or kept on any land in the subdivision except by special permit issued by the Board of Directors. However, a reasonable number of dogs, cats, or other common household pets may be kept without the necessity of obtaining such permit."

DECREE — A court order or declaration announcing the legal consequences of the facts.

DECREE OF FORECLOSURE — A decree issued by the court upon completion of a foreclosure of a lien, or a mortgage or a deed of trust foreclosed as a mortgage.

DEDICATION — The dedication of privately-owned land to the public for no consideration, with the intent that the land will be accepted and used for public purposes. A landowner may dedicate the entire fee simple interest, or an easement such as a public right-of-way across his/her property. Lands thus dedicated are normally taxed at a preferential rate.

There are two types of dedications: statutory and common law. A statutory dedication is accomplished by recording a subdivision map approved by county officials and expressly indicating on the map areas dedicated to the public, such as parks and streets. A common law dedication is a matter of contract and thus requires an offer, evidenced by an intention and an unequivocal act of dedication on the part of the owner, and an acceptance on the part of the public. The dedication may be either express, as where a developer or subdivider deeds his/her roads to the county, or implied, as where the owner has acquiesced to the public use of his/her property, usually for the prescriptive period (ten years).

For example, in order to prevent the public from claiming a dedication, the owner will often close off his/her street or sidewalk for one day out of the year. This is done to prove that the public's right to use the property is a mere license and that the owner has a definite intention not to dedicate his/her property to the public. Some owners imbed in their sidewalk a plaque stating "Private Property, Permission to Use Revocable." "No Trespassing" signs may be insufficient for purposes of preventing the public from claiming a dedication.

The fee interest acquired by dedication is similar to a qualified fee; for example, upon an abandonment of the dedicated public use, the fee goes to the owner under a possibility of reverter, while the government is usually prevented from diverting the property to a new use.

Dedication of property such as streets and open spaces is sometimes made a prerequisite to governmental approval of a proposed development. In some cases, the developer can pay a fee rather than dedicate land. (*See* TRANSFER DEVELOPMENT RIGHTS.)

DEDUCTION — An ordinary and necessary expense paid or incurred in a taxable year which is related to a business or the production of income. Such deductions are in addition to any other deduction permitted by law and depend upon the accounting method used by the taxpayer. Except where specifically authorized by the Internal Revenue Code, expenses for personal or family purposes are usually not deductible. A deduction has the effect of reducing the amount of taxable income and thereby reducing a taxpayer's tax liability. If a person owns a house which serves as his/her personal residence, the IRC permits a portion of mortgage interest, property taxes and casualty losses as allowable deductions. Owners of investment real estate are entitled to deductions for maintenance expenses, minor repairs, insurance premiums and deprecation. (*See* HOME OFFICE.)

DEED — A written instrument by which a property owner/grantor conveys and transfers to a buyer/grantee an ownership interest in real property. There are many types of deeds, including a gift deed, guardian's deed, executor's deed, sheriff's deed, quitclaim deed, tax deed and trustee's deed, among others. The major difference, besides the obvious one of different grantors, is the type of covenants made by the grantor. In Washington, the most commonly used deed is the general warranty deed. (*See* COVENANT.)

In order to be valid, a deed must contain the following elements:

1. **Grantor**. There must be a grantor named in the deed. He/she must be at least 18 years of age and of sound mind. A mistake in the spelling of his/her name or his/her signature will not invalidate the deed if his/her identity is otherwise clear. If there are multiple grantors, each must be named as a grantor in the deed to convey his/her interest, or each may convey separately in separate deeds. In Washington, both husband and wife must sign as grantors in order to convey community real property. In the event that the grantor is a minor or an incompetent, a deed can be executed only by a guardian appointed and acting under the supervision of a court. If the grantor is a Washington corporation, the president and secretary may sign as grantors; however, a resolution of authority must be obtained from the board of directors or shareholders. If the grantor is a partnership, joint venture, limited liability partnership or limited liability company, the name or names under which the ownership entity took title should be used. If the grantor has legally changed his/her name after obtaining title to the property, both the current name of the grantor and the name under which the grantor was formerly known should appear. (See GRANTOR.)

2. **Grantee**. There must be an actual grantee. Thus a deed delivered to an artificial entity, e.g., a corporation prior to its coming into legal existence by filing its articles of incorporation, is void for lack of a grantee. A deed delivered to the estate of a dead grantee is void, although a deed delivered to a minor or an incompetent is valid. While a grantor

cannot be the sole grantee, the grantor could convey the deed jointly to the grantor and another person or a legal entity wholly owned by the grantor.

A deed, even though signed and acknowledged by the grantor and delivered to the grantee, is not operative as a valid conveyance until the grantee's name is inserted in it by the grantor personally, by someone at his/her request and in his/her presence, or by his/her agent (duly authorized in writing).

In the granting clause of a deed, the grantee should be designated as precisely and clearly as the grantor. Inquiry should be made as to how the grantee wishes to take title. This is particularly important if a married woman or man is to be a grantee. There is a presumption in Washington that all property acquired during a marriage is community property. If the married person is purchasing property as separate property that should be stated (e.g., Mildred Johnson, wife of Wilbert Johnson, as her separate property). If the grantee is acting in a fiduciary capacity, usually the name of the administrator, guardian, trustee, etc., is listed first, followed by a statement showing fiduciary relationship (e.g., Mary Mallien, as executrix under the will of Peter Mallien, deceased). If the grantee is a corporation, the correct corporate name should be used, and the state of incorporation should be shown. If the grantee is a partnership, title may be taken either in the name of the individual partners or in the name of the partnership (e.g., Hock and Erickson, a partnership composed of Jacob Hock and Haldor Erickson).

3. **Consideration**. A deed should recite some consideration, although in most instances it need not be the actual consideration. Most deeds recite a nominal consideration, such as, "for $10 and other good and valuable consideration." Deeds granted by fiduciaries, however, must state the actual consideration. Regardless of what is stated, the state excise tax must accurately reflect the true purchase price if it is not an exempt transaction. (*See* EXCISE TAX ON REAL ESTATE.)

4. **Words of Conveyance**. There must be words of conveyance such as "hereby grant and convey." The deed can thus be distinguished from a mortgage instrument.

5. **Legal Description**. There must be a legal description of the land conveyed. The legal description must be in metes and bounds, Government Survey, or by lot, block and subdivision of a recorded plat.

Note that if the deed attempts to convey more property than the seller actually owns (through an incorrect legal description), the deed is not void but is valid for that portion of the description actually owned by the grantor.

6. **Signature**. The grantor must sign the deed and such execution must be acknowledged before a properly authorized officer, e.g., a notary.

7. **Delivery**. A deed must be delivered to be valid. Delivery is the final act of the grantor, signifying his/her intention that the deed shall currently take effect. There is no delivery unless it is the intention of grantor to deliver it. However, when transferring Torrens registered property, it is the registration of the deed and not the act of delivery which conveys title.

Upon valid delivery of the deed by the grantor and acceptance by the grantee, title passes and the deed ceases to be an operative instrument. Title cannot be reinvested in the grantor by the grantee destroying the deed even with the intent to restore the grantor's original title. (*See* DELIVERY.) Therefore, in law, it is merely evidence of title and thus its loss or destruction does not adversely affect the grantee's title as between the grantor and the grantee and all those who had actual knowledge of the deed.

Though not essential for validity, a deed is normally recorded to protect the grantee against claims of any third party. To be validly recorded, a deed must by properly recorded in the chain of title.

Delivery must be made during the lifetime of the grantor. Assume, for example, that a grantor entered the hospital and delivered a deed to his/her brother saying, "the property is yours in case I die" (as opposed to "when I die"). There is no delivery since the grantor still has title to the property should he/she live. In this case, the grantor could have written a last will and testament to assure that his/her brother would succeed to the property in the event of his/her death.

The delivered deed must be accepted by the grantee. This requirement is often presumed by the courts where beneficial to the grantee (called "constructive acceptance"), as in cases of a beneficial conveyance to a person incapable of consenting, such as a deed to a minor or an incompetent person. The acceptance can be presumed by the grantee retaining the deed, recording the deed, encumbering the title, or any other act of ownership.

In the normal sale of real property, the Purchase and Sale Agreement generally includes a clause stating the type of deed that will be required to convey title, usually a general warranty deed, a statutory deed or a warranty deed. However, in some transactions, different types of deeds may be found due to the nature of the grantor.

Different types of deeds: (1) Administrator's or Executor's Deed — Any deed (usually a special warranty) that is given to a grantee by the administrator or executor of an estate. (2) Bargain and Sale Deed — A deed which warrants only ownership and the right to convey. (3) Correction or Reformation Deed — Any deed (usually a quitclaim) that is used to correct an error in a previous deed. (4) Deed of Trust — A security instrument which imposes a lien on the real property of the debtor. As such, the purpose of the lien is to secure the repayment of a debt or obligation owing from a borrower to a lender. (5) Deed Release — A clause contained in a real estate contract wherein the vendor agrees to

execute deeds to portions of the property with satisfactory partial debt reduction as provided by the contract, thereby permitting the vendee to subdivide and sell portions of the property. (6) General Warranty Deed — Grantor warrants that he/she will defend the title given to the grantee from lawful claims by others and that the property is free and clear of encumbrances except for those mentioned in the deed at the time of conveyance. (7) Gift Deed — A deed for which the only consideration is love and affection. (8) Quitclaim Deed — A deed used to convey whatever interest a grantor may have in real estate to grantee, but which contains no warranties. (9) Reconveyance Deed — A deed executed by Trustee upon request of the beneficiary upon full payment of a note secured by a Deed of Trust. (10) Sheriff's Deed — A deed, by court order, to be delivered by the Sheriff to the holder of a Certificate of Sale after the termination of the statutory period of redemption; contains no warranty, but affords good title. (11) Special Warranty Deed — This deed limits the liability of the grantor to defending the title only from claims arising from himself/herself, his/her heirs and assigns. (12) Statutory Warranty Deed — A short form of general warranty deed where the covenants are implied. (13) Tax Deed — A deed executed by the County Treasurer to a grantee after a tax sale of the property; no warranties are contained, but affords good title. (14) Trustee's Deed — Deed executed by the Trustee under a Deed of Trust when defaulted property is sold at Trustee's Sale. (15) Warranty Deed — same as a general Warranty Deed, but property must be free and clear of all encumbrances. (*See* ACCEPTANCE, CHAIN OF TITLE, COMMUNITY PROPERTY, CONSIDERATION, CONTRACT, CORPORATION, CORRECTION DEED, COVENANT, DELIVERY, EXCISE TAX ON REAL ESTATE SALES, GIFT DEED, INDENTURE DEED, MERGER, PARTNERSHIP, RECORDING.)
Reference: RCW 23.08, RCW 23.36, RCW 25.04, RCW 28.45, RCW 64.04, RCW 64.08, RCW 82.20.

DEED IN LIEU OF FORECLOSURE — A deed to a lender given by a borrower/owner conveying mortgaged property in which the mortgage is in default. It is an alternative to a foreclosure action. Its main disadvantage to a lender is that the deed does not wipe out junior liens, as a foreclosure action would; therefore the terms and conditions of a deed in lieu must be negotiated before the lender will accept such a deed. (*See* FORECLOSURE.)

DEED OF CONVEYANCE — *See* DEED OF TRUST, FULL RECONVEYANCE.

DEED OF TRUST — A deed of trust is the main security device used in Washington creating an interest in property as security of payment of debts or the fulfillment of obligation on real estate, which is almost always in the form of a promissory note. (*See* LIEN THEORY STATES.)

In 1965 the deed of trust became a recognized security device in Washington only after years of effort by leaders of the mortgage industry whose objective was to place Washington in a position of equality in attracting out-of-state investment capital. The greatest advantages of the deed of trust over a mortgage are: an out-of-court sale can be conducted by which overcrowded court dockets are avoided and any statutory redemption period is eliminated and title is vested immediately in the purchaser at a Trustee's sale upon the issuance of a Trustee's Deed. The simpler procedure and the shorter time period required to release on the security of the defaulting debtor is attractive to lenders who deal on a national scale.

Under the deed of trust, authority to sell the real estate upon default of the debtor is transferred to a third party (trustee) by the grantor (borrower) to protect the beneficiary (lender). Upon the default, the trustee, following a statutory procedure, conducts a trustee's sale. If the grantor (borrower) pays the promissory note secured by the deed of trust in full, the trustee executes a full reconveyance back to the grantor.

A deed of trust must be in writing, signed and acknowledged, and it should be recorded promptly. No excise tax is required to be paid because it does not constitute a conveyance of property. (*See* LOAN COMMITMENT, LOAN SUBMISSION, LOAN TO VALUE RATIO, MORTGAGE.)
Reference: RCW 61.24.

DEED RESTRICTION — A limitation placed in a deed limiting or restricting the use of the real property. (*See* COVENANT.)

DE FACTO — Latin for "in fact."

DEFAULT — The nonperformance of a duty or obligation that is part of a contract. The most common occurrence of default on the part of a buyer or lessee is nonpayment of money when due. A default is normally a breach of contract and the nondefaulting party can seek legal remedies to recover his/her loss. Defaults in long-term leases or real estate contracts other than nonpayment might be failure to renew insurance policies, failure to pay real estate taxes, bankruptcy, and so forth.

Note that a buyer's good faith inability to obtain financing under a contingency provision of a Real Estate Purchase and Sale Agreement is not considered a default (the performance of the contract depends on the buyer getting the property financed), and in such a case the seller must return the buyer's deposit.

A junior mortgage or deed of trust usually contains a clause authorizing the junior mortgagee/beneficiary to advance money to cure any default the debtor may make on the first lien (mortgage or deed of trust). Were the first mortgage/deed of trust to remain in default and the lender to foreclose, it would have the effect of wiping out the junior mortgage/deed of trust. (*See* JUNIOR MORTGAGE, NOTICE OF DEFAULT.)

DEFAULT JUDGMENT — A court order in favor of the plaintiff resulting from defendant's failure to answer the complaint or appear in court to defend the action.

DEFEASANCE CLAUSE — A clause used in leases, deeds of trust and mortgages to defeat or cancel a certain right upon the happening of a specified condition. Automatic defeasance was important under the common law and in title-theory states where title is transferred under a mortgage or deed of trust. Washington is a lien theory state, meaning that title remains with the borrower, and the mortgagee/beneficiary receives a security interest in the property. Some Washington deeds of trust and mortgages nevertheless contain defeasance language, even though it has no effect. (*See* LIEN THEORY STATES.)

A document which is called a deed or a sale-leaseback by the parties might be treated as a mortgage if it contains a defeasance clause permitting reconveyance back to the grantor upon full satisfaction of a debt.

DEFEASIBLE FEE SIMPLE — A fee estate in real property subject to being divested upon the occurrence of specified conditions. (*See* FEE SIMPLE DEFEASIBLE.)

DEFECT OF RECORD — Any encumbrance on a title that is made a part of the public record. Some recorded defects are easements, judgments, deeds of trust, and mortgages or other liens. (*See* CLEAR TITLE.)

DEFENDANT — The person being sued by the plaintiff in a lawsuit; the one charged with the wrong, and from whom recovery is sought. (*See* DAMAGES, RESPONDENT.)

DEFERRED COMMISSIONS — Commissions which are earned but not yet fully paid.

A salesman may not ordinarily receive compensation from anyone other than his/her present broker. In the case of deferred commissions from a previous broker, however, the salesman may receive such commissions direct from his/her former employing broker. A cash basis taxpayer-salesman would not have to pay income tax on the amount earned until he/she actually receives it.

Often commissions are deferred when not enough cash has been paid as a down payment to the seller. For example, in the sale of a condominium to be constructed, the broker may receive part of his/her commission from the down payment and the remainder when the project is completed and the buyer pays in full and receives his/her title. Sometimes in large commercial or investment transactions, part of the sales commission is deferred due to the size of the commission. In these cases, an interest bearing note is executed by the party owing the money, and it is common to secure this debt by a second mortgage or deed of trust on real estate. The salesperson would be wise to have a provision in his/ her contract with the broker that the salesperson is named in both the promissory note and deed of trust. Some brokers tell their salesperson that the salesperson cannot be named under the license law, but this is not true. (*See* COMMISSION, COMPENSATION.)
Reference: RCW 18.85.

DEFERRED MAINTENANCE — Physical depreciation or loss in value of a building resulting from postponed maintenance to the building. This is a type of depreciation which is normally curable by making the necessary repairs and improvements. It is sometimes called **curable physical depreciation**.

A prospective purchaser of a building in which there is a significant amount of deferred maintenance should be especially careful to compute the estimated repair and replacement costs into his/her investment analysis of the property.

DEFERRED OR DELAYED EXCHANGE — A IRC Section 1031 exchange where the "exchange" of properties is not simultaneous. As a result of a limited number of federal court rulings (the "Starker" cases), tax practitioners set up elaborate procedures to put the sales proceeds in a trust to be used to purchase properties in the future. In 1991, the Treasury issued regulations establishing strict guidelines which if followed provide a "safe harbor" for a delayed exchange.

In a delayed exchange:

1. The cash proceeds of the sale of the relinquished property must be deposited with a Qualified Intermediary;

2. The "like-kind" replacement property must be designated in writing within 45 calendar days (not business days) of the initial sale closing;

3. The sale/purchase of the replacement property must be closed by the 180th day after the closing of the relinquished property.

In Washington, the entity holding the funds in trust and the title to the property (a qualified intermediary) is usually called a facilitator. (*See* EXCHANGE.)

DEFERRED PAYMENT METHOD — An accounting method of reporting taxable income on a deferred basis. (*See* INSTALLMENT SALE.)

DEFICIENCY — In the event of a foreclosure of a mortgage or a deed of trust foreclosed as a mortgage, there is a deficiency when the highest bid in a foreclosure sale is less than the outstanding balance of the debt plus foreclosure-related costs.

DEFICIENCY JUDGMENT — A judgment against a borrower, endorser or guarantor for the balance of the debt issued when the security for a loan is insufficient to satisfy the debt. A deficiency occurs when the foreclosure sale of a property produces less than the amount needed to pay the costs and expenses of the action and to satisfy the obligation secured by the foreclosed mortgage or a deed of trust foreclosed as a mortgage. For such deficiency, a personal judgment is entered against the original mortgagor. The judgment operates as a lien on the judgment debtor's assets and is enforceable and collectible in the same manner as any judgment at law.

In Washington, the commonly used **nonjudicial** foreclosure under a deed of trust will not result in a deficiency judgment because the jurisdiction of a court is not invoked.

The parties can agree that the lender can look only to the collateral (the mortgaged property) in the event of a default. To accomplish this, the parties place in the note language to the effect that "this note is without recourse," which has the effect of preventing a deficiency judgment. In some states, like California, the mortgagee cannot recover a deficiency judgment on a purchase money mortgage; these states have enacted anti-deficiency legislation.

If a purchaser assumes the seller's existing mortgage, he/she thereby becomes personally liable (along with the seller) for any deficiency. However, when the purchaser buys the property "subject to" the existing mortgage, he/she cannot be held personally liable for any deficiency; thus, upon default, his/her liability would extend only to the loss of the property. (*See* DEED OF TRUST, FORECLOSURE, JUDGMENT LIEN, MORTGAGE.)

DEFLATED MORTGAGE — A mortgage in which the parties agree to reduce the amount of the principal debt and increase the interest rate. In this way, the seller receives the same amount of dollars but the buyer obtains a greater interest deduction.

DEGREE — A surveying term meaning one/360th part of a full rotation about a point in a plane. (*See* ANGLE.)

DELAYED EXCHANGE — *See* DEFERRED OR DELAYED EXCHANGE.

DELINQUENT — The status of a financial obligation such as a promissory note when payment is past due.

DELINQUENT EXCISE TAX PENALTY — The real estate excise tax must be paid within thirty days after the date of the sale, even if the document is not recorded. A 1988 law imposes a penalty on delinquent real estate excise taxes in addition to a one percent per month interest charge. The penalty is 5% of the amount of the tax if not paid within thirty days of the date due, 10% if not paid within sixty days, and 20% if not paid within ninety days. (*See* EXCISE TAX ON REAL ESTATE SALES.)
Reference: RCW 82.45.100

DELIVERY — The legal act of transferring ownership. A deed must be delivered **and** accepted before becoming valid. Legal delivery does not refer to the act of manually transferring the document; rather, it refers to the **intention** of the grantor. The grantor must intend that the deed is currently operative and effective to transfer the title to the grantee, and that the grantee become the legal owner. For example, a grantor may voluntarily hand over a deed to a grantee only for review by the grantee's attorney. This would not be a valid delivery since the grantor did not have the intention to relinquish all control over the deed. To be a legal delivery, the grantor must have been competent, not only at the time of signing and acknowledging the deed, but also at the time of its delivery.

If this requisite intention is present, there is a valid delivery of the deed even though the grantee's right to possession and enjoyment of the property is deferred to a future date. Thus, where the deed is given to a third person with instructions to give it to the grantee upon satisfaction of a condition which is certain to occur, there is an effective delivery and the third person holds the deed as agent for the grantee. For instance, where George Mallien gives a deed to an escrow agent with instructions to deliver it to Richard Mallien "when I die," with no other conditions being imposed on the "delivery," then it is a valid delivery and effectively transfers title to Richard with possession and enjoyment delayed until George's death. But if George had instructed the agent to give the deed to Richard "in case I die," then there is no valid delivery since George did not intend a present transfer of title. When the grantor makes a constructive delivery to an agent, he/she must relinquish all control over the deed; otherwise there is no effective delivery. There is no valid delivery upon an unauthorized delivery by an escrow agent prior to full performance of the stated escrow conditions.

Once there is a valid delivery and acceptance, the act of the grantee in surrendering the property or the deed is not effective to put title back in the original grantor. To accomplish this, the grantee must execute a new deed back to the original grantor.

While a deed does not have to be recorded to be valid, the standard form Purchase and Sale Agreement normally provides that escrow shall not close a transaction and disburse the proceeds of sale until the deed (or assignment of lease or real estate contract, etc.) is recorded. Thus the transaction is finally closed at the time title has passed to the buyer. Title to Torrens registered property, however, is not transferred upon delivery of the deed. It is transferred only upon registration of the deed on the certificate of title with the registrar of titles and the issuance of a transfer certificate of title to the new owner.

A deed is presumed to have been delivered if the deed is found in the possession of the grantee, or the deed is recorded. A deed still in the possession of the grantor is presumed not to have been delivered. Examination of the deed itself, circumstances surrounding its execution, and the words and conduct of the parties may well determine the issue of delivery. (*See* ACCEPTANCE, DEED, ESCROW.)

Historically, title to real property was transferred by "livery of seisin," the act of giving possession of the property over to the grantee. This act was sometimes symbolized by the grantor's standing on the property and handing the grantee a twig or a handful of earth. Sometimes a witness recorded the act on a document. Today, the transferring of possession is represented by delivery of the document reflecting the grantor's intent to transfer title to the property.

DEMAND — 1. A letter from a creditor requesting payment of the amount due, as in a loan or lease.

2. The quantity of economic goods that can be bought at a certain price, in a given market, at a particular time; what the market place will demand. Effective demand is the desire to buy, coupled with the ability to pay. Demand is an essential element of value.

DEMAND DEPOSIT — Funds in a checking account or regular savings account at a bank.

DEMAND NOTE — A promissory note that permits the holder to call in the loan at any time upon notice; by comparison a term note is not payable until the time specified.

DEMISE — A conveyance of an estate or interest in real property to someone for a certain number of years, for life, or at will - most commonly for years, as in a lease. A lease often refers to the "demised premises." The use of the word demise often implies a covenant of quiet enjoyment by which the lessor undertakes to guarantee that the lessee will not be disturbed in his/her use of the premises by superior claims of others. Demise is commonly used as a synonym for the term "let" in a lease.

DEMISED PREMISES — The part of a property which is leased to a tenant. (*See* LEASE.)

DEMISING WALL — A partition or dividing wall found in a building which houses two or more tenants, separating the area leased by one party from that leased by others.

DEMOGRAPHY — The statistical study of human populations, especially in reference to size, density, and distribution. Demographic information is useful in evaluating commercial locations, shopping center sites, and so on.

DEMOLITION LOSS — 1. A loss in value due to physical destruction of the premises. Generally, a loss due to the voluntary demolition of a building is deductible as an ordinary loss. However, if an owner purchases the property with the intent of demolishing the existing building, the demolition loss is not an ordinary loss but a cost which must be allocated to the basis of the land. In addition, the cost of demolishing a certified historic structure cannot be deducted; such costs must be treated as an additional land cost.

2. Some leases contain a clause which, upon proper notice, gives the lessor the right to cancel the lease in the event that the lessor chooses to demolish the building. The clause is usually only required by owners of older buildings who want to leave their options open for new construction at some unknown future date.

DENSITY — When used in connection with zoning requirements, a term meaning the number of building units per acre or the number of occupants or families per unit of land area (acre, square mile, and so on); usually the ratio of land area to improvement area. For example, if a parcel of real property were zoned R10, the maximum density per net usable acre would be ten units. (*See* FLOOR AREA RATIO, LAND USE INTENSITY, ZONING.)

DENSITY ZONING — A type of zoning ordinance, generally associated with subdivisions, that restricts the average maximum number of houses per acre which may be built within a particular subdivision or area. For example, if a subdivision were zoned at a 15,000 square-foot-lot-minimum, the developer could build only 2.5 houses per acre. On the other hand, if the area is density zoned at an average maximum 2.5 houses per acre, the developer is free to achieve an open, clustered effect by slightly reducing individual lot sizes. Regardless of lot size or the number of units clustered, the subdivider will be in compliance with the ordinance as long as the average number of units in the development remains at or below the maximum density. This average is called gross density.

Developers frequently work closely with zoning boards and commissions to develop ordinances and standards most beneficial to living comfort and aesthetic values.

DEPARTMENT OF HOUSING AND URBAN DEVELOPMENT (HUD) — *See* HUD, INTERSTATE LAND SALES.

DEPARTMENT OF LICENSING — One of the major administrative agencies of the State of Washington. The Real Estate Program is one of the divisions which make up the Department. (*See* DIRECTOR OF LICENSING, LICENSING LAW.)

DEPLETION — Reduction in size or quantity. The exhaustion of an asset, such as can happen with gas, oil, mineral oil, or timber-producing real estate.

DEPOSIT — Money offered by a prospective buyer as an indication of his/her good faith in entering into a contract to purchase; earnest money; security for the buyer's performance of a contract. An earnest money deposit is not necessary to create a valid purchase contract because the mutual promises of the parties to buy and to sell are sufficient consideration to enforce the contract. If the buyer completes the purchase, the deposit money is applied toward the purchase price. If the buyer defaults, the seller can elect to retain the deposit money as liquidated damages; sometimes he/she would split the amount retained with his/her broker, up to an amount not exceeding the broker's commission (per the terms of the Purchase and Sale Agreement). If the seller defaults, the deposit is returned in full to the buyer.

In order to protect himself/herself, the seller should require a deposit large enough to cover the broker's commission, cost of title search and an amount to cover his/her loss of time and opportunity to sell elsewhere. A deposit of ten percent of the purchase price should be adequate; however, as the price of real property has increased, a deposit of ten percent is seldom made. If the seller requires too substantial a deposit, however, a defaulting buyer might seek a return of part of the deposit money claiming that the deposit did not accurately serve as liquidated damages, but rather was a forfeiture or penalty. However, most Purchase and Sale Agreements in Washington have a safe harbor provision which provides that a deposit up to five (5) per cent will not be considered excessive.

The question sometimes arises as to whom the deposit belongs. If the seller authorizes his/her broker to accept deposit money on his/her behalf, the deposit money belongs to the seller when the broker accepts it. It never belongs to the broker, although the broker may share in the deposit money if the buyer defaults and the seller retains the deposit as liquidated damages. The question of who owns the deposit sometimes arises in cases where the broker absconds with the deposit money. If the seller has not authorized the broker to accept the deposit money, the broker is acting as the buyer's agent in handling the money until such time as the seller accepts the buyer's offer to purchase. Thus the buyer would suffer the loss in the event the broker steals the money. If the seller has authorized the broker to accept deposits on his/her behalf, the seller would suffer such loss. (*See* ADDITIONAL DEPOSIT, CLIENT TRUST ACCOUNT, LICENSING LAW, LIQUIDATED DAMAGES, REAL ESTATE PURCHASE AND SALE AGREEMENT.)

DEPOSITION — The formal testimony made prior to trial of a witness or a party to a lawsuit, called the deponent. Any party may take the testimony of any person by a deposition using an oral examination or written questions (called interrogatories) for the purpose of discovery (ascertaining evidence) or for use as evidence or for preserving testimony in the legal action or for both these purposes.

DEPRECIABLE LIFE — For an asset, the time period over which depreciable cost is to be allocated. For tax returns, depreciable life may be shorter than estimated service life. (*See* DEPRECIATION (TAX).)

DEPRECIABLE REAL PROPERTY — Depreciable property must be of a type that is subject to wear and tear, and must consist of property used in a trade or business, or held for investment. Consequently, land and the taxpayer's personal residence are not depreciable. If, however, the taxpayer uses part of his/her residence for business purposes, he/she can allocate such use and take a pro rata depreciation deduction. The Internal Revenue Code imposes stringent requirements on the business purpose deduction. (*See* HOME, USED FOR BUSINESS.)

Depreciation rules for real property changed dramatically under the 1986 Tax Reform Act. Cost recovery periods are lengthened and accelerated cost recovery methods are no longer available. It is not essential that the property actually produce income; it is sufficient that the property is held with the expectation of producing income or making a profit.

Only improvements to real property can be depreciated, such as buildings, sidewalks, fences, and so on. (*See* ACCELERATED COST RECOVERY SYSTEM, DEPRECIATION (TAX), HOME, USED FOR BUSINESS.)

DEPRECIATION ALLOWANCE — The accounting charge made to allow for the fact that the asset may become economically obsolete before its physical deterioration. The purpose is to write off the original cost by distributing it over the estimated useful life of the asset. It appears in both the profit and loss statement and the balance sheet. (*See* DEPRECIATION (TAX).)

DEPRECIATION (APPRAISAL) — A loss in value due to any cause; any condition which adversely affects the value of an improvement. For appraisal purposes, depreciation is divided into three classes according to its cause: **physical** deterioration, **functional** obsolescence, and **economic** obsolescence — also referred to as **external** obsolescence. The most common method of measuring depreciation was once the straight-line method, but today most appraisers use the breakdown method in which depreciation is broken down into all three classes with each class measured separately, whether curable or incurable.

Physical deterioration of an improvement is indicated by decay or disintegration, cracks, wear and tear, settling of foundations, structural defects, actions of the elements, any loss of physical soundness, and termite damage.

Functional obsolescence (inside property lines) is indicated by obsolete boilers, ancient plumbing, unnecessarily high ceilings, out-of-date lighting fixtures and outmoded architecture.

External (economic) obsolescence (outside property lines) is indicated by population decreases, incongruous uses of property, legislative action — city, state, and national changes in a neighborhood, and invasion of extraneous conditions that lower values.

Accrued depreciation, also called **past depreciation**, is depreciation existing as of the date of appraisal. In contrast, future depreciation is an estimation of the loss in value which is likely to occur in the future.

Because of depreciation factors, it isn't likely that any two properties will be valued exactly alike. Assume, for example, that two buildings were constructed at the same time, using similar materials. After two years, the properties would have different values due to the independent effect of depreciation forces on the separate buildings; for example, one of the buildings may now have termites. (*See* APPRAISAL, COST APPROACH.)

DEPRECIATION RECAPTURE — A provision contained in the Internal Revenue Code that makes excess depreciation taken on real property subject to income tax upon the sale or disposition of the property.

DEPRECIATION (TAX) — For tax purposes, depreciable property is property used in trade or business or held for the production of income which is subject to physical decay or obsolescence and has a definite useful life. It isn't necessary that the asset be earning income or bringing in money as long as it is used in a trade or business or held for the production of income.

Land is not depreciable (although the cost of landscaping may be depreciated in certain cases). So, when you buy improved property, you have to allocate your purchase price among the land and the buildings and other improvements. Some taxpayers use the allocation as set by the county tax assessor; however, before doing so, the owner should review the allocation with an appraiser due to the fact some assessors over value the land and under value the improvements.

The annual amount of the depreciation deduction results from an arbitrary apportionment of the investment in the building systematically spread over its useful life. Thus, tax depreciation occurs even though the property itself may have actually appreciated in value.

The 1986 Tax Reform Act eliminated accelerated depreciation (called "cost recovery" since 1981) on investment real estate. The 1986 Act established a new Modified Accelerated Cost Recovery System (MACRS) for all investment real estate acquired after 1986 which is used in trade or business or held for the production of income. (*See* MODIFIED ACCELERATED COST RECOVERY SYSTEM (MACRS).)

If the taxpayer does not take depreciation, the IRS will compute the allowable straight-line depreciation for him/her, and apply it to reduce the basis upon the sale of the property. The taxpayer who is entitled to take the depreciation deduction is the one who suffers the economic loss due to the decrease in value. Usually this is the owner, though bare legal title alone is not sufficient. For example, a life tenant is entitled to the deduction as if he/she were the absolute owner of the property. When the life tenant dies, the depreciation deduction, if any, passes to the remainderman.

DEPTH TABLES — Mathematical devices used in appraisal of real estate to measure differences in value between lots of different depths and corner lots. One of the earliest depth tables established was the 4-3-2-1 rule, which provided that the front quarter of the lot holds 40 percent of the value; the second 30 percent; the third 20 percent; and the fourth 10 percent. This rule has been recently expanded to provide percentages for each few feet of the lot. In Washington, depth tables are not frequently used, because property is usually valued on a square foot rather than a front foot basis. (*See* APPRAISAL.)

DESCENT — The acquisition of an estate by inheritance, where an heir succeeds to the property by operation of law. Descent literally means the hereditary succession of an heir to property of an ancestor who dies intestate (leaving no will), partial intestacy (pretermitted and unmentioned children in a will) or lapse (inability or unwillingness of the named taker to take).

Washington laws of descent provide for the distribution of an intestate person's property according to established formulas, as described in the following example: If a husband dies without a will, leaving a wife, two daughters and two grandsons (sons of a deceased son), the distribution is as follows: the wife takes community property, both personal and real, and one-half of any separate property of the deceased husband; the two daughters and the two grandsons take one-half of any separate property. As to both real and personal property, each daughter takes a 1/6 interest and each grandson takes a 1/12 interest (the grandchildren taking their share per stirpes, according to right of representation through the deceased son, their father). (*See* INTESTATE, PROBATE.)
Reference: RCW 11.04, RCW 11.12.

DESCRIPTION — The portion of a conveyance document which defines the property being transferred. Documents such as assignments of leases, leases, real estate contracts, deeds, deeds of trust and mortgages must contain a full legal description of the property to be valid. A contract for the sale of real property (e.g. a Real Estate Purchase and Sale Agreement) must have a full and complete legal description. The land must always be described according to one of following methods, known as a record description: metes and bounds, Government Survey (section and township), or lot, block and subdivision of a recorded plat.

In a deed, the description is normally divided into two parts: the general and the specific descriptions. The general description identifies the parcel in question usually by location, name or reference to previous known owners. It leads into the specific description with the phrase "more particularly described as follows," or by reference to public maps, plats or other recorded information. (*See* DEED, GOVERNMENT SURVEY, LEGAL DESCRIPTION, PLAT.)

DESIGNATED BROKER — The licensed broker in charge of all brokerage activities for a partnership (must be a partner), a corporation (must be an officer), a limited liability company (must be a manager or member) or a limited liability partnership (must be a partner.). (*See* BROKER, LICENSING LAW.)
Reference: RCW 18.85.

DESIGNATED REAL ESTATE INSTRUCTOR (DREI) — A professional designation awarded to members of the Real Estate Education Association who meet high standards involving educational, experience, examination, and teaching skills demonstration.

DETACHED SINGLE FAMILY HOME — A free-standing structure designed for one family unit.

DETERIORATION — A loss in value due to physical wear and tear, negligent care and damage.

DETERMINABLE FEE — *See* FEE SIMPLE DETERMINABLE.

DEVELOPER — One who attempts to put land to its most profitable use by the construction of improvements, such as a condominium or a subdivision project. The developer organizes and supervises the entire project, usually from the acquisition of land all the way through construction and final sales, and sometimes continuing with the maintenance of the project. While his/her financial rewards are sometimes substantial, the risks are also high. All aspects of development are becoming so specialized and highly technical that developers frequently retain consultants, such as planning, construction and finance experts, to assist them throughout the various stages of development.

DEVELOPMENT IMPACT FEE — An amount of money charged a developer by a local governmental body to cover the costs of providing essential services to the proposed project, such as fire and police protection, and road maintenance.

DEVELOPMENT LOAN — A loan to cover the cost of improving property; an interim loan. In the usual case, a subdivider acquiring land seeks financing to cover the costs of both on-site and off-site improvements (site preparation, roads, sewer, water, drainage) to bring the individual lots up to a standard so that they can be profitably marketed. Often the development loan will specify a schedule of partial releases to permit individual lots to be sold free and clear from the lien of the loan. Development loans on large subdivisions are often structured in phases to match the incremental development of the project.

DEVELOPMENT PLAN — *See* LAND USE MAP.

DEVELOPMENT RIGHTS — The rights a landowner sells to another to develop and improve the property. In some areas, where residential units are to be built on land to be leased at economic or market levels, development rights are the premium paid by the developer for the privilege of improving the property and bringing the future seller and the landowner together to create the leasehold estate. Sometimes only the development rights themselves are sold, and, after the improvements are built and sold, the purchasers lease the land directly from the landowner. Often the developer purchases a master lease in conjunction with the development rights and then subleases the improved lots to the ultimate purchasers. Development rights may be sold by the developer to a sub-developer, provided the landowner consents to such assignment. (*See* TRANSFER OF DEVELOPMENT RIGHTS.)

DEVISE — Traditionally a gift of real property made under a will. The donor is the devisor and the recipient is the devisee. Where there is no will, the real property "descends" to the heirs. (*See* BEQUEATH, DESCENT.)

DIFFUSED SURFACE WATERS — Those waters that come from rain, snow, or underground springs and are diffused over the surface of the ground.

DILUVION — The gradual and imperceptible washing away and resultant loss of soil along a watercourse; opposite of alluvion.

DIRECTIONAL GROWTH — The direction or location toward which a community appears destined to grow. This directional growth is considered in mortgage underwriting and appraisal, as it plays a role in determining the present and future value of real estate.

DIRECTOR OF LICENSING — An official appointed by the Governor to administrate the Department of Licensing; one of its divisions is the Real Estate Program. In addition to his/her administrative responsibilities, he/she sits as chairman of the Washington Real Estate Commission. (*See* LICENSING LAW, REAL ESTATE COMMISSION, REAL ESTATE DIVISION.)

DIRECT REDUCTION MORTGAGE — A mortgage that requires a fixed payment of principal each period. The total payment will vary, as the interest portion will reduce with each payment.

This type of mortgage is occasionally seen when private financing is used.

Under the direct reduction payment plan, the mortgagor is able to easily calculate how much has been paid on the principal since this amount remains the same each month. What varies is the amount applying to interest. Thus, in the early years of the loan, the combined monthly principal and interest payments are larger than in a constant or level mortgage payment plan.

DIRECT SALES COMPARISON APPROACH — A method of appraising or evaluating real property based on the principle of comparison. Using this method the value of property is figured by comparing the prices paid for similar properties and establishing the value accordingly. The three main steps in what was formerly called the market-date approach are:

1. Locate comparable properties (properties with the same "highest and best use") which have sold recently, usually within the last three months, in "arm's length transactions." This excludes certain sales, such as bankruptcy or foreclosure sales, sales by the government, sales between relatives, and so on. The contract sales price must be adjusted to an effective sales price, considering unusual seller concessions and changes in market conditions since the sale.

2. Compare these properties with the subject property and make all necessary adjustments in the sales prices for any significant differences in the property, such as age, location, and physical characteristics. There should be similarities in the number of rooms, bathrooms, bedrooms, size of lot, building age, style and condition. Adjustments are necessary even in comparing vacant land, such as hookups for utilities, soil composition, and location.

3. Reconcile all the comparable information and draw a conclusion of value.

The direct sales comparison approach is the most reliable gauge of the market and is most frequently used in appraising residential property, where the amenities are often so difficult to measure. This approach is also a component for use in the other two methods of determining value. In the cost approach, market data is used to determine the depreciation figure, and in the income approach, market data is used to determine the capitalization rate. The Direct Sales Comparison approach requires an active real estate market for the type of property being appraised. (*See* APPRAISAL, COMPARABLES.)

DISABILITY — A physical or mental impairment that substantially limits one or more major life activities, such as walking, seeing, learning and working. Disability includes a record of such impairment or the fact of being regarded as having such impairment. The Americans with Disabilities Act (ADA) protects individuals with disabilities from various forms of discrimination in employment, public services, transportation, public accommodations and telecommunication services. A person abusing illegal drugs or alcohol is not covered, but a person who is rehabilitated in these areas may be protected under ADA. (*See* AMERICAN WITH DISABILITIES ACT.)

DISAFFIRM — To repudiate or revoke a contract. If a voidable contract, the injured party may elect to disaffirm the contract.

DISBURSEMENTS — Money paid out or expended in an accounting process, such as an escrow closing. Disbursements may represent a credit on the ledger, such as when the net proceeds of sale are disbursed to the seller, or a debit, as when the attorney's fees or title search are paid for. (*See* CLOSING, CLOSING COSTS.)

DISCHARGE OF BANKRUPTCY — The date a bankruptcy is finally discharged. This date is important for loan underwriting purposes since certain programs require a minimum amount of time to have transpired from the date of bankruptcy before an application can be considered for approval.

DISCHARGE OF CONTRACT — Cancellation or termination of a contract. Some of the common grounds in which the obligations of a contract may be discharged are: mutual cancellation; rescission; performance or nonperformance; accord and satisfaction; illegality; and, in certain circumstances, to the extent a court will not enforce the contract, by the Statute of Limitations, the Statute of Frauds, and the Bankruptcy Act. This is no discharge in the event of a breach of contract, but there are remedies to the nonbreaching party.

DISCLAIMER — A statement denying legal responsibility, frequently found in the form of: "There are no promises, representations, oral understandings or agreements except as contained herein" or "as is." Such a statement, however, would not relieve the maker of any liabilities for fraudulent acts or misrepresentations. Also called an exoneration clause or exculpatory clause.

A common disclaimer found in broker information fact sheets may be: "The information contained on this fact sheet is taken from sources deemed reliable. However, we cannot guarantee the accuracy of such information." Note that this type of disclaimer may be effective to protect one against an innocent misstatement of fact but will not protect one from making an intentionally false statement. (*See* "AS IS", EXCULPATORY CLAUSE.)

DISCLOSURE STATEMENT — 1. An information report required under the Federal Truth-in-Lending law to be given consumer borrowers by creditors.

2. Any statement of fact required by law, such as the settlement disclosure required under the Federal Real Estate Settlement Procedures Act. State law requires certain disclosures in the sale of recreational lots. (*See* WASHINGTON LAND DEVELOPMENT ACT.)

3. In Washington in the late 1980s, many multiple listing services adopted a property condition report form patterned after those adopted in a number of states and in particular, California. Since the form was given the number of 17, one of many forms made available by a multiple listing service to its members, it became known as Form 17.

The Washington Legislature in 1994 adopted a required form entitled "Residential Real Property Transfer-Seller's Disclosure" which is a five page long, fill-in-the-blanks form which the real estate industry refers to as "The Real Property Transfer Disclosure Statement" and is still referred to as Form 17. The seller of residential real property (one to four units) is required to deliver this form, completed to the best of the seller's knowledge, within five days after all parties to a Purchase and Sale Agreement have signed it. (*See* CAVEAT EMPTOR, REAL PROPERTY TRANSFER DISCLOSURE STATEMENT.)
Reference: RCW 64.06

DISCOUNT — To sell at a reduced value; the difference between face value and cash value. There are companies which specialize in buying mortgages, deeds of trust and real estate contracts (often referred to as "paper") at a discount. Often the original lender will want to cash out on the loan and will thus sell his/her mortgage at the lowest discount rate he/she can find. If the discount rate were 12%, for example, the lender could sell his/her $100,000 mortgage at 88% of its worth ($88,000 or 12% below par). Discounting any type of loan will increase its effective yield to the lender.

In tight money situations, a developer seeking permanent take-out financing in a condominium project might have to "buy down" permanent mortgages to a set interest rate for purchasers of the units, by paying a discount charge to the lender. For example, to get a lender to agree to provide the financing for individual purchasers at nine percent interest, the developer may have to buy down the commitment by paying the lender a discount of five percent of the loan amount. (*See* BUY-DOWN LOAN, END LOAN, ORIGINATION FEE, POINTS, TAKE OUT FINANCING, USURY.)

DISCOUNT BROKER — A licensed real estate broker who specifically provides brokerage services at lower rates than most brokers. Some discount brokers limit their services; for example, they do not sit open houses or pay for advertising.

DISCOUNT DEPARTMENT STORE — A specialized type of shopping center or large single store with emphasis on lower prices. Some discount stores ("closed door discount stores") are open only to qualifying members.

DISCOUNT POINTS — An added loan fee charged by a lender to make the yield on a lower-than-market interest VA or FHA loan competitive with higher interest conventional loans. By law, the buyer may pay any discount points on an FHA loan. The amount of discount points is set by each individual lender, and usually reflects the spread between the conventional rates and FHA/VA rates at the time the loan is made. Each point represents an approximate equivalent increase in the FHA/VA interest rate of 1/8 percent. For example, if a lender charges a discount of eight points on a $100,000 loan at nine percent interest, this increases the lender's effective yield from 9% to 10% (1/8 x 8 = 1%). The entire discount fee is collected from the seller at the start of the loan. (*See* BASIS POINTS, POINTS.)

DISCOUNT RATE — Interest rate used to convert future payments to present values. (*See* INTERNAL RATE OF RETURN.)

DISCOUNTED CASH FLOW — Used in measuring return from a real estate investment; it is the present value of a future income stream as determined by a given discount rate (using present value tables). This measure weighs dollars received early in the life of an investment more heavily than those received later. Two common methods are the internal rate of return method and the net present value method. Also known as present value analysis. (*See* INTERNAL RATE OF RETURN, PRESENT VALUE.)

DISCOUNTING — The appraisal process of mathematically computing the value of a property based on the present worth of anticipated future cash flows or income. (*See* INTERNAL RATE OF RETURN, PRESENT VALUE OF ONE DOLLAR.)

DISCOVERY — The legal process by which lawyers preparing for trial can require witnesses for the other side to produce documents and answer written or oral questions.

DISCRIMINATION — The act of making a distinction against or in favor of a person on the basis of the group or class to which the person belongs; the failure to treat people equally. The Washington State Law Against Discrimination is designed to prevent discrimination in any real estate transaction in Washington. The law lists various types of prohibited discriminatory practices but generally covers all prejudice in real estate transactions, including related financial practices, based on race, sex, color religion, ancestry, and marital status. (*See* WASHINGTON STATE HUMAN RIGHTS COMMISSION.)

DISCRIMINATION

Washington laws on discrimination effectively prevents any discrimination in the rental, lease or sale of real property. Many people believe they can legally discriminate under certain conditions. Three commonly cited examples are:

1. The rental of a duplex if the lessor or a member of his/her immediate family resides there;

2. The rental of rooms in an owner's home as long as it is not run as a commercial facility; and

3. The preference given by a religious institution to members of the same religion, or of one sex, in a real estate transaction.

In none of the above examples may a person discriminate in Washington.

Brokers as well as property owners are charged with upholding the discrimination law. The prudent broker would inform his/her principal of the provisions of the discrimination law, and if the principal still insisted on discriminating, the broker should terminate the agency. A broker is sometimes accused of discrimination for failure to show specific properties to certain parties. In such cases, the broker's strongest defense is an assertion that the complaining party was not a qualified buyer. In order to best establish proof for his/her assertion, it would be prudent for the broker to use a standard buyer's qualification form as a normal procedure in showing **all** properties to all prospects.

The law makes void all discriminatory restrictive covenants and conditions in real estate agreements. Discriminatory practices may not be inserted into any real estate documents, and those discriminatory provisions in documents which were written before the discrimination law was enacted are now inoperative. A real estate document containing such a provision is still valid; however, the discriminatory portion is voided.

Neither real property owners or real estate licensees may discriminate against an individual with AIDS. (*See* AIDS.)

The Washington State Human Rights Commission enforces the discrimination law, and has power to receive, initiate, investigate and rule on complaints alleging any violation. An aggrieved person must file a written complaint with the Commission within six (6) months of the alleged discriminatory practice. The Commission then immediately forwards a copy of the complaint to the "respondent" (person charged with the violation). The Commission reviews the charges, makes efforts to get the parties to conciliate and, if not successful, has a full hearing procedure to determine the merits of the complaint. Thus far, there have been few discrimination complaints in Washington and most of these have been successfully settled by conciliation, without the need for a full hearing.

If the Commission finds that a discriminatory practice has occurred, it is empowered to issue a cease and desist order, and to take affirmative action to compel the respondent to sell or lease to the complainant. The Commission may also post or publish the name of the respondent, and require payments of damages, which may be assessed at $1,000 for each violation, unless greater damages are proven. The Commission's actions are subject to judicial review if requested by one of the parties.

The Civil Rights Act of 1866 provides that: "All citizens of the United States shall have the same right, in every state and territory, as is enjoyed by white citizens therewith to inherit, purchase, lease, sell, hold, and convey real and personal property." In the case of **Jones vs Mayer**, decided in 1968, the U.S. Supreme Court held that the 1866 law prohibits "all **racial** discrimination, private as well as public, in the sale or rental of property." Also in 1968 the federal fair housing law was enacted to eliminate discrimination in housing. (*See* FEDERAL FAIR HOUSING LAW.)
Reference: RCW 18.85, RCW 49.60.

Discrimination in financing transactions is further regulated under the Federal Equal Credit Opportunity Act.

The Federal Fair Housing Act of 1968 also prohibits "blockbusting" and "steering".

The National Association of Realtors® and HUD and the Justice Department have created affirmative marketing agreements to assure minorities free and open access to housing via comprehensive, voluntary programs. NAR has adopted a Code for Equal Opportunity. The code includes suggested conduct for Realtors® belonging to member boards who have adopted it and who wish to comply with both the letter and the spirit of the fair housing laws. (*See* BLOCKBUSTING, FEDERAL FAIR HOUSING LAW, STEERING.)

Some deeds and other written instruments pertaining to real property contain covenants and restrictions which restrict or forbid the conveyance, encumbrance, occupancy, or lease of property to individuals of a particular race, creed, color, national origin, or with any sensory, mental, or physical handicap. These covenants, while void and unenforceable, are repugnant to many property owners and interfere with their free enjoyment of ownership.

A 1987 State law allows an owner of property subject to a discriminatory covenant or restriction to have the provision removed from the public records by bringing an *in rem* declaratory judgment action in the superior court of the county in which the property is located. The title of the action shall be the description of the property, and the necessary party to the action shall be the property owner. The fee for filing the action is $20. If the court finds any provision of the written instrument pertaining to the real property void, it shall enter an order striking the provision from the public records and eliminating it from the property title.
Reference: RCW 49.60.224.

In 1992, the Americans with Disabilities Act, a federal law, became effective. ADA is designed to eliminate discrimination against individuals with disabilities by mandating equal access to jobs, public accommodations, government services, public transportation and telecommunications. (*See* AMERICANS WITH DISABILITIES ACT, DISABILITY, DISPARATE IMPACT.)

DISINTERMEDIATION — The process of individuals investing their funds directly instead of placing their savings with banks, savings and loan associations, and similar institutions for investment by such institutions. It occurs in varying degrees when rates of return on direct investments rise above rates paid by thrift institutions on savings deposits. This bypassing of financial institutions occurs when proportionately higher yields are available on secure investments (such as high grade corporate bonds and government securities) than can be obtained on savings deposits. Disintermediation has a direct influence on the scarcity of mortgage money since diverted savings rarely find their way into mortgages.

DISPARATE IMPACT— A legal doctrine used in federal discrimination cases to show a violation even when the defendant's actions have no apparent relationship to a protected class. In a disparate impact case, an intent to discriminate is not necessary. The disparate impact doctrine prohibits a neutral restriction that has a statistically greater effect on a protected class than on other classes. Once a plaintiff shows that there is a substantial disparate impact on a protected class, the burden is shifted to the defendant to show that there is a valid nondiscriminatory reason for the statistical imbalance.

For instance, the U.S. Supreme Court has held that aptitude tests that are a prerequisite to employment and that fail substantially more blacks than whites constitute a disparate impact. A disparate impact analysis might be applied to a condominium association's house rules and their impact in a familial status or handicap case. (*See* FEDERAL FAIR HOUSING LAW.)

DISPOSAL FIELD — A drainage area, not close to the water supply, where waste from a septic tank is dispersed. The waste is drained into the ground through tile and gravel.

DISPOSSESS PROCEEDINGS — Legal action to evict someone not legally in possession. (*See* EVICTION, SUMMARY POSSESSION.)
Reference: RCW 59.18.

DISTRAINT — The right of a landlord, pursuant to a court order, to seize a tenant's belongings for rents in arrears.

In 1973, the Washington Legislature amended the Landlord Tenant Act to provide that when a tenant had quit the premises wrongly and abandoned personal property, the landlord, after following a statutory procedure, could take possession and eventually sell the

abandoned personal property. Where the tenant leaves possessions on the premises, after a reasonable period of time, the landlord can, in effect, treat them as being abandoned. (*See* ABANDONMENT, LANDLORD TENANT ACT.)
Reference: RCW 59.18.

DISTRESSED PROPERTY — Property that brings an insufficient return to the owner or is in difficulty for other reasons. Sometimes, property which must be sold due to pending foreclosure or probate of an insolvent estate is referred to as distressed property.

DIVIDED INTEREST — An interest in various parts of a whole property, such as the interest of the fee owner, lessee, or mortgagee.

DOCK-HIGH BUILDING — An industrial building in which the floor level of the main floor is constructed at a height sufficient to permit direct loading onto the beds of trucks parked at ground level outside.

DOCUMENTS — Legal instruments, such as conveyancing documents, (deeds, leases, deeds of trust, mortgages), contracts (options, exchange, and purchase and sale agreements), and other legal forms (wills and bills of sale).

DOMICILE — The state where an individual has his/her true, fixed, permanent home and principal business establishment and to which place he/she has the intention of returning whenever he/she is absent. Once established, a domicile is never lost until there is a concurrence of specific intent to abandon the old domicile, intent to acquire a specific new domicile, and actual physical presence in the new domicile. "Domus" is the Latin word for "house."

Though a person may have houses in different states and reside there at different times of the year, he/she can have only one domicile. Since domicile consists of physical presence plus an intention to make Washington one's permanent abode, such factors as local registration of autos, driver's license, voting, paying taxes, membership in local organizations, local bank accounts, local business interest, etc., are all important in establishing the requisite intent. (*See* LICENSING LAW, RESIDENCE.)

DOMINANT ESTATE (TENEMENT) — The estate which is said to attach to and derive benefit from the servient estate in reference to an easement appurtenant, as where an easement road passes over an owner's land (the servient estate) to give access to an adjacent parcel (the dominant estate). The dominant estate usually adjoins the servient estate. (*See* EASEMENT, EASEMENT IN GROSS.)

DONOR — One who gives or makes a gift. The recipient of the gift is called a donee. (*See* GIFT TAX.)

DOORSTOP — A device attached to the wall or floor to prevent a door from opening too far and damaging the wall.

DORMER — A projection built out from the slope of a roof, used to house windows on the upper floor and to provide additional headroom. Common types of dormers are the gable dormer and the shed dormer.

DOUBLE CORNER STUD OR POST — Two vertical studs joined at right angles to form the corner of the frame. The resulting double studs are stronger than regular studs and thereby give greater support.

DOUBLE DECLINING-BALANCE — *See* DECLINING-BALANCE METHOD.

DOUBLE ESCROW — An escrow set up to close the sale of property and the concurrent resale of the same property. Usually means a person is selling real property which he/she does not own but has a right to purchase under an option or is purchasing under a Purchase and Sale Agreement. Often the seller who sets up a double escrow uses the buyer's funds in the second escrow to complete the seller's purchase in the first escrow, usually at a profit.

A real estate licensee would be under a duty to fully disclose to his/her principal what was transpiring. Failure to do so could result in suspension or loss of the real estate license. (*See* ESCROW.)

DOUBLE LOAD CORRIDOR — A building term used to describe a design in which the apartment units are located on both sides of the corridor, as in many hotels. As one walks down the corridor, there are units on both sides, as opposed to a single load corridor with units on only one side.

DOUBLE OR CAP PLATES — Two horizontal boards on top of and connecting the studs. The plate serves as a foundation for the rafters and ceiling joists.

DOUBLE TAXATION — Paying a tax at the corporate level and then paying another tax on the same income at the personal level. Double taxation is a term often used in discussions of corporations. Under the corporate form of ownership, one is subject to a double tax, e.g., the corporation must pay a corporate income tax on its earnings and a shareholder must pay a second tax when he/she draws earnings out of the corporation in the form of dividends. One method of avoiding this double taxation is to have much of the earnings passed through to the key employees in the form of large salaries. However, one must be careful not to pay excessive compensation because the IRS will take a very close look at whether or not the compensation paid is reasonable for the work performed. If the IRS determines the compensation to be excessive, it will treat such excess as dividends and thus not deductible to the corporation.

S Corporations, Real Estate Investment Trusts (REIT's), mutual funds, partnerships, limited liability companies and limited liability partnerships avoid this double taxation by allowing profits and losses to "pass through" to the individual investors with no tax being paid by the corporate entity. (*See* CORPORATION, LIMITED PARTNERSHIP, S CORPORATION.)

DOUBLE WINDOW HEADER — Two boards laid on edge that form the upper portion of a door or window.

DOWN PAYMENT — The amount of cash a purchaser will pay at the time of purchase. While it usually includes the earnest money deposit, the terms are not synonymous. The earnest money is applied to the total amount of cash down payment due at the closing. (*See* DEPOSIT, EARNEST MONEY.)

DOWNSIDE RISK — The risk that an investor will lose his/her money in a particular venture.

DOWNSPOUT — A vertical pipe made of cement, metal, clay, or plastic which carries rainwater down from the eaves to the ground.

DOWNSTROKE — Slang real estate term for the amount of money needed to enter into an investment. In the purchase of real property, it would include the total down payment plus closing costs.

DOWN ZONING — A change in zoning from a higher to a lower or from a more active to less active classification, such as from residential to conservation, or multifamily to single-family use. In these cases, there is no taking under eminent domain and thus no compensation paid to the affected landowner who helplessly sees the property reduced in value. (*See* ZONING.)

In recent years, residents of certain areas of our larger metropolitan cities have attempted and, in some cases, have reversed the zoning for a particular area so that the new zoning would not allow as high a density of population or as tall buildings as previously permitted. This is popularly referred to as down zoning. For example, the residents of the south slope of Queen Anne Hill in Seattle have been successful in down zoning the area so that high rise apartments and condominiums cannot be built to block the view. (*See* POLICE POWER.)

DRAGNET CLAUSE — A clause in a mortgage which extends the lien of the mortgage to secure repayment of other debts of the mortgagor, past, present or future. Dragnet clauses are strictly construed by the courts who may require a direct relationship between the original debt and the other debts. Problems for a buyer could arise where a buyer purchases property subject to a mortgage containing a dragnet clause.

DRAINAGE — A system of gradually drawing off water and moisture from land naturally, or artificially by means of pipes and conduits. A landowner may not obstruct or divert the natural drain of water to the detriment of another landowner.

DRAW — An advancement of money. A brokerage company will sometimes advance money to its more experienced salesmen to be applied either against commissions earned but not paid, or future commissions. Also refers to a "construction draw" or the periodic advancing of funds under a construction loan agreement.

DREI — *See* DESIGNATED REAL ESTATE INSTRUCTOR.

DRILL TRACK— That segment of rail track which is intermediary between a main line and the individual industry tracks (spurs) which serve private industrial property.

DRUG ENFORCEMENT ACT — A 1988 federal law establishing the right of federal drug enforcement authorities to seize real property on which illegal drug activity is taking place. To avoid forfeiture, owners have the burden either to prove that they had no knowledge their property was used for illegal drug activity or that they had knowledge and made reasonable efforts to stop the illegal use. Real estate agents acting as property managers for absentee owners should be diligent in notifying owners of illegal drug activity on managed property. At the same time, the manager should avoid wrongly accusing a tenant of illegal drug activity.

DRY MORTGAGE — A mortgage or deed of trust in which the lender looks solely to the real property for recovery of the debt in case of default; i.e., there is no personal liability for any deficiency upon foreclosure, a nonrecourse mortgage. (*See* DEFICIENCY JUDGMENT.)

DRY ROT — Fungus-caused decay in timber, which reduces the wood to a fine powder. The term is actually a misnomer in that moisture must be present, even though it may not be obvious. (*See* ROT.)

DRYWALL CONSTRUCTION — Any type of interior wall construction not using plaster as finish material. Wood paneling, plywood, plasterboard, gypsum board, or other types of wallboard are usually used for drywall.

DUAL AGENCY — Representing both principals to a transaction. Washington State License Law provides that a real estate licensee can have his/her license revoked or suspended for representing both parties to a real estate transaction without informing them of his/her dual agency. The License Law requires the licensee to inform the principals in writing, in case he/she needs to prove that he/she did so. Though this statute seems to imply that it would be permissible to represent both parties as long as each consents in writing, it merely states that the Real Estate Program will not take disciplinary measures in such a case.

The fact that a broker is getting paid by one party does not necessarily make the broker the exclusive agent of that party, although it may be evidence of that fact.

A cooperating broker who acts as a subagent of the listing broker would have the same conflict of interest/dual agency problem in trying to also act as the buyer's agent (*See* AGENCY, SUBAGENT.)

Historical background

Common law agency principles stressed the fiduciary duties of loyalty an agent owes to his/her principal. In the minds of many who considered the problems of dual agency, there definitely was a conflict with the principles of agency law and the occurrence of a dual agency. Often debate on the subject turns on a practical problem, that is the traditional real estate practice of the seller listing his/her property and paying a commission. Rarely did the buyer of a piece of property agree to pay a commission to a real estate licensee if the real estate licensee found a property fitting the buyer's needs. However, it became a growing phenomenon where a buyer retains a real estate licensee to represent him/her that the buyer and seller were working with different salespeople from the same brokerage company. The most practical solution was to obtain written consent. The selling broker would state clearly to the buyer that he/she was the seller's agent and owed his/her first loyalty to the seller, but that he/she would also assist the buyer according to the highest ethical standards of the real estate profession. Dual agency rules apply similarly when a real estate brokerage company has a listing on a property and one of its salespeople wants to represent the buyer. In such a case, the brokerage company had to specifically disclose to the buyer that the company's first loyalty was to the seller. From 1987 until 1996, a Rule and Regulation of the State Real Estate Commission required that a selling agent provide the principals involved in a real estate transaction with oral and/or written disclosure of whom the agent represents in the transaction. Any Purchase and Sale Agreement had to contain the following acknowledgment: AGENCY DISCLOSURE: At the signing of this agreement the selling agent represented _________ Each party signing this document confirms that prior oral and/or written disclosure of agency was provided to him/her in this transaction. (*See* AGENCY DISCLOSURE, LICENSING LAW.)
Reference: RCW 18.85, WAC 308-124B-040

During the 1980s, it became evident that the common law principal regarding the **selling** broker as an agent of the seller with the same fiduciary duties to that person as the **listing** broker was contrary to the belief of most buyers. As the real estate industry struggled to adapt, the Na-

> tional Association of Realtors® on the national level, the Washington State Real Estate Commission and then the Washington Association of Realtors® on the state level studied how to adapt to the reality that most buyers thought "their" agent represented them. As a first step, the Washington State Real Estate commission adopted the written disclosure Rule and Regulation in 1987.

In 1996, Washington State, at the urging of the Washington Association of Realtors®, adopted legislation called the "Real Estate Brokerage Relationships Act." This law adopted a statutory set of definitions and structure which replaces the common law structure of agency law as it applied to real estate licensees, sellers and buyers. As part of the change, a statutory definition of dual agency was set forth: "Dual Agent means a licensee who has entered into an agency relationship with both the buyer and seller in the same transaction."

"In a transaction in which different licensees affiliated with the same broker represents different parties, the broker is a dual agent and must obtain the written consent of both parties as required under RCW 18.86.060. In such a case, each licensee shall solely represent the party with whom the licensee has an agency relationship, unless all parties agree in writing that both licensees are dual agents."

RCW 18.86.060 sets forth a detailed list of duties of any licensee who will be acting as a dual agent.

DUCT — A tube, pipe, or channel for conveying or carrying fluids, cables, wires, or tempered air. Underfloor duct systems are commonly used to provide for telephone and electrical lines.

DUE DATE — The specific date on which a payment is to be paid. If the payment is not made on or before the due date, then it is past due. Most real estate loans carry with them a first of the month due date as well as a grace period up to ten to fifteen days during which time the payment can be made without penalty. The last day of the grace period is known as the delinquency date and payment after that date normally must also include a past payment charge.

DUE DILIGENCE — 1. A fair, proper, and due degree of care and activity. An expressed or implied requirement in certain real estate contracts stating that a person use good faith efforts to perform that person's obligations under a contract. A buyer who makes an offer contingent on obtaining financing must use due diligence in seeking such financing.

2. Also, a term used in securities law to refer to the duty of the issuer or broker to insure that the offering prospectus is accurate and does not misstate or omit material information.

3. The investigation and analysis of all the risks and benefits of a purchase and/or development of a parcel of property. (*See* FEASIBILITY STUDY.)

DUE ON SALE CLAUSE — An acceleration clause (sometimes called an alienation clause) found in mortgages, deeds of trust and real estate contracts requiring the borrower to pay off the debt when he/she sells the secured property (this has been expanded in some cases to make the debt due and payable if the borrower moves out of the property or puts it up for rent), thus resulting in automatic maturity of the note at the lender's option. This clause effectively eliminates the possibility of a new buyer assuming the mortgage unless the lender permits the assumption, in which case the lender might increase the interest rate and/or charge an assumption fee. It was a growing practice in Washington, by the late 1970's for lenders to have due on sale clauses in their mortgages and deeds of trust. By the end of the 1980's, all institutional real estate loans and most private ones include a "due on sale" provision. Real estate licensees must carefully read all mortgages, deeds of trust and real estate contracts before they assert they can be assumed. (*See* ACCELERATION CLAUSE.)

In Washington, a sale on a real estate contract is a conveyance within the meaning of the covenant not to assign the contract or convey the property without the seller's consent.

Both the Federal National Mortgage Association (FNMA) and the Federal Home Loan Mortgage Corporation (FHLMC) require what is now known as Paragraph 17, a "due on sale" provision, on a loan either corporation may buy, whether it is a FHA, VA or conventional loan. FNMA will enforce the due on sale provision for all conventional loans sold under commitments dated November 10, 1980, or after. (*See* BALLOON PAYMENT.)

DUMMY — A person who buys property for another to conceal the identity of the true purchaser; also called a **straw man** or **nominee**. If a broker or a salesman attempts to use a dummy buyer to purchase for himself/herself property which is listed with him/her, he/she must specifically disclose in writing to the seller his/her interest or relationship to the buyer. Failure to do so will result in suspension or revocation of his/her license. The seller may also sue the licensee for any secret profit.
Reference: RCW 18.85.

DUPLEX — A structure that provides housing accommodations for two families and supplies each with separate entrances, kitchens, bedrooms, living rooms, and bathrooms. A two-family dwelling with the units either side-by-side or one above the other. A duplex apartment is one in which there are rooms on two floors.

In subdivisions which are restricted to single-family dwellings, some duplex owners argue that a duplex is merely the combining of two separate single-family dwellings with a party wall. To prevent arguments of this type, many subdividers restrict use to "detached single-family dwellings."

DURESS — Unlawful force or action by one person against a person whereby the person is forced to perform some act against his/her will. The threat of force is called menace. A contract entered into under duress is void. To qualify as duress, the threats must be unlawful; therefore, it would not be duress to threaten to bring a good faith lawsuit. (*See* UNDUE INFLUENCE, VOIDABLE.)

DWELLING — Any building, or structure, or part thereof, used and occupied for human habitation or intended to be so used, including any appurtenances.

DWELLING UNIT — As defined in many zoning codes, a room or rooms connected together, constituting an independent housekeeping unit for a family and containing a single kitchen.

Under the Federal Fair Housing Act, the term "dwelling" includes residences and land intended for a residence, but excludes hotel and motel accommodations.

E

E/M - An abbreviation used to indicate a Purchase and Sale Agreement for real property. Also referred to as an Earnest Money Agreement. (*See* EARNEST MONEY, REAL ESTATE PURCHASE AND SALE AGREEMENT.)

EARLY OCCUPANCY - The practice of allowing the buyer to take possession of the real property prior to closing. Such a practice should be carefully evaluated because of the risks of mechanics liens, inadequate insurance coverage, the costs of eviction and "buyer's remorse" (a term referring to the reluctance of some buyers to close on a Purchase and Sale Agreement). If a seller decides to allow early possession, an early possession agreement stating all the terms and conditions should be signed by all parties.

EARNEST MONEY - The cash deposit (including initial and additional deposits) paid by the prospective buyer of real property as evidence of his/her good faith intention to complete the transaction; called **hand money** or a **binder** in some states. Earnest money does not usually exceed ten percent of the purchase price, and its primary purpose is to serve as a source of payment of damages should the buyer default. Earnest money is not essential to make a purchase agreement binding if the buyer's and seller's exchange of mutual promises of performance (that is, the buyer's promise to purchase and the seller's promise to sell at a specified price and terms) constitute the consideration for the contract. When a purchaser makes an earnest money deposit through a real estate office, the check should be made out to the real estate company, never to the salesperson, or to the escrow company that will conduct the closing.

The deposit, or earnest money, is usually given to the broker at the time the offer is written. The broker then has the responsibility of depositing this money into a trust account; or, with the knowledge and consent of both parties, the broker may hold the earnest money (if it is in the form of a check) until the offer has been accepted. The broker may not, however, commingle this money with his/her own general funds. When the transaction is consummated, the earnest money is credited toward the purchase price and costs.

In the majority of real estate transactions, the real purpose of the earnest money is to serve as a source of payment of damages to the seller if the buyer defaults. However, exact ownership of an earnest money deposit is often uncertain. Until a real estate transaction is closed, the earnest money is the buyer's. However, once there is acceptance of the offer by the seller, the buyer loses control of the earnest money. The seller is not entitled to the money until the transaction is closed. If a party defaults on the transaction, the other party may be entitled to the earnest money. However, that party may not want the earnest money, e.g., a buyer sues for specific performance. At no time does the earnest money belong to the broker. Therefore, the uncertain nature of the earnest money deposit makes it necessary for the money to be deposited in a trust account so they are protected pending a final answer as to where they are to go. The broker's authority to hold this money on behalf of the seller should be specifically set forth in the listing, since such authority is not implied in law.

The usual rule is that a real estate broker places an earnest money deposit in his/her trust account or deposits it with the escrow closer. If it is deposited to the broker's trust, the escrow agent's trust or the title company's trust account, it is a non-interest bearing demand account. If the earnest money deposit is large and will be held for a period of time, the buyer and seller may make special arrangements by written authorization signed by both parties instructing the broker to deposit the money in an interest bearing account. The written authorization must specify to whom the interest belongs. In some cases it goes to the seller if the transaction is consummated and to the purchaser if it is not consummated. At other times, it goes to the purchaser regardless. At no time is the broker entitled to the interest. (*See* ADDITIONAL DEPOSIT, BINDER, CLIENT TRUST ACCOUNT, COMMINGLING DEPOSIT, DEPOSIT, DOWN PAYMENT, ELECTION OF REMEDIES, REAL ESTATE PURCHASE AND SALE AGREEMENT.)

EARNEST MONEY ACCOUNT - *See* CLIENT TRUST ACCOUNT

EARNEST MONEY AGREEMENT (E/M) - A contract for the purchase of real estate. (*See* REAL ESTATE PURCHASE AND SALE AGREEMENT.)

EASEMENT - A nonpossessory right which one property owner (the benefited party) has in land owned by another (the burdened party), entitling the holder of the interest to limited use or enjoyment of the other's land. Because an easement is an actual interest in land, the Statute of Fraud applies and an express grant of easement must be in writing, usually taking the form of a separate deed, a reservation in a deed or an easement agreement. Easements may also be created by necessity, as in "landlocked" situations, by implication, dedication, condemnation, or by prescription. (*See* EASEMENT BY NECESSITY, EASEMENT BY PRESCRIPTION.)

Easements are either appurtenant or encumbering. An easement appurtenant is a right in another's land (servient estate) which benefits and attaches to the owner's land (dominant estate). Such an easement is a burden to or an encumbrance upon an owner's property. In Figure A, Lot 3 has a 30-foot roadway easement across Lot 1. This easement is appurtenant to and passes with the land, regardless of whether the owner of Lot 3 expressly transfers the easement when he/she sells Lot 3, the dominant estate. It also binds the succeeding owner of Lot 1, whether or not the deed to Lot 1 refers to the easement. Where an easement or right of way is located by a grant which does not define its width, the width is that suitable and convenient for the ordinary uses of free passage. Common examples of easements appurtenant are the right to travel over another's property, party walls, and shared driveways. In a condominium, the right to walk over the parking area, or the right to have utility lines running through the walls or a sewer pipe running beneath the land surface are also examples of easement appurtenant.

FIGURE A

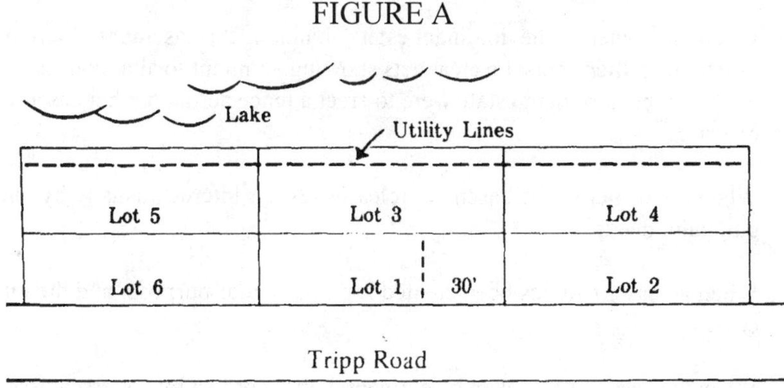

An easement in gross is personal in nature and does not pass with the land because it does not benefit or attach to any dominant estate. Common examples are utility easements, power lines easements, and the like. (*See* EASEMENT IN GROSS.)

In Figure A, the owners of Lots 5 and 6 may agree that the owner of Lot 5 will not build a building so high that it cuts off the view of the lake which the owner of Lot 6 enjoys. This is called a negative easement.

Easements should not be confused with profits or licenses. A profit is the right to take the soil, mineral or products of the land. A license is not an interest in land; it is merely permission to use the land of another for some limited purpose, and it can be revoked at any time.

Some of the major sources of litigation involving easements are the initial easement grant's failure to adequately define the easement area (the floating easement problem), the uses to which it may be put, or which party has responsibility for repair and upkeep.

Since the easement is both a benefit to the holder and a burden to the servient property owner, it significantly affects the value of the respective properties, and therefore, extent of the easement should be clearly understood. Since most easements originate by express grant, the drafter should clearly express the rights and duties associated with the easement. An easement can be an affirmative easement, such as a right of way to cross the property, or a negative easement, such as a restriction on height of a fence. It can also be created for different periods of time — for a terms of months, years, or for life.

Easements may be terminated:

1. When the owner of the dominant estate becomes the owner of the servient estate. The easement is thus terminated by merger;

2. When the owner of the dominant estate abandons the easement. Mere nonuse is insufficient; there must be clear acts showing an intent to abandon, such as if the owner of the dominant estate were to erect a fence across his/her easement right-of-way;

3. When the owner of the easement releases his/her interest, usually by means of a quitclaim deed;

4. When an easement has been created for a particular purpose, and the purpose ceases;

5. When the easement is taken by eminent domain or lost by adverse possession; or

6. When the grantee makes use of the easement for an improper purpose (called "overburdening").

Note that an easement cannot be terminated due to any inconvenience or hardship experienced because the owner of the servient tenement cannot develop the property without added expense. The owner of the servient tenement cannot relocate the easement simply to suit personal needs — to do so would be, in essence, a private right of eminent domain. (*See* EASEMENT BY NECESSITY, EASEMENT BY PRESCRIPTION, EASEMENT IN GROSS, IMPLIED EASEMENT, LICENSE, SCENIC EASEMENT, SERVIENT EASEMENT.)

EASEMENT APPURTENANT - An easement that runs with the land. (*See* EASEMENT.)

EASEMENT BY NECESSITY - An easement created by a court of law in cases where justice and necessity dictate it, especially in the classic landlocked situation. Two essential elements are: (1) there must have been a common grantor of the dominant and servient estates; and (2) there must be a reasonable necessity for the easement, not just mere convenience. For example, if Mr. Wayne had owned Lots 1-6 Figure A in Easement and then conveyed Lot 3 to Mr. Lee without mention of any easement of passage across Lot 1, most courts would imply an easement by necessity. This easement is based on the presumed intention of the parties. Since it is created by operation of law, the Statute of Frauds is not applicable and no writing is required. Also called an easement by implied grant.

EASEMENT BY PRESCRIPTION - A right acquired by an adverse user to use the land of another. As with acquiring title through adverse possession, the use must be adverse, hostile, open, notorious and continuous for the statutory period (10 years). An easement by prescription cannot be acquired on public land. Unlike easements by express or implied grant, an easement by prescription may be extinguished by nonuse for the prescriptive period without evidence of actual abandonment. (*See* ADVERSE POSSESSION, EASEMENT.)

EASEMENT IN GROSS - The limited right of one person to use another's land (servient estate), where such right is **not** created for the benefit of any land owned by the owner of the easement; that is, there is no dominant estate, as the easement attaches personally to the owner, not to the land. The easement in gross does not pass as an appurtenance to the servient estate, and must be expressly transferred. If there is uncertainty as to whether an easement is appurtenant or in gross, most courts favor the interpretation that it is an easement appurtenant.

An easement in gross is similar to a license, except that it is irrevocable for the period of the owner's life; that is, the owner of Lot 3 in Figure A in Easement may give his friend, Mr. Lee, a nonrevocable right to cross over Lot 3 and fish in the lake. The right, or easement in gross, will terminate upon the death of Mr. Lee, or upon the conveyance of Lot 3 to a new owner, whichever occurs first. Mr. Lee may not assign his right to anyone else. A personal easement in gross may not be assigned by the owner to a third party. Commercial easements in gross, however, such as rights given utility companies to install pipe lines and power lines, are a more substantial property interest and are assignable.

EAVE - The overhang of a sloping roof that extends beyond the walls of the house. Also called roof projection.

EAVE TROUGH or GUTTER - A channel, often a separate metal, wood or vinyl channel placed at the edge of the eaves to carry rain water to the downspout. It can also be a channel built into the roof itself.

ECONOMIC-BASE ANALYSIS - An appraisal term to describe a means of measuring the economic activity of a community which enables it to attract income from outside its borders; the study of the relationship between basic and nonbasic employment patterns as a means of predicting population, income, and other variables having an effect on real estate and land utilization. This term refers to the ways in which people in a community make their livings.

ECONOMIC LIFE - The estimated period over which an improved property may be profitably utilized so that it will yield a return over and above the economic rent attributable to the land itself; the period during which an improvement has value in excess of its salvage value. In the case of an older structure or improvement, economic life refers to the period during which the remaining improvements to the real property (not land) are depreciated for tax purposes. The economic lives of such improvements are normally shorter than their actual physical lives. (*See* USEFUL LIFE.)

ECONOMIC OBSOLESCENCE - A loss of value resulting from factors existing outside of the property itself and which are not under the control of the property owner. Usually referred to as external obsolescence. (See EXTERNAL OBSOLESCENCE.)

ECONOMIC RENT - The rental income which real estate can command in an open, competitive market at any given time, as contrasted with contract rent or the income actually received under a lease agreement. For example, if there is a new manufacturing plant being built, yet there is no new housing being built, the appraiser should consider this fact since rents will increase due to normal supply and demand principles. (*See* CONTRACT RENT.)

EFFECTIVE AGE - The age of the improvements to real property at the time of inspection, which differs from actual age by such variable factors as depreciation, quality of maintenance and the like. Thus, remodeling can extend the economic life of a structure by reducing or mitigating the impact of actual age and increase its life expectancy.

EFFECTIVE GROSS INCOME - The estimated potential gross income from a rental property, less an allowance for vacancy and bad debts.

EFFECTIVE INTEREST RATE - The actual rate or yield of a loan, regardless of the amount stated on the debt instrument. (*See* ANNUAL PERCENTAGE RATE.)

EFFECTIVE RATE - The average lease rate of a property per square foot after deducting negotiated concessions such as free rent, construction allowances over and above the cost of building standard items, or the costs of the landlord's assumption of a tenant's existing lease.

The actual rate of return to the investor. It may vary from the contract rate for a variety of reasons. Also called yield.

Also used to describe a payment amount on certain mortgage notes, usually buy-down types, that offer lower payment amounts calculated with an "effective rate" that is less than the face rate.

EFFECTIVE RATE OF INTEREST - The percentage determined by dividing the dollar cost to borrow money for one year by the amount borrowed. The effective rate of interest usually differs from the stated interest rate if there is a discount or premium on the debt, a change in required interest payments, lender-required compensating balance or lender participation.

EFFECTIVE YIELD - A calculation of the return on investment that considers the price paid, the time held and the interest charged. The effective yield on a discounted mortgage loan is greater than the interest charged. Suppose a lender charges four discount points on a $10,000 loan for one year at 10% simple interest. Rather than receiving $10,000, the borrower receives $9,600 but is obligated to pay back $10,000 plus $1,000 in interest. This makes an effective yield of $1,400 ÷ $9,600 or 14.6%, rather than 10%.

EFFICIENCY UNIT OR APARTMENT - A small, compact apartment unit, sometimes called a studio apartment. It consists of a combination living room, bedroom, kitchenette, and bathroom areas.

EFFICIENT AND PROCURING CAUSE - The legal test to determine if in fact a real estate licensee is entitled to a sales commission when property sells other than through an exclusive right to sell agreement. The licensee must be able to show that he/she procured the buyer and, as a result of the licensee's action, a sale took place. The primary reason for the exclusive right to sell listing agreement among real estate brokers is that under such an agreement, the broker has earned the commission if and when the property sells regardless of whether the broker actually sold the property. (*See* PROCURING CAUSE.)

EFFLUENCE - An out flowing; excrement deposited by a soil-absorption waste system that may seep or flow out onto the ground or into a creek, stream, river, or lake, particularly in times of flooding or high groundwater levels. (*See* DISPOSAL FIELD.)

EGRESS - A way to exit from a property; the opposite of ingress.

EJECTMENT - A legal action by an owner to regain possession of real property where there is no landlord-tenant relationship between the owner and the occupant; an action to oust someone who is not legally in possession of real property, such as a trespasser or a tenant at sufferance whose lease has expired. (*See* EVICTION.)

ELDERLY HOUSING - Housing occupied by persons age 62 or older, or housing specially designed for occupants age 55 or older. Under the federal housing law, elderly housing does not have to be made available to families.

ELECTION OF REMEDIES - Making a selection from several alternative courses of action to remedy a breach of contract. For example, if the buyer defaults under the terms and conditions of a real estate purchase and sales agreement, the seller must elect whether to retain the deposit as liquidated damages, to tender the deed and sue for specific performance, or to sue for damages. The seller must elect to pursue one of the remedies.

The retention of the earnest money deposit by a seller on the default of a buyer may be interpreted by a court to be an election of that remedy, and foreclosure the election of either of the other two remedies.

Under the terms of many purchase and sale agreements used in Washington, if the seller elects to retain the deposit as liquidated damages, he/she sometimes splits the deposit with the broker (up to the amount of the previously agreed-upon commission.) (*See* CONTRACT OF SALE, LIQUIDATED DAMAGES, PURCHASE AND SALE AGREEMENT, SPECIFIC PERFORMANCE.)

ELECTRICAL SYSTEM - The typical minimum requirement for a residential dwelling is a 100-amp, 120/240-volt service. Houses with central heating and air-conditioning need a minimum of 100 - 150 amps. The utility meter will state the volt and wire service, such as 240V, 3W, which means 240-volt, 3-wire service. FHA will not accept a 120-volt, 2-wire service.

ELEEMOSYNARY CORPORATION - A corporation formed for charitable and benevolent purposes and subject to special statutory controls. (*See* NONPROFIT CORPORATION.)

ELEVATION - The height of land above sea level. In a set of blueprints, elevation designates drawings of side views of a structure; for example, a front elevation shows the appearance of the front of a building.

ELLWOOD TECHNIQUE - An advanced method of developing a capitalization rate that is based on the ratio of investment represented by debt and by equity. (*See* INTERNAL RATE OF RETURN.)

EMBLEMENT - A growing crop (called fructus industriales), such as grapes and corn, which is produced annually through labor and industry. Emblements are regarded as personal property even prior to harvest; thus, a tenant has the right to take the annual crop resulting from his/her labor, even if the harvest does not occur until after tenancy has ended. A landlord cannot lease land to a tenant farmer and then terminate the lease without giving the tenant the right to reenter the land to harvest any crops grown by the tenant.

EMINENT DOMAIN - The right of government (both state and federal), public corporations (school districts, sanitation districts), public utilities, and public service corporations (railroads, power companies) to take private property for a necessary public use, with just compensation paid to the owner. Generally, however, the law will not allow compensation for loss of profits, inconvenience, loss of good will, and the like, although severance damages may be awarded for a loss in value to adjacent property which is not actually condemned. Through eminent domain, the state may acquire land (either fee, leasehold, or easement) for streets, parks, public buildings, public right-of-way, and similar uses. No private property is exempt from this exercise of governmental power.

If the owner and the government cannot negotiate a satisfactory voluntary acquisition of the property, the government can initiate a condemnation action to take the property. In such a case, an owner's main grounds for complaint would usually be that the intended use is not a sufficient public use or that the valuation given his/her property in the condemnation proceeding is not a just valuation.

Eminent domain differs from the taking of land through police power in that eminent domain is an outright acquisition of property with payment of compensation. It is not an uncompensated regulation of the use of property as in the case of restrictive zoning. Generally speaking, the courts will not permit a taking in fee if an easement will do; e.g., an entire parcel can't be taken if only a part is needed.

Whether a taking is for a public purpose is broadly construed. For example, a public purpose exists in condemnation for urban renewal purposes. The government can, for instance, condemn a blighted area and then sell it to a private developer for private purposes.

Upon the vesting of title in the government, all preexisting liens and encumbrances are extinguished; anyone affected by this change, such as mortgagees, must look to the award of condemnation money for satisfaction of their claims.

Generally, when an owner's property is taken by eminent domain, recognition of gain realized from the condemnation money can be deferred if qualified replacement property is purchased within three years from the end of the year in which the taxable gain is realized. In most cases, in order for the replacement property to qualify, it must be similar or related in use ("like kind" property).

A lessee is usually given the right to cancel his/her lease when a large portion of the leased premises is taken. Some long-term leases provide for a condemnation award to be apportioned between lessor and lessee, according to the value of the parties' respective estates. (*See* CONDEMNATION, POLICE POWER, SEVERANCE DAMAGES.)

EMPLOYEE - One who works under the supervision and control of another. For purposes of state licensing law, the real estate salesperson is employed by the broker. For federal tax purposes, the salesperson may qualify as an independent contractor. (*See* INDEPENDENT CONTRACTOR.)

EMPTY NESTER - An older individual or couple whose children have grown and left home. Statistics show that such families are major condominium buyers.

ENCROACHMENT - An unauthorized invasion or intrusion of an improvement or other real property wholly or partly onto another's property, thus reducing the size and value of the invaded property. Common examples of encroachments are the roof of a building which extends over the property line or the front of a building that extends over the building setback line or extends onto a neighbor's property. Most encroachments are the result of carelessness or poor planning rather than bad intent, as in the case of a driveway or fence built without a survey to find the lot line.

Since an undisclosed encroachment could render the title unmarketable, its existence should be noted in the listing, and the Purchase and Sale Agreement should be made "subject to" the existence of the particular encroachment.

An encroachment is a **trespass** if it encroaches on the land, and a **nuisance** if it violates the neighbor's air space, such as the overhanging branches of a tree. The injured party can seek a judicial remedy in ejectment, quiet title, or injunction and damages. A court is empowered to order the removal of the encroachment. However, if the encroachment is slight, the cost of removal is great, and it was created unintentionally, the court might decide to award money damages in lieu of ordering removal.

An accurate land survey will disclose most encroachments, and is usually required by lenders and buyers of any substantial parcel of real property. A prudent purchaser will obtain a survey when purchasing property if there is any doubt as to possible encroachments. If such a survey reveals any encroachments not previously disclosed by the seller, the buyer may compel the seller to pay for the survey to remove the encroachment, or reduce the purchase price accordingly.

Encroachments are not normally revealed in the chain of title. Also, most standard title insurance policies do not insure against matters which an accurate survey would reveal. An extended coverage title policy (an ALTA extended policy) will insure against encroachments. (*See* ALTA EXTENDED, EXTENDED COVERAGE, SURVEY, TRESPASS.)

ENCUMBRANCE - Any claim, lien, charge, or liability attached to and binding on real property which may lessen its value, or burden, obstruct, or impair the use of a property but not necessarily prevent transfer of title; a right or interest in a property held by one who is not the legal owner of the property. There are two general classifications of encumbrances: those that affect the title, such as judgments, mortgages, mechanics liens, and other liens which are charges on property used to secure a debt or obligation; and those that affect the physical condition of the property such as restrictions, encroachments, and easements.

A covenant against encumbrances guarantees that there are no encumbrances against the property except those specifically disclosed. If no encumbrances are disclosed as "exceptions" in the Purchase and Sale Agreement but the preliminary title report discloses encumbrances, the purchaser need not go through with the transaction.

Encumbrances may be noted on the deed following the property description. Assumed mortgages and deeds of trust normally appear on a deed. (*See* DEED, EASEMENT, LIEN.)

END LOAN - Permanent mortgages which consumers use to finance the purchase of a new condominium unit or a lot within a developed subdivision; often called **takeout** financing. Normally, the lender who makes the development or interim loan for a construction project will also provide the permanent financing to individual unit buyers to **take out** the developer after the project is completed and sold. Hence the terms takeout financing and end loan. (*See* PERMANENT FINANCING.)

ENDORSEMENT - A method of transferring the title to a negotiable instrument, such as a check or promissory note, by signing the owner's name on the reverse of such instrument. A blank endorsement guarantees payment to subsequent holders. An endorsement which states that it is **without recourse** does not guarantee payment to subsequent holders. A special endorsement specifies the person to whom or to whose order the instrument is payable. Sometimes spelled indorsements.

In FHA loans, a notation placed on the note by the FHA indicating that the loan is insured under the National Housing Act.

A notation is added to an instrument after execution to change or clarify its contents. In insurance, coverage may be restricted or enlarged by endorsing a policy. (*See* AFFIRMATIVE COVERAGE, HOLDER IN DUE COURSE.)

ENERGY-EFFICIENT HOUSING - Housing built with advanced technology that reduces home energy costs.

ENFORCEABLE - Any agreement, such as a valid contract, in which the parties to it can be compelled to perform.

ENGINEERING BREAKDOWN METHOD - An appraisal method of estimating accrued depreciation, which considers separate estimates of each major building component, such as roof, elevators and air conditioning.

ENJOIN - To forbid performance of an act or, in some cases, to command performance of an act. Courts can issue injunctions against a pattern of discrimination in real estate transactions. Both federal and state agencies have injunctive powers against subdividers who sell land in violation of the land sales law. (*See* INJUNCTION.)

ENTERPRISE ZONE - A new concept for urban renewal in which business firms receive special tax and government regulatory breaks for locating their business in certain depressed neighborhoods. (*See* URBAN ENTERPRISE ZONE.)

ENTIRETY, TENANCY BY - A form of joint ownership of property between husband and wife with the right of survivorship which does not exist in the State of Washington. (*See* COMMUNITY PROPERTY.)

ENTITLEMENT - The portion of the loan the Veterans Administration guarantees a lender if the veteran defaults. (*See* V.A. MORTGAGE (G.I. LOAN).)

ENTITY, LEGAL - A person, actual or artificial, that is recognized by law. Usually refers to an artificial being such as a corporation, partnership, limited liability partnership or limited liability company. There are many tax considerations for a buyer in choosing the appropriate entity to hold title to a real estate investment. (*See* OWNERSHIP.)

ENTREPRENEUR - One who takes the initiative to organize and manage an enterprise or business, usually assuming a substantial portion of risks, losses and profits; a promoter; a developer. He/she solves real estate problems for himself, whereas a real estate broker or a real estate counselor solves them for others. (*See* LICENSING LAW.)

ENVIRONMENTAL FORCES - One of the four categories of forces that, according to appraisal theory, affect property values. Examples of environmental forces include climate, topography, soil and natural barriers. The remaining three forces are economic, social and political (governmental).

ENVIRONMENTAL IMPACT STATEMENT - A report which includes a detailed description of a proposed development project with emphasis on the existing environmental setting, viewed from both a local and regional perspective, and a discussion of the probable impact of the project on the environment during all phases.

The National Environmental Policy Act (NEPA), enacted in 1969, requires federal agencies to file environmental impact statements with the Federal Council on Environmental Quality and obtain the council's approval for all proposed government actions. Government actions have been interpreted as including anything from approval of a federal license or permit to policy determinants, provisos, and proposed legislation. Such impact statements must include the following information: (1) a detailed description of the proposed action; (2) a discussion of the direct and indirect impact on the environment that might result from the action; (3) identification of unavoidable adverse environmental effects; (4) an assessment of any feasible alternatives to the proposed action; (5) a description of the action's cumulative and long-term effects on the earth's surface; and (6) identification of any irreversible commitment of resources that might result from the action. (*See* ENVIRONMENTAL PROTECTION AGENCY (EPA), STATE ENVIRONMENTAL POLICY ACT (SEPA).)

ENVIRONMENTAL PROTECTION AGENCY (EPA) - A federal agency created in 1970 by bringing together various federal pollution control activities that had been scattered among a number of federal departments and agencies. The EPA is involved with environmental problems of air and water pollution, solid waste management, pesticides, radiation and noise. In these areas, EPA sets standards, determines how much pollution is tolerable, establishes timetables to bring polluters into line with the standards, and enforces environmental laws. EPA conducts an extensive environmental research program, as well as providing technical, financial, and managerial help to State, regional and municipal pollution control agencies and allocates funds for sewage treatment facilities. The original authority of EPA has been subsequently increased by the passage in 1970 of the Clean Air Amendments and the Resource Recovery Act; in 1972, the Federal Water Pollution Control Act Amendments, the Federal Environmental Pesticide Control Act, the Noise Control Act and the Marine Protection, Research and Sanctuaries Act; and in 1974, the Safe Drinking Water Act. The State of Washington is in Region 10 of EPA; the Regional Office is in Seattle. (*See* ENVIRONMENTAL IMPACT STATEMENT.)

EQUAL CREDIT OPPORTUNITY ACT - In 1974, Federal Legislation was passed to insure that the various financial institutions and other firms engaged in the extension of credit exercise their responsibility to make credit available with fairness, impartiality, and without discrimination on the basis of sex or marital status. The Act applies to all who regularly extend or arrange for the extension of credit. Regulation B, implementing the Act, contains partial exemptions from procedural provisions for business, securities and public utilities credit.

Principal provisions of Regulation B are that: (1) Creditors may not make statements discouraging applicants on the basis of sex or marital status. (2) Creditors may not refuse, on the basis of sex or marital status, to grant a separate account to a creditworthy applicant. (3) Creditors may not ask the marital status of an applicant applying for an unsecured separate account, except in a community property state or as required to comply with state law governing permissible finance charges or loan ceilings. (4) Neither sex nor marital status may be used in credit scoring systems. (5) Creditors may not inquire into childbearing intentions or capability, or birth control practices, or assume from an applicant's age that an applicant or an applicant's spouse may drop out of the labor force due to childbearing and thus have an interruption of income. (6) With certain exceptions, creditors may not require or use unfavorable information about a spouse or former spouse where an applicant applies for credit independently of that spouse and can demonstrate that the unfavorable history should not be applied. (7) A creditor may not discount part-time income, but may examine probable continuity of an applicant's job. (8) A creditor may inquire about and consider whether obligations to make alimony, child support or maintenance payments, affect an applicant's income. (9) A creditor may ask to what extent an applicant is relying on alimony, child support or maintenance payments to repay the debt. The applicant must first be informed that such disclosure is unnecessary if the applicant does not rely on such income to obtain the credit. (10) Creditors must provide the reasons for terminating or denying credit to applicants who so request. (11) Creditors must inform holders of existing accounts of their rights to have credit history reported in both names. (12) Creditors must, with certain exceptions, give applicants the following written notice: "The Federal Equal Credit Opportunity Act prohibits creditors from discriminating against credit applicants on the basis of sex or marital status. The Federal agency which administers compliance with this law concerning this (insert appropriate description bank, store, etc.) is (name and address of the appropriate agency)." (13) With certain exceptions, creditors may not terminate credit on an existing account because of a change in an applicant's marital status without evidence that the applicant is unwilling or unable to pay.

The legislation provides for civil liability for violations of this Act. Types of liabilities are: (1) Any creditor who fails to comply with any requirement imposed under this title shall be liable to the aggrieved applicant in an amount equal to the sum of any actual damages sustained by such applicant acting either in an individual capacity or as a representative of a class. (2) Any creditor who fails to comply with a requirement imposed under this title shall be liable to the aggrieved applicant for punitive damages in an amount not greater than $10,000 as determined by the court, in addition to any actual damages provided in section 706(a). Provided, however, that in pursuing the recovery allowed under this subsection, the applicant may proceed only in an individual capacity and not as a representative of a class. (3) Section 706(b) notwithstanding, any creditor who fails to comply with any requirement imposed under this title may be liable for punitive damages in the case of a class action in such amount as the court may allow, except that as to each member of the class no minimum recovery shall be applicable, and the total recovery in such action shall not exceed the lesser of $500,000 or one percent of the net worth of the creditor.
Reference: 15 USC 1691 et seq

EQUAL DIGNITIES RULE - A rule of agency law which stipulates that when a contract is required by law to be in writing, the authority of an agent to enter into such a contract on behalf of his/her principal must also be in writing. For example, a power of attorney for real estate contracts must be in writing because the State's Statute of Fraud requires that all real estate contracts be in writing and that the agent's authority likewise be in writing. The power of attorney must also be recorded if the real estate contract is expected to be recorded. (*See* AGENCY, POWER OF ATTORNEY, STATUTE OF FRAUDS.)

EQUALIZATION BOARD - See BOARD OF EQUALIZATION.

EQUITABLE CONVERSION - A rule of law created to give the buyer under an executory contract of sale title for certain purposes prior to the date set for closing. Because a court of equity "regards as done that which ought to be done," the doctrine of equitable conversion operates upon the execution of a real estate contract involving real estate and converts the interest of the seller who has legal title of the real property to an interest in personal property, and it converts the interest of the buyer who owes money to an interest in real estate. Thereafter, the seller holds his/her legal title only as security for the purchase price. The doctrine applies in cases involving the valuation of the seller's interest at his/her death, and also in cases involving risk of loss or destruction of the premises. For example, assume the seller had agreed to sell his/her farm for $100,000 but died before closing; also assume he/she had willed his/her personal property to Jamie and his/her real property to Nicholas. Through the doctrine of equitable conversion, the seller's interest in the farm is treated as personal property and thus the proceeds from the sale would pass to Jamie. (*See* REAL ESTATE CONTRACT, RISK OF LOSS.)

EQUITABLE LIEN - A lien arising out of a written contract which shows an intention of the parties to charge some particular property with a debt or obligation. An equitable lien may be implied by a court out of principles of fairness and justice, such as where the parties intended to create a lien but there was a defective execution of a loan instrument. A vendee's lien, which the buyer has against the property when the seller defaults in his/her performance of the sales contract, is an equitable lien. In Washington, if community funds of a married couple are expended on real property claimed by one spouse to be separate property, the other spouse will have an equitable lien. (*See* COMMUNITY PROPERTY.)

EQUITABLE SERVITUDE - An easement of use enforced in equity which permits restrictive covenants not running with the land to be enforced as though they did run with the land. To enforce these equitable servitudes it must appear that the restrictive covenants are designed for the benefit of the lot owners in a particular subdivision or tract; that there is a dominant or benefited land; that there is a general scheme or plan of improvement or development for the entire tract; and that the covenants are intended as restrictions on the land conveyed and incident to its ownership, the purchaser accepting the lot subject to that burden. The doctrine of equitable servitudes might be asserted against a person attempting to build an apartment building by a homeowner in a tract designed for single family homes. (*See* COVENANTS, RESTRICTIVE COVENANTS, SERVITUDE.)

EQUITABLE TITLE - The interest held by a vendee under a real estate contract; the equitable right to obtain absolute ownership to property when legal title is held in another's name. Though the vendor retains the bare legal title, the vendee has the right to demand the legal title be transferred upon payment of the full purchase price. This interest is transferable by deed, assignment, contract, or mortgage and passes to the vendee's heirs and devisees upon death. Thus, the vendee will benefit from any increase in value between the date of the purchase agreement and delivery of the deed. The vendee will, however, also take the risk of any adverse circumstances, such as a change in zoning. (*See* EQUITABLE CONVERSION, REAL ESTATE CONTRACT.)

EQUITY - 1. That interest or value remaining in property after payment of all liens or other charges on the property. An owner's equity in his/her property is normally his/her monetary interest over and above the mortgage indebtedness. If the property is encumbered with a long-term mortgage, the mortgagor's equity in the property increases with each monthly mortgage payment. In the early years of the mortgage, the equity buildup is gradual, as most of the monthly payment is applied to interest on the loan rather than to principal. The greater an owner's equity, the less risk for a mortgagee who lends money based on the security of the property.

If the real property is maintained in the condition in which it was acquired, or improved and the neighborhood in which it is located is not deteriorating, appreciation must be figured in when considering an owner's equity. (*See* SWEAT EQUITY.)

EQUITY BUILDUP - The gradual reduction of outstanding principal due on the mortgage through periodic amortized payments. (*See* EQUITY.)

EQUITY, COURT OF - A court of equity is a court originally set up under the early English court structure to handle those types of complaints for which there was no adequate remedy in the law courts, particularly cases where money damages would not adequately compensate the injured party. For example, if a seller refuses to perform his/her contract to sell his/her farm to the buyer, the buyer's only remedy at law is to sue for money damages. A court of equity could, however, force specific performance of the contract. As in most states, Washington does not have separate courts of equity and law, but the distinction between legal and equitable remedies such as regards specific performance and proceedings without injury is still of importance. (*See* COMMON LAW, SPECIFIC PERFORMANCE.)

EQUITY MORTGAGE - A line of credit made against the equity in the borrower's home. The equity is based on a percentage of the appraised value of the home, minus any outstanding mortgage. It is secured by a second open end mortgage or deed of trust on the home. The interest rate may be fixed or tied to the prime rate. (*See* DEED OF TRUST, MORTGAGE.)

EQUITY OF REDEMPTION - The right given to the mortgagor (borrower) by statute in Washington to redeem his/her real property within a specified time after a foreclosure sale (sometimes referred to as a statutory redemption right). The borrower (mortgagor) retains title after the sale, and he/she may redeem the property from the purchaser by paying, within the allowable redemption period, the amount bid at the sale, plus interest and costs. The statutory period of redemption in Washington is generally one year. If the security instrument contains a **nonagricultural provision**, and if the right to a deficiency judgment is waived, then the period of redemption is only eight months. When nonagricultural property improved with a structure is abandoned for six months or more, and no payments are made on the debt during such period, the borrower forfeits his/her rights of redemption. Ordinarily, the borrower must yield possession to the successful bidder on the date of the sale, but if the property is the borrower's "homestead," he/she is entitled to retain possession through the entire period of redemption. If the security device is a deed of trust, and the beneficiary chooses to foreclose against a defaulting borrower in an out-of-court sale under the authority of the Washington Deed of Trust Act, then the borrower has no right of redemption after the sale. (*See* FORECLOSURE, MORTGAGE, REDEMPTION PERIOD.)

EQUITY PARTICIPATION - Refers to the arrangement between a purchaser/owner and a lender in which the lender shares an equity interest in a real property purchase in exchange for assisting with the financing of the acquisition. The lender may provide all or part of the down payment, closing costs, or monthly payments. Lenders may be private parties, corporations, mortgage lenders, or even the seller. May be used in the financing on the original acquisition or on refinancing.

EQUITY PURCHASER - One who purchases another's equity in a property without necessarily assuming personal liability for the loan.

EQUITY RATIO - The percentage relationship between the down payment and the total purchase price or equity value at any point in time to total property value.

EQUITY SHARING LOAN - A loan where a resident-owner splits his/her equity or the increase in the value of the home with an investor-owner, who contributes toward the down payment and may also contribute to monthly payments and benefits by being able to share in the tax write-offs. (*See* SHARED APPRECIATION LOAN.)

EQUITY SKIMMING - In 1988 Washington adopted a law prohibiting equity skimming. Equity skimming practices are used to obtain title to properties for the purpose of refinancing the property with the buyer receiving the refinance funds or obtaining rents or payments without ever satisfying any of the underlying obligations that may exist on a property.

This bill prohibits various types of equity skimming. Any person who willfully engages in a pattern of equity skimming is guilty of a class B felony punishable by a maximum fine of $20,000 and/or confinement in a state correctional institution for up to ten years. A pattern of equity skimming is defined as at least three acts of equity skimming within any three-year period with at least one act of equity skimming occurring after the effective date of the act.
Reference: RCW 61.34

EQUITY TRUST - A real estate investment trust (REIT) that acquires income producing properties, as contrasted with a mortgage REIT, that makes or purchases loans on real estate. (*See* REAL ESTATE INVESTMENT TRUST (REIT).)

EQUITY YIELD RATE - The internal rate of return on an equity investment calculated without regard to the impact of federal income taxes. An equity yield rate reflects the effect of financing on the investor's rate of return.

EROSION - The gradual loss of soil due to the operation of currents, tides or winds; the opposite of accretion. (*See* ACCRETION, AVULSION.)

ERRORS AND OMISSIONS INSURANCE - A form of insurance which covers liabilities for errors, mistakes and negligence in the listing and selling activities of a real estate office or escrow company. Errors and omissions insurance policies are typically written on a **claims-made** basis, i.e., the insured is covered only if the claim is made during the period of the policy and within a stated time of the insurer (the broker) becoming aware of the claim, e.g. 30 days. When a broker or salesman considers the enormous exposure to liability he/she has, as stated in many of the consumer interest cases decided over the last few years, the premium for errors and omissions insurance seems slight. It does not cover fraudulent behavior.

Under the rules and regulations of some of the MLS's in Washington, every member of the MLS is encouraged to carry errors and omissions insurance in amounts which will adequately protect the public against damage from any misconduct or negligence of the member. The Washington Association of Realtors offers a specifically designed errors and omissions policy to its members. *(See* CAVEAT EMPTOR.)

ESCALATOR CLAUSE - 1. A clause in a contract permitting an adjustment of certain payments up or down to cover certain contingencies. Many fixed-rental net leases, particularly long-term commercial leases, contain a clause in which the parties agree to an adjustment of rent based on set increases in such items as taxes, insurance, maintenance and other operating costs. Similarly, the rent may be tied to the cost of living index and raised at stated intervals (e.g., every five (5) years). An escalator clause protects the lessor's investment position against an erosion of his/her rate of return over the term of the lease by maintaining his/her yield during periods of inflation. *(See* CONSUMER PRICE INDEX, GRADUATED RENTAL LEASE.)

2. A clause contained in some mortgages permitting the lender to increase or decrease the agreed upon interest rate based on fluctuations in prevailing interest rates or the prime rate. Some lenders reserve the right to increase the monthly payments and/or interest rates upon the happening of a certain event; for example, an increase in the interest rate in the event of late payment or default. The escalator clause should not be confused with the alienation or due on sale clause. Often, a borrower who is selling the mortgaged property will "voluntarily" agree to an increase in the stated interest rate rather than have the lender call in the loan under the due on sale provision. *(See* ADJUSTABLE RATE LOAN.)

3. A clause in a Purchase and Sale Agreement that says the offeror will match or beat any other bona fide offer by a specific dollar amount, e.g., $500.00. (*See* SELLERS MARKET.)

ESCAPE CLAUSE - A clause in a contract relieving a party of liability for failure to perform, as where a stated contingency does not occur. If such a clause allows the party to cancel the contract for no reason whatsoever, there really is no enforceable contract since mutuality of obligation is lacking. *(See* CONTINGENCY.)

ESCHEAT - Whenever any owner of real or personal property dies leaving property subject to the jurisdiction of this State, and is not survived by any person entitled to the property, the private ownership of the property lapses and the ownership "escheats" (reverts) to the State by legal process.

Since a presumption exists that some heirs capable of taking title exist in every case, the process of escheat is not automatic, but awaits legal proceedings in the form of a decree of distribution by a probate court. This decree is not entered until at least eighteen months after the issuance of letters testamentary or of administration. Heirs may appear and claim the estate (the dollar value) from the State at any time within fifteen years of the date of issuance of the above letters. *(See* ABANDONMENT.)
Reference: RCW 11.08

ESCROW - The process by which money and/or documents are held by a disinterested third person (a "stakeholder") until the satisfaction of the terms and conditions of the escrow instructions (as prepared by the parties to the escrow). When these terms have been satisfied, there is a delivery and transfer of the escrowed funds and documents. In Eastern Washington, most closings are done by attorneys. In Western Washington, the common practice is to employ the services of a licensed escrow company, title company, lending institution or an attorney to carry out the escrow functions.

Under the Washington Escrow Agent Registration Act, escrow is formally defined as:

"Any transaction wherein any person or persons, for the purpose of effecting and closing the sale, purchase, exchange, transfer, encumbrance or lease of real or personal property to another person or persons, delivers any written instrument, money, evidence of title to real or personal property, or other thing of value to a third person to be held by such third person until the happening of a specified event or the performance of a prescribed condition or conditions, when it is then to be delivered by such third person, in compliance with instructions under which he/she is to act, to a grantee, grantor, promisee, promisor, obligee, obligor, lessee, lessor, bailee, bailor, or any agent or employee thereof."

Escrow can be used to close all types of real estate transactions involving the sale of real estate, the mortgage of real estate, an exchange of real estate, a sale by means of a real estate contract, and a long-term lease of real estate. In all cases, the escrow holder acts as a fiduciary and retains documents and assets entrusted to him/her until specified conditions are fulfilled. He/she is the special agent for **both** parties and acts in accordance with the escrow instructions given by both. The Purchase and Sale Agreement serves as primary escrow instructions for both seller and buyer as it contains (or should contain) the agreement of the parties as to who pays for what expenses, proration date, and the like. This underscores the critical role of the real estate salesman or broker whose responsibility it is to advise the parties and properly prepare the Purchase and Sale Agreement. If the Agreement has been unprofessionally prepared, the escrow company may be delayed or even be prevented from closing the transaction. If an established escrow company is not involved in the transaction, an attorney should be consulted about the preparation of proper escrow instructions.

Because of the escrow's limited duties of disclosure and the confidentially of the escrow in general, facts known to the escrow holder are normally not imputed or implied to the other party. Escrow is a limited agent for both parties, but once the conditions to the escrow transaction have been performed, the nature of the dual agency changes — escrow then becomes the agent for the seller for the money and the buyer for the deed. Escrow acts as the "clearing house" for the details of the transaction. Escrow cannot be unilaterally revoked and in the event of disagreement the escrow can only be amended, changed, or revoked by mutual agreement.

The escrow agent is not authorized to comply with any instructions or demands of any third person who is not a party to the escrow. Thus, if the broker makes a demand upon the escrow agent for his/her commission, the escrow agent should ignore the demand and close the escrow according to his/her instructions since the broker is not a party to the escrow.

In closing a real estate transaction, the escrow company performs duties such as ordering the title policy, having new documents prepared, drawing up closing statements, obtaining necessary signatures, recording documents and receiving and disbursing funds. The buyer is thus assured of receiving a clear title and the seller is assured of receiving his/her proceeds, after payment of their respective closing costs. Escrow fees are typically split equally between buyer and seller. A borrower (purchaser) under a VA mortgage may not pay escrow fees and a borrower (purchaser) under FHA financing is restricted as to how much he/she may pay.

Some special situations to which an escrow arrangement is most appropriate are: (1) closing of a sale and immediate resale or purchase; (2) closing when several lenders are involved either in new mortgages or releases of prior encumbrances; (3) closing an entire condominium project where purchaser's funds must be escrowed under state law; (4) closing for out-of-state sellers who insist on escrow's controlling the disbursement of their funds.

Real estate brokers may close escrows for transactions which they have negotiated as long as no fee for the escrow service is charged. Independent escrow companies may close escrows under authority of the Escrow Agent Registration Act, by registering the company as an escrow agent and employing a licensed escrow officer to supervise transactions. The escrow agent is required to maintain errors and omissions insurance and a fidelity bond covering its employees. Real estate brokers are not required by statute to maintain a fidelity bond or errors and omissions insurance.

However, **no** individual may select, prepare, and complete legal documents incident to the closing of a real estate and personal property transaction unless certified as provided by Admission to Practice Rule (APR) 12 of the Washington Supreme Court. APR 12 was adopted after the Washington Supreme Court ruled that the selection and completion of legal documents by anyone other than an attorney constituted the unauthorized practice of law. The unauthorized practice of law is a misdemeanor offense.

Legal documents include deed, promissory notes, guarantees, deeds of trust, reconveyances, mortgages, satisfactions, security agreement, releases, Uniform Commercial Code, documents, assignments, contracts, real estate excise tax affidavits, and bills of sale.

Those individuals and institutions exempt from registration under the Escrow Agent Registration Act are not exempt from certification under APR 12 if they select, prepare, and complete legal documents incident to the closing of a real estate or personal property transaction. APR 12 only exempts lenders holding security interest in the subject property from the certification requirement.

Real estate brokers must be certified under APR 12 if they select, prepare, and complete legal documents incident to the closing of real estate or personal property transactions. Registration under the Escrow Registration Act does not exempt escrow officers from the certification requirements of APR 12.

When a valid escrow has been set up with a binding and enforceable Purchase and Sale Agreement deposited with the escrow holder along with a fully executed deed, the death or incapacity of one of the parties to the escrow will not terminate the escrow. Upon performance of his/her part of the contract, the surviving party is entitled to have escrow concluded according to the terms of the contract. *(See* CLOSING COSTS, COLLECTED FUNDS, DELIVERY, DOUBLE ESCROW, ESCROW AGENT REGISTRATION ACT, HOLDING ESCROW, INTEREST, INTERPLEADER, RELATION BACK DOCTRINE.) *Reference:* RCW 18.44, RCW 2.48.180, WAC 308-124D

ESCROW AGENT - An independent third party legally bound to carry out the written provisions of an escrow agreement. (*See* ESCROW AGENT REGISTRATION ACT.)

ESCROW AGENT REGISTRATION ACT - Any person in Washington who wishes to engage in the business of performing for **compensation** the duties of an escrow agent in real estate transactions, except for limited exceptions, must be appropriately registered with the Department of Financial Institution. *(See* ESCROW.)

The registration and licensing requirements do not apply to: (1) banks, trust companies, mutual savings banks, savings and loan associations, credit unions, insurance companies, title insurance companies or federally approved lenders; (2) attorneys; (3) real estate brokers (provided no compensation is received for escrow services); (4) receivers, trustees in bankruptcy, executors, administrators, guardians or other persons acting under the supervision of a Court; (5) disbursement of funds by a joint control agent under a construction draw arrangement.

Under provisions of the Registration Act, a certified escrow agent is identified as the company engaged in the escrow business. The term "company" includes corporations, firms, co-partnerships and sole proprietorships.

To receive the certified escrow agent certificate, a corporate officer, partner or the sole proprietor must have passed the Escrow Agent Examination and as well as provided the Department of Financial Institution with an application form, an annual fee, a commercial credit report showing a good credit rating, a copy of a fidelity bond providing fidelity coverage and an errors and omissions policy. If an assumed business name is to be used, a certified copy of the certificate of the assumed name must be provided. If a corporation, Articles of Incorporation and a copy of the Annual Report as filed with the Secretary of State must be provided. If a partnership, a copy of the partnership agreement must be provided.

A certified escrow agent may employ qualified escrow officers to perform the escrow function. To be eligible for an escrow officer's license, the individual must: be a resident of the State of Washington; have attained eighteenth birthday; pass the Washington State Escrow Officer Examination. The examination cannot be waived. An escrow officer's license is valid only when acting for or in behalf of a certified escrow agent. The examination given shall encompass the following: (1) Appropriate knowledge of the English language, including reading, writing and arithmetic. (2) An understanding of the principles of real estate, conveyancing, the general purpose legal effects of deeds, mortgages, deeds of trust, contracts of sale, exchanges, rental and optional agreements, leases, earnest money agreements, personal property transfers, and encumbrances. (3) An understanding of the obligations between principal and agent. (4) An understanding of the meaning and nature of encumbrances upon real property.

Every certified escrow agent shall keep adequate records of all transactions handled by or through him/her, including itemization of all receipts and disbursements of each transaction, which records shall be open to inspection by the Director of Licenses or his/her authorized representatives. Every certified agent shall keep a separate escrow fund account in a recognized Washington State depository authorized to receive funds, in which shall be kept, separate, apart and segregated from the agent's own funds, all funds or moneys of clients which are being held by the agent pending the closing of a transaction. Such funds shall be deposited not later than the first banking day following receipt thereof. Violation of this section shall constitute grounds for suspension or revocation of the registration and the certificate thereof of any person under this chapter.

The Director of Financial Institutions may, upon his/her own motion, and shall, upon verified complaint in writing by any person, investigate the actions of any licensed certified escrow agent or escrow officer and may temporarily suspend or permanently revoke or deny such license for any holder who is guilty of the following: (1) Obtaining a license by means of fraud, misrepresentation, concealment, or through the mistake or inadvertence of the Director. (2) Violating any of the provisions of this chapter or any lawful rules or regulations made by the Director pursuant thereto. (3) A crime against the laws of this or any other state involving moral turpitude or dishonest dealings. (4) Knowingly committing or being a party to, any material fraud, misrepresentation, concealment, conspiracy, collusion, trick, scheme, or device whereby any other person lawfully relying upon the word, representation, or conduct of the licensee acts to his/her injury or damage. (5) Conversion of any money, contract, deed, note, mortgage, abstract or other evidence of title to his/her own use or to the use of his/her principal or of any other person, when delivered to him/her in trust or on condition, in violation of the trust or before the happening of the condition; and failure to return any money or contract, deed, note, mortgage, abstract or other evidence of title within thirty days after the owner thereof is entitled thereto, and makes demand therefor, shall be prima facie evidence of such conversion. (6) Failing, upon demand, to disclose any information within his/her knowledge to, or to produce any document, book, or record in his/her possession for inspection by the Director of Financial Institutions or his/her authorized representatives acting by authority of law. (7) Committing any act of fraudulent or dishonest dealing, and a certified copy of the final holding of any court of competent jurisdiction in such matter shall be conclusive evidence in any hearing under this chapter. (8) Accepting, taking or charging any undisclosed commission, rebate or direct profit on expenditures made for the principal.

An escrow agent shall not make disbursements on any escrow account without first receiving deposits directly relating to the account in the amounts at least equal to the disbursements. The deposits shall be in one of the following forms:

1. Cash;

2. Interbank electronic transfers such that the funds are unconditionally received by the escrow agent or the agent's depository;

3. Checks, negotiable orders of withdrawal, money orders, cashier's checks, and certified checks that are payable in Washington State and drawn on financial institutions located in Washington State;

4. Checks, negotiable orders of withdrawal, money orders, or;

5. Any depository check, including any cashier's check, certified check, or teller's check, which is governed by the provisions of the Federal Expedited Funds Avail ability Act, 12 U.S.C.

No real property lender, escrow agent, or officer or employee of any escrow agent or real property lender may give or agree to pay or give any money, service, or object of value to any real estate agent or broker, to any real property lender, or to any officer or employee of any agent, broker, or lender in return for the referral of any real estate escrow services. *Reference:* RCW 18.44

ESCROW INSTRUCTIONS - In a sales closing, those documents signed by buyer and seller that detail the procedures necessary to close a transaction and direct the escrow agent how to proceed. Sometimes the buyer and seller execute separate instructions.

ESTATE - 1. The degree, quantity, nature and extent of ownership interest which a person has in real property. The term "estate" is often used simultaneously with the word "interest." To be an estate, an interest must be one that is (or may become) possessory, and whose ownership is measured in terms of duration. A freehold estate (a fee simple or a life estate) is an interest in land for an uncertain duration. All other interests are "less-than-freehold" or leasehold interests, such as an estate or tenancy for years or an estate at will. Not all interests in land are estates. For example, a mortgage or deed of trust is a lien or charge on land, but is not a part of ownership and thus is not an estate. *(See* FEE SIMPLE, FEE SIMPLE DEFEASIBLE, FEE TAIL, FREEHOLD.)

2. The property owned by a decedent and which may be subject to federal and state tax and probate administration.

ESTATE AT WILL - Leasehold estate that can be terminated at any time by either landlord or tenant. *(See* TENANCY AT WILL.)

ESTATE FOR YEARS - A conveyance of realty for a definite period of time. This is the most common type of leasehold and is one that has a specified beginning date and ending date to the term. Although the leasehold is called an estate for years, it may in fact be for a shorter time. The term may be one month, one week, or even one day. During the terms of the lease, a tenant has a right to possess, control, enjoy, and dispose of the property rights. If the tenant were to die during the term of the leasehold, the property interest would pass to the tenant's estate. If the tenant retains possession of the property after the expiration of the term, this is referred to as holding over. The landlord has the option to treat the holdover tenant as a trespasser and proceed to dispossess him/her from the property, or he/she may elect to treat the term of the lease as renewed, thereby converting the leasehold into a periodic tenancy, or in some states into a tenancy at will.

ESTATE FROM YEAR TO YEAR - A leasehold interest in real estate also known as a periodic tenancy or an estate from period to period, which is automatically renewed for the same term as in the original lease; thus, the conveyance is for an indefinite period of time. If the lease term is for more than one year, the term upon renewal is considered to be for one year.

For example: If Scott signs a lease for a five-year period with an automatic renewal provision, then at the end of the term, if Scott has failed to give proper notice to terminate the lease, the tenancy will automatically renew for an additional term of one year.

Where no term is specified, the manner and time that the rent is paid establishes the term by implication. For example, if the rent is paid monthly, the implication is that the term is from month to month.

ESTATE OF INHERITANCE - A freehold estate that can be passed by descent or by will after the owner's death, such as a fee simple absolute. A life estate is not an estate of inheritance.

ESTATE TAX, FEDERAL - A tax imposed by the federal government upon the transfer of property from the estate of a deceased to a beneficiary. All property in which the deceased had an interest, including jointly held property and life insurance proceeds, is subject to federal estate tax. The Tax Reform Act of 1976 reflected substantial change in the area of federal estate taxation. Three of the major changes include: (1) No longer would lifetime transfers (gifts) receive preferential treatment over transfers effective at death; in addition, gift taxes and estate taxes were set up under a common rate schedule. Gift tax rates had previously been three-fourths of estate tax rates. (2) Lifetime transfers (gifts) and transfers effective at death would be cumulated for determining estate tax; however, any gift tax paid would be subtracted from any estate tax due. (3) Under certain conditions, real property used for farming or trade or business may be valued on the basis of its use instead of on the basis of "highest and best" use.

The Economic Recovery Act of 1981 adopted the following changes in the area of federal estate taxation: (1) The amount exempt from taxation was increased up to $600,000 in 1987 (the amount has been increased, see next paragraph); (2) after 1981 unlimited amounts of property may be transferred to a spouse tax free; (3) generally, the value of gifts (other than gifts of life insurance) made by a decedent within three years of death is not includible in the gross estate. In addition, post-gift appreciation will not be included in the gross estate. However, transfers made within three years of death (other than gifts qualifying for the annual gift tax exclusion) are includible in the gross estate for purposes of determining the estate's qualification for special use valuation, deferral of estate taxes and stock redemptions and for purposes of determining property that is subject to estate tax liens.

Under the Taxpayer Relief Act of 1997, the amount excluded from federal estate taxes was increased to $625,000 in 1998; the amount increases $25,000 per year until it tops off at $1,000,000 in 2006 and later years.

The basis of inherited property is the value at the time of the death of the decedent or six months later.

The federal estate tax is due and payable within nine months after the decedent's death. Extension on payment of the tax may be granted upon petition showing that the estate would have to sell an asset at a "sacrifice" price. Beneficiaries inheriting a family farm or business may be granted an extension to pay the estate tax. Where this extension is granted, the U.S. Treasury has a lien on the property. Lenders are reluctant to lend money to owners of such real estate. Now, the Treasury may subordinate its lien to that of a bank. In the sale of real property, the preliminary title report will raise the exception of unpaid estate taxes.

Competent legal advice, careful estate planning, the proper choice of form of ownership, and the use of inter vivos trusts can serve to eliminate much of the estate tax burden and the cost of probate administration. *(See* CONSIDERATION, GIFT TAX, INHERITANCE TAX, PROBATE. STEPPED-UP BASIS.)

ESTOPPEL - A legal doctrine by which a person is prevented from asserting rights or facts which are inconsistent with a previous position or representation made by act, conduct, or silence. For example, a mortgagor who certifies that he/she has no defenses against the mortgagee would be estopped to later assert any defenses against a person who purchased the mortgage in reliance on the mortgagor's certificate of no defense, e.g., the mortgagor/borrower signs a letter agreeing that the balance due is $115,000 cannot later assert that the actual balance was lower when the letter was signed. An estoppel differs from a waiver in that a waiver generally refers to a voluntary surrender or relinquishment of some known right, whereas estoppel creates an inability to assert a defense or right.

If the conduct of one party to an agreement is such that it misleads another, and the first party relies on that conduct, an estoppel will be created to prevent the first party from denying the effect of his/her conduct. When a grantor conveys more interest in land than he/she in fact has, and later acquires the full title, such grantor can be barred by estoppel from denying the grantee's full interest in the land. When a real estate owner allows another person to act as if he/she is the true owner, and an innocent purchaser buys the land from that other person, the true owner is estopped from asserting ownership.

In boundary cases, a landowner is sometimes estopped to assert that the true boundary line is different from the line previously agreed upon by the owner and his/her neighbor. This is especially true if the neighbor has acted in reliance on the landowner's representations of the location of the line and built a fence or driveway, planted crops, made improvements, or the like.

Sometimes a seller under an oral contract of sale is estopped to assert the statute of frauds as a defense to the buyer's suit for specific performance when the buyer has entered into possession, paid money, or made improvements and the buyer can show that he/she would suffer irreparable injury and hardship if the contract were not enforced.

Equitable estoppel may be asserted by a developer who obtained a building permit but then finds the government has down zoned the parcel or changed the land use. *(See* NONCONFORMING USE, VESTING.)

A purchaser of rental property might have the existing tenants execute estoppel statements acknowledging their obligation to pay the proper amount of rent according to the specified terms of their leases. *(See* CERTIFICATE OF NO DEFENSE, LACHES, REDUCTION CERTIFICATE.)

ESTOPPEL BY DEED - A legal doctrine under which one who, without having legal title to a property, deeds the property to another and then subsequently obtains good title to the property. The grantor is then estopped from denying his/her lack of title at the time of the original conveyance, thus automatically vesting complete legal title in the grantee. *(See* AFTER-ACQUIRED, QUITCLAIM DEED.)

ESTOPPEL CERTIFICATE OR LETTER - A statement that in itself prevents the issuer from later asserting different facts. *(See* CERTIFICATE OF NO DEFENSE, REDUCTION CERTIFICATE.)

ET AL. - Latin abbreviation for **et alii** meaning "and others."

ET UX. - Latin abbreviation for **et uxor** meaning "and wife."

ET VIR. - Latin abbreviation for "and man," generally meaning "and husband."

ETHICS - A system of moral principles, rules and standards of conduct. High ethical standards are more important in real estate than in other transactions where the clients may be more familiar with the services performed. Good ethics is concerned with fidelity, integrity and competency. *(See* CODE OF ETHICS.)

ETHNIC GROUP - People belonging to the same race and having a common heritage of language, culture, and customs. *(See* DISCRIMINATION.)

EVICTION - The disturbance of a tenant's enjoyment of all or any material part of the leased premises by act of the landlord or by claim of a superior title by a third party.

Typical grounds for the eviction of a tenant by a landlord, include nonpayment of rent, unlawful use of the premises violating the use provision of the lease (such as conducting a business in a rental unit leased strictly for residential purposes), and noncompliance with health and safety code.

Under the Landlord Tenant Act, if a tenancy has been terminated and the tenant refuses to move out voluntarily, the landlord may not remove or exclude the tenant from the premises, except by court order served by the sheriff. If the landlord does so, he/she may be liable for actual damages which the tenant sustains and the prevailing party may recover cost of suit and reasonable attorney fees.

If the tenant refuses to move out, the landlord must go to court and get a court order directing the sheriff to remove the tenant, physically, if necessary.

If the landlord has to bring an unlawful detainer action to evict the tenant, and the court finds for the landlord, the tenant may be liable for all rent the court finds that is due, any damages or expenses accrued by the landlord during the proceedings, and the court costs and attorney's fees involved.

The unlawful detainer is a special statutory proceeding which is supposed to speedily restore to the plaintiff (landlord or tenant) possession of the disputed premises. Each step is prescribed by the statute and must be strictly complied with in order to confer jurisdiction.

The statute provides the court only with jurisdiction to decide who is entitled to possession. The action is not available for the purpose of litigating the title to real property or the question on title to or the conversion of personal property.

Eviction procedures under the new Washington Landlord Tenant Act are complicated. If the landlord pushes the eviction as fast as possible and the hearings are held within the shortest possible time, the period of time from the point which the tenant gets the first notice of eviction until the tenant's belongings are placed in storage can be from 20 to 30 days. *(See* ABATEMENT, EJECTMENT, LANDLORD TENANT ACT.)
Reference: RCW 59.18

EVIDENCE OF TITLE - Proof of ownership of property. Common examples of such evidence are a certificate of title, title insurance policy, or, with Torrens registered property, a Torrens certificate of title.

A person who contracts to sell property must furnish the buyer with a marketable title to the property. In Washington, the seller normally pays for a title insurance policy as evidence of good title at closing. *(See* CERTIFICATE OF TITLE, TAX AND LIEN SEARCH, TITLE INSURANCE.)

EXAMINATION, ESCROW LICENSING - *See* ESCROW AGENT REGISTRATION ACT.

EXAMINATION, REAL ESTATE LICENSING - All persons seeking a Washington real estate license must take a written examination and demonstrate a reasonable knowledge of general real property laws and principles, documents, and state licensing laws. Under no circumstances is the examination requirement waived. A separate examination is given for salesmen and for brokers, and each is entirely objective, multiple choice in format.

Each application for a real estate examination must be accompanied by a nonrefundable application fee for either a salesman's examination or for a broker's. An unsuccessful candidate may take as many examinations as he/she can endure, although a new application must be made for each successive reexamination. Application for salesman and broker examinations must be filed with the Real Estate Program of the Department of Licensing.

The following are prerequisites for sitting for the Commission's written licensing examinations for salesperson:

1. **General**. The applicant must be at least 18 years of age.

2. **Education**. An applicant must have successfully completed a sixty-hour course in real estate fundamentals approved by the Real Estate Commission. Proof of successful completion must be submitted with the application.

3. **Waiver of Education**. The Real Estate Program may allow substitution of the clockhour requirement if the individual is otherwise qualified by reason of completion of equivalent educational course work in an institution of higher education.

The following are prerequisites for sitting for the Commission's written licensing examinations for brokers:

1. **General**. The applicant must be at least 18 years of age.

2. **Education**. An applicant for a broker examination must have a high school diploma or have passed a GED examination, have successfully completed 120 "clock hours" of education in real estate courses approved by the Real Estate Commission, which should include 30 hours in Brokerage Management, 30 hours in Real Estate Law, 30 hours in business management and one elective 30 hours course. Proof of successful completion must be submitted with the application.

3. **Waiver of Education**. The Real Estate Program will recognize certain equivalent education in lieu of approved courses, such as university credits in real estate or law school credits for real property courses. Likewise, the Real Estate Program will waive the education requirement for a broker or salesman from a state which has educational standards similar to Washington's, although only a few states qualify for this waiver.

4. **Experience**. A person applying for the real estate broker examination must have been engaged in the real estate business as a full-time real estate salesman for a period of two years or have had other experience and/or education in the selling or management of real estate, in order to obtain a waiver of all or part of the two-year requirement. It is possible for a part-time salesperson to accumulate enough experience to qualify to sit for the broker

examination. E.g., a part-time salesperson averaging at least 20 hours per week could qualify with 4 years experience.

5. **Waiver of Experience.** Waivers are granted to candidates who, in the opinion of the Director, are otherwise and similarly qualified, or are otherwise qualified by reason of practical experience in a business allied with or related to real estate. The following guidelines should help a candidate to determine whether or not an application would be considered: (1) attorney; (2) three years experience closing real estate transactions; (3) five years experience as a real property appraiser; (4) five years experience in construction; and (5) five years experience at a lending institution, title company or mortgage company. The Department usually considers experience within the seven (7) years preceding application.

A waiver of experience is not a waiver of the educational requirements.

A broker candidate can only receive one waiver. If the candidate is unsuccessful, a second waiver will be granted only under very unusual circumstances. *(See* BROKER, LICENSING LAW, SALESMAN.)
Reference: RCW 18.85, WAC 308-124

EXCEPTION - 1. As used in a conveyance of real property, an exception is the exclusion from the conveyance of some part of the property granted. The title to that withdrawn part remains vested in the grantor by virtue of his/her original title. A conveyance by Miss Rae to Mr. Hoyt of a ten-acre parcel, "excepting therefrom a strip of land ten feet wide running along the northerly boundary," constitutes a legal exception. An exception is to be distinguished from a reservation, which is the creation on behalf of the grantor of a new right issuing out of the thing granted, such as the reservation of an easement by the grantor to cross the property or the reservation of a life estate in the conveyed property.

2. Liens and encumbrances specifically excluded from coverage under a non-extended coverage title insurance policy. (*See* EXTENDED COVERAGE.)

3. Those matters noted in the "subject to" clause of the Purchase and Sale Agreement, in which the seller agrees to convey clear and marketable title "subject to the following exceptions." *(See* RESERVATION.)

EXCHANGE - A transaction in which all or part of the consideration for the purchase of real property is the transfer of property of a "like kind" (i.e., real estate for real estate). The original attraction of an exchange was in those cases where it was difficult to produce a cash buyer.

The exchange has become a popular device for deferring capital gains taxes. The **tax-free exchange**, as it is sometimes wrongly called, involves the exchange of property held for investment or the production of income for property of a like kind (which includes improved and unimproved property). In such an exchange, payment of any tax is not avoided but, rather, is deferred until the property is later disposed of in a taxable transaction. The underlying philosophy behind an exchange is that income tax should not apply as long as an investment remains intact in the form of real estate. The exchange of a personal residence does not qualify for this tax-deferred treatment. A leasehold with 30 or more years remaining under the lease can be exchanged for a fee title to improved or unimproved property. One disadvantage to an investor in a tax-free exchange is that the basis in the new property is the basis in the old property, it is lower than it would have been had the new property been purchased and the old property been sold in separate transactions. Such a reduced basis thus results in smaller depreciation deductions. It is important that the Purchase and Sale Agreement indicates the taxpayer's intention to exchange rather than to sell the property.

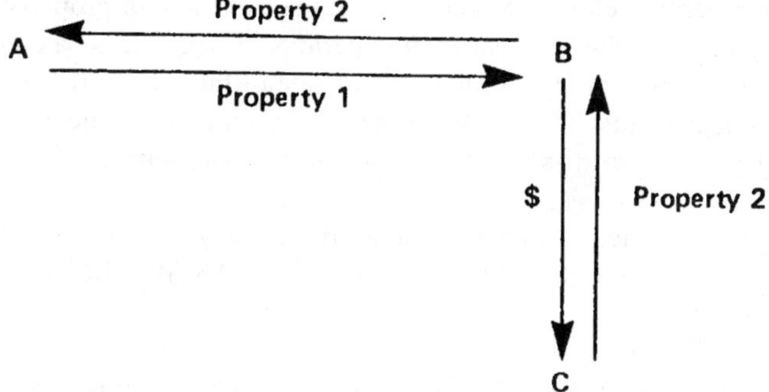

Prior to the creation of the deferred or delayed exchange, the most frequent types of exchanges were the "three-way" exchanges. In one type, the exchanging party (A) conveys his/her property (1) to the purchaser (B) in exchange for new property (2) which the purchaser obtains pursuant to the exchanging party's directions.

In another type, the exchanging party (a) conveys his/her property (1) to the purchaser (B) in exchange for new property (2) received directly from a third-party seller (C).

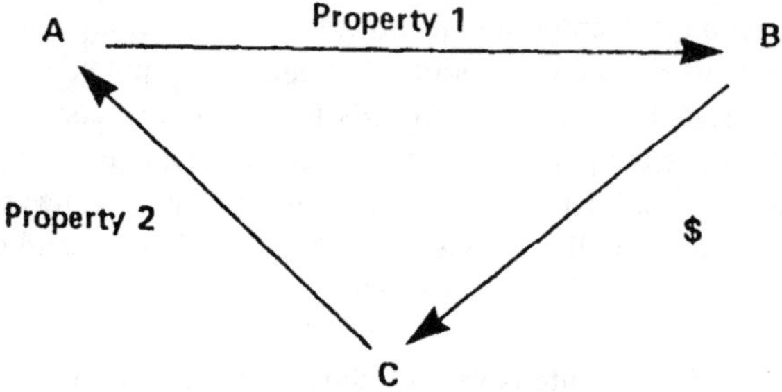

It is rare to find two properties of equal value; therefore, to balance the equities, one party usually also pays some money or assumes a larger amount of underlying debt. If received by the party seeking the tax-free exchange, this money or additional debt from which a person is relieved would be treated as boot, and gain will be taxable to the extent of that boot. For example, David John Smith wants to exchange his $500,000 apartment building subject to a $400,000 mortgage lien for Hoyt Brock's apartment building, valued at $450,000 with a $400,000 mortgage. Smith's equity is $100,000 and Brock's equity is $50,000. Therefore, Brock would have to pay $50,000 in boot to equalize the equities. Or, if the equities were the same, but Brock's property had only a $350,000 mortgage (so that David John was relieved of $400,000 but assumed only $350,000), then David John would again be considered to have received $50,000 of boot.

In many cases the exchangor needs time to locate the replacement ("up-leg") property. Under special deferred/delayed exchange rules, the exchange of property need not be simultaneously, although there are strict time periods in which to locate and close the replacement property measured from the time of sale of the "relinquished property." The replacement property must be located within the United States if the exchanged property is U.S. property. (It is permissible to exchange foreign property for foreign property.)

If an exchangor is married, the spouse should release any marital rights in the exchange deed. *(See* BOOT, DEFERRED OR DELAYED EXCHANGE, LIKE KIND, MULTIPLE ASSET EXCHANGE.)

EXCISE TAX ON REAL ESTATE SALES - A county tax imposed on the transfer or conveyance of realty or any interest therein by means of deed, lease, sublease, assignment of purchaser's contract and deed, a real estate contract or similar instrument. The tax was authorized by the State Legislature to provide for funding of necessary school revenues. One side effect has been to furnish reliable data on the fair market value of the property to help establish more accurate real property tax assessments. The seller, grantor, or lessor is liable for the tax. An unpaid, overdue tax is a lien on the property. The amount of the tax may be recovered either by personal action against the seller, grantor or lessor or by foreclosure against the property.

Where the transaction is exempt, the document must be accompanied by an affidavit setting forth the grounds for the exemption. Exempt from the tax are mortgages, deeds of trust, correction deeds and fulfillment deeds for real estate contracts which have been recorded and the excise tax paid, transfers between husband and wife or parent and child, seller's assignment of contract and deed, a deed where the seller has received no funds for his/her equity and he/she will continue to pay the debt service, and deeds resulting from probate or divorce action and sheriff's deeds.

The enforceability of the statute is very effective since the county auditor will not accept for filing any deed or instrument of sale of an interest in real estate without the stamp of the county treasurer showing that the real estate sales tax has been paid, or that the transfer is not taxable. An affidavit referring to the transfer is executed by one of the parties or his/her agent and presented to the county treasurer. If a tax is due it is then paid, and the instrument of conveyance is stamped by the treasurer. If no tax is payable, the instrument is so marked. It is only at this point that the county auditor will accept the instrument for recording.

The amount of the Washington excise tax is based on the "actual full consideration," which means the price or amount, whether cash or otherwise, actually paid or ultimately required to be paid for real property, including the value of any mortgages, liens or encumbrances thereon at the time of transfer. *(See* RECORDING.) For years, the excise tax was 1%; however, the present rate exceeds 1% in all counties. In recent years, it has been increased and now varies from county to county. A phone call to the county treasurer in the county where the property is located will give you the local rate. *(See* DELINQUENT EXCISE TAX PENALTY.)
Reference: RCW 28.45

EXCLUSIVE AGENCY - A written listing agreement giving one broker/agent (real estate office) the right to sell property for a specified time, but reserving to the owner the right to sell the property himself/herself without payment of any commission. The exclusive agent will be entitled to a commission if the property is sold by himself/herself or anyone else other than the seller. In Washington, an exclusive agency is used much less frequently than the exclusive right-to-sell listing. Some multiple listing services are starting to accept exclusive agency listings. *(See* EXCLUSIVE RIGHT-TO-SELL)

EXCLUSIVE LISTING - A written listing of real property in which the seller agrees to appoint only one broker to sell his/her property for a specified period of time. This does not necessarily mean, however, that only one company can show the property to prospective buyers, due to the fact, most brokers belong to a multiple listing service. The two types of exclusive listings are the exclusive agency and the exclusive right-to-sell. All exclusive listings must stipulate a termination date to avoid having a listing continue indefinitely. A listing for an indefinite period is frowned on by the courts and is generally poor practice. This is to protect sellers who, unaware the listing is still in effect after the end of the initial listing period, may list the property with another broker and thus may find themselves liable for the payment of two full commissions. *(See* EXCLUSIVE AGENCY, EXCLUSIVE RIGHT TO SELL, EXTENDER CLAUSE.)

EXCLUSIVE RIGHT-TO-SELL - A written listing agreement appointing a broker as the exclusive agent for the sale of property for a specified period of time. The listing broker is entitled to a commission if the property is sold by the owner, by the broker, or by anyone else. In many cases, the listing broker is a member of a multiple listing service and the listing is shared with all members of the MLS. If the listing office is not the selling office, it usually receives one-half of the commission as a listing commission. The vast majority of homes listed in Washington are listed under an exclusive right-to-sell. The phrase "right to sell" really means the right to find a buyer; it does not mean that the agent has a power of attorney from the owner to sell the property.

There is a growing trend for owners of commercial-investment real estate to give exclusive right-to-sell listings. In a commercial-investment listing, it may provide that the property can only be exchanged and not sold. *(See* EXCHANGE, LISTING, TERMINATION OF LISTING.)

EXCULPATORY CLAUSE - (1) A clause sometimes inserted in a promissory note in which the lender waives the right to a deficiency judgment. Also called a non-recourse note. The creditor can look only to the real property to satisfy the debt in case of default. (2) As used in a lease, a clause that intends to clear or relieve the landlord from liability for tenants' personal injury and property damage. It may not, however, protect the landlord from injuries to third parties. *(See* DISCLAIMER.)

EXECUTE - The act of making a document legally valid, such as formalizing a contract by signing, or acknowledging and delivering a deed. In some cases, execution of a document may refer solely to the act of signing; in other cases, it may refer to complete performance of the document's terms.

EXECUTION - A judicial process whereby the court directs an officer of the law to levy upon (seize) the property of a judgment debtor in satisfaction of a judgment. Certain property may be exempted from execution due to a homestead. *(See* HOMESTEAD.)

EXECUTOR - A person appointed by a testator (the person making the will) to carry out the directions and requests in his/her last will and testament, and to dispose of the property according to the provisions of the will. A female executor is called an executrix. In Washington, whether or not the executor must post a bond prior to performing his/her duties depends on whether or not the will provides for it.

The executor is entitled to possession and control of the testator's real estate pending determination of heirs and distribution of the property. Unless the power to sell the decedent's real property is given to the executor in the will, he/she must request court approval prior to selling the property. The executor does not need a real estate license in order to sell the property. When the will authorizes the executor to sell real property, he/she may sell it either at public auction or private sale, without any notice to the court (however, title does not pass until the sale is confirmed by the court). *(See* ADMINISTRATOR, PROBATE.)

EXECUTORY CONTRACT - A contract in which one or both of the parties has not yet performed, such as in a Purchase and Sale Agreement. An "executed" contract, on the other hand, is one in which there is nothing left to be done by either party; it has been completely performed by both parties. The instrument is no longer a contract but rather is evidence of an executed agreement. The distinction is important. For example, the Statute of Frauds does not apply to an executed oral agreement; thus, one who conveys property by deed in accordance with an oral contract of sale cannot later assert the Statute of Frauds to try to rescind the contract and get back the property. If executory, however, the seller could not be forced to convey the deed under the oral contract.

EXECUTORY INTEREST - An interest in property which shifts title from one transferee to another. A fee simple subject to an executory interest is an estate where, upon the happening of an event designated in the grant, the fee simple is automatically transferred to a third person and not to the original grantor or his/her heirs. For example, Peter Desportes grants his farm "to L. Hebert so long as it is used during the next 20 years to grow wheat, and if not so used, then to W. Fournier and his heirs."

The distinction between an executory interest and a **possibility of reverter** (when the property reverts to the grantor) is important because the executory interest must generally become possessory within the period allowed under state law. *(See* FUTURE INTEREST, POSSIBILITY OF REVERTER, RULE AGAINST PERPETUITIES.)

EXEMPLARY DAMAGE - *See* PUNITIVE DAMAGES.

EXHIBIT - A document or section of a document presented as part of the supporting data for the principal document. For example, a Purchase and Sale Agreement may have a legal description attached as an exhibit; an inventory of furniture may also be attached as an exhibit. *(See* ADDENDUM.)

EXPANSION OPTION - A provision in a lease granting a tenant the option to lease additional adjacent space after a specified period of time.

EXPERT WITNESS - A witness in a lawsuit or arbitration qualified to render testimony by virtue of specialized knowledge and/or experience. For example, an experienced real estate broker may be asked to testify as to the standard of care of brokers in the community; or an appraiser may testify as to the value of property involved in a legal proceeding.

EXPOSURE - 1. Where and/or how a property is situated in terms of compass direction or its accessibility to air, light, or facilities. For example, residential properties are offered as having a southern exposure or a high degree of exposure to sunlight.

2. In marketing terms, a property must be exposed for sale in the open market. A property's exposure to the market includes how it is displayed, exhibited, and/or allowed to be seen by qualified buyers.

EXPROPRIATION - The taking of private land for a public purpose under the government's right of eminent domain, as exercised in a condemnation suit. *(See* EMINENT DOMAIN.)

EXTENDED COVERAGE - 1. A term used in fire insurance to include wind damage and other perils.

2. A title insurance policy which covers risks normally excluded by most standard coverage policies. The standard policy normally only insures against the title as shown by the public records. It does not cover such off-record matters as might be discovered by an inspection of the premises. Most lenders will require this added coverage, usually in the form of an "American Land Title Association Extended Coverage Policy." Extended coverage indemnifies the insured against such things as defects, liens, encumbrances, easements, rights of parties in possession, tax liens, and encroachments, none of which is disclosed by the public records. *(See* AMERICAN LAND TITLE ASSOCIATION, ALTA EXTENDED TITLE INSURANCE, HIDDEN RISK, TITLE INSURANCE.)

EXTENDED MORTGAGE TERM - The traditional residential loan is usually written for a thirty year period. In times of high inflation, in an effort to counter higher monthly loan payments caused by higher interest rates, some lenders will make loans for terms which may be up to forty years. The longer term of years lowers the monthly payment with principal reduction being lower in the early years of the loan. *(See* CREATIVE FINANCING.)

EXTENDER CLAUSE - 1. A clause, once found in listing forms, which provides that the listing will continue for a set period of time, such as 90 days, and then will be automatically renewable until the parties agree to terminate it. Most multiple listing services no longer use an extender clause in their standard listing form since the use of such a clause by an organization may be a violation of the antitrust laws. Such clauses, however, do not violate antitrust laws if inserted by individual brokers in their own exclusive listing forms, though the clause must state a final termination date.

2. A **carry over** clause (referred to as a safety clause) contained in a listing which provides that a broker is still entitled to a commission for a set period of time after the listing has expired if the property is sold to a prospect of the broker introduced to the property during the period of listing.

Most multiple listing services' standard form listing provides that the seller agrees to pay the broker his/her cash commission as follows: "If within 90 days after expiration of the listing agreement, the property is sold to or exchanged with any person who physically inspected the property with the broker or any cooperating broker during the listing period and if the broker gave seller the name of such person in writing within five days after the stated expiration date of this listing agreement." The owner should disclose to any broker seeking a listing whether there are any expired listings. Unless careful disclosure is made of any extended clauses in such expired listings, the owner could be faced with a claim for commissions from both the former broker who had shown the buyer the property and the new broker. *(See* NEGOTIATION, OVERRIDE.)

EXTENSION - An agreement to continue the period of performance beyond the specified period. For example, the parties to a real estate sale may mutually agree to extend the time of closing of the transaction.

A lease extension is an agreement by which the lease is made effective for an additional period of time beyond its effective date; it is often referred to as a lease renewal.

In periods of tight money, when buyers with maturing real estate contracts find it difficult to sell or refinance their property prior to the maturity date of their contract for deed, many buyers are willing to pay a premium in order to extend the agreement and thus avoid a default. However, care should be taken by a mortgagee in extending a debt since, in the case of deed assumptions, an extension may have the effect of changing the original contract so that guarantors and prior grantees are released from liability.

EXTERNAL OBSOLESCENCE - A loss of value (typically incurable) resulting from extraneous factors that exist outside of the property itself; a type of depreciation caused by environmental, social or economic forces over which an owner has little or no control. If there is a change in zoning, external obsolescence is likely to occur, as in the following examples: to a residence if a business locates next to it; to a well-maintained house in a deteriorating neighborhood; and to a motel if a new highway is built that results in difficult access to the motel. Other causes might be proximity to nuisances and changes in land use or population. Also called locational or environmental obsolescence. *(See* COST APPROACH, OBSOLESCENCE.)

F

FACADE - The exposed or front face of a building; often used to describe an exterior that features a unique architectural design or concept.

FACE LIFT - Non-structural changes that result in an improved appearance of a building. Such things as repairs, paint, new windows, and general cleaning all serve to improve the appearance of a building.

FACE RATE OF INTEREST - The stated interest rate in a promissory note. Also known as the **contract rate or nominal rate**, the face rate of interest will be less than the **annual percentage rate** (APR) if additional charges such as origination fees and discount points are charged by the lender. (*See* ANNUAL PERCENTAGE RATE.)

FACE VALUE - The amount due at the maturity of an instrument; the par value as shown on its face, not the real value or the market value. Mortgage notes are often sold at a discount below their face value. Also, the dollar amount of insurance coverage.

FACILITATOR - One who assists another. This term has no precise legal meaning in the State of Washington. However, it is used in two contexts: (1) A real estate licensee who assists a buyer and seller in reaching an agreement in a real estate transaction and the licensee claims to be a facilitator and not an agent of either party. In some cases, dual agents refer to themselves as facilitators because they provide limited agency services to their respective principals. (2) The legal entity holding funds in trust under an IRC 1031 Exchange. (*See* AGENCY, DEFERRED OR DELAYED EXCHANGE, DUAL AGENCY.)

FAIR CREDIT REPORTING ACT - A federal law designed to protect the public from the reporting of inaccurate information by credit agencies. Under the Fair Credit Reporting Act, an individual has the right to inspect information in his/her file at the credit bureau, to correct any errors, and to file explanatory statements as a supplement to the file. The act also requires that if a seller of real estate refuses to sell to a particular prospective buyer and/or a lender refuses to extend credit because of the buyer's credit report, the seller or lender must disclose to the prospective buyer the identity of the credit agency making the report. Most adverse information about a debtor is dropped after seven years (except bankruptcy information which can be shown for up to ten years). (*See* EQUAL CREDIT OPPORTUNITY ACT.)

FAIR HOUSING ACT - *See* FEDERAL FAIR HOUSING LAW.

FAIR HOUSING AMENDMENT ACT OF 1988 - A federal act which amended the *Federal Fair Housing Act of 1968* to include two new protected classes, the handicapped and the "familial" status, or families with children under eighteen. The amendment became effective March 12, 1989. (*See* FAMILIAL STATUS, FEDERAL FAIR HOUSING ACT OF 1968.)

FAIR MARKET VALUE - The highest monetary price which a property would bring, if offered for sale for a reasonable period of time in a competitive market, by a seller who is willing but not compelled to sell, to a buyer, willing but not compelled to buy, both parties being fully informed of all the purposes to which the property is best adapted and is capable of being used.

Fair market value is used as a basis for determining property taxes. In Washington, the assessed valuation of real property for tax purposes is an amount representing 100 percent of the assessor's estimate of fair market value. As an appraisal term, it usually stated as **market value**.

FALSE ADVERTISING - Advertising which contains blatantly false or misleading information. False advertising by a seller constitutes misrepresentation and gives the buyer grounds for canceling his/her contract to purchase. In certain cases, false advertising may constitute fraud and would support a legal action to recover a money judgment for any damages suffered. Generally, a real estate licensee responsible for false advertising is subject to suspension or revocation of his/her real estate license. (*See* ADVERTISING, BLIND AD, LICENSING LAW, RESCISSION.)

FAMILIAL STATUS - As provided for in the Fair Housing Act, a situation in which one or more individuals under age 18 lives with a parent or legal guardian or another person given written permission from a parent. Specifically covered are pregnant women or a person in the process of securing legal custody. (*See* FAIR HOUSING AMENDMENT ACT OF 1988.)

FAMILY - In the traditional sense, family refers to persons related to each other by blood or marriage. In the more modern sense, the term family is being given a broader interpretation, to include certain nontraditional living arrangements. It is important to check definitions under local zoning ordinances to see whether "single-family dwellings" permit unmarried, unrelated groups such as the elderly or disabled to live together. (*See* RELATED PARTIES.)

FANNIE MAE - Nickname of the Federal National Mortgage Association (FNMA). (*See* FEDERAL NATIONAL MORTGAGE ASSOCIATION.)

FARM AND LAND INSTITUTE - The former name of a national organization that is a section to the National Association of Realtors®. Now known as the Realtors® Land Institute (RLI). (*See* ACCREDITED LAND CONSULTANT.)

FARM AREA - A selected geographical area or one specific building (e.g., a high-rise office building) to which a real estate salesperson devotes special attention and study. A good salesperson learns everything there is to know about his/her farm area, including all recent comparables, and tries to solicit listings from this community. The salesperson is thus an expert on his/her farm area.

FARM ASSETS - The true concept of the ranch or farm offered for sale or exchange, separated into its component assets (particularly for income tax purposes) consists, among other things of: (1) farmland; (2) personal residence; (3) other residences and structures used in the business of farming or ranching; (4) vines, trees, pipelines, fences, irrigation systems, livestock; and (5) unharvested crops sold to the purchaser.

These assets are subject to special treatment for income tax purposes, as provided for in the Internal Revenue Code and the Regulations of the Internal Revenue Service. Therefore, the importance of price allocation upon a sale, exchange or lease of the whole ranch or farm property, or some part thereof is important.

FARM CREDIT SYSTEM - A federal program inaugurated under the Federal Farm Loan Act of 1916, designed to serve the unique financial requirements of farmers, ranchers, producers and harvesters of agricultural products, rural homeowners, and owners of selected farm-related businesses. The 50 states are divided into 12 Farm Credit Districts, operating independently under the supervision of the Federal Farm Credit Administration. (*See* FARM LAND BANK.)

FARMERS HOME ADMINISTRATION (FmHA) - A former federal agency of the U.S. Department of Agriculture designed to handle farm financing. This agency was replaced in 1994 by the Rural Housing and Community Development Services. (*See* RURAL ECONOMIC AND COMMUNITY DEVELOPMENT.)

FARMLAND - Land used specifically for agricultural purposes, in the raising of either crops or livestock. Also land so designed in zoning laws for agricultural purposes.

FEASIBILITY STUDY - An analysis of a proposed project with emphasis on the attainable income, probable expenses, and most advantageous use and design. A feasibility study is often used by a developer to entice investors to put up the front money for a proposed development. Such a study is required by some mortgage investors and lending institutions prior to granting a loan commitment. However, it is different from a marketability study which is more concerned with demand for the contemplated use. (*See* ABSORPTION RATE, FRONT MONEY.)

The purpose of a feasibility study is to estimate the rate of return obtainable for a specific project and to determine whether the proposed project is economically feasible.

FEDERAL CONSUMER CREDIT PROTECTION ACT - *See* TRUTH-IN-LENDING ACT.

FEDERAL DEPOSIT INSURANCE CORPORATION (FDIC) - The name of an independent executive agency which insures the deposits of all banks entitled to federal deposit insurance. Individual accounts are insured up to $100,000. FDIC is now an arm of the U. S. Treasury Department assigned by FIRREA to the management of SAIF and BIF, two federal deposit insurance funds. (*See* BANK INSURANCE FUND (BIF), FINANCIAL INSTITUTIONS REFORM, RECOVERY AND ENFORCEMENT ACT (FIRREA), SAVINGS ASSOCIATION INSURANCE FUND (SAIF).)

FEDERAL FAIR HOUSING LAW - Congress enacted Title VIII of the Civil Rights Act in 1968, which is usually called the federal fair housing law, declaring a national policy of providing fair housing throughout the United States (Reference Sections 3601-3631 of Title 42, United States Code). This law makes discrimination based on race, color, sex, religion, or national origin illegal in connection with the sale or rental of most housing and any vacant land offered for residential construction or use. The federal law does not prohibit discrimination in other types of real estate transactions, such as those involving commercial or industrial properties. The law is administered by the Office of Equal Opportunity (OEO) under the direction of the Secretary of the Department of Housing and Urban Development (HUD).

As amended in 1972, the law requires that equal opportunity posters (11" x 14") be displayed at brokerage houses, model home sites, mortgage lenders' offices, and other related locations. Failure to display the poster constitutes prima facie evidence of discrimination if a broker who does not display the sign is investigated by HUD on charges of discrimination. The poster must have the equal housing opportunity slogan: Equal Housing Opportunity. It must also carry the equal housing opportunity statement: "We are pledged to the letter and spirit of U.S. policy for the achievement of equal housing opportunity throughout the Nation. We encourage and support an affirmative advertising and marketing program in which there are no barriers to obtaining housing because of race, color, religion, or national original." There must also be the following equal housing opportunity logo on the poster:

The fair housing law provides protection against the following acts of discrimination, if they are based on race, color, sex, religion, or national origin:

- Refusing to sell or rent to, or deal or negotiate with any person.
- Discriminating in terms or conditions for buying or renting housing.
- Misrepresentation in terms or conditions for buying or renting housing.
- Discriminating by advertising that housing is available only to persons of a certain race, color, sex, religion, or national origin.
- Denying that housing is available for inspection, sale, or rent when it really is available. (This includes a practice called steering, whereby certain brokers may steer members of minority groups away from some of their listings in racially mixed areas.)
- Blockbusting, a practice whereby a broker hopes to make a profit through persuading owners to sell or rent housing by telling them that minority groups are moving into the neighborhood.
- Denying or requiring different terms or conditions for home loans made by commercial lenders, such as banks, savings and loan associations, and insurance companies.
- Denying to anyone the use of or participation in any real estate service, such as brokers' organizations, multiple listing services, or other facili ties related to the selling or renting of housing.

The Fair Housing Act applies to the following:

- Single-family housing owned by private individuals when a broker or other person in the business of selling or renting dwellings is **employed** (includes use of MLS) and/or discriminatory advertising is used.

- Single-family housing not owned by private individuals, such as those owned by development corporations.

- Single-family housing owned by a private individual who owns more than three such dwellings or who, in any two-year period, sells more than one dwelling in which he/she was not the most recent resident.

- Multifamily dwellings of five or more units.

- Multifamily dwellings containing four or fewer units, if the owner does not reside in one of the units.

Exceptions: The following situations are exempt from the fair housing law (but covered by the post-Civil War 1866 anti-discrimination civil rights law, if based on race):

- The sale of real property if neither a broker nor discriminatory advertis ing is used, and no more than one dwelling in which the owner was not the most recent resident is sold during any two-year period.

- The rental of rooms or units in owner-occupied multiple dwellings for two to four families, if discriminatory advertising is not used and the services of a broker are not employed (the "Mrs. Murphy exemption"). However, this practice in unlawful in Washington. (*See* WASHING TON STATE HUMAN RIGHTS COMMISSION.)

- The sale, rental, or occupancy of dwellings owned and operated by a religious organization for other than commercial purposes to persons of the same religion, if membership in that religion is not restricted on ac count of race, color, sex, or national origin.

- The restriction of lodgings owned or operated by a private club for other than a commercial purpose to rental or occupancy by its own members.

There are two separate remedial avenues, one administrative and one judicial. An aggrieved person may take his/her complaint directly to a U.S. district court within 180 days of the alleged discriminatory practice, whether or not a verified complaint has been filed with the Secretary of the Department of Housing and Urban Development. However, in states with equivalent anti-discrimination judicial rights and remedies, such a suit would have to be brought in the state court. The burden of proof is on the complainant. The court can grant permanent or temporary injunctions, temporary restraining orders, or other appropriate relief, and may award actual damages and not more than $1,000 in punitive damages. Criminal penalties are provided for those who coerce, intimidate, threaten, or interfere with a person's buying, renting, or selling housing, making a complaint of discrimination, or exercising any rights in connection with this law. Licensees should keep detailed records of all transactions and rentals in order to defend themselves against possible discrimination complaints. Violations are frequently proven through the use of "testers" and the courts have ruled that there is no requirement that the testers actually be bona fide purchasers or renters. (*See* BLOCKBUSTING, DISCRIMINATION, PANIC PEDDLING, STEERING.)

Discrimination in federally subsidized housing projects is prohibited under Title VI, Civil Rights Act of 1964, which states that: "No person in the United States shall, on the ground of race, color or national origin, be excluded from participation in, be denied the benefits of, or be subject to discrimination under any program or activity receiving federal financing assistance." (*See* DISPARATE IMPACT.)

FEDERAL HOME LOAN BANK SYSTEM (FHLB) - Established by Congress in 1932 to help restore the nation's depression-wracked savings system. At the same time, Congress created a new class of federally chartered savings associations (prior charters were issued only by the states) and set up 12 regional Federal Home Loan Banks to provide a credit reserve for its members. From the beginning until 1989, the banks functioned under the supervision of the Federal Home Loan Bank Board. In that year the board was abolished and replaced by the Federal Housing Finance Board.

FEDERAL HOME LOAN MORTGAGE CORPORATION (FHLMC or FREDDIE MAC) - A federally chartered corporation established in 1970 for the purpose of purchasing mortgages in the secondary market. Its 15 million shares of preferred stock are owned by 3,000 savings associations and 100,000 shares of common stock are owned by the Federal Home Loan Bank. While Freddie Mac may purchase loans from any source, its policies and practices are designed to meet savings association needs. For example, its dominant commitments are for immediate purchases of loans: those already existing in an association's portfolio. And it purchases loan participations, meaning from 50 to 85 percent of a block of loans, with the remainder held in portfolio by the selling association.

To sell a loan to Freddie Mac, the loan originator must comply with the seller/servicer requirements and the loan must be written on FHLMC uniform documents. FNMA and FHLMC have jointly developed a series of documents to standardize their mortgage loan purchases and these have become known as "conforming" loans.

To raise money for the purchase of loans, Freddie Mac may sell its own securities. However, from its beginning, Freddie Mac has been a leader in the use of mortgage-backed securities for its cash. Rather than borrow money through the sale of an issue of bonds, Freddie Mac has converted blocks of mortgage loans into securities, thus passing the interest risk on to the security investor. The vehicle that Freddie Mac uses is the Mortgage Participation Certificate (known as "PC's" in the financial markets) which represents an undivided interest in a large, geographically diversified group of residential mortgages and is unconditionally guaranteed by FHLMC. This is an "agency" type of guarantee, **not** a federal government guarantee.

In 1983, Freddie Mac introduced a variation of the mortgage-backed security called a Collateralized Mortgage Obligation (CMO). The CMO segments the cash flows from the underlying block of mortgage loans into usually four basic classes of bonds with differing maturities. (*See* COLLATERALIZED MORTGAGE OBLIGATIONS, PARTICIPATION SALE CERTIFICATE, SECONDARY MORTGAGE MARKET.)

FEDERAL HOUSING ADMINISTRATION (FHA) - The FHA was established in 1934 under the National Housing Act to encourage improvement in housing standards and conditions, to provide an adequate home financing system through the insurance of housing mortgages and credit, and to exert a stabilizing influence on the mortgage market. The FHA was the federal government's response to lack of housing, excessive foreclosures, and a collapsed building industry during the depression.

Important achievements of the FHA program have been general acceptance of the amortized loan, standardization of appraisal processes, and better planning and land utilization by developers. Additionally, the introduction of high loan-to-value ratios combined with a small down payment requirement expanded significantly the number of potential home buyers.

FHA loans have traditionally played an important part in the financing of housing even though such loans have never exceeded 30 percent of the total loans made. In recent years, FHA loans have received heavy competition from conventional loans which have a high loan-to-value ratio backed up by private mortgage insurance (such as MGIC).

Mutual Mortgage Insurance: The FHA, which operates under the Department of Housing and Urban Development (HUD), neither builds homes nor lends money itself. Rather it insures loans on real property, including condominiums, made by approved lending institutions. Should the homeowner default on his/her mortgage, the lending institution will not incur any significant losses since FHA has insured the lender against that risk. This is accomplished under a mutual mortgage insurance plan. The more common types of FHA programs are Title I - Home Improvement and Title II - Home Mortgage.

For most programs, a FHA borrower pays a one-time premium of the closing of the loan and annual premiums thereafter. The one-time premium paid at the closing of the loan is called the OTMIP (one-time mortgage insurance premium) or the UFMIP (up front mortgage insurance premium) in some trade publications.

The amount of the one-time premium varies depending on the loan amount and the term of the loan. For a loan with a repayment term of 15 years or less, the premium is two percent. For a loan with a term over 15 years, the premium is 2.25%. This premium may be paid by the borrower in cash or it may be financed. If the premium is paid in cash at closing, the amount paid is rounded down to the last $50.00 multiple; if financed, the rounding down rule does not apply.

If an FHA loan is paid off early (due to a sale or a refinance), the borrower may be entitled to a refund of part of the premium since the FHA has not fully earned the fee. If paid off early, the unearned portion will be refunded according to a FHA schedule. In the case of a sale of the property and an **assumption** of the FHA loan, there is no refund.

The amount of the annual fee will be .25% or .50% of the original loan amount depending on the loan term. One-twelfth of the annual premium is paid monthly with the normal mortgage payment.

How long the annul premium must be paid depends on the loan to value ratio of the loan and the term of the loan; e.g., a loan to value ration of 90% to 95% with a term of 15 years or less would require a .25% annual premium for four years; while a loan to value ratio of 90% to 95% with a term of 30 years would require a .50% annual premium for twelve years.

FHA financing of a condominium does not have either the one-time mortgage insurance premium or the annual premiums; rather, the borrower pays what is called a "monthly premium," sometimes called a "periodic premium," for the full term of the loan at the rate of .50% of the loan balance per year.

In 1987, the FHA altered its policy for payment of its insurance in the event of a loan default. Under prior procedures, the FHA allowed the mortgagee to elect to either retain the property after foreclosure, or to submit its claim for mortgage insurance along with title to the foreclosed property. If title is delivered to the FHA, the mortgagee receives interest bearing government bonds (debentures), cash or a combination of both. Under the newer procedures, the mortgagee is allowed to submit a claim for mortgage insurance benefits without granting title to the FHA on the property. To implement this rule, the FHA sets an "adjusted market value" for the property in the event of foreclosure. Then the lender takes title to the property and can only claim the difference between the FHA's adjusted market value and the amount of the insured commitment. This rule applies to property insured after November 30, 1983. An additional rule requires the lender to seek a deficiency judgment against the defaulted borrower. The "claims without conveyance" rule allows this to be done.

For properties that the FHA takes title to in foreclosure actions, they are resold generally under one of two methods: (1) as-is on a bid basis, or (2) at a market price as set by the FHA after the property has been rehabilitated. With the increase in foreclosures that resulted from economic declines in the 1980s in several sections of the country, the FHA resorted to auction sales of some of its properties. At these auctions, a potential home buyer could be pre-qualified for a loan to assist in bidding successfully.

Interest Rates and Loan Amounts: Prior to 1982, the maximum allowable interest rate for an FHA insured loan was set by the Secretary of Housing and Urban development. Since it was normal for the FHA loan originator to adjust the yield on such loans by discounting so as to meet market requirements, the cost often became a part of the price of the house. In 1982, the FHA began a phaseout of the interest ceilings and allowed rates to be set at whatever level was agreed upon between borrower and lender. However, the practice of requiring a loan discount remains as a negotiable cost of borrowing money. It may be paid for by either the buyer or the seller.

Thus the borrower must be prepared to pay in cash at closing the difference between the cost of the property and the amount of the insured commitment (which becomes the amount of the loan). In addition, for most programs, the borrower must pay for all prepaid items at closing - this is generally the escrow requirements for property tax and hazard insurance. FHA offers an assistance to home buyers by allowing the inclusion of closing costs (subject to FHA limitations) as a part of the insured commitment. Thus the insured commitment is based on a percentage (varies with the different programs) of the sum of the property value plus closing costs.

In fact, the borrower must provide evidence of the needed funds before FHA will make its commitment to insure the loan. There is no prohibition against placing secondary financing on the property after the FHA mortgage is closed and FHA has issued FHA mortgage insurance to the lender.

Loan Fees and Discount Points: An FHA loan applicant is allowed to pay a loan origination fee of not more that one percent of the amount borrowed (or 2 1/2 percent for construction loans when the lender makes inspection and partial disbursements during building construction). The buyer is also permitted to pay any loan discount points.

Programs: Title 1 FHA loans are granted for home improvements, alterations, and repairs. These loans are for relatively low amounts with a repayment term of no longer than seven years and thirty two days.

Title II FHA loans are granted for construction or purchase of a home. They may also be obtained to refinance existing mortgage debt. While there are a number of Title II programs, the most popular are:

Section 203(b): The most widely used program (in some years, this program accounts for up to two-third of all FHA loans), this mortgage is available for both owner-occupants and nonowner occupants purchasing or refinancing one-to four-family homes. The maximum loan-to-value ratio is 95 percent.

Section 203(b) - Veteran: Qualified veterans may purchase one-to four-family homes as owner-occupants with a loan-to-value ration which may exceed 97 percent due to a slightly lesser down payment (the "required investment") than the standard 203(b) loan requires. Sometimes called an FHA/VA loan, which is incorrect due to the fact that the Veteran's Affairs is not involved.

Section 234(c) - Condominiums are covered under this program, which in most respects is similar to the basic 203(b) program. To obtain an FHA loan in a condominium, it is necessary that the condominium itself be FHA approved.

Section 245: The Graduated Payment Mortgage was introduced by FHA in 1978 to permit lower monthly payments in the early years of the mortgage for the purpose of offering easier qualifications of home buyers. Qualification on the borrower's income is based on the first year's monthly payment amounts rather than what income it will take to amortize the loan. The lower initial monthly payments are achieved with a calculation that reduces the initial payment sufficiently to allow a set percentage of increases each succeeding year until it reaches a level that will fully amortize the remaining balance of the loan. Unpaid interest resulting from the lower early monthly payments is added to the principal balance each year resulting in "negative amortization."

The FHA offers five different payment plans with their Plan III being the most popular. Plan III offers the lowest initial payment amount, increasing 2 1/2 percent each year for five years, reaching a payment amount that amortizes the loan over the next 25 years. To offset the possibility that the increase in the loan amount in the early years might result in a loan greater than the initial property value, these plans require higher down payments.

Assumptions: FHA loans may be assumed subject to certain restrictions. Two methods can be used. One is a **simple** assumption that allows the loan to be assumed without notification to the FHA. With this method, there is no change in the interest rate or underlying conditions of the loan and the original borrower remains fully liable for repayment in the event of a subsequent default. Further, the original obligor can be reported to national credit bureaus as the delinquent party in the event of a delinquency or a default. Simple assumptions are not permitted during the first two years of the loan.

The other method is a **formal** assumption that requires FHA approval of the new buyer. To qualify for such an assumption the loan must be current, the new buyer must meet FHA qualification standards for creditworthiness, and the new buyer must agree to the loan assumption. If these conditions are met, the loan can be assumed with no change in the interest rate or underlying conditions and the original borrower (the seller) is released from further liability.

All loans made before December 15, 1989 can be assumed without approval.

For loans originated on or after December 15, 1989, the creditworthiness of the new buyer must be ensured prior to conveyance of title in **all** assumptions. The due-on-sale rules apply to transactions using a real estate contract, lease option or a wraparound note.

Commitments: A developer or builder sometimes seeks an FHA commitment to insure the mortgage on a project to be constructed. In such cases, the FHA may give a conditional commitment to ensure that is dependent upon the structures or houses being satisfactorily completed according to FHA standards as verified by FHA inspection. Some commitments are dependent upon the sale of the building to a purchase satisfactory to FHA. (*See* CLOSING COSTS, COMMITMENT, CONVENTIONAL LOAN, DEBENTURE, GRADUATED PAYMENT MORTGAGE, IN-SERVICE LOAN, INSPECTION, MINIMUM PROPERTY REQUIREMENT, MUTUAL MORTGAGE INSURANCE FUND, PRIVATE MORTGAGE INSURANCE, VA MORTGAGE.)

FEDERAL LAND BANK - Regional banks established as part of the Farm Credit Administration which are a source of long-term mortgages to farmers. The Federal Land Banks make first mortgages through local federal land bank associations to farmers, ranchers, rural residents and farm-related businesses. A majority of the funds used to make these loans come from the selling of securities by the Federal Land Banks to investors.

FEDERAL NATIONAL MORTGAGE ASSOCIATION (FNMA) - "Fannie Mae" is the popular name for the Federal National Mortgage Association, established as a federal agency in 1938 for the purpose of purchasing FHA loans from loan originators. The reason was to provide some liquidity for government-insured loans in a depression-wracked economy when few lending institutions would undertake this type of loan. In 1944, VA loans were added to their purchase program. Fannie Mae became a major source of funds for mortgage companies that offered FHA and VA loans. Mortgage companies hold no deposit assets and must sell their loans quickly to replenish their available cash.

In 1968 Congress partitioned Fannie Mae into a continuing government agency known as the Government National Mortgage Association (under the Department of HUD), and issued a federal charter to Fannie Mae to operate as a private corporation. Its stock is freely traded on the New York Stock Exchange. However, Fannie Mae as a private corporation retained certain ties to the federal government, such as five of its 18 directors are named by the President of the United States, and it has the right to borrow up to $2.25 billion from the U. S. Treasury. These close ties give Fannie Mae a financial market status as an "agency" of the federal government which enhances its credit allowing it to borrow funds at a slightly lower cost than other corporations.

As a private corporation, Fannie Mae expanded its purchase programs, adding conventional loans in 1972. It has continued its close relationship with mortgage companies, most of whom service FNMA loans that they originate. Fannie Mae no longer sets a servicing fee for its seller/servicers, but expects them to earn 25 to 35 basis points included in the interest rate charged to the borrower. Fannie Mae periodically sets its yield requirement in accordance with market rates, advising its seller/servicers by phone contact. Loan originators, such as mortgage companies, savings associations and banks, may obtain firm commitments for funds for up to 60 days in advance of their requirements.

Thus, a loan originator knows how much it must charge a borrower if the loan is to be sold to FNMA.

Fannie Mae purchases a variety of loans including standard fixed interest rates, adjustable rates, and graduated payment plans. It offers such groups as large builders and real estate companies "master commitments" in $25 million minimum amounts for funds for up to 12 months in advance. In many ways, Fannie Mae provides assurance to the mortgage market of available funds.

Loans sold to Fannie Mae must be written in accordance with Fannie Mae's specific requirements. To simplify these requirements for loan originators, Fannie Mae has worked in cooperation with Federal Home Loan Mortgage Corporation to develop a series of uniform mortgage instruments. Since both Fannie Mae and Freddie Mac (FHLMC) follow national housing policies, they adhere to similar limitations on the size and kinds of loans they will buy. Thus, these agencies have brought into the market a new kind of conventional loan, identified as a "conforming loan."

To obtain money to buy loans, Fannie Mae from its beginning has sold bonds, mostly shorter term debenture bonds that still carry the status of "agency issues," but are not guaranteed by the federal government. Fannie Mae's principal source of income has been the margin between what it paid for its funds, and what it could earn on its portfolio of mortgage loans. When this margin dried up in the early 1980s as its cost of funds exceeded its return on the mortgage loans, Fannie Mae turned to various financial services to earn a fee income. Also, in 1983 Fannie Mae shifted its dependence from borrowed funds to buy loans to a new procedure: it became a converter of mortgage loans into mortgage-backed securities. By pledging large blocks of mortgage loans as collateral, Fannie Mae issues mortgage-backed securities that are sold to a broad market of investors. With this procedure, Fannie Mae shifts the risk of interest rate fluctuations to the security investor and retains for itself a small margin on the cash flows passed through to the holder of the security.

FEDERAL RESERVE SYSTEM - The national central banking system designed to control the nation's economy via the control of the money supply, availability of credit and interest rates. It is divided into 12 districts, each served by a federal reserve bank. The "Fed" has a great impact on real estate investment activity through its regulation of member banks' reserves, which includes reserves required for all institutions handling transaction accounts (checking accounts, i.e., money unavailable for loans or any other use; determination of discount rates, the rate that the district banks charge member banks for the use of the Feds' money (thus impacting interest rates); decisions to buy or sell government securities; and the supervision of truth-in-lending and equal credit opportunity laws.

FEDERAL SAVINGS AND LOAN ASSOCIATION - In 1989 the Federal Savings and Loan Insurance Corporation was replaced by the Savings Association Insurance Fund

(SAIF). (*See* SAVINGS AND LOAN ASSOCIATION, SAVINGS ASSOCIATION INSURANCE FUND.)

FEDERAL TAX LIEN - A federal lien which attaches to real property, if the federal estate tax is not paid, or if the taxpayer has violated the federal income tax or payroll tax laws in some fashion.

Under the Federal Tax Lien Act of 1966, a junior federal tax lien will not be divested by a nonjudicial foreclosure proceeding (under a power of sale) taken under state law unless; (a) the federal government consents, in writing, to the sale, or (b) written notice of the proposed sale is given, thus giving the federal government an opportunity to collect its lien from the proceeds of the sale. Accordingly, most attorneys obtain a current title report prior to commencing a nonjudicial foreclosure in order to be sure there are no outstanding federal tax liens on the subject property.

In Washington, notices of federal tax liens need to be filed with the Clerk of Court for the county. The federal tax lien is generally subject to the interest of purchasers and creditors who record their interest in the Office of the County Auditor prior to the date the notice of the federal tax lien is recorded. As with other liens, the federal tax is subject to the priority of liens of real property taxes and special improvement assessments owed to the state or county, regardless of whether they are recorded before or after notice of the federal tax lien is recorded.

The above rules do not apply, however, if the taxpayer becomes "insolvent." In such cases, the federal government may assert different rules, claiming priority of its lien over previously recorded liens.

The Tax Act providing for the priority of federal tax liens, is conditioned on public indexing of the liens at Internal Revenue Service offices. An index of liens affecting real property will be maintained in the district office for the area in which the property is located. An index of liens affecting personal property will be maintained in the district office for the area in which the taxpayer resides at the time of the filing of the notice of a lien.
Reference: 31 U.S.C.A. Section 191

A tenant in common could be surprised to find the real property sold or partitioned to satisfy a federal tax lien against a co-tenant in common. This potential threat of partition is also a concern to a purchaser in a timesharing project.

FEDERAL TRADE COMMISSION (FTC) - A federal agency created to investigate and eliminate unfair and deceptive trade practices or unfair methods of competition in interstate commerce. Deceptive practices generally include such actions as an affirmative misstatement of fact — an express statement that is false, as well as any false implication that may reasonably be implied from such a statement. This could encompass a developer's misleading representations of his/her intent to resell property for purchasers. Unfair practices would generally include any practice in which the following three elements are present: the practice offends public policy; it is immoral, unethical, oppressive, or unscrupulous; it causes injury to consumers. This would include such actions as inducing purchasers to buy through scare tactics or high-pressure gimmicks. The FTC also enforces the truth-in-lending laws as they relate to brokers. (*See* ANTITRUST.)

The FTC monitors the Equal Credit Opportunity, Fair Credit Reporting and the Home Mortgage Disclosure Acts.

FEDERALLY RELATED TRANSACTION - Any sale transaction that ultimately involves a federal agency in either the primary or secondary mortgage market. Under FIRREA, state-certified or state-licensed appraisers must be used for certain loans in federally related transactions.

FEE APPRAISER - An appraiser who makes appraisals on a professional basis and charges a fee. An appraiser who operates as an independent contractor and is not part of a company staff. Appraisal services include valuation, review and/or consultation.

Fee appraisers who are approved by FHA are said to be on the "HUD fee panel." For FHA loans, the 1990 Housing Bill allows lenders to select their appraisers rather than use an appraiser assigned by HUD.

FEE SIMPLE - The maximum possible estate one can possess in real property. A fee simple estate is the least limited interest and the most complete and absolute ownership in land; it is of indefinite duration, freely transferable, and inheritable. Fee simple title is sometimes referred to as "the fee." All other estates may be created from it, which means that all other estates must be something less than fee simple (such as life estates, leaseholds, etc.). Any limitations that exist on the control and use of the land held in fee do not result from the nature of the estate itself, but are founded on public or private controls governing the use of the land (zoning ordinances and building codes or restrictions and conditions). The fee may also be encumbered, either by voluntary (e.g., mortgages or deeds of trust) or involuntary (e.g., tax lien) encumbrances. Such encumbrances tend to reduce the value of the fee interest. (*See* FREEHOLD, RESTRICTIONS.)

FEE SIMPLE DEFEASIBLE - An estate in land in which the holder has a fee simple title subject to being divested upon the happening of a specified condition; also called a **qualified fee** or a **defeasible fee**. For example: Jeffery Dee grants his farm to Chris Emil as long as Emil does not build a liquor store on the premises. Emil has a fee simple estate, but if he were to build a liquor store, the property would revert to Dee. Any transaction involving a fee simple defeasible estate should be referred to an attorney for a professional opinion.

Fee simple defeasible estates may be categorized as follows: **fee simple determinable**, in which case the property would automatically revert to the grantor upon the occurrence of the specified condition; or **fee simple subject to a condition subsequent**, in which case the grantor would have to exercise his/her right of entry and actually take possession of the property in order to get his/her reversion. The law does not favor unreasonable restrictions on use or ownership of property where property has been purchased; however, where the property has been acquired by a gift or inheritance, unreasonable restrictions may be recognized. Problems arise under changing circumstances: e.g., Rose Fournier gives property to a Church for so long as property is used for church services. The congregation moves to the other side of town and wants to sell the old church and build a new one with the proceeds. They cannot sell it, because once they stop using the property the property reverts to the original grantor or to her heirs. (*See* POSSIBILITY OF REVERTER, RIGHT OF RE-ENTRY.)

FEE TAIL - A freehold estate which has the potential of continuing forever, but will necessarily cease if and when the first fee tail tenant's lineal descendants die out. At common law, words of inheritance and procreation were needed to create a fee tail estate, that is, "to Harry and the heirs of his body." Washington does not recognize this type of estate and converts all fee tail estates into fee simple estates. A fee simple estate is an estate of inheritance which can pass to both collateral and lineal heirs.
Reference: RCW 11.12, RCW 64.04

FELT JOINT COVER - A covering of tightly woven wool treated with a bitumen tar derivative that prevents seepage at the joints of plumbing pipes.

FHA - A popular reference to the Federal Housing Administration, a federal agency. (*See* FEDERAL HOUSING ADMINISTRATION.)

FHA INSURANCE - An insurance fee charged the borrower on all FHA mortgages. The insurance payment is retained by FHA for use in buying any mortgage in default that is being held by a lender. (*See* FEDERAL HOUSING ADMINISTRATION.)

FIABCI - The acronym for the "Federation Internationale de Biens Consuls Immobliers," the former name for the International Real Estate Federation which has its home office in Paris, France. FIABCI-USA is the United States Chapter and was formerly affiliated with the National Association of Realtors®. The relationship was terminated by NAR in the early 1990s as part of a movement in NAR to more directly control the "Voice of Real Estate" in international real estate.

FICTITIOUS NAME - For business purposes an "assumed business or fictitious company name" is permitted in the State of Washington. An assumed business name may be selected by an individual, partnership, corporation. limited liability company or limited liability partnership transacting business in the State. The two general guidelines when an

assumed business name may be used are: (1) that fraud would not be committed on the public, and (2) that the assumed name is not deceptively similar to some other company's name.
Reference: RCW 19.80

In the State of Washington there are three ways to protect the use of an assumed business name: (1) The completion of an affidavit to be filed with the Clerk of Court in the county in which you wish to protect the name. The affidavit of an assumed business name may be filed in as many counties as a person believes is necessary. (2) The registration of a **trademark** with the Secretary of State's Office which protects the use of the assumed business name for the State of Washington. (3) An incorporation with the assumed business name taken as the corporate name.

In addition, if the assumed business name is to be used for a real estate company, there must be compliance with the Rules and Regulations of the Real Estate Commission. The Real Estate Program of the Department of Licensing may prevent a real estate firm from using the same name or a name deceptively similar to that of a real estate firm which is licensed and operating in the State of Washington if it is believed that the interest of the public will be endangered. However, a bona fide franchisee may be licensed using the name of the franchisor in conjunction with an identification as to the firm's name. This identification must appear in all advertisements, letterheads, stationery, envelopes, forms, signs, web sites and business cards, etc.
Reference: WAC 308-124B

FIDELITY BOND - A bond taken out by a business covering all losses resulting from dishonest actions of any of the principals or employees of the organization. Most real estate companies in the State of Washington have a fidelity bond. A fidelity bond in the amount of $200,000 is required for all escrow companies in the State. Also known as a surety bond.
Reference: RCW 18.44

FIDUCIARY - A relationship which implies a position of trust or confidence wherein one is usually entrusted to hold or manage property for another. The term "fiduciary" describes the relationship owed by an attorney to his/her client, or a broker (and salesperson) to his/her principal. Among the obligations a fiduciary owes to his/her principal are duties of loyalty; obedience; full disclosure; the duty to use skill, care and diligence; and the duty to account for all moneys. During the course of a real estate transaction and the fiduciary relationship that is established thereby, a real estate licensee often learns confidential information about the real properties and the financial abilities of the principals involved in the transaction. This information cannot be used by the real estate licensee even after the transaction is closed and the fiduciary relationship is dissolved. One of the reasons it is so difficult to adequately represent both parties in a real estate transaction is that the broker has a duty to keep confidential that information learned from the principal and also a duty to disclose all pertinent information to the principal. (*See* AGENCY, DUAL AGENCY, SUBAGENT.)

When an agent breaches his/her fiduciary duties, the principal can usually: (1) bring action for money damages, (2) sue to impress a constructive trust upon any secret profit, and/or (3) compel the agent to forfeit or repay the real estate commission.

FIFTEEN-YEAR MORTGAGE or DEED OF TRUST - A loan with a less than traditional payback period, specifically one of fifteen years. During the past thirty years, the vast majority of long-term residential loans have been made with thirty year payouts. However, in recent years more and more home buyers have opted for loans with shorter maturity periods, such as fifteen-year mortgages or deed of trust. The primary advantage of an early-payoff loan is the fact that considerably less interest is paid over the life of the loan since the principal is borrowed for a shorter period of time. However, offsetting this advantage is the fact that since the principal is borrowed for a less than normal period of time, the principal repayment each period is greater than with thirty-year loan. Thus, higher monthly payments eliminate many people from qualifying for fifteen-year loan. For example, $80,000 borrowed at a ten percent rate of interest requires a monthly payment of $702.06 to fully amortize the loan over thirty years. However, the monthly payment increases to $859.68 (22% more) if the loan is amortized over a fifteen-year payback.

FILE - To place an original document on public record. Most legal documents are **recorded**, e.g. kept in the form of a literal copy produced by electrostatic process and microfilm. After documents pertaining to real estate transactions have been recorded in the Office of the County Auditor, the originals are returned to the individual who requested that they be recorded, unless the Office of the County Auditor is directed otherwise. (*See* RECORDING.)

FILES - A popular reference to the required records which a real estate broker must maintain under the requirements of the Real Estate License Law.
Reference: RCW 18.85

FILLED LAND - An area where the grade has been raised by depositing or dumping dirt, gravel or rock. The seller, and thus the seller's agent, of such land has, under most circumstances, a duty to disclose to the buyer the fact that the property is filled land. Failure to disclose would risk liability to an unaware buyer who subsequently suffers damages (for example, if the land were to slip or subside during construction) and seeks to rescind the transaction when he/she discovers the property is on filled land. Naturally, this disclosure rule does not apply if it is obvious that the entire community or a substantial portion is on filled land which has been utilized for a relatively long period of time without any adverse problems, as in the downtown waterfront area and Pioneer Square area of Seattle. (*See* CAVEAT EMPTOR.)

FINANCE CHARGE - The total of all costs imposed directly or indirectly by the creditor/lender and payable either directly or indirectly by the customer/borrower, as defined by the federal truth-in-lending laws. (*See* ANNUAL PERCENTAGE RATE, TRUTH-IN-LENDING LAWS.)

FINANCE FEE - A mortgage brokerage fee to cover the expenses incurred in placing the mortgage with a lending institution; a mortgage service charge or origination fee. With VA and FHA loans, this placement fee is limited to one percent of the loan amount, except in special cases. The normal conventional loan finance fee is approximately 1 to 1 1/2 percent of the loan amount for an existing building and 2 percent for new construction. The finance fee is sometimes stated in "points," with each point being equal to one percent of the loan amount: for example, two percent would commonly be called two points. (*See* POINTS.)

FINANCIAL ACCOUNTING STANDARDS BOARD (FASB) - Independent full-time committee of accountants, recognized by the accounting profession and the Securities and Exchange Commission as an official body to establish standards of financial reporting and accounting.

FINANCIAL FEASIBILITY - An analysis which concludes that a proposed project will attain a cash flow of sufficient quantity, quality and duration to allow investors to recover the capital invested and achieve the necessary and expected rate of return. Factors to be considered are the timing of inflows and outflows of cash, revenues, costs, debt service, and the proceeds of a sale or refinancing.

FINANCIAL INSTITUTIONS REFORM, RECOVERY, AND ENFORCEMENT ACT (FIRREA) - Federal legislation enacted in 1989 that changed the regulatory framework of financial institutions in the United States. It was the most sweeping overhaul of laws governing real estate lending in 55 years. Commonly referred to as the "savings and loan bailout bill," FIRREA was a direct result of the insolvency problems felt by many savings and loan associations during the middle and late 1980s. Included in the act was the creation of the Savings Association Insurance Fund (SAIF), which insures thrift deposits, and the Bank Insurance Fund (BIF) which insures commercial bank deposits. Both funds are administered by the Federal Deposit Insurance corporation (FDIC). FIRREA also established the Resolution Trust corporation (RTC), an agency created to manage the assets and liabilities of savings and loan associations that became insolvent both before and after the enactment of the act.

FINANCIAL LEVERAGE - The use of borrowed money to complete the acquisition of an investment. If the asset purchased with borrowed money offers annual financial benefits at a rate in excess of the loan's interest rate, leverage is said to be positive or favorable. The investor makes money by borrowing. Conversely, if an asset purchased with borrowed money fails to increase in value or if it fails to provide benefits in excess of the interest rate paid on the borrowed money, the leverage is negative. Leverage is neutral when the property earns at the same rate as the interest rate on borrowed money. (*See* LEVERAGE.)

FINANCIAL MANAGEMENT RATE OF RETURN (FMRR) - A modified internal rate of return model designed to remedy some of the deficiencies of the internal rate of return (IRR) technique. Two rates are considered by the FMRR: (1) a safe, liquid after-tax rate, and (2) a run-of-the mill reinvestment rate. (*See* RATE OF RETURN.)

FINANCIAL RISK - The uncertainty resulting from the financing of an investment. The investment may not generate adequate cash flow to repay the underlying borrowed debt.

FINANCIAL STATEMENT - A formal statement of the financial status and net worth of a person or company, setting forth and classifying assets and liabilities as of a specified date. Sometimes the requester of the financial statement may stipulate that it must be certified by a recognized CPA firm. In some areas of the country, the recent trend among mortgage bankers is to require certified financial statements from all loan applicants.

Under Washington's Land Development Act of 1973, the developer of a registered subdivision must file a yearly report which includes a current financial statement on the development. At present these financial statements do not need to be certified.

Federal registration under the Interstate Land Sales Act requires that the necessary financial statements must be certified if over 300 lots are involved. (*See* FULL DISCLOSURE, INTERSTATE LAND SALES, LAND DEVELOPMENT ACT.)
Reference: RCW 58.19, WAC 308-126

FINANCING - That part of the purchase price for a property which is exclusive of the down payment paid by the buyer. The function of negotiating the loan of funds for a real estate purchase.

It has often been said by experienced real estate salespeople that selling real estate, as far as price goes, is usually selling the down payment and the financing terms (the monthly mortgage or deed of trust and real property tax payments).

Examples of financing instruments are mortgages, deeds of trust and real estate contracts.

Funds for real estate financing may be obtained from the following groups of lenders: (1) savings and loan associations, which operate either under federal or state charter; (2) banks and trust companies; (3) trust funds; (4) savings banks; (5) insurance companies; (6) mortgage companies; (7) the sale of registered securities to private investors; and (8) private individuals. The private individual is often ready to accept a greater risk than a lending institution. However, interest rates, service charges and closing fees are likely to be higher than that charged by an institution. A large proportion of secondary financing, that is second mortgages and deeds of trust, is done by individuals.

Normally there are several instruments used in financing real estate. There is a note, evidencing the obligation of the borrower to repay, and the security instrument, which in Washington may be a mortgage or deed of trust. In the case of a purchase under a real estate contract, there is no note. The cost of financing real estate may include some or all of the following: (1) appraisal fee; (2) credit report fee; (3) title insurance fee; (4) correspondent's fee; (5) attorney's fee; (6) survey charge; (7) closing fee; (8) recording fee and (9) broker's fee. The cost to a borrower in obtaining the financing varies directly with the availability of money seeking investments in real estate. (*See* DEED OF TRUST, MORTGAGE, REAL ESTATE CONTRACT.)

FINANCING PACKAGE - The total of all loans used to develop and/or purchase a real estate project. For example, the financing package assembled by a builder might include the loan to purchase the land, a construction loan, gap financing and prearranged permanent loans for the purchasers of the finished homes or condominium units.

Can also refer to the documents assembled by the lender for a home loan applicant. The "package" is submitted to the underwriter for review and approval/disapproval.

FINANCING STATEMENT - A brief document (required under the Uniform Commercial Code) generally filed with the Secretary of State's office to perfect or establish a creditor's security interest in a chattel with the exceptions of (1) farm equipment; (2) consumer goods; and (3) fixtures and goods that will become fixtures which require filing at the County Auditor's Office. It is important in real estate to protect the creditor's interest in personal property which is security for a debt, but which becomes a fixture when attached to realty. For example, if Mr. McIntrye buys a sink from Sears Roebuck and Company on a conditional sales contract and then installs the sink in his home, the sink becomes a fixture subject to all existing recorded liens. Sears, however, may protect its security interest by immediately filing a financial statement (Form UCC1), which would give it a prior secured right to the sink superior to that of the home mortgagee. Thus, Sears has a prior right to the sink in the event Mr. McIntrye defaults on his home mortgage, and the bank forecloses on the realty.

It is the security agreement between debtor and creditor, not the financing statement, that creates the lien. However, it is the filing of the financing statement that "perfects" the lien, i.e., makes the lien effective against later creditors. While the use of a financing statement is usually not applicable to real property, the purchaser of a real estate contract from the original seller (vendor) should file a financing statement. When filed, the financing statement is effective for five years from the date of filing unless it has an earlier maturity date. Also, a continuation statement can extend the five (5) year period. (*See* FIXTURE, SECU-

RITY AGREEMENT, UNIFORM COMMERCIAL CODE.)
Reference: RCW 62A-9

FINDER'S FEE - A fee paid to someone for producing a buyer to purchase or a seller to sell or list property; also called a referral fee.

A finder is a person who finds, interests, introduces, or bring together parties in a deal, even though the finder has no part in negotiating the terms of the transaction. In Washington, a broker can split his/her commission **only** with another Washington real estate licensee, or a real estate broker from another state who referred the eventual purchaser or seller to him/her or one or both of the principals to the transaction.

The question sometimes arises as to whether an owner can pay a finder's fee to an unlicensed person. In accepting such a fee, the finder runs the serious risk of being classified as a real estate salesperson and found in violation of the Washington Real Estate Law and therefore guilty of a gross misdemeanor which is punishable by up to one year in a county jail and/or a fine of up to $1,000. (*See* LICENSING LAW.)
Reference: RCW 18.85

FINISH FLOORING - The visible interior floor which is usually made of a decorative hardwood such as oak. The finish flooring may be laid in strips or in a block design such as parquet.

FIRE INSURANCE - A form of property insurance covering losses due to fire, often including additional coverage against other hazards, such as smoke or windstorm. (*See* INSURANCE.)

FIRE SPRINKLER SYSTEM - A fire protection system activated by heat within a given building area, which automatically provides a flow of pressurized water from overhead nozzles when the temperature exceeds a certain predetermined level. To prevent the water-supply pipes from freezing, they are often filled with compressed air to hold the water behind the dry valve; the system is called a dry system.

FIRE STOP - Short boards placed horizontally between the studs or joists that decrease draughts and thus help retard fires.

FIRE WALL - A wall constructed of fire-retardant materials, the purpose of which is to prevent the spread of fire within a building. The fire wall carries a standard rating that designates its ability to constrain fire in terms of hours.

FIRE YARD - An area, the length of one or more sides of a building, which must be kept clear in order to facilitate the passage of fire vehicles, according to certain building codes.

FIRM COMMITMENT - A definite undertaking by a lender to loan a set amount of money at a specified interest rate for a certain term. Also, a commitment by the FHA to insure a mortgage on certain property to a specified mortgagor (as opposed to a commitment conditioned on approval of a yet to be determined mortgagor).

A real estate lender has a duty to see that financial obligations and commitments regarding real estate transactions are in writing and express the exact agreements of the parties, and that copies of such agreements are placed in the hands of all parties involved at the time the agreements are executed. (*See* CONDITIONAL COMMITMENT.)

FIRREA - *See* FINANCIAL INSTITUTIONS REFORM, RECOVERY AND ENFORCEMENT ACT OF 1989 (FIRREA).

FIRST MORTGAGE OR DEED OF TRUST - The mortgage/deed of trust on property that is superior in right to any other mortgage/deed of trust. It is not enough that a mortgage is the first to be executed or that the parties call it a first mortgage; absent subordination, it must be recorded first. The same is true of a first deed of trust. (*See* SECOND MORTGAGE, SUBORDINATION AGREEMENT.)

FIRST REFUSAL, RIGHT OF - The right of a person to have the first opportunity either to purchase or lease real property. Unlike an option, however, the holder of a right of first refusal has no right to purchase until the owner actually entertains an offer to purchase from some third party. In a lease situation, a right of first refusal might give the tenant the right either to purchase the property if offered for sale, or to renew the lease. This right is clearly more advantageous to the tenant than it is to the landlord. A property burdened with a right of first refusal is less marketable than one without such right.

In an option to purchase, the tenant can decide to exercise or not to exercise the option at a fixed price during the option period. In a right of first refusal, however, the holder can exercise his right only if the owner has offered to sell the property or has received a bona fide offer from a third person to purchase the property. At that point, the holder can seek to purchase the property by matching the offer. If the owner first offers the property to the tenant and he/she refuses, then the owner is free to offer to any third party on the same terms and conditions.

In some older condominiums, the association of unit owners retains the right of first refusal on any sale of a unit; however, in HUD-FHA qualified condominiums and in condominiums eligible for FNMA financing, restrictions such as the right of first refusal are not permitted.

FISCAL YEAR - A business year used for tax, corporate or accounting purposes, as opposed to a calendar year. For example, a commonly used fiscal year is the 12 month period from July 1 through June 30 of the following calendar year. It may not coincide with a calendar year. Individuals and partnerships ordinarily use a calendar year.

FIXED EXPENSES - Those recurring expenses which have to be paid regardless of whether or not the property is occupied, such as real property taxes, hazard insurance, and debt service. As opposed to operating expenses necessary to maintain the production of income from the operation of a property. (*See* OPERATING EXPENSES.)

FIXED RATE LOAN - A loan with the same rate of interest for the life of the loan. Until the late 70's and early 80's, the fixed rate loan was the typical real estate loan. With the arrival of highly volatile interest rates, lenders attempted to adjust interest rates with a variety of new different type loans. As the quasi-governmental agencies changed their guidelines establishing a market place for these new adjustable interest loans, it became evident that the fixed rate loan would be seen less and less in the real estate market for a period of time in the late 1980s.

Since the early 1990s the fixed rate loan has dominated the real estate financing market again. However many of the adjustable rates are still in the market place and will return to popularity as the economy changes. (*See* ADJUSTABLE RATE LOAN, ADJUSTABLE RATE MORTGAGE (ARM), BUY DOWN LOAN, EQUITY-AIDE/HOME PARTNERS, EQUITY SHARING LOAN, EXTENDED MORTGAGE TERM, FLEXIBLE LOAN INSURANCE PROGRAM (FLIP), GRADUATED-PAYMENT ADJUSTABLE-RATE MORTGAGE, GRADUATED-PAYMENT MORTGAGE, MORTGAGE SUBSIDIES, RENEGOTIABLE-RATE MORTGAGE, REVERSE ANNUITY, SHARED APPRECIATION LOAN, VARIABLE-RATE MORTGAGE, WRAP AROUND MORTGAGE.)

FIXTURE - An article which was once personal property but has been so affixed to the real estate that it has become real property (e.g., stoves, bookcases, plumbing, track lighting and tile). Whether an article is a fixture depends on the intention of the parties as may be determined by the manner of annexation, the type of article and its adaptability to the real property, the relationship of the parties and the purpose served.

Generally, the test of whether or not an item is a fixture as a result of its method of attachment depends more on the firmness of its installation rather than on the size of the hole that might be caused by its removal. The fact that removal leaves a dirty or unpainted spot is irrelevant. If removal of the item would cause much damage to the structure, then it is probably a fixture. If determined to be a fixture, then the article passes with the property even though it is not mentioned in the deed. Some articles are so closely associated with the structure that they are deemed to be fixtures under a constructive annexation theory, such as keys to a house which pass to the buyer upon sale of the property.

When a fixture is wrongfully removed from real property, the proper measure of damages is the value of the fixture in place as part of the realty, and not what it would sell for on the open market after removal from the building.

An exception to the fixture rule is made for **trade** or **tenant** fixtures. A business tenant can normally remove his/her fixtures at the termination of the lease. The courts reason that the parties did not intend that the tenant's fixtures would become a permanent part of the building. The trade fixture rule applies only to articles installed by the tenant and not those installed by the landlord. If the tenant fails to remove his/her fixtures, the landlord takes title to the abandoned property. (*See* ABANDONMENT.)

The question of whether an item is a fixture has gained special importance in modern transactions because of the different rules of lien priority for fixtures and non-fixtures under the Uniform Commercial Code.
Reference: RCW 62A9

A seller must deliver all fixtures unless noted as exceptions in the Purchase and Sale Agreement. This applies to non-owned fixtures as well. A broker would be advised to inspect the premises carefully and inquire whether any of the apparent fixtures such as a hot water heater, air conditioner, T.V. satellite dish are rented or being purchased under a UCC financing statement. The Purchase and Sale Agreement (E/M) should specify who is to own certain doubtful items such as television antennas, security system, blinds and mirrors. In the uncertain category are: wall-to-wall carpeting (may depend on whether the flooring underneath is finished or just plywood), light bulbs (especially large fluorescent tubes), trellises, kitchen appliances attached to the wall (can opener), fancy door chimes and standard size curtain rods. (*See* EMBLEMENTS, FINANCING STATEMENT, PERSONAL PROPERTY, TRADE FIXTURES.)

FLAG LOT - A land parcel having the configuration of an extended flag and pole. The pole represents access to the site which is usually located to the rear of another lot fronting a main street. A parcel may be subdivided into one or two flag lots as shown below:

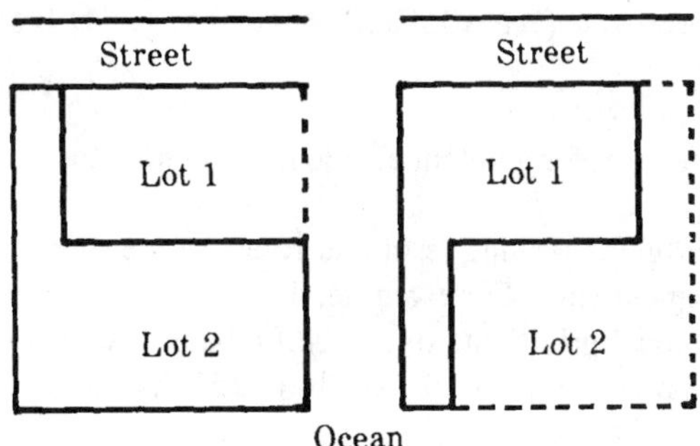

FLASHING - Sheet metal or other impervious material used in roof and wall construction to protect a building from seepage of water.

FLAT - An apartment unit or entire floor of a building used for residential purposes. Not a commonly used term in Washington.

FLEXIBLE LOAN INSURANCE PROGRAM (FLIP) - The Federal Home Loan Bank has authorized federally chartered savings and loan associations to make flexible-payment mortgages provided that each monthly payment at least covers interest costs and the loan payments become fully amortized by the end of the fifth year. (*See* VARIABLE PAYMENT PLAN.)

Under the Flexible Loan Insurance Payment, or FLIP, potential buyers could reduce their monthly payments by as much as 20 percent during the initial year of the mortgage and then graduate upward over the next five years. The buyer places the down payment in an interest-bearing savings account as pledged cash collateral. Only the lender can draw on the pledged account and the moneys can be used to supplement the buyer's monthly payment or to apply against principal if the borrower defaults or the property is sold. Private mortgage insurance covers the top 20 percent of the loan, thus reducing the lender's risk. Also called a pledged account mortgage.

FLEXIBLE PAYMENT MORTGAGE - A loan in which the payment schedule is based on the borrower's particular financial condition. Often, interest rates are initially lower than ordinary mortgages and the initial payments are below those of an amortized mortgage. This mortgage repayment plan enables younger buyers to purchase homes by allowing them to make smaller payments in the early years and larger payments later, when their incomes have increased. (*See* GRADUATED PAYMENT MORTGAGE.)

FLIP - 1. A FLIP mortgage is a flexible loan insurance program mortgage. (*See* FLEXIBLE LOAN INSURANCE PROGRAM.)

2. A flip transaction is one in which one party contracts to buy a property with the intention to quickly transfer (flip) the property over to another buyer, or the buyer quickly rehabs and sells the property. (*See* ASSIGNMENT, BACK-TO-BACK ESCROW, TRADING ON EQUITY.)

3. A slang real estate term for a potential sale that did not close.

FLOAT - 1. A mortgage banking term that refers to the spread of the variable interest rate on a loan; the **pegged rate**. For example, the interest on a development loan might be set at 3% above the local prime rate of a specific bank. A float can have a "floor" or a "ceiling" such as, "in no event below 9% or above 15%"; or it can have no limitation, as in a "full float."

2. A banking term that indicates a check has not yet been cleared for collection. Local checks may "float" for two or three days before clearing and East Coast checks for up to one to two weeks. Also may refer to the bank's use of the money prior to the check's clearing. (*See* COLLECT FUNDS, ESCROW, PRIME RATE, VARIABLE INTEREST RATE.)

FLOOD INSURANCE - Insurance offered by private companies and subsidized by the federal government, designed to provide coverage for damage from floods or tidal waves. Primary and secondary lending institutions regulated by the federal government require flood insurance on any financed property located within certain flood prone areas as identified by the Federal Emergency Management Agency. Because the law places the sole responsibility on the lending institutions to initiate, maintain, and renew the flood insurance, lenders are very conservative in interpreting whether or not a property is in such a zone.

Real estate licensees have an obligation to inform potential purchasers of homes and other buildings in a designated 100-year flood plain area that federal law requires them to obtain flood insurance.

The phrase "100-year flood plain" in itself may impart a false sense of security to some people. After all, it means such an area is likely to be flooded only once every 100 years on the average. However, the possibility of flooding obviously varies from one flood plain area to another. Owners of property in such an area have no way of knowing when or how often the law of averages will catch up with them.

Much of Western Washington and significant portions of the eastern part of the state are in flood plain areas. Real estate licensees can determine if a particular parcel of property is located in a flood plain by checking the appropriate Flood Hazard Boundary Map issued by the Federal Insurance Administration.

In 1968, Congress enacted a National Flood Insurance Act and expanded it in 1973 with the Flood Disaster Protection Act. The legislation is designed to provide flood insurance at affordable rates through federal subsidization. This goal is achieved through the National Flood Insurers Association.

FLOOD PLAIN - The flat portions of land located along watercourses and streams which are subject to overflow and flooding; building in these areas is usually restricted by governmental controls.

FLOOD-PRONE AREA - A flood-prone area is one having a one percent annual chance of flooding, or a likelihood that a flood may occur once every 100 years. (*See* FLOOD PLAIN.)

FLOOR AREA RATIO - The ratio of floor area to land area, often land on which the building sits. It may be expressed as a percent or decimal and is determined by dividing the total floor area of the building lot by the lot area; used as a formula in zoning ordinances to regulate building volume; a restriction on the amount of building per lot area; a density restriction.

FLOOR DUTY - A frequent practice in real estate brokerage offices of assigning one sales agent the responsibility for handling all telephone calls and office visitors for a specified period of time. The person **on floor** gets exposed to new clients if the caller does not ask to speak to a particular salesman (known as an "up" call). This person must be a licensed real estate agent, not a secretary.

FLOOR JOIST - Horizontal boards laid on edge resting on the beams and foundation that provide the main support for the floor. The subflooring is nailed directly to the joists. Joists are also found in ceilings.

FLOOR LOAD - The pounds per square foot of weight that the floor of a building is capable of supporting, assuming such weight is evenly distributed.

FLOOR LOAN - A loan amount which is below the maximum loan approved. For example, a lender may agree to make a $2,000,000 permanent loan as follows: $1,200,000 upon closing and the balance of $800,000 provided the premises are 75 percent leased by a certain date. The $800,000 "gap" will only be funded if the occupancy level specified is attained within the specified period after the funding of the floor loan. If this occupancy is not obtained, the developer must seek "gap financing," which can be very expensive because of the high risks involved. *(See* GAP FINANCING.)

FLOOR PLAN - The architectural drawings showing the floor layout of a building. Under the Washington condominium law, the developer must file a set of floor plans and elevations of the building together with a verified statement of the architect or engineer showing the layout, when he/she records the declaration. (*See* CONDOMINIUM MAP.)

An examination of the floor plan is an important consideration in the appraisal valuation process. A poor floor plan or room layout could result in a devaluation for incurable functional obsolescence.

FLUE - An enclosed passage in a chimney or any duct or pipe through which smoke, hot air, and gases pass upward. Flues are usually made of fire clay or terra cotta pipe.

FOOT-CANDLE - A determination of light intensity. One foot-candle is the illumination measured on a surface one foot distant from the source of one candle. Therefore, the light level in an office space may be described as, say, 85 foot-candles.

FOOTING - A concrete support under a foundation, chimney, or column that usually rests on solid ground and is wider than the structure being supported. Footings are designed to distribute the weight of the structure over the ground.

FOR SALE BY OWNER (FSBO) - A situation in which the owner attempts to sell his/her property without listing with a real estate broker. Many owners will cooperate with and compensate a broker representing a buyer. Experienced brokers actively solicit listings from FSBOs (pronounced "fizz-bows"). The FSBO often gets discouraged in a short time, especially after having to deal with unqualified buyers, flaky offers and mere lookers. The broker receiving a commission from an owner must clarify in writing whether the broker represents the owner or the buyer. This is also true when the broker buys directly for his/her own account. (*See* AGENCY, LICENSING LAW, REAL ESTATE BROKERAGE RELATIONSHIPS ACT.)

FORBEARANCE - The act of refraining from taking legal action despite the fact that a mortgage or deed of trust is in arrears. It is usually granted only when a borrower makes a satisfactory arrangement by which the arrears will be paid at a future date. (*See* CONSIDERATION, WORKOUT.)

FORCE AND EFFECT OF LAW - A phrase referring to the fact that an administrative regulation has the same legal significance as a legislative act. When the Real Estate Commission adopts a rule and regulation implementing the licensing law, the rule and regulation has equal validity as the licensing law itself. (*See* LICENSING LAW, REAL ESTATE COMMISSION.)
Reference: RCW 18.85

FORCE MAJEURE - A term, originally used in insurance law, meaning a superior or irresistible force, one that cannot be foreseen or controlled (a "vis major"). It refers to a clause found in many construction contracts that is designed to protect the parties when part of the contract cannot be performed or the time of performance must be delayed due to causes which were outside the control of the parties and could not have been prevented by the exercise of due care and prudence. For example: a subcontractor agreed to pay $500 a day damages for each day past December 31 that his/her installation of the plumbing was not complete, except where the delay was caused by Acts of God, labor disputes, inability to obtain materials, fire and the like. Thus, if a shipping strike caused a 30 day delay in the arrival of the plumbing pipes, the subcontractor would not have to pay the $500 per day, at least through January 30. (*See* ACT OF GOD.)

Sometimes a force majeure clause is inserted in a ground lease to protect a tenant obligated to complete an improvement by a certain date from a default caused by unavoidable delays in completing the project.

FORECAST - Estimate of the outcome of future occurrences; particularly, financial statements of future periods based on such estimates.

FORECLOSURE - A legal procedure whereby property used as security for a debt is sold to satisfy the debt in the event of default in payment of the note representing the debt or default of other terms in the mortgage document. (In Washington, a deed of trust may be foreclosed as a mortgage; however, it is rarely done.) The mortgage foreclosure action is brought in the Superior Court of the county in which the real property is located. The court orders a sale of the property to the highest bidder. Anybody wishing to bid on the property may do so by depositing their bid price with the County Clerk. The mortgagee (lender) may bid in the unpaid principal balance of the mortgage. The highest bidder receives a Certificate of Sale. After the **equity of redemption** period has run, the sheriff executes a deed to the holder of the Certificate of Sale.

Under early common law, the defaulting mortgagor/borrower had a right to redeem the foreclosed property at any time upon paying his/her debt. This left the mortgagee in a very uncertain position with respect to the property. The foreclosure action was designed to foreclose or terminate this equitable right of the mortgagor to redeem; in this way, the mortgagee would be certain that the mortgagor could not thereafter regain title to the property. In Washington there are limited redemption periods which vary, depending upon certain circumstances. (*See* REDEMPTION, EQUITABLE RIGHT OF.)

In a mortgage foreclosure, the lender/mortgagee generally has the right upon default by the borrower "to accelerate" the indebtedness. This means that the lender declares the entire amount of the note due immediately and the borrower has no right to nullify the foreclosure action merely by paying the delinquent installments and accrued interest.

If there are any excess proceeds of the foreclosure sale after deducting all expenses and costs, they are paid to the mortgagor/borrower. If, on the other hand, the proceeds from the sale are not sufficient to repay the foreclosed debt, recourse may be had against the debtor/borrower for the deficiency. As a matter of practice, deficiency judgments are rarely sought on the foreclosure of residential property.

A borrower who files bankruptcy can effectively interfere with the foreclosure proceedings. Once bankruptcy is filed, no creditor can take any action against the debtor outside of bankruptcy court. Therefore, any foreclosure action is automatically stayed (or delayed) while the bankruptcy is pending. Also, if the foreclosure sale takes place within one year before the filing of the bankruptcy, the sale can be voided if the foreclosure sale price is substantially less than the actual fair market value of the secured property.

An alternative to foreclosure would be for the mortgagee to accept a deed in lieu of foreclosure from the mortgagor. This is sometimes known as a friendly foreclosure since it is settled by agreement rather than civil action. The major disadvantage to this type of default settlement is that the mortgagee takes the real estate subject to all junior liens, whereas foreclosure eliminates all such liens. (*See* BANKRUPTCY, DEED OF TRUST, DEFICIENCY JUDGMENT, EQUITY OF REDEMPTION, FEDERAL TAX LIEN, MORTGAGE, UPSET PRICE.)

FOREIGN CORPORATION - A corporation doing business in a state in which it was not created or incorporated is known as a foreign corporation. It must comply with certain terms and conditions imposed by any other state in which it does business. The state statutes make no distinction between a foreign and an alien corporation (a corporation organized outside the United States and its territories); both are regarded as foreign. (*See* ALIEN, CORPORATION.)

Foreign corporations seeking to do business in Washington must qualify and obtain a certificate of authority and appoint a resident agent for the purpose of service of process. If the corporation later withdraws, the Secretary of State may accept service for the corporation in an action based on corporate activities while here.

An unqualified foreign corporation (not registered with the Secretary of State's Office) is unable to bring a court action in Washington, but can defend itself if sued. If an unregistered foreign corporation should file a lawsuit, the lawsuit will not be dismissed if the corporation qualified by time of trial.
Reference: RCW 32.01

FOREIGN INVESTMENT IN REAL PROPERTY TAX ACT OF 1980 (FIRPTA) - The purpose of the law is to subject nonresident aliens and alien corporations to U.S. income tax upon their gain from the disposition of a United States real property interest: (1) an interest in real property located in the U.S., and (2) an interest in any domestic corporation that was a "United States real property holding corporation" at any time during the five-year period prior to the disposition of the interest, or during the period the taxpayer held the interest after June 18, 1980, if shorter. A United States real property corporation is a domestic or foreign corporation, whose interest in U.S. real property is 50 percent or more of its total assets. The test as to the percentage of its assets can apparently be made on any day of the calendar year. (*See* FOREIGN CORPORATION.)

For purposes of computing the tax, a nonresident alien or foreign corporation is treated as being "engaged in a trade or business within the United States," and the gain is treated as "effectively connected" with the U.S. trade or business. Thus, a foreign investor is subject to tax at regular rates. Expenses attributable to the gain may be deducted, and nonresident aliens are allowed the capital gains deduction.

The gain of nonresident alien individuals for the sale of an interest in U.S. real property is taxed at a minimum rate of 21% of the lesser of the taxpayer's alternative minimum taxable income or the net real property gains for the taxable year. In general, unless otherwise provided, a 10% tax must be withheld by the purchaser from the gross proceeds from the sale of a U.S. real property interest by a nonresident alien. If requested, the IRS can determine the seller's maximum tax liability, if any, and that amount would be withheld. Withholding is not required if the property is to be used as a residence by the purchaser and the selling price is less than $300,000.

The prudent listing broker will require that a foreign seller sign an affidavit if the seller is a resident alien. Otherwise, the broker may be liable for failing to advise the buyer to withhold the required 10% amount. These rules are complicated and brokers should develop a clear policy on handling listings and sales from foreign sellers. (*See* AGRICULTURAL FOREIGN INVESTMENT DISCLOSURE ACT, FIABCI.)

FORESHORE LAND - Land that is above sea level only at low tide. (*See* SHORELINE.)

FOREST PRACTICES - The State Forest Practices Appeals Board has ruled that a buyer of logged land assumes responsibility to reforest the land at the moment of purchase, and may not shift it to the previous owner or logger. Brokers offering logged-off forest lands should disclose to buyers that they are responsible to reforest the land.

Prospective buyers should inspect the land, inquire of the seller, or inspect the approved harvest application on file with the Department of Natural Resources to determine if logging has occurred since 1975 when the Forest Practices Act first required reforestation.

Brokers should research the question of the new owner's responsibility as part of their preparation for selling. A title insurance policy will not show the requirement.

FORFEITURE - The loss of a right to something as a result of nonperformance of an obligation or condition. A forfeiture loss usually bears no true relationship to the amount of damages allowed by law, and thus there is a strong public policy against enforcing forfeitures. Courts may refuse to enforce provisions in contracts which require the defaulting party to forfeit, or give up, all amounts paid in under an installment purchase contract (real estate contract). In these cases the courts will allow a suit for damages. (*See* RESCISSION.)

Real property may be acquired by forfeiture, such as when a grantor has conveyed real estate subject to a condition subsequent. Should the condition be breached, the grantor can reacquire the property by forfeiture by exercising the right of reentry.

A real estate license may be lost through forfeiture when the licensee fails to pay the appropriate renewal fees or to fulfill any continuing education requirements.

FORGERY - A false signature, alteration or falsification. A forged deed is void and ineffective to transfer any title to the grantee and recording will not make it valid. Even if a later purchaser for value acquires the property with no notice of the prior forged deed, he/she does not obtain valid title. A title insurance policy will compensate such a purchaser for his/her loss from forgery in the chain of title.

FORM 17 - *See* RESIDENTIAL REAL PROPERTY TRANSFER DISCLOSURE STATEMENT.

FORMICA - A trade name for a plastic material used primarily for the top of counter areas, but which is also used for wall covering, as a veneer for plywood panels, or as a wallboard where a fire-resistive material is desirable. Similar and competitive materials are produced under other trade names.

FORUM - A place or jurisdiction where disputes are heard; such as a court, a public administrative agency (e.g., Department of Licensing), or a private group (e.g., Board of Realtor®'s Arbitration Panel).

FORUM SHOPPING CLAUSE - The clause in an agreement specifying the state in which the parties agree lawsuits may be brought and designating which state law may apply. Typical language is:

"This contract shall be interpreted and construed under and governed by the laws of the State of Washington and any lawsuit arising out of or because of this contract shall be brought in the state courts of Washington. The judgment of the State Supreme Court shall be final and binding on all parties hereto."

Such a clause will generally be upheld if the state designated as the one whose laws govern the transaction and the state in which the lawsuit is filed bear some relationship to the place of making or place of performance of the original contract.

FORWARD COMMITMENT - An agreement by a lender or investor to either make or purchase a loan within a certain period of time into the future. For example, a builder might receive a commitment from a lender to borrow a certain sum of money at an agreed upon rate and the commitment might be good for a specified period of time, such as 90 days. By having this forward commitment the builder knows how much money can be borrowed plus what the money will cost. For such a commitment, the lender may charge the builder a fee such as so many points if and when the money is actually borrowed.

FOUNDATION DRAIN TILE - A pipe, usually clay, placed next to the foundation footing to aid in water runoff.

FOUNDATION WALL - The masonry or concrete walls below or at ground level that serve as the main support for the frame structure. Foundation walls usually form the side walls of the basement.

FOUR-THREE-TWO-ONE RULE (4-3-2-1) - *See* DEPTH CHART

FRACTIONAL APPRAISAL - An appraisal of a portion of a property, such as the value of a leasehold interest, value of an improvement without land, etc. (*See* APPRAISAL.)

FRANCHISE - (1) A right or privilege conferred by law, such as the state charter authorizing the formation and existence of corporations. The privilege granted to conduct certain service business, such as operating a taxicab company, is a franchise. (2) Private contractual right to operate a business using a designated trade name and the operating procedures of a parent company (the franchisor), such as Century 21 Real Estate Office. In the financing of income property, a franchise may have value as additional security to a loan. It may also be assigned to the lender.

Since the early 1970's, a development in real estate brokerage business is the advent and growing popularity of the franchised brokerages. Such firms as Century 21, ERA, and Re/Max operate franchised brokerages on a national level. These organizations do not own and operate the individual offices outright; rather, they license their standardized trade names, reputations, operating procedures, and referral services to independently owned and operated brokerages. These referral services take the multiple-listing-service idea one step further, having the capability to refer prospects across town or across the country. There are several successful Washington based franchise organizations. In the 1970s, the real estate business was divided on whether or not belonging to a real estate franchise organization had long term benefits for an established broker. This question has now been settled with franchise organizations dominating the real estate brokerage marketplace.

An independent broker's decision to become a franchisee or continue doing business as usual, or pursue some other alternative course of action, will depend on his/her evaluation of his/her goals and objectives and how they can best be achieved. A very general summary of the major advantages and disadvantages usually cited for real estate franchises is shown below.

ADVANTAGES

1. Market identification is available through the use of a tradename and trademark.
2. A market image is provided through mass advertising techniques.
3. Association with a successful operation can be beneficial in several ways.
4. A referral system by which franchise members trade leads and listings has certain advantages.
5. Brokers can receive volume discounts not otherwise available (e.g. advertising).
6. Recruitment of sales personnel is easier.
7. Management help and services are provided.
8. Franchisees may obtain good sales training programs not otherwise available.

DISADVANTAGES

1. Fees, whether initial or a royalty override, may be higher than necessary in terms of the benefits derived.

2. There is an original identity loss which cannot be recaptured.

3. There are certain bookkeeping requirements which many brokers feel are unnec essary.

4. Because of the necessity of group approval for certain activities — specifically those related to marketing — there can be difficulties in agreeing on concerted unified actions.

5. Referrals can sometimes lead to tensions between individual franchisees in large market areas.

6. There can be reduced ability to choose business associates, particularly where franchisors are often more interested in quantity than quality.

7. In some instances, a franchisor may not live up to its promises.

8. A tradename and trademark may turn out to be a poor substitute for a long estab lished local name.

Washington is one of the states that regulates the sale of franchises. The Washington law is based on the principle of full disclosure (disclosure of all necessary financial and business data to make an informed business decision by a franchisee).

The Federal Trade Commission has adopted a business and franchise rule designed to alleviate "widespread evidence of unfair practices in connection with the sale of franchises" where the franchisee operates under the trade name of a franchisor or where the franchisor has significant control or gives significant assistance to the franchisee. The FTC rules goes far beyond the Washington law governing franchises and creates a whole new set of protection for franchisees. The FTC rule was designed to curb abuses by franchisors, while allowing continued development of the franchise system which is growing into a dynamic and mature business activity.
Reference: RCW 19.10

FRAUD - Any form of deceit, trickery, breach of confidence or misrepresentation by which one party attempts to gain some unfair or dishonest advantage over another. Unlike negligence, fraud is a deceitful practice or material misstatement of a material fact, known to be false, and done with intent to deceive, or with reckless indifference as to its truth, and relied upon by the injured party to his/her damage. For example, in response to a buyer's question regarding a possible structural problem, the seller produces a falsified inspection report. Not disclosing known defects or remaining "silent" can be considered fraud; in some cases, silence may not be golden.

It is important to distinguish between fraud in the inducement and fraud in the execution of a contract. If the party knows what he/she is signing but his/her consent to sign is induced by fraud, the contract is voidable by him/her. If the party does not actually know what he/she is signing because he/she is deceived as to the nature of his/her act and he/she doesn't intend to enter into a contract at all, then it is void. The voidable contract is binding until rescinded, whereas the void contract is of no force or effect whatsoever. The state statute of limitations for a court action based on fraud is general computed from the date of the fraud or from the time at which the defrauded person could discover or should have discovered the fraud.

It is the duty of a real estate agent to protect the public against fraud, misrepresentation or unethical practices in the real estate field. A broker's or salesperson license can be suspended or revoked for any fraudulent act. (*See* LICENSING LAW, MISREPRESENTATION.)
Reference: RCW 18.85

FREDDIE MAC - Popular name for Federal Home Loan Mortgage Corporation. (*See* FEDERAL HOME LOAN MORTGAGE CORPORATION.)

FREE AND CLEAR TITLE - Title to real property which is absolute and unencumbered by any liens, mortgages, clouds or other encumbrances, especially voluntary liens (mortgages or deeds of trust). (*See* MARKETABLE TITLE.)

FREEHOLD - An estate in real property, the exact termination date of which is unknown (for a described, yet indefinite period of time); those estates that have a potentially indefinite duration (**fee simple**) or a period of years incapable of exact determination (**life estate**). Freehold estates may be categorized as **estates of inheritance**, such as fee simple, and lesser estates for life, which extend only for the life of an individual. Nonfreehold (**leasehold**) estates can be measured in calendar time. In the Old English court system, only an owner of freehold property could bring a real action (as opposed to a personal action for money damages). Thus, only freehold estates were regarded as real property. The two principal elements of a freehold estate are actual ownership of real property and unpredictable duration.

FREEHOLDER - One who owns land that he/she can transfer without anyone's permission.

FREE STANDING BUILDING - A building containing one business rather than a row of stores or businesses with a common roof and side walls.

FRIEZE BOARD - A horizontal exterior band or molding, often decorated with sculpture resting directly below the cornice.

FRONT-END FEE - Charges made by a lender to a borrower for expenses incurred in determining whether or not a loan will be made. Such expenses would include credit report, appraisal, survey, structural inspection and sometimes legal fees. The fee may be stated as a set amount or as a percentage of the requested loan. Such fees are not payment for the use of money and thus are not considered to be interest.

FRONT-ENDING or FRONT-LOADING - Recognition of profit from a transaction prior to periods during which it is earned or despite significant risks which could result in subsequent losses. Some real estate syndications are heavily front loaded; that is, the syndicator receives a good share of his/her proposed profit at the time the investor initially funds the syndication.

FRONT FOOT - A measurement of property frontage abutting the street line or waterfront line, with each front foot presumed to extend the depth of the lot. Lots of varying depth but with the same front foot may be compared for valuation purposes by use of a depth table. When a lot measurement is given as "Lot A is 75' x 150'," the first figure (75') refers to the front feet. If Lot A were valued at $22,500, it would be worth $300 per front foot. (*See* APPRAISAL, DEPTH TABLES, SPECIAL ASSESSMENT.)

FRONT MONEY - A popular expression in the real estate development business referring to the hard money (cash, as opposed to borrowed moneys) the developer must come up with to purchase the land, pay attorney's fees, loan charges and other initial expenses prior to actually developing a project. Front money is sometimes called **start-up costs** or **seed money**. **End money** is a reserve in case project costs exceed estimates.

FRONTAGE - The length of a property abutting a street or body of water; that is, the number of feet that "front" the street or water. Frontage differs from width, which sometimes decreases or increases as the lot extends back from the street or water. (*See* APPRAISAL.)

FRONTAGE ASSESSMENT - An assessment made by a local government to pay for improvements such as roads. Improvements such as roads or sidewalks can be paid for by assessing the property facing or abutting the road based on the proportion of a particular property's frontage to the total distance being improved.

FROSTLINE - The depth of frost penetration in the soil. The frost line varies throughout Washington and footings should be placed below this depth to prevent movement of the structure.

FRUCTUS NATURALES - Uncultivated crops and perennial plants such as trees and bushes, which are generally classified as real property. **Fructus industriales,** on the other hand, are annual plants requiring cultivation and are classified as personal property. (*See* EMBLEMENTS.)

F.T.C. - *See* FEDERAL TRADE COMMISSION.

FULL DISCLOSURE - A requirement to reveal fully and accurately all material facts. A broker is under a fiduciary obligation to disclose in full to his/her client all known, relevant facts affecting a proposed transaction. Washington's Land Development Act requires a developer to disclose fully all material facts of a project to each prospective purchaser through required distribution of the public report. In 1994, it became a requirement that the seller of residential real property (one to four units) in Washington complete a full disclosure statement of the real property being sold. (*See* AGENCY, DISCLOSURE, LICENSING LAW, REAL PROPERTY TRANSFER DISCLOSURE STATEMENT.)
Reference: RCW 58.19, WAC 308-126, RCW 64.06

FULL RECONVEYANCE - Upon payment in full of the debt secured by a deed of trust, the trustee reconveys the property to the person or persons entitled thereto on written request of the grantor and the beneficiary, or upon satisfaction of the obligation secured and written request for reconveyance made by the beneficiary or his/her assignee. It is acknowledged by the trustee and should be recorded immediately. (*See* DEED OF TRUST.)
Reference: RCW 61.24.

FUNCTIONAL OBSOLESCENCE - A loss in value of an improvement due to functional inadequacies, often caused by age or poor design. For example, functional obsolescence may be attributable to such things as outmoded plumbing or fixtures, inadequate closet space, poor floor plan, excessively low ceilings, or antiquated architecture. Thus, a warehouse with nine-foot ceilings would probably suffer a loss in value because a modern forklift could not operate in such a small space. (*See* APPRAISAL.)

FUNDING FEE - A fee paid to secure certain types of mortgage protection, such as the fee paid to the Veterans Administration for it to guarantee the veteran's loan.

FURRING - Thin strips of wood used to level up a wall and provide air space between the wall and the plaster. Furring is often used to give the wall a thicker appearance.

FUTURE ADVANCES - Money which is advanced by a mortgagee (lender) to a mortgagor (borrower) and is intended to be secured by a prior mortgage. If the mortgage document specifically states the amount of such advances, and the mortgagee is contractually obligated to make such advances, then the mortgage lien is superior to that of any other lien which intervenes between the time of recordation of the original mortgage and the time the future advances are made. For example, a construction loan is usually disbursed in installments as the project progresses. These payments are called "obligatory advances" and take priority from the date of recordation of the construction mortgage, regardless of intervening liens. In other cases, like an open mortgage, the lender might have the privilege of making additional advances. These advances are "optional advances" and do not have priority over intervening recorded liens and thus an examination of the title is essential prior to making any advances.

FUTURE INTEREST - A person's present right to an interest in real property, which will not result in possession or enjoyment until some time in the future. Future interests include reversions, right of entry, executory interests, possibility of reverters, and remainders, both vested and contingent. (*See* GIFT TAX, REMAINDER ESTATE.)

GAIN - The profit received upon the sale of an asset. If it is a depreciable capital asset, then the gain technically consists of two elements: recapture of excess depreciation, if any, and capital gain (the balance of the gain after deducting excess depreciation). Favorable long-term capital gains treatment was re-established in the Taxpayers Relief Act of 1997. (*See* CAPITAL GAIN, RECAPTURE OF DEPRECIATION, TAX PREFERENCE.)

GAMBREL ROOF - A curb roof, having a steep lower slope and a flatter one above, as seen in Dutch Colonial architecture.

GAP FINANCING - The financing used to make up the difference between the underlying loan (floor loan) and the total amount required. Gap financing usually fills a temporary need until permanent financing is obtained, and thus is sometimes called a **bridge mortgage**. (*See* FLOOR LOAN.)

Gap financing may also be used when permanent take out financing is difficult to obtain or is too expensive. By obtaining gap financing and waiting, it is possible that more favorable terms may be reached. (*See* RENT UP.)

GAP IN TITLE - A break in the chain of title, such as when the records do not reflect any transfer to a particular grantor. This could happen if that grantor had failed to record his/her deed. (*See* CHAIN OF TITLE.)

GARDEN APARTMENT - A type of multiple-unit dwelling providing for a lawn and/or garden area.

GARNISHMENT - A legal process designed to provide a means for creditors to safeguard for themselves the personal property of a debtor which is in the hands of a third party ("garnishee"). In Washington, the creditor may have to post a bond payable to the debtor to cover all attorney fees, court costs, and double the amount claim if the creditor should be found to have wrongfully brought the garnishment action.

The types of properties which may be garnisheed include goods or effects of the debtor concealed in the hands of third parties, debts owed to the debtor by the garnishee, wages payable by the garnishee as allowed by law, and security interests of the debtor in the hands of the garnishee. The procedures usually require the service of a writ of garnishment upon the garnishee who must secure in his/her hands all property of the creditor to pay the creditor-plaintiff the amount of judgment the plaintiff may recover. The debtor may obtain release of the garnisheed property by filing a bond with the court in the amount sufficient to pay the claim of the creditor, together with costs and interest and conditioned upon judgment in favor of the creditor.

If garnishment is **after** judgment, then the property is paid over to the creditor. If the debt is disputed, then the garnishee should deposit the property with the court. Generally, the complaint and writ of garnishment are issued pursuant to the creditor's petition for process, or by subsequent motion of the creditor requesting the court to insert in the process a direction to the officer servicing the same to leave a copy with the garnishee and to summon the garnishee to answer certain questions. Because of U.S. Supreme Court decisions requiring notice and a hearing prior to a deprivation of a person's property with prejudgment security remedies, the entire garnishment process **prior** to a judgment and without a hearing may be unconstitutional.
Reference: RCW 7.33.

GAZEBO - An ornamental garden structure, often constructed of light metal or wood, from which a view or garden may be enjoyed,.

GENERAL AGENT - One who is authorized to perform any and all acts associated with the continued operations of a particular job or a certain business of the principal. The essential feature of a general agency is the continuity of service, such as that provided by a property manager of a large condominium project. Almost all real estate brokers are not general but special agents. (*See* AGENCY, ATTORNEY-IN-FACT, SPECIAL AGENT.)

GENERAL CONTRACTOR - A construction specialist who enters into a formal construction contract with a land owner or master lessee to construct a real estate building or project. Also called the **prime contractor**, he/she often negotiates individual contracts with various subcontractors specializing in particular aspects of the building process, such as plumbing, electrical, air conditioning, drywall, and the like. If the general contractor fails to pay them, the subcontractors can assert mechanics' liens against the entire project. To become a general contractor, one must obtain a license from the state. (*See* CONTRACTOR, MECHANIC'S LIEN, PERFORMANCE BOND.)

GENERAL LIEN - A right of a creditor to have all of the debtor's property sold to satisfy a debt. Unlike a specific lien against certain property, a general lien is directed against the individual debtor and attaches to all of his/her property. Common examples of general liens are judgment liens and government tax liens arising from unpaid taxes such as income, gift, estate, inheritance and franchise taxes. A general lien will be effective in those counties where copies have been filed with the County Clerk. (*See* LIEN.)

GENERAL PARTNER - A partner in a partnership who is empowered to enter into contracts on behalf of the partnership and who is fully liable for all partnership debts. In a limited partnership, the general partner is in charge of managing the partnership, and is accountable to the limited partners as a fiduciary. (*See* LIMITED PARTNER, PARTNERSHIP, UNIFORM PARTNERSHIP ACT.)

GENERAL PARTNERSHIP - A form of business organization in which two or more co-owners carry on a business for profit. All the owners are general partners and share a full liability for the debts and obligations of the partnership. Although advisable, a written partnership agreement with a buy-sell provision between the partners is not required. A general partnership may be subject to dissolution by reason of the death, withdrawal, bankruptcy, or legal disability of any general partner. (*See* PARTNERSHIP.)

GENERAL PLAN - A long-range governmental program to regulate the use and development of property in an orderly fashion; a plan aimed at a well-balanced community growth.

In planning a subdivision, a developer might establish a general building scheme, or general plan, in order to achieve a degree of uniformity in the subdivided community. When a general plan exists, the subdivider will make each conveyance subject to recorded restrictions in order to keep the general plan in operation. Then, any lot owner can enjoin any other lot owner from violating the general plan. For example, in a subdivision generally planned for residential use only, one lot owner could prevent another lot owner from constructing a restaurant. (*See* EQUITABLE SERVITUDE, GROWTH MANAGEMENT, RESTRICTION.)

GENERAL SERVICES ADMINISTRATION (GSA) - An independent agency organized in 1949 to manage, lease and sell buildings belonging to the United States Government.

GEODETIC SYSTEM - The United States Coast and Geodetic Survey System. The skeleton of the system consists of a network of bench marks covering the entire country. Each bench mark is located by its latitude and longitude. The system was initiated to identify tracts of land owned by the federal government, but has gradually been extended throughout the nation. The term "geodetic" deals with the science of measuring the earth and exactly locating points on its surface. (*See* GOVERNMENT SURVEY.)

GIFT DEED - A deed in which the consideration is "natural love and affection." Because the deed is not supported by a valuable consideration, the donee may not be able to enforce against the donor certain promises or agreements contained in the deed. A gift deed is valid unless made to defraud creditors. (*See* DEED, EXCISE TAX ON REAL ESTATE SALES, GIFT TAX.)

GIFT LETTER - A letter provided to a lender or government agency (FHA or VA) acknowledging that the money being used (often the down payment) to purchase real property was a gift from a relative with no obligation to repay.

GIFT TAX - A graduated federal tax paid by a donor upon making a gift. For the purposes of the gift tax, a gift is defined as the transfer by an individual of any type of property for less than adequate consideration in money or money's worth ("detached and disinterested generosity"). There is a $10,000 per year per donee exclusion which can be made tax free. An interest-free or low-interest loan to a family member may be subject to income tax and gift tax. Regardless of value, a gift tax return must be filed if the gift is of a future interest, such as a remainder fee. A gift return generally must be filed for a gift made to an individual other than a spouse if it exceeds $10,000 or is a gift of a future interest (regardless of value). A return does not have to be filed for gifts qualifying for the tuition or medical expense exclusion. Also, to the extent that his/her gifts exceed this exclusion, each donor has a set once in a lifetime exemption that can be applied to gifts, regardless of the donee. This exemption is set at $625,000 in 1998 and increases at the rate of $25,000 per year until it tops out in 2006 at $1,000,000. Effective in 1997 there is no estate or gift tax on taxable transfers aggregating $600,000 or less. For example, assume that Lynn Gauthier gave each of her five children a gift of $10,000 in 1997. There would be no gift tax because of the $10,000 per donee exemption. Now assume that in 1998, Lynn Gauthier gave $200,000 to each of her five children ($1,000,000 total). There would be no gift tax on the first $50,000 ($10,000 x 5), and no gift tax on the next $625,000, assuming that Lynn Gauthier had not used up any of her onetime cumulative $625,000 exclusion in any prior years. But there would be a gift tax on the remaining $325,000 and she would have to file a gift tax return and pay a gift tax. A gift tax return must also be filed if individual gifts exceed the annual exclusion, even if there is no tax in the event that the donor has not yet used the unified credit exemption.

Under the provisions of the Tax Reform Act of 1976, there was a major overhaul of our federal gift tax law. Some of the major changes include:

1. No longer would lifetime transfers (gifts) receive preferential treatment over trans fers effective at death; in addition, gift taxes and estate taxes were set up under a common rate schedule. Gift tax rates had previously been three-fourths of estate tax rates.

2. Lifetime transfers (gifts) and transfers effective at death would be cumulative for determining estate tax; however, any gift tax paid would be subtracted from any estate tax due.

3. A unified credit replaces the gift tax exemption. Any part of the credit used to offset gift tax is not available to offset federal estate tax.

4. The marital deduction is liberalized by providing an unlimited deduction for life time gifts between spouses.

If the donor is unable to pay the gift tax due, the donee may be held responsible for the tax under the theory of "transferee liability."

One of the primary purposes of the $10,000 annual exclusion is to avoid the necessity of determining the motivation involved in relatively small transfers between persons, regardless of relationship.

Where real estate has been given, the possibility of gift tax liability may be raised as a cloud on the title when the donee requests a title report on an eventual sale. Therefore, all documentation as to when and where a gift tax was paid, and if it did not have to be paid and why not, should be obtained by the donee for his/her records.

The donee's tax **basis** in property acquired by gift is the same as the donor's basis. Both the basis and the holding period follow the property. If, however, there is a loss upon the transfer of the property, then the basis is the lower of the donor's basis or the fair market value as of the date of the gift. Though the donor is obligated to pay the tax, the donee may pay it, in which case that amount is added to his/her basis. (*See* ESTATE TAX.)

GI LOAN - Government-guaranteed loan. (*See* VETERANS AFFAIRS (VA) LOAN.)

GINNIE MAE - Nickname of the Government National Mortgage Association.

GIRDER - A heavy wooden or steel beam supporting the floor joists in a building. The girder provides the main horizontal support for the floor.

GOING CONCERN VALUE - The value existing in an established business as compared to the value of selling the real estate and other assets of a concern whose business is not yet established. The term takes into account the good will and earning capacity of a business. Sometimes used in the test of determining solvency or insolvency or in computing value for purposes of corporate merger or issuance of stock. (*See* BUSINESS OPPORTUNITIES, GOODWILL.)

GOOD FAITH - Bona fide. An act is done in good faith if it is in fact done honestly, whether it be done negligently or not.

Under the Landlord Tenant Act, both landlord and tenant have an obligation of good faith in the performance of the rental agreement. Under Washington's anti-discrimination law it is a discriminatory practice to refuse to receive or transmit a bona fide offer to engage in a real estate transaction if based on race, sex, color, religion, ancestry or marital status.

Sometimes an act done in "bad faith" is punishable as a crime. For instance, if an investor-borrower applies for an owner-occupant loan and lies about his/her intent to occupy, this type of falsehood is punishable as a misdemeanor under the National Banking Act. *(See* BONA FIDE, RECORDING.)

GOOD FAITH ESTIMATE - The Real Estate Settlement Procedures Act requires a lender to promptly give (within three business days of an application) to loan applicants a good faith estimate of closing costs. (*See* BUYING YOUR HOME.)

GOOD WILL - An intangible, salable asset arising from the reputation of a business. When a business is sold, the sales price often includes a valuation for the good will of the business. Good will is not a depreciable asset, although it is a capital asset. Thus the seller favors a large value placed on the good will and the buyer prefers a lesser value. (*See* BUSINESS OPPORTUNITIES, CONDEMNATION, GOING CONCERN VALUE, NON-COMPETITION CLAUSE.)

GOVERNMENT LOT - See QUARTER SECTION.

GOVERNMENT NATIONAL MORTGAGE ASSOCIATION (GNMA) - A federal agency created in 1968 when the Federal National Mortgage Association (FNMA) was partitioned into two separate corporations. "Ginnie Mae," as it is popularly called, is a corporation without capital stock and is a division of the United States Department of Housing and Urban Development (HUD). The GNMA operates the special assistance aspects of federally aided housing programs and has the management and liquidating functions of the old FNMA. The FNMA is authorized to issue and sell securities backed by a portion of its mortgage portfolio, with the GNMA guaranteeing payment on such securities. The GNMA also guarantees similar securities issued by other private offerors (banks, mortgage companies, savings and loan associations) if they are backed by accumulated pools of VA or FHA mortgages. For an initial fee of $500 plus an annual fee paid to the GNMA, the private issuer can obtain the guaranty of the GNMA, backed by the full faith and credit of the United States Government.

Under the so-called tandem plan, the GNMA generally acquires from lenders the kinds of mortgage loans that would not otherwise be made because either their high-risk factors or low interest rates (such as those offered under government-subsidized housing programs) make them uneconomical for the private lending community. If the GNMA did not commit itself to purchasing such loans at prevailing market yields, lenders would not make them, particularly in low and moderate-income areas. For example, a lender may agree to issue a mortgage at an interest rate of six percent, well below the current market. The GNMA buys the mortgage, then resells it at a discounted price which will yield the buyer eight percent. The two point spread represents a federal government subsidy which enables a home purchaser to finance his/her home at a more affordable rate.

Now gaining popularity among investors is the "Ginnie Mae pass-through." This is a security interest in a pool of mortgages that provides for a monthly pass-through of principal and interest payments directly to the certificate holder. Such certificates are guaranteed by Ginnie Mae. (*See* GUARANTEED MORTGAGE CERTIFICATE, MORTGAGE-BACKED SECURITY, TANDEM PLAN.)

GOVERNMENT PATENT - The original United States land grant which conveyed government-owned land to the people.

GOVERNMENT SURVEY - A system of land description that applies to much of the land in the United States, particularly in the Western States; also called the geodetic or rectangular survey system. It is based on pairs of principal meridians and base lines, with each pair governing the surveys in a designated area. Principal meridians are north and south lines, and base lines extend east and west. The government survey method was designated to create a checkerboard of identical squares covering a given area. The largest squares measure 24 miles on each side and are called quadrangles. Each quadrangle is further divided into 16 squares called townships, whose four boundaries each measure 6 miles. A column of townships extending north-south is called a range and is numbered numerically east and west according to its distance from the principal meridian. There are now 36 principal meridians located in different parts of the United States. Washington is one of 30 states which utilizes the Federal Government Survey's system. The Willamette Meridian was used in the Government Survey of Washington. (*See* BASE LINE, MERIDIAN.)
Reference: RCW 58.20.

Because of the curvature of the earth, the north-south lines or ranges converge as they extend toward the north pole. To keep the range lines six miles apart as nearly as possible, the lines are laid out for approximately 24 miles, and then adjusted so that they are again six miles apart, to preserve as nearly as may be the square shape of the township.

A township is six miles square, or 36 square miles. Townships are numbered north and south from the base line. Each square mile, which is equivalent to 640 acres, is designated as a section. Sections within a township are numbered from the northeast corner, following a back and forth course, until the last section (36) in the southeast corner is reached. This method of numbering insures that any two sections with contiguous numbers also have contiguous boundaries. For purposes of land description, sections are commonly divided into half-sections containing 320 acres, quarter-sections containing 160 acres, etc. Land acreage descriptions are then generally made by referring to a particular quarter of a particular township or tier either north or south of a particular base line, and either east or west of a particular meridian.

A section is the smallest subdivision usually surveyed by government surveyors, and at each section corner there is a marker known as a "Survey Monument". A typical government survey description would be:

> "The E. 1/2 of the N.W. 1/4 of the S.E. 1/4 of Section 17, and the S.W. 1/4 of the S.E. 1/4 of the N.E. 1/4 of Section 17, and the N. 1/2 of the N.E. 1/4 of the S.E. 1/ 4 of Section 17, and the N.W. 1/4 of the S.W. 1/4 of Section 16."

Note that generally, the longer the description, the smaller the parcel of land. This method is good for identifying large parcels, but not for pinpointing small lots. (*See* GEODETIC SYSTEM.)

GOVERNMENT SURVEY SYSTEM

TOWNSHIP GRID

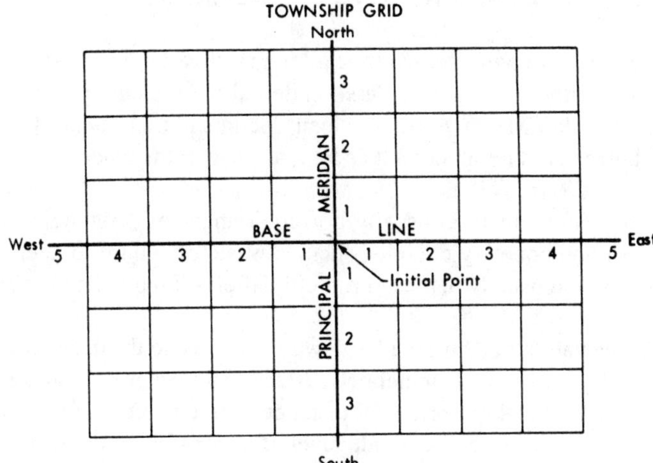

NUMBERING OF SECTIONS IN TOWNSHIP

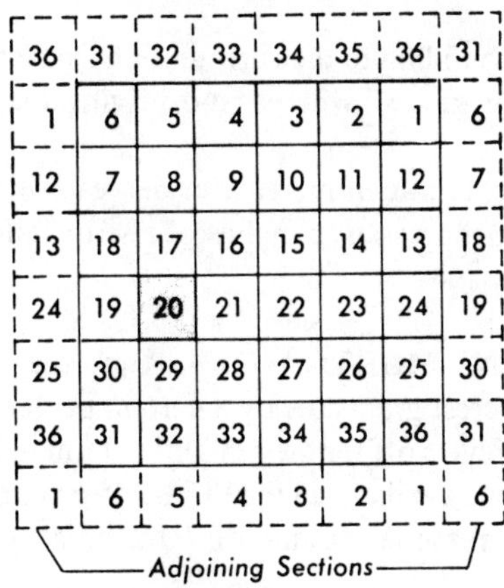

SECTION 20

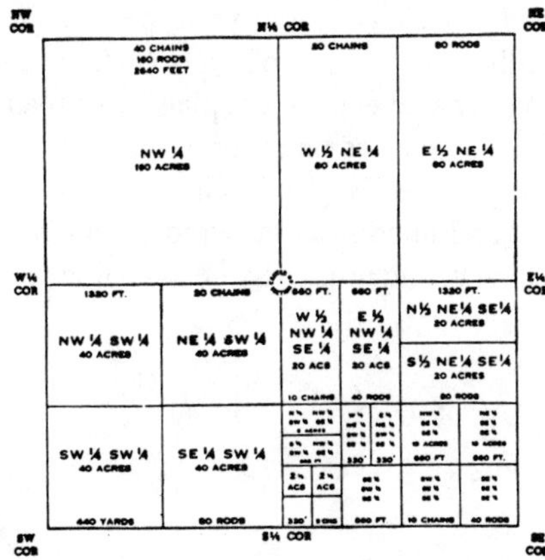

GRADUATE, REALTOR®'S INSTITUTE - See GRI.

GRACE PERIOD - An agreed-upon time after an obligation is past due during which a party can perform without being considered in default. For example, a mortgage or deed of trust payment is due March 1, but the loan documentation contains a ten-day grace period, so the borrower is not in default as long as payment is made by March 10.

With monetary defaults, there is usually no requirement of prior written notice to the debtor. But with nonmonetary defaults, such as waste or failure to keep a property insured, the grace period usually begins to run only after written notice is given.

GRADE - The elevation of a hill, road, sidewalk, or slope to the degree that it is inclined from level ground. The slope of an inclined surface of a road or lot is generally expressed as a percentage of the level or horizontal distance; a five percent grade rises five feet in each 100 feet of level distance. The grade level of a lot refers to the general elevation of the land. Rough grade is a surface on which topsoil will be spread to bring the lot up to a finished grade.

The relation of space in a building to the surrounding surface of the earth; for example, a basement is usually "below grade," whereas most living space is "above grade."

GRADIENT - The slope, or rate of increase or decrease in elevation, of a surface, road, or pipe. Gradient is often expressed in inches of rise or fall per horizontal linear foot of ascent or descent.

GRADUATED PAYMENT MORTGAGE - A mortgage in which the monthly payment for principal and interest graduates by a certain percentage each year for a specific number of years and then levels off for the remaining term of the mortgage. There are five different versions of the plan available in the FHA-245 program. The most popular is Plan III in which payments increase at the rate of 7 1/2 percent per year for five years *(See* chart).

The FHA-245 program is especially attractive to persons just starting their careers and anticipating increases in their incomes to obtain a home with an initially lower payment then would be available under a level payment plan. This plan helps borrowers qualify for loans by basing repayment schedules on salary expectations and anticipated home price appreciation. Since FHA underwriting guidelines are based on the first year's monthly requirement for principal and interest amortization, persons using FHA-245 can qualify for larger loan amounts than would ordinarily be available under other forms of financing.

Comparison of Payment Schedules of Level Payment Mortgage
and FHA Graduated Payment Mortgage (Plan III)
$100,000 loan, 11 1/2% interest, 30-year term
(rounded to nearest dollar)

Year	Level Payment	Graduated Payment	Difference
1	$991	$760	-231
2	991	817	-174
3	991	878	-113
4	991	944	- 47
5	991	1014	+ 23
6-30	991	1091	+ 100

GRADUATED RENTAL LEASE - A lease in which the rent payments commence at a fixed, often low rate, but "step up" or increase at intervals as the lease term matures. Such increases might be based on a percentage of the increased value of the land based on a periodic appraisal. This gives long-term commercial tenants an opportunity to get started in business without a heavy rental burden during the early years. A graduated rental lease is often an excellent device for soliciting tenants in a tough market or in a difficult to lease facility. (*See* CASH FLOW, ESCALATOR CLAUSE.)

GRANDFATHER CLAUSE - Common expression used to convey the idea that something which was once permissible continues to be permissible despite changes in the controlling law. For instance, a developer with prior county planning approval to build on 10,000 sq. ft. minimum size lots can build on the lots even if the current zoning regulations are amended to require 12,000 sq. ft. minimum size lots. The developer is "grandfathered" under the originally approved subdivision plan. Similar to "nonconforming use." (*See* VESTING.)

GRANT - The act of conveying or transferring title to real property. The operative words in a conveyance of real estate are to **grant, bargain, sell, warrant and convey**. The grantor delivers the grant, in the form of a deed or a Purchaser's assignment of contract and deed, to the grantee. (*See* DEED.)

GRANT DEED - A type of deed in which the covenants are created by statute and are contained in the deed merely by using the word grant.

The grant deed as an instrument of conveyance is not used in the State of Washington.

GRANTEE - The person who receives from the grantor a conveyance of real property. The grantee must be a legal person, either an individual or legal entity, who exists at the time of the conveyance and is capable of taking title. As a general rule, a grantor cannot convey title to himself/herself alone. He/she may, however, convey title to himself/ and others; for example, John Reilly conveys title to John Reilly and George Ant as joint tenants.

Some general applications of the above principles are:

1. If the grantee is dead at the time of delivery of the deed, the deed is void. (Deliv ery is deemed to have taken place when the executed deed is placed in escrow, not necessarily when it is actually delivered to the grantee.)

2. If the grantee is an entity or an informal club or society which had not filed its incorporation papers or had not been legally organized before delivery of the deed, the deed is void for lack of a grantee.

3. A deed conveying an estate to the heirs of a living person is void since no person can be an "heir" during the lifetime of his/her ancestor. (The correct wording would be "to Wayne Mark and his heirs and assigns ...")

4. When the grantee's name has been omitted, the deed generally is ineffective to convey title until the name is filled in with the grantor's permission. (*See* DEED, GRANT, OWNERSHIP, FORM OF.)

GRANTOR - The person transferring title to, or an interest in, real property. A grantor must be competent to convey; thus, an insane person cannot convey title to real property. In Washington, a deed from a minor is voidable (not void) and may be disaffirmed within 3 years after the grantor reaches majority (18 years old). A corporate grantor must have legal existence, be authorized to hold and convey title to real property and be represented by a duly authorized officer of the corporation.

The grantor must be clearly identified in the deed. Misspellings do not render the deed inoperative unless the discrepancy is so extensive that the grantor cannot reasonably be identified. The grantor should convey title under the same name in which he/she acquired the title. If he/she has changed his/her name, the grantor should reflect such change; e.g., "John Henry, who acquired title under the name John H. Adams ..."

When title is vested in two or more persons, each must convey his/her separate interest. Usually all co-owners will join in one deed, although separate deeds are perfectly valid to transfer the complete title to the grantee. (*See* COMMUNITY PROPERTY, DEED, SEPARATE PARTY.)

Even though she may not be a co-owner of the property, a wife should join in the deed conveying her husband's property, to prevent anyone from raising the question of her community property interest. The marital status of the grantor should be inserted in the deed; e.g., married, single, unmarried (divorced), widow. (*See* DEED, GRANT, OWNERSHIP, FORM OF.)

GRANTOR-GRANTEE INDEX - Public record books which are maintained in the Office of the County Auditor, listing all recorded instruments and the liber and page number where the complete document can be found in the record books. Separate index books are maintained for grantors and grantees so that a document can be located by searching under either name. These books are indexed by year and are in alphabetical order of the grantor in the grantor index and the grantee in the grantee index books.

The grantor-grantee indexes contain the following information: kind of instrument, name of grantor, name of grantee, date of instrument, book, page and date of recording. The book and page number refer to the record book in which can be found a literal copy of the recorded instrument.

An example of one method to search a title using the grantor-grantee indexes is as follows: Assume A owned a farm in 1890. In 1925, A conveyed the farm to B by deed. In 1950, B conveyed the farm to C by deed. In 1960, C borrowed $50,000 from the Bank of Colfax and gave a mortgage on the property. In 1974, C conveyed the farm to D by deed and now D enters into a contract to sell the property to E.

The basic title search procedure is that each owner is traced back through the grantee index to the source of his/her ownership. Thus, the title searcher would start by looking in the grantee index under D's name from the present back to 1974 when he/she finds the deed to D from C, then under C's name from 1974 back to 1950, where he/she finds the deed from B to C, then under B's name back to 1925 when he/she finds the deed from A to B, then under A's name from 1925 backward. The searcher will then look in the grantor index under A's name from 1890 and "search up" to 1925, then under B's name from 1925 to 1950, then under C's name from 1950 to 1974, then under D's name from 1974 to present. This way the searcher will pick up the mortgage to the Bank of Colfax which is recorded in 1960 in the grantor's index under C's name. However, if the deed from C to D, even though subject to C's mortgage, made no reference to C's mortgage, the searcher would not pick up the mortgage. The searcher would pick it up during his/her search of the book of real estate loans. (*See* RECORDING, TITLE SEARCH.)

GREENBELT - An area of land in a real estate development which is set aside by local government planning regulations upon which nothing can be built. Usually the purpose of such an undertaking is to establish a buffer between certain types of land uses. (*See* BUFFER ZONE.)

GRI (GRADUATE, REALTOR®'S INSTITUTE) - The professional designation of Graduate, Realtor®'s Institute (GRI) which may be earned by any member of the Washington Association of Realtors® who has been licensed for two years and successfully completes the prescribed three week (90 hour) educational courses. The GRI program is presented in all 50 states by the State Association of Realtors® under authority granted to the State Association by the National Association of Realtors®.

GROSS AREA - The total floor area of a building measured from the exterior of the walls (excluding those unenclosed areas like decks). In commercial leasing, the gross floor area is the entire square footage within the floor's perimeter, measured to the inside finish of the permanent outer building walls or to the glass line in newer buildings, with no allowance made for structural projections and with a required minimum ceiling height of 7 1/2 feet.

GROSS INCOME - The total income derived from a business or from income producing property, before deductions for expenses, depreciation, taxes, and similar allowances. Also, the income used by lenders for qualifying purchasers for loans.

GROSS INCOME MULTIPLIER - *See* GROSS RENT MULTIPLIER.

GROSS LEASE - A lease of property under which the lessee pays a fixed rent and the lessor pays the taxes, insurance, and other charges regularly incurred through ownership; also called a **fixed** or **flat** lease. In a net lease, the lessee pays some or all of these charges. Most residential and office leases are gross leases. Most residential ground leases and commercial and industrial building leases are net leases. (*See* NET LEASE, TRIPLE NET LEASE.)

GROSS RENT MULTIPLIER - A rule of thumb for estimating the market value of income-producing residential property. The multiplier is derived by using comparable sales divided by the actual or estimated monthly rentals in order to arrive at an acceptable average. By multiplying the estimated rent of the property under consideration by the multiplier, one can compute a rough estimate of the property's market value. Only a rough estimate of value is thus produced because the gross rent does not allow for variations in vacancies, uncollectible rents, property taxes, management, and similar unpredictable circumstances.

The use of the gross income multiplier, sometimes called the gross rent multiplier, has slowly been going out of use in recognition of the fact that it is a very crude guideline and does not take into consideration tax ramifications of different possible investors, nor does it recognize alternate methods of financing. (*See* APPRAISAL, INTERNAL RATE OR RETURN.)

GROUND COVER - Plants grown to keep soil from washing away, e.g., grass, ivy and other low growing plants.

GROUND LEASE - A lease of land alone, sometimes secured by improvements placed on the land. Also called a **land** lease. The ground lease is a means used to separate the ownership of the land from the ownership of the buildings and improvements constructed on the land. In most areas, it is a net lease that creates a tenancy for years, typically for a term of 55, 75, or 99 years. Ground leases do not generally run for longer than 99 years due to some early state laws that held leases of 100 years or longer to be transfers of fee simple title rather than leases. The lease rent (called ground rent) normally is fixed for an initial period of years (calculated as a percentage of the assessed valuation of the land on the date of lease execution), with the balance of the rent to be renegotiated on or before the expiration date of the fixed term. The new rent is usually based on a set percentage of return to the ground owner of the then appraised value of the property minus the cost of on-site and off-site improvements. Sometimes the rent increase is determined at the time of execution of the lease, and a graduated lease, with fixed increases at stated intervals, is agreed upon. In some states a ground lease is used in both residential and condominium developments; however, it is also popular in commercial property development. (*See* NET LEASE, PERCENTAGE LEASE, RENEGOTIATION OF LEASE.)

GROUNDWATER - Water under the surface of the earth, regardless of the geological structure in which it is standing or moving. Groundwater does not include water flowing in underground streams with identifiable beds and banks.

GROWTH MANAGEMENT - The process of controlling the size, time and direction of growth in a community. Growth management is accomplished through the use of zoning regulations and other types of police power, eminent domain, taxation and capital budgeting by the community.

GUARANTEED MORTGAGE CERTIFICATE (GMC) - A debt instrument issued by Freddie Mac to raise money for its activities in the secondary market. Each GMC represents an undivided interest in a large, geographically diversified group of residential mortgages and is unconditionally guaranteed by Freddie Mac. Payment of interest is made to the security holder every six months. Principal is paid once a year.

GUARANTEED SALE PROGRAM - A service offered by some brokers in which they agree to pay the owner of a listed property a predetermined price if the property is not sold within a specified period of time. This enables the owner to purchase a replacement property regardless of how long it takes to sell the listed property.

The broker generally charges a fee in addition to the sales commission — usually a percent of the sales price. Brokers should be aware that the Internal Revenue Service will consider the property acquired through a guaranteed sales program as dealer property per the Internal Revenue Code. (*See* DEALER.)

The guaranteed sale agreement must be well drafted to cover all rights and obligations of all parties. State licensing officials take a close look at these programs since owners have complained that some brokers refuse to perform their promises. (*See* LICENSING LAW.)

GUARANTY - An undertaking or warranty by one person (guarantor) to insure that another person (obligor) shall perform his/her contract or fulfill his/her obligation to a third person (obligee). In the event the obligor defaults and doesn't perform, the guarantor is legally responsible for completing the obligation; e.g., repaying the loan. (*See* PERSONAL JUDGMENT.)

GUARDIAN - A person, appointed by court or by will, who is given the lawful custody and care of the person (called a ward) or property of another. The ward might be a minor, an insane person or a spendthrift. The guardian may, upon court approval and without necessity of obtaining a real estate license, sell the ward's real property, if it is in the best interest of the ward. The grantee would receive valid title under a guardian's deed. A guardian ad litem is one appointed by a court to bring or defend a legal action on behalf of his/her ward.

GUEST-CAR RATIO (GCR) - For purposes of site planning of an apartment complex or a condominium, the number of parking spaces required for each living unit for use of guests.

GUTTER SYSTEM - The total gutter system for a structure for carrying off rainwater, including downspouts, either splash blocks or elbow extensions, and in some cases even ground wells. Gutters should be free of rust, tightly secured to the structure and slanted enough so that water will drain and not become stagnant. Downspouts should not empty at the base of the foundation walls but should have either splash blocks or elbow extensions to prevent basement leaks and soil erosion from the foundation walls and flower and shrub beds.

HABENDUM CLAUSE - That part of the deed beginning with the words "to have and to hold," following the granting clause and reaffirming the extent of ownership that the grantor is transferring. The habendum clause defines or limits the extent of ownership in the estate granted (e.g., a fee simple, or life estate, or easement). "To have and to hold unto the said Jane Henley, grantee, a life estate in ..." If there is a discrepancy between the extent of ownership as specified in the granting clause and that specified in the habendum clause, the granting clause prevails. Consequently, the habendum clause is not an essential part of the deed. (*See* QUANTUM.)

HABITABLE - Being in a condition that is fit to live in. The residential landlord has an obligation to keep the leased premises in a habitable condition. If any condition within the premises renders the dwelling unit uninhabitable or poses imminent threat to the health or safety of any occupant, the tenant may terminate the rental agreement by following certain procedures prescribed in the Landlord Tenant Act. (*See* ABATEMENT, LANDLORD TENANT ACT.)

Courts are now enforcing implied warranties of habitability against builders of new residences, where the defects render the building uninhabitable. (*See* CAVEAT EMPTOR, IMPLIED WARRANTY OF HABITABILITY.)
Reference: RCW 59.18

HABITABLE ROOM - A room used for living purposes, such as a den, bedroom, or kitchen, as opposed to a bathroom or hallway. Usually, habitable rooms are the only ones counted in the number of rooms in a house.

HALF SECTION - A land area of 320 acres (128 hectares), constituting one-seventy-second of a township.

HANDICAPPED PERSON, REMOVAL OF BARRIERS FOR - The Tax Reform Act of 1976 provided a special incentive to make more accessible and usable by the handicapped and elderly any facilities used in trade or business. (*See* AMERICAN DISABILITY ACT.)

HANGOUT - A balloon loan that occurs when a long-term loan exceeds the term of a lease for the same property. If a lender makes a commitment to a 24-year loan on a property with a 20-year lease, the four-year difference is called a hangout. When the terms call for the balance of the loan to be paid at the expiration of the lease, the loan is called a balloon loan.

HARD MONEY MORTGAGE - Any real estate loan given to a borrower in which the borrower receives cash (hard money) to be used for any purpose, as opposed to a real estate loan given to finance a specific real estate purchase. Often, a hard money loan will take the form of a second deed of trust given to a private mortgage company in exchange for the cash needed to purchase an item of personal property or solve some personal financial crisis. The borrower in this case would pledge the equity in his/her property as collateral for the hard money deed of trust. (*See* SECOND MORTGAGE, SOFT MONEY.)

HARDPAN - A compacted layer of soil, usually containing clay, through which it is difficult to drain or dig.

HARDWARE - In construction, the metal accessories, such as doorknobs, hinges, locks, etc.

HARDWOOD - Wood used for interior finish, such as oak, maple, and walnut. Originally referred to the type of tree (deciduous) and not the hardness of wood; modern usage often refers to the hardness of the wood.

HAZARD INSURANCE - A property insurance policy which indemnifies against loss resulting from physical damage to property due to hazards such as fire and windstorm. (*See* INSURANCE.)

HAZARDOUS SUBSTANCE OR WASTE - Material that poses a threat to the environment or to public health or is inherently dangerous to handle or dispose of. The Environmental Protection Agency lists hundreds of hazardous substances that are either toxic (leads to death), corrosive (acidic), ignitable (danger from heat or smoke), or reactive (can lead to explosions). The EPA regulates the disposal of such hazardous material. (*See* TOXIC CONTROL ACT.)

HEARING - An administrative legal proceeding with definite issues of fact to be determined and with parties having the right to be heard much the same as at a trial.

Under the provisions of the Real Estate Licensing Law, a procedure has been formulated for the revocation or suspension of a license, for a refusal to renew a license or for the refusal to accept application for licensing. The Director of Licenses sets the matter for hearing at a specific time and place. The individual who is the subject of the hearing is served with a verified statement stating the reason or reasons the hearing was called, at least twenty (20) days before the scheduled hearing. The Real Estate Program and the accused may be represented by counsel. The provisions of the Washington Administration Procedure Act apply to the hearing. The Director or his/her authorized representative appoints the hearing officer. If the accused does not appear, the hearing officer may proceed and determine the facts of the accusation in his/her absence. Rules of Evidence pertain to the hearing and there is a transcript of the proceedings. If the Director finds the State's accusations to be supported by fair preponderance of the evidence, he/she shall notify the licensee and take what he/she considers appropriate action.

If the decision is to suspend or revoke a license, or to not issue a license, an order to that effect is signed and forwarded to the affected party. Such an order is not operative for a period of ten (10) days. The affected party is entitled to a judicial review in a Superior Court. If the affected party institutes an appeal, he/she must post a $500 bond within thirty (30) days, pay the cost of having a transcript prepared of the disciplinary hearing and pay for it within 15 days of the filing of the transcript in the appellate action. The appeal and posting of bond makes the action to revoke or suspend a license inoperative until the appeal is decided. (*See* LICENSING LAW.)
Reference: RCW 18.85, RCW 34.04.

HEARTH - The floor of the fireplace. The front hearth, which extends out into the room, may be made of brick or decorative stone. The back hearth inside the fireplace is usually made of fire brick.

HECTARE - A metric unit of land measurement equal to 2.471 acres, or 100 ares. An are is 100 square meters. The prefix hect- means "100 times;" thus, a hectare is 100 ares.

HEIGHT, BUILDING - Vertical distance measured from curb or grade level, whichever is the higher, to the highest level of a flat roof or to the average height of a pitched roof, excluding penthouse or other roof appendages occupying less than 30 percent of the roof area.

HEIR - A person who inherits under a will or a person who succeeds to property by the laws of descent if the decedent dies without a will (intestate). Washington has established a preferential method for determination of heirs for purposes of distributing an intestate decedent's estate. In descending order of preference are children, surviving spouse, parents, children of parents and grandparents.

Where real and personal property descends to more than one heir, the heirs take title as tenants in common. The words "heirs and assigns" are no longer necessary to convey or devise title in fee simple. (*See* DESCENT, TENANT IN COMMON.)
Reference: RCW 11.02, RCW 11.04.

HEIRS AND ASSIGNS - Heirs are recipients of an inheritance from a deceased owner, whereas assigns are successors in interest to a property. The phrase "heirs and assigns" is customarily inserted in deeds and wills and is considered to be words of limitation and not words of purchase. Words of limitation in a conveyance indicate what type of estate is created. Words of purchase indicate who takes the estate. For example, in a conveyance "to Harry and his heirs," the words "to Harry" are words of purchase. The words "and his heirs" are words of limitation indicating a fee simple estate; they would not be present in the transfer of a life estate. Heirs and assigns are also generally responsible for the contracts of their predecessors, such as leases, options, deeds of trust, mortgages and real estate contract.

HEREDITAMENT - Every kind of inheritable property, including real, personal, corporeal, and incorporeal; those things appurtenant to the land. An incorporeal hereditament would be the right to receive future rents or insurance proceeds.

HETEROGENEOUS - Different or diverse. Heterogeneity is one of the major physical characteristics of real estate. Because no two parcels of land are the same, investors should carefully evaluate the characteristics of a particular site for suitability for proposed uses since a use that works on one parcel of land may fail for another. In addition, heterogeneity makes specific performance a viable remedy for breaches of contract involving real estate. If a person contracts for a particular parcel of land, receiving its value in money or receiving another similar parcel does not substitute for the original land.

HIATUS - 1. A gap in the chain of title. 2. A space existing between adjoining parcels due to a faulty legal description, sometimes called a "gap."

HIDDEN AMENITIES - Features of a property which, even though they may not be easily recognizable, add to the value of the property. Examples would include extra wall insulation, high quality paint and better grade materials.

HIDDEN DEFECTS - A title defect which cannot be ascertained from an examination of the public records. The most common hidden defects include forgery or lack of delivery in the chain of title; corporate forgery (the execution by the appropriate officers of an unauthorized instrument); minority of a party to an instrument; death of a principal prior to execution of an instrument by his/her attorney-in-fact; conveyance in fraud of creditors; community property rights of the spouse of a first party who falsely represented himself or herself to be single. All such hidden defects are covered under standard coverage policies of title insurance. (*See* EXTENDED COVERAGE, TITLE INSURANCE.)

HIGHEST AND BEST USE - An appraisal term meaning that reasonable use which, at the time of the property's appraisal, is most likely to produce the greatest net return to the land and/or the building over a given period of time. The use must be legal and in compliance with regulations and ordinances within the police power of the county and state, including health regulations, zoning ordinances, building code requirements, and other regulations. The highest and best use is determined by evaluating the quantity and quality of income from various alternative land uses. Net return normally is interpreted in terms of money, though consideration may be given to such things as amenities.

For example: vacant land in a central business district currently used as a parking lot may or may not be employing its highest and best use, depending on whether the surrounding market is ready for further commercial development. A gas station site may be more effective as a fast-food facility or a dry cleaners. (*See* APPRAISAL.)

HIGH RISE - A popular expression for a condominium or apartment building generally higher than six stories. However, there is no national height standard.

HIGH WATER MARK - That line on the shore reached by the shoreward limit of the rise of medium tides "between the spring and the neap." In most states, this mark, also called "mean high water," is the dividing line between public and private property. In Washington, however, in a 1961 U.S. Supreme Court decision, the "line or ordinary high tide" is defined as being the average elevation of all high tides as observed at a location through a complete tidal cycle of 18.6 years.''

The high water mark may be very important due to the fact that all patents issued after November 11, 1889, were restricted by the State's Constitution whereby everything below the high water mark belongs to the State of Washington. (*See* PATENT, TIDE LANDS.)

HIP ROOF - A pitched roof with sloping sides and ends.

HOLDBACK - (1) That portion of a loan commitment not funded until some additional requirement such as a certain percentage of rental or completion is attained. (2) In construction or interim lending, a percentage of the contractor's draw held back to provide additional protection for the interim lender, often an amount equal to the contractor's profit paid out when the interim loan is satisfied. (*See* FLOOR LOAN.) (3) Money held in escrow until a repair delayed, say, by weather, is completed to satisfy work orders by the appraiser/lender.

HOLDER IN DUE COURSE - A person who has obtained a negotiable instrument (promissory note, check) in the ordinary course before it is due, in good faith and for value, without knowledge that it has been previously dishonored and without notice of any defect or set-off at the time it was negotiated.

A holder in due course enjoys a favored position with respect to a negotiable instrument because the maker cannot raise certain "personal defenses" in refusing payment. Personal defenses include lack of consideration, setoff and fraud. This facilitates trade and commerce because people are more willing to accept such instruments without careful investigation of the maker's credit or the circumstances surrounding the creation of the instrument.

A holder in due course is insulated against a claim by the maker that the promissory note has been paid in part or in full or has been forged. Thus the maker of the note should have the note marked "paid" and returned to him/her in order to avoid the risk of the holder's negotiating it to another holder in due course who could force the maker to pay it again. (*See* NEGOTIABLE INSTRUMENT.)

It was in the area of consumer purchases that the doctrine had its harshest effects when consumers had to pay for defective or undelivered goods or services, and the legal gimmickry that protected the financiers was almost always included in the boilerplate terms of the contract, rarely read and rarely understood by the consumer.

On May 14, 1976, the doctrine almost disappeared due to the adoption of the "Preservation of Consumers' Claims and Defenses." The whole impact of the rule can be understood by the notice which must now appear in all credit agreements:

"Any holder of this consumer credit contract is subject to all claims and defenses which the debtor could assert against the seller of goods or services obtained pursuant hereto or with the proceeds hereof. Recovery hereunder by the debtor shall not exceed amounts paid by the debtor hereunder."
(*See* FEDERAL TRADE COMMISSION.)

HOLD HARMLESS CLAUSE - A clause inserted in a contract whereby one party agrees to indemnify and protect the other party from any injuries or lawsuits arising out of the particular transaction. Such clauses are usually found in leases wherein the lessee agrees to "indemnify, defend and hold harmless" the lessor from claims and suits of third persons for damage resulting from lessee's negligence on the leased premises. Hold harmless clauses are also found in property management contracts where the owner holds the agent harmless for all damages except those caused by the agent's own negligence.

HOLDING COMPANY - A controlling company which owns or directs the operations of one or more other corporations; a corporation organized to hold the stock of other corporations, such as a bank holding company.

HOLDING ESCROW - An arrangement whereby an escrow agent holds the final title documents (a deed) to a real estate contract until paid in full. This terminology is seldom heard in the State of Washington, where it is usually referred to as true escrow. (*See* TRUE ESCROW.)

HOLDOVER TENANT - One who stays on the leased premises after his/her lease has expired. The landlord normally has the choice of evicting the holdover tenant or permitting him/her to remain and continue to pay rent.

Under the Washington Landlord Tenant Act, the holdover tenant is liable for a sum equal to the monthly rent under the previous rental agreement, computed and prorated on a daily basis, for each day he/she remains in possession for any period up to one month. If the tenant stays over longer than one month and the landlord fails to bring proceedings for recovery of possession of the rental unit within a reasonable time, then the acceptance of rent shall create a month-to-month tenancy in the absence of an agreement between the parties to the contrary at the time of such acceptance. (*See* LANDLORD TENANT ACT, TENANCY AT SUFFERANCE.)

HOLIDAYS - The following is a list of significant holidays recognized by most banks and many businesses, as well as state and federal offices. (S=State, F=Federal):

New Year's Day	January 1	SF
Martin Luther King's Birthday	3rd Monday/January	SF
President's Day	3rd Monday/February	SF
Memorial Day	last Monday/May	SF
Independence Day	July 4	SF
Labor Day	1st Monday/September	SF
Columbus Day	2nd Monday/October	F
Veterans' Day	November 11th	SF
Thanksgiving	3rd Thursday/November	SF
Day after Thanksgiving	3rd Friday/November	S
Christmas	December 25th	SF

Legal public holidays recognized by the federal government are specified in Section 6103(a) of Title 5 of the United States Code.

Usually, whenever an act is to be performed upon a particular day which happens to fall upon a holiday, the act may be performed upon the next business day with the same effect as if performed upon the day appointed. This rule is generally not true where the parties have **clearly indicated** that "time is of the essence." In any event, a prudent contract drafter should foresee possible problems and make the appropriate adjustments.

HOLOGRAPHIC WILL - A will which is entirely written, dated and signed in the testator's handwriting, and which was not witnessed. A holographic will is not valid in Washington where all wills must be attested to by two or more competent witnesses subscribing their names to the will in the presence of the testator. It is the lack of witnessing signatures, not the handwritten form, which renders the holographic will invalid in Washington.
Reference: RCW 11.12.

HOME EQUITY LOAN - A second mortgage or deed of trust on a personal residence which is based on the equity in a home. The loan has a normal repayment schedule that includes interest and principal. Sometimes, proceeds from home equity loans go toward an addition or improvement to the home. (*See* SECOND MORTGAGE.)

HOME INSPECTION - A professional inspection of a property to ascertain the condition of the improvements. In Washington, it is usually paid for by the buyer and made a contingency to the buyer's obligation to buy under the terms and conditions of the Purchase and Sale Agreement. Some sellers authorize a home inspector to complete a report in the hopes this will make the property more marketable. Buyers and sellers should review the scope of services covered - some inspectors check roofs and foundations whereas others do not.

It is recommended that all buyers obtain a home inspection regardless of the age of the home or condominium, even if it is new. Washington does not license home inspectors. The Department of Licensing has recommended that agents recommend the use of engineers as inspectors.

HOME MORTGAGE DISCLOSURE ACT - A federal law that requires lenders with federally related loans to disclose the number of loans made in different parts of their service areas with the design of eliminating the discriminating practice of "redlining." (*See* REDLINING.)

HOME OWNERS WARRANTY PROGRAMS - Warranty and insurance protection programs offered by private insurance companies.

The major provisions of the program are that a new home is warranted for a specific period of time, e.g., ten years, against major structural defects. The first year or two of the warranty is the builder's obligation. The next period of time is covered by the insurance company. For example, during the first year the builder may provide a warranty that materials and workmanship in the new home meet an approved standards. During the second year the builder continues to be responsible for the wiring, piping, and duct work on the systems in the home. During the first two years, the insurance company assumes the builder's responsibilities to the homeowner if, for any reason, he/she cannot or will not meet the warranty's obligations.

The builder usually pays a onetime insurance premium and warranty administration fee per thousand of the home's selling price.

HOME OWNERSHIP - The status of owning the residence in which one lives. There are certain tax advantages derived from owning a home, such as deduction of real estate taxes and interest payments, no tax on the gain upon the sale of the residence and certain casualty losses. (*See* INTEREST, RESIDENCE, SALE OF.)

HOME OWNER POLICY - A combined property and liability insurance policy designed for residential property. There are a variety of these packaged policies designed for owners of single-family dwellings, for tenants and for condominium owners. The homeowner policy can be endorsed for additional coverage, such as an inflation guard or an art collection.

HOME OWNER'S ASSOCIATION (HOA) - A nonprofit association of homeowners organized pursuant to a declaration of restrictions or protective covenants for a subdivision, a PUD, or a condominium. Like other nonprofit associations, a homeowner's association does not have shareholders, but rather it has members.

The Washington State Homeowners Association Act (H.O.A.) which became effective July 23, 1995 applies to membership associations in planned unit developments and subdivisions where all association members own residential real property and pay assessments for common expenses associated with the real property that is owned by the association. The H.O.A. specifically excludes condominiums.

The H.O.A. contains a broad grant of power to the board of directors of the association subject to limitation or expansion in the association's governing documents. These powers were patterned after the Washington Condominium Act and include the power to adopt rules, power to regulate the use, maintenance, repair, replacement and operation of the common areas, and the power to levy fines, after notice and an opportunity for a hearing, according to due process procedures and a previously published fine schedule. The governing documents can contain other powers not enumerated in the H.O.A., and associations are granted broad implied powers to exercise any other powers necessary and proper for the governance and operation of the association. Officers and directors of a homeowner's association are held to the same standard of care and loyalty required of an officer or director of any other non-profit corporation.

Several key areas of the H.O.A. provide for a budget ratification procedure which involves owner review of all assessments adopted by the board. Additionally, owners by majority vote of the voting power in the association may remove a member of the board of directors with or without cause. The H.O.A. also provides that all board meetings except for some narrow exceptions are open to owners and their agents. Executive sessions are allowed if a vote is taken in an open meeting on a motion of the specified purpose of the closed meeting and any action taken in a closed meeting must be voted on by the directors in a subsequent open session before it becomes effective. The H.O.A. requires the association or its managing agent to keep financial and other records sufficiently detailed to enable the association to fully declare to each owner the true state of its financial status. The Act also provides open access by members, lenders, and their agents to all records of the association excluding any unlisted telephone numbers of owners.

The H.O.A. Act grants a great deal of protection to members of homeowners associations which was previously only available under the Washington Condominium Act to owners of condominium units.
Reference: RCW 64.

In a typical subdivision development, a developer will record a declaration of restrictions, covenants and easements to insure the orderly and harmonious development of the subdivision, and to protect against future depreciation of values resulting from deterioration of the neighborhood. After sales of the lots have commenced, the developer will normally transfer the right of enforcement of the restrictions, liens, and covenants from himself to the Homeowner's Association. In connection with condominiums, the Homeowner's Association also sees that the common elements are maintained, such as the swimming pools and elevators, and normally hires a managing agent to implement its policies. (*See* CONDOMINIUM ASSOCIATION, UNINCORPORATED ASSOCIATION.)

The Tax Reform Act of 1976 allows two types of housing associations — condominium management associations and residential real estate management associations - to elect to be treated as tax-exempt organizations for taxable years beginning after 1973. But this tax-exempt status will protect the association from tax only on its exempt function income, such as membership dues, fees, and assessments received from member-owners of residential units in the particular condominium or subdivision involved. On any net income that is not exempt function income, the association is taxed at corporate rates but is not permitted the corporate surtax exemption granted to regular domestic corporations.

HOMESTEAD - A home which is used as a personal residence.

Homestead laws have been enacted as public policy to promote property ownership and family stability. The Washington State Constitution states: "The legislature shall protect by law from forced sale a certain portion of the homestead and other property of all heads of families." It is deemed important to protect a family's home even from just demands of creditors.

The Homestead Law protects a homestead from attachment and from forced sale for the debts of the owner up to $30,000 or the total net value of the lands, mobile home, and improvements, whichever is less. There are five exceptions to this protection. These include: (1) mechanic's and materialmen's liens; (2) mortgages, deeds of trust or real estate contracts; (3) certain debts arising out of a bankruptcy filed by one spouse within six months of the other spouse's bankruptcy; (4) child support debts; and (5) a condominium or homeowners association assessment.

Prior to 1981 a **declaration of homestead** had to be filed in the Office of the County Auditor. In 1981, the Legislature made the homestead automatic once the property is occupied as a true permanent residence and thereby is protected from execution and a forced sale to satisfy a judgment debt except as otherwise set forth in the statute. The homestead consists of the dwelling house in which the claimant resides, together with all the appurtenant buildings and the land supporting and surrounding the structures, or land that is purchased without improvements with the intention of building a dwelling house in which to live or placing a mobile home on it. If a claimant is married, the homestead may be selected from community property or from the separate property of one of the spouses if the other spouse agrees. The property remains a homestead until it is conveyed or abandoned in accordance with the statute.

A homestead declaration is an exemption allowed by law against "unsecured" creditors. It has no legal effect on prior encumbrances of record such as mortgages, trust deeds and mechanic's liens since they are secured.

One may have a homestead on only one property at a time. Moving from the property does not abandon the homestead but it may be abandoned by the sale of the property or recording a Declaration of Abandonment.
Reference: RCW 6.12, RCW 11.52.

HOME, USED FOR BUSINESS - The Tax Reform Act of 1976 placed tighter restrictions on deducting rent, utility bills and other expenses attributable to an office at home. Such deductions will be allowed only when part of the home is used exclusively and regularly as a taxpayer's principal place of business or as a place to meet clients, patients or customers. Deductions will not be permitted to exceed the income produced in that office. As of January 1, 1999, a home office will meet the principal place of business test if it is used to conduct administrative or management activities and the taxpayer can show that there is no other fixed location where the taxpayer conducts substantial administrative of managerial activities for his/her business.

HOMOGENEOUS - An appraisal term meaning of same or similar kind. As used in appraisal, this term describes an area or neighborhood in which the property types or uses are similar and harmonious, and the inhabitants have similar cultural, social, and economic backgrounds, it tends to stabilize property values in the area.

HORIZONTAL PROPERTY REGIMES ACT - The name given to the statute adopted in 1963 pertaining to condominiums in the State of Washington, permitting ownership of a specified horizontal layer of air space as opposed to the traditional method of vertical ownership of property from the earth below to the sky above. In a condominium, the horizontal planes appear as the floor and ceiling and the vertical planes appear as the walls. In order to come under the umbrella of the regime, that is, to be able to have an individual apartment have the individual rights of private property as to taxation and conveyance, a developer has to fully disclose all his/her plans by recording a Declaration with the County Auditor. Once the condominium building has been completed, it is turned over to the owners (owners' association) to operate and manage according to bylaws which have been established according to general guidelines imposed by the law. (*See* CONDOMINIUM, CONDOMINIUM ASSOCIATION, CONDOMINIUM OWNERSHIP.)
Reference: RCW 64.32

In 1990, Washington adopted the Condominium Act which applies to all condominiums created after July 1, 1990. However, the Horizontal Property Regimes Act still applies to all condominiums created prior to July 1, 1990. Some of the new Condominium Act provisions apply to condominiums created before July 1, 1990. (*See* CONDOMINIUM ACT.)
Reference: RCW 64.34

HOSTILE POSSESSION - Possession of real property by a person which is in contradiction, or adverse to, the possession of the true title owner. The word "hostile" does not mean there is any real hatred or force. It means that the possessor's claim neither recognizes the title of the true owner nor is subordinate to that title. Hostile possession is one of the essential elements to establish a claim to title under adverse possession. (*See* ADVERSE POSSESSION.)

HOTEL - As defined in many zoning codes, a building or group of attached or detached buildings containing dwelling or lodging units in which 50 percent or more of the units are lodging units, usually distinguished by a front desk, dining room and other common facilities.

HOUSE RULES - Rules of conduct adopted by a board of directors of a condominium or planned unit development and designed to promote harmonious living among the owners and occupants. Such rules are usually enforced by the resident manager or managing agent with the support of the board. Since it is easier to change the House Rules than to amend the Bylaws (which often needs 60 percent owners' approval), most condominium associations use the House Rules to regulate the use of the condominium such as the promulgation of rules for use of certain common areas like the swimming pool, rules prohibiting pets, guest parking or loud noises. (*See* CONDOMINIUM, HOMEOWNER'S ASSOCIATION, LANDLORD TENANT ACT.)

Landlords of apartment buildings usually require their tenants to abide by the published House Rules. The House Rules must be fair and apply equally to all tenants.
Reference: RCW 64.32, RCW 64.34

HOUSING AFFORDABILITY INDEX - An index published monthly by the National Association of Realtors showing the financial ability of the median income family to purchase the median-priced home with an 80 percent loan. An index greater than 100 means that the median income family could qualify for more than the median-priced home with an 80 percent loan. A less than 100 index means that the same median income cannot qualify to buy the median-priced home, which is normally the case during times of inflation and higher than normal interest rates.

HOUSING FOR THE ELDERLY - A project specifically designed for elderly persons (55 years of age or older) which provides living-unit accommodations and space for common use by the occupants in social and recreational activities and sometimes when needed, incidental facilities and space for health and nursing services for the project residents.

HOUSING STARTS - Housing units placed under construction, as distinguished from building permits issued. The use of national and regional statistics in housing starts is helpful in analyzing real estate and real estate loan trends; it is a key economic indicator. (*See* STARTS.)

HOUSING TRUST FUND ACCOUNT - See WASHINGTON HOUSING TRUST FUND

HUD - A federal cabinet department officially known as the Department of Housing and Urban Development. HUD is active in the area of national housing programs; among its many programs are urban renewal, public housing, model cities, rehabilitation loans, new FHA subsidy programs, and water and sewer grants. The Office of Interstate Land Sales Registration is under HUD's jurisdiction, as are the Federal Housing Administration (FHA) and the Government National Mortgage Association (GNMA). (*See* DEPARTMENT OF HOUSING AND URBAN DEVELOPMENT.)

HUD PROGRAMS GENERALLY IDENTIFIED BY NUMBER

Title	
I	Home Improvement Loans Mobile Home Loans
1	Community Development Block Grants (Housing and Community Development Act of 1974)
VI	Equal Opportunity in HUD-Assisted Programs (Civil Rights Act of 1964)
VIII	Fair Housing (Civil Rights Act of 1968)
Section	
8	Lower-Income Rental Assistance (U.S. Housing Act of 1937)
23	Low-Rent Leased Public Housing (U.S. Housing Act of 1937)
202	Direct Loans for Housing for the Elderly or Handicapped (Housing Act of 1959)
203(b) and(i)	One-to-Four Family Home Mortgage Insurance (National Housing Act of 1934)
207	Multi-family Rental Housing (National Housing Act (1934))
213	Cooperative Housing (National Housing Act (1934))

221(d)(2)	Home ownership for Low Moderate and Income Families (National Housing Act (1934))
221(d)(3) and(4)	Multi-family Rental Housing for Low and Moderate Income Families (National Housing Act (1934))
223(f)	Existing Multifamily Rental Housing (National Housing Act (1934))
231	Mortgage Insurance for Housing for the Elderly (National Housing Act (1934))
232	Nursing Homes and Intermediate Care Facilities (National Housing Act (1934))
234	Condominium Housing (National Housing Act (1934))
235	Home ownership Assistance for Low and Moderate Income Families (National Housing Act (1934))
244	Single-Family Home Mortgage Coinsurance (National Housing Act (1934))
244	Multifamily Housing Coinsurance (National Housing Act (1934))
245	Graduated Payment Mortgage (National Housing Act (1934))
312	Rehabilitation Loans (Housing Act of 1964)
701	Comprehensive Planning Assistance (Housing Act of 1954)

Executive Order

1246	Equal Employment Opportunity (September 24, 1965)
11063	Fair Housing (Title VIII) (Civil Rights Act of 1968)

The various HUD programs identified are not always in existence/funded at any one time. A specific program will be funded for a period of time and then will not be funded for a period of time.

HUI - Originally referred to a Chinese family investment group, it now is a common Hawaiian expression for an association or joint venture of friends (such as several married couples) or business associates in a real estate or business enterprise. The expression is sometimes heard in Washington. A hui often takes the form of a partnership, and sometimes refers to a "syndication." The members of the hui hold title as tenants in common in proportion to their respective ownership of shares. If a real estate licensee forms or is involved in a hui, particular care must be taken to not violate Washington's Securities Laws. (*See* REAL PROPERTIES SECURITIES REGISTRATION.)

HUNDRED-PERCENT LOCATION - Generally refers to the location in the downtown business district which commands the highest land value. This type of location usually reflects the highest rental prices and the highest traffic and pedestrian count. This term sometimes refers to the site which is ideal for the requirements of a specific user.

HYPOTHECATE - To put up specific real or personal property as security for an obligation, without surrendering possession of it.

In a typical purchase of a house, the buyer pays a portion of the purchase price with his/her own money and borrows the balance from a lending institution. The lender requires the buyer to hypothecate the property as security for repayment of the loan, which is accomplished by use of a mortgage or deed of trust. The borrower retains the rights of possession and control, while the lender secures an underlying lien right in the property. (*See* COLLATERAL, DEED OF TRUST, MORTGAGE, PLEDGE.)

I

I-BEAM - An iron or steel structural framing member, in cross-section forming the letter I.

IDEM SONANS - Sounding the same. Legally, names improperly spelled will not void an instrument, provided the written name sounds the same as the correctly spelled name and there is no evidence of any intent to deceive by incorrect spelling.

ILLIQUIDITY - An asset that may be difficult to sell for full value on short notice. The lack of assets that can be quickly converted to cash.

IMPACT FEES - A municipal or county assessment against new residential, industrial, or commercial development projects to compensate for the added costs of public services generated by the new construction. Such indirect service requirements could be to cover hookup costs for water and sewer lines, road construction and building of schools.

IMPLIED AGENCY - An actual agency, the existence of which as a fact is proved by deduction or inferences from facts and circumstances of a particular case, including the words and conduct of the parties. Sometimes called ostensible agency. (*See* AGENCY, REAL ESTATE BROKERAGE RELATIONSHIPS ACT.)

IMPLIED CONTRACT - An unwritten contract inferred from the actions of the parties. An unwritten agreement is determined by the conduct of the principals. Also, a contract in which the terms are understood and agreed to, but not fully stated in the document. In Washington, all contracts pertaining to real estate must be in writing to be legally enforceable. (*See* ESTOPPEL, STATUTE OF FRAUD.)

IMPLIED EASEMENT - An easement arising by implication from the acts or conduct of the parties. For example, a person acquiring mineral rights on a property also acquires an implied easement to enter the property for the purpose of removing the minerals. (*See* EASEMENT.)

IMPLIED LISTING - A listing which arises by operation of law as implied from the acts of the parties. In some states, a listing which arises by implication from the conduct of the broker and seller may be enforceable even though not in writing; however, in Washington all listing contracts **must be in writing** and a copy delivered to all parties signing it. (*See* CONTRACT, LISTING, STATUTE OF FRAUDS.)

IMPLIED WARRANTY OF HABITABILITY - A legal doctrine imposing on the landlord a duty to make all residential premises acceptable to live in and ready for occupancy and to continue to maintain them in a state of repair throughout the entire term of the rental period. This is a reversal of the common law, where the landlord was shielded by the "caveat emptor" doctrine, under which the tenant took the premises "as is" regardless of habitability.

Washington's Landlord Tenant Act specifically provides that the landlord shall make all repairs and arrangements necessary to put and keep the premises in a habitable condition. The landlord must protect the tenant from all latent defects (e.g., hidden conditions of which the tenant is unaware and could not be expected to know).

The implied warranty of habitability has recently been applied to the seller or the builder of a new home, who can be held liable for defects making the dwelling unfit. (*See* ABATEMENT, CAVEAT EMPTOR, LANDLORD TENANT ACT.)
Reference: RCW 59.18.

IMPLY - To infer; actions and conduct which indicate or suggest, as something naturally to be inferred, without express statement. Real estate agreements must be expressed, as opposed to implied and must be in writing. (*See* STATUTE OF FRAUDS.)

IMPOUND ACCOUNT - A trust account established to set aside funds for future needs relating to a parcel of real property. Many lenders require an impound account to cover future payments for taxes, assessments, and insurance so as to protect their security from defaults and tax liens. Many lenders on real estate loans require a tax reserve of six months and an insurance reserve of one year. (*See* BUDGET MORTGAGE, CUSTOMER TRUST FUND.)

When the property is sold and the loan assumed, the lender usually does not return the account balance to the owner. The money remains with the lender, and it is a matter between the buyer and seller as to prorating the account balance between them at closing. Impound accounts are required for FHA loans, and although VA regulations do not require an impound account for taxes and insurance premiums on GI loans, many lenders customarily require that such accounts be established and maintained. Under RESPA, the amount of reserves in the impound account is limited to one-sixth of the estimated amount of taxes and insurance that will become due in the twelve month period beginning at settlement.

Sometimes, part of the purchase price due the seller may be impounded or put aside by escrow to meet a post-closing expense of clearing title or repairing the structure. (*See* CUSTOMER TRUST FUND.)

IMPROVED LAND - Real property whose value has been enhanced by the addition of on-site and off-site improvements such as roads, sewers, utilities, buildings, etc.; as distinguished from raw land. It could also be an alteration of the land's surface, such as an irrigation channel.

IMPROVEMENTS - Valuable additions made to property, amounting to more than repairs, costing labor and capital and intended to enhance the value of the property. Improvements of land would include grading, sidewalks, sewers, streets, utilities, etc. Improvements on land would include buildings, fences, and the like.

Under modern appraising methods, the value of improvements is generally determined by what the improvements add to the land in the production of income or amenities. A reasonable relationship should exist between a site and the character of the improvement placed upon it. An over-improvement, under-improvement, or misplaced improvement detracts from the combined value of a lot and the building on it.

For income tax purposes, improvements to investment properties must generally be capitalized, with deductions taken over a period of years, whereas maintenance and repairs which do not add to the value of the property can be deducted as business expenses in the year incurred. (*See* BASIS, REPAIRS.)

IMPUTED INTEREST - An interest rate implied by law. Where an installment contract fails to state an interest rate or sets a rate unreasonably low, the IRS will impute or create interest at a prescribed rate percent per year (computed semiannually).

IMPUTED NOTICE - An agent's knowledge that is binding upon the principal because of the agency relationship between them. If, for example, the buyer's agent is notified of the seller's acceptance of the buyer's offer, the buyer could not thereafter withdraw the offer even though the buyer had not actual notice yet of the accepted contract.

Under the Real Estate Brokerage Relationships Act, unless agreed to in writing, a principal does not have knowledge or notice of any fact known by an agent unless actually known by the principal. However, the most common Purchase and Sale Agreements provide for a limited imputed knowledge as it pertains to notices. (*See* AGENCY, REAL ESTATE BROKERAGE RELATIONSHIPS ACT.)
Reference: 18.86.100

INACTIVE LICENSE - In Washington, a real estate licensee can place his/her license in an inactive status with the Real Estate Program of the Department of Licensing. During this time the licensee cannot transact any real estate business on behalf of anyone, including splitting fees with active licensees for referrals. The licensee must continue to pay license fees. If the license is inactive for more than three years. the licensee must show proof of successfully completing an approved thirty clock hour course in real estate prior to application for active status. (*See* LICENSING LAW.)

INCAPACITY TO CONTRACT - Certain classes of persons are prohibited by law from making contracts while they are under certain disabilities and with a few exceptions such contracts are void. (*See* CAPACITY OF PARTIES, INCOMPETENT, INFANT, MINOR.)

INCH (WATER MEASURE) - An inch, or miner's inch, is that amount of water which will flow through an orifice one inch square in a position vertical to the flow of water under a head specified either by custom or statute.

INCHOATE - Incomplete, imperfect, begun but not completed. In some states a wife's interest in the lands of her husband during his life is an inchoate dower interest. This right does not exist in Washington, which is a community property state. (*See* COMMUNITY PROPERTY.)

Also describes a mechanic's lien that has not yet been filed but will take effect when filed and is effective as of the date of the commencement of work.

INCLUSIONARY ZONING - A land-use concept in which local zoning ordinances require residential developers to include a certain percentage of dwelling units for low and moderate-income households as a condition to governmental approval of development of the project.

INCOME APPROACH - An approach to the valuation or appraisal of real property as determined by the amount of net income the property will produce over its remaining economic life. The four main steps in calculating the income approach to valuation requires one to:

1. Estimate the potential annual gross income, that is, the income that would accrue if all units were rented at their fair market value.

2. Determine the effective gross income by deducting an allowance for vacancy and collection loss.

3. Determine the annual net operating income by then deducting the annual expenses of the operation.

4. Apply the appropriate capitalization rate to the annual net operating income.

The most difficult step in this process is the application of the appropriate capitalization rate. This rate must be selected to reflect accurately the recapture of the original investment over the economic life of the improvement, give the investor an acceptable rate of return on his/her original investment, plus provide for the return of borrowed capital. Note that an income property that carries with it a great deal of risk will generally require a higher rate of return than a safe investment. The appraiser must use residual techniques to provide for the recapture of the investment in the improvement but not the land because land is not a wasting asset. The main advantage of using this approach is that its best approximates the expectations of the typical investor of commercial property who is looking for a money return on the investment. It is rarely used on single-family residential properties. (*See* APPRAISAL, BUILDING RESIDUAL TECHNIQUES, CAP RATE, ECONOMIC RENT, LAND RESIDUAL TECHNIQUE, PROPERTY RESIDUAL TECHNIQUES.)

INCOME PROPERTY - Property purchased primarily for the income to be derived plus certain tax benefits. Income property can be commercial, industrial or residential. (*See* INCOME APPROACH.)

INCOME TAXES - See BASIS, DEPRECIATION, PROPERTY TAX, RESIDENCE, TAX.

INCOMPETENT - A person who is not legally qualified to perform a valid act; one who lacks the power to act with legal effectiveness; any person who is impaired by reason of mental illness, physical disability, drugs, age, or other cause to the extent that he/she lacks sufficient understanding or capacity to make or communicate responsible decisions concerning his/her person. Thus, insane, and in certain cases, intoxicated people, are incapable of entering into valid contracts. A corporation not authorized by its articles of incorporation to purchase real property is incompetent to contract for the purchase of real estate. Similarly, an officer not so authorized by the board of directors is incompetent to sell corporate real estate. An illiterate person, however, is not incompetent to contract as long as he/she understands the nature of his/her acts. If a person is adjudged incompetent, the court will generally appoint a guardian to contract with all persons doing business with the incompetent. (*See* CAPACITY OF PARTIES, GUARDIAN, INFANT, MINOR.)

INCORPORATE - The act of forming a legal corporation by preparing the necessary articles of incorporation and filing them with the Office of the Secretary of State in Olympia. (*See* ARTICLES OF INCORPORATION, CORPORATION.)

INCORPORATION BY REFERENCE - A method of including all the terms of one document into another document merely by reference. For example, a Purchase and Sale Agreement may refer to an addendum or an exhibit and incorporate the terms of such addendum or exhibit to the same extent as if it were fully set forth. A short-form deed of trust, mortgage or lease may refer to a previously recorded lengthy document containing the many "boiler plate" provisions of the mortgage or lease transaction.

INCORPOREAL RIGHTS - Intangible or non-possessory rights in real property such as easements, licenses, profits and the like.

INCREMENT - An increase in quantity or size, commonly used to refer to the development of large subdivisions in phases or in "increments." (*See* UNEARNED INCREMENT.)

INCUBATOR SPACE - An industrial park building divided into small units of different sizes to accommodate newer, growing companies that want to combine office and industrial space at one location.

INCUMBRANCE - *See* ENCUMBRANCE.

INCURABLE OBSOLESCENCE - All items physically deteriorated are treated in an appraisal of real property as incurable if it appears to be not economically feasible or profitable to cure the deterioration on the date of the appraisal. If the depreciation is due to functional obsolescence, it is treated as incurable if it is not profitable to cure it. Economic obsolescence is generally incurable. (*See* APPRAISAL.)

INDEMNIFY - To reimburse or compensate someone for a loss already suffered by him/her. (*See* HOLD HARMLESS CLAUSE.)

INDENTURE DEED - A deed in which both grantor and grantee bind themselves to reciprocal obligations. Normally, a deed need only be signed by the grantor (called a "deed poll") but an indenture deed is signed by the grantee as well, who might thereby agree to assume or agree to special covenants. The word "indenture" stems from an ancient custom whereby deeds were made for each of the parties on the same sheepskin and then cut apart on an uneven line creating an "indented" agreement. They could later prove genuineness by matching up their indentures. Some leases to be signed by both lessor and lessee also begin with the words "This Indenture ..."

INDEPENDENT APPRAISAL - An estimate of value performed by a qualified, disinterested party. (*See* APPRAISAL.)

INDEPENDENT CONTRACTOR - One who is retained to perform a certain act, but who is subject to the control and direction of another only as to the end result and not as to how he/she performs the act. The critical feature, and what distinguishes an independent contractor and an employee or agent, is the degree of **control**. (*See* AGENCY.)

An employer, as defined or interpreted by the FICA and income tax laws, must withhold income tax and pay social security from commissions paid to an employee, but not to an independent contractor, who must personally pay FICA and taxes.

Almost all Washington brokers treat their salespeople as independent contractors and do not withhold federal taxes. Brokers should be aware, however, that it is not sufficient merely to label a salesperson as an "independent contractor" in a written agreement (incidentally, not to be entitled an "employment agreement").

Current Treasury regulations require three conditions for an independent contractor status to exist: (1) a written contract, (2) a real estate license, and (3) the salesperson is paid on the basis of performance, not the number of hours worked.

A person who hires an independent contractor is not usually liable for injuries caused by the negligence of the independent contractor. An employer, however, is liable for acts of his/her employees done within the scope of their employment. Thus, an employer would be liable for automobile accidents of employees while driving on their employer's business. In view of the complex issues involved in determining whether real estate salespeople are employees or independent contractors, most brokers carry liability insurance covering all their salespeople and office personnel. In addition, most brokers require their salespeople to name the broker as "also insured" on their personal automobile insurance policy.

Because Washington's licensing law makes the broker responsible for many of the activities of his/her salespeople, many brokers want to exercise a high degree of control over these activities. However, the Washington licensing law does not preclude the establishment of independent contractor status for tax purposes. (*See* SALESPERSON.)
Reference: IRS Revenue Rules 76-136, 76-137

INDEX LEASE - A lease that provides for adjustments of rent according to changes in a price index such as the consumer price index. (*See* CONSUMER PRICE INDEX, LEASE.)

INDEX RATE - The rate to which the interest rate on an adjustable rate loan is tied. At set adjustment periods, the borrower's interest rate will move up or down as the index rate changes. One of the most popular indices is the interest rate on one-year U.S. Treasury securities.

INDEX TO RECORDS OF TITLE - An index is one of the facilities to be used in making a search for a record. Its object is to point out the book and page in which a particular record may be found in the Office of the Clerk of Court or County Auditor. (*See* GRANTOR-GRANTEE INDEX.)

INDICATED VALUE - The worth of a subject property as shown by recent sales of comparable properties.

INDIRECT COSTS - Development costs not related to the land or structures, such as legal and architectural fees, financing, and insurance costs during construction.

INDIRECT LIGHTING - The light which is reflected from the ceiling or other object external to the fixture.

INDIVIDUAL RETIREMENT ACCOUNT (IRA) - A retirement savings program which an individual may institute if he/she is not covered under a qualified retirement plan or is self-employed (such as an independent contractor). For tax purposes, persons establishing and maintaining such accounts are allowed to deduct IRA contributions from their gross income up to a certain amount in each year they qualify. A person maintaining an IRA is, in effect, creating a tax-sheltered retirement fund, the contributions to and earnings of which are not taxable until retirement.

Real estate salespeople who are independent contractors and salespeople who are employees but not covered by a company retirement plan can set up their own IRA and deduct from their taxable income a maximum of $2,000 of their commission income or salary for contributions to their retirement account.

The Tax Reform Act of 1986 made dramatic changes in the deductibility of IRA contributions. The Act limits or eliminates deductions for IRA contributions by taxpayers who are active participants in an employer-provided retirement plan, with a phaseout of the deduction based on the taxpayer's adjusted gross income. Workers who are not covered by company-sponsored retirement plans may still deduct their IRA contributions, according to established limits. Taxpayers who cannot take an IRA deduction under the new rules may still make a nondeductible contribution of up to $2,000 annually, thus deferring income tax on the earnings of the IRA funds until withdrawal. (*See* KEOGH PLAN.)

INDORSEMENT - *See* ENDORSEMENT

INDUSTRIAL PARK - An area zoned industrial that contains sites for many separate industries and is developed and managed as a unit, usually with provisions for common services for the users; a relatively modern real estate concept which has proven very successful.

Typically, an industrial developer will acquire a large parcel of land, obtain industrial zoning, and bring in streets, water, sewer systems and utilities. Then he/she records a declaration of restrictions setting up a property owners' association and regulating setback lines, landscaping, architecture of buildings, etc. The developer might sell a site to a particular industry which will build its own plant, or the developer might build the plant and lease it to the industry. The advantage to the industry is that it avoids the headaches and costs of acquiring prepared industrial property and saves money by sharing common expenses for items such as sewer, security, utilities, and the like.

INFANT - In Washington, legally a person is an infant until he/she reaches the age of eighteen. A contract by an infant is not void but generally may be disaffirmed by the infant. An infant is legally incompetent to effect a sale, lease, or mortgage of his/her property. He/she may, however, act through his/her duly appointed guardian. If a guardian claims to act as a representative of an infant in real estate transactions, it is important to obtain proof of the guardian's authority to act in the particular instance. (*See* CAPACITY OF PARTIES, INCOMPETENT, MINOR.)

INFLATION GUARD - An endorsement to an insurance policy that automatically increases coverage during the life of the policy at a certain percentage at regular intervals, e.g, every six months or once a year.

INFORMED CONSENT - Consent to a certain act that is given after a full and fair disclosure of all facts needed to make a conscious choice. Licensing law requires that the broker obtain the consent of buyer and seller when the broker intends to act as their dual agent. A seller who signs a written consent to dual agency but later discovers that the broker concealed the facts that the buyer was the broker's relative, the property was underpriced or the buyer already had a resale buyer lined up, could allege that the consent was not fairly given. If successful, the seller could rescind the transaction based on an unlawful dual agency. (*See* DUAL AGENCY.)

INFRASTRUCTURE - The man-made physical features of an urban area such as roads, highways, sewage and drainage systems, and utility facilities necessary to support a concentration of the population.

INGRESS - A way to enter a property; access. The opposite of egress.

INHABITABLE - Being fit to live in. (*See* HABITABLE, IMPLIED WARRANTY OF HABITABILITY, LANDLORD TENANT ACT.)

IN-HOUSE SALE - Refers to a sale in which the listing salesperson and the selling salesperson in the transaction are both with the same real estate office and there is no outside salesperson involved as in a cooperative sale. Either the listing salesperson finds the buyer, or another salesperson working for the listing broker finds the buyer.

INITIALS - Abbreviation of a name. Initials are effective as a person's signature so long as the signer intends them to be equivalent to his/her legal signature.

Any changes made in a contract (such as in a Purchase and Sale Agreement) should be initialed by all parties and dated. A notary must initial all erasures to a document; otherwise, the document may not be accepted for recordation. A conservative approach to signing a lengthy document is to have all parties initial each page. (*See* LEGAL NAME, SIGNATURE.)

INJUNCTION - A legal action whereby a court issues a writ which forbids a party defendant from doing some act, or compels the defendant to perform an act; it requires a

person to whom it is directed to refrain from doing a particular thing. For example, if a person engages in the escrow business without being appropriately registered, the State's Department of Financial Institution can bring an action in a Superior Court seeking an injunction to cease the action.
Reference: RCW 18.84

INNOCENT MISREPRESENTATION - A misstatement of material fact given without any intent to deceive. (*See* MISREPRESENTATION.)

INNOCENT PURCHASER FOR VALUE - One who purchases real property without notice, actual or constructive, of any superior rights or interests in the real property. The recording statutes are designed to protect an innocent purchaser for value who first records from the secret claims of a prior purchaser. Also called a bona fide purchaser for value. (*See* POSSESSION, RECORDING.)

INQUIRY NOTICE - Legal notice which is presumed by law where there exist facts which would make a reasonable man inquire further. For example, if someone is in possession of property prior to closing, the purchaser is charged with knowledge of whatever an inspection of the property would have disclosed and would therefore take title subject to the rights of the occupant. (*See* ACTUAL NOTICE, CONSTRUCTIVE NOTICE, POSSESSION.)

INSIDE LOT - Any lot located between the corner lots on a given block.

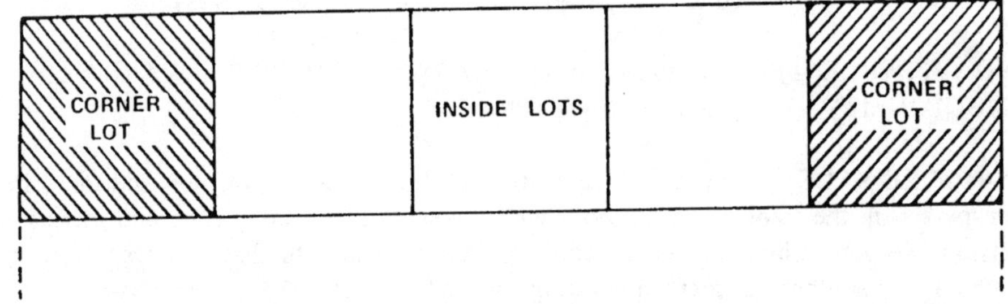

INSPECTION - A visit to and review of the premises. A prudent purchaser of property always inspects the premises during daylight hours before closing. Since possession of property gives constructive notice of any claims of ownership, an inspection is important to reveal any possible claims of others. An inspection might also reveal any encroachments or unrecorded easements. It is good practice for a broker to inspect the listed premises so he/she can be sure his/her representations to prospective buyers are accurate and not just exaggerations of the seller. (*See* INQUIRY NOTICE.)

Many brokers recommend inserting a clause in the Purchase and Sales Agreement to the effect that all appliances and electrical and plumbing fixtures will be in normal working order and shall be inspected by the buyer prior to closing. The buyer should make such an inspection within a few days before the closing. If such a clause is inserted in the contract when the transaction is to be closed in escrow, the escrow company will not close until it has received an inspection approval letter from the buyer. Both the VA and FHA require inspections to insure that a buyer does not have to make major repairs in the first year of occupancy (roof, wiring). However, the buyer receives only an assurance and **not a guarantee**. The VA permits a buyer to pay for any inspection costs and a seller should be aware that he/she might have to make repairs prior to VA approval. (*See* FEDERAL HOUSING ADMINISTRATION, VA MORTGAGE.)

A title insurance company issuing an owner's extended policy may have one of its inspectors search for easements not shown in the public records, building restrictions, and improvements not within the stated lot lines. (*See* ALTA EXTENDED COVERAGE.)

Except in cases of abandonment or emergency, a landlord has no legal right to enter a tenant's dwelling without a court order, arbitrator's award, or consent of the tenant. Unless it is impractical to do so (e.g., emergency), a landlord must give a tenant two days advance notice before entering a dwelling unit. The tenant must not unreasonably refuse to allow the landlord access to the dwelling for legitimate purposes. Legitimate purposes for entrance by the landlords to a dwelling are: (1) to inspect the premises; (2) make necessary or agreed repairs, alterations, or improvements; (3) supply necessary agreed services; or (4) exhibit the dwelling unit to prospective or actual purchasers, mortgagees, tenants, workmen, or contractors. (*See* LANDLORD TENANT ACT.)
Reference: RCW 59.18

Often a purchaser will make an offer on a commercial-investment improved property without having had an opportunity to inspect the complete facility. So the broker or salesperson preparing the Purchaser and Sale Agreement inserts a clause (contingency) to the effect that the purchaser has a right to inspect the complete facility, unit by unit, prior to closing. If such a clause is inserted in the E/M, the escrow company should not close the transaction until it has received an inspection approval letter from the buyer.

Due to the legal liability imposed on real estate licensees by courts for failure to adequately point out structural problems in residences that they have sold in the early 1980s, a growing number of brokers instructed their salespeople to insert an inspection provision in all Purchase and Sales Agreements. The inclusion of a physical inspection contingency is now standard practice in Washington.

INSTALLMENT METHOD OF REPORTING INCOME - An exception to the cash or accrual method of reporting income is the installment method. The Internal Revenue Code permits return of income from the sale or other disposition of real property, with certain limitation, to be structured so the installment method can be used by a seller. (*See* ACCRUAL METHOD, CASH METHOD, INSTALLMENT SALE.)

INSTALLMENT NOTE - A promissory note providing for payments in two or more definite stated amounts at different times. (*See* INSTALLMENT SALE.)

INSTALLMENT SALE - An income tax method of reporting income received from the sale of real estate where the sales price is paid in installments, i.e., where at least one payment is to be received after the close of the taxable year in which the sale occurs. No down payment is required. Section 453 of the Internal Revenue Code no longer requires there be two installments of principal; i.e., the buyer could make a down payment of prepaid interest only, and a balloon payment of principal in a later year. If the seller provides any financing, it is an installment sale. Some or all of the purchase price must be paid in a year(s) subsequent to the tax year of the sale.

If certain conditions are met, the taxpayer can postpone reporting income to future years when other income may be lower and thus lessen the tax bite. In short, a taxpayer can avoid paying the entire tax in the year of sale. In addition to cash received, the "sales price" includes the fair market value of any property received from the buyer, notes, and any existing mortgage on the property whether or not assumed by the buyer. The year of the sale is the tax reporting year of the seller and the date of the sale is the date of transfer of title to the property or possession under a real estate contract.

Money received in the year of sale includes option money even if paid in a prior year, down payment, payment of seller's indebtedness, excess of mortgage over basis, and subsequent principal payments. Mortgages assumed by buyer are not normally included in computing payments in the year of sale. However, if the amount of the mortgage exceeds the seller's basis in the property, the excess is treated as payment in the year of sale.

Reportable income from a sale only includes money paid on the purchase price of property. Interest is not a payment made on the purchase price but a payment made in consideration of the right to defer all or part of such payment. Interest, of course, is fully taxable as ordinary income.

Because the seller can defer all or a substantial part of his/her gain until he/she actually receives the unpaid balance of the purchase price, he/she can accept a small cash down payment thus expanding the market of potential buyers. He/she may also be in a position to negotiate for a higher sales price. In addition, the seller pays only a tax on a portion of each installment payment; that portion that represents the return of his/her capital investment (his/her basis) is not taxable, only that portion of principal that represents gain is taxable. The seller thus retains a larger amount of each payment, which he/she can use for further investments.

For example, assume a property is sold for $105,000 by a seller who has owned the property for 18 months or longer. The buyer pays $20,000 down and gives the seller a purchase money note for $85,000 payable at 10 percent over 10 years. The seller's basis in the property is $50,000 and he/she incurs selling expenses of $5,000. The seller's gain from this transaction is calculated as follows:

Gross selling price:	$105,000
Less selling expenses:	5,000
Net selling price:	$100,000
Less adjusted basis:	50,000
Gain:	$50,000

The seller's taxable gain under the installment method is computed as follows:

Gain:	$50,000	
		= 48 percent
Gross selling price:	105,000	

In the year of sale the seller would pay a capital gain tax on 48 percent of $20,000 (the down payment) or $9,600. Assuming an effective capital gain rate of 20 percent there would be due a tax of $1,920.

In each subsequent year he/she will pay a capital gain tax on 48 percent of the principal amounts received (approximately 48 percent of $8,500 or $4,080). If the entire tax had been paid in the year of sale, it would have been approximately $12,500.

Sellers should receive competent tax advice if they contemplate taking advantage of the tax deferring benefits of installment sale reporting.

A seller may elect to report the total gain in the year of the sale and pay taxes due on the total gain.

If the gain in the year of the sale is a long-term capital gain, the gain in later years is also long term; short term treatment in the year of sale applies also to later years. Interest payments received on the deferred sale installments are reported with your other interest income.

If the seller makes an installment sale of depreciable property, any depreciation recapture is reported as income in the year of disposition.

Generally, dealers must report gain in the year of sale for real estate held for resale to customers sold on an installment plan. However, the installment method may be used by dealers of certain time shares (generally time shares of up to six weeks per year) and a limited number of residential lots, but only if an election is made to pay interest on the tax deferred by using the installment method.

A taxpayer cannot report a loss on the installment method.

The Installment Sales Revision Act of 1980 eliminated the long-standing requirement that no more than 30 percent of the selling price from a sale of realty could be received in the tax year of the sale. Also, the IRS rule that the installment method was available only for a sale that involved payments in at least two tax years has also been eliminated. Now, a lump-sum payment received in the year following the sale or in a later year can qualify for the installment method of reporting gain.

Since 1980, the I.R.C makes the installment method of reporting automatic for sales of real property unless the taxpayer elects to the contrary. An election for non-installment treatment is to be made on or before the due date of the return (including extensions) for the tax year of sale. It is made by reporting the entire gain for the tax year of sale. An election to report on the installment basis is no longer required; it is now automatic.

Under the 1986 Tax Reform Act installment gain treatment is limited by the "proportional disallowance rule" based on the ratio of the taxpayer's overall debts to assets. The reason for this limitation is that the IRS does not want to allow taxpayers to defer gain by using the installment method to the extent that they are concurrently receiving cash from borrowings. The rule applies to installment sales of (1) property held for sale to customers, and (2) real property used in a trade or business or held for the production of rental income with a sales price exceeding $150,000. It does not apply to installment sales of personal use property and certain farm property.

The amount that is "proportionately disallowed" in a particular year is called Allocable Installment Indebtedness (AII). AII is considered a payment received on the installment notes held by the taxpayer and is calculated as follows:

$$AII = \frac{\text{Amt. of installment note} \times \text{Taxpayer's average quarterly indebtedness}}{\text{Adjusted basis of taxpayer's assets including the installment note}}$$

All types of indebtedness are covered, including bank loans, accounts payable, and accrued expenses. AII is adjusted to reflect actual payments received on the note, which will not result in recognition of additional gain.

Installment sale treatment may be denied for transactions in which the proportionate disallowance rule would otherwise be avoided by using related parties, pass-through entities, or intermediaries. (*See* BASIS, IMPUTED INTEREST, REAL ESTATE CONTRACT.)

INSTITUTE OF REAL ESTATE MANAGEMENT (IREM) - A national organization established to promote and encourage professionalism in real estate property management. IREM sponsors various education programs, publishes and distributes numerous publications and awards three professional designations: (1) Certified Property Manager (CPM), (2) Accredited Resident Manager (ARM), and (3) Accredited Management Organization (AMO).

INSTITUTIONAL LENDER - Financial institutions such as banks, insurance companies, savings and loans or any lending institutions whose loans are regulated by law. Such institutions invest depositors' and customers' money in mortgages, as contrasted with private lenders such as pension and trust funds which invest their own funds. Institutional lenders are frequently represented by mortgage brokers who act as loan correspondents for out-of-state institutional lenders. Because they are actually lending other people's money, institutional lenders are heavily regulated by the government.

For years life insurance companies ranked first among institutional lenders for total mortgage investments. However, savings banks and savings and loan associations have closed the gap. Savings and loan associations usually lend on 1 to 4 family buildings; life insurance companies are big lenders on multifamily structures and life insurance companies and commercial banks lend heavily on commercial properties.

INSTRUMENT - A formal legal document such as a contract, deed, or will. The term document is a more comprehensive term referring to any paper relied upon as the basis, proof, or support of anything else. (*See* STATUTE OF FRAUDS.)

INSULATION - Pieces of plasterboard, compressed wood-wool, fiberboard, or other material placed between inner and outer surfaces, such as walls and ceilings, to protect the interior from heat loss. Insulation works by breaking up and dissipating air currents.

INSULATION DISCLOSURE - The Federal Trade Commission requires that real estate brokers, builders and sellers of **new** houses must disclose in their sales contracts the type, thickness and R-value of the insulation installed in the house. In addition, brokers are required to show the required facts in all listing agreements and Purchase and Sales Agreements.

INSURABLE INTEREST - A right or an interest in property of such a nature that the occurrence of the event insured against would cause financial loss to the insured. Such interests, for example, may be that of an owner, a mortgagee, a lessee, or a trustee. To collect damages from an insurance policy, one must be able to prove an insurable interest at the time of loss. (*See* INSURANCE.)

INSURABLE TITLE - A title on which a title insuring company is willing to issue its policy of insurance. (*See* TITLE INSURANCE.)

INSURANCE - Indemnification against loss from a specific hazard or peril. There are many kinds of insurance available to cover property or liability against various risks.

Fundamentally, insurance may be written on objects such as buildings, contents of buildings, and equipment. Or it may be written to cover activities such as loss of income resulting from damage or some other unforeseen happening. Insurance can also be obtained to cover the insured's legal liability to other people. Note that when a building is insured under an insurance policy, it is insured against specific risks, such as fire, windstorm, and explosion. All risk-coverage is available under some circumstances so that one policy provides complete coverage for the owner in the event that the insured object is damaged. Property and liability insurance policies are personal contracts made by an insurer with a particular insured person. Such policies, therefore, do not run with the land and cannot be assigned without the consent of the insurer. If a loss occurs, however, the right to the insurance proceeds may be assigned. When a loss of property does occur, the policy may be reduced by the amount of the loss. An additional premium is then required to reinstate the policy back to the full amount of insurance.

Most insurance policies contain a pro rata liability clause which usually provides "that the insurer is not liable for a greater portion of any loss than the amount insured against bears to the total insurance carried on the property against the peril involved, whether collectible or not." This prevents the owner from collecting a greater amount than the actual loss by carrying policies with several insurance carriers.

Public liability insurance covers the risk which an owner assumes when the public may enter his/her building. A situation that might be covered by such a liability policy would be a claim made for hospital expenses and doctor's bills submitted by a person who was injured in a building and claimed that the injury was due to the landlord's negligence in not properly maintaining the stairs. These policies are usually referred to as owners', landlords', and tenants' liability insurance.

When a claim is made under a policy that insures a building or other physical object, there may be two possible methods of determining the amount of the claim. One is based on the depreciated value, or actual cash value, of the damaged property, and the other is based on the replacement cost. If a part of a thirty-year-old building is damaged, the timbers and the materials are thirty years old and therefore do not have the same value as new material. In determining the amount of the loss according to actual cash value, the cost of new material would be obtained, and this would be reduced by the estimated depreciation which the item had suffered during the time it had been in the building. The alternate method is to cover replacement cost. This would represent the actual amount a builder would charge to replace the damaged property at the time of the loss.

Insurance rates are set by rating bureaus which are supervised by state authorities. Under this system, the cost of the risk of possible damage is spread over all properties in the state by the establishment of a premium rate based upon the losses experienced during the past year or several years for the risk involved. Rates are revised by underwriting bureaus and are kept current in accordance with the loss ratio and cost of repairing the damage.

If a person owned a $1 million building and thought the building was in such fine condition and so well protected and cared for that it would be impossible to suffer a loss for more than $100,000, he/she might decide to buy a policy for $100,000. The building is underinsured since the policy on a commercial building will include what is called a coinsurance clause. This clause requires that in the event of loss, the total insurance carried on the building must equal the stated percentage of the value of the insured building. The penalty for not carrying the proper amount of insurance is a reduction in the amount of the claim which the insurance company is required to pay. For instance, most commercial properties include an 80 percent coinsurance clause. If the building owner carries the proper amount of insurance at the time of loss, his/her claim will be paid in full to the limit of the amount of the policy. Residential insurance policies also contain a coinsurance clause. The purpose of a coinsurance clause is to require the insured to carry the proper amount of insurance so that he/she will pay an adequate premium for this coverage.

In order to obtain hazard insurance, one must have an insurable interest in the property. Both vendor and vendee have an insurable interest in property sold under a real estate contract. Most real estate contracts require that the buyer maintain insurance to a stated amount and make the loss payable to the seller. If the Purchase and Sale Agreement provides for the assignment and proration of the seller's insurance policy, the transfer should be made at the closing. The seller then signs a form called an assignment of policy. This form is not effective until it has been accepted by the insurance company or by its authorized agent. (*See* COINSURANCE.)

INTER VIVOS TRUST - A trust which takes effect during the life of the creator, as opposed to a testamentary trust, which does not take place until the death of the creator. Inter vivos transfers are those made between living persons (for example, deeds and leases).

The inter vivos trust is frequently utilized to allow the trustee to provide investment services where the trustor is unsophisticated or unwilling to administer his/her assets or as a vehicle for a trustor to dispose of insurance proceeds, pension benefits and his/her estate ("pour-over trust"), this latter being a way to avoid probate proceedings. (*See* ESTATE TAX, GIFT TAX.)

INTEREST - The sum paid or accrued in return for the use of money. Interest is usually stated in terms of an annual rate, although the parties may not always call this payment "interest" since it may be disguised in the form of points or a prepayment penalties. Interest on a promissory note is usually charged and due in arrears, at the end of each payment period (monthly, semiannually, etc.) Interest payments are deductible for income tax purposes with certain restrictions.

Interest rates are quoted for a one-year period. This annual interest amount is divided by 12 to find the interest due for one month. A shortcut to finding a month's interest charge is to multiply the principal balance of the loan by the interest factor show in the following table:

INTEREST FACTOR TABLE

RATE(%)	FACTOR	RATE(%)	FACTOR
8 %	.66667	9 1/4%	.777083
8 1/4%	.68750	9 1/2%	.79167
8 1/2%	.70833	9 3/4%	.81251
8 3/4%	.72917	10 %	.83333
9 %	.75000	10 1/4%	.85417

Interest payments on principal residences and second, or vacation, homes are fully deductible as long as the debt does not exceed the original cost of the residence plus the cost of improvements. Interest paid on amounts borrowed against the appreciated equity in first or second homes is deductible only if the borrowed amount is used for educational or medical expenses or for home improvement.

Note that there is a difference between nominal interest, the amount (percentage) an annual interest stated in the loan document, and effective interest, the amount of interest the borrower actually pays. The difference usually results from the manner in which the debt is collected, such as the use of discount points to increase the gross rate or principal plus interest (add-on) methods. In addition, see the explanation under **TRUTH-IN-LENDING LAWS** for the difference between interest and the annual percentage rate. (*See* ACCRUAL METHOD, BLOCK INTEREST, BUY DOWNS, COMPOUND INTEREST, IMPUTED INTEREST, POINTS, PREPAID INTEREST, USURY.)

INTEREST IN PROPERTY - A legal share of ownership in property, whether the entire ownership, as in a fee simple interest, or partial ownership, as in a leasehold estate.

INTEREST RATE CAP - The maximum interest rate charge allowed on an adjustable rate loan for any one adjustment period during the life of the loan. In addition, the loan may have a lifetime cap on interest.

INTERIM FINANCING - A short-term loan usually made during the construction phase of a building project; often referred to as a construction loan. The proceeds from the interim loan are disbursed in increments as the construction progresses. Long-term or permanent financing is usually arranged to "take out" the interim loan. (*See* CONSTRUCTION LOAN, TAKEOUT FINANCING.)

INTERLOCUTORY DECREE - A judicial order that does not take final effect until a specified time or the occurrence of a certain event. Besides divorce decrees, which often have a bearing on the division of real property, condemnation actions also frequently involve interlocutory decrees.

INTERNAL RATE OF RETURN (IRR) - A rate of discount at which the present worth of future cash flows is exactly equal to the initial capital investment. Also called discounted cash flow. An investor in real estate or any other investment is interested in two factors when analyzing a potential investment: the return of the original invested capital and a return on the original investment. Usually this return on investments is expressed as an annual return, or yield. The internal rate of return is a sophisticated mathematical measurement which, in the last few years since its inclusion in the Realtors® National Marketing Institute commercial investment courses, has seen a growing popularity. The advantages of the use of the internal rate of return as a measurement of an investment's worth is that all types of investments, stocks, bonds, real estate, and business ventures can be analyzed so they can be compared in an objective manner. Internal rate of return is calculated on the basis of the projected cash flows from the initial investment.

Although the internal rate of return is becoming more and more widely used, it does present some problems. The primary one does not directly relate to the validity of the IRR but probably presents the greatest difficulty — it is that most real estate sales personnel and investors do not understand what it entails. The particular problem with the use of the IRR mathematical formula is that it requires the assumption that the investments being analyzed have similar risk factors, and the projected cash flows used as measurements are only as good as the person preparing the projections.. (*See* INWOOD TABLES, PRESENT VALUE OF ONE DOLLAR.)

INTERNAL REVENUE CODE (IRC) - The body of statutes codifying the federal tax laws and administered by the Internal Revenue Service (IRS), an agency which issues its own regulations interpreting those laws.

INTERNATIONAL COUNCIL OF SHOPPING CENTERS (ICSC) - A trade organization of shopping center owners, managers and major tenants that functions as a medium for the interchange of information about shopping center practices and operations.

INTERNATIONAL REAL ESTATE FEDERATION - *See* FIABCI.

INTERPLEADER - A legal proceeding whereby an innocent third party (stakeholder) can deposit property or money which he/she holds and which is subject to adverse claims with the court so that the court can distribute it to the rightful claimant.

The distribution of an earnest money deposit held in escrow is often a problem when the buyer and seller are in dispute over the purchase contract. The escrow agent will not release the funds until all of the parties, including the broker, sign a cancellation of escrow form. When one of the parties refuses to cancel the escrow, and the escrow agent cannot get the parties to agree on the disposition of the deposit money, the only recourse for the escrow agent is to file an interpleader action asking the court to accept the money and distribute it to the rightful claimant. Under such circumstances, escrow agents strongly urge the parties to compromise because the total costs of the interpleader action incurred by both parties often exceeds the amount of the deposit; thus nobody gets any money. When the broker is holding the earnest money, he/she may originate the interpleader. (*See* ESCROW.)

INTERSTATE LAND SALES - The Interstate Land Sales Full Disclosure Act is a federal law, enacted in 1968, which regulates interstate land sales by requiring registration of real property with the Office of Interstate Land Sales Registration (OILSR) of the United States Department of Housing and Urban Development (HUD). The main purpose of the act is to require disclosure of full and accurate information regarding the property to prospective buyers before they decide to buy. To comply with the act, the developer must prepare a statement of record and register the subdivision with HUD. After the registration is effective, the developer must deliver to the purchaser (and obtain a receipt for) the property report prior to execution of the purchase agreement. The developer must give prospective buyers a cooling-off period of three business days (formerly forty-eight hours) to consider the material contained in the property report. Some larger Washington subdivisions are registered with HUD because HUD regulations apply if the developer uses the mails or any other means of interstate commerce in the sale of lots.

There is an intrastate exemption to the regulations of this act that is limited in scope and very narrowly construed. If the subdivision contains fewer than 300 lots which are offered and advertised only to residents of the state in which the subdivision is located (leeway is given so that 5 percent or less of sales in any one year may be made to residents of another state), the subdivider may apply for the exemption.

Some of the more common exemptions from HUD filing requirements are:

1. Subdivisions in which there are fewer than 50 lots;

2. Subdivisions in which all the lots are five acres or more in size;

3. Subdivisions in which a lot is improved with a building or in which there is a contract obligating the seller to erect such a building within a period of two years;

4. Subdivisions in which the lots are free and clear of all liens and encumbrances (HUD interprets this to include covenants, conditions, and restrictions of record) at the time of the sale and the purchaser has personally inspected the property.

It should be noted that condominium units are considered by HUD to be lots "in the sky," and thus the developer may have to register a condominium with HUD. The risk of noncompliance is greatest in those larger projects in which the developer is building in separate increments but promotes the use of common facilities which may not be completed for more than two years (such as a golf course).

A developer need not register with HUD a condominium in which each unit has been completed prior to sale. In this regard, completed means habitable and ready for occupancy. The developer can also avoid registration (and thus not be required to furnish buyers with a property report) if the unit is sold under a contract that obligates the seller to complete construction of the development within two years following the sale, as long as construction is not delayed by conditions beyond the developer's control. Also, the developer does not have to give a prospective buyer a HUD property report before the buyer signs a reservation but only before he/she signs a contract to buy.

Note that even though a particular subdivider or subdivision may be exempt from registration under the law, it is still unlawful to make false statements regarding such sales by means of interstate commerce. (*See* PROPERTY REPORT, STATEMENT OF RECORD, WASHINGTON LAND DEVELOPMENT ACT.)

INTERVAL OWNERSHIP - A popular system of timeshare ownership in which the owner acquires title to a specific unit for a certain week or weeks of every year. (*See* TIMESHARING.)

INTESTATE - To die without a will or with a will which is defective in form. The decedent's property passes to his/her heirs according to the priorities set forth under the laws of descent. These laws of descent vary from state to state, and determine who is entitled to the decedent's property which passes through probate; descent laws do not affect the distribution of jointly held property or life insurance proceeds.

If the decedent was single, all the property passes to the parents equally or to the surviving parent if only one parent is alive. If no parents are surviving, then it passes equally to the brothers and sisters. If the decedent was married with no children, half of the property passes to the surviving spouse, and half passes equally to the parents or the surviving parent. If no parents are surviving, then half passes equally to the brothers and sisters. If the decedent is married with children, then the wife receives all the community property and the wife and children will share equally in the decedent's separate property. (*See* DESCENT, WILL.)
Reference: RCW 11.04.

INTRASTATE EXEMPTION - A security offering which is exempt from federal registration requirements because it is part of an issue offered and sold only to residents of one particular state, where the issuer of the security is a resident of and doing business within that state, or if a corporation, is incorporated by and doing business within that state. Though exempt from the burdensome registration requirements of the Securities and Exchange Commission, the intrastate offering is still subject to the full-disclosure and antifraud provisions of the Securities Act of 1933. The intrastate exemption is strictly construed and enforced. If one sale or resale is made to a nonresident, the exemption will be lost; the issuer will then have to register the entire issue and offer rescission rights to prior purchasers. (*See* PRIVATE OFFERING, REAL PROPERTY SECURITIES REGISTRATION, RULE 147.)

INTRINSIC VALUE - The result of a person's individual choices and preferences for a given geographical area based on the features and amenities the area has to offer. For example, to most people, property located in a well-kept suburb near a shopping center would have a greater intrinsic value than similar property located near a sewage treatment plant. As a rule, the greater the intrinsic value, the more money a property can command upon its sale. Most land speculation is based on this principle of present versus future intrinsic value. What was a suburban site a few years ago could very well be in a booming community in the future, and it is the wise investor who knows how to spot, buy, and sell such speculative properties at the most advantageous times.

INVENTORY - An itemized list of property. Many brokers recommend that their clients attach to the listing contract or Purchase and Sale Agreement an inventory of personal property to be included in the sale of a residential property, including a condominium dwelling. Such a procedure lessens misunderstandings as to what items in the seller's home will pass to the buyer with the sale. Of course, an inventory should definitely be included in the sale of income producing property such as a furnished apartment building, and the agent should verify the inventory. (*See* BULK SALES, DEALER.)

INVERSE CONDEMNATION - An action for just compensation brought by a person whose property has been effectively taken, substantially interfered with, or taken without just compensation by the government. For example, when a governmental authority announces it will condemn an owner's property and then unduly delays in taking the property, the owner can bring legal action to force a condemnation and payment in the taking. Or, if the noise of low flying aircraft damages the owner in the use of the land, there may be inverse condemnation, or a taking of property for which compensation must be paid. It is referred to as inverse condemnation because it is started by an owner who seeks compensation from the condemning agency. (*See* CONDEMNATION.)

Courts have held that a zoning action which merely decreases the market value of property does not constitute a compensable taking actionable under a theory of inverse condemnation as long as a reasonably viable economic use exists. An inverse condemnation suit is not available before there has been an actual taking or physical interference with the subject property.

Inverse condemnation is the flip side of eminent domain. It occurs when a public entity directly "condemns" private property by acting (e.g., a restrictive use regulation like down zoning), or failing to act when it should have, and property loss or damage results. It is irrelevant whether the act or failure to act was negligent. The taking is not by legal action, but by inverse condemnation conduct.

INVESTMENT CONTRACT - A contract, transaction, or scheme whereby a person invests money in a common enterprise and is led to expect profits solely from the efforts of the promoter or a third party. The sale of real property using "investments contracts" is deemed to be the sale of a security thus requiring compliances with federal and state securities laws. (*See* REAL PROPERTY SECURITIES REGISTRATION.)

INVESTMENT INTEREST - The amount of interest incurred to purchase or carry investment property. This does not include interest incurred in the financing of a residence or passive activity interest. Investment property includes that producing income defined as interest, dividends, annuities, or royalties, and any trade or business in which the taxpayer does not materially participate, so long as that activity is not treated as a passive activity. Investment interest is deductible to the amount of the investment income.

INVOLUNTARY CONVERSION - A tax term referring to a loss through destruction or condemnation of property. In the event that property has been condemned and the owner replaces the property, the basis in the replacement property is deemed to be the same as that which is replaced, except that it is increased by any debt assumed above the amount of the condemnation award, and gain is recognized to the extent that the award exceeds the price paid for the replacement property.

In case of involuntary conversion the taxpayer may elect to postpone tax on the full gain provided he/she invests the proceeds in replacement property the cost of which is equal to or exceeds the net proceeds from the conversion. The replacement period for personal-use property is two years; for business and investment property it is two or three years depending on the type of involuntary conversion; for a residence and its contents involuntarily converted due to a Presidentially declared disaster it is four years. If the taxpayer finds that he/she cannot buy a replacement by the end of the period, an extension may be requested from the I.R.S.

INVOLUNTARY LIEN - A charge or claim against real property imposed by the operation of law, such as a lien for delinquent taxes, a mechanic's lien or a judgment.

INWOOD TABLES - A set of interest tables widely used by appraisers before the popularity of calculators or computers in computing the present value of an annuity for a number of years at various interest rates. Among its many uses, it enables an appraiser to estimate the value of a leasehold interest when the income stream (cash flow) is constant. Also referred to as the Inwood coefficient.

The principle underlying the system is that a series of equal annual payments to be made in the future is not an annuity's present worth. The annuity is worth only that amount which, if deposited today at a fixed rate of interest compounded annually, would provide for the withdrawal at the end of the year of an amount equal to one annual payment. (*See* INTERNAL RATE OF RETURN, PRESENT VALUE OF ONE DOLLAR.)

IRONCLAD AGREEMENT - An agreement that cannot be broken by the parties to it.

IRREVOCABLE - Not capable of being changed.

IRRIGATION DISTRICTS - Quasi-political districts created under special state laws to provide water services to property owners in the district and given the power to levy assessments to finance its operations.

J

JALOUSIES - Adjustable glass louvers in doors or windows used to regulate light and air or exclude rain.

JAMB - A vertical surface lining the opening in the wall left for a door or window.

JERRY RIGGED OR BUILT - A slang expression implying construction of all or a portion of the improvements is of an inferior workmanship or quality. Also known as/ derived from "jury rigged," a nautical term.

JOINT - In construction, this term means the point that two objects or surfaces join or meet.

JOINT AND SEVERAL LIABILITY - A situation in which more than one party is liable to repay a debt or obligation and a creditor can obtain compensation from one or more parties, either individually or jointly, whichever he/she chooses. Partners are jointly and severally liable for partnership debts and obligations, as are grantee and grantor for any unpaid common expenses in the sale of a condominium unit. Employees, affiliates, and agents of a subdivider violating the Washington Land Development Act may be liable jointly and severally and to the same extent as the subdivider. There is normally a right of contribution among persons held jointly and severally liable so that the person who is actually forced to repay the debt can collect equal amounts from the others who also are liable, if they have the resources to pay. (*See* RIGHT OF CONTRIBUTION, WASHINGTON LAND DEVELOPMENT ACT.)

JOINT TENANCY - A form of property ownership. An estate or unit of interest in real estate that is owned by two or more natural persons with rights of survivorship. Only one title exists, and it is vested in two or more persons, all owning equal shares. Four unities are required to create a joint tenancy: unity of title, unity of time, unity of interest, and unity of possession. Unless all four of the unities are present, a joint tenancy is not created. Such unities are present when title is acquired by one deed, executed and delivered at one time, and conveying equal interests to all the grantees who hold undivided possession of the property as joint tenants. A joint tenancy can be created only by grant or purchase (by a deed of conveyance), or by devise (will) — it cannot be created by operation of law. The grantees or devisees must be specifically named as joint tenants.

A distinctive feature of the joint tenancy is the right of survivorship by which the surviving joint tenant(s) succeeds equally to the interest of the deceased joint tenant. The death of one of the joint tenants does not destroy the owning unit, it only reduces by one the number of persons who jointly own the unit. No formal probate proceedings are necessary. Where there are two joint tenants and one dies, the survivor takes no new title but rather holds the entire estate under the original grant of title. Where there are more than two joint tenants and one dies, the survivors continue to own the property in equal undivided interests. When the last surviving joint tenant dies, the property passes to his/her heirs. A corporation cannot be a joint tenant since a corporation has perpetual existence and, at least in legal theory, never dies.

A joint tenancy may be severed or terminated by:

1. Mutual agreement of the joint tenants.

2. Bankruptcy of a joint tenant.

3. Conveyance of a joint tenant's interest, since this destroys the unities of title and time. Thus, if Joe and Harry own a property as joint tenants and Joe sells his interest to Bill, the joint tenancy is severed and Bill and Harry now own an undivided one-half interest in the property as tenants in common. The conveyance severs the survivorship rights so that the grantee is a tenant in common free of the survivorship rights in the other cotenants. If Joe, Harry and Dick owned the property as joint tenants and Joe sold his interest to Bill, then Bill would own an undivided one-third interest as a tenant in common with Harry and Dick; Harry and Dick would own the remaining two-thirds as joint tenants.

One of the principal advantages of joint tenancy is avoidance of the delay and expense of probate proceedings since the surviving joint tenant immediately becomes the sole owner of the property. Thus the current value of the property is not included in the total value of the estate on which probate fees are assessed. In addition, the survivor holds the property free from debts of the deceased joint tenant and from heirs against his/her interest.

These advantages should be weighed against the fact that the savings in probate fees are partly offset by legal costs of terminating the joint tenancy of record, and may be totally offset by the added taxes. Typically, the probate delay is not unreasonably long. There sometimes have to be probate proceedings anyway to cover the furnishings and personal property of the deceased which is normally not held in joint tenancy. In addition, the joint tenant gives up his/her right to dispose of his/her interest by will and, as a result, precludes the use of estate planning procedures to minimize the effect of death taxes. These death taxes can be substantial since the value of the jointly held property is included in the decedent's estate for estate tax purposes even though it doesn't pass through probate proceedings. In fact, the federal estate tax is applied to the entire value of all jointly held property, not the original cost, except to the extent that the surviving joint tenant can provide detailed records clearly proving the extent of his/her contribution (Reference Section 2040, IRC). Joint tenancies are subject to gift taxes, income taxes, and inheritance taxes in addition to federal estate taxes.

The prudent purchaser will discuss these tax consequences with experienced tax counsel before deciding whether to hold title to the property in joint tenancy. The prudent real estate licensee will not recommend any specific type of ownership form to any purchaser(s). If there is a recommendation and a problem arises, the licensee may be sued for the unauthorized practice of law. If a purchaser(s) requests a recommendation, refer the purchaser(s) to an attorney. Under Washington law, a joint tenancy must be specifically described or the intention to create a joint tenancy be manifestly apparent. If it is not, then the conveyance is construed to create a tenancy in common.

Upon the death of a joint tenant, the survivor(s) should, as a matter of good title practice, record an affidavit of death and a death certificate in the Office of the County Auditor in all counties where property was held in joint tenancy. (*See* COTENANCY, GIFT TAX, INHERITANCE TAX, PROBATE, PROPERTY TAX, SEVERANCE, STRAW MAN, TENANCIES, UNDIVIDED INTERESTS, UNITY.)

JOINT TENANTS - Those holding joint tenancy. (*See* JOINT TENANCY.)

JOINT VENTURE - The joining of two or more people in a specific business enterprise such as the development of a condominium project or a shopping center. It is necessary that there be an agreement, express or implied, to share in the losses or profits of the venture. Joint ventures are a business form similar to partnerships and they are treated as partnerships for tax purposes. The main difference between the two is that a joint venture is a special joining of the parties for one specific project with no intention on the part of the parties to enter into any continuing partnership relationship. If the joint parties combine their efforts on several different projects, the relationship becomes more like a general partnership than a joint venture. (*See* LIMITED PARTNERSHIP, PARTNERSHIP.)

JOINTURE - A form of property ownership which does not exist in the State of Washington.

JOIST - A heavy piece of horizontal timber, to which the boards of a floor, or the lath of a ceiling, are nailed. Joists are laid edgewise to form the floor support.

JUDGMENT - The formal decision of a court of law concerning the respective rights and claims of the parties to an action or suit. In Washington, a judgment includes a decree and any order from which an appeal lies. After a judgment has been entered and recorded in the Office of the Clerk of Court, it becomes a general lien on the property of the defendant. It is a general lien only in the county where the judgment is rendered unless a copy of the decree is filed with another county clerk. (*See* EXECUTION.)

If an individual has no assets, he/she is sometimes referred to as "judgment proof," which means it makes no financial sense to sue the person. Under the Real Estate Brokerage Relationship Act adopted in 1997, the theory of vicarious liability on the part of a principal was greatly limited; however, if the agent or subagent responsible for the act giving rise to a lawsuit is not able to pay a judgment and the principal benefited from the act, then there may be vicarious liability and the principal can be sued.
Reference: RCW 18.86.

JUDGMENT LIEN - A purely statutory general lien binding on all the real estate of a judgment-debtor and giving the holder of the judgment a right to levy (e.g., seize) the land for satisfaction of his/her judgment. (*See* ATTACHMENT, HOMESTEAD, JUDGMENT.)

JUDICIAL FORECLOSURE - A method of foreclosing upon real property by means of a court supervised sale. After an appraisal, the court determines an upset price below which no bids to purchase will be accepted. (*See* FORECLOSURE, MORTGAGE, UPSET PRICE.)

JUDICIAL PRECEDENT - A legal term describing the legal principals established by prior appellate court decisions (called "case law"). Under the doctrine of "Stare Decisis," lower courts must follow the prior decision of higher courts. (*See* COMMON LAW.)

JUMBO LOAN - A mortgage loan that has a principal balance greater than the amount eligible for purchase by Fannie Mae or Freddie Mac. A jumbo loan sometimes has a higher interest rate.

JUNCTION BOX - A metal box used to enclose the meeting (junction) of electrical circuits, wires and cables.

JUNIOR DEED OF TRUST OR MORTGAGE - A mortgage or deed of trust which is subordinate in right or lien priority to a prior existing security instrument on the same realty, e.g., a second mortgage. Since this security contains more risk than a first deed of trust or mortgage, it usually carries a higher interest rate. Institutional lenders, such as savings and loan associations, are not permitted by law to make loans which are secured by junior deeds of trust or mortgages. As a general rule, the foreclosure of a senior lien **extinguishes** all junior liens, whereas the foreclosure of a junior lien has no effect on a senior lien, that is, the purchaser at the junior foreclosure sale buys the property subject to the senior lien. There is no legal limit on the number of junior mortgages that can be placed on a property. Sometimes a first deed of trust will specifically state that no junior security may be placed against the property and if it is done, the first security can be foreclosed. (*See* SECOND MORTGAGE, SECONDARY FINANCING, SUBORDINATION CLAUSE.)

JURAT - The clause written at the bottom of an affidavit by a Notary Public stating when, where, and before whom such affidavit was sworn.

JURISDICTION - The authority or power to act, such as the authority of a court to hear and render a decision that binds both parties. Real estate matters are usually within the jurisdiction of the court of the county in which the property is located. The Real Estate Program of the Department of Licensing has jurisdiction over the licensing and conduct of real estate salesmen and brokers. (*See* LICENSING LAW, POLICE POWER.)
Reference: RCW 18.85.

JUST COMPENSATION - An amount of compensation to be received by a party for the taking of his/her property by a governmental entity under the power of eminent domain. Under both the federal and state constitutions, private property may not be taken for public use without just compensation being paid to the owner or if the value is disputed by having it first been determined by a court. This determination of just compensation is the most difficult problem in condemnation proceedings. A condemnee can accept the offered compensation or he/she can request and receive a court hearing (a trial) for determining the appropriate amount of compensation. In Washington, the principal of eminent domain is well established with the question of valuation being a battle of the experts, the appraisers retained by both sides. (*See* BEFORE AND AFTER METHOD, CONDEMNATION, EMINENT DOMAIN, POLICE POWER, REVERSE CONDEMNATION, SPECIAL BENEFITS.)

KEOGH PLAN - A federal tax law designed to encourage businesspeople to set money aside for retirement years by giving them a substantial tax advantage. The plan permits a self-employed individual to set aside a certain percentage of his/her compensation into a trust each year and to deduct this amount on his/her tax return as an ordinary business expense. This money can be invested by the trust on behalf of the individual and all earnings and gains on these investments are compounded tax free. When the individual retires, he/she can take a lump-sum distribution of the whole fund. A tax is due when the fund is distributed upon retirement, by then the taxpayer is probably in a lower tax bracket, and if the money is distributed over a ten-year period, a special ten-year averaging formula will reduce the tax even further. (*See* INDIVIDUAL RETIREMENT ACCOUNT, INDEPENDENT CONTRACTOR.)

A Keogh may be either a defined-benefit or defined-contribution plan. A defined-contribution plan lets the taxpayer contribute a set amount — say, five to ten percent of earnings — to the plan a year, limited to the lesser of $30,000 or 25 percent of non-deferred earnings. Contributions to the more complicated defined-benefit plan constitute an amount necessary to fund an eventual payout based on actuarial tables for the taxpayer's life expectancy. The annual contribution cannot exceed the lesser of $90,000 or 100 percent of average earnings for the three consecutive years of highest earnings.

An individual who works for someone else may still be eligible for a Keogh if he or she has any self-employment earnings, for example from director's fees, or consulting.

One major change under the 1986 Tax Reform Act for defined plans disallows full benefits until age sixty-five, while the former law mandated a minimum age of sixty-two.

KEY LOT - A lot that has added value because of its strategic location, especially where it is needed for the highest and best use of contiguous property. Also a residential lot with more than one backyard facing it.

KEY MAN INSURANCE - A life insurance policy purchased by a company or partnership to cover the estimated cost of replacing a key man in the company; it may be either a key man life or a disability policy, or a combination of both. Some lenders require key man insurance where the borrower is a corporation or partnership relying primarily on the talents of its executive officer. It is often the source for funding a mandatory buy/sell agreement on the death of a partner or stockholder in a closely held corporation.

KEY TENANT - A major office building tenant who leases several floors; a major department store in a shopping center. (See ANCHOR TENANT.)

KICK PLATE - A metal or plastic strip, placed at the lower edge of a door or on a riser of a step, to protect it from damage by accidental kicking.

KICKBACK - A payment made to someone for referral of a customer or business. Generally speaking, kickbacks are illegal. The reason is that, unlike a commission, a kickback is made without the customer's knowledge; thus, the referral could have been made without the customer's best interest at heart. Secret kickbacks to a real estate licensee by a provider of escrow services or a lender are specifically prohibited by the *Real Estate Settlement Procedures Act.* (*See* FINDER'S FEE.)

KICKER - Different types of equity participations a lender may seek as a condition for lending money, such as participation in rentals, profits, or extra interest. (*See* DEED OF TRUST, INTEREST, MORTGAGE, PARTICIPATION LOAN, USURY.)

Also, a sub-panel beside the main electrical panel.

KILN - A large oven-like chamber used for baking, drying, and hardening various materials such as lumber, brick and lime.

KILOVOLT - 1,000 volts.

KILOWATT - 1,000 watts.

KILOWATT HOUR - 1,000 watt-hours.

KIOSK - A small structure usually constructed of wood with one or more sides open and typically used as a newsstand, photo film center or ice cream stand. Such an enterprise usually pays rent on a fairly high percentage lease basis. (*See* PERCENTAGE LEASE.)

KITCHENETTE - Space, less than 60 sq. ft. in area, used for cooking and preparation of food.

KITE WINDER - The steps at the curvature of a circular stairway, which are triangular, or kite-shaped

KNOCKDOWN - Any parts of a building which can be easily assembled, installed, or removed, such as certain types of window frames, partitions, etc.

KNOLL - A small rounded hill.

L

LACHES - An equitable doctrine used by courts to bar a legal claim or prevent the assertion of a right because of undue delay or failure to assert the claim or right. For example, a property owner cannot watch the construction of an adjacent thirty-story building and, after the building reaches the twenty-ninth floor, assert a claim that the building encroaches five feet onto his/her property and demand that it be torn down. Laches could be compared with the statute of limitations, which is the legal doctrine used to bar a claim asserted after the passing of a statutory period of time. (*See* STATUTE OF LIMITATIONS.)

LAMINATED - Layers of wood or other material bonded together to form a single unit, e.g., a laminated beam.

LANAI - Popular term in the western states for a balcony, verandah, porch, or covered patio.

LAND - The surface of the earth extending down to the center and upward to the sky, including all natural things thereon such as trees, crops, or water; plus the minerals below the surface and the air rights above. The term **real property** includes the land and all artificial things attached to the land such as houses, fences, fixtures and the like, together with all rights appurtenant to the property such as easements, rents, profits, etc. In customary usage, the term **land** has become synonymous with **real property** and **real estate**.

LAND ACQUISITION LOAN - A loan to acquire land that is to be held for future development by a commercial developer. The person or enterprise that uses this type of loan is speculating on a future change in the zoning or an alteration in the present use of the land that will make it more valuable. These loans are risky and hard to acquire.

LAND BANK - Refers to the practice of some large corporations of purchasing land and holding the land in an undeveloped state for future development.

LAND CONTRACT - Another name for an installment purchase contract, by which the buyer obtains **equitable title** (the right to use the property) while the seller retains **legal title** (record title) as security for payment of the balance of the purchase price. In Washington, land contracts are referred to as **real estate contracts**. (*See* EQUITABLE CONVERSION, REAL ESTATE CONTRACT.)

LAND DESCRIPTION - A description of a particular piece of real property. In the case of a Purchase and Sale Agreement, an assignment of lease, a deed of trust or mortgage, and other legal documents dealing with real estate, the description of the property must be a complete legal description. (*See* LEGAL DESCRIPTION.)

LAND DEVELOPMENT ACT - *See* WASHINGTON LAND DEVELOPMENT ACT.

LAND DEVELOPMENT LOAN - A short term loan used primarily by subdivision developers. This loan is for the purposes of acquiring the land and developing it for a specific use that can be either residential, commercial, or industrial.

LAND ECONOMICS - The scientific study of land and the methods of determining and implementing it for the highest and best use.

LAND LEASE - A lease of the ground or land but none of the improvements. A lease for the use of the land.

LAND LEASEBACK - A creative financing device often used with raw land which a developer wants to improve, in which the developer sells the land to an investor who leases the land back to the developer under a long-term net lease and subordinates his/her fee ownership to the lender providing development financing. The net effect of the land leaseback transaction is to obtain maximum leverage, including 100 percent land financing, and, since the land is subordinated to development financing, probably 100 percent development financing as well. (*See* SALE AND LEASEBACK, SUBORDINATION AGREEMENT.)

LAND POOR - The financial condition of being short of money because of owning an excess of real property which does not produce income but which results in ongoing out of pocket expenses.

LAND RESIDUAL TECHNIQUE - A method of real property appraisal similar to the building residual technique of capitalization, except that the amount of income earned by the improvements (the return on and recapture of the capital investment) is deducted from the annual net income, and the resulting figure (the land residual) is capitalized and is then added to the improvement cost to arrive at the appraised value of the real property. (*See* INCOME APPROACH, RESIDUAL PROCESS.)

LAND, TENEMENTS AND HEREDITAMENTS - A feudal phrase used to describe all types of immovable realty including the land, buildings and all appurtenant rights thereto; the complete ownership of all the bundle of rights in a freehold estate.

LAND TRUST - A trust originated by the owner of real property, in which real estate is the only asset. As in all trusts, the legal title to the property is in the trustee's name. The beneficial interest in the trust property is in the beneficiary, who is usually the trustor (that is, the person who created or established the trust). Generally, only living persons may create a land trust, but corporations as well as living persons can be the beneficiaries. The beneficial interest in real estate held in a land trust is considered to be personal property. The beneficiary has the rights to the possession, income, and proceeds of the sale of such property. Under a land trust agreement, the trustee deals with the property only upon written direction of the beneficiary. The land trust agreement is executed by the trustor and the trustee. A beneficial interest under a land trust can be transferred merely by assignment, without the necessity of a deed and all its formal requirements. It can be pledged as collateral for a loan without a mortgage being placed on record (through a collateral assignment). Courts have held that real estate held in a land trust cannot be partitioned by the beneficiaries because their interest is not one in real estate, but one in personal property.

A land trust generally continues for a definite term, such as 20 years. At the expiration of the term, if the beneficiary does not extend the trust term, the trustee is usually obligated to sell the real estate and to return the net proceeds to the beneficiary.

LAND USE INTENSITY - A system of land use under county zoning codes designed to relate land, building coverage of the land, and open space to one another. The land use intensity (LUI) scale provides a series of density ratings (percentages) which include floor area, open space, living space, and recreation space. In applying land use intensity, the floor area ratio creates a maximum amount of floor area in a building in relation to the land area of the lot upon which the building is to be constructed. Open space requirements are minimum requirements based upon and computed from a percentage of the actual floor area to be developed in a particularly zoned lot. The LUI has become an important tool in the development of Planned Unit Developments (PUD). (*See* PLANNED UNIT DEVELOPMENT, ZONING.)

LAND USE MAP - A development plan for a specific part of the overall county general plan, depicting the types of land uses permitted in the area, such as residential, medium density apartment, resort, and the like. In Washington, the county building department is usually responsible for matters concerning the general plan and the development plan. The development plan provides the detailed scheme for placement or use of specific facilities within a defined area so as to insure the most beneficial use of such area. A development plan is within the framework of and implements the general plan.

LANDLOCKED - Real property having no access to a public road or way, such as parcel C in the drawing below.

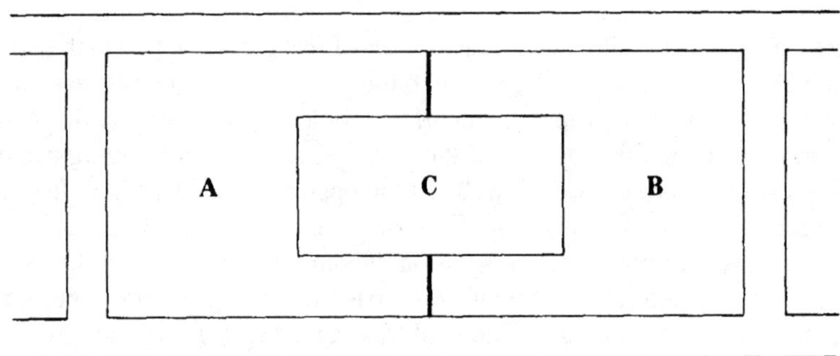

If parcel C had ever been a part of parcel A or B, a court would grant the owner of parcel C an easement of necessity over the parcel with which it had once been joined. This easement of necessity continues only during the period of necessity. Landlocked parcels are sometimes created as a result of condemnation for a limited access highway. (*See* EASEMENT BY NECESSITY.)

LANDLORD - The lessor or the owner of leased premises. The landlord retains a reversionary interest in the property so that when the lease ends, the property will revert to him/her.

LANDLORD TENANT ACT - Washington's Landlord Tenant Act went into effect July 16, 1973. The Act was designed to revise the law governing residential landlord and tenant relationship by changing it from one based on the law of conveyance to a relationship that is primarily contractual in nature, and setting forth in detail the rights, obligations and remedies of both tenant and landlord.

Under the Act, minimum habitability standards and procedures for the correction of housing defects were established; new notice periods were instituted; the ills of absentee landlordism were minimized; unfair reprisals and lock outs were expressly prohibited; procedures for arbitration of disputes were established; and damage deposits were protected by requiring trust or escrow accounts for such funds, and a specific time period was established for either reimbursement or notice of the reasons for withholding of same.

Some of the highlights of the Act are:

1. Generally it applies to all rental units in homes and apartment houses. It does not apply to residences which are incidental to some other service being rendered, such as a hospital, college dormitory, religious facility, correctional facility, hotel, motel or the like.

2. Both Washington district and superior courts may exercise jurisdiction over any landlord or tenant with respect to any conduct within the State governed by the Act.

3. The landlord must keep the unit fit for human habitation. The Act is quite specific in what the landlord must do.

4. If the landlord does not reside in the State of Washington, he/she must designate a person who resides in the county where the premises are located who is authorized to act as his/her agent for the purposes of service of notices and process. If no one is designated by the landlord, then the person to whom the rental payment is made shall be considered the agent.

5. If the landlord fails to maintain the premises in the manner defined in the Act, the tenant must notify the landlord of the defective condition and, depending on the nature of the deficiency, the Act states how rapidly the landlord must correct the deficiency. (*See* ABATEMENT, ABANDONMENT.)

6. In order for a tenant to use any of the remedies of the Landlord Tenant Act, he/she must be current in the payment of rent.

7. The landlord is required to give the tenant 30 days notice of any increase in rent. After receiving the notice, the tenant has 10 days to decide whether to pay the increase at the beginning of the next rental period or to give the landlord the required 20 days notice to terminate the tenancy.

8. Either the landlord or tenant may terminate the tenancy by written notice of twenty (20) days or more before the end of any monthly rental period (e.g., within the first eleven (11) days of any thirty-one (31) day month and within the first ten (10) days of any thirty (30) day month.)

9. The landlord must give a tenant at least ninety-days written notice of any condominium conversion or the adoption of a policy excluding children. The ninety-day notice is in lieu of the twenty-day notice for termination of a month-to-month tenancy unless the change is delayed beyond the ninety days. In such a case, the tenant is entitled to receive the regular twenty-day notice unless that right has been waived. (*See* ABANDONMENT, ACCESS, CONSTRUCTIVE EVICTION, DISTRAINT, HABITABLE, LANDLORD, LEASE, MOBILE HOME LANDLORD TENANT ACT, MONTH-TO-MONTH TENANCY, NOTICE, PREMISES, RENT, RENTAL AGREEMENT, RENT CONTROL, RETALIATORY EVICTION, SECURITY DEPOSIT, SINGLE-FAMILY RESIDENCE, SUBLEASE, SURRENDER.)
Reference: RCW 59.18

LANDSCAPING - The art of arranging or modifying ground forms and plant materials, and designing spaces around buildings or other areas, to secure pleasing or advantageous effects.

Under certain circumstances, landscaping costs can be depreciated. According to a recent IRS ruling, apartment building developers can take depreciation for landscaping over the life of the building. The general rule, however, is that land itself is not depreciable for tax purposes. (*See* DEPRECIATION.)

Landscaping is required as an integral part of all new multifamily, commercial, industrial, public and institutional development in many municipalities and counties in Washington. The location and type of landscaping required depends on the adjacent zoning. Generally, the proposed use must buffer less intensive uses permitted in the adjacent zone. Additions and remodeling of existing structures may require landscaping, depending on the cost of construction.

LAP SIDING - The siding used for exterior finishes of a house or other structure. Each board overlaps another in a fashion similar to clapboard siding.

LARGER PARCEL - A term used in condemnation cases when the court considers the extent of severance damages in cases where a partial taking has occurred. There is usually a requirement of unity of ownership, use, and contiguity. However, it has been held that integrated use, not physical contiguity, is the test of whether condemned land is part of a single tract that would warrant an award of severance damages. (*See* CONDEMNATION, SEVERANCE DAMAGES.)

LATE CHARGE - An added charge required to be paid as a penalty for failure to pay a regular loan installment when due or in a lease when rent isn't paid on time. It is generally not treated as interest, but as a service charge for the extra work and inconvenience suffered by the creditor. The courts, however, will not enforce excessive late charges (such as 10 percent or more of the unpaid principal).

LATENT DEFECTS - Hidden structural defects presumably resulting from faulty construction, known to the seller but not to the purchaser and not readily discoverable by inspection. If the owner or the broker is aware of such defects, such as a defective water heater, he/she must disclose them to the prospective purchaser. If a latent defect is great enough, failure to disclose such information is a tacit misrepresentation and may be grounds for the buyer to rescind the contract. (*See* "AS IS," MISREPRESENTATION, REAL PROPERTY TRANSFER DISCLOSURE STATEMENT.)

LATERAL AND SUBJACENT SUPPORT - The support received by a parcel of real property from the land adjoining it is called lateral support. Subjacent support is that support which the surface of the earth receives from its underlying strata. The basic rules of support are the same for both. In essence, an adjoining landowner (or holder of mineral or other rights beneath the land of another) owes a duty to support his/her neighbor's land in its natural state. This duty of support does not run specifically to any of the improvements on the land, but does impose liability for damage to improvements on the neighbor's land if the land would have subsided as a result of the landowner's excavation even without the weight of the improvements. In general an owner of property can lessen his/her exposure to liability by giving his/her neighbors adequate notice of his/her intent to perform excavation work on his/her property so his/her neighbor can shore-up and take other precautions.

LATH - Thin strips of wood or metal nailed to rafters, ceiling joists, or wall studs to form a groundwork for slates, tiles, shingles, or plaster.

LAW - That body of rules by which society governs itself. Real estate law is derived from the English common law, state and federal constitutions, state and federal legislation, county and municipalities ordinances and appellate court decisions. In addition there is "private law" which refers to "law"' the parties create for themselves in their legal documents. For example, the bylaws and house rules of a condominium set forth detailed private rules of conduct for the owners and violation of these rules gives the owners legal recourse against the violator. (*See* COMMON LAW, LICENSING LAW.)

LAW DAY - The date an obligation becomes due; sometimes refers to the closing date. Under the common law, the mortgagor had to pay off the mortgage debt by the law day. In the past, failure to pay on time would result in the mortgagor automatically losing his/her property to the mortgagee. If payment was made by the law day, the mortgage became void and the mortgagee would be divested of any title to the property pursuant to the defeasance clause. (*See* DEFEASANCE, REDEMPTION, EQUITABLE RIGHT OF.)

LEACHING CESSPOOL - In plumbing, any cesspool which is not watertight and permits waste liquids to pass into the surrounding soil by percolation.

LEAD-BASED PAINT - Houses built before 1978 (per FHA regulations) should be checked for lead-based paint. Lead-based paint is hazardous to a person's health. Lead-based paint should only be cleaned by a contractor trained to deal with it. To permanently remove lead-based paint, only a "lead abatement" contractor should be hired.

The Residential Lead-Based Paint Hazard Reduction Act of 1992 requires affirmative action on the part of the sellers, landlords and real estate agents to ensure that lead-based paint hazards are addressed in the sale and leasing of homes and apartments constructed prior to 1978. All prospective buyers or tenants of such property must be provided a pamphlet published by the U.S. Environmental Protection Agency entitled "Protect Your Family From Lead in Your Home."

LEAD LENDER - Typically, a local lender who funds the initial portion of a large loan and arranges for an institutional lender(s) to fund the balance of the financing. The lead lender handles the servicing of the loan. (*See* PARTICIPATION MORTGAGE.)

LEASE - An agreement, written or unwritten, transferring the right to exclusive possession and use of real estate for a definite period of time from the land owner (lessor) to the renter (lessee). To create a valid lease, the lessor must retain a reversionary right; that is, the lessor (landlord) grants the right of possession to the lessee (tenant), but retains the right to retake possession after the lease's term has expired. The lease is, in effect, a combination of both a conveyance (to transfer the right of occupancy) and a contract (to pay rent and assume other obligations). The lessor's interest is called the **leased fee estate** and consists of the right to recover the contract rent plus the reversion. The lessee's interest is called the **leasehold estate** and consists of the right to the exclusive use and occupancy of the estate. An "agreement for a lease" contemplates the execution of a lease at a later time.

The law controlling landlord-tenant relations originally developed from early agricultural leases. With such leases, the landlord's obligation was limited to providing the tenant with peaceful possession; in return the tenant agreed to pay rent. Under this agreement the landlord was not expected to assist in the operation of the land. Rather, leased lands were under the exclusive control of the tenant without interference from the landlord. In the simplest terms, the tenant-landlord relationship was a strict possession-rent relationship. If a tenant defaulted in his/her rent payment, eviction would be forthcoming. In a rural setting, this was a workable arrangement.

In modern times, however, the courts apply the rules governing contracts in determining the validity of a lease. Usually, no special wording is necessary to create the relationship of landlord and tenant. A lease should be in writing; however, if it is not written, the law will write it for the parties involved, just as the law writes a will for someone who dies intestate. Although, depending on the circumstances, the lease may be written, oral, or implied. The lessor, being the owner of the real estate, is usually bound by an implied covenant of quiet enjoyment for the benefit of the lessee. By this covenant, the lessor asserts that the lessee will not be evicted by a person who successfully claims to be the real owner of the premises with a title which is paramount to the lessor's. The requirements for a valid lease are similar to those of a contract and are generally as follows:

Capacity to Contract: The parties must be legally capable of entering into a contract. (Note, however, that a minor can generally enter into binding contracts for necessities, of which essential housing may be considered one of the most basic needs.)

Mutual Agreement: The parties must reach a mutual agreement and support it by valid consideration.

Legal Objectives: The lease's objectives must be legal; that is, it would generally be illegal to lease a building as a house of prostitution, so a lease for such a purpose would be invalid.

Statute of Frauds: Washington's statute of frauds generally applies to leases. The statute provide that leases for more than one year (one year plus one day) or leases which will not be fully performed within one year from the date of making must be in writing. Note that a lease for exactly one year could fall under the statute of frauds if the lease period commences subsequent to the date of entering into the agreement. Similarly, a lease for less than one year may fall under the statute of frauds if more than one year elapses between the signing of the lease and its termination date. Even though a lease might be for a term of less than one year, as a matter of good business practice, it should be put into writing to lessen the chances of dispute and misunderstanding between the parties. A lease not in conformance with the statute of frauds is generally considered unenforceable. Even a short-term lease should be put in writing because: it will be good proof in case of trial, usually falls under a longer statute of limitations, provides for attorney's fees, and acts as a preliminary screening device for spotting potentially troublesome tenants.

Signatures: The lease must be signed by the landlord because the courts consider the lease as a conveyance of real estate. When the lessor holds his/her interest in a community property status, the spouse is required to join in signing the lease. A lease need not be signed by the lessee (although it is good practice for the tenant to do so), since his/her taking possession and paying rent constitutes an acceptance of the lease terms. When a lease is signed by two or more tenants, they become jointly and severally liable and can only avoid this by signing separate leases specifying their separate obligations.

Description of the Premises: A description of the leased premises should be clearly stated. Usually, this involves only a street address and/or apartment number for residential, apartment, and small commercial properties. Large commercial site leases, on the other hand, must be more detailed, including such things as a floor plan, total square footage, storage areas, parking, and the like. It is not clear in Washington whether a complete street and town address is sufficient, or whether the complete legal description must be used. Therefore, the prudent draftsman will include the full legal description in his/her lease.

Use of the Premises: The lessor may restrict the use of his/her property through provisions included in the lease. This is particularly important with leases for stores or commercial space. For example, a lease may contain a provision that the property is "to be used for the purpose of a Freddie the Derelict's Fantastic Fun Palace restaurant, and no other." If the lease does not state a specified purpose, the tenant may use the premises for any lawful purpose.

Term of the Lease: The term of the lease is the period for which the lease will run, and it should be stated precisely. Good practice requires that the beginning and ending of the term dates be stated, together with a statement of the total period of the lease. For example, "for a term of thirty years beginning June 1, 1968 and ending May 31, 1998." Courts do not favor leases with an indefinite term and will hold that such perpetual leases are not valid unless the language of the lease and the surrounding circumstances clearly indicate that such is the intention of the parties. The maximum long-term lease is traditionally 99 years, since there were some early state court decisions holding that a lease of 100 years or more actually passed fee simple title to the lessee.

Possession of the Leased Premises: In most states, the landlord must give the tenant actual occupancy or possession of the leased premises. Thus, if the premises are occupied by a holdover tenant, or adverse claimant, at the date of a new lease, the landlord owes a duty to the new tenant to bring whatever action is necessary to recover possession and to bear the expense of this action. In a few states, however, the landlord is bound to give the tenant only the right of possession, and then it is the tenant's obligation to bring any necessary court action to secure actual possession. In Washington, this point has not been decided and the tenant would have several alternative courses of action: sue the landlord for damages, claim an offset against rents due until possession is gained, sue for possession or specific performance of the lease, or in the extreme case rescind the lease.

Consideration: Rent is the usual consideration granted for the right to occupy the leased premises. The payment of rent, however, is not essential as long as consideration was granted in the creation of the lease itself. Some courts have construed rent as being any consideration which supports the lease, thus not limiting its definition to the monthly payment of a specified amount. After a lease has been executed and is in force, most courts will not enforce an agreement to reduce or increase the rent during the term for which the lease was originally drawn. These courts consider the lease to be a contract and therefore not subject to change unless the changes are in writing and tantamount to cancellation of the original lease. Under common-law principles, the rent was payable at the end of the lease term unless the parties agreed otherwise. This was based on the concept that rent is a return for the lessee's enjoyment of the use of the land and thus not payable until after the enjoyment had occurred. Modern leases, however, provide for rent to be paid in advance. Most land leases and long-term leases provide, in addition to the payment of rent, that the tenant will be required to pay all property charges, such as real estate taxes, special assessments, water and sewer taxes, and all necessary insurance premiums to protect the property. Most leases provide for some form of security. This security for payment of rent may be established: (a) by contracting for a lien on the tenant's property, (b) by requiring the tenant to pay a portion of the rent in advance, (c) by requiring the tenant to post security, and/or (d) by requiring the tenant to have a third person guarantee the payment of the rent.

There are three main classifications of leases:

1. Leases based on the type of realty involved, such as office leases, ground leases, proprietary leases, residential leases.

2. Leases classed according to the term of the lease, such as short-term and long-term leases. Most short-term leases are gross leases requiring the landlord to pay all taxes, assessments, and operating costs (such as most apartment leases). Long-term leases are often net leases that give the tenant greater rights and responsibili ties. Particularly in long-term leases, attention should be given to the rights of both parties in the event of condemnation of the leased premises.

3. Leases classed according to the method of rent payment, such as fixed-rental leases, graduated leases, percentage leases, gross leases or net leases.

Washington requires that leases for a term of two years or more, or the assignment of such a lease, be recorded with the county auditor of the county in which the land is situated. If the property is registered land, leases for a term of three years or more must be recorded. (*See* TORRENS SYSTEM.) If the term is uncertain for some reason or where renewals or extension options might run over, one should record or register the lease. As a practical matter, the complete lease is seldom recorded, rather a memorandum of lease is recorded which provides the public notice that the property is leased and that a prudent person interested in the property will investigate further.

A lessee may assign his/her lease or sublet the premises if the terms of the lease do not prohibit it. A tenant who transfers the entire remaining lease term assigns the lease. A tenant who transfers most of the term, but retains a small part of it, sublets. Most leases prohibit a lessee from assigning or subletting without the landlord's permission.

If the landlord sells the property, the grantee takes title subject to the lease and becomes liable for all covenants in the lease. Tenants who make improvements to a landlord's property usually do so for the benefit of the landlord. Such improvements, if classified as fixtures, become part of the real estate. A tenant, however, may be given the right to install trade fixtures or chattel fixtures by the terms of his/her lease. It is customary to provide that such trade fixtures may be removed by the tenant before the expiration of the lease provided he/she puts the building back into the condition it was when he/she took possession.

In land leases involving agricultural land, the courts have held that damage or destruction of the improvements does not relieve the tenant from the obligation to pay rent to the end of the term. This ruling has been extended in most states to include leases of land on which the tenant has constructed a building. It also has been extended in many instances to include leases which give possession of an entire building to the tenant. Since the tenant is leasing an entire building, the courts have held that he/she is also leasing the land on which that building is located. In those cases where the leased premises are only a part of the building (such as office or commercial space or an apartment in an apartment building), upon destruction of the leased premises, the tenant may not need to continue to pay rent. Under the Residential Landlord-Tenant Act, because the landlord has a duty to maintain the premises in condition fit for human habitation, destruction of the premises would seem to give the tenant a power to terminate, though termination would not occur automatically.

A lease may be terminated by:

1. expiration of the term

2. merger of the leasehold and fee estates

3. destruction or condemnation of the premises

4. abandonment

5. agreement of the parties (surrender)

6. forfeiture due to default or breach of the leasing terms and conditions.

(*See* ABANDONMENT, CONTRACT, EVICTION, FIXTURE, FLAT LEASE, GRADUATED RENTAL LEASE, GROSS LEASE, GROUND LEASE, LANDLORD, LANDLORD-TENANT ACT, LEASEHOLD, LEASE OPTION, MONTH-TO-MONTH TENANCY, NET LEASE, PERCENTAGE LEASE, SECURITY DEPOSIT, SURRENDER, TRADE FIXTURE.)

LEASE INSURANCE - Insurance available to a landlord that protects against loss in income due to the tenant(s) not paying rent. Such coverage is normally available only for commercial real estate.

LEASE OPTION - *See* LEASE PURCHASE.

LEASE PURCHASE - A lease-purchase is a lease with an option to buy. A seller enters into an agreement with a buyer to purchase property with all or a portion of the rental payments to apply to the sales price, usually in the form of a down payment. In residential property, when a purchaser does not have sufficient funds for a minimum down payment, he/she can enter into a lease and have a part of the rental payment accumulate into an amount that is sufficient for the required down payment. Some lenders have guidelines for this type of purchase plan. Usually the lender will require that the rental portion of the lease-purchase payment to be a fair market rent and not an artificial, below-the-market rental used to create the required down payment. If the rent is not a fair market rent, the lender views the transaction as the seller giving the buyer the down payment in the form of a reduced rent.

Often, the appraiser making an appraisal on the property involved in a lease-purchase will be asked to estimate the fair market rent. If the lease-purchase rental payments are at a fair market rent, the lender can credit the overage as accumulating towards the required down payment.

For example, a seller, leases/sells a property to a tenant/buyer, who lacks the sufficient down payment, for an $80,000 residence. The tenant/buyer will be required to make monthly payments of $1,100 per month with $800 as rent and $300 as an accumulating down payment. At the end of 27 payments the buyer will have accumulated slightly more than a 10% down payment.

In a lease-purchase, it is advisable that parties enter into two separate agreements, a lease contract and a Purchase and Sale Agreement. The two contracts are tied to one another, but the agreements and responsibilities are specified for each contract. Often if the tenant violates the rental agreement, the breach is treated as a breach of the Purchase and Sale Agreement and terminates both contracts.

LEASED FEE - The interest and rights of the lessor in real estate that the lessor has leased is called a leased fee. The lessor has a right to receive rental income and a right to possess the property at the end of the lease. The value of the rent payments plus the remaining property value at the end of the lease period (the reversionary interest) is the leased fee interest, which may be sold or mortgaged subject to the rights of the tenant. In valuing the leased fee, the appraiser usually will capitalize the present value of the income received by the lessor and add the reversionary value of the land, or land and building, at the expiration of the lease term (the annuity method of capitalization). The reversionary value of the land is difficult to predict so it is usually calculated to be the same as its present value, discounted to its present value by multiplying the value times the appropriate Inwood factor. (*See* INTERNAL RATE OF RETURN, INWOOD TABLES.)

LEASEHOLD - A less-than-freehold estate which a tenant possesses in real property. In a lease situation, the tenant possesses a leasehold and the landlord possesses the reversion estate (that is, when the lease terminates, the property will revert to the landlord). Leasehold estates are generally classified as estates in personal property. Under common law, an estate for years was termed a "chattel real" and classified as personal property. The four principal types of leasehold estates are the estate for years, the periodic tenancy (estate from year to year), the tenancy at will, and the tenancy at sufferance. The estate for years runs for a specific period of time; the periodic tenancy runs for an indefinite number of time periods; the estate at will runs for an indefinite time; an estate at sufferance runs until the landlord takes some action.

Unlike other uses of land, the leasehold is a transfer of the exclusive right to possession, as opposed to the mere privilege to use the land. Thus, a hotel guest is different from a tenant. The significance between various types of authorized usage's of property (licenses, easements, profits, and leases) becomes important in terms of the remedies available upon breach of contract. The tenant in a leasehold can only be removed from the property by following strict statutory eviction procedures, whereas a license can usually be revoked at any time.

The term or duration of the leasehold estate varies, depending on the purposes of utilization of the land. Many residential apartment leases are short-term, that is, for one year or month-to-month. Most ground leases usually run for 55 years, while some run for 75 years or longer. For FHA and VA leasehold-mortgage purposes, it is required that leases have a minimum of 55 years, with a fixed rental for the first 30 years. These long-term leases are transferred by assignment of lease rather than by deed. Both the assignor and assignee of a leasehold estate must sign the assignment of lease since the assignee assumes the obligations of the assignor under the lease.

Under common law, improvements constructed by the lessee on the leased premises would revert to the landlord at the termination of the leasehold estate. Many ground leases, however, specifically provide in the reversion clause for the right of the lessee to remove all improvements at the end of the lease term. This provision simplifies the arrangement of financing and negotiation for an extension or renewal of the lease.

The valuation of a lessor's interest is a complex procedure that involves the use of capitalization rates and present value tables to ascertain the present value of the landlord's reversion interest and the present value of the rental income. In comparing properties for valuation purposes, leaseholds should only be compared with other leaseholds and not with fee simple properties.

In areas where leaseholds are popularly used, it is common practice to make leasehold estates subject to a recorded declaration of restrictions, usually by reference in the lease to the book and page number of the declaration. A purchaser should examine the lease and all referenced documents well in advance of closing in order to ascertain exactly what he/she is buying. (*See* ASSIGNMENT OF LEASE, GROUND LEASE, LEASE, LEASEHOLD MORTGAGE, LESS-THAN-FREEHOLD ESTATE, PERIODIC TENANCY, TENANCY AT SUFFERANCE, TENANCY AT WILL.)

LEASEHOLD IMPROVEMENTS - Fixtures and other improvements to leased property, made by or for a specified tenant, sometimes called tenant improvements. (*See* FIXTURES, LEASEHOLD, TENANT IMPROVEMENT COSTS (T.I.s).)

LEASEHOLD MORTGAGE - A mortgage placed upon the lessee's interest in the leased premises. Leasehold mortgage financing is a specialized form of secondary financing because the mortgage is subordinate to the position of the fee owner. The prime lenders in leasehold financing are life insurance companies, major mutual savings banks, and major commercial banks.

In the development of a large project, the fee owner will sometimes lease the land to a developer and subordinate his/her fee to the leasehold mortgage. The subordination may be limited to loans of a certain type or term (such as a construction loan but not any refinancing), or the subordination might take place only upon full completion of construction of the proposed improvement. Often, the lender will attempt to persuade the fee owner to mortgage the fee along with the leasehold mortgage. (*See* SUBORDINATION CLAUSE.)

LEGACY - A disposition of money or personal property by will, as in a bequest.

LEGAL AGE - The age at which one attains majority and is no longer a minor; in Washington, it is 18 years of age. (*See* MINOR.)

LEGAL DESCRIPTION - A description of a parcel of real property which is complete enough that a court of law will accept it as an adequate description. It is usually complete enough that an independent surveyor could locate and identify the specific piece of real property. Oral testimony is not admissible to describe the property more fully, except in certain cases involving fraud or mistake. In general usage there are three kinds of legal descriptions; those based on government surveys, those based on recorded plats, and those using a metes and bounds description.

A legal description is required on all Purchase and Sale Agreements, real estate contracts, deeds, deeds of trust, mortgages, and the like. Street addresses or general descriptions (e.g., "the Old Homestead Farm") are inadequate to use in real estate documents. (*See* GOVERNMENT SURVEY; LAND DESCRIPTION; LOT, BLOCK AND SUBDIVISION; METES AND BOUNDS; PLAT.)

LEGAL NAME - The given or **Christian** name in combination with the surname or family name. Under common law principles the insertion, omission, or mistake in middle name or initial is immaterial.

An application for the state examination or licensing of real estate salesmen or brokers must contain the applicant's full legal name. The use of initials is strongly discouraged, especially with common surnames such as Smith, Johnson, Wong, etc. This policy is designed to eliminate confusion and misidentification over applicants with similar names. (*See* INITIALS, NAME, CHANGE OF, SIGNATURE.)

LEGAL NOTICE - That notice which is either implied or required by law. Constructive notice under the recording laws is also referred to as legal notice. (*See* ACTUAL NOTICE, CONSTRUCTIVE NOTICE.)

LEGEND STOCK - A security certificate which has a notation on its face indicating that its transferability is restricted; normally it cannot be transferred for a certain period of time or until registered. Securities which claim exemption from SEC registration under the intrastate exemption (Rule 147) or the private offering exemption (Rule 146) must contain a restricted transfer legend.

LESSEE - The person to whom property is rented or leased; called a **tenant** in most leases.

LESSOR - The person who rents or leases property to another. In residential leasing, he/she is often referred to as a **landlord**.

LESS-THAN-FREEHOLD ESTATE - An estate held by one who rents or leases property. This classification includes an estate for years, periodic tenancy, estate at will, and estate at sufferance. (*See* FREEHOLD, LEASEHOLD.)

LET - To rent out.

LETTER OF CREDIT - An agreement or commitment by a bank ("issuer") made at the request of a customer ("account party") that the bank will honor drafts or other demands of payment from third parties ("beneficiaries") upon compliance with the conditions specified in the letter of credit. Through the issuance of its letter of credit, the bank undertakes to pay the seller's draft, thereby substituting the bank's credit for that of the buyer. This often takes the form of a letter from a bank in one area of the country to a bank or merchant in another area introducing the person named and vouching for him/her and specifying a sum of money to be extended to him/her.

A letter of credit might be used where a long-term tenant has to put up a substantial security deposit, or a borrower seeking a large mortgage commitment might be required to put up a substantial deposit in the form of a letter of credit, forfeitable if the commitment is not exercised. The account party prefers a letter of credit in lieu of having to place cash in escrow on deposit, thereby incurring borrowing costs or losing return on such funds. Sometimes it is necessary for a developer of a large hotel or other large development project to obtain a letter of credit at the start of the project to cover the costs of furniture which won't be needed for another 18 months. This gives assurance to the mortgagee and others that the developer will have adequate funds to complete the project when it comes time to fund the furniture purchase.

The bank charges a small annual fee for issuing the letter of credit which, naturally, is issued only to its customers with the highest credit ratings. Unlike direct loans, the bank need not report obligations under letters of credit as liabilities in its financial statements, nor is the bank required to maintain a certain amount of bank reserves to back up its letter of credit obligations.

Article 5 of the Uniform Commercial Code covers extensively the law concerning letters of credit. (*See* LINE OF CREDIT.)

LETTER OF INTENT - An expression of intent to invest, develop or purchase without creating any firm legal obligation to do so. It may refer to a specific project, or it may be a general letter of intent without regard to any specific project. The following is the kind of language used in a letter of intent to negate any legal duty to carry out the terms of the letter:

"Since this instrument consists only of an expression of our mutual intent, it is expressly understood that no liability or obligation of any nature whatsoever is intended to be created as between any of the parties hereto. This letter is not intended to constitute a binding agreement to consummate the transaction outlined here in nor an agreement to enter into contract. The parties propose to proceed promptly and in good faith to conclude the arrangements with respect to proposed development, but any legal obligations between the parties shall be only those set forth in the executed contract and lease. In the event that a contract and lease are not executed, we shall not be obligated for any expenses of the developer or for any charges or claims whatsoever arising out of this letter of intent or the proposed financing or otherwise and, similarly, the developer shall not be in any way obligated to us." (*See* REAL ESTATE PURCHASE AND SALE AGREEMENT.)
Reference: RCW 65.08

LETTER OF PATENT - A legal instrument transferring title to real property from either the United States or an individual state to the person named in the patent.

LETTER REPORT - A short appraisal report limited to the property characteristics, valuation, and recommendations. (*See* APPRAISAL.)

LEVEL PAYMENT MORTGAGE - A mortgage which is scheduled to be repaid in equal periodic payments which include both principal and interest. Since payments are credited first against interest on the declining principal balance, the amount of money credited to principal gradually increases while that credited to interest gradually decreases. Under most conventional VA and FHA loans, the mortgage payments include taxes and insurance in addition to principal and interest. (*See* AMORTIZATION, AMORTIZATION SCHEDULE, BUDGET MORTGAGE.)

LEVERAGE - The use of borrowed funds to purchase investment property with the anticipation that the property acquired will increase in return so that the investor will realize a profit not only on his/her own investment, but also on the borrowed funds. The employment of a smaller investment to generate a larger rate of return through borrowing. The term "high leverage" often is used when the investor has made a very low down payment. For example, Mrs. Anderson purchases a $75,000 parcel of raw land for $4,000 down on April 1. Mrs. Anderson sells the property for $85,000 on November 1, thus making a profit from the use of other people's money (leverage). Her profit on the purchase price of $75,000 is 13%, but the profit on her principal investment of $4,000 is 250%. While the foregoing example may occur, the unsophisticated real estate investor should exercise caution and seek expert counsel before speculating.

The basic principle of investing is that there is a direct correlation between the degree of risk and the rate of anticipated earnings. Care must be taken that each investor decides for himself/herself the degree of risk he/she is willing to assume. (*See* INTEREST, MISREPRESENTATION.)

LEVY - To assess; seize; collect. To levy an execution is to officially seize the property of a person to satisfy an obligation. Usually the sheriff levies upon and brings within his/her control the personal property of a judgment debtor. Levying is not a judicial act, but rather a ministerial act. To levy a tax is to assess a property and set the rate of taxation. (*See* ATTACHMENT, WRIT OF EXECUTION.)

LIABILITY - Legal responsibility for an act. (*See* DAMAGES.)

LIABILITY INSURANCE - Insurance which protects against claims by third parties due to damages or injuries caused by the insured on his/her property. While it is normal practice for owners and commercial tenants to purchase liability insurance, it is recommended that residential tenants also purchase liability insurance. (*See* INSURANCE.)

LIABILITY OF LANDOWNERS (RECREATIONAL USE) - Washington has extended the immunity of landowners for permitting public use of land for recreational purposes.

A landowner is immune from liability for unintentional injury to persons permitted to use rural property for outdoor recreational purposes. This immunity protection now applies to urban lands as well. Furthermore, the definition of "outdoor recreation" is expressly expanded to include horseback riding, bicycling and clam digging. Such permitted use of the land, however, would not support a claim for adverse possession.

LIBOR (LONDON INTERBANK OFFERED RATE) - An average of daily lending rates from several major London banks. LIBOR has been used as an index for Adjustable Rate Mortgages.

LICENSE - 1. Permission or authority to do a particular act upon the land of another, usually on a nonexclusive basis. A license is a personal, revocable and nonassignable right, but unlike an easement, it is not considered to be an interest in the land itself. If a right to use another person's land is given orally, it will generally be considered to be a license rather than an easement. A license ceases upon the death of either party and is revoked by the sale of the land by the licensor. A commercial parking lot gives its customers a license to park for a fixed fee. Also, a movie theater authorizes its customers to use the premises for a certain limited purpose. (*See* EASEMENT.)

Usually, the question of the use of a parcel of real property whether it is with a license or some claim of adverse use when the property owner tells the licensee to stop use of the property. (*See* ESCROW AGENT REGISTRATION ACT, ADVERSE POSSESSION, PRESCRIPTIVE EASEMENT.)

2. Formal permission from a constituted authority (such as the Real Estate Program of the Department of Licensing) to engage in a certain activity or business, such as real estate brokerage. (*See* LICENSING LAW.)
Reference: RCW 18.85

LICENSEE - A person who has a valid license. A real estate licensee can be a salesperson, associate broker or a broker. (*See* LICENSE, LICENSING LAW.)

LICENSING LAW - In Washington, it is unlawful for anyone to act as a real estate broker or salesman without first obtaining a license from the Real Estate Program of the Department of Licensing. In addition, in a lawsuit to collect compensation for rendering real estate brokerage service, the real estate broker/plaintiff bringing the action must allege and prove that the plaintiff was duly licensed prior to the time of offering to perform the brokerage service. Except as specifically exempted, all persons engaged in the business of real estate, including telephone solicitors, must be licensed. All applicants must first demonstrate their competence by passing a written examination; in no case will this be waived. Applicants, however, who have passed the multi-state examination in another state may be eligible to take only the Washington State law section of the examination. (*See* EXAMINATION, REAL ESTATE LICENSING.) It is not necessary that an applicant be a United States citizen and even a legal residence in Washington. To be eligible for a salesperson's or broker's license, an applicant must have attained the age of eighteen (18); broker applicants must show proof of graduation from high school or the equivalent (G.E.D.-General Education Development examination which may be taken at any Community College in the State). A salesperson applicant must successfully complete an approved sixty clock hour course prior to obtaining a first license. A broker applicant for an examination must have completed successfully 120 clock hours of approved education, which must include 30 hours of brokerage management, 30 hours of real estate law, 30 hours in business management and one elective course.

In mid-1976, there were approximately 18,000 active licensed brokers, associate brokers and salespeople operating out of approximately 3,500 real estate offices in Washington. At the same time, there were approximately 14,000 inactive brokers and salespeople.

In mid-1981, there were approximately 30,500 active licensed real estate brokers, associate brokers and salespeople operating out of approximately 4,200 real estate offices in Washington. At the same time, there were approximately 27,000 inactive brokers, associate brokers and salespeople.

In mid-1988, there were approximately 24,800 active licensed real estate brokers, associate brokers and salespeople operating out of approximately 3,700 real estate offices in

Washington. At the same time, there were approximately 27,000 inactive brokers, associate brokers and salespeople.

In mid-1998, there were approximately 27,000 active licensed real estate brokers, associate brokers and salespeople operating out of approximately 3,600 real estate offices in Washington. At the same time, there were approximately 18,000 inactive brokers, associate brokers and salespeople.

Exemptions from Licensing: The following persons are exempt from any license requirements:

1. A person buying or selling for his/her own account;

2. Any duly authorized attorney-in-fact who receives no compensation for the brokerage services rendered;

3. An attorney-at-law in the performance of his/her duties or a person acting as a receiver, trustee, executor or otherwise acting under court authorization or a person selling under a deed of trust;

4. A residential manager of a single apartment complex.

A residential manager, however, must have a real estate license if property for more than one owner's property is managed or if the property is in more than one complex, even if owned by one owner. In this regard, there is a question if an unlicensed individual could manage property lawfully if the single complex was not in a single city block, or ownership of the property was in any form other than a sole ownership (community property would be included), corporate or partnership. As this is a gray area, it is recommended that guidance as to whether or not a license is required be sought from the Real Estate Program of the Department of Licensing.

Broker's License: An individual who has been a Washington active licensed salesman for two years and passes the state broker's examination (*See* EXAMINATION, REAL ESTATE LICENSING.) may open his/her own brokerage office. An application must be submitted with the appropriate fee. A broker must maintain an office or be employed by or associated with a licensed broker as an associate broker. The place of business must comply with local zoning; when required, a broker applicant must produce written verification from the city or county Zoning Department that any such place of business is located in an area zoned to allow such a business.

A broker's license may be issued to a sole proprietorship. An individual broker may be appointed a "designated broker" for a corporation, general partnership, limited liability partnership or limited liability company. In each case, application is as stated above. The broker must be an officer in the corporation; in a partnership, the broker must be a full general partner. In a limited liability company the broker must be the manager or a member, or a partner of the limited liability partnership. All officers, partners and members must provide a current credit report. Only the designated broker has to have a license; no other officer or partner need have any type of real estate license in Washington. An officer or partner who does not have a valid real estate license may not engage in the real estate business by virtue of the corporation, partnership, limited liability company or limited liability partnership being licensed. The designated applicant must submit a certified copy of documents creating the legal entity. For example, with a corporation a copy of the Articles of Incorporation; a copy of the corporation's annual report and a copy of the corporate meeting minutes designating an individual the corporation's broker and specifying the duties as such. The designated broker partnership applicant must submit a copy of the Partnership Agreement designating an individual the partnership's broker and specifying the duties as such. In a corporation, partnership, limited liability partnership or limited liability company, the licensed broker must have full management and supervisory responsibility. A finding in an administrative hearing that the broker did not have full management and supervisory responsibility could result in the broker having his/her license revoked or suspended. It could also result in all corporate officers and partners:

1. Being charged with a gross misdemeanor for violating the real estate license law, and

2. Being permanently prohibited from owning any interest in a licensed real estate office in Washington.

Salesperson's and Associate Broker's License: Unless a salesperson has an inactive license, he/she must be employed by a licensed broker and only one. Unless a broker has an active broker's license or an inactive license, he/she must be employed by a licensed broker as an associate broker. Neither one can accept any commission or other compensation (finder's fee) from anyone other than his/her broker. If either one decides to change brokers, his/her license must be returned to the Department of Licensing with a release form where it will be retained until his/her new broker applies for it to be reissued and pays a transfer fee.

A brokerage office may establish a branch office only when an associate broker who is in direct management of the branch office is designated as a "branch manager." The branch manager is under the overall supervision of the broker.

Temporary Permit: In certain limited circumstances, the Division may issue a temporary broker's permit to the legally accredited representative of a deceased broker, the senior qualified salesman in that office or other qualified representative of the deceased, which shall be valid for a period not exceeding four months.

Term of License: Salesperson, associate broker and broker licenses (sole proprietorship) must be renewed on or before the birthday of the individual. Licenses issued to corporations, general partnerships, limited liability partnerships and limited liability companies expire December 31st. Renewal fees paid by mail are considered as paid when due if the envelope bears a postmark on or before the individual's birthday for individuals or January 1 for corporations, partnerships, limited liability companies and limited liability partnerships.

Before renewing a salesperson's license (active or inactive) for the second time, a salesperson must submit proof of satisfactorily completing thirty (30) clock hours of approved real estate education completed specifically for the renewal. Salesperson's renewal example: First license issued September 1, 1998. Next birthday, December 1, 1998 is the first renewal of the license. December 1, 1999 will be the second renewal and the 30 hours educational requirement must be fulfilled prior to that date. Failure to submit proof prior to the second renewal date will cause a mandatory suspension of the license. There can be no waiver of this requirement. A list of approved courses is available from the Real Estate Program of the Department of Licensing.

Any person who has passed the examination for real estate broker or real estate salesperson must become licensed within one year from the date of such examination in order to become eligible for such license. Failure to comply with this provision will necessitate the taking and passing of another examination. An individual may have his/her first license under an **inactive status** by submission of the proper form and payment of the proper fee.

Continuing Education: After the second renewal, a licensee must successfully completed 30 clock hours of approved education every two years before being permitted to renew his/her license.

Inactive Status: Any license may be placed on inactive status (generally referred to as "on ice"). Upon passing the state examination, an individual may apply for a first license on inactive status. While on inactive status, the individual may not engage in any activity which requires a real estate license. A license may remain on inactive status indefinitely by paying the annual renewal fee. Failure to pay a license renewal timely will result in a late delinquency penalty. The holder of an inactive license for over three (3) years must successfully complete an approved 30 clock hour course within one year **prior** to becoming actively licensed.

Grounds for Suspension or Revocation of License: The license of a salesperson, associate broker or broker may be revoked, after an administrative hearing, under the following circumstances:

1. Obtaining a license by means of fraud, misrepresentation or concealment.

2. Violating any provision of the License Law or any Rule or Regulation made by the Real Estate Commission.

3. Being convicted of forgery, embezzlement, bribery, larceny, obtaining money under false pretenses, extortion, conspiracy to defraud or similar offenses.

4. Making, causing, authorizing, or knowingly permitting the making or causing of any false statement, description or promise of such character to reasonably in duce any person to act thereon, and knew or could have known the falsity of the statements.

5. Being a party to any material fraud, misrepresentation, conspiracy, collusion, concealment, trick, scheme or device whereby any person lawfully relies on same.

6. Continuing as a salesperson after a license has been revoked or during the sus pension thereof.

7. Conversion of any money, note, contract, etc., to his/her own use or that of his/ her principal.

8. Failing to disclose any information within the licensee's knowledge or produce any other document, book or record demanded by the Division.

9. Continuing to sell real estate or operate according to a plan whereby the interests of the public are endangered after the Division has objected in writing.

10. A finding by a court that the licensee has committed an act of fraudulent or dis honest dealing or a crime involving moral turpitude.

11. Advertising in any manner without affixing the broker's name as licensed.

12. Failing to tell a principal that the earnest money was other than cash prior to acceptance.

13. Charging or accepting compensation from more than one party in any one trans action without full disclosure of all the facts to all parties.

14. Accepting, taking or sharing any undisclosed commission, rebate or direct profit on expenditures made for a principal.

15. Appraising real estate contingent upon reporting a predetermined value.

16. Issuing an appraisal report in which the licensee has an undisclosed interest in the real estate.

17. Misrepresenting membership in a local, state or national real estate association.

18. Discrimination against any person in hiring or in sales activity, on the basis of race, color, creed or national origin.

19. Failure to keep trust account records as prescribed by the Division.

20. Failure to preserve for three (3) years all business records.

21. Failing to furnish a copy of any document signed by an individual at the time of execution.

22. Acceptance by a salesperson, associate broker or branch manager of any commission or any valuable consideration from anyone except from the licensed real estate broker with whom he/she is licensed.

23. Acceptance of any undisclosed rebate or kickback from any organization by a licensee where he/she directed business.

24. Failing to disclose any interest in any real estate being sold or purchased through the licensee.

25. Failure by a broker to exercise adequate supervision over those licensed to the broker.

26. Any conduct in a real estate transaction which demonstrates bad faith, dishonesty, untrustworthiness or incompetency.

Reference: RCW 18.85.230

Violations - Penalty: Any person acting as broker, associate broker or salesperson, without a license, or violating any provision of the License Law, shall be guilty of a gross misdemeanor. If found guilty of violating a provision of the License Law, a licensee's license may be suspended or revoked. Or fined up to $1,000 per violation. Additionally the licensee can be required to satisfactorily complete a 30 hour educational course. In addition to revocation or suspension, the matter may be referred to a county prosecutor for criminal prosecution. In the case of a **non-licensee**, the matter is referred to the county prosecutor in the county in which the offense occurred.
Reference: RCW 18.85 and WAC 308-124

LIEN - A charge or claim which one person (lienor) has upon the property of another (lienee) as security for a debt or obligation. Liens can be created by agreement of the parties (mortgage) or by operation of law (tax liens). They may be general (thus affecting all the debtor's property, as in a judgment lien) or specific (thus affecting only a particular property, as in a mortgage or deed of trust given on one piece of property). Liens can be statutory or equitable, voluntary or involuntary. For example, a mechanic's lien is an involuntary, statutory, special lien, whereas a mortgage or deed of trust is a voluntary, equitable, special lien. If the mortgage lien, however, was foreclosed upon and there was a deficiency, the resulting deficiency judgment, when recorded, would be a general lien upon all of the debtor's property. Certain statutory liens become unenforceable after a lapse of time, e.g., judgment liens after 10 years, mechanics' liens after 90 days from date the court orders the lien to attach, unless suit is filed. Liens do not transfer title to the property; until foreclosure, title remains in the debtor.

The priority of a lien is normally determined by the date of recordation; thus it is important to record the appropriate document as soon as the lien has been created. State property tax liens and assessments, however, take priority over all liens, even those previously recorded. Since the lien is an encumbrance on the title, the lienor should (at the lienee's expense) execute and record a satisfaction of the lien as soon as the lien has been paid, in order to remove this cloud on the title. (*See* DEED OF TRUST, ENCUMBRANCE, JUDGMENT LIEN, MECHANIC'S LIEN, MORTGAGE, TAX LIEN.)

LIEN THEORY STATES - Those states, like Washington which treat a mortgage/deed of trust solely as a security interest in the secured real property with title remaining in the mortgagor/grantor who has use of the property and is entitled to all rents and profits. The lien theory, or equitable theory, regards the debt as the principal fact and the mortgage/deed of trust merely as holding a lien as security for the debt. This differs from a title theory state, wherein legal title is transferred to the lender subject to being reconveyed back to the borrower when the debt is satisfied. (*See* DEED OF TRUST, LIEN, MORTGAGE.)

LIFE-CARE FACILITY - A residential development designed to provide medical and skilled nursing care for senior citizens. Residents are offered a continuing care contract, including independent living units at a periodic rent.

LIFE ESTATE - Any estate in real or personal property which is limited in duration to the life of its owner or by the life of some other designated person. If the estate is measured by the lifetime of a person other than its owner, it is called **life estate per autre vie**. Although classified as a freehold estate (since it is a possessory estate of indefinite duration), a life estate is not an estate of inheritance. For example, Ben Hurst conveys his home to his grandson, Jim, and reserves a life estate to himself. Ben (the life tenant) has a life estate and Jim a reversionary interest in the property. When Ben Hurst dies, the fee simple property reverts to Jim.

A life estate may arise by agreement of the parties, in which case it is called a conventional life estate.

A life tenant:

1. Is entitled to possession and ordinary uses and profits of the land, just as if he/she were the fee owner.

2. Is obligated to keep the premises in a reasonable state of repair and free from waste so that the realty will later revert to the grantor or the remainderman in approximately unchanged condition in terms of its characteristics and value.

3. Is obligated to pay the ordinary taxes, interest on encumbrances (not mortgage principal amortization), and his/her apportioned share of special assessments.

4. Is barred from creating any interest in the property which extends beyond the measuring life.

5. Is under no obligation to insure the premises for the benefit of the future interest holders, each of which has a separate, insurable interest and is responsible for obtaining his/her own insurance.

The life tenant may sell his/her interest or encumber it subject to any deed restrictions to the contrary, and the interest is subject to execution sale if there is a money judgment against him/her. The **transferee** receives no greater interest than the life tenant had, that is, an estate which ends at the expiration of the measuring life. Thus it is difficult to sell or mortgage a life estate. The mortgagee of a life tenant's interest would therefore probably require the life tenant to make the mortgagee the beneficiary of a term life insurance policy.

For tax depreciation purposes, a life tenant deducts depreciation over the useful life of the property and not on the tenant's life expectancy. After the death of the life tenant, the remainderman gets the deduction.

Where a taxpayer makes a gift of real property but retains a life estate, the entire value of the property is includable in the deceased taxpayer's estate for federal estate tax purposes.

A life estate is terminated by the death of the person whose existence is the measuring life. While no probate proceeding is necessary to establish title in the remainderman, it is good title practice to record a death certificate to show the fact of death. If the life tenant acquires the fee simple title to the property, the life estate is terminated by merger. (*See* DEPRECIATION, TAX; FREEHOLD, PER AUTRE VIE, REMAINDERMAN, WASTE.)

LIFE TENANT - A person possessing a life estate.

LIFTING CLAUSE - A clause included in a junior loan instrument that allows the underlying mortgage or deed of trust (senior loan) to be replaced or refinanced as long as the amount of the new senior loan does not exceed the amount of the first lien outstanding at the time the junior loan was made. (*See* SUBORDINATION AGREEMENT.)

LIGHT AND AIR - An owner has no natural right to light and air and cannot complain when a neighbor erects a structure which cuts off his/her light and air. To eliminate this possibility, some abutting owners attempt to purchase an easement for **light and air** over their neighbor's property. Such easement should, of course, be granted in writing and recorded. For example, an owner with a beautiful view of Puget Sound might seek to obtain an easement of light and air from his/her neighbor over the neighbor's property. If granted, then neither the neighbor nor any successor could build a structure in this air-space. One cannot acquire a light and air easement by prescription; that is, one cannot claim that he/she has acquired a prescriptive right to the air space because he/she has used the view for the prescriptive statutory period of 10 years. (*See* AIR RIGHTS.)

In 1971 the State of Washington adopted legislation to protect the public's right to the natural beauty of the State along its highway system. (*See* SCENIC VISTA ACT.)

In some areas of the larger metropolitan cities of the country, including Seattle, efforts have been made to prevent high-rises, thereby protecting the public's right to light and air. (*See* DOWN ZONING.)

LIGHT INDUSTRY - A zoning designation for industrial use encompassing mostly unobjectionable light manufacturing, as opposed to those industries which cause noise, air or water disturbances and pollution. It includes such "clean" industries as bakeries, dry cleaning and food processing.

LIKE-KIND PROPERTY - A federal tax term relating to the nature of real estate rather than its quality or quantity. Only like-kind quality will qualify for a real estate exchange and the resulting tax benefit.

Like-kind property is any real property, whether improved or unimproved, held and to be held by the taxpayer for investment or income-producing purposes, thus excluding dealer property and residence. The property need only qualify as like property to the party seeking the tax-deferred benefit of the exchanges of like property. (*See* CONDEMNATION, EXCHANGE.)

One property may be improved and the other raw land, one can be domestic and the other foreign realty, or one a shopping center and the other an apartment building. Both properties must, however, be of the same ownership interest. Thus, a fee simple interest could not be exchanged for a leasehold. However, an IRS regulation does state that a leasehold interest of 30 years or more is to be deemed a fee simple. The Tax Court has upheld the exchange of general partnership interests in partnerships with substantially the same kind of underlying assets.

LIMITATIONS OF ACTIONS - Time within which legal actions must be commenced or else be barred. (*See* LACHES, STATUTE OF LIMITATIONS.)

LIMITED COMMON AREA OR ELEMENTS - That special class of common elements in a condominium reserved for the use of a certain apartment(s) to the exclusion of other apartments. This would include assigned parking stalls, storage units, or any common areas and facilities available for use by at least one, but less than all, unit owners.

Any amendment of the declaration affecting the limited common elements requires the unanimous consent of all those to whom the use is reserved. Additions to or alterations of a limited common element require prior approval of the Board of Directors on behalf of the Homeowners Association. (*See* CONDOMINIUM.)
Reference: RCW 64.32

LIMITED LIABILITY COMPANY (LLC) - A hybrid business entity which combines characteristics and benefits of both a limited partnership and a S corporation. Unlike a corporation, however, an LLC does not have perpetual existence. The principal governing document of an LLC is its operating or management agreement, which is similar to a corporation's bylaws. (*See* S CORPORATION.)

LIMITED PARTNERSHIP - A partnership agreement in which one person (or group of persons) organizes, operates, and is responsible for, the entire partnership venture. This person is called the general partner and often referred to as the managing partner. The other members of the partnership are merely investors and have no say in the organization and direction of the operation. These passive investors are called limited partners. The limited partners share in the profits and compensate the general partner for his/her efforts out of such profits. Unlike a general partnership, in which each member is responsible for the total losses (if any) of the syndicate, the limited partners only stand to lose as much as they invest — usually nothing more. The general partner, then, is totally responsible for any large-scale losses incurred by the investment. Note, however, that when a limited partner receives cash distributions, either upon dissolution of the partnership or during the investment period, and the partnership's creditors' obligations remain unsatisfied, he/she may be required to return such distributions in order to satisfy the creditors' claims.

The limited partnership has been popularly used in the syndication of real estate ventures because it permits investors with only small amounts of capital to participate in real estate projects that require much capital and expertise in management, restricts the potential liability to their contribution, and also permits "pass-through" of tax benefits of real property ownership.

It is important for the organizer of a limited partnership to be careful that the partnership is not treated by the IRS as an association taxable as a corporation (resulting in "double taxation" of income). Careful drafting of the limited partnership agreement by an experienced real estate attorney will usually achieve for the partnership its preferred tax status, in which all profits or losses "pass through" the partnership and are taxed only at the individual level. Partnership status thus combines the direct tax advantages of an immediate write-off of losses, if any, plus the elimination of the second tax at the corporate level.

The 1976 Tax Reform Act provides that fees paid in connection with syndicating a partnership must be capitalized. Organizational expenditures, which are those expenditures incidental to the creation of the partnership, may be capitalized or amortized over a 60-month period commencing with the month that the partnership begins business. The Act also provides that it is no longer permissible to allocate a full share of a partnership loss for the entire year to a partner who did not hold his/her interest the entire year. A partnership share of income or losses must correspond to the portion of the year that a partnership interest is held.

Washington has adopted the Uniform Limited Partnership Act to regulate the formation and operation of limited partnerships in this State. Under this Act, a certificate stating any assumed name, if any, names of all participants, amount of capital contributed by each, terms of partnership, shares of profit to each limited partner, must be filed with the Secretary of State's office in Olympia. The name may not contain the surname of any limited partner. An interest of a limited partner is personal property and fully assignable, so long as the filed certificate is amended.

Under the 1986 Tax Reform Act, partnerships are subject to the passive loss rules. Thus, losses from limited partnerships can be used only to offset income from other "passive investments," and cannot be used to shelter income from salary, interest, and dividends as under previous law. Passive investments are defined as any trade or business in which the taxpayer does not materially participate, and any rental activity, whether or not the taxpayer materially participates. Any interest held by a limited partner is automatically treated as passive.

In 1981, Washington adopted some significant changes in its limited partnership law, which now:

1. Simplifies the addition and withdrawal of partners.

2. Allows greater operating flexibility for limited partnerships.

3. Allows for reservation of names of limited partnerships.

4. Recognizes that a partnership's agreement and not the certificate of partnership is the basic document of the partnership. The certificate is a statutory required prerequisite to the formation of a partnership, but serves only as notice that the partnership is limited and that certain partners are limited partners.

5. Deals significantly with the important issue of the powers and liabilities of limited partners. The basic test for limited partner liability, i.e., whether there has been participation "in the control of the business," is retained. However, a limited partner who has exercised "control" becomes liable only to third parties who have transacted business with the partnership with actual knowledge of the exercise of control, unless the exercise was in "substantially the same" manner as a general partner in which case liability is the same as that of a general partner. An important change is made with respect to the liability of people erroneously believing themselves to be limited partners. The act preserves, for a limited period, the liability of such equity participants to third parties who transact business with the partnership with the good faith belief that the participant is a general partner. The period of such liability may be terminated by the equity participant by with drawing from the enterprise or by filing the appropriate certificate showing the equity participant's status as a limited partner.

6. Provides several changes regarding the financing and dissolution of limited partnerships. It allows the contribution of services in return for a limited partnership interest.

7. Makes explicit the ability to issue a limited partnership interest in exchange for a promise of future cash payments, property contributions, or performance of services.

8. Provides the courts with considerable authority to judicially dissolve a limited partnership. Dissolution may be granted upon a showing by any partner that "it is not reasonably practicable to carry on the business in conformity with the partnership agreement," or that "other circumstances render dissolution equitable."

9. Clarifies previous law which was unclear as to whether or not limited partnerships operating in more than one state retain limited liability status in any other state than the state of organization. The act provides for registration of foreign limited partnerships and specifies choice-of-law rules.

Since a limited partner's interest is personal property, his/her death will not dissolve the partnership. Also, judgment and federal tax liens against a partner do not affect the partnership property, although it may affect the partner's right to receive profits.

Under 1987 Amendments, a limited partner may participate in a number of activities in the operation of the partnership without incurring the liability of a general partner; these activities include: taking any legal action permitted or required by law, requesting or attending a meeting of partners; winding up the partnership, exercising a right or power permitted to limited partners by law, or proposing or making decisions relating to the admission or removal of either a limited or general partner, a transaction involving a conflict of interest between the partnership and a general partner, an amendment to the partnership agreement or certificate, and matters the partnership agreement permits the limited partners to approve or disapprove.

A foreign limited partnership must register in this state, but is not required to disclose the general nature of its business. The registration must include the names and addresses of all general partners and the address at which the names and addresses of the limited partners may be found. The foreign domestic partnership must also promise to retain those records until the registration in this state is canceled.

The sale of a limited partnership interest involves the sale of a security and thus is subject to applicable state and federal laws dealing with the sale of securities and would have to be registered unless exempt. (*See* AT-RISK RULES, DOUBLE TAXATION, FICTITIOUS NAME, INTEREST, NET WORTH, REAL PROPERTY SECURITIES REGISTRATION, SAFE HARBOR RULE.)
Reference: RCW 19.80, RCW 25.08

LIMITED POWER OF ATTORNEY - A power of attorney that is limited to a particular task, such as the transfer of a specific parcel of property. Most lenders and title insurance companies prefer the use of limited or special powers of attorney in real estate transactions as opposed to the use of general powers of attorney. (*See* POWER OF ATTORNEY, SPECIAL AGENCY.)

LIMITED PRINCIPAL'S LICENSE - *See* DIRECT PARTICIPATION PROGRAM LICENSES

LIMITED SERVICE BROKER - A broker who offers the consumer less than the full line of services usually provided by a real estate broker. Such limited services might include explaining the standard offer form, writing ads, assisting a buyer to obtain financing, and following up in escrow, but might not include advertising, showing, or holding open houses.

LINEAL - (1) As it relates to family relationships, **lineal** means direct-line descendants, such as children or grandchildren, as opposed to collateral (nephews, cousins, etc.); living descendants (blood or adopted), however remote from the deceased; (2) as it relates to measurements, **lineal** means having length only. The lineal measure of a square four feet on each side is 16 feet. Also called a **linear** measure.

LINE OF CREDIT - A maximum amount of money a bank will lend one of its more reliable and credit worthy customers without need for any formal loan submission. The borrower is thus assured of quick loan service without experiencing any delaying credit review prior to disbursement of any funds. Lines of credit are subject to periodic review of the customer's credit standing and overall banking relationship. (*See* LETTER OF CREDIT.)

LINE OF CREDIT LOAN - A loan in a second lien position established to provide cash to the borrower on an as-needed and on-going basis. In recent years homeowners have used this type of loan as a source of cash for medical expenses, education and consumer purchases. The interest rate charged is normally an adjustable or variable rate and is only charged on the outstanding balance, not on the total line of credit. Since the Tax Reform Act of 1986, such loans, also known as home equity loans, have become very popular, primarily due to the fact that interest paid by the borrower is normally tax deductible.

LINE STAKES - Ordinarily refers to those stakes set along the boundary lines of a parcel of land surveyed by metes and bounds.

LINTEL - A horizontal board that supports the load over an opening such as a door or window.

LIQUIDATED DAMAGES - An amount predetermined by the parties to an agreement as the total amount of compensation an injured party should receive in the event the other party breaches a specified part of the contract. Often in building contracts the parties will anticipate the possibility of a breach (for example, a delay in completion by a set date) and will specify in the contract the amount of the damages to be paid in the event of the breach. To be enforceable, the liquidated damage clause must set forth an amount which bears a reasonable relationship to the actual damages as **estimated** by the parties, otherwise, the court will treat the amount as a penalty for failure to perform. The courts look with disfavor upon penalty clauses and will probably declare them to be void and unenforceable. The clause should therefore specify for what damage the party is being compensated (for loss of rent, attorney fees, etc.). As a general rule, a court will not enforce a liquidated damage clause in an installment contract or real estate contract where the clause tends to work a forfeiture of all installment payments made.

The liquidated damage provision in the Purchase and Sale Agreement provides for a loss of the deposit if the buyer defaults (the broker may be entitled to a portion of this deposit). Generally, a cash deposit placed with the seller or with escrow is considered to be liquidated damages in the event of the buyer's default; the seller could, however, elect to pursue his/her other legal remedies. The theory is that a buyer is not likely to give up money as a deposit unless the amount is a reasonable estimate of the damages that the seller will suffer if the buyer breaches the contract. (*See* DAMAGES, ELECTION OF REMEDIES, UNJUST ENRICHMENT.)

LIQUIDITY - The ability to sell an asset and convert it into cash at a price close to its true value. Stocks that are traded publicly (not stocks in small or closely held corporations) are a relatively liquid investment. Real estate is traditionally considered to be a longer term investment, as it is not highly liquid.

One test of the liquidity of a person or company is a ratio which measures the immediate debt-paying ability of the person. It considers cash in hand and anything that can be instantly turned into cash, called quick assets. A 1:1 ratio is generally acceptable for a business firm. The ratio is: **Quick Assets: Current Liabilities.**

LIS PENDENS - A legal document recorded in the Office of the County Auditor which gives constructive notice that an action has been filed in either a state or federal court affecting a particular piece of property. "Lis Pendens" is a Latin term which means "action pending" and is in the nature of a quasi-lien. A person subsequently acquiring an interest in that property takes it subject to any judgment that may be entered; that is, a purchaser is bound by the result of the lawsuit.

A notice of lis pendens is not the same as placing a lien on or attaching real property. It is only notice of a pending action involving title or possession of real property. A lien, however, is a charge or security interest against the property, and an attachment is a procedure to preserve the property for collection purposes. The end result of filing a lis pendens, however, is the same; that is, the property may not be freely sold or encumbered and title is thereby effectively rendered unmarketable during the litigation.

The notice of pendency of action must contain the names of the parties, the object of the action and a description of the property affected thereby. From and after the time of recording the notice, the purchaser or encumbrancer of the property affected shall be deemed to have constructive notice of the pendency against parties designated by their real names. Naturally, an attorney should be consulted prior to filing a lis pendens. (*See* ATTACHMENT, SLANDER OF TITLE.)

LISTING - A written employment agreement between a property owner and a broker authorizing the broker to find a buyer or a tenant for certain real property. Oral listings are not illegal, they are just unenforceable. Even though an oral listing may be unenforceable, it still imposes fiduciary duties on a broker.

Listings can take the form of **open listings, net listings, exclusive agency, or exclusive right-to-sell** (*See* those topics herein). In Washington, the commonly accepted form is the **exclusive right-to-sell listing.**

The contract is between the seller and the broker. The seller does not have to be the owner. Someone holding an option may list such property with a broker for sale, intending to exercise the option only if a buyer is found. If a salesperson quits a real estate company, the listing remains the property of the broker.

The professional broker will be careful to check the ownership of the property to be listed to avoid getting listings signed by unauthorized persons. The broker has a legal and ethical duties to check the property and be sure that all the information on the listing contract

is accurate and complete. He/she shouldn't ask the owner to warrant the accuracy of technical or detailed matters about which the owner could not really know. (*See* REAL PROPERTY TRANSFER DISCLOSURE STATEMENT.)
Reference: RCW 64.06

Listings are personal service contracts, and as such, they may not be assigned to another broker. This does not, however, prevent the broker from delegating to his/her sales staff the task of procuring buyers for the property. In addition, the listing may provide that the broker will use the services of other brokers via a multiple listing service. In a buyer's listing, the buyer employs the broker to locate a property. Due to the fact that it is a personal service contract, the death of the buyer/seller or broker terminates the contract.

The time limit included in the listing agreement is extended by implication if negotiations to sell the property are in progress at the time the listing expires.

The broker must give a copy of the listing to all the parties signing it at the time of signing. The broker should not show the listing contract (including MLS listings) to the buyer, since the listing is an employment contract strictly between the seller and broker. A buyer who has read the listing might then be able to sue the seller if the buyer had relied on misstatements or omissions in the listing and thereby suffered damages.

The listing states the amount of commission the seller will owe the broker upon the happening of certain stated conditions. If a listed property is transferred by way of an involuntary sale, such as a foreclosure, condemnation, or tax sale, the broker is usually not entitled to a commission. (*See* AGENCY, CONTRACT, EXCLUSIVE AGENCY, EXCLUSIVE RIGHT TO SELL, EXTENDER CLAUSE, MULTIPLE LISTING SERVICE, NET LISTING, OFFER, OPEN LISTING, REAL ESTATE BROKERAGE RELATIONSHIP ACT, TERMINATION OF LISTING.)
Reference: RCW 18.85

LISTOR - A real estate broker or salesperson who obtains the listing on a particular property. In most brokerage companies, the listor will receive a certain percentage (perhaps 25 percent) of the total commission if the property is sold. The listor will receive more if he/she also is responsible for making the sale (the **selling** salesperson).

LITIGATE - To dispute or contend in the form of a lawsuit; to settle a dispute or seek relief in a court of law; to carry on a suit.

LITIGATION - A lawsuit. Legal action, including all proceedings therein.

LITTORAL LAND - Land bordering on the shore of a sea or ocean and thus affected by the tide currents. Littoral land is different from riparian land, which borders on a bank of a watercourse or stream. *(See* RIPARIAN.)

LIVABILITY SPACE RATIO (LSR) - For purposes of site planning, the minimum square feet of non-vehicular outdoor area which is provided for each square foot of total floor area.

LIVE LOAD - A moving or variable weight which may be safely added to the intrinsic weight of a structure. For example, a modern high rise office building may have a live load capacity of 60 lbs. per square foot to accommodate office furniture, equipment and people.

LIVING TRUST - An arrangement in which a property owner (trustor) transfers assets to a trustee who assumes specified duties in managing the asset. After payment of operating expenses and trustee's fees, the income generated by the trust property is paid to or used for the benefit of the designated beneficiary. A trust established by a will is called a testamentary trust. (*See* LAND TRUST.)

LOAD - Weight supported by a structural part such as a load-bearing wall.

LOADING DOCK - The area, either within an industrial building and adjacent to its loading doors, or outside of the structure, which is used for the shipping or receiving of merchandise and the movement of merchandise between the warehouse area and trucks or rail cars.

LOAN BALANCE TABLE - A table showing the balance remaining to be paid on an amortized loan; also called a remaining balance table.

LOAN COMMITMENT - A written commitment by a lender of the amount he/she will loan to a qualified borrower on a particular piece of real estate for a specified amount of time under specified terms. It may be a conditional or qualified commitment or it may be a firm commitment. It is more formal than preliminary loan approval. The lender usually decides after reviewing the borrower's loan application whether to make a commitment to loan the requested funds. This application contains information such as the name and address of the borrower, his/her place of employment, salary, bank accounts, credit references, and the like. (*See* LOAN SUBMISSION.)

LOAN CONSTANT - *See* CONSTANT.

LOAN CORRESPONDENT - One who negotiates loans for conventional lending institutions or other lenders. Many life insurance companies, pension funds, and real estate investment trusts do not have their own mortgage loan departments and rely on loan correspondents. The correspondent may continue to service the loan for the lender and acts as the collecting agent. (*See* MORTGAGE BANKER.)

LOAN ORIGINATION FEE - A charge incurred by a borrower to cover the administrative costs of the lender in making a loan. The amount is typically stated as a percentage of the loan, for example, one percent.

LOAN SUBMISSION - A package of pertinent papers and documents with regard to a specific property or properties, which a lender receives for his/her review and consideration for the purpose of making a mortgage loan. The following papers and documents are generally included: (a) letter of transmittal, (b) appraisal, (c) financial statements, (d) credit reports and/or Dun and Bradstreet reports, (e) application, (f) sales or purchase agreements on existing properties, (g) leases, if applicable, (h) photographs, (i) plat plan and survey, (j) cost breakdown, if applicable, (k) set of plans and specifications on proposed construction, (l) such as zoning ordinances, utilities map, strip maps, aerial photographs and the like, and (m) other pertinent information which would help the lender in considering a particular submission. (*See* LOAN COMMITMENT.)

LOAN-TO-VALUE RATIO - The ratio that the amount of the loan bears to the appraised value of the property or the sales price, whichever is lower (the amount of the loan is divided by the lower figure). Loan-to-value ratios depend on the individual lender's policy. Most lenders realize that the greater an equity the borrower has in the property the less inclined he/she is going to be to default and lose it through foreclosure. Of all commercial lenders, savings and loan associations traditionally allow the highest loan-to-value ratio. The maximum loan-to-value ratio for commercial lenders is often set by law, by the state or federal regulatory agency that oversees the particular commercial lender. When private mortgage insurance is used, the lender can sometimes offer 90-95 percent loan-to-value ratios (usually restricted to owner-occupants). Investors might qualify for 80 percent financing. FHA loan ratios are fixed by statute. There are no ratios for VA loans. A maximum loan-to-value ratio is set by law for institutional lenders, such as commercial banks and savings and loan associations. (*See* PRIVATE MORTGAGE INSURANCE.)

LOBBY - (1) A public waiting area or meeting place in hotels, motels, apartment buildings, office buildings, or other similar structures. (2) To work for or against passage of a bill or resolution pending before a legislative body.

LOCAL REALTORS® ASSOCIATION OR BOARD - A local city or county-wide organization which is a member of the Washington Association of Realtors® and the National Association of Realtors®, which is composed of real estate licensees holding Realtor® status. There are 32 local Association/Board of Realtors® in the State of Washington. The membership size of the boards vary from 4,800 in the Seattle-King County Association to 59 in the Grant County Association of Realtors®. There is one statewide (considered a local) Association composed of Commercial-Investment Realtors®.

A local Association of Realtors® focuses attention on the areas of professional standards and conduct, education and local legislative problems. In some cases, it has a committee that performs a multiple listing service function. (*See* NATIONAL ASSOCIATION OF REALTORS®, WASHINGTON ASSOCIATION OF REALTORS®.)

LOCAL IMPROVEMENT DISTRICT - These districts are activated under state law by the local city or county or by vote of the inhabitants of a particular geographical area. Upon activation, the district becomes a separate legal entity governed by a board of directors and possessing many of the characteristics of a city, particularly in the field of taxation. As a rule, the district issues its own bonds to finance particular improvements such as water distribution systems, drainage structures, irrigation works, parking facilities and a host of other types of developments. To repay the funds borrowed through the issuance of bonds, these districts have the power to assess all lands included in the district on an ad valorem basis, such assessments constituting liens on the land until paid. These liens can be foreclosed by sale similar to a tax sale and are prior to private property interests.

LOCATION, LOCATION, LOCATION - A commonly used real estate expression to denote the "three" most important factors in determining the success of a real estate project.

LOCK BOX - A special lock placed on the door of a listed property designed to facilitate the showing by real estate licensees of that property. A cooperating broker, who usually is a member of a MLS, who wanted to inspect or show the property quickly need not go to the listing broker's office to get the house keys. Some lock boxes have locks that open with keys. Others operate with a code.

Lack of ordinary care in installing the lock box could result in liability for property damage, theft, or personal injury. Some errors and omissions insurance policies now have a special lock box liability endorsement.

LOCK-IN - 1. The prohibition of prepayment of a loan secured by a mortgage or deed of trust, so that the borrower is " locked in"' to the loan for a specified period.

2. The period of time (often 30 days) that the interest rate and other terms and conditions of a loan commitment is guaranteed by a lender.

LOCUS SIGILLI (L.S.) - Latin for "under seal," used in the abbreviated form, "L.S.," at the end of signature lines in some formal legal documents; used instead of the actual seal. At one time, individuals and corporations had seals, and documents were invalid unless the seal was affixed. Now, signatures are notarized and only corporations in certain circumstances must affix a seal.

LOFT - Building area which is unfinished; also refers to open space, normally on the first or second floor and typically used for a low-cost manufacturing operation. The tenant pays a lower rent for loft space than for finished space, and amortizes the cost of finishing the area over the term of the lease.

LONG TERM CAPITAL GAIN - Gain on the sale of a capital asset which has been held for a specified time or longer. Long term capital gains are taxed at a special rate and not as ordinary income. (*See* CAPITAL GAIN.)

LONG TERM FINANCING - A mortgage or deed of trust for a term of ten years or more, as distinguished from construction loans or interim loans. (*See* ADJUSTABLE RATE LOAN, ADJUSTABLE RATE MORTGAGE (ARM), BUY DOWN LOAN, EQUITY-AIDE/HOME PARTNERS, EQUITY SHARING LOAN, EXTENDED MORTGAGE TERM, FLEXIBLE LOAN INSURANCE PROGRAM (FLIP), GRADUATED-PAYMENT ADJUSTABLE-RATE MORTGAGE, GRADUATED-PAYMENT MORTGAGE, MORTGAGE SUBSIDIES, RENEGOTIABLE-RATE MORTGAGE, REVERSE ANNUITY, SHARED APPRECIATION LOAN, VARIABLE-RATE MORTGAGE, WRAP AROUND MORTGAGE.)

LONG TERM LEASE - A lease covering a period of ten years or more. (*See* LEASE.)

LOOP - A looped roadway having two access points off the same roadway.

LOSS FACTOR - A commercial leasing term, also known as the **load factor** or **partial floor factor**, which is the square footage difference between the rentable area and the usable area expressed as a percentage. For example, an office building floor with a rentable area of 16,000 square feet and a usable area of 14,400 square feet has a load factor of 10 percent. The 1,600 square feet is used up by bathrooms, corridors and elevator shafts.

The loss factor is a simple gauge for a tenant to use in evaluating separate rental sites which may have comparable rents but greatly different loss factors.

LOSS PAYEE - The person designated on an insurance policy to be paid in case the insured property is damaged or destroyed. A secured lender often requires the borrower to carry adequate insurance on the property used as security and to name the lender as a loss payee. (*See* INSURABLE INTEREST.)

LOT - Generally, any portion or parcel of real property. Usually refers to a portion of a subdivision.

LOT, BLOCK AND SUBDIVISION - A description of real property that identifies a parcel of land by reference to lot and block numbers appearing on maps and plats of subdivided land recorded in the Office of the County Auditor. For example, the description might read:

"Lot 19, Block 70, Brock's Addition to the City of Olympia, according to plat thereof recorded in Volume 19 of Plats, Page 40, records of Thurston County, Washington."

A lot is an individual parcel of land generally intended to be conveyed in its entirety to a prospective buyer. A block is typically a group of contiguous lots bounded by streets, such as a city block. Blocks are generally separated by roads. (*See* PLAT, SUBDIVISION.)
Reference: RCW 58.08

LOT LINE - The boundary line of a lot in a subdivision.

LOUVER - Affixed or adjustable formation of slats in a wall, ceiling, door, etc., to let in light and air, allow ventilation of fumes from within and yet keep out rain. A finned sunshade on a building. The diffusion grill on fluorescent light fixtures. Also spelled louvre.

LOVE AND AFFECTION - A type of consideration. Love and affection is a good and sufficient consideration when a gift is intended. It is different from a valuable consideration, and the difference is important in those areas of the law requiring a valuable consideration, such as under the recording act which protects the rights of bona fide purchasers for value. A common example of a deed (usually a quitclaim in Washington) supported by love and affection is a gift transfer of the family home by a father to his son "for love and affection." In Washington, the grantor(s) and grantee(s) must be related to avoid the payment of excise tax. (*See* CONSIDERATION, GIFT TAX, NATURAL AFFECTION, VALUABLE CONSIDERATION.)

LOWBALL OFFER - An offer to purchase a property that is significantly less than the listed price. Such an offer, if accepted, allows the buyer to acquire the property at a price that appears to be below market value. (*See* MARKET VALUE.)

LOW-RISE - A two or three-story building.

LUMINOUS CEILING - A ceiling emitting light from its entire surface, through the use of fluorescent light above translucent glass or plastic.

M

MACRS - See MODIFIED ACCELERATED COST RECOVERY SYSTEM.

MAGGIE MAE - Nickname for the first non-federal secondary market for conventional mortgages, the Mortgage Guaranty Insurance Corporation (MGIC). It provides a market where a lender can sell MGIC-insured mortgages to other investors.

M.A.I. - The initials M.A.I. stands for Member of the American Institute of Real Estate Appraisers. An MAI must be at least 28 years of age, have a college degree and a minimum of five years of "creditable appraisal experience," and must submit two acceptable demonstration appraisal reports, as well as pass certain required examinations. MAI appraisers subscribe to a high code of professional standards and ethics. Most lenders requiring an appraisal will request a report done by an MAI or another professional, such as a SREA (Society of Real Estate Appraisers) or an ASA (American Society of Appraisers). (*See* APPRAISAL.)

MAIL, USE OF - *See* ACCEPTANCE, REAL ESTATE PURCHASE AND SALE AGREEMENT.

MAIN LINE - The principal or through track of a railroad line on which traffic moves through yards or between stations. The main line is operated by timetable or train order and governed by block signal indication.

MAINTENANCE - The care and work put into a building to keep it in operation and productive use; the general repair and upkeep of a building. If maintenance is deferred, the building will suffer a loss in value. (*See* DEFERRED MAINTENANCE, PROPERTY MANAGEMENT.)

MAINTENANCE FEE - A charge or lien levied against property owners to maintain their real estate in operation and productive use, especially in condominiums. In condominium living, the amount of the maintenance fee is usually determined by the board of directors upon review of the budgets. There are usually two budgets. The first is designed to anticipate the month-by-month needs with totals by category for the year. Financial statements are usually prepared each month. These statements compare the actual receipts and disbursements with the operating budget figures, giving a clear financial picture for basing management decisions.

A second budget called a five-year capital budget is prepared or updated yearly. This budget is designed to anticipate major expenditures such as painting the building, purchasing association insurance for the common areas, recarpeting corridors, and replacing any items of substantial cost. The income for these expenditures is obtained from monthly maintenance fee assessments, and is processed in the monthly financial statement through the condominium reserve fund. This reserve fund money is kept in regular savings accounts or higher yield time certificate deposits, and is withdrawn for disbursements when the need arises. (*See* CONDOMINIUM ASSOCIATION, OPERATING EXPENSES.)

MAJORITY - The age at which a person is no longer a minor and is thus able to freely enter into contracts. The age of majority in Washington for contract purposes is 18. (*See* MINOR.)

MAKER - The person (borrower) who executes a promissory note and thus becomes primarily liable for payment to the payee (lender). The maker of a check is known as the drawer.

MALL - A landscaped public area set aside for pedestrian traffic. Malls are popular features of large retail shopping centers. They are now also being created in established downtown retail areas to revitalize existing businesses and are being built in suburban areas to generate new business.

MANAGEMENT - *See* PROPERTY MANAGEMENT.

MANAGEMENT AGREEMENT - A contract between the owner of income-producing property or condominium project and the individual or firm who will manage that property. The management agreement establishes the scope of the agent's authority, his or her duties, compensation, termination procedures, and other matters, such as payment of expenses. In addition to the essential elements of a valid contract, the written management agreement should contain, at a minimum, the legal description of the property to be managed, "hold harmless" clauses, scope of services, rate and schedule of compensation, accounting and report requirements, the starting date, the termination date and any provisions for renewal options. (*See* CONTRACT, MAINTENANCE FEE, PROPERTY MANAGEMENT.)

MANAGEMENT SURVEY - A detailed analysis of the economic, physical and operational aspects of a property with recommendations as to changes and improvements to enhance the profitability of the project. (*See* PROPERTY MANAGEMENT.)

MANDAMUS - An emergency writ issued from a high court ordering or prohibiting performance of a certain activity by a public official. A court might, for example, order a reluctant public official to issue a real estate license provided the complainant is qualified.

MANSARD ROOF - An architectural style in which the top floor or floors of a structure are designed to appear to be the roof. Such a roof has two slopes on each of the four sides of the building with the upper slope less steeply inclined.

MANTEL - The decorative facing placed around a fireplace. Mantels are usually made of ornamental wood and topped by a shelf.

MANUFACTURED (OR FACTORY BUILT) HOUSING - A residential living unit that is constructed in sections in a factory. The house is built in two or more sections. In the factory there are usually two production lines, one for each half of the house. When the sections come off the assembly line they are carried to the building site by a flat-bed truck. At the building site, the foundation has been laid (either a slab or a crawl space foundation), and the plumbing, wiring and any heating and air conditioning ducts are in place. The sections are then placed onto the foundation and joined together for the finished product. Manufactured housing is often called modular housing.

The quality of construction and the materials used for manufactured housing are very similar to a house built by conventional methods; therefore, it is distinguished from a mobile home. When the unit is permanently affixed to a foundation, it assumes the characteristics of a site-built residential dwelling and can be legally classified as real property. When a loan is issued on a manufactured house, an ALTA 7 endorsement (title insurance) is usually required if loan closing instructions indicate that the secured property is improved by a manufactured housing unit.

MANUFACTURED HOUSING INSTITUTE - This trade organization represents the manufacturers and dealers of mobile and modular homes throughout the United States and is based in Arlington, Virginia.

MAPS AND PLATS - Surveys of particular pieces of land prepared by registered surveyors or civil engineers, showing monuments, boundaries, area, ownership, and the like.

A subdivider must submit maps and plats of the proposed subdivision with his/her application for registration of the subdivision. The subdivider must also record the subdivision map and plat at the County Auditor's; thereafter, when lots are sold in the subdivision, the legal description need only refer to the subdivision lot and block number, name of the subdivision and the Volume and Page of the County records in which it was recorded.

It is illegal to subdivide a tract into lots and sell them by lot or block number without first recording a map or plan of the subdivision. The County Auditor will not accept a plat for

recording until it has been approved by the appropriate legislative or planning authority. (*See* LOT, BLOCK AND SUBDIVISION, PLAT, SHORT PLAT.)
Reference: RCW 58.08, RCW 58.16.

MARGINAL LAND - Land which is of little value because of some deficiency, such as poor access, lack of adequate rainfall, or steep terrain. Modern land reclamation and development techniques have successfully converted some marginal lands into attractive and functional developments.

One of the earliest attempts to improve marginal land in Washington was Henry Yesler's use of sawdust from his sawmills on Skid Road to fill the low lying area where Pioneer Square is now located in Seattle.

MARINA - A docking and mooring facility for boats which is generally equipped with repair facilities, gas, supplies, and other conveniences; a boat basin.

MARITAL DEDUCTION - A deduction against federal estate tax due equal to the value of property passing (in certain ways) to the surviving spouse, up to a maximum of approximately one-half the decedent spouse's estate. (*See* ESTATE TAX, FEDERAL.)

MARK - A symbol used for a signature. (*See* X.)

MARKETABLE TITLE - Title that is free from defects or flaws that may disturb the purchaser's peaceful possession and enjoyment of the property or its market value if he/ she desires to sell it.

Good or clear salable title reasonably free from risk of litigation over possible defects; also referred to as marketable title, or as "merchantable title," or "saleable title."

A seller under a Purchase and Sale Agreement (E/M) is required to deliver marketable title at closing; e.g., title that is so free from significant defects, other than those specified in the E/M that the purchaser can be assured against having to defend the title. Title would not be marketable if there were a significant risk of litigation; the buyer cannot be forced to buy a lawsuit.

Sometimes a buyer will insert in the E/M a provision to the effect that the seller shall deliver title "free from all defects or encumbrances." A seller should be aware that in such a case the buyer could probably reject title even if there were only a small or insignificant encroachment or defect. Unless the E/M provides otherwise (usually contained in the "subject to" clause), any of the following could render title unmarketable: easements, restrictions, violations of restrictions, zoning ordinance violation, existing leases and encroachments.

Although an unmarketable title does not mean that the property cannot be transferred, it does mean that there are certain defects in the title which may limit or restrict its ownership, and the purchaser cannot be forced to accept a conveyance which is materially different from the one bargained for in the Purchase and Sale Agreement.

Questions of marketable title must be raised by the purchaser prior to acceptance of the deed. Once the buyer accepts the deed, his/her only recourse is to sue on the covenant of warranty, if any, contained in the deed. (*See* MERGER, SUBJECT CLAUSE, UNMARKETABLE TITLE.)

MARKET DATA APPROACH - A method of appraising or evaluating real property based on the principle of substitution, that is, the value of property tends to be established by the prices paid for similar properties more commonly referred to as **direct sales comparison** approach. The three main steps in the market data approach are:

1. Locate comparable properties (properties with the same "highest and best use") which have sold recently, usually within the last three months;

2. Compare these properties with the subject property and make all necessary adjustments in the sales prices for any significant differences in the property, such as age, location and physical characteristics; and

3. Correlate all the comparable information and draw a conclusion of value.

The market data approach is the most reliable gauge of the market and is most frequently used in appraising residential property, where the amenities are often so difficult to measure. This approach is also a component for use in the other two methods of determining value: market data is used to determine the depreciation figure to be used in the cost approach, and the capitalization rate to be used in the income approach. The market data approach requires an active real estate market for the type of property being appraised. (*See* APPRAISAL, COMPARABLE, DIRECT SALES COMPARISON APPROACH.)

MARKET VALUE - The highest price, estimated in terms of money, which a property will bring if exposed for sale in the open market, allowing a reasonable time to find a purchaser who buys with knowledge of all the uses to which the property is adapted and for which it is capable of being used; often referred to as the price at which a willing and informed seller would sell and a willing and informed buyer would buy, neither being under any pressure to act.

Under guidelines published by federal lending institutions (FNMA, FHLMC, FHLBB), market value is the most probable price which a property should bring in a competitive and open market under all conditions requisite to a fair sale, the buyer and seller each acting prudently, knowledgeably and assuming the price is not affected by undue stimulus. Implicit in this definition is the consummation of a sale as of a specified date and the passing of title from seller to buyer under conditions whereby:

1. Buyer and seller are typically motivated;

2. Both parties are well informed or well advised, and each acting in what he/she considers his/her own best interest;

3. A reasonable time is allowed for exposure in the open market;

4. Payment is made in terms of cash in U.S. dollars or in terms of financial arrangements comparable thereto; and

5. The price represents the normal consideration for the property sold unaffected by special or creative financing or sales concessions granted by anyone associated with the sale. (*See* FAIR MARKET VALUE.)

MARKETING PLAN - A study detailing the means by which a parcel(s) of real estate (improved or unimproved) will be sold. The plan, if developed properly, will identify the target market, establish how and when the property will be shown and, generally, cover the total marketing of the property. Such a plan, while it may be used for a single parcel such as a home, is very commonly used in association with timesharing and second home sites. The marketing plan should be developed prior to the property being available for purchase.

MARRIED WOMAN - Until 1972, a married woman had a disability under Washington community property laws. Under the 1972 amendments to the community property laws, women became equal in dealing with the community's property. Specifically, the law was changed to provide that: (1) Neither spouse shall sell, convey, or encumber the community real property without the other spouse joining the execution of the deed or other instrument by which the real estate is sold, conveyed, or encumbered, and such deed or other instrument must be acknowledged by both spouses. (2) Neither spouse shall purchase or contract to purchase community real property without the other spouse joining in the transaction of purchase or in the executing of the contract to purchase. (*See* COMMUNITY PROPERTY.)
Reference: RCW 26.16.030.

MASTER FORM INSTRUMENT - An instrument containing many covenants and other clauses in a deed of trust may be recorded with the county auditor as a master form instrument. Such an instrument need not be acknowledged. It is indexed under the name of the person recording same. Thereafter, all of the provisions in the master form instrument may be incorporated by reference in any other deed of trust by reference to the county, and the date when recorded and the Auditor's File Number, volume and page where such master is recorded, and by furnishing a copy of the master form to the person who is executing the deed of trust.

MASTER LEASE - The dominant lease in a building or development. For example, a developer might lease land from a fee owner, construct a building or condominium, and then sublease space to others. The subleases will generally have provisions that conform to the terms of the master lease, since the sublease is subject to the terms of the master lease. (*See* SUBLEASE.)

MASTER PLAN - A comprehensive plan to guide the long-term physical development of a particular area.

MASTER SENIOR APPRAISER - The senior designation granted by the National Association of Master Appraisers. To become designated, an individual must have completed a series of courses in appraising residential, rural and commercial/investment properties, and submit three appropriate demonstration appraisals. Each member must subscribe to the Uniform Standards of Professional Appraisal Practice and a set of professional ethics. Members may use the initials "MSA" after their name to indicate membership.

MASTER SWITCH - An electrical wall switch which controls more than one fixture or outlet in a room.

MATERIAL FACT - Any fact that is relevant to a person making a decision. Agents must disclose all material facts to their clients. Buyer agents must disclose to their principals material facts about the condition of the property, such as known: structural defects, building code violations and hidden dangerous conditions. Brokers are often placed in a no-win situation of trying to evaluate whether a certain fact is material enough that it needs to be disclosed to a prospective buyer, such as the fact a murder occurred on the property ten years ago or the fact the neighbors have loud parties. It is sometimes difficult to distinguish between "fact" and "opinion." The statement "Real property taxes are low" is different from "Real property taxes are $500 per year." Even though brokers act in good faith, they may still be liable for failure to exercise reasonable care or competence in ascertaining and communicating pertinent facts that the broker know. (*See* AGENCY, MISREPRESENTATION, REAL ESTATE BROKERAGE RELATIONSHIP ACT.)

Consumers should pay particular attention to the definition of "material fact" in the brochure agents must provide buyers, sellers and tenants. (*See* REAL ESTATE BROKERAGE RELATIONSHIP ACT.)

MATERIALMAN - The supplier of material used in the construction of an improvement. The materialman is entitled to a lien on the property for moneys overdue, whether they be due from the owner or the prime contractor, and he/she must file a lien within 60 days from date furnished. With respect to materials or supplies used in the construction, alteration, or repair of any single family residence or garage, the notice must be given not later than ten days after the date of the first delivery of the materials. (*See* MECHANIC'S LIEN.)

MATURITY - The time when an indebtedness, such as a promissory note, becomes due and is extinguished if paid in accordance with the agreed upon schedule of payments. (*See* CURTAIL SCHEDULE.)

MAXIMUM LOAN AMOUNT - The largest dollar figure in terms of how much money can be borrowed under a specific government loan program, such as subsidized housing program or an FHA project.

MEANDER LINE - An artificial line used by the surveyors to measure the natural, uneven, winding property line formed by rivers, streams and other watercourses bordering a property. The meander line is primarily a device to measure area, not to determine a boundary line. Surveyors sometimes use straight lines on courses approximating the natural line. In a conveyance of land described as bounded by a meander line, the true boundary is the streams or waters themselves (which for oceanfront property in Washington is the line of ordinary high tide, which has been defined as "the average elevation of all high tides as observed at a location through a complete tidal cycle of 18.6 years"). (*See* BEACH, HIGH WATER MARK, TIDE LANDS.)

MEASURE OF DAMAGES - The rule of law set by statute or case law as to the amount of damages a plaintiff can recover against a defendant for a breach of contract or other civil wrong. (*See* BENEFIT OF BARGAIN, DAMAGES.)

MEASUREMENT TABLES - Some U.S. measurements and their metrical equivalents that might be useful to anyone in the real estate business.

Unit	**U.S. Measurement**	**Metric Equivalent**
mile	5,280 feet; 320 rods; 1,760 yards	1.609 kilometers
rod	5.50 yards; 16.5 feet	5.029 meters
hectare	2.47 acres	10,000 sq. meters
sq. mile	640 acres	2.590 sq. kilometers
acre	4,840 sq. yards; 160 sq. rods;	4.047 sq. meters
	43,560 sq. feet	0.405 hectares
sq. yard	9 sq. feet	0.836 sq. meters
sq. foot	144 sq. inches	0.093 sq. meters
kilometer	0.62 mile	1,000 meters
chain	66 feet or 100 links	20.117 meters

ACRE EQUIVALENT One Acre Equals a Rectangle of the Following Size

LENGTH (FEET)*		WIDTH (FEET)*
16.5	by	2640
33	by	1320
50	by	871.2
66	by	660
75	by	580.8
100	by	435.6
132	by	330
150	by	290.4
208.7	by	208.7

*Note - multiply by 0.3048 to arrive at the equivalent measurement in meters.

CONVERSION CHART FROM CUSTOMARY TO METRIC AND VICE VERSA

When you know:		You can find:	If you multiply by:
LENGTH	inches	millimeters	25.4
	feet	centimeters	30.48
	yards	meters	0.9
	miles	kilometers	1.6
	millimeters	inches	0.04
	centimeters	inches	0.4
	meters	yards	1.1
	kilometers	miles	0.6
AREA	square inches	square centimeters	6.5
	square feet	square meters	0.09
	square yards	square meters	0.8
	square miles	square kilometers	2.6
	acres	square hectometers (hectares)	0.4
	square centimeters	square inches	0.16
	square meters	square yards	1.2
	square kilometers	square yards	0.4
	square hectometers (hectares)	acres	2.5
MASS	ounces	grams	28.35
	pounds	kilograms	0.45
	short tons	megagrams (metric tons)	0.9
	grams	ounces	0.035
	kilograms	pounds	2.2
	megagrams(metric tons)	short tons	1.1

LIQUID VOLUME	ounces	milliliters	28.35
	pints	liters	0.47
	quarts	liters	0.95
	gallons	liters	3.8
	milliliters	ounces	0.034
	liters	pints	2.1
	liters	quarts	1.06
	liters	gallons	0.26

MECHANIC'S LIEN - A statutory lien created in favor of materialmen and mechanics to secure payment for materials supplied and services rendered in the improvement, repair or maintenance of real property. This right did not exist in common law. Note that materialmen are suppliers, while mechanics are laborers.

The underlying theory of a mechanic's lien is that the materialman has enhanced the value of the property, and he/she should therefore be able to follow the material into the property to assert a claim for payment. The lien accrues in favor of subcontractors, materialmen and laborers independently of the original contractor, and not by way of subrogation to the rights of the latter. Thus, any person or association of persons furnishing labor or material for the improvement of real estate can assert a mechanic's lien provided there is a valid contract. The lien is for work and materials which became a permanent part of the building, and thus dues not cover certain costs for furnishing tools, or office overhead like telephone, stationery and other similar expenses.

The mechanic's lien attaches to the improvement as well as to the interest of the owner of the real property who contracts for the improvement, including the equitable interest of a buyer under a real estate contract. The term "owner" also includes a lessor whose lease requires the erection of buildings, even though only the lessee contracted for the building.

A notice of mechanic's lien for labor or services must be filed within ninety (90) days from the date of the cessation of the performance of labor or the furnishing of materials. If only materials are furnished, there is a sixty (60) day requirement. Notice must be given within ten days after the first day of delivery to a single family residence. (*See* MATERIALMAN.) A lien is filed for record in the Office of the County Auditor. The lien must specifically state a great deal of information, such as: the time of commencement of performing labor or furnishing material, time of cessation, name of person who performed labor or furnished material, the description of the property to be charged with the lien, the name of the owner or reputed owner, the value, the amount for which the lien is claimed and the like.

A lien or a right of lien may be assigned.

The property remains subject to the lien only for a period of eight calendar months after the claim has been filed for record, or, if credit is given and the credit terms are stated in the claim of lien, then eight calendar months after the expiration of such credit.

The mechanic or materialman enforces his/her lien by bringing an action to foreclose the lien some time within the above period. The foreclosure action is similar to the action to foreclose a mortgage. If another foreclosure of lien action on the same property is pending, the lienor who wishes to foreclose his/her lien may either await the outcome of the prior action or be made a party to that action and have his/her lien foreclosed along with another party's lien. No two separate foreclosure of lien actions may be brought at the same time.

Mechanics' and materialmen's liens date back to the commencement of the performance of the labor or furnishing of the materials, and thus have priority over any encumbrance which may attach after that time and all encumbrances attaching before that time of which the lien claimant had neither actual nor constructive notice.

In the event the property is transferred after the lien is effective, but before filing notice of lien, the mechanic's lien has priority. Thus, a good faith purchaser for value without notice of the visible commencement of operations takes title subject to the possibility of a subsequent notice of lien. A prudent purchaser should obtain proper title insurance (an extended ALTA coverage policy) to protect himself or herself against this type of risk. (*See* AMERICAN LAND TITLE ASSOCIATION.)
Reference: RCW 60.04.

MEDIATION - *See* ALTERNATIVE DISPUTE RESOLUTION PROCESS.

MEETING OF THE MINDS - Mutual assent or agreement between the parties to a contract regarding the substance of the contract. Whether there has been a meeting of the minds is an objective test; e.g., did the parties by their words and acts manifest an intention to be bound to a contract. Thus, while a party may not intend to bind himself/herself to a contract, he/she may be deemed to be bound in law because of his/her outward indications of assent. Whether or not there has been a meeting of the minds is measured by observed standards (by the observed statements and conduct) and not that of a person's hidden intention. There can be no contract unless there is a meeting of the minds; e.g., there must be a valid offer which is properly accepted.

The question of whether there has been a meeting of the minds sometimes arises in cases where the broker is claiming he/she has produced a ready, willing and able buyer and is thus entitled to his/her commission despite the fact the seller decides not to accept the buyer's offer (assuming the offer matched the listing terms). (*See* ESTOPPEL, OFFER AND ACCEPTANCE.)

MENACE - The threat of violence used to obtain agreement to a contract. Like duress and undue influence, menace is grounds to void a contract. (*See* DURESS.)

MERCHANTABLE TITLE - *See* MARKETABLE TITLE.

MERCHANTS' ASSOCIATION - An organization for shopping center tenants structured to facilitate joint advertising, promotion and other activities beneficial to the entire center.

MERGER - The uniting or combining of two or more interests or estates into one.

An easement may be extinguished upon the merger of the servient and dominant estates. For example, the owner of Lot One (Mr. Anderson) gives the owner of the adjacent Lot Two (Mr. Corner) an easement to cross over Lot One, and then subsequently Mr. Corner acquires title to Lot One. If Mr. Corner later sells Lot Two to Ms. Lewis the easement is not revived; it has been merged into Lot 1 and would have to be created anew.

As a general rule, when a greater and lesser estate become vested in the same person, the lesser estate merges into the greater estate; thus, if the landlord sells the property to the tenant, there is a merger of the leasehold estate, the lease is terminated, and the tenant is relieved of his/her duty to pay rent.

When a deed is delivered pursuant to a Purchase and Sale Agreement, all the terms of the E/M are merged into and superseded by the deed, unless otherwise provided in the real estate contract or the deed. Thus, if the vendor wants representations, warranties or restrictions in the E/M to continue and survive the deed, he/she must insert them in the deed or specify which covenants and conditions in the E/M are to survive delivery of the deed or assignment of the lease. For example, when the E/M calls for something to be done after closing and delivery of the deed, such as the installation of a sewer system, this requirement would survive the deed and be enforceable.

A merger clause in a contract states; "this writing constitutes the entire agreement between the parties and all other prior negotiations and representations are not a part of the contract." (*See* SURVIVAL CLAUSE.)

MERIDIAN - One of a set of imaginary lines running north and south used by surveyors for reference in locating and describing land under the government survey method of property description. (*See* GOVERNMENT SURVEY METHOD.)

MESNE CONVEYANCE - An intermediate or middle conveyance; any conveyance between the first or initial conveyance and the most recent conveyance in the chain of title.

MESNE PROFITS - Profits derived from the wrongful possession of land. Usually mesne profits are recoverable by the lawful owner.

METES AND BOUNDS - A common method of land description that identifies a property by specifying the shape and boundary dimensions of the parcel, using terminal points and angles. A metes and bounds description starts at a well-marked point of beginning and follows the boundaries of the land by courses and metes (measures, distances and compass direction) and bounds (landmarks, monuments) and returns to the true point of beginning. Generally, however, in verifying such a description, monuments prevail over courses and distances. A description which fails to enclose an area by returning to the point of beginning is defective. If there is any discrepancy in the distance between monuments and linear measurements, the actual measured distance between the monuments prevails.

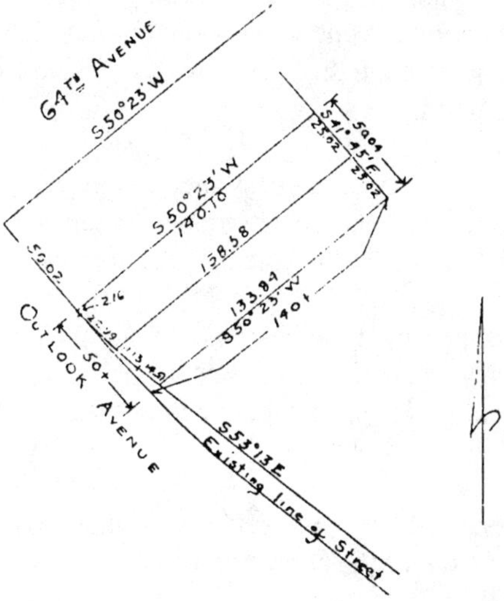

A metes and bounds description is required in any subdivision file plan sought to be registered with the Office of the County Auditor. Anyone who subdivides a tract into lots and sells by a lot number without filing a metes and bounds file plan is subject to a fine. (*See* LEGAL DESCRIPTION, MONUMENTS, POINT OF BEGINNING, SUBDIVISION.) *Reference:* RCW 58.17.

METRIC MEASUREMENT - The basic unit of measuring length in the metric system is a meter. A meter equals 39.37 inches. (*See* MEASUREMENT TABLES.)

METROPOLITAN AREA - The area in and around a major city. For example, the Seattle metropolitan area is often construed to include that certain area from Lynnwood in the north, Federal Way to the south and Issaquah on the east.

MEZZANINE - An intermediate floor between two main stories of a building or between the floor and ceiling of a one-story structure. A mezzanine usually covers a relatively small portion of the total floor space.

MGIC (MORTGAGE GUARANTY INSURANCE CORPORATION) - An independent insurance corporation which will insure the top 12 to 30 percent of the principal of a loan made by approved lenders to qualified borrowers. When regulations limit a lending institution's mortgage loans to a definite percentage of appraised value (80 percent, for example), it is possible to obtain a larger loan with an MGIC or, as it is sometimes called, MAGIC guarantee without violating those regulations. MGIC is the largest company of approximately ten companies who offer this type of service. The MGIC guidelines will be used as an example of the typical program. There are several coverage plans available depending upon the ratio of the loan to the appraised value. For example, if a residence is appraised at $90,000, and a qualified purchaser wishes to make a cash payment of only $9,000, he or she will need a 90 percent conventional mortgage loan of $81,000. Even though the lender's limit is 80 percent, this loan may be obtained with an MGIC guarantee under one of the following plans:

1. The borrower must pay a onetime insurance charge at the time of closing, with the exact percentage of the charge determined by the number of years it will take to reduce the loan balance to 80 percent of the appraised value.

2. The borrower must pay an initial charge of .35% on a 15% down loan to as high as .9% for a 3% down loan, and 1/4 of one percent of the remaining loan balance must be paid annually until the outstanding mortgage debt is reduced to 75 to 80 percent of property value.

In addition, the borrower is charged an appraisal fee with either payment plan if the amount of the loan is 80 percent or more of the appraised value.

In consideration of either of these plans, MGIC guarantees, at its option, either to take possession of a foreclosed property and pay the insured lender the outstanding debt, including defaulted interest and foreclosure costs, or to pay the insured percentage of this amount without taking possession of the property. In many cases, MGIC chooses the latter alternative, thus avoiding the problems associated with maintenance and resale of the property. (*See* PRIVATE MORTGAGE INSURANCE.)

MID-RISE - A four to seven-story building.

MILE - A linear measurement of distance equal to 1,760 yards or 5,280 feet, or 1.609 kilometers. (*See* MEASUREMENT TABLES.)

MILITARY CLAUSE - A clause inserted in some residential leases to allow the military tenant to terminate the lease in case of transfer, discharge or other circumstances making termination appropriate. Example:

"It is expressly agreed that if the lessee herein should receive official orders relieving him/her from duty at Fort Lewis or from active duty in the Army or ordering him/her to live in service quarters, he/she may terminate this lease upon written notice of his/her intention to do so, and such termination shall become effective 30 days after the date of the service of the notice upon the lessor, and if the date of such termination shall fall between the days on which rent becomes due, there shall accrue on the first day of the rental period in which such termination shall take effect a proportionate part only of the rent which would be due but for such termination." (*See* SOLDIER'S AND SAILOR'S CIVIL RELIEF ACT.)

MILL OR MILLAGE RATE - One-tenth of a cent. Term used in real estate taxation. A one mill rate is one-tenth of one percent of the assessed value. Washington uses a mill rate to compute property taxes. For example, if the mill rate is 42 and the property is assessed at $20,000, the tax would be .0042 x $20,000, or $84. Many counties calculate the tax rate in mills but express them in dollars on the annual Real Estate Tax Statement.

MINERAL RIGHTS - Rights to subsurface land and profits. Normally, when real property is conveyed, the grantee receives all rights and title to the land including everything above and below the surface, unless reserved by the grantor. (*See* OIL AND GAS LEASE.)

MINIMUM LOT AREA - A zoning restriction establishing a minimum lot size upon which a building may be erected. For example, RS-7200 zoning for King County provides an area for a single family dwelling of a minimum lot size of 7,200 square feet with a minimum lot width of 60 feet, a front yard depth of 20 feet (key and transitional lots, 15 feet), with side yards of five (5) feet. The maximum height of the dwelling may be 35 feet to roof ridge. If restrictions as to minimum lot area are contradictory in County or City Zoning, or a restrictive covenant in plat or deed restrictions, the **more** restrictive will prevail. (*See* CLUSTER DEVELOPMENT, ZONING.)

MINIMUM PROPERTY REQUIREMENTS - Under FHA loan requirements, a property must be livable, soundly built, and suitably located as to site and neighborhood before the agency will underwrite a residential mortgage loan.

MINIMUM SETBACK REQUIREMENT - *See* SETBACK REQUIREMENT.

MINI-WAREHOUSE - A one-story structure partitioned into small, secure individual units for use by individuals and businesses to store personal or business property. Individual units are normally rented on a month-to-month basis with the rent charged varying with the unit size. Units vary in size from 50 or 60 square feet up to 500 square feet. (*See* ABANDONMENT, SELF STORAGE.)

MINOR - A person who is under the legal age of majority, which in Washington is 18 years of age; a legal infant who is not a completely competent legal party. Most contracts, except those for necessities such as food and clothing, entered into by a minor are voidable at his/her option; however, if the minor does not disaffirm the contract within a reasonable time after attaining majority, then the contract will become fully enforceable against him/her. For example, if a minor lists property with a broker, the broker would not be able to collect his/her earned commission if, when he/she finds a ready, willing and able buyer, the minor decides to repudiate the listing contract. Note that, in any event, the minor could not sell the property without court approval since a minor does not have the legal capacity to transfer title to property. Nor does a minor have power to make a valid will.

Since the grantor of a deed must be competent, a deed by a minor is voidable, although a minor may be a grantee, and may receive real property by gift or inheritance. A minor is deemed incapable of appointing an agent to sell his/her property, thus any power of attorney he/she executes is void.

If it is necessary that land owned by a minor be sold for the minor's maintenance or for investment, court proceedings appointing a guardian must be instituted. The court can grant the guardian a special license to sell the property upon the guardian's posting a bond. The guardian does not need a real estate license.

Title by adverse possession cannot be established against a minor unless the adverse possession continues three years after the minor becomes 18 years old. (*See* ADVERSE POSSESSION, GUARDIAN, INFANT, VOIDABLE.)

MISDEMEANOR - A crime less than a felony or a gross misdemeanor punishable by up to ninety (90) days in jail and/or a fine up to $500. Acting as an escrow agent or real estate agent without being properly registered or licensed is a misdemeanor. (*See* ESCROW AGENT REGISTRATION ACT.)
Reference: RCW 18.44.140.

MISNOMER - A mistake in name. When a misnomer occurs in a deed, the proper procedure is to prepare and record a correction deed so as to avoid future title disputes. The misnomer of a corporation in a deed is not material if the corporation can be reasonably identified, as where the deed states "Abby, Ltd." whereas the true name is "Abby, Limited." A seller can be compelled to execute a correction deed if his/her deed to the grantee contained a covenant of further assurance. (*See* COVENANT.)

MISPLACED IMPROVEMENT - A poorly located improvement; an improvement that is poorly planned in that it is either too costly or does not conform to the best utilization of the site. (*See* OVERIMPROVEMENT.)

MISREPRESENTATION - A false statement or concealment of a material fact made with the intention of inducing some action by another party. A court can grant relief in the form of damages or rescission of contract if the misrepresented fact is material to the transaction. Misrepresentation can be an affirmative statement, such as "this house does not have termites." It can also be a concealment of a material fact known to one party which that party knows is not reasonably ascertainable by the other party. An example of this would be a case where a seller knows of a serious defect in the support beams, yet does not disclose this fact to the buyer. This is sometimes called "negative fraud." However, if the buyer clearly does not believe or rely on the misrepresentations, or makes his or her own inspection and relies only on this investigation, the contract cannot be rescinded due to misrepresentation.

Statements of opinion are not normally material facts, and thus are not actionable. For example, "this house is a great buy at $150,000 since it is worth much more than that," is a statement of opinion, often known as "puffing." However, if the person making the representation possesses some superior knowledge, then the representation, though opinion, is treated as one of fact. If a builder, for instance, says, "the foundation appears to be properly laid," he or she is liable if, in fact, it is not. Courts have held that when a broker represents that he or she does not think the property is on filled land, he or she may be liable if it turns out that the land is fill and the buyer thereby suffers damages. Although misrepresentations usually take the form of verbal or written statements, they could be such things as a nod of the head, pointing out false boundaries, or displaying a forged map — in other words, any action that may tend to convey a false message.

Any broker who may become involved in a "Shown by Owner" sales promotion must be extremely cautious in advertising. Real Estate License Law forbids the making of false promises through advertising which are intended to influence, persuade or induce others, or any other conduct which constitutes untrustworthy or improper dealings. Advertising "For Sale by Owner" or "Sale by Owner" when the negotiation, either in whole or in part, is through or by a licensed real estate person is misrepresentation.

It is not necessary that a person actually intend to misrepresent a fact. A broker or salesperson is liable if he/she knows of the falsity of a statement. Thus, if a real estate licensee makes a negligent misrepresentation of a material fact to induce the buyer to buy, and the buyer relies on this fact to his/her detriment, then the real estate licensee is liable. The seller may also be liable because the statement was made by his/her agent within the scope of authority of the agency. Under these circumstances, an aggrieved buyer may generally have a successful case against the broker if:

- The real estate licensee has knowledge of facts unknown to or beyond the reach of the buyer which materially affect the value or desirability of the property, and he/she fails to disclose these facts;
- The real estate licensee intends to defraud the buyer by such nondisclosures;
- The buyer suffers actual damages as a result of the misrepresentation;

Some of the consequences of misrepresentation are:

- The broker or salesperson guilty of misrepresentation can have his/her license suspended or revoked;
- Have the contract rescinded or the defrauded party can collect damages;
- The principal may not have to pay a commission to a misrepresenting broker;
- Under the federal Interstate Land Sales Act, a broker making a misrepresentation may be jointly and severally liable to the purchaser;
- The buyer may be able to keep the property and sue the seller for the difference between the purchase price and the lesser actual value;
- The buyer may be able to collect damages for expenditures made in reliance upon the misrepresentation.

(*See* AGENCY, "AS IS", LATENT DEFECTS, PUFFING, REAL ESTATE BROKERAGE RELATIONSHIPS ACT, SCOPE OF AUTHORITY.)

MISTAKE - An error or misunderstanding. A contract is voidable if there is a mistake that is mutual, material, unintentional, and free from negligence. Innocent mistakes seldom serve to void a contract. A party cannot claim mistake to get out of a contract on the basis that he/she did not read the contract he/she signed and was therefore mistaken as to its material terms. Neither ignorance nor poor judgment is a mistake of fact. Nor can a he/she claim a mistake in that he/she did not know the legal consequences of signing the contract (mistake of law).

When there is an ambiguity known by one party who fails to explain the mistake to the innocent party, the innocent party's interpretation generally will prevail. (*See* ADHESION CONTRACT.)

MITER - In carpentry terminology, the ends of any two pieces of board of corresponding form cut off at an angle and fitted together in an angular shape.

MITIGATION OF DAMAGES - A principle of contract law that refers to the obligation of an injured party to take reasonable steps to reduce or eliminate the amount of damages that party may be entitled to. For example, a landlord has a duty to try to locate a replacement tenant for space vacated or abandoned by a prior tenant in breach of the lease.

MIXED USE - The use of real property for more than one use, such as a condominium building that has residential and commercial units. It could combine retail, office and residential, or industrial, office and residential.

MOBILE HOME - Prefabricated trailer-type housing units that are semi-permanently attached to land, either the owner's fee land or a leasehold, such as in a mobile home park. Mobile homes are usually affixed to a concrete foundation and connected to utilities. Although they may not be as mobile as the word implies, they may be removed from such attachments and hauled to a new location. In this respect, mobile homes possess the features of both real and personal property. They are like real property when the units are attached to the earth's surface, and like personal property when they are detached and moved. The courts, however, generally consider a mobile home a fixture, and thus treat it as real property.

Many areas of the U.S. have initiated zoning legislation restricting mobile homes and mobile home parks within the community. While some restrictions single out mobile homes by name, others may restrict them indirectly by prohibiting any housing unit containing less than a prescribed area of living space.

Currently, mobile homes represent 20 to 25 percent of all housing units built each year. Mobile home financing is similar to automobile financing. However, loan terms are generally longer for mobile homes, running 10 to 12 years. Such loans are generally secured by a lien on the mobile home's title registered with the State Licensing Department. Mobile home loans may be underwritten by either the VA or FHA. Because depreciation is so high in the early years of mobile home ownership, these homes, if held for investment purposes, are usually depreciated for income tax purposes based on a ten-year useful life. (*See* DEPRECIATION [TAX], USEFUL LIFE.)

In some counties like King County, a mobile home may be placed on any legal residential lot or within any approved mobile home park licensed by the County Health Department.

The construction of a mobile home must be approved by the Washington State Department of Labor and Industries (LI) or the U.S. Department of Housing and Urban Development (HUD) and have the appropriate insignia with identification (ID) number affixed to the unit. Those units not bearing the appropriate insignia must meet additional requirements imposed by the county and state.

In King County, a mobile home may be temporarily placed on a legal residential lot of 15,000 square feet or more which is already occupied with a dwelling, subject to obtaining a temporary use permit, provided the mobile home:

1. Is used to accommodate an individual(s) requiring daily care, as established by a physician's certification, and

2. Meets the minimum yard, height, building placement and lot coverage provisions of the zone, and

3. Is removed when the hardship is over.

The Real Estate License Law authorizes a broker and salespeople licensed to the broker to negotiate the sale of a used or new mobile home together with the underlying land, rental or lease interest so long as he or she is not operating as an agent of a vehicle dealer.

The homestead exemption applies to mobile homes; this homestead exemption is subject to execution or satisfaction in execution of a judgment of a debt secured by a purchase money security agreement with the mobile home as collateral. The homestead exemption may be waived in writing in consideration for the landlord not terminating the tenancy if the tenant has defaulted in rent. (*See* HOMESTEAD.)

A community property interest is recognized in a mobile home. (*See* COMMUNITY PROPERTY.)
Reference: RCW 18.85, RCW 46.12, RCW 46.70.

MOBILE-HOME PARK - An area zoned and set up to accommodate mobile homes. Mobile-home parks are also called trailer parks.

MODEL HOUSE - A house built as part of a land development program to demonstrate style, construction, and possible furnishings of similar houses to be erected and sold. A model house is also known as a "demonstration house." It is an excellent selling aid if properly handled, and is often sold with some of the furnishings after it has served its purpose. The first house completed in the development may be used as the model.

MODIFICATION - 1. The influence on land use and value resulting from improvements made by man to surrounding parcels.

2. A change to a contract. A contract can be modified at any time with the consent of both parties.

MODIFIED ACCELERATED COST RECOVERY SYSTEM (MACRS) - The 1986 Tax Reform Act modified the ACRS structure of depreciation by lengthening the cost recovery periods for depreciable real estate assets. Effective for property placed in service after December 31, 1986, the accelerated method was no longer available for real estate; straight-line is the only allowable method. Note that the 1981 Tax Act used the word "recovery" where pre-1980 laws used "depreciation." As a matter of practice, the term "recovery" never caught on, whereas, the term "depreciation" is commonly used.

The new rules do not distinguish between new or used property, nor is any salvage value considered. The method used for additions or improvements is identical to that used for the underlying property. No matter when the property is placed in service, it is deemed to have been placed in service at the middle of the month.

The recovery period for residential rental property placed in service after December 31,

1986, is 27.5 years. Residential rental property is a rental building or structure for which 80% or more of the gross rental income for the tax year is rental income from dwelling units. If the owner occupies any part of the building, the gross rental income includes the fair rental value of the unit occupied.

The method of recovery for nonresidential and residential property is the straight-line method:

1. For nonresidential real property placed in service after December 31, 1986, but before May 13, 1993, the depreciation recovery period is 31.5 years.

2. For nonresidential real property placed in service after May 12, 1993, the recovery period is 39 years. Under a transition rule, the 31.5 year recovery period rather than the 39-year recovery period applies to a building placed in service before 1994 if before May 13, 1993, there was a binding, written contract to buy or build it.

Under the 1986 Act, depreciation/cost recovery is still subtracted from basis when calculating the amount of gain or loss on the sale. There is no recapture of straight line MACRS depreciation for buildings and improvements acquired or built after 1986. However, there can be a recapture of depreciation on the sale of real estate placed in service prior to 1987. (*See* CAPITAL GAINS.)

MODULAR HOUSING - A relatively recent concept in building homes which aims at producing housing at a cheaper and faster rate through prefabricating processes. Modular methods expedite construction because the house itself can be built in the factory while the building site is being prepared, thus eliminating costly delays. (*See* MANUFACTURED or FACTORY BUILT HOUSING.)

MODULE - A common dimensional element that influences the placement of window mullions, ceiling tiles, light fixtures, columns, electrical distribution systems, partitions, and like things. The module selected may greatly enhance the flexibility of office design.

MOISTURE BARRIER - Any treated material, or even paint, used to retard or prevent moisture or water vapor from seeping into or through walls or floors of a building.

MOLDING - The cornice; wood molding applied to cover the junction of roof boards and outside wall. On the interior, the picture molding is often fastened where the wall joins the ceiling, whereas toe molding is placed to cover any gaps where the floor and wall meet.

MONEY - *See* COMMINGLING, TRUST ACCOUNT.

MONTH-TO-MONTH TENANCY - A periodic tenancy where the tenant rents for one month at a time. In the absence of a rental agreement (oral or written), a tenancy is deemed to be month-to-month. Under such a tenancy, the estate continues for an indefinite period of time until either lessor or lessee gives the statutory notice of termination. Under the Landlord Tenant Act, notice to terminate a month-to-month tenancy must be written and must be given 20 days in advance of the anticipated termination by either landlord or the tenant. A notice to increase rent requires 30 days notice. As a matter of good business practice, the notice should be personally delivered or sent by Certified Mail, Return Receipt Requested.

A month-to-month tenancy may be created when a tenant holds over after his/her lease term expires. When no new lease agreement has been made, the landlord may either evict the tenant if he/she chooses, or acquiesce in the holdover tenancy.

A landlord's acceptance of rent in advance after the first month of a holdover, after the expiration of a lease, creates a month-to-month tenancy in the absence of an agreement to the contrary between the parties at the time of such acceptance. (*See* LANDLORD TENANT ACT, PERIODIC TENANCY, RENT.)

MONUMENTS - Visible markers, both natural and artificial objects, which are used to establish the lines and boundaries of a survey. Monuments include artificial immovables like stakes, iron pins or posts, and stone markers, as well as natural objects such as marked trees, streams and rivers. A possible problem with natural monuments is the fact that they sometimes move from their original locations. An example of an intangible monument would be the corner of a section in a government survey system. While not visibly identifiable, it can still be accurately located by survey. The use of monuments is essential to the accuracy of a metes and bounds description. A metes and bounds description commences with a point beginning at a monument such as an iron pin or the intersection of two streets. (*See* METES AND BOUNDS.)

In a contested issue as to who owns a particular property, monuments prevail in the event that courses or distances as set forth in a metes and bounds description in deeds or other documents show otherwise.

In surveying a new subdivision, the surveyor establishes survey monuments from which to take measurements.

MORAL CHARACTER - The ability on the part of the person licensed to serve the general public in a fair and honest manner.

Persons who have been convicted of a crime within ten years of application may be required to submit fingerprint identification on a form provided by the Department of Licensing, Real Estate Program, prior to issuance of a real estate license.
Reference: WAC 308-124A-020.

MORAL TURPITUDE - An act of baseness, evilness or depravity in private social duties contrary to the accepted customary rule of right and duty between fellow men, conduct contrary to justice, honesty, modesty, or good morals. For example, embezzlement, larceny, robbery, rape, obtaining money by false pretenses, kidnapping, perjury, the sale of drugs and blackmail are crimes of moral turpitude whereas possession of small amounts of marijuana or income tax evasion probably is not. Felonies are crimes of moral turpitude.

The Washington Real Estate Licensing Law provides that the Real Estate Program of the Department of Licensing may revoke or suspend the license of any individual who is convicted of a crime involving moral turpitude. Disciplinary action may be taken even though the individual pleads guilty or nolo contendere (I will not contest it) and the sentence is deferred or suspended. The Real Estate Program may also refuse to issue a license to an applicant who has been found guilty of a crime of moral turpitude. (*See* FELONY, LICENSING LAW, MORAL CHARACTER.)
Reference: RCW 18.85.

MORATORIUM - A temporary suspension, a period during which a borrower is granted the right to delay fulfillment of an obligation. During the so called Boeing depression in Seattle in the early 1970s, a number of lending institutions gave moratoriums to apartment owners on mortgage payments. In some cases, it was only a moratorium of the principal portion of the monthly payment. In other cases, it was a moratorium of the principal payment and part of the interest payment.

Some communities unable to finance necessary community improvements, e.g., sewers, sewer treatment plants, water systems and schools, have put a moratorium on building until their financial problems can be cured. In some cases, moratoriums have been instituted by communities, not because of financial problems, but because of environmental or social concern.

MORE OR LESS - When used in a legal description of land, it denotes that the total acreage given in the description is an approximation. For example, a legal description may read "_____ , containing 100 acres more or less." Inclusion of these words allows for slight differences which may arise; for example, the exact acreage may be 99 acres or 101 acres. However, the use of "more or less" in a legal description does not insure the validity of the description if substantial differences exist between the actual dimensions and what has been included in the description.

MORTGAGE - A legal document used to secure the performance of an obligation. The term mortgage is derived from the French word "mort" meaning dead and "gage" meaning pledge. Thus, the pledge is extinguished when payment of the debt is made. In the usual real estate transaction, the buyer of real estate needs or wants to borrow money to pay the seller the difference between the down payment and the purchase price. When the lender (mortgagee) loans the money, the buyer-borrower (mortgagor) is required to sign a promissory note for the amount borrowed and execute a mortgage to secure the debt. The purpose of the mortgage note is to create a personal liability for payment on the part of the mortgagor; the purpose of the mortgage is to create a lien on the mortgaged property. The note and the mortgage may appear in the same document, though it is customary to have separate instruments. The mortgage is not effective until and unless there is a valid debt, and this debt must be described and identified in the mortgage document. The mortgage document is frequently lengthy and contains many clauses such as provisions for acceleration, subordination, release schedule, purchase money, waivers; and covenants to pay taxes, to keep the premises in repair and to maintain adequate insurance.

In effect, the mortgage states that the lender can look to the property in the event the borrower defaults in payment of the note. The lender (mortgagee) can bring foreclosure proceedings to sell the property and retain that part of the proceeds representing the moneys still due on the note. If the proceeds of sale are less than the amount owed, the mortgagee could obtain a deficiency judgment against the mortgagor for the balance under certain conditions.

The rules of contract law apply to mortgages. The mortgage must be in writing and must name the parties (who must be competent to contract), legally describe the mortgaged property, state a consideration, contain a mortgaging clause, state the debt and terms of repayment, and be signed by the borrower (mortgagor). In addition, the mortgagor should state his/her marital status and, if married, the spouse must also sign the mortgage (because of his/her community property interest in the property). The mortgage must be acknowledged and then recorded in the Office of the County Auditor in the county where the property is located, with the priority of the lien determined by the date of recordation. *Reference:* RCW 64.04.

In Washington, the lien theory has always been a basic premise in the law of mortgages. In a mortgage under this theory, the title remains with the mortgagor and is not transferred to the mortgagee. The mortgage placed on the property is only a charge or a lien on the title.

Any interest in real property can be mortgaged. Thus, the owner of the fee, or leasehold, or even a life estate can mortgage his/her interest. The owner of a cooperative apartment, however, cannot mortgage his/her apartment since his/her ownership is not an interest in real property; it is stock ownership which is personal property (though this stock may sometimes be used as collateral for a loan).

When property is sold, the existing mortgages may be assumed or made subject to (unless restricted by a "due on sale" clause) or paid off. When paid in full, the mortgagor should be sure to record a satisfaction of mortgage as notice that the mortgage is no longer a lien on the property.

The 1980s witnessed a variety of types of mortgages such as the adjustable mortgage loan, the graduated payment mortgage, the wraparound mortgage, the shared appreciation mortgage, the flexible loan insurance plan, and the buydown mortgage, among many others.

There are many types of mortgages which are discussed herein under their individual headings, such as blanket mortgages, budget mortgages, open-end mortgages, package mortgages, participation mortgages, and purchase money mortgages, among others. (*See* CERTIFICATE OF NO DEFENSE, CREATIVE FINANCING, DEFEASANCE, DEFICIENCY JUDGMENT, FORECLOSURE, LIEN THEORY, LOAN COMMITMENT, LOAN SUBMISSION, LOAN TO VALUE RATIO, MORTGAGE LIEN, PROMISSORY NOTE, REDEMPTION, SATISFACTION OF MORTGAGE, SUBORDINATION CLAUSE.)

In Washington, the deed of trust has substantially replaced the mortgage as the security instrument for a real estate loan. (*See* DEED OF TRUST.)

MORTGAGE-BACKED SECURITY - Securities that are secured by pools of mortgages and are used to channel funds from securities markets to housing markets. Ginnie Mae has a popular MBS program recognized for its low risk and high yield. The Ginnie Mae MBS security is a pool of VA and FHA mortgages put together as a bond. Freddie Mac and Fannie Mae also have MBS programs. (*See* PARTICIPATION SALE CERTIFICATE.)

MORTGAGE BANKER - A person, corporation, or firm not otherwise in banking and finance which normally provides its own funds for mortgage financing as opposed to savings and loan associations or commercial banks that use other people's money — namely that of their depositors — to originate mortgage loans. Although some mortgage bankers do supply permanent (long-term) financing, the majority of mortgage bankers specialize in supplying short-term and interim financing, either through their own resources or by borrowing from commercial sources. The mortgage banker often advances his/her own funds to close the loan, often without a takeout loan. His/her objective is to ultimately sell the loan at a profit, but he/she is underwriting the risk himself/herself as opposed to the mortgage broker who will not act without his/her principal's consent.

The activities of mortgage bankers have been greatly expanded due to the development of the mortgage correspondent system. Under this system, a mortgage banker or mortgage banking company will seek to originate a large number of loan transactions and then sell these mortgages at a discount to large investors, such as insurance companies, commercial banks, and retirement and pension funds. There are specialists in originating FHA and VA loans in capital short areas and selling them to financial institutions, often located in another part of the U.S. where there is surplus savings, for an origination fee. The mortgage banker normally remains in the picture and services the underlying mortgage for his/her major investor clients. Such services include collecting monthly payments, disbursing the funds to pay taxes and property insurance, supervising the loan, preventing any delinquencies, and taking proper remedial action in the event of delinquency. (*See* LOAN CORRESPONDENT, MORTGAGE BROKER, WAREHOUSING.)

MORTGAGE BROKER - A person or firm which acts as an intermediary between borrower and lender; one who, for compensation or gain, negotiates, sells or arranges loans and sometimes continues to service the loans. Loans originated by the mortgage broker are closed in the lender's name, and are usually serviced by the lender. This is opposed to mortgage bankers, who not only close loans in their own names, but continue to service them as well.

In 1987, Washington adopted the Mortgage Broker Practices Act which governs the business practices of any person who for compensation or in the expectation of compensation either directly or indirectly makes, negotiates, or offers to make or negotiate a residential mortgage loan. "Residential mortgage loan" means any loan primarily for person, family, or household use secured by a mortgage or deed of trust on residential real estate upon which is constructed or intended to be constructed a single family dwelling or multiple family dwelling of four or less units.

There are a number of exceptions to the Act:

1. Any person doing business under the laws of this State of the United States relating to banks, bank holding companies, mutual savings banks, savings and loan associations, credit unions, consumer finance companies, industrial loan companies, insurance companies, or real estate investment trusts;

2. An attorney licensed to practice law in this State who is not principally engaged in the business of negotiating residential mortgage loans when such attorney renders services in the course of his/her practice as an attorney;

3. Any person doing any act under order of any court;

4. Any person making or acquiring a residential mortgage loan solely with his or her own funds for his/her own investment without intending to resell the residential mortgage loans;

5. A real estate broker or salesperson licensed by the State who obtains financing for a real estate transaction involving a bona fide sale of real estate in the performance of his/her duties as a real estate broker and who receives only the customary real estate broker's or salesperson's commission in connection with the transaction;

6. Any mortgage broker approved and subject to auditing by the Federal National Mortgage Association, the Government National Mortgage Association, or the Federal Home Loan Mortgage Corporation;

7. Any mortgage broker approved by the United States Secretary of Housing and Urban Development for participation in any mortgage insurance program under the National Housing Act.

A mortgage broker covered by the Act must, upon receipt of a loan application and before the receipt of any moneys from a borrower, make a full written disclosure to each borrower containing an itemization and explanation of all fees and costs that the borrower will be required to pay in connection with obtaining a residential mortgage loan. A good faith estimate of a fee or cost shall be provided if the exact amount of the fee or cost is not determinable.

The written disclosure must contain the detailed information on the terms and conditions of the loan. The annual percentage rate, finance charge, amount financed, total amount of all payments, amount of each payment, amount of points or prepaid interest and the conditions and terms under which any loan terms may change between the time of disclosure and closing of the loan, and, if a variable rate, the circumstances under which the rate may increase, any limitation on the increase, the effect of any increase, and an example of the payment terms resulting from an increase.

There must be itemized costs of any credit report, appraisal, title report, title insurance policy, mortgage insurance, escrow fee, property tax, insurance, structural or pest inspection, and any other costs associated with the residential mortgage loan.

Every contract between a mortgage broker and a borrower shall be in writing and shall contain the entire agreement of the parties.

A mortgage broker shall have a written correspondent or loan brokerage agreement with a lender before any solicitation of, or contracting with, the public.

A mortgage broker shall deposit, prior to the end of the next business day, all moneys received from borrowers for services in a trust account of a federally insured financial institution located in this State. The trust account shall be designated and maintained for the benefit of borrowers.

Except as permitted by the Act, a mortgage broker shall not receive a fee, commission, or compensation of any kind in connection with the preparation, negotiation, and brokering of a residential mortgage loan unless a borrower actually obtains a loan from a lender on the terms and conditions agreed upon by the borrower and mortgage broker.

A mortgage broker may not solicit, advertise, or enter into a contract with a borrower that provides in substance that the mortgage broker may earn a fee or commission through the mortgage broker's "best efforts" to obtain a loan even though no loan is actually obtained for the borrower; or solicit, advertise, or enter into a contract for specific interest rates,

points, or other financing terms unless the terms are actually available at the time of soliciting, advertising, or contracting.
Reference: RCW 19.146

MORTGAGE COMMITMENT - An agreement to lend a specific amount of money over stated terms and conditions, including time. Mortgage commitments are usually conditional on approval of various segments of a loan application. Some of the more common conditions for approval that are incorporated into the mortgage commitment are: acceptable income and credit for the borrower, an appraisal supporting the value and approving the condition of the property, sufficient funds to close the loan and good title to the property used for collateral. A mortgage commitment can be issued for a period of time, e.g., for 30 days.

MORTGAGE CONSTANT - Factor or multiplier used for rapid computation of the annual payment needed to amortize a loan. (*See* CONSTANT.)

MORTGAGE DISCOUNT - *See* DISCOUNT POINTS.

MORTGAGE GUARANTEE INSURANCE CORPORATION - *See* MGIC.

MORTGAGE INSTRUMENT - In general, any document related to the making of a real estate loan. It can refer to the deed of trust, mortgage or promissory note.

MORTGAGE INSURANCE - A kind of insurance plan which will pay off the mortgage balance in the event of the death or, in some plans, disability of the insured mortgagor. In essence, mortgage insurance is decreasing-term life insurance. The premiums are paid with the regular monthly mortgage payment. Protection for a $140,000 policy over a 30-year loan period for a 35-year-old mortgagor would, for example, cost approximately $214.00 per year. Before purchasing mortgage insurance, an individual should review coverage with a knowledgeable insurance agent.

Mortgage insurance is not the same as **private mortgage insurance** which provides coverage to lenders for a loan in excess of 80% of value. (*See* MGIC (MORTGAGE GUARANTY).)

Some insurance agents assert a term life policy in the same amount will carry a lower monthly premium and give the estate more flexibility on how to use the proceeds on the death of the insured.

MORTGAGE INSURANCE CERTIFICATE - A certificate issued by HUD/FHA as evidence that the mortgage has been insured. This certificate is evidence that a contract of mortgage insurance exists between HUD/FHA and the lender.

MORTGAGE INSURANCE PREMIUM - *See* FEDERAL HOUSING ADMINISTRATION, PRIVATE MORTGAGE INSURANCE.

MORTGAGE INTEREST DEDUCTION - An allowable tax deduction for persons who itemize their federal and state income tax returns.

MORTGAGE LIEN - A lien or charge on the real property of a mortgagor which secures the underlying debt obligation. As with other liens affecting real property, the mortgage lien receives its priority by proper recording. Until recorded, the mortgage operates only as a contract between the parties and creates no lien affecting any recorded mortgage or lease. Whether a recorded mortgage is entitled a "first mortgage," a "second mortgage," or a "third mortgage," it has priority over all subsequent recorded mortgages or other liens, unless it is subordinated to such subsequent liens. As with all liens, a mortgage lien becomes junior to any real estate tax liens or liens for special assessments.

Sometimes a mortgage is intended to secure future advances which the mortgagee may make to the mortgagor, as in a construction loan, when obligatory progress payments are made as various stages of the construction are completed. Such future advances would be superior in priority to mortgages, or other liens taking effect between the date of recording of the mortgage and the future advance, only where the future advance relates to the same transaction or series of transactions and the mortgage specifically refers to this particular advance as being secured by the previously recorded liens.

In Washington, a deed of trust may also be used whenever a mortgage would be used. (*See* DEED OF TRUST, FUTURE ADVANCES, LIEN, RECORDING, SUBORDINATION CLAUSE.)

MORTGAGE LOAN SERVICING - The process of collecting the periodic mortgage payments and escrow funds, paying property taxes and insurance and overseeing the administration of a loan over its life.

MORTGAGE LOAN UNDERWRITING - The process of reviewing an application from a prospective borrower for a loan and making a recommendation as to the risk to the lender making the loan. The underwriting process is an integral part of the lending process.

MORTGAGE NETWORK - The use of computers to search and apply for mortgage loan money. A more modern system of keeping current on mortgage rates than the old weekly loan sheet. In addition, some computers can prequalify the buyer, match the buyer with a loan and even print out the loan application papers.

MORTGAGE PROTECTION INSURANCE - *See* MORTGAGE INSURANCE.

MORTGAGEE - In a mortgage transaction, the one who receives and holds a mortgage as security for a debt; the lender; a lender or creditor who holds a mortgage as security for payment of an obligation.

MORTGAGOR - The one who gives a mortgage as security for a debt; the borrower; usually the landowner, though it could be the owner of a leasehold estate; the borrower or debtor who hypothecates or puts up his/her property as security for an obligation. (*See* HYPOTHECATE.)

MOST FAVORED TENANT CLAUSE - A provision in a lease which assures a tenant that any negotiating concessions given to other tenants will also be given this tenant. Such a clause is especially helpful in the early stages of renting a building, since the tenant is assured that later tenants will not get better concessions.

MOTEL - A structure designed to provide convenient rental quarters for transients. Motels sometimes have common facilities for guests such as dining rooms, meeting rooms, and the like.

MUD ROOM - A vestibule or small room used as the entrance from a play yard or alley. The mud room frequently contains a washer and dryer.

MUDSILL - The lowest horizontal component of a structure, such as a foundation timber placed directly on the ground or foundation.

MULLION - Thin vertical strips inside the window sash that divide the window glass into panes.

MULTIPLE ASSET EXCHANGE - An exchange of property for income tax purposes, usually involving two businesses, in which the values of many related assets — land, buildings, machinery, goodwill — are added together to reach a composite figure on which to compute the exchange.

Even if the individual component values differ in a multiple asset exchange, income tax on any gain realized from the transaction can be deferred if the composite values are the same. For example, Company A exchanges all of its operating assets for like-kind assets of Company B. The following breakdown of each company's assets occurs:

	Company A	Company B
Land	$150,000	$100,000
Buildings	175,000	200,000
Machinery	75,000	50,000
Goodwill	50,000	100,000

Traded on an asset-by-asset basis, Company A would be taxed on boot valued at $75,000 — the $25,000 difference in the building values, plus the $50,000 difference in goodwill values. However, classified as a multiple asset exchange, both composite values are the same and no boot is involved. Note that multiple asset exchanges are generally complicated and are subject to many tax laws and rulings. Please seek competent tax counsel. (*See* BOOT, EXCHANGE.)

MULTIPLE DWELLING - Any structure for the accommodation of two or more families or households in separate living units. An apartment house. (*See* APARTMENT BUILDING.)

MULTIPLE LISTING (MLS) - A listing agreement used by a real estate brokerage company which is a member of a multiple-listing organization. The multiple-listing agreement is, in effect, an exclusive right to sell with an additional authority and obligation on the part of the listing broker to distribute the listing to other brokers making up the multiple-listing membership. Under this plan there is an exchange of listings among a group of real estate brokers or members of a real estate board, subject to regulations mutually agreed upon. The procedure is generally as follows: A broker in the group, receiving a listing, sends it to the group's central office; he/she is now the listing broker. The central office relays the listing to all brokers in the group. In large multiples, the information is placed in a computer data base to which all brokers and sales people have access. When a purchaser is found by a member of the group, he/she becomes the selling broker. The selling broker communicates with the listing broker and the transaction is consummated. The central office, informed of the sale, notifies all other brokers there is a pending sale. The listing broker may, under the rules of the group, be entitled to a flat fee or to a percentage of the commission. The central office may receive a small percentage of the commission for operating expenses; the rest of the commission goes to the selling broker. The essential advantage of multiple listing is that the chances of finding a prospect purchaser are multiplied. Although a broker may have an exclusive right-to-sell listing agreement with an owner, other brokers may still have an opportunity to find a buyer for the property under a multiple listing system. In fact, according to the rules of most Multiple Listing Services (MLS), all listings that are to be interchanged must be exclusive.

Listings submitted to the MLS must include all information on the standard listing form approved by the MLS, including:

a) Name and address of owner;

b) Signatures of all parties authorizing the sale, exchange, or other disposition of the property and signature of the listing broker or his/her representative;

c) If other than cash, complete terms of sale;

d) Complete information on location or availability of utilities and all other information required to give a complete description of the property;

e) All matters which would not be apparent to a layman from a physical inspection of the property, such as building setback lines, easements, restrictions and covenants running with the land, whether or not sewers and utilities are connected, assessed values for land and improvements, taxes, and any other restriction, reservation or condition materially affecting value;

f) A photo of the improvements, if any.

In Washington, a majority of the MLS's are committees of Local Associations of Realtors®. However, in the Puget Sound area it is a separate incorporated association which is not affiliated with a Realtor® Association. Under a 1969 amendment to the Washington Real Estate Licensing Law, an MLS must submit its entrance requirements and initiation fee schedule to the Washington Real Estate Commission for approval. The Commission may not approve any entrance requirement which is more restrictive than the standards of the 1969 amendment. An MLS may require the applicant: (1) To be a licensed broker. (2) To obtain and maintain a policy of insurance. (*See* ERRORS AND OMISSION INSURANCE.) (3) To pay an initiation fee based upon a mathematical formula. However, in no case, may the initiation fee exceed $2,500. (Initiation fees are considered capital expenditures and are not a deductible business expense.) (4) To have been a broker in the territory of the MLS for one year prior to application or an associate broker in the territory of the MLS for one year and one year's experience as a broker some place else in the state. (5) To follow any rules of the association which do not violate federal or state law. (*See* COMMERCIAL BROKERS ASSOCIATION, CONTINGENCY LISTING, COOPERATING BROKER, LISTING, NORTHWEST MULTIPLE LISTING SERVICES, OFFICE EXCLUSIVE, POCKET LISTING, SUBAGENT.)
Reference: RCW 18.85.400.

MUNICIPAL ORDINANCES - Enactments by the governing body of a municipality providing for proper and safe use of structures by their owners, such as building codes and zoning regulations. These ordinances may regulate sanitary conditions, fire hazards, overcrowding and the like.

MUNIMENT OF TITLE - A legal document showing or providing title to real property, such as a deed or contract, which is evidence of ownership and enables an owner to defend his/her title.

MUNTIN - The narrow vertical strip that separates two adjacent window sashes.

MUTUAL MORTGAGE INSURANCE FUND - One of four FHA insurance funds into which all mortgage insurance premiums and other specified revenue of the FHA are paid and from which losses are met. (*See* FEDERAL HOUSING ADMINISTRATION (FHA).)

MUTUAL RESCISSION - The termination of a contract when each party agrees to release the other party in exchange for his/her or own release. For example, a buyer makes an offer on real property subject to obtaining financing within 30 days and closing within 45 days, which is accepted by the seller. Twenty-five (25) days later when the buyer is rejected for a loan, the buyer and seller execute a mutual rescission agreement and the earnest money is refunded to the buyer.

MUTUAL WATER COMPANY - A water company organized by or for water users in a given district with the object of securing an ample water supply at a reasonable rate. Stock is purchased by and issued to users.

MUTUALITY OF CONSENT - A meeting of the minds; a mutual asset of the parties to the formation of the contract. (*See* OFFER AND ACCEPTANCE.)

N

NAME, CHANGE OF - Use of a new name. A person may change his/her name merely by using another name with the intention to make that his/her legal name, as long as the change is not done to defraud anyone. However, because of all the problems which arise from not having proper identification in the new name, most parties desiring to change their names go through a formal name change, a relatively simple procedure. A name change can also be embodied in a divorce decree permitting the married woman to resume the use of her maiden name, or the name of a former husband. (*See* CHANGE OF NAME.)

If a person uses one name as a grantee of property and then grants/sells the same property under another name, there will be a potential defect in the record title; e.g., when the second deed is recorded, it will not be recorded in the chain of title and therefore will not give constructive notice to the world of its contents. For example, if Britt Rae, a single woman receiving title as such and later marrying, should convey title as Britt Shannon, there would be a defect in the record title. Britt Rae should convey title as "Britt Shannon, formerly known as Britt Rae." An appropriate entry would therefore be made in the grantor-grantee index so a title company searching the title would be able to see that the new deed was derived from the chain of title in which Britt Rae was the grantee.

It is helpful to title searchers if a married woman continues to use the name given her by her parents. For instance, Britt Lea Rae would become Mrs. Britt Lea John or Mrs. Britt Rae John and not Mrs. Robert John. (*See* LEGAL NAME.)

NAME, FICTITIOUS - Not a true name, usually the name of a company such as "The Washington Group." If the fictitious (business) name of a broker is to be used to advertise real property, the name must be first approved by the Real Estate Program.

While a deed to a fictitious person is void, a deed to a real person using a fictitious name is valid. (*See* ASSUMED BUSINESS NAME, FICTITIOUS NAME, LICENSING LAW.)

NAME, RESERVATION OF - The exclusive right to the use of a trade name. A tradename may be reserved by any person intending to organize a corporation, partnership, limited partnership, limited liability company or limited liability partnership. Reservation of a name is made by filing an application for reservation with the Secretary of State's Office and paying a fee. A name reservation is good for sixty (60) days and is not renewable. After the single reservation, the appropriate fees must be paid to permanently obtain the name. Additionally the trademark must be renewed every ten years. The Secretary of State will not reserve a name which might be confused with another registered name. At the present time there is no method of reserving a name with the Real Estate Program for a real estate company or with the Department of Financial Institutions for an escrow company.

NAMED INSURED - The person named in an insurance policy as the one protected.

NARELLO - The Association of Real Estate License Law Officials was formerly known as the National Association of Real Estate License Law Officials. (*See* ASSOCIATION OF REAL ESTATE LICENSE LAW OFFICIALS.)

NATIONAL ASSOCIATION OF INDEPENDENT FEE APPRAISERS - A professional association of appraisers with over 2,000 members nationally. It offers the specialty designations, I.F.A. (member), I.F.A.S. (senior member), I.F.A.C. (appraiser-counselor).

NATIONAL ASSOCIATION OF MASTER APPRAISERS (NAMA) - A professional association of appraisers formed by real estate educators to improve the practice of real estate appraising through mandatory specific education. It grants two specialized and one general designation. Specialty designations, Master Residential Appraiser (MSA) and Master Farm and Land Appraiser (MFLA) recognize individual achievement in a specific area of appraising. The senior designation, Master Senior Appraiser (MSA) is awarded to those individual members who have completed requirements in all aspects of real estate appraising. Companies may also be granted the designation Certified Appraisal Organization (CAO), to those organizations employing only designated appraisers.

NATIONAL ASSOCIATION OF REAL ESTATE BROKERS - *See* REALTIST.

NATIONAL ASSOCIATION OF REALTORS (NAR) - The largest and most prestigious real estate organization in the world. NAR has over 700,000 members, and includes Realtors® and Realtor-Associates® representing all branches of the real estate industry. The national organization functions through state and local real estate boards/associations, which in Washington is the Washington Association of Realtors and its 30 Local Boards/Associations. Active brokers who have been admitted to membership in NAR are allowed to use the trademark "REALTOR." Salesmen are admitted on a "Realtor" or "Realtor-Associate" status. The Washington Association of Realtors has elected to be an all "Realtor" state, which means all its members are "Realtors." Members of NAR subscribe to a Code of Ethics. (*See* CODE OF ETHICS, LOCAL ASSOCIATION OF REALTORS, REALTOR, WASHINGTON ASSOCIATION OF REALTORS.)

The national professional organizations directly affiliated with the National Association of Realtors are the: Realtor National Marketing Institute; Society of Industrial Realtors; Institute of Real Estate Management; Realtor's Land Institute; American Institute of Real Estate Appraisers; American Society of Real Estate Counselors; and Women's Council of Realtors.

NATIONAL ASSOCIATION OF REVIEW APPRAISERS AND MORTGAGE UNDERWRITERS (NARA/MU) - A national organization whose members review appraisals and underwrite mortgages. This nonprofit organization has approximately 7,000 members and is thus one of the largest "consumers" of appraisals in the nation. It offers the designations C.R.E.A. (Certified Real Estate Appraiser) and R.M.U. (Registered Mortgage Underwriter.)

NATIONAL HOUSING PARTNERSHIP - A private, profit-making company, in conjunction with its sole and general partner and administrative arm, the National Corporation for Housing Partnership, which specializes in housing for low to moderate income families, the handicapped, and the elderly. It has some 350 multifamily projects in the United Sates.

NATIONAL SOCIETY OF REAL ESTATE APPRAISERS - A professional real estate organization whose members are involved in the appraisal of real estate. The society awards three designations: (1) Residential Appraiser (RA), (2) Certified Real Estate Appraiser (CRA), and (3) Master Real Estate Appraiser (MREA).

NATURAL AFFECTION - The feeling that naturally exists between close relatives such as a parent and child or a husband and wife. In law, such is regards as good consideration and may appear in a deed when property is being transferred. In a deed in Washington it is often expressed as "love and affection."

NATURAL MONUMENT - An object such as a river, shore, or beach which exists as it was placed by nature. Such objects are used to denote boundaries in the description of legal boundaries. (*See* MONUMENT.)

NATURAL PERSON - An individual; a private person, as distinguished from an artificial entity such as a corporation or partnership.

NEGATIVE AMORTIZATION - A financing arrangement in which the monthly payments do not pay the monthly interest on the loan and the loan balance increases over the term of the loan rather than decreases.

NEGATIVE CASH FLOW - The investment situation where cash expenditures to maintain an investment (taxes, mortgage payments, maintenance, etc.) exceed the cash income received from the investment.

Some investors will purchase real estate investments that operate on a negative cash flow basis with the expectation that the favorable yield on their investment will come in the form of appreciated value upon the sale of the property.

Under the 1986 Tax Reform Act rental real estate activities which are considered to be "passive investments" and losses generated can only be used to offset other passive income. Individuals with adjusted gross incomes (AGI) of $100,000 or less may deduct up to $25,000 of net losses from rental of residential or commercial property against regular income. This deduction phases out for taxpayers with AGI's between $100,000 and $150,000. Also known as "negative carry." If the investor is not involved in active management of the investment, the loss will be a **passive loss**. (*See* PASSIVE LOSS.)

NEGATIVE EASEMENT - An easement, such as a building restriction or a view easement, which has the effect of preventing the servient landowner from doing an act otherwise permitted. (*See* SCENIC EASEMENT.)

NEGLIGENCE - The failure on the part of someone to perform with due care.

NEGOTIABLE INSTRUMENT - Any written instrument which may be transferred by endorsement or delivery so as to vest legal title in the transferee. Common examples of negotiable instruments are checks, public stocks, and promissory notes. To be negotiable, a promissory note must be an unconditional promise, made in writing by one person to another and signed by the maker, engaging to pay on demand or at a fixed or determinable time, a certain sum of money, to order or to bearer. It is essential to use words of negotiability such as "pay to Todd Edwin, or order, or bearer."

One who takes a negotiable instrument in good faith, for a valuable consideration and without notice of any defect, is a holder in due course, against whom the maker of the note cannot assert personal defenses (such as lack of consideration) in order to refuse payment.

Under the Uniform Commercial Code, a transferor implies certain warranties concerning the negotiable instrument, such as: that it is genuine and is what it purports to be; that the transferor has good title; that all involved parties have the capacity to contract; and that the transferor does not know of any fact that would impair the validity of the contract or make it valueless. (*See* ENDORSEMENT, HOLDER IN DUE COURSE, UNIFORM COMMERCIAL CODE.)

NEGOTIATION - The transaction of business aimed at reaching a meeting of the minds among the parties; bargaining.

The sale of real estate illustrates the negotiation process. At times the first offer is considered to be just an indication of an intention to deal and thereafter a series of counteroffers follow, leading up to consummation of the transaction.

Most listing forms contain a safety clause allowing the broker to recover his/her commission for a specified period of time after the termination of the listing if the listed property is sold to anyone with whom the broker was negotiating prior to the time the listing ended. In this regard, "negotiation" means more than putting the parties in touch; it means actually transacting business, bargaining and arousing interest to effect a purchase and sale.

Real estate commission rates are not fixed by law but are the subject of negotiation between the parties. (*See* PROCURING CAUSES.)

NEIGHBORHOOD - Adjacent areas showing common characteristics and homogeneity of land use.

NEIGHBORHOOD SHOPPING CENTER - A group of retail business, usually 15 to 20, providing a limited variety of convenience stores (barbershop, dry cleaning), having common parking and management, and catering to 1000 families or more.

NET AFTER TAXES - The net operating income after all charges, including federal income taxes, have been deducted.

NET INCOME - The sum arrived at after deducting from gross income the expenses of a business or investment, including taxes and insurance, and allowances for vacancy and bad debts; net income is what the property will earn in a given year's operation. Generally net income is calculated before depreciation.

NET LEASE - A lease, usually commercial, whereby the lessee pays not only the rent for occupancy, but also pays maintenance and operating expenses such as taxes, insurance, utilities and repairs. Thus the rent paid is "net" to the lessor. Popular with investors who want to obtain a steady stream of income without having to handle the problems associated with management, maintenance and the like. Commercial or industrial leases, ground leases, and long-term leases are typically net leases.

Because the common interpretations given to the term "net lease" are so broad, it is essential to review the lease document to determine what expenses the tenant is to pay. In a true net lease the tenant is responsible for expenses relating to the premises exactly as if the tenant were the owner. Examples of such expenses are real estate taxes; special assessments; insurance premiums; all maintenance charges, including labor and materials; cost of compliance with governmental health and safety regulations; payment of claims for personal injury or property damage; and even costs of structural, interior, roof, and other repairs.

It is helpful to distinguish between the net rent, called "base rent," and the total of base rent and expenses, called "effective rent." (*See* GROSS LEASE, PERCENTAGE LEASE, TRIPLE NET LEASE.)

NET LISTING - An employment contract in which the broker receives as his/her commission all excess moneys over and above the minimum sales price agreed upon by broker and seller. Because of the danger of unethical practices in such a listing, its use is discouraged in most states, including Washington. In some states, such as Massachusetts, New Jersey, Michigan and New York, the use of a net listing is illegal.

NET NET - - *See* NET LEASE.

NET NET NET - *See* NET LEASE.

NET OPERATING INCOME (NOI) - The income/balance remaining after deduction of all operating expenses and replacement reserves, but before deducting any debt service or depreciation.

NET RATE - The interest rate an investor receives after a servicing fee is deducted.

NET RETURN - The net cash received for an investment. It is a rate of interest based on a "cash-on-cash" method. When an investor deducts all costs and expenses associated with making an investment from what is received from the investment, the investor is looking at the net return.

NET SPENDABLE - The money remaining each year after collecting rents and paying operating expenses and mortgage payments.

NET USABLE ACRE - That portion of a property which is suitable for building. A 20 acre parcel may have 20 gross acres and only 15 net usable or building acres. Density requirements under local zoning regulations are based on the net usable acreage of the property.

NET WORTH - The value remaining after deducting liabilities from assets. Many private real estate syndication offerings establish their own suitability standards for prospective investors, such as requiring that the investor maintain a net worth of at least $75,000.

Federal law sometimes requires a corporation to have a certain minimum net worth before it can manage the funds of others. For example, in real estate syndications, a corporate general partner must have and maintain a fair market value net worth (without considering its interest in the partnership) equal to the lesser of $250,000 or 15% of the amount invested by the limited partners if the amount so invested is $2,500,000 or less; or equal to 10 percent of the amount so invested if that amount exceeds $2,500,000 (the "safe harbor" rule). If the general partner of the "partnership" does not maintain this minimum net worth the effect is that the Internal Revenue Service will not give a favorable written ruling that this partnership will be treated as a partnership, rather than an association taxable as a corporation. Where a limited partner joins a partnership and cannot ascertain if the partnership will be taxed as an association or not, he/she is taking a substantial risk. Most general partners, therefore, try to comply with this safe-harbor rule. (*See* LIMITED PARTNERSHIP.)

NET YIELD - The return on an investment after subtracting all expenses.

NETTING OUT - A slang expression that describes the amount of money the seller wants to receive on a sale of property; the amount that can be put in the seller's pocket after all expenses and payment of liens.

"NO ACTION" LETTER - A written opinion from the Securities and Exchange Commission (SEC) informing an applicant that the SEC will not require, based on the facts presented in the request for opinion, that a proposed project be registered as a security. If a project is classified as a security, it is subject to various complicated restrictions and regulations. It is advantageous, then, for project developers to avoid this classification in order to avoid these regulations. For example, the developer of a proposed resort condominium may seek an interpretation from the commission that his/her project does not involve the offering of a real estate security. The developer will do this in the form of a request for a "no action" letter in accordance with the procedure set forth in the Securities Act. A developer must also request a "no action" letter to certify that his/her property is exempt from registration in accordance with federal interstate land sales subdivision regulations. (*See* REAL PROPERTY SECURITIES REGISTRATION.)

"NO DEAL COMMISSION" CLAUSE - A clause inserted in a listing contract which stipulates that a commission is to be paid **only if and when title passes**. This nullifies the generally accepted principle that a broker earns a commission when the broker has brought an acceptable "ready, willing, and able," buyer to the seller for the price and under the terms specified in the listing agreement.

NOMINAL CONSIDERATION - A consideration bearing no relation to the real value of the contract. A deed often recites a nominal consideration, such as "ten dollars and other valuable consideration." Such nominal consideration raises a presumption that the grantee is a "purchaser" rather than a donee and thus is protected under the recording act as a subsequent good faith purchaser.

A broker must not be a party to the naming of a false consideration in any document, unless it is the naming of an obviously nominal consideration. To do so would not only violate the Realtor's Code of Ethics but would also be cause for suspension or revocation of the broker's license. (*See* DUAL CONTRACT, EXCISE TAX ON REAL ESTATE SALES, RECORDING.)

NOMINAL INTEREST RATE - The interest rate stipulated in a note or contract, which may differ from the true or effective interest rate, especially if the lender discounts the loan and advances less than the full amount. (*See* ANNUAL PERCENTAGE RATE, EFFECTIVE INTEREST RATE.)

NOMINEE - One designated to act for another as his/her representative in a limited sense. A nominee corporation is sometimes used to purchase real property where the principals do not wish to be known. Care should be taken in structuring a purchase through the nominee corporation so that there are no adverse tax consequences.

The term nominee is not a synonym for assignee.

The nominee form is often used by a real estate syndicator who is the buyer but not the ultimate purchaser. It is also used in a Section 1031 tax-free exchange situation for acquiring the replacement property. (*See* ASSIGNMENT.)

NON-BEARING WALL - A wall that does not help to support the structure of a building.

NON-COMPETITION CLAUSE - A provision in a contract or lease prohibiting a person from operating or controlling a nearby business which would compete with one of the parties to the contract. The courts will enforce such a provision as long as it is reasonable as to time and location. Non-competition clauses are frequently found in percentage leases for shopping centers, as where a shoe store tenant agrees to not establish a competing shoe store across the street. Sometimes referred to as a no-compete clause. If a value is placed on it, then it is considered ordinary income to the seller and its value could be capitalized by the buyer, amortizable over the life of the covenant. (*See* COVENANT NOT TO COMPETE.)

NONCONFORMING LOAN - Normally usage of the word "nonconforming" implies loan amounts and underwriting practices that are outside those used by Freddie Mac and Fannie Mae guidelines.

NONCONFORMING USE - A permitted use which was lawfully established and maintained at the time of its original construction but which no longer conforms to the current use regulations because of a change in the zoning. The nonconforming use might be the structure itself, the size of the lot, the use of the land, or the use of the structure. The use will eventually be eliminated, although the nonconforming use status is not necessarily discontinued upon the sale or lease of the property. By allowing the use to continue for a reasonable time, the government can assure itself that the use will not continue indefinitely and, at the same time, avoid having to pay just compensation for taking the property through condemnation.

When purchasing a nonconforming structure, a person should be made aware that in case of substantial destruction by fire or otherwise, zoning may bar reconstruction. Suppose a fire damages the structure so that it will cost more than 50% of the assessed value for tax purposes to rebuild; then it cannot be rebuilt. A buyer should discuss demolition insurance with his/her agent before buying. (*See* VARIANCE.)

NONDISCLOSURE - The failure to reveal a fact, with or without the intention to conceal it. (*See* MISREPRESENTATION.)

NONDISTURBANCE CLAUSE - A clause inserted in a mortgage whereby the mortgagee agrees not to terminate the tenancies of lessees who pay their rent if the mortgagee forecloses on the mortgagor-lessor's building. Without such a clause, a lessee whose lease was signed subsequent to the mortgage could have the lease terminated by a foreclosure action.

NONJUDICIAL FORECLOSURE - The process of selling real property under a power of sale in a deed of trust which is in default. (*See* DEED OF TRUST, FORECLOSURE.)

NON OWNER OCCUPIED - A property that is not occupied by the owner is said to be non owner occupied. Usually a non owner loan will carry a higher interest rate.

NONRECOURSE LOAN - A loan in which the borrower is not held personally liable on the note. The lender on a nonrecourse loan generally feels confident that the collateral property will be adequate security for the loan. (*See* DEFICIENCY JUDGMENT.)

NO PAY FOR DELAY CLAUSE - These clauses typically provide that the contractor, subcontractor, or supplier is not entitled to any additional compensation or damages resulting from a delay in the completion date of the project which is caused by the contracting party or someone acting for the contracting party. Washington has declared no pay for delay clauses void as against the public policy of the state.

NORMAL WEAR AND TEAR - That physical deterioration which occurs in the normal course of the use for which a property is intended, without negligence, carelessness, accident or abuse of the premises (or equipment or chattels) by the occupant, members of their household, or their invitees or guests. The tenant of residential property is not responsible for loss in value due to normal wear and tear. An important element in determining the reasonableness of a unit's wear and tear is the length of the tenant's residency. For instance, if an apartment has been inhabited by the same renter for three years, it may be reasonable to expect that the walls need to be painted and that the carpeting needs to be cleaned. The landlord, then, cannot hold back the security deposit for such damage.

Normal wear and tear is deterioration or depreciation in value by ordinary and reasonable use, but specifically does not include items which are missing from the dwelling unit. Normal wear and tear is a major cause of property depreciation.

NORTHWEST MULTIPLE LISTING SERVICE - A multiple listing service (MLS) is an organization that pools the listings of all member companies. Members of the MLS are authorized to show any of the properties in the pool which greatly expands the offerings any one member may show to a prospective buyer, as well as extends the marketing of their own listings. NWMLS was formed in 1996 to provide services to real estate licensees in King, Pierce and Snohomish counties. Owned by its member brokers, the NWMLS was created to replace the Puget Sound Multiple Listing Association, which had been established in 1984 through a combining of four independent multiple listing services. (*See* WASHINGTON INFORMATION NETWORK (WIN))

NOSING - The rounded outer edge of a stair tread.

NOTARY PUBLIC - A public officer, an official witness, whose function is to administer oaths and to attest and certify documents by his/her signature and official seal, thereby giving them credit and authenticity. In the absence of a seal, the notarization is void. One who has a beneficial interest cannot act as a Notary Public to the same document, e.g., a grantee or mortgagee. (*See* ACKNOWLEDGMENT.)

NOTE - A document signed by the borrower of a loan, stating the loan amount, the interest rate, the time and method of repayment and the obligation to repay. The note is the evidence of the debt. (*See* PROMISSORY NOTE.)

NOTICE - 1. Legal notice is notice which is required to be made by law, or notice which is imparted by operation of law as a result of the possession of property or the recording of documents. When deeds are recorded in the Office of the County Auditor, subsequent purchasers are thereby put on notice as to the contents of such documents; this is called **legal** or **constructive notice**.

2. Notice which is required by contract, for example, when the parties agree to terminate a contract by the written notice of either party 30 days prior to termination. Though notice can be oral, it is always advisable to give notice in writing, in such a manner that is easy to prove that necessary notice was given. Such written notice should be sent Certified Mail, Return Receipt Requested, or should be personally delivered with a receipt from the receiving party.

3. The Landlord Tenant Act provides that twenty (20) days notice must be given to terminate a month-to-month tenancy. (*See* ACTUAL NOTICE, CONSTRUCTIVE NOTICE, LANDLORD TENANT ACT, NOTICE OF DEFAULT.)
Reference: RCW 59.18

NOTICE OF ASSESSMENT - A notice sent by the County Assessor's Office to the owner of real property specifying the assessed value of the property and the amount of the real estate tax due. In many cases, this is sent to the mortgage or deed of trust lender for payment. A property owner should request that the lender forward it after payment, if the lender does not do it as a matter of policy. (*See* ASSESSED VALUATION, EXCISE TAX ON REAL ESTATE SALES, PROPERTY TAXES, REAL ESTATE TAX STATEMENT.)

NOTICE OF CONSENT - A legal procedure that allows a state official to receive legal process for nonresidents. As a condition to doing business in a state, an out-of-state subdivider or broker must often file a notice of consent.

NOTICE OF DEFAULT - A notice to a defaulting party that there has been a default in the performance of a term or condition of a contract, usually providing a grace period in which to cure the default. Notices of default are usually provided in real estate contracts and mortgages and are sometimes required by operation of law as in Washington's deed of trust legislation. Care should be taken to make the grace period at least five **business** days; otherwise a defaulting party receiving a notice of default sent on Thursday before a long holiday weekend might not have sufficient time in which to cure.

Under a real estate contract, in order to avoid a forfeiture of the property through an inadvertent default, the prudent purchaser will insert in the real estate contract a clause requiring that notice of default be given along with a grace period to correct the default. Such notice should be in writing and sent to the defaulting party by Registered or Certified Mail, Return Receipt Requested, at an address specified in the contract, or such address as the purchaser shall provide the seller by registered mail. (*See* NOTICE.)
Reference: RCW 61.24

NOTICE OF LIEN - A specific written notice for a mechanic's lien to be recorded in the Office of the County Auditor in which the real property is located. (*See* MECHANIC'S LIEN.)

NOTICE OF PENDENCY - *See* LIS PENDENS.

NOTICE TO QUIT - A written notice given by a landlord to his/her tenant, stating that the landlord intends to regain possession of the leased premises and that the tenant is required to quit and remove himself/herself from the premises either at the end of the lease term or immediately if there is a breach of lease or if the tenancy is at will or by sufferance; sometimes refers to the notice given by the tenant to the landlord that he/she intends to give up possession on a stated day.

Under the Landlord Tenant Act, a landlord is required to give a tenant written notice to pay rent before bringing summary proceedings to evict the tenant. (*See* LANDLORD TENANT ACT, SUMMARY POSSESSION.)

NOVATION - The substitution of a new obligation for an old one; substitution of new parties to an existing obligation, as where the parties to an agreement accept a new debtor in place of an old one. For example, in an assumption of a loan, the lender may release the seller and substitute the buyer as the party primarily liable for the mortgage debt. A novation requires an intent to discharge the original contract, and, being a new contract, a novation requires its own consideration and other essentials of a valid contract.

NUISANCE - Conduct or activity which results in an actual physical interference with another person's reasonable use or enjoyment of his/her property for any lawful purpose. A private nuisance is one affecting only a limited number of people, whereas a public nuisance is one affecting the community at large (such as excessive noise from jet airliners). If a use is considered to be a nuisance, the injured party can seek either an abatement of the nuisance by way of an injunction, or damages. Common examples of nuisances are activities resulting in unreasonable noise, odors, fire hazards, and the like. (*See* ATTRACTIVE NUISANCE, TRESPASS.)

NULL & VOID - Having no legal force or effect; of no worth; unenforceable; not binding. Discriminatory restrictive covenants contained in a deed or other instrument are null and void. (*See* VOID.)

NUNCUPATIVE WILL - An oral will declared by the testator in his/her final sickness, made before witnesses and afterwards reduced to writing. Such a will is valid in Washington under very restricted circumstance; however, real property cannot be devised by a nuncupative will.
Reference: RCW 11.12

OATH - A solemn pledge made before a notary public or other officer. A person taking an oath is often referred to as the "affiant." An oath often takes the form of an appeal to a Supreme Being to attest to the truth of a person's statement. An example of an oath would be: "You do solemnly swear that the contents of this affidavit, which you subscribe to, are true as therein stated." In Washington, the notary does not have to require the affiant either to raise his/her hand or to place it on a Bible before administering the oath. If the affiant cannot or will not use the term "swear," an affirmation is permissible. (*See* AFFIRMATION.)

OBLIGOR - A promisor; one who has incurred a lawful obligation to another (the obligee). The maker of a promissory note is an obligor. In a performance bond, the contractor is the obligor. One who guarantees the performance of the obligation is a surety. (*See* SURETY.)

OBSOLESCENCE - A cause of depreciation in a property. Functional obsolescence is a loss of value due to a perceived defect in a structure, such as outmoded plumbing, or inadequately designed fixtures. An example of functional obsolescence would be one bathroom in a 5-bedroom house. External (economic) obsolescence is a loss in value from causes in the neighborhood, but outside the property itself, such as a change in zoning, loss of job opportunities and other external detrimental conditions.

OCCUPANCY AGREEMENT - An agreement to permit the buyer to occupy the property prior to the close of escrow (sometimes referred to as **early possession**) in consideration of paying the seller a specified rent, usually on a daily prorated basis. An occupancy agreement should be in writing to avoid the possible friction which could arise between buyer, seller and broker over the right to early occupancy and the amount of rent to be paid. It is not prudent for the buyer to be allowed to occupy the premises prior to the close of escrow without having a written occupancy agreement. It would also be prudent to have the buyer waive any contingencies to the purchase. The buyer in this situation should take out a homeowner's insurance policy, or at least receive an endorsement on the seller' policy in order to be properly covered. Due to past bad experiences, many brokers feel that the buyer should be allowed early possession only in cases of emergency. (*See* EARLY OCCUPANCY.)

If it is important for the buyer to have physical occupancy on an agreed date, the Purchase and Sale Agreement may provide that a portion of the purchase price be held in escrow to guarantee delivery of occupancy and to be paid to the buyer as liquidated damages if the seller does not deliver occupancy as agreed. (*See* CLOSING.)

OCCUPANCY PERMIT - The Uniform Building Code (UBC) classifies all buildings by type of occupancy or use. There are many classifications, but they all fall into three general categories: (1) residential, such as homes and apartments; (2) commercial, such as banks, office buildings, restaurants, and (3) industrial, which includes factories, service stations, garages.

A Certificate of Occupancy is required for all types of new construction. For residential construction, when the building permit is signed off at final inspection it becomes the Certificate of Occupancy. For new commercial or industrial construction, a separate Certificate of Occupancy is issued after the building passes final inspection.

A Certificate of Occupancy is a certification that a building meets the Code requirements for its intended use. Building code, fire code and other safety-related requirements differ for the various types of occupancies defined in the UBC. Consequently, when use of a structure changes, the type of occupancy changes and a new Certificate of Occupancy is required.

OFFER - A promise by one party to act or perform in a specified manner provided the other party will act or perform in the manner requested. An offer demonstrates an intention to enter into a contract (e.g., Purchase and Sale Agreement) as opposed to merely inviting offers from others (e.g., a listing contract). An offer must be a certain and definite promise and state what is demanded in return; it must be communicated to offeree and made with serious intent to contract. An offer creates the power of acceptance in the other party until withdrawn.

The Purchase and Sale Agreement is a vehicle to transmit to the seller a prospective buyer's offer to purchase the seller's property. An offer must be definite and certain. If it is illusory, it may be held void for lack of certainty. Thus, it must actually bind the offeror if it is accepted. (*See* CONTRACT, OFFER AND ACCEPTANCE.)

OFFER AND ACCEPTANCE - The two components of a valid contract; a meeting of the minds. An offer is a proposal or a manifestation of an intention to enter into a contract. The offer must be communicated to the offeree and must be definite and certain, with all terms reduced to writing when dealing with real estate. The offer creates a power of acceptance in the person to whom it is communicated. Upon the acceptance by the offeree of all the terms of the offer, a valid contract is created. The offeror can revoke his/her offer at any time before the offeree has communicated his/her acceptance to the offeror, but the revocation is not effective until received by the offeree. Immediately upon revocation, the offeree no longer has the power to accept the contract. An offer may be terminated by lapse of time, communication of notice of revocation, qualified acceptance (counteroffer), rejection, death or insanity of the offeror.

The acceptance of an offer must be definite, unambiguous and unqualified. If the acceptance is qualified in any way or changes the terms of the offer in any way, then it constitutes a counteroffer and a contract can only be created when this counteroffer is accepted by the original offeror. In real estate transactions, the acceptance should be in writing and signed by the party to be bound. At a minimum, the date the acceptance is made should be noted. Some brokers suggest the exact time (e.g., 1:35 p.m., October 20th, 1998) should be noted.

Most offers to purchase real property are made on the standard Purchase and Sale Agreement. It is common for the offeror, the prospective buyer, to give the offeree until midnight of ______(usually 2, 3, or 4 days or longer if offer must be submitted by mail) in which to accept the offer. The purpose is to limit the time in which the seller has the power to accept. The offeror could, nevertheless, withdraw the offer any time during the specified period since an offer can be revoked any time prior to notification of acceptance, except where the offeror's agreement to hold the offer open is supported by independent consideration. If accepted after the specified deadline, the acceptance would constitute a counteroffer.

A written offer which was mailed to the offeree is deemed to be accepted and a contract created when the offeree places his/her acceptance in the mail. If the offeror attempts to revoke his/her offer after the offeree has mailed his/her acceptance but before the acceptance is received by the offeror, the revocation would be ineffective. The rationale is that the offeror has chosen the mail as his/her agent. (Sometimes referred to as the "Mail Box Rule.") When the offeree delivers to the agent, e.g., puts the acceptance in the mail, it is deemed to be effectively communicated to the offeror, even if the acceptance is lost in the mails. (*See* ACCEPTANCE, CONTRACT, COUNTEROFFER, OFFER, OPTION.)

OFFER TO SELL - Broadly defined in most statutes to include any inducement, solicitation, or attempt to encourage a person to buy property or acquire an interest in property.

Under the Washington licensing laws, one who offers to sell, buy or rent any real estate or any options on real estate for others for compensation is required to have a real estate license. (*See* LAND DEVELOPMENT ACT, LICENSING LAW.)
Reference: RCW 18.85, RCW 58.19.

OFFERING SHEET - A one-page loan summary that assists the investor in evaluating the real estate loan being submitted by the loan correspondent.

OFFEROR - The party who makes an offer. The party to whom an offer is made is the offeree.

OFFICE - The space in which the clerical work of a business establishment is transacted.

A real estate brokerage office must be located in an area **commercially** zoned. A Rule and Regulation of the Real Estate Commission allows an office in a residence if the office is separate from any living quarters, is identified as a real estate office by a sign at the office entrance and the office entrance is open to the public and does not lead through any living quarters and there is only one licensee, the broker. Each real estate office must prominently display the name of the real estate firm as it appears on the license issued by the Real Estate Program of the Department of Licensing. (*See* BRANCH OFFICE.)
Reference: WAC 308-124F

Licenses of the real estate broker and all other licensed personnel must be prominently displayed in the office to which the individual is licensed. A real estate broker must promptly notify the Real Estate Program of the Department of Licensing of a change of location or mailing address of the main office or any branch office. (*See* HOME, USED FOR BUSINESS, LICENSING LAW.)
Reference: RCW 18.85, WAC 308-124B.

OFFICE BUILDING - A building which obtains a large percentage of its revenue from the rental of commercial offices, in addition to income derived from ground-floor store space, if any. Office buildings are almost invariably multiple-story structures, containing two or more elevators, and arranged so that rows of offices open onto hallways extending through the building.

An office building is appraised, in general, like other income property. (*See* APPRAISAL.) It is, however, a complex appraisal, involving special problems. In evaluating an office building, the appraiser must consider particularly the factors involved in the economic background of the city and the district in which the property is located, for they are almost as important as data regarding the property itself. These economic factors include: population growth, monthly payrolls, total bank clearances, building permits over a period of years, school enrollment, public utilities and transportation facilities, office space normally required, rentable office space available in the locality, rentals of competitive properties, percentage of vacancies and nature of tenancies. Information regarding the property itself, which must be carefully collected and examined by the appraiser, may be grouped as follows: (1) the site, (2) the building, and (3) the income from the property.

OFFICE EXCLUSIVE - A listing in which the seller refuses to submit the listing to a Multiple Listing Service, even after being informed of the advantages of MLS, and signs a certification to that effect. The seller, in essence, wants only the listing broker to show the property. It is a listing which is retained by one real estate office to the exclusion of other cooperating brokers. Office exclusives, in some MLS's, must be filed in the MLS office but are not disseminated to other members. This has been successfully challenged.

In certain cases, the MLS may write to the seller concerning the advantages of MLS and request that the seller reconsider listing with MLS. A copy of any such letter must be sent to the listing broker. An office exclusive does not relieve the listing broker who is a Realtor from the obligation to cooperate fully with other members in selling the property in accordance with the ByLaws of the Board and the Code of Ethics of the National Association of Realtors. (*See* MULTIPLE LISTING SERVICE.)

OFFICE IN THE HOME - *See* HOME, USED FOR BUSINESS; OFFICE.

OFFICE OF EQUAL OPPORTUNITY (OEO) - The federal agency under the direction of the Secretary of the Department of Housing and Urban Development which is in charge of administering the Fair Housing Act. (*See* FEDERAL FAIR HOUSING LAW.)

OFFICE OF INTERSTATE LAND SALES REGISTRATION (OILSR) - The federal agency which enforces federal legislation on interstate land sales. Since establishment of OILSR, as part of HUD in 1969, many of the abuses and frauds perpetrated on the public in the sale of recreational property across state lines have ended. However, anyone considering buying recreational property out-of-state should only do so after consulting with knowledgeable real estate agents in the area of the property. (*See* INTERSTATE LAND SALES.)

OFF-RECORD TITLE DEFECT - A defect in title which is not apparent from an examination of the public records. A recorded document may not effectively transfer title to property if it was forged or was never delivered to the grantee or was signed by incompetent parties. A party whose signature has been forged to a deed still retains legal title to the property and can enforce his/her title even against a good faith purchaser for value who records the forged deed. (*See* ADVERSE POSSESSION.)

To protect against losses incurred as a result of off-record risks, a buyer should obtain an extended coverage title insurance policy. (*See* AMERICAN LAND TITLE ASSOCIATION, TITLE INSURANCE.)

OFFSITE COSTS - Costs for such items as sewers, streets, utilities, etc., which are incurred in the development of raw land, but are not connected with the actual construction of the buildings (on-site costs).

OFF-SITE MANAGEMENT - Those property management functions that can be performed away from the premises being managed, e.g., accounting for rents collected and paying bills. Examples of on-site management functions are showing rental units, making repairs and handling evictions. (*See* LICENSING LAW.)

OFF-STREET PARKING - Parking spaces located on private property, usually on an area provided especially for such use; provides vehicular parking spaces with adequate aisles for maneuvering to provide access for entrance and exit.

OIL AND GAS LEASE - A grant of the sole and exclusive right to develop the land described in the lease for oil and gas, or a lease for a designated term of years for the purpose of such development, subject to the condition of a payment of royalty in the event of production, of the commencement of drilling operations on or before a specified date and of the performance within a prescribed time of a certain amount of development work. Typically, there is an express or implied easement to enter the property in order to drill. (*See* IMPLIED EASEMENT, PROFIT A PRENDRE, ROYALTY.)

OMITTED PROPERTY - Property which has escaped taxation. Property of a decedent omitted in the assessment of inheritance and/or estate tax. Lands omitted in the original assessment of a local improvement. (*See* PROPERTY TAXES.)

ONE HUNDRED PERCENT COMMISSION - A commission arrangement between a real estate broker and a salesperson, usually an independent contractor, in which the salesperson receives the full net commission on certain real estate sales provided the salesperson meets specified sales quotas and/or pays the broker for specified administrative overhead costs. The Real Estate Program scrutinizes such arrangements to be certain that there is compliance with the licensing law requirement of adequate supervision by the managing broker of all salespeople.

ON-SITE IMPROVEMENT - The construction of a building or other improvements within the boundaries of a property, thus increasing the value of the property. (*See* OFF-SITE IMPROVEMENTS.)

ON-SITE MANAGEMENT - Those property management functions that must be performed on the premises being managed, such as showing rental units. (*See* LICENSING LAW, OFF-SITE MANAGEMENT.)

OPEN AND NOTORIOUS POSSESSION - Possession which is sufficiently clear that a reasonable person viewing the property would know that the occupant claimed some title or interest in it. An owner does not lose his/her property by adverse possession unless he/she has notice, actual or constructive, of the occupant's claim to the property. The construction of buildings or the fencing and cultivating of the land would certainly be sufficiently open and notorious possession. The mere posting of a no trespassing sign probably would not be sufficient. (*See* ADVERSE POSSESSION.)

OPEN-END MORTGAGE OR DEED OF TRUST - A mortgage or deed of trust in which the borrower is given a limit up to which he/she may borrow, with any incremental advances of money up to but not exceeding the original borrowing limit to be secured by the same mortgage or deed of trust. It allows a borrower to reborrow any part of the amount paid back on the underlying loan without the need of writing a new mortgage or deed of trust. Usually the interest rate on the new money will be at the market rate at the time of disbursement and there may be some closing costs on the new funds. However, there are reduced costs, such as minimized refinancing and appraisal costs. The lender should require a title insurance update prior to each incremental advance since intervening recorded liens may have priority over the mortgage or deed of trust. An open-end real estate loan is relatively rare in Washington these days. (*See* EQUITY MORTGAGE, FUTURE ADVANCES.)

OPEN HOUSE - The common real estate practice of showing a listed home to the public during established hours, frequently on Sunday afternoons. In Washington, open house signs may not be placed on public property in some cities and prior consent should be acquired from private land owners. (*See* SIGNS, SITE OFFICE.)

OPEN HOUSING LAWS - Housing which is free from discrimination based on race, sex, color, religion or national origin. Both federal and state anti-discrimination laws are designed to insure that housing is made available to all who can afford it. (*See* DISCRIMINATION, FEDERAL FAIR HOUSING LAW, WASHINGTON STATE HUMAN RIGHTS COMMISSION.)

OPEN LISTING - A listing given to any number of brokers who can work simultaneously to sell the owner's property. The first broker who secures a buyer ready, willing and able to purchase at the terms of the listing is the one who earns the commission. In the case of a sale, the seller is not obligated to notify any of the brokers that the property has been sold. Unlike an exclusive listing, an open listing need not contain a definite termination date, in which case it terminates after a "reasonable" time (what is customary in the community); however, either party can in good faith terminate the agency at will. Many times, there is a provision in an open listing allowing a broker to register a prospective purchaser. This registration enables the broker to collect a commission if a registered purchaser buys the property within a specified time period (e.g., up to one year on commercial-investment) of registration or termination of the listing. (*See* PROCURING CAUSE.)

OPEN MORTGAGE OR DEED OF TRUST - One which may be repaid at any time with no prepayment penalty. This term is not generally used in Washington. There is no general terminology used in Washington in common usage which speaks to the idea.

OPEN SPACE - A certain portion of the landscape which has not been built upon and which is sought either to be reserved in its natural state or is used for agricultural or recreational purposes, such as parks, squares and the like. In addition, open space is park land within a subdivision, usually designated as such by a developer as a condition for receiving a building permit from the city or county. HUD provides funds to communities for up to 50 percent of the cost of acquiring, developing and preserving land for parks, recreation, conservation, science and historic uses. (*See* OPEN SPACE TAXATION LAW.)

OPEN SPACE TAXATION LAW - The Open Space Act is designed to encourage the preservation of qualified lands through the application of current use assessment.

Certain types of agricultural, timber land and just unused lands qualify for a lower assessment which results in a significant reduction in assessed valuation, which in return results in lower taxes.

Once the land is classified it shall not be applied to any other use. A change of use will result in removal from classification. Upon removal of land from classification, an additional tax shall be imposed. This additional tax shall be the difference in the amount of tax paid as open space and the amount that would have been paid if the land was not so classified, plus interest, for a maximum of seven years prior to removal from classification. In addition, there is a penalty of 20% of this total amount. This 20% penalty can be avoided if the owner requests removal, in writing, after eight years of classification. This request, which is irrevocable, must be made two years prior to the date of withdrawal. (*See* REAL PROPERTY TAXES.)
Reference: RCW 84.34.

OPERATING BUDGET - An itemized statement of income, expenses and net operating income before debt services and cash flow. Expenses consist of fixed costs, such as employee salaries, taxes and insurance premiums; and a cash reserve fund for variable expenses, such as repairs, supplies and replacements. A property manager for an investment property typically is charged with the responsibility of developing an operating budget to give the owner an idea of the cash yield to expect from the property during a fixed period, typically a year. The budget is also helpful as a guide to the manager for the future operation of the property and as a measure of past performance. The budget should incorporate the long-term goals of the owner for the property. The property manager should be conservative in forecasting income for future periods.

OPERATING EXPENSES - Those periodic and necessary expenses which are essential to the continuous operation and maintenance of a property. For the purpose of preparing a reconstructed operating statement in connection with the appraisal of real estate, operating expenses are to be distinguished from fixed expenses, reserves for replacements, and other charges. Operating expenses will include: administration costs, general payroll, custodian, cleaning costs, cost of supplies, rubbish and ash removal costs, structural and exterior maintenance, maintenance of grounds, alterations, decorating and embellishments, air conditioning, electricity, heat, gas, water and miscellaneous variable costs. Operating expenses do not include items such as mortgage payments, capital expenditures and depreciation.

OPERATION OF LAW - The application of established rules of law upon a particular fact situation. For example, a principal-agent relationship will be terminated through operation of law by such things as expiration of the term of a listing, death of either party, destruction of the subject matter, material change in circumstances.

OPINION OF ATTORNEY GENERAL - An opinion prepared by the Washington State Attorney General by way of advising the executive and administrative heads of the state government upon questions of law touching their official duties. There is an assistant attorney general assigned to the Real Estate Program of the Department of Licensing who acts as legal counsel for the both the Department of Licensing and the Real Estate Commission. This individual will also act as prosecutor in administrative hearings concerning potential disciplinary actions.

OPPORTUNITY COST - Earnings available on alternative investments. (*See* BENEFIT OF BARGAIN RULE, DAMAGES.)

OPTION - An agreement to keep open, over a set time period, an offer to sell or purchase property. The option must be supported by its own actual consideration, separate and independent from the purchase price of the property. If not based on consideration, it can be revoked or withdrawn by the seller prior to acceptance by the buyer; it is nothing more than an offer to sell. A mere recital of consideration alone is not sufficient except in a lease-option situation, in which the provisions of the lease are themselves sufficient consideration to support the option. (*See* LEASE PURCHASE.)

The option must contain all the essential terms of the underlying contract of sale so that a complete binding contract is created immediately upon the optionee's election to exercise his/her right to purchase or sell. Necessary information includes: (1) the names and addresses of the parties; (2) the date of option; (3) consideration; (4) words granting the option; (5) the date the option expires; (6) a statement of purchase price and principal terms (usually a copy of the purchase agreement is attached and incorporated by reference); (7) a statement as to the method of notice of intent to exercise the option; (8) provisions for the forfeiture of option money upon failure to exercise; and (9) acknowledged signatures of optionor (the prospective buyer) and optionee (the prospective seller). (*See* BILATERAL CONTRACT, CONTRACT, LEGAL DESCRIPTION, STATUTE OF FRAUDS.)

Sometimes an option to buy is exercised only when the property has appreciated in value during the option period at which time the optionee may feel that, in retrospect, he/she made a bad bargain. In trying to find grounds to get out of the contract, the optionee might have his/her attorney closely scrutinize the provisions of the option to see if it contains all the essential terms of purchase. If the option fails to cover all the material terms and leaves some for future agreement, then the option is not enforceable. For example, if the option agreement detailed the parties, the property, price and method of payment, but omitted the interest rate on the mortgage, a court would not enforce the contract. Thus, an experienced real estate attorney should be consulted **before** the parties enter into an option agreement.

It is sometimes difficult to distinguish between an option and a Purchase and Sale Agreement. Since a listing contract often provides a broker does not earn a commission on an option unless and until the option is exercised, the distinction has a practical importance. If both parties are obligated to perform, then it is a Purchase and Sale Agreement. If just one party is obligated to perform, then it is an option. An option is thus a unilateral contract in which the optionee/offeree agrees to make the offer irrevocable for a certain time in return for the optionor/offeror's performance of payment of the option money. When the optionor gives the appropriate notice of intent to exercise the option, he/she in effect accepts the offer and there is then a bilateral contract of sale with both parties bound to perform. If the optionor gives notice to exercise the option, yet changes the terms, it is a counteroffer. The option money is usually non-refundable but applied toward the purchase price.

If the optionor elects not to exercise the option, the optionee keeps the option money and neither party is obligated to perform. Since "time is of the essence" in an option agreement, the option automatically expires if not exercised on or prior to the termination date. Death of the optionee does not affect the optionor; he/she can still exercise his/her right to purchase and the contract is binding on the optionee's heirs and assigns. An extension of option for an additional period of time must be written and supported by additional consideration.

Sometimes an option is recorded since the rights of the optionor will relate back to the date of the option and take priority over all intervening rights of third parties with notice of the option. Good title practice requires that a release of option be recorded in the event a recorded option is not exercised. Otherwise, the lapsed option will constitute a cloud on the title.

If a tenant pays rent with the understanding that he/she has an option (the right must be in written form) to purchase and that if he/she exercises the option, the option may provided that a certain part of the rent paid will be credited to the purchase price. The failure to exercise the option does not entitle him/her to get back any of the rent he/she has paid, not even the part which would have been credited on the purchase price if the option had been purchased.

An option is not an interest in land and is therefore not capable of being security for a mortgage or deed of trust. Similarly, an optionor is not eligible for "just compensation" if the underlying property is taken in a condemnation proceeding.

No state excise tax need be paid when recording an option since it is not a present transfer of real estate. The option merely contemplates and provides for a future transfer in the event that the option is exercised.

It should be emphasized that when the subject matter of the option is community property, both husband and wife must execute the option in Washington. If only the husband has signed and executed the option and the optionor elects to exercise the option, the optionee cannot force the wife to execute a deed; and therefore, the optionor will be precluded from purchasing the property. (*See* COMMUNITY PROPERTY.)

Some relevant tax features of an option are:

1. The cost of the option may be added to the basis of the property when the option is exercised. Thus, an optionor who pays $5,000 for the three month right to purchase a farm for $200,000 will have a basis of $205,000 upon exercise of the option assuming the option money is not applied toward the purchase price.

2. The option money is not taxable upon receipt. If the option is not exercised within the specified time, the option consideration is taxed as ordinary income in the year the option expires.

3. An option is an asset and any profit made on the sale of the option is taxable income.

4. On a lease with an option to buy, where all or a substantial portion of the rent is applied to the purchase price and the tenant has the right to purchase the property for a nominal amount at the end of the lease, there is a strong possibility that the Internal Revenue Service will construe this as a disguised real estate contract and assert that it was not a lease with an option but actually a sale. In such a case, the lease rent payments would not be deductible; they are treated as installment payments which the **tenant** must capitalize and for which he/she must take deductions in the form of depreciation deductions. The **landlord** runs the risk of being taxed on the entire gain in the year of sale (the year the lease was entered into) unless the transaction can qualify for installment reporting. (*See* HOLDING PERIOD, LEASE OPTION.)

OPTION TO RENEW - A lease provision giving the tenant the right to extend the lease for an additional period of time on set terms. (*See* LEASE, OPTION.)

"OR MORE" CLAUSE - A provision in a mortgage, deed of trust, or real estate contract permitting a larger monthly payment than the normal monthly payment without having to pay a prepayment penalty. Sometimes there is a limitation (e.g., 15 percent of the original amount per year) on how much may be paid under an "or more" clause.

ORAL CONTRACT - A verbal unwritten contract. All real estate contracts must be in writing except leases for a period of one year or less. Even short-term leases should be in writing to lessen the chances of dispute between lessor and lessee. (*See* STATUTE OF FRAUDS.)

ORDINANCES - The rules, regulations and codes enacted into law by local governing bodies. Generally, such governing bodies enact ordinances regulating such things as building standards, zoning standards, motor vehicle standards, and subdivision requirements. (*See* MUNICIPAL ORDINANCE, ZONING.)

ORDINARY AND NECESSARY BUSINESS EXPENSE - An expense incurred through the normal course of business, such as rent or expenditures for supplies, as opposed to expenses for a specific project or venture. Under federal income tax laws, ordinary and business expenses may be deducted in the year they are incurred, rather than spread over two or more years as with a capital expenditure. (*See* CAPITAL EXPENDITURE, REPAIRS.)

ORGANIZATIONAL EXPENSES, PARTNERSHIP - Under the Tax Reform Act of 1976, partnerships and partners can not claim deductions for amounts paid or incurred to promote the sale of a (or to sell a) partnership interest (called syndication expenditures), or for amounts, except as noted below, incurred to organize a partnership.

Syndication expenditures are those connected with the issuing and marketing of interests in a partnership, such as commissions, professional fees and printing costs.

However, a partnership may elect to capitalize its organizational expenditures and to amortize and deduct these expenses ratably over a period of not less than 60 months, commencing with the month that the partnership begins business. (*See* SYNDICATION.)

ORIENTATION - Placing a house on its lot with regard to its exposure to the sun, prevailing winds, privacy from the street and neighbors, and protection from outside noises.

ORIGINATION FEE - The finance fee charged by a lender for placing a mortgage or deed of trust. The origination fee is generally computed as a percentage of the face amount of the loan. For example, the lender's fee for originating a $50,000 loan might be 1.5 percent, or $750. The origination fee is not tax deductible as interest on borrowed money, but rather treated as a cost for services rendered and must be capitalized. Origination fee to a borrower on a FHA or VA loan cannot exceed 1% of the loan amount. (*See* FINANCE FEE, POINTS.)

OSTENSIBLE AGENCY - An actual agency relationship that arises by the actions of the parties rather than by express agreement. For example, an owner knows a broker is showing the owner's vacant lot to prospective buyers without authority to do so. Unless the owner takes some steps to stop such unauthorized showings, the law will consider that third parties have just cause to believe that the broker is the owner's agent. Thus the owner could become liable for certain acts of the "owner's broker." It is called an ostensible agency because on the surface it appears to exist. Once this type of agency is created, the owner is prevented (by estoppel) to deny its existence. (*See* AGENCY, IMPLIED AGENCY, REAL ESTATE BROKERAGE RELATIONSHIP ACT.)

OUTSIDE OF CLOSING - The payment of certain closing costs to someone directly and not through the closing process, as reflected by the notation "POC" (Paid Outside of Closing) on the settlement statement.

OUTSTANDING BALANCE - The amount of a loan that remains to be paid. An outstanding note is one in which there is still a liability.

OVERAGE - In retail store leases, the lessor/owner often sets a minimum monthly base rent, with a percentage of the volume of business the store does over a specified amount constituting additional rent. This added rent, or overage, should be treated as excess income. (*See* PERCENTAGE LEASE.)

When use by a lender, overage simply means profit, or additional profit, which may be created by increasing a certain fee for a time.

OVERALL RATE - The direct percentage ratio between net annual operating income and sales price. The overall rate is calculated by dividing the net income by the price. (*See* CAP RATE, INCOME APPROACH.)

OVERHANG - The part of a roof that extends beyond the exterior wall.

OVERIMPROVEMENT - An improvement which, by reason of excess of size or cost, is not the highest and best use for the site on which it is placed. Examples of overimprovements are a $500,000 home in a neighborhood comprised of mostly $100,000 homes, or a $5,000 pool in the backyard of a $25,000 home. In neither case would the owner be able to recapture his/her total expenditure. The term overimprovement usually means that the owner has over-built for the neighborhood and will take a loss at time of sale. (*See* HIGHEST AND BEST USE.)

OVERRIDE - A commission paid to managerial personnel (e.g., a branch manager) on sales made by their subordinates, usually calculated as a percentage of the gross sales commissions earned by the salesmen. A rental amount paid by a tenant on monies generated by the tenant's business in excess of certain amounts, such as $.01 per gallon of gas sold by a gas station tenant over 50,000 gallons each month.

OVERRIDING ROYALTY - A royalty fee retained by a lessee of an oil and gas lease when the property is subleased. (*See* OIL AND GAS LEASE.)

OWELTY - Compensation paid by a favored cotenant to the other members of the tenancy where there is a physical partition of the real estate into unequal shares. Such payments are usually court-ordered. (*See* PARTITION.)

OWNER/OCCUPANT - Property owner who physically occupies the property; the opposite of an absentee landlord or owner. An owner/occupant can usually get a lower loan rate over an investor/owner.

OWNER'S POLICY - A title insurance policy provided by a grantor/seller for a grantee's/buyer's benefit which insures the grantor's title as it appears of record. This is the normal policy provided by sellers and accepted by purchasers of real estate in Washington. The lender on the real estate normally obtains an extended coverage policy to protect his/her security interest. If there is a lender's policy, the owner can obtain a combined owner/lender policy for a reduced fee. (*See* EXTENDED COVERAGE, TITLE INSURANCE.)

OWNERSHIP - An owner is defined as one who has complete dominion over particular property. The person in whom the legal or equitable title rests. Commonly understood as the person who, in case of the destruction of property, must sustain the loss.

OWNERSHIP, FORM OF - A broker is often asked by his/her buyer or clients to advise them on the appropriate form of ownership of real property. The form of ownership is important because:

1. The existing form of ownership determines who must sign the various documents involved in the sale, such as listing, option, earnest money agreement or deed.

2. The form affects many future rights of the parties. How one takes title to property may have consequences involving income taxes, real property taxes, gift taxes, estate and inheritance taxes, transferability, exposure to creditor's claims and probate or its avoidance.

A broker should be well versed in the differences between the various methods of owning property, for example: joint tenancy, tenancy in common, community property, tenancy by severalty, or ownership by a created legal entity such as a partnership, corporation, limited liability company or limited liability partnership. However, though the broker can discuss these differences with his/her client, he/she may not recommend a specific form of ownership, as that would constitute the practice of law without a license. Rather, the broker should recommend that the client consult experienced tax or legal counsel, especially if there will be multiple owners, to determine the most advantageous form of ownership for the particular parties. A broker may be doing a client a disservice by not recommending that the client receive experienced legal or tax counsel as to the method of ownership. (*See* ABSENTEE OWNER, GRANTEE, COMMUNITY PROPERTY, JOINT TENANCY, TENANCY IN COMMON, TENANCY IN SEVERALTY, PARTNERSHIP.)

P

PACKAGE MORTGAGE - A method of financing in which the loan that finances the purchase of a home also finances the purchase of personal items such as appliances. The mortgage instrument describes the real property and declares the enumerated home accessories to be fixtures and, thus, part of the mortgaged property. As in a budget mortgage, the monthly payments include principal, interest, and pro rata payments for the appliances. Some lenders feel that the use of a package mortgage results in fewer defaulted loans. This is because a buyer can pay for essential furnishings over an extended period of time without an additional down payment, rather than exhaust his/her resources by buying them outright. The package mortgage is sometimes used in the sale of new subdivision homes and in the sale of certain condominium developments. Most package mortgages also require the mortgagor to sign and file a financing statement in accordance with the provisions of the Uniform Commercial Code. In a package mortgage, the interest is paid only on the remaining balance and not on the original debt as in the typical consumer installment loan. (*See* BUDGET MORTGAGE, FINANCING STATEMENT.)

PAD - The area in a mobile home park allocated for the placement of a mobile home unit. Also means a foundation, or site particularly suited for a specific type of improvement, such as "a convenience store pad" in a retail development.

PANIC PEDDLING - The illegal practice of soliciting sales or rental listings by making written or oral statements that create fear or alarm, transmitting written or oral warnings or threats, soliciting prospective minority renters or buyers, or acting in any other manner so as to induce or attempt to induce the sale or lease of residential property, either:

1. through representations regarding the present or prospective entry of one or more minority residents into an area, or

2. through representations that would convey to a reasonable person under the circumstances, whether or not overt reference to minority status is made, that one or more minority residents are or may be entering the area.

The term minority means any group that can be distinguished because of race, sex, religion, color, or national origin. Vigorous solicitation of sellers in a rapidly changing neighborhood is called panic peddling. (*See* DISCRIMINATION, FEDERAL FAIR HOUSING LAW, WASHINGTON STATE HUMAN RIGHTS COMMISSION.)

PAPER - A business term referring to a mortgage or a deed of trust and note, or a real estate contract, which is usually taken back by a seller from the buyer when real property is sold. Land developers sometimes sell subdivided recreational lots by way of ten-year contracts for deed with down payments as low as ten percent. They then sell these contracts, or "papers," at a discount to a lender, or pledge it as security for a loan. (*See* DEED OF TRUST, DISCOUNT, MORTGAGE, NOTE, PURCHASER MONEY MORTGAGE.)

PARAGRAPH 17 - The provision which contains a "due on sale clause" is in Paragraph 17 of the FNMA/FHLMC Uniform Instrument. As a practical matter, almost all mortgages, deeds of trust and real estate contracts drafted after the early 1980s contain a "due on sale clause". Whether a real estate sale of a single family residence will occur in a tight money market often depends on whether or not there is a "due on sale clause" in the seller's note and underlying mortgage or deed of trust. (*See* ASSUMPTION OF MORTGAGE, ASSUMPTION SALE.)

PARALLEL - Lines of latitude encompassing the earth. (*See* BASE LINE AND MERIDIAN.)

PARAMOUNT TITLE - Title to real property which is better or superior to any other alleged title to the same property. (*See* TITLE.)

PARAPET - The part of the wall of a house that rises above the roof line.

PARCEL - A lot or a specific portion of a larger tract of land.

PARITY CLAUSE - A provision which allows for a mortgage or trust deed to secure more than one note, providing that all notes be secured equally by the mortgage without any priority or preference.

PARKING INDEX OR RATIO - The relationship between the number of off street parking spaces and the number of building units or buildable square footage in a particular development. Local zoning codes often specify minimum ratios.

PAROL - Verbal; not in writing. In Washington, the general rule is that all agreements and contracts pertaining to real property must be in writing to be enforceable. (*See* PAROL EVIDENCE RULE, STATUTE OF FRAUD.)

PAROL EVIDENCE RULE - A rule of evidence designed to achieve a degree of certainty to a transaction and to prevent fraudulent and perjured claims. When the parties to a real estate contract put their agreement into final written form, the parol evidence rule prevents the admission into court of evidence of any prior or contemporaneous oral or written negotiations or agreements which vary or contradict the terms of the written contract. Thus, if the buyer and seller orally agree that the buyer will pay the broker's commission, but the final contract states the seller will pay, then the written contract prevails and evidence of the prior oral agreement is not admissible. Note that the rule does not prohibit proof of oral contracts entered into subsequent to the formal written contract.

There are many exceptions to the parol evidence rule. For example, parol evidence is always admissible to show that the parties did not in fact intend to create a contract; to show that the contract was illegal in its inception; to show that there were certain conditions precedent to the creation of a contract; or to clarify any ambiguities in the contract. In other words, a party can still challenge the validity of a contract, as opposed to trying to vary, change, or add new terms. (*See* CONTRACT, STATUTE OF FRAUDS.)

PARQUET FLOOR - A floor made of short pieces of hardwood laid in various patterns, as opposed to traditional wood floorings; not a strip floor.

PARTIAL PAYMENT - In loan collection, less than the full payment due, usually not credited until the balance of the payment is received.

PARTIAL RECONVEYANCE - An instrument filed when part of the secured property is released from the lien of the deed of trust. (*See* DEED OF TRUST, PARTIAL RELEASE).

PARTIAL RELEASE - A clause found in a mortgage or deed of trust which directs the mortgagee/beneficiary to release certain parcels from the lien of the blanket mortgage or deed of trust upon the payment of a certain sum of money. The clause is frequently found in tract development construction loans. The instrument filed is called a "partial satisfaction of mortgage." A mortgagee or beneficiary cannot be compelled to release a portion of the realty from the lien of the mortgage or deed of trust unless provided for in the security document. (*See* BLANKET MORTGAGE, RELEASE CLAUSE.)

PARTIAL TAKING - In condemnation, when only a part of a privately owned property is taken for public use. Special benefits or damages to the part remaining must be considered in determining the just compensation to be paid for the part taken. (*See* BEFORE AND AFTER METHOD, CONDEMNATION, SEVERANCE DAMAGES, SPECIAL BENEFITS.)

PARTIALLY AMORTIZING - Loan repayment schedule that provides for equal payments of principal and interest up to a certain stop-date, (referred to as a "call" or a "call date") at which time the balance of the principal is due in full. (*See* BALLOON PAYMENT.)

PARTICIPATING BROKER - 1. A brokerage or its agent who obtains a buyer or prospective buyer for a property which is listed with another brokerage company. Usually called a cooperating broker, the participating broker normally splits the commission with the seller's broker in an agreed upon amount, typically 50 percent.

2. A broker who assists the listing broker on behalf of the seller, whether or not such broker is an agent of the seller, the listing broker or the buyer. Sometimes a condominium developer lists his/her condominium for sale with several brokerage companies, which are referred to as the participating brokers in the project. (*See* COOPERATING BROKER.)

PARTICIPATION LOAN - A loan in which the lender participates in the income of the venture beyond a fixed return, or receives a yield on the loan in addition to the straight interest rate. The lender may participate in the income of the property, the profits of the venture, or take an equity position in the project. Sometimes called an "equity kicker," a participation loan is mainly used in large commercial loans. Used by lenders as a hedge against inflation and to increase their total yield on the loan, such as participation on gross rents over a fixed base of 90%. These participations usually occur when an institutional lender, such as a life insurance company, makes loans on commercial properties or multifamily units during periods of high interest rates and tight money. (*See* KICKER.)

PARTICIPATION SALE CERTIFICATE - A mortgage-backed security sold by the Federal Home Loan Mortgage Corporation (FHLMC — "Freddie Mac") to fund its purchases of mortgages in the FHLMC and represent ownership interests in pools of mortgages purchased by FHLMC and serviced by the sellers. They are freely transferable so they may be sold among investors in much the same way as bonds. (*See* MORTGAGE BACKED SECURITIES.)

PARTITION - The dividing of common interests in real property owned jointly by two or more persons. It sometimes happens that one of several tenants in common desires to sell the property while the other tenants think it best to hold on to the investment. If the parties cannot reach an agreement, an action in partition is often the solution. The main purpose of partition is thus to provide a means by which people, finding themselves in an unwarranted common relationship, can free themselves from the relationship incidental to such common ownership.

When two or more persons hold or possess real property as tenants in common, in which one or more of them has an estate in fee, or a life estate in possession, a suit in equity may be brought by any one or more of them in the county in which the property is situated, requesting a partition of the property according to the respective rights of the parties interested therein. If it appears that a partition in kind cannot be made without great prejudice to the owners, the court can order the sale of all or part of the property. The verified petition for partition fully describes the property, and specifically sets forth the rights of all interested parties. The petitioner should immediately file a lis pendens against the property to give constructive notice of the pending action.

The court in equity has the power in a partition to remove any clouds on title, to vest titles by decree, to cause the property to be divided among the parties as they agree or by the drawing of lots, to divide and allot portions of the premises to some or all of the parties and order a sale of the remainder, or to sell the whole and use the proceeds to equalize the general partition. The court can, by decree, invest the purchasers with title to the property. (*See* COTENANCY, OWELTY.)

A partition action has no effect on the rights of a mortgagee of all the former co-owners. The fact of partition may make the mortgagee's position so insecure that it can accelerate the interest rate and/or exercise the option under a due on sale clause and assert that the remaining balance is due, depending on the language in the security instrument.

Because partition is expensive, lengthy and burdensome, tenants may choose to negotiate the division among themselves, or conduct an auction sale (even with only themselves as bidders and a third party as the auctioneer). Many attorneys recommend that individuals purchasing property for investment take title as partners and that the partnership agreement have a buy-sell provision. A well drafted buy-sell agreement will avoid problems associated with an partition action. (*See* BUY-SELL.)
Reference: RCW 7.52.

PARTNERSHIP - "An association of two or more persons to carry on as co-owners of a business for profit," as defined in the Uniform Partnership Act, which is in force in a majority of the states and has been adopted in Washington. It is a contractual arrangement and does not require the approval of the State as a corporation does. A partnership is considered to be a collection of individuals without a separate collective existence. The partnership in and of itself is not a separate entity.

There are no legal requirements concerning the name of a partnership, but Washington's Assumed Name Statute requires a partnership, unless it is doing business under the surname of all partners, to file a certificate of assumed name with the Secretary of State's office. (*See* ASSUMED BUSINESS NAME, FICTITIOUS NAME.)
Reference: RCW 19.80.010.

In Washington, a partnership is sometimes formed to take title to real property which is being held for business use or investment purposes. Normally the partnership is not too large, with a maximum number of eight in most cases. The reason for this limitation is that each partner is equal to each and every other partner; therefore, it is often difficult to obtain the necessary unanimous agreement in arriving at management decisions. In addition, each partner has an interest in the partnership property as a whole with an undivided interest in the partnership profit after all partnership debts have been paid; the partner who works receives no more compensation than those who are passive, which is often cause for arguments. For the above reasons, in partnerships of more than 3 or 4 people, a limited partnership arrangement is normally established with one partner acting as the general partner. This general partner is charged with management responsibilities and is compensated for it.

In Washington, a partnership can be issued a real estate broker's license provided the designated individual holds a valid Washington broker's license. If the designated broker of the partnership engages in criminal activity, it is possible for other partners to be held responsible. If disciplinary license action is taken, it may be possible for an unlicensed partner to be included; and he/she could lose the right to be involved in any other legal entity licensed by the Real Estate Program of the Department of Licensing. (*See* GENERAL PARTNER, JOINT VENTURE, LICENSING LAW, LIMITED PARTNERSHIP, ORGANIZATIONAL EXPENSES, PARTITION, TENANCY IN PARTNERSHIP.) *Reference:* RCW 25.04, RCW 18.85.

PARTY DRIVEWAY - A driveway located on both sides or on side line of a property line and used in common by the owners of each abutting property. It is best for the owners to have a recorded, written agreement detailing the rights and duties of both parties, rather than for them to rely solely on the general law of easements. Often the parties enter into a maintenance agreement which provides a procedure as to when and how maintenance will be performed and the method of paying for it. (*See* EASEMENTS.)

PARTY TO BE CHARGED - The person referred to in the Statute of Frauds as the one against whom the contract is sought to be enforced; the one who is being sued (the defendant) and is thus being charged with the obligations of the contract that person has signed; the one to be bound or held to the contract. (*See* STATUTE OF FRAUDS.)

PARTY WALL - A wall which is located on or at a boundary line between two adjoining parcels and is used or is intended to be used by the owners of both properties in the construction or maintenance of improvements on their respective lots. It often is designed to serve simultaneously as the exterior wall of two adjacent structures. Though most often centered, the party wall may be entirely located on one lot. It is often built and maintained under a recorded agreement. The party wall is typically a perimeter wall joining two attached houses giving structural support to both, and is most frequently encountered in townhouses or tract houses in highly developed urban areas where property owners wish to make full use of the width of their lots. The duty to repair a party wall falls equally on both owners, and one owner may not use his/her rights to the wall in such a way as to damage his/her neighbor.

Each owner holds in severalty that cross portion of the wall on his/her tract, subject to an easement (called a cross easement) in the other owner for use of the wall as a perimeter wall of his/her respective building, and for its support. A party wall may be created by agreement, deed, or implied grant; and since a party wall involves an easement, the agreement should be in writing as required by the Statute of Frauds. The right to a party wall can also arise by prescription, as where a surveyor's error causes a wall to encroach on adjoining land and such encroachment continues for the 10-year prescriptive period. (*See* ADVERSE POSSESSION, COMMON WALL, PRESCRIPTION.)

When one property owner decides to build, he/she may enter into a party wall agreement with his/her neighbor. Under the typical agreement, Gordon will build first, and then such time as his neighbor, Graham, decides to build on his lot and use the wall, Graham will pay Gordon for one-half the cost of the wall. A party wall is also used, for example, where Gordon owns two lots and builds a house on each with one wall dividing the two houses and serving as the perimeter wall of each. (*See* COMMON WALL.)

PASSIVE INVESTOR - An investor who invests only capital and does not take an active role in the packaging, building, or managing of a project; the opposite of an active investor. (*See* LIMITED PARTNERSHIP, PASSIVE LOSS.)

PASSIVE LOSS - Refers to rules established by the Tax Reform Act of 1986 designed to eliminate the prior practice of allowing losses and credits from **passive** investments to offset other sources of income (also called tax shelter). The law now disallows the deduction of passive activity losses and passive activity credits against other active sources of income. Losses or credits disallowed in any year may be carried forward to the succeeding year and treated as a deduction or credit allocable only to passive activities, carry-backs are not permitted. Any unrealized losses from an activity are allowed in full upon a taxable disposition of the activity.

The term "passive activity" means any activity that involves the conduct of any trade or business in which the taxpayer does not materially participate in any rental activity. A taxpayer is deemed to be materially participating in an activity only if the taxpayer is involved in the operation on a regular, continuous and substantial basis. Any interest held by a limited partner is automatically treated as passive because limited partners do not participate in management. Passive income does not include interest, dividends not derived in the ordinary course of business, or gain or loss from the disposition of property producing interest or dividends. The taxpayer may use up to $25,000 of real estate rental losses to off set ordinary income.

There is a limited exception for real estate rental activities in which an individual taxpayer actively participates. (*See* LIMITED PARTNERSHIP, PARTNERSHIP, PASS-THROUGH, PASSIVE INVESTOR, PASSIVE LOSS.)

PASS THROUGH - Tax advantage of a limited partnership that permits income, profits, losses, and deductions, especially depreciation, to "pass through" the legal structure of the partnership directly to the individual investors. Also called "flow through." Also found in real estate investment trusts. (*See* LIMITED PARTNERSHIP, PASSIVE LOSS.)

A pass-through security is the type issued by the Government National Mortgage Association (Ginnie Mae) to mortgage investors. It means that cash flows from the underlying block of individual mortgage loans are "passed through" to the holders of the securities in a pro rata share, including loan prepayments. With a mortgage-backed security, the timely payment of principal and interest is guaranteed by Ginnie Mae. In 1982, the Federal National Mortgage Association (Fannie Mae) instituted its own mortgage-backed securities program designed to attract billions of dollars into the conventional mortgage market from pension funds and other investors. (*See* MORTGAGE-BACKED SECURITIES.)

PAST PERFORMANCE - Performance of a contract that is less than the full performance required. (*See* BREACH OF CONTRACT.)

PATENT - The name of the instrument which conveys ownership of public land by either State or Federal government to a private individual.

PAYEE - The receiver of a note (a mortgagee under a mortgage or beneficiary under a deed of trust) or check. (*See* MAKER.)

PAYMENT BOND - The part of a performance bond which assures an owner that material and labor furnished in the construction of a building will be fully paid for, and that no mechanics' liens will be filed. The payment bond protects subcontractors and materialmen from nonpayment by the prime contractor or owner. (*See* COMPLETION BOND, PERFORMANCE BOND.)

PAYOFF - The payment in full of an existing loan, usually at the time of refinancing or upon the sale or transfer of a secured property. Escrow will contact the mortgagee seeking the "payoff figures."

PAYOR - One who signs and gives a note (a mortgagor under a mortgage or a grantor under a deed of trust) or check.

PEDESTRIAN TRAFFIC COUNT - A systematic study and analysis of the numbers and kinds of people passing by a particular location, to determine potential buying power in a given area. A pedestrian traffic count is especially important in planning, developing and leasing shopping centers or retail outlets. (*See* TRADE AREA.)

PENALTY - A punishment imposed for violating a law or an agreement. Some of the penalties for violations of real estate related laws are:

1. Escrow Registration Act: Any person who engages in business as an escrow agent, who has not received of Certificate of Registration issued by the Department of Financial

Institutions, is guilty of a misdemeanor, punishable by imprisonment for not more than 90 days or by a fine of not more than $250 or by both.
Reference: RCW 18.44.140.

2. Washington State Securities Act: Any individual who willfully violates the Act or makes any false or misleading statements on any documents required by the Act should be fined not more than $5,000 or imprisoned not more than 10 years or both.
Reference: RCW 21.20.400.

3. Real Estate Licensing Law:

a. Any person acting as a real estate broker, associate real estate broker, or real estate salesman, without a license, shall be guilty of a gross misdemeanor. Punishment may be up to one year in jail, a fine up to $1,000 or both.

Reference: RCW 18.85.340

b. If a real estate licensee is found to have violated the Real Estate Licensing Law or a Rule and Regulation of the Real Estate Commission, the Director of the Real Estate Commission may suspend the license for a period of time, revoke the license, levy a fine not to exceed $1,000 for each offense or require the licensee to complete an education course in the selected area which the licensee violated.

Reference: RCW 18.85.230

4. Washington State Law Against Discrimination: When a determination is made by the Washington State Human Rights Commission that an unfair practice involving real property has been committed, in addition to relief action (such as a decease and desist order or an affirmative action plan) it may award the injured party up to $10,000 by the offending party for the first offense, $25,000 for two offenses within five years and $50,000 for three offenses within seven years. (*See* WASHINGTON STATE HUMAN RIGHTS COMMISSION.)
Reference: RCW 49.60.225.

5. Sometimes, a court will not enforce a liquidated damages clause if the amount of damages is so excessive that it bears no true relationship to the real damages which are suffered upon a breach. In such a case, the court will treat the damages clause as a penalty and, therefore, not enforceable. The court will then award the proper measure of damages to the injured party. (*See* LIQUIDATED DAMAGES.)

PENSION FUND - An institution that holds assets invested in long-term mortgages, deeds of trust and high grade stocks and bonds having acceptable yields and security. The purpose of a pension fund is to accumulate funds to hold and invest in such a manner that it will provide retirement income to individuals entitled to the benefits of the fund (e.g., labor unions, federal, state and county employees) under an agreed upon plan.

A practice among attorneys and real estate brokers as well as other professional business people, is to incorporate and set up their own pension and profit-sharing plans because of favorable tax treatment given to qualified plans. (*See* KEOGH PLAN.)

PENTHOUSE - An apartment or condominium unit located on the roof of a building, or more commonly, an apartment or condominium unit on the top floor of a building. A penthouse apartment normally rents, and a condominium unit normally sells for a premium above the prices of most other units in the building.

PER AUTRE VIE - For another's life. A life estate per autre vie is a life estate that is measured by the life of a person other than the grantee. For example, Hrin grants to Slater a life estate in his mansion for the life of Craig. Also called pur autre vie. (*See* LIFE ESTATE.)

PERCENTAGE LEASE - A lease whose rental is based on a percentage of the monthly or annual gross sales made on the premises; also covers sales to employees, mail order sales, sales taxes, and installment sales. Percentage leases are common with large retail stores, especially shopping centers. There are many types of percentage leases: straight percentage of gross income, without minimum; fixed minimum rent plus a percentage of the gross; fixed minimum rent against a percentage of the gross, whichever is greater, or fixed minimum rent plus a percentage of the gross, with a ceiling to the percentage rental.

The Institute of Real Estate Management, the International Council of Shopping Centers, the Urban Land Institute, and other real estate management organizations publish percentage lease tables (See sample table that follows), which can be used as general guides when negotiating lease terms. For example, the percentage range of bowling lanes might be 8 to 10 percent; for cocktail lounges, 7 to 10 percent; and movie theaters, 10 to 12 percent.

Most percentage leases are based on a percentage of gross sales, not gross profits, because of the difficulty in determining what is a "profit." Utmost care must be taken to define adequately and fully "gross sales." It is particularly necessary to differentiate the applicability of the percentage to credit sales, sales made at other store locations, trade-ins, gift certificates and interstore transactions. The definition of gross income usually excludes sales and excise taxes. A generally acceptable definition of gross sales is "the gross amount of all sales made in, from, or at the leased premises, whether for cash or on credit, after deducting the sales price of any returned merchandise where a cash refund is given."

The landlord should consider protective provisions to cover the following: tenant's obligation to act in good faith; tenant's obligation not to compete with himself by opening a nearby store; periodic reports of sales volume; inspection of books and records; prohibition of assignment or subletting without consent; recapture of premises. The percentage rent requires detailed auditing procedures which are difficult to apply to small business operations, difficult to enforce, and do not apply to personal service businesses, such as Realtors or attorneys.

The sample chart is provided as an example only. Please obtain a current chart from one of the organizations listed above. Do not make any business decisions based on this chart.

SAMPLE PERCENTAGE LEASE RATES

	%		%
Auto Accessories.........	3-4	Hardware.........................	5
Books and Stationery.....	5-7	Leather Goods...........	5-6
Bowling Lanes.............	8-9	Motion Picture Theaters...	10-11
Cocktail Lounges...........	8	Office Supply.................	4-6
Department Stores...........	3-4	Parking Lots & Garages (Attendant)...	40-60
Drug Stores (Individual).	4-6	Photography..................	7-9
Electrical Appliances....	5-6	Restaurants......................	6-7
Furniture........................	5-8	Women's Dress Shops....	6-7
Gas Stations, ¢ per gallon	11/2-2		
Grocery Stores (Individual)	1-2		
Grocery Stores (Chain).... .	2-4		

(*See* BASE RENT, GROSS LEASE, NET LEASE, NON-COMPETITION CLAUSE, RECAPTURE RATE, SHOPPING CENTER.)

PERCOLATION TEST - A hydraulic engineer's test of soil to determine the ability of the ground to absorb and drain water. This information helps to determine the suitability of a site for certain kinds of development, and for the installation of a septic tank or an injection well for a sewage treatment plant. A subdivider registering his/her subdivision with HUD must include a percolation report in his/her application.

PER DIEM - Daily, e.g., interest calculated on a daily basis. This term is normally heard at closing when the interest on the real estate loan is charged on a daily or per diem basis.

PERFECTING TITLE - The process of eliminating a particular claim or all claims against a title. (*See* QUIET TITLE ACTION.)

PERFORMANCE BOND - A bond, usually posted by one who is to perform work for another, which assures that a project or undertaking will be completed as per agreement or contract. A performance bond is frequently requested of a contractor to guarantee the completion of a project. The bond usually provides that if the contractor fails to complete the contract, the surety company can itself complete the contract, or pay damages up to the limit of the bond. A performance bond is normally combined with a labor and materials bond, which guarantees the owner that all bills for labor and materials contracted for and used by the contractor will be paid by the surety company if the contractor defaults. Thus the performance bond is the best device to protect the owner against mechanics' liens filed by subcontractors. A performance bond typically costs about one percent of the total construction costs, and a contractor must have a good "track record" in order to obtain such a bond. (*See* COMPLETION BOND, PAYMENT BOND, SURETY.)

PERIODIC COSTS - The fixed property expenses (like taxes, insurance) that occur on a regular but infrequent basis.

PERIODIC TENANCY - A leasehold estate which continues from period to period, such as month to month, year to year. All conditions and terms of the tenancy are carried over from period to period, and continue for an uncertain time until proper notice of termination is given.

A periodic tenancy may arise by express agreement of the parties, but usually arises by implication, in situations in which no definite time of possession has been set but rent has been fixed at a certain amount per week, per month, or per year. (*See* LANDLORD TENANT ACT, MONTH-TO-MONTH TENANCY, TENANCY AT WILL.)

PERMANENT FINANCING - A long-term loan, as opposed to an interim loan. Certain lenders specialize in lending short-term money to finance the construction of a condominium, a shopping center or other major project. Other lenders specialize in lending long-term money to "take-out" the interim or construction lender. Permanent loans typically range 20-30 years at fixed interest rates. Today a variable interest rate may be used or a rate may be set for an initial period and then renegotiated. (*See* TAKEOUT FINANCING.)

With construction loans, there is often a tri-party agreement covering the permanent lender, interim lender, and borrower so that: there is a joint use of documents; the interim lender will agree not to assign the loan to another lender; and the interim loan will be assigned to the permanent lender within a stated time upon completion of construction and satisfaction of specified conditions.

PERSON - Statutes vary as to the definition of "person" because a legal person may be not only an individual, but also a corporation, a government or governmental agency, a business trust, an estate, a trust, an association, a partnership, a joint venture, a limited liability company, two or more persons having a joint or common interest, or any other legal or commercial entity.

PERSONAL LIABILITY - The obligation to satisfy a debt to the extent of one's personal assets. Shareholders in a corporation and limited partners in a limited partnership syndication are usually protected against personal liability for debts of the corporation or syndication. A borrower under a nonrecourse loan also avoids personal liability on the loan (the lender must look solely to the sale of secured property for recovery of amounts owed). A guarantor is personally liable for the default of the borrower. (*See* NONRECOURSE.)

In Washington the general rule is that the purchaser of real property which is subject to a mortgage or deed of trust is personally liable for the mortgage debt if the purchaser assumes the mortgage or deed of trust. If the purchaser takes it subject to the underlying debt, there is no personal liability for a possible deficiency. Even in those cases where the purchaser assumes the debt, the mortgagee (lender) may look to both parties to satisfy any deficiency judgments. There is no release of the original mortgagor unless a release is negotiated at the time of sale and assumption of the loan. (*See* DEED OF TRUST, MORTGAGE.)

PERSONAL PROPERTY - Things which are tangible and movable; property which is not classified as real property, such as chattels, also called personalty. Title to personal property is transferred by way of a bill of sale, as contrasted with a deed for real property.

Items of personal property frequently become the object of dispute between buyer and seller, most often due to whether an item is considered a "fixture" or due to the seller's attempt to substitute a similar item. Some cautious buyers insert a clause in their purchase contracts to the effect that the buyer will get the appliances "as currently installed and used in the premises."

A tree is real property while it is rooted in the ground, but when it is severed, it is transformed into personal property. When lumber is assembled, however, and used as material to construct a house, it once again becomes a fixture, or real property. (*See* FIXTURE, REAL PROPERTY, UNIFORM COMMERCIAL CODE.)

PER STIRPES - To take a share under the law of descent by right of representation, as opposed to taking per capita or in one's individual right. For example, assume Mr. Shield dies without a will, leaving $60,000. He leaves no wife, but has two surviving children (Pat and Mike) plus two grandchildren by a deceased third child. Pat and Mike take their per capita share of 1/3 each, and the two children of the deceased child would take per stirpes (by right of representation) equally of the deceased child's 1/3 share; e.g., each grandchild takes a 1/6 share, or $10,000. (*See* DESCENT, INTESTATE.)

PER UNIT COST METHOD - A method of computing a property management fee based on the direct cost of managing a specific number of rental units.

PETITION - A formal request or application to an authority, such as a court, generally seeking specific relief or redress of some wrong. Petitions frequently encountered in real estate include: a petition to a superior court for partition of real estate; a petition filed in a superior court by a respondent in a state discrimination hearing, seeking judicial review of an adverse determination of the State's Human Rights Commission; a petition to a planning commission for a zoning change.

PHYSICAL DETERIORATION - A reduction in utility or value resulting from an impairment of physical condition, which deterioration can be divided into either curable or incurable types. A form of depreciation caused by the action of the physical elements, such as wind or snow, or just ordinary wear and tear.

Two common methods of calculating physical depreciation are the observed condition method and the straight-line or age-life method. (*See* APPRAISAL, DEPRECIATION.)

PHYSICAL INSPECTION - Since the late 1980's, it has become a standard marketplace condition that a residential Purchase and Sale Agreement offer by a buyer is subject to a physical inspection by a professional inspection company. Many home inspectors belong to the American Society of Home Inspectors (ASHI). An inspection is recommended even with a new house or condominium. (*See* CONTINGENCY, SPECIAL CONDITIONS.)

PHYSICAL LIFE - The actual age or life span of a structure, as opposed to its economic life. (*See* ECONOMIC LIFE.)

PIER - A column, usually of steel reinforced concrete, evenly spaced under a structure to support its weight. Foundation piers may be formed by drilling holes in the earth to a prescribed depth and pouring concrete into them. Foundation piers that support some structures, such as bridges, may be above the ground. The term may also refer to the part of a wall between windows or other openings that bears the wall's weight.

PIGGYBACK LOAN - A joint loan with two lenders sharing a single mortgage or deed of trust. For example, a bank may originate a loan at 85 percent of the appraised value of the property. The originating bank would supply 70 percent of the money and a private lender would supply the top 15 percent. The private lender would most likely obtain private mortgage insurance to cover its loan, and the insurance would continue in effect until the loan was reduced to 70 percent of the appraised value. The private lender is the piggyback lender and is subordinated to the senior lender. A piggyback loan is distinguishable from a second mortgage or deed of trust in that there is only one mortgage or deed of trust on the property. This distinction is important because many institutional lenders can lend only on first mortgages or deeds of trust. (*See* PARTICIPATION LOAN.)

PILASTER - An upright, architectural member or vertical projection from a wall, on either one or both sides, used to strengthen the wall by adding support or preventing buckling.

P.I.T.I. - Abbreviation for principal, interest, taxes, and insurance, as commonly found in an all-inclusive mortgage or deed of trust payment.

PLACE - A cul-de-sac serving more than three lots and exceeding 125 feet in length.

PLAINTIFF - The person who commences a lawsuit, the complainant. (*See* DEFENDANT.)

PLANNED UNIT DEVELOPMENT (PUD) - A housing design to produce a high density of dwellings and maximum utilization of open spaces. This efficient use of land allows greater flexibility for residential land and development. It also usually results in lower priced homes and minimum maintenance cost. Often, PUDs are specifically provided for in zoning ordinances or are listed as a conditional permitted use.

The developer plans the project and seeks local governmental approval of the proposed PUD zone. He/she then organizes a nonprofit community association to provide for maintenance of the common areas, records a declaration of covenants and restrictions, and records a subdivision plat reserving common areas to the members of the association but not to the general public.

The PUD concept is really an "overlay" zoning which enables a developer to obtain a higher density (and sometimes a mixed-use) than is permitted by the underlying zoning. Because the buildings are usually clustered together, there is more green area left open for parks and recreation. For example, compare the two illustrations below. The first is a rendition of a conventional-design subdivision, containing 368 housing units. Note that it uses 23,200 linear feet of street and leaves only 1.6 acres open for parks. Contrast this with the PUD pictured directly below it. Both subdivisions are equal in size and terrain. However, by minimally reducing lot sizes and clustering them around limited-access cul-de-sac streets, the number of housing units remains nearly the same — 366; the street areas are reduced — 17,000 linear feet; and open space is drastically increased — 23.5 acres. In addition, using modern building designs, this clustered plan could be modified to comfortably accommodate 550 patio homes or 1,100 townhouses.

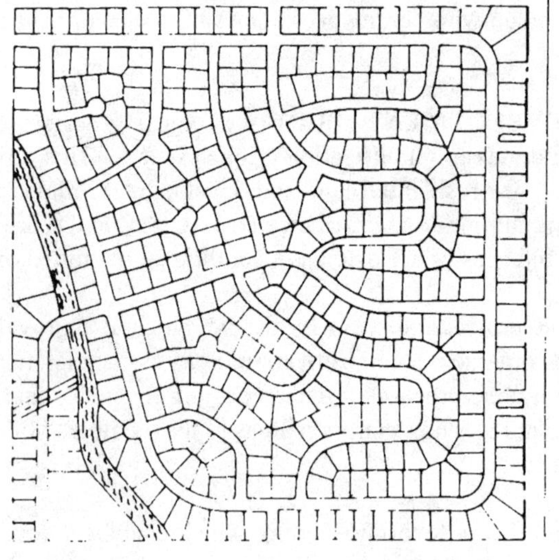

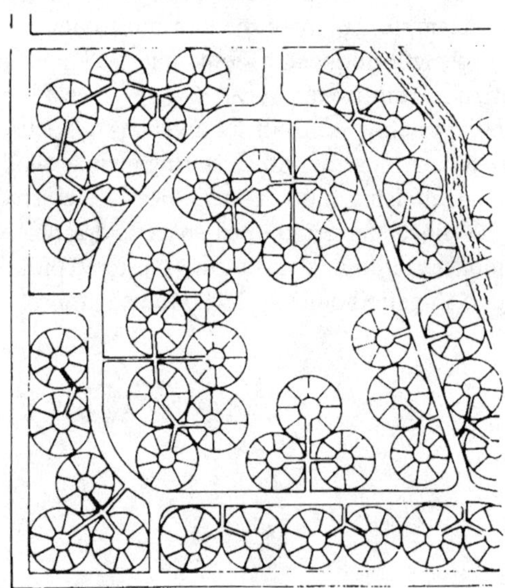

Though similar in some respects, a PUD is quite different from a condominium. In a PUD, the unit is a lot, there is no direct interest in the common areas and the PUD is created by covenants in the deed or master lease. In a condominium, the unit is a space of air, there is a percentage of ownership interest in the common areas, the association of owners is usually incorporated, and the condominium is created by recording a declaration pursuant to state condominium laws. PUDs are also used in resort housing and even shopping center projects. (*See* DENSITY ZONING.)

PLANNING COMMISSION - An official governmental agency on the city or county level, created to direct and control the use, design and development of land. Members of the Commission serve without pay, but are often advised by a salaried Planning Director and staff. Often the planning department prepares and the commission adopts a comprehensive, long-term general plan for the physical development of the city-county area or region. The plan may be referred to as the Master or General Plan upon its adoption by the planning commission and legislative body.

PLANS AND SPECIFICATIONS - All the drawings pertaining to a development under consideration, such as the building drawings, the mechanical drawings, the electrical drawings, and the like (plans); together with the written instructions to the builder containing all the information pertaining to dimensions, materials, workmanship, style, fabrication, colors, and finishes which supplement the details appearing on the working drawings (specifications). (*See* WORKING DRAWINGS.)

PLASTER FINISH - The last thin layer of fine grain plaster applied as a decorative finish over several coats of coarse plaster over the lath base. Finishing plaster usually has a high ratio of lime to sand, while coarser plasters have more sand. Plaster is pasty when applied to the wall but hardens as it dries. In newer buildings drywall (also called sheetrock or gypsum board) is often used as a substitute for plaster.

PLAT - A map of a town, section, or subdivision indicating the location and boundaries of individual properties. On the face of the map will be shown lot numbers, area, block numbers, section, streets, public easements, monuments, North arrow, date, scale, etc. Plats and platting are an important part of subdivision procedures which often require the subdivider to submit a preliminary plat for consideration. The subdivider subsequently files a final plat after the improvements have been completed and approved by the appropriate officials.

A short plat is four or less lots that have been subdivided, approved and recorded in Department of Records and Elections.

Plats are recorded in the Office of the County Auditor. They are entered into the County Plat Book Records and are assigned a volume number, depending upon which volume they are recorded in and the page number which then becomes part of the reference to the plat in the future, e.g., Bel Glenn Addition to the City of Bellevue according to plat thereof recorded in Volume 48 of Plats, page 22, records of King County, Washington. (*See* PLAT BOOK, SHORT PLAT SUBDIVISION.)

PLAT BOOK - A public record of maps of subdivided land showing present ownership and the division of the land into blocks, lots and parcels, and indicating the approximate dimensions of individual parcels. Plat books are available for inspection in the Office of the County Auditor.

PLATE - A horizontal piece (usually a piece of wood) which forms a base for supports. The sill or sole plate rests on the foundation and forms the base for the studs. The wall plate or cap plate is laid along the top of the wall studs and forms a support base for the rafters.

PLATTED LAND - Land that has been subdivided with each lot within the subdivision numbered and the land recorded as a subdivision. (*See* PLAT BOOK, SUBDIVISION.)

PLEDGE - The transfer or delivery of property to a lender to be held as security for a debt, e.g. a pawn shop. A hypothecation differs from a pledge in that when one hypothecates property, he/she puts up the property as security but does not surrender possession of it (e.g. a deed of trust or a mortgage).

Some savings and loan associations will loan an amount over their authorized limit when the borrower pledges sufficient funds to cover such excess amount. The pledge account is like a savings account, although the pledgor cannot withdraw his/her funds except in accordance with the pledge agreement. (*See* COLLATERAL, COMPENSATING BALANCE.)

PLEDGED-ACCOUNT MORTGAGE - *See* FLEXIBLE LOAN INSURANCE PROGRAM (FLIP).

PLOT PLAN - A plot plan is an accurate drawing or map of an individual property site that shows the size and configuration of the property and the size and precise location of most man made features (buildings, driveways, walkways) on the property.

Plot plans show both what currently exists on your property and what physical changes you wish to make which will change the physical appearance of the land or man made features.

Plot plans are required to accompany most land use applications or construction permit applications in order to obtain approval to change how the property will be used or in order to construct something on the property.

PLOTTAGE - The merging or consolidating of adjacent lots into one larger lot, with the consequent result of improved usability and increased value; also called assemblage.

Problems involving plottage value are usually encountered in assembling land for a major building improvement that requires the use of more land than is usually represented by the average-sized lot in the locality where the improvement is contemplated. (*See* ASSEMBLAGE.)

POCKET LICENSE CARD - Evidence of licensure, sometimes called a "wallet card," issued by the Real Estate Program of the Department of Licensing. This card should be carried by a licensee at all times and should be presented when requested by any person with whom the licensee is dealing with regards to real estate.

POCKET LISTING - A listing which is retained by the listing broker or salesman and which is not made available to other brokers in the office or to other Multiple Listing Service members. This practice is strongly discouraged by the profession and is forbidden by many brokerages. Under residential MLS rules, a member must report any new listing (except for commercial listings, which are optional) within a specified time period (e.g., two or three days). (*See* MULTIPLE LISTING SERVICE.)

POINT OF BEGINNING - The starting point in a metes and bounds description of property, which is usually a street intersection or a specific monument. To effectively complete a legal description of a property, the description must always return to the point of beginning in order to enclose the described area. (*See* METES AND BOUNDS.)

POINTING - The filling up of joints in a masonry wall (e.g., the exterior wall of a fireplace) such as found between bricks so that the appearance is more attractive and the wall has more support. Sometimes called tuck pointing.

POINTS - A generic term for a percentage of the principal conventional loan amount. A lender often charges a borrower service charge points for making the loan. Each point is equal to one percent of the loan amount. In the initial stages of a loan application, the lender often does not know what loan amount will be approved, so he/she cannot state the finance charge in dollars and cents. Thus, it is convenient to state the charge as a set percentage of the loan amount, such as five points.

The term "points" has taken on numerous meanings in everyday practice and is a common source of confusion. Although used interchangeably, the term "points" and "discount charges" are not synonymous. A point is technically a unit of measure. It measures not only the amount of "discount" but also other costs such as mortgage insurance premiums and origination fees. The borrower should insist on each cost item being properly identified.

With a VA loan, the buyer by law may pay only the origination fee, and the seller must pay all of the remaining discount charges or discount points. These discount charges have the effect of increasing the yield on the mortgage. Since the discount is a means of raising the effective interest rate, the buyer would be paying a higher interest rate than the law allows on FHA and VA loans if he/she were allowed to pay the discount. When a seller pays the discount points, then it really amounts to a discount in the sales price he/ she will receive.

An agreement to pay points should be in the Real Estate Purchase and Sale Agreement (an earnest money agreement) and should be covered by the broker in the listing agreement. Where an earnest money agreement is silent on the payment of points, a seller cannot be held liable to pay points on a buyer's mortgage. In addition, where a seller pays points, they should be made aware that they might have to pay more than originally anticipated due to such variables as: an appraisal at a value lower than the seller originally thought; property repairs, as required per FHA, calling for building permit fees and other costs; and, market changes which may cause a higher point structure.

Points are a one time charge paid for the use of money. The Tax Reform Act of 1976 provides that where points are paid as compensation for the use of borrowed money (and thus qualify as interest for tax purposes rather than as payment for the lender's services), the points are a substitute for a higher stated annual interest rate. As such, points are similar to a prepayment of interest and are to be treated as paid over the term of the loan for purposes of the prepaid interest rule. This also applies to charges that are similar to points, such as a loan processing fee or a premium charge. Note, however, that discount charges paid by the seller for an FHA loan are not interest and therefore are not deductible; however, it may be deducted as a selling expense and reduce the amount realized on the sale.

The deductibility of points paid on home purchase loans and improvement loans paid by a cash-basis taxpayer on any indebtedness incurred in connection with the purchase or improvement of, and secured by, his/her principal residence are deductible in the year of payment if four conditions are met. First, the payment of points must be paid pursuant to an established business practice in the area where the loan is incurred. Second, the deduction is allowed only to the extent that the amount of the payment does not exceed the amount generally charged in the area. Third, the amount of points is computed as a percentage of the loan and specifically earmarked on the loan closing statement either as "points, " "loan origination fees" or "loan discount;" and fourth, the points are paid directly to the lender. (*See* DISCOUNT POINTS, FHA, PREPAID INTEREST.)

Homeowners who have refinanced existing loans solely to get a lower interest rate cannot fully deduct the points charged in connection with paying off their loans (the points must be amortized over the term of the loan).

Under federal Truth-in-Lending, the borrower's payment of points must be reflected in the annual percentage rate and fully disclosed to the consumer. (*See* ANNUAL PERCENTAGE RATE.)

POLICE POWER - The constitutional authority and inherent power of a state to adopt and enforce laws and regulations to promote and support the public health, safety, morals and general welfare. Police power is derived from the State Constitution, which also vests in the counties, cities and municipalities the power to adopt and enforce appropriate local ordinances and regulations not in conflict with general laws. Some examples of police power are the right to tax, the right to regulate land use through zoning, the right to require persons selling real estate to be licensed, the right to regulate pollution, and environmental control. In many ways, police power could be more accurately described as policy power by various legislative bodies. It is the right of the government to pass and to enforce laws to provide for the general public welfare. The laws must be uniform in operation, must not discriminate and cannot be to the advantage of any particular person or group.

Also derived from the police power is the right to damage or destroy private property (without compensation to the owner) when such an act is necessary to protect the public interest. This may happen, for example, when a condominium unit is on fire and the fire department must destroy an adjoining unit to extinguish the fire and save the rest of the building. While the government would not be required to compensate an owner for such destruction, a valid claim may be filed against the insurance policy covering the burning unit, or against the owner's own policy. Although police power permits the state to regulate the use of an individual's property in order to protect public health, safety and welfare, such regulation has its limits; if it goes too far, it will be recognized as a "taking" requiring the individual affected to receive just compensation. (*See* CONDEMNATION, EMINENT DOMAIN.)

PORTE COCHERE - A roofed structure extending from the entrance of building over an adjacent driveway to shelter those getting into or out of vehicles.

POSITIVE CASH FLOW - Refers to the number of dollars remaining after collecting rental income and paying operating expenses and debt payments. If more money is owed than is earned, it is called a negative cash flow (or an "alligator").

POSSESSION - The act of either actually or constructively possessing or occupying property. There is a presumption of ownership of property arising from the possession of property, and such possession imparts constructive notice of the rights of the party in possession. Therefore, when someone is in possession of property under a claim of ownership and another purchases the property from the owner of record, the subsequent purchaser for value is **not** protected under the recording laws since possession imparts constructive notice in much the same way as does the recording of a deed. It is said the purchaser should have inquired into the claims of the person in possession; thus, it is sometimes called "inquiry notice." Also, possession of a property often cures an indefinite description in deeds, leases, contracts of sale, and the like. The right to possess real property typically passes to the buyer upon the closing of a sales transaction. (*See* ADVERSE POSSESSION, CONSTRUCTIVE NOTICE, INQUIRY NOTICE, OCCUPANCY AGREEMENT, RECORDING.)

POSSIBILITY OF REVERTER - A possibility that property granted under a deed may revert back to the grantor if the grantee breaches a condition subject to which the property was granted. For example, Angie Sheron deeds her farm to Britt Burgess and her heirs, so long as Britt Burgess does not permit the consumption of alcohol on the property. Upon Ms. Burgess' breaching the condition by allowing alcoholic beverages on the property, the property would automatically revert back to Ms. Sheron.

Such contract conditions which violate Washington's discrimination law are automatically void, and, in fact, case law in Washington indicates that the courts will not recognize a possibility of reverter in certain conveyances. (*See* DEFEASIBLE FEE SIMPLE.)

POSTDATED CHECKS - A check which has on its face a date later than the actual date of signing, and which is therefore not negotiable until the later date arrives. A check is not invalid solely because it is antedated or predated, provided this is not done for an illegal purpose. When a broker accepts a postdated check as an earnest money deposit, he/she must disclose this fact to his/her principal in writing in the Purchase and Sale Agreement.

POTABLE WATER - Water which is capable of being safely and agreeably used as a drink. A public offering statement used in the sale of subdivided land must disclose whether potable water is available.

POWER OF ATTORNEY - A written instrument authorizing a person (the attorney-in-fact) to act as the agent on behalf of another to the extent indicated in the instrument. Highlights of pertinent practice with respect to the use of powers of attorney for the sale or purchase or real estate are:

1. A person acting under power of attorney from an owner of real estate does not need a real estate license to sell the owner's property. An exception to this would occur if the attorney-in-fact is engaged in real estate brokerage and is purposely evading the licensing law. (*See* LICENSING LAW.)
Reference: RCW 18.85.

2. Good title practice requires that the power of attorney be recorded, otherwise the signed document, such as the deed, will not be effective as against third parties. Naturally, the power of attorney must be acknowledged to be recorded. A notice of revocation is needed to revoke a recorded power of attorney.

3. Good title practice also requires that the parties use a **special or limited** power of attorney rather than an all-inclusive general power of attorney to convey real estate. The power of attorney is strictly construed and thus must specifically authorize the attorney-in-fact to carry out the full transaction. A power to **sell** does not grant the power to convey. A legal description must be inserted prior to execution and cannot be inserted later by the attorney-in-fact.

4. Any instrument signed with a power of attorney should be executed as follows: "Leland John, Principal, by Hoyt John Agent, his attorney-in-fact." The agent's name should never be signed first. It is permissible for the attorney- in-fact to type the name of the principal.

5. One spouse can be the attorney-in-fact for the other spouse for the purchase of property, but a husband should not be his wife's attorney-in-fact (or vice versa) for the sale of their property. (*See* COMMUNITY PROPERTY.)

6. Normally, death of either the principal or attorney-in-fact revokes the power of attorney. Most title companies are extremely cautious with power of attorney documents because of the revocation by death rule. If the power of attorney, however, clearly states that it is a durable power of attorney and continues even in the case of incapacity or death of the signor, the power of attorney will not be terminated by the death of a principal. (*See* AGENCY.)

7. Under the equal dignities rule, the power of attorney must be in writing since the real estate document to be signed must be in writing.

8. When the transaction is to be closed in escrow, the original power of attorney should be forwarded to escrow. (*See* ATTORNEY-IN-FACT, EQUAL DIGNITIES RULE, PRACTICE OF LAW.)

9. It is recommended to obtain the approval of a title company as to the form which a party plans to use; often it is only at the closing of a transaction the parties find out that an out-of-state form or one provided by a governmental entity is not accepted by the title company in the State.

POWER OF SALE - Authority given to a trustee under a deed of trust to sell property in the event of a default in one of the terms of the deed of trust or nonpayment by the grantor.

PRACTICE OF LAW - Rendering services which are peculiar to the law profession such as preparing legal documents, giving legal advice and counsel or construing contracts by which legal rights are secured. A broker can have his/her license suspended or revoked by practicing law, regardless of whether or not he/she charges a fee. The broker also has an ethical duty to recommend that legal counsel be obtained when the interest of either buyer or seller requires it.

It is permissible for a broker or salesperson to complete certain standard forms such as a Purchase and Sale Agreement; however, the licensee has a duty to do so with accuracy and with the certainty of an attorney. The Purchase and Sale Agreement must be approved by an attorney as to form and content. Such completion of forms is permissible only where it is incidental to the licensee earning his/her commission and not where he/she makes a separate charge for filling in the form. In no event can a real estate licensee prepare documents such as real estate contracts, deeds, options and certain leases.

Only attorneys and the parties to a transaction are authorized to prepare legal instruments. The National Association of Realtors considers it unethical and the unlawful practice of law for a Realtor to draft a power of attorney for his/her client.

Washington does permit institutions (lending institutions and title companies) which have traditionally selected, prepared, and completed documents relating to the sale or transfer of real property to do so provided that: (1) no additional fee is charged; (2) parties to the transaction are given written notice that the documents may substantially affect legal rights and that any questions regarding legal rights should be referred to an attorney of their choice; and (3) no attorney has previously been selected by the party involved. Any person operating under this act will be held to the same standard of care as an attorney would be under like circumstances.

PRECLOSING - A preliminary meeting preceding the formal closing where documents are prepared and signed, and estimated prorations are made well in advance of the closing date. Preclosings are often used in the conversion of entire apartment buildings to condominiums, as there may be many separate units to finally close on one day.

PREEMPTION CLAUSE - A clause sometimes inserted in a deed of subdivided land in which the developer either retains the right of first refusal on a resale of the property or gives that right to the owner of an adjacent lot who may exercise the right when the property is offered for sale. Also contained in some condominium documents in which any condo owner has the right of first refusal upon the resale of another unit in the building. (*See* FIRST REFUSAL, RIGHT OF.)

PREFAB HOUSING - *See* COMPONENT BUILDING, MODULAR HOUSING.

PRELIMINARY REPORT - A title report is normally issued when escrow is opened. A preliminary report or policy of title insurance reports only those documents having effect upon such title. (*See* TITLE INSURANCE.)

Abstracts are not used in Washington.

PREMISES - (1) A specific section of a deed which states the names of the parties, the recital of consideration and the legal description of the property. (2) The subject property which is deeded or the unit that is leased. Under the Washington Landlord Tenant Act, "premises" refers to the dwelling unit, appurtenances thereto, grounds, facilities held out for the use of tenants generally, and any other area or facility whose use is promised to the tenant. "Premises" is sometimes synonymous with land. (*See* DEED, SUBJECT PROPERTY.)

PREMIUM - (1) The consideration given to invite a loan or a bargain, such as the consideration paid to the assignor by the assignee of a lease or contract. In leasing property, sometimes part of the rent is capitalized and this premium is paid in a lump sum at the time the lease is signed. (2) In insurance terminology, a premium is the amount paid for an insurance policy. The unearned premium is that portion which must be returned to the insured upon cancellation of the policy.

PREPAID EXPENSES - Expenses which are paid before they are currently due. Most fire insurance premiums are paid one year in advance; rent is normally paid a month in advance. At closing, the seller is normally credited with prepaid expenses and charged for prepaid income, such as rent received.

PREPAID INTEREST - The paying of interest before it is due. Prior to 1975, the prepayment of interest was a tax saving technique because the IRS allowed a taxpayer to deduct the prepayment of interest under certain circumstances. The 1976 Tax Reform Act, however, provides that interest cannot be deducted as prepaid (whether it, in fact, was or not). Interest must be deducted over the life of the loan. Mortgage service points are also subject to the prepayment rules. However, mortgage service points paid in connection with the financing of a principal residence may be deducted in the year paid. (*See* POINTS.)

PREPAYMENT - Early payment of a debt. If a homeowner is offered a discount to prepay the balance due on his/her mortgage, deed of trust or real estate contract, the Internal Revenue Service has ruled that the taxpayer must recognize income by the amount of the discount.

PREPAYMENT PENALTY - The amount set by the creditor as a penalty to the debtor for paying off the debt prior to its maturity; an early withdrawal charge. The prepayment penalty is charged by the lender to recoup a portion of interest that he/she had planned to earn when the loan was made. It covers the lender for initial costs to set up the loan, service it, and carry it in the early years of high risk. The reason most lenders are willing to allow prepayment after five years without penalty is that much of the total note's interest has been paid in by that time. (*See* REQUIRED NET YIELD.)

Sample language concerning prepayment is "additional principal payments may be made with any monthly installment, but prepayments made in any calendar year in excess of 10 percent of the original amount of this note shall be subject to a charge of one percent of such prepayments." A few loans contain a prepayment and coasting clause, under which the buyer can pay before the money is due and then "coast" so long as there is a surplus built up. The amount of the penalty varies, but it is often an amount equal to the interest that would have been paid on the balance for a specified period of, for example, 90 days.

Real estate loans with **savings and loan institutions** can be prepaid at any time and, by law, the penalty may not exceed an amount greater than one percent of the prepayment amount. The amount of the prepayment penalty is usually specified in the promissory note. A reasonable prepayment charge, however, is not considered interest since it is payable only in connection with the borrower's exercise of an option given him/her by the lender.

PREPAYMENT PRIVILEGE - The right of the debtor to pay off part or all of the debt without penalty prior to maturity, such as in a mortgage, deed of trust or a real estate contract. If the debtor prepays part of the loan, the payment is applied to the last payments due. Thus, if the debtor in January prepays for six months, he/she still has to make the February payment.

If a seller/vendor under a real estate contract wants to take advantage of the tax benefits of installment sale reporting of income, he/she must be sure to restrict the amount of principal payable by the vendee in any given year. Otherwise the vendee would be free to pay any amount of additional principal and the vendor might lose the tax advantage.

No right to prepay exists unless agreed upon, as, for example, when monthly payments are in a stated amount "or more" or "not less than" such as "$200 or more per month." Where there is a right to prepay, it is called an "open mortgage."

Where there is no right to prepay a mortgage, it is called a "closed mortgage." If the seller won't consent to a prepayment, the buyer cannot force a prepayment by purposely defaulting on several installments and then tendering the balance due with interest to the date of payment while maintaining that the default in the mortgage automatically triggered the acceleration clause. Courts have ruled that an acceleration clause is for the benefit of the creditor, and the creditor can elect whether or not to enforce it.

An increasingly popular practice is to have a time period in the first part of the mortgage in which there can be no prepayment. This is generally known as a "lock-in." Note that a lender may not charge a prepayment penalty on any FHA insured or VA guaranteed loan. (*See* ACCELERATION CLAUSE, INSTALLMENT SALE, "OR MORE" CLAUSE.)

PRESALE - A preconstruction sales program by a condominium developer who is required to sell a certain percentage of units before a lender will commit to finance construction of the project. Also when a home buyer commits to a sale on a single family structure to be built.

PRESCRIPTION - The acquiring of a right in property, usually in the form of an intangible property right such as an easement or right-of-way, by means of adverse use of property that is continuous and uninterrupted for the prescriptive period. Possession need not literally be continuous provided use is on a regular basis. (*See* ADVERSE POSSESSION, EASEMENT.)

Prescriptive rights are not favored in the law since they necessarily work corresponding forfeitures on the rights of other persons. Thus, when one enters into the possession of another's property there is a presumption that he/she does so with the true owner's permission and in subordination to the latter's title. A use which is permissive in its inception cannot ripen into a prescriptive right no matter how long it continues, unless there has been a distinct, positive assertion by the "dominant tenant" of a right hostile to the owner of the "servient tenement." The burden of proving prescriptive rights rests upon the one who is to be benefited by the establishment of such a right. The claimant must prove that his/her use of the other's land has been open, notorious, continuous, uninterrupted, over a uniform route, adverse to the owner of the land, and with the knowledge of such owner at a time when he/she was legally able to assert and enforce his/her rights. However, proof that the use of another's land has been open, notorious, continuous, uninterrupted, and for the required period of time, creates a presumption that the use was adverse unless otherwise explained, and the burden of explanation is on the owner of the "servient tenement" to prove that use was permissive.

Prescriptive rights cannot be obtained against city, county, state or federal real property.

PRESCRIPTIVE EASEMENT - An interest in the property of another obtained through the open, notorious, hostile, and continuous use of the land for a statutory period of time. (*See* ADVERSE POSSESSION, EASEMENT BY PRESCRIPTION, PRESCRIPTION.)

PRESCRIPTIVE TITLE - *See* ADVERSE POSSESSION, EASEMENT BY PRESCRIPTION, PRESCRIPTION.

PRESENT VALUE OF ONE DOLLAR - A doctrine which is based on the fact that money has a time value. The present worth of a payment to be received at some time in the future is the amount of the payment less the loss of interest; thus, the present value of one dollar receivable one year from now is equal to one dollar less the loss of interest for one year. For example, if interest is six percent a year, then the value of the dollar next year is $.94.

Tables (such as the Ellwood or Inwood tables) have been devised to set forth a list of factors to be used to discount money to be received in the future at various interest rates over various periods of time. These tables are most frequently used to compute the value of a reversion, especially in long-term lease valuations. The present value of one dollar is also used in computations related to the sale of a building in determining the present value of the assigned leases. (*See* INTERNAL RATE OF RETURN, INWOOD TABLE.)

PRESERVATION DISTRICT - A zoning district established to protect and preserve park land, wilderness areas, open spaces, beach reserves, scenic areas, historic sites, open ranges, watersheds, water supplies, fish and wildlife, and to promote forestry and grazing.

PRESUMPTION - A rule of law which provides that a court will draw a particular inference from a certain fact or evidence unless and until the truth of such inference is disproved or rebutted. For example, the date on a deed is presumed to be the date of delivery, and a transfer to two or more people with no tenancy stated is presumed to be a tenancy in common with equal interests. (*See* ADVERSE POSSESSION, DELIVERY, POSSESSION.)

PREVAILING RATE - A general term to describe the average interest rate presently being charged by banks and lending institutions on real estate loans.

PRICE FIXING - The practice of conspiring to establish fixed fees or prices for services rendered or goods sold. In the past, the setting of commission percentages and management fees by local realty associations has been successfully attacked as price fixing and thus a violation of the Sherman Antitrust Act. (*See* ANTITRUST.)

PRIMA FACIE EVIDENCE - A legal term used to refer to evidence which is good and sufficient on its face ("at first view") to establish a given fact or prove a case. This kind of evidence will prove a case unless it is rebutted or contradicted; presumptive evidence.

PRIME CONTRACTOR - A construction supervisor who contracts with the owner to perform and oversee a job and then subcontracts the work to various skilled trades people. Owners should not make the final payment to the prime contractor until written assurances (lien releases) are received that all subcontractors have been paid. (*See* HOLDBACK, MECHANICS' LIEN.)

PRIME RATE - The minimum interest rate charged by a commercial bank on short-term loans to its largest and strongest clients (those with the highest credit standings). Prime rate is often used as a cost of money indicator. Prime rates are determined in part by the rates banks have to pay for the money they lend to their prime rate borrowers. Interest rates obtainable on other types of loans and the return on investments, such as federal government securities, also have considerable influence on the setting of prime rates. The supply of money and the demand for loans causes the prime rate to fluctuate, sometimes on a daily basis. The decisions of the Federal Reserve Bank to increase or decrease the supply of money cause prime rates to increase or decrease, as does the Federal Reserve Bank's rediscount rate.

On many large loans the interest rates float with the prime rate. For example, the interest rate may be stated as three percent above the prime rate of the Bank of Spokane, determined as of the first banking day of each month. In a very volatile money market, such as where the prime rate changes six or seven times in a month, some lenders structure their loans using the daily prime rate average for the month. (*See* FLOAT.)

PRIME TENANT - A tenant (or related group of tenants) who is the largest single occupant of a building. Such occupancy is usually for 25 percent or more of the building's aggregate square footage. The prime tenant may be the principal tenant of a property by virtue of name and reputation. A tenant who occupies the largest amount of floor space leased, or who possibly owns the building it occupies, is also considered a prime tenant. In a sublease situation, the original lessee is sometimes referred to as the prime tenant. (*See* ANCHOR TENANT.)

PRINCIPAL - 1. One of the main parties to a transaction. For example, the buyer and seller are principals in the purchase of real property.

2. In a fiduciary relationship, the principal is the person who hires an agent to work on his/ her behalf, e.g., seller hires a real estate broker to represent him/her in the sale of property. (*See* AGENCY, FIDUCIARY, REAL ESTATE BROKERAGE RELATIONSHIP ACT.) *Reference:* RCW 18.86.

3. The capital sum; interest is paid on the principal. NOT principle.

4. The phrase "principals only" often found in ads is meant to exclude real estate agents from contacting the person placing the ad.

PRINCIPAL MERIDIAN - The prime meridian intersecting the initial reference marker of a survey which is used as a reference line for numbering ranges. The meridian used in Washington is the Willamette Meridian. (*See* BASE LINE AND MERIDIAN, DESCRIPTION, LEGAL DESCRIPTION, METES AND BOUNDS.)

PRINCIPAL RESIDENCE - A structure that has been actually and physically occupied by the taxpayer. No minimum period of occupancy is required. The tax laws give special preferential treatment to taxpayers who sell their principal residence if they meet certain guidelines. (*See* RESIDENCE, SALE OF.)

While taxpayers may occupy several residences, they can have only one **principal** residence. Some factors to consider include time occupied, voting address, real property tax treatment, and similar factual proof.

PRIORITY - The order of position, time or place. The priority of liens is generally determined by the order in which the lien documents are recorded, except that real property tax liens have priority over even prior recorded liens. Thus the old adage: "first in time is first in right." (*See* RECORDING.)

PRIVATE MORTGAGE INSURANCE - Private mortgage insurance insures a portion of the loan against default, commonly called "PMI." A special form of insurance designed to permit lenders to increase their loan to-market-value ratio, often up to 95 percent of the market value of the property. Many lenders are restricted to 80 percent loans by government regulations, special loss reserve requirements, or internal management policies related to mortgage portfolio mix. A lender may, however, loan up to 95 percent of the property value if the excess of the loan amount over 80 percent of value is insured by a private mortgage guaranty insurer. A private mortgage insurer insures both mortgages and deeds of trust.

If it approves the loan, the mortgage insurance company will issue a commitment to insure the lender under a policy carrying 20 percent of the loan balance, minimum settlement option coverage. Upon receipt of the Certificate of Insurance, the lender may increase the loan amount to a higher percentage of the value of the property (usually 95 percent for owner-occupied projects in Washington).

The borrower pays the premiums for the insurance, e.g., usually at the rate of 1 percent of the loan for the first year and 1/4 of 1 percent of the principal balance each year thereafter. The amount varies depending on the organization issuing the mortgage insurance. If the loan is prepaid, a portion of the premium may be rebated to the borrower.

Note that the FHA mortgage insurance premiums is 1/2 of 1 percent on the unpaid balance of the loan. This higher rate is due to the fact that FHA is insuring more than just the top 20 percent of the loan; it is insuring the entire loan. In the case of a serviceman, the government may pay the mortgage insurance premium while the mortgagor remains on active duty. It should be noted that on 95 percent FHA loans the Federal Home Loan Bank Board insists that federal savings and loan associations set up a special reserve fund or require insurance for that portion of the loan above 80 percent — this insurance would be private mortgage guaranty insurance.

There are special private mortgage insurance programs for commercial properties and for lease guarantees. (*See* CLIC.)

Since a private mortgage insurance company cannot insure two mortgages on the same property, many lenders try to structure piggyback loans to create only one mortgage. (*See* MGIC, PIGGYBACK LOAN.)

PRIVATE OFFERING - An offering of a real estate security which is exempt from registration with state and/or federal regulatory agencies because it does not involve a public offering. In 1974, the Securities and Exchange Commission adopted guidelines (Rule 146) on what constitutes a private offering, in the hopes of bringing certainty to this area. Washington's Securities Division has not adopted Rule 146.

Washington's private offering exemption was amended in 1975 to provide that an issuer may make 10 security sales to persons in this state within any twelve consecutive month period. In addition to the limitation upon the number of sales allowed in this state, there is a $100,000 limitation upon the total amount of the sales within any consecutive twelve month period. Under prior Washington law, a security which was limited to less than 20 offerees was treated as a private offering and exempt from registration with the Washington Securities Division. It is important to note, however, that even though the private offering security may be exempt from the expensive and burdensome registration requirements, it is still subject to the full disclosure and anti-fraud provisions of the securities laws. (*See* ANTI-FRAUD PROVISION, INTRASTATE EXEMPTION, REAL PROPERTY SECURITIES REGISTRATION, RESTRICTED REAL ESTATE SECURITIES.)
Reference: RCW 21.20, WAC 460-44A.

PRIVITY - The mutual or successive relationship to rights in the same property, as in privity of contract (mortgagor — mortgagee) or privity of estate (landlord — sublessee).

PROBATE - The formal judicial proceeding to prove or confirm the validity of a will. The will is presented to the probate court, and creditors and interested parties are notified to present their claims or to show cause why the provisions of the will should not be enforced by the court. In Washington, a will is probated in the Superior Court of the county where the testator resided. If a nonresident, the will is probated in the Superior Court of the county where the real property is located.

Even if the decedent dies without a will, his/her estate is still subject to a probate action. The court determines the rightful heirs, pays legal claims of creditors, and appoints an administrator to distribute the real and personal property according to the court's decree.

If a creditor claims an interest in the decedent's estate, he/she must assert his/her claim within a specified period of time or be forever barred, except, however, when a secured creditor such as a mortgagee forecloses upon the decedent's property held as security even though he/she has not previously filed a claim.

The executor or administrator of an estate must file a final accounting with the Superior Court showing all income, expenses and the remaining assets, and he/she is discharged upon court approval of the final accounting. When this process has been completed, the real property is fully transferable free from debts, claims or taxes of the decedent.

A broker entering into a listing arrangement with the executor or administrator of an estate in probate should be aware of the following: (1) the amount of commission may be fixed by the court; and (2) commissions are payable only from the proceeds of sale. Thus a broker is not entitled to a commission unless the court approves the sale, even if he/she produces a ready, willing and able buyer. (*See* ADMINISTRATOR, EXECUTOR, INTESTATE, TESTATOR, WILLS.)

PROCEEDS - The net sum of cash realized from sale of property or the net sum of cash given to a borrower by the lender in a loan transaction.

PROCESSING - The production segment between loan application and before loan closing. Loan processing begins after a loan application is taken by a representative of a real estate lender, who is usually called a loan officer. Employees in real estate loan companies who work on the verifying and assembling of the paperwork necessary to close are called processors.

PROCURING CAUSE - The direct action by a person that results in the successful completion of some objective. In real estate brokerage, the term is used to denote the action(s) by a real estate licensee that results in the owner selling her or her property.

Under an open listing, the broker who is the procuring or effective cause of the sale is the one entitled to the commission. A broker can be the procuring cause even though it is only indirectly through his/her efforts that the property is sold. For example, if the broker sent to the owner's home a prospect to whom the owner then sold the property, the broker may be considered to have been the procuring cause of the sale.

In Washington, the most commonly used listing is the exclusive right-to-sell. With this type of listing, the broker is entitled to his/her commission if the property is sold "by you, by me, or by anyone else," thus eliminating most procuring cause controversies. Procuring cause issues do sometimes arise, however, in disputes between the cooperating broker and the listing broker where both advise the buyer without knowledge of the other's involvement.

In Washington, an exclusive right-to-sell listing is not always given on commercial-investment property. When it is not given, a broker who exposes the property to potential purchasers on an open listing basis normally provides a method of registering the prospects he/she exposes to the property. The open listing agreement provides that when a registered prospective purchaser actually purchases, the broker will be paid a commission.

Given the factual situation where one real estate licensee introduces a prospect to the property as the "procuring cause," and another licensee consummates the sale, which results in a dispute as to the sharing of commission, the Washington Association of Realtors has not adopted a policy statement to solve such a dispute. Several other state associations have adopted a policy statement, and the guidelines from the Hawaii Association of Realtors are one accepted method of settling such a dispute. The guidelines are as follows:

1. A member who accompanies a prospect on the first inside inspection of an improved property or first on-site inspection of an unimproved property shall be deemed the procuring cause of the sale and shall be entitled to share in the commission, if:

   a. the member had the right to show the property for sale through a valid listing from the owner or through a cooperative arrangement with the listing member; and

   b. the inspection, together with diligent and reasonable pursuit of the prospect by that member, produces a series of events which, without break in continuity directly results in consummation of the sale with that prospect.

2. In the absence of a prior arrangement by or on behalf of prospect's broker with listing member, each of the following events by itself does not constitute a procuring cause:

   a. submission or introduction of a property by voice or mail; or

b. the giving of information on a property; or

c. the making of an appointment to show the property; or

d. registration of the name of the prospect with the listing member; or

e. referring prospects to a property or open house; or

f. attending open house but not showing prospect open house.

One or more of these events; however, if coupled with first inspection and/or diligent pursuit to consummation of sale with the prospect, may satisfy the test of procuring cause.

3. Buyers attending an open house by themselves for the first time are the prospect of the open house showing member who can become the procuring cause if he/she diligently pursued consummation of the sale with that prospect.

4. If member A in arbitration successfully establishes all of the requirements under paragraph one above, he/she shall be entitled to a cooperating broker's share of commission, even though Member B was not informed of Member A's contribution to the sale. Further, in case of fraud or collusion between buyer and Member B, or grossly unfair and unethical conduct by Member B, the Professional Standards Arbitration Committee of the local Board may award the entire commission to Member A.

The foregoing policy is one approach used to avoid disputes or misunderstandings. However, there is no substitute for good salesmanship, professional service to clients and customers and common courtesy and consideration in dealings between licensees. (*See* EXCLUSIVE LISTING, LISTING, OFFER, TERMINATION OF LISTING.)

PROFIT - A right to take part of the soil or produce off the land, such as the right to take coal, fruit, timber. Also called an **a prendre**. Since a profit is an interest in land, it can only be created by written grant or by prescription, and not by custom or oral agreement. The basic difference between an easement and a profit is that an easement confers only the right to **use** another's land, whereas a profit confers the right to **remove** the soil or products thereof. (*See* FRUCTUS NATURALES.)

PROFIT AND LOSS STATEMENT - A detailed statement of the income and expenses of a business, which reveals the total financial picture as of a certain date. Commonly referred to as a "P & L."

PRO FORMA STATEMENT - A projection of future income and expenses. A pro forma statement is frequently found in a prospectus for an offering of a real estate security, such as a limited partnership to own rental property. A pro forma statement should be clearly labeled as a projection, and distinguished from operating figures which are based on actual past performance.

PROGRESS PAYMENTS - Payments of money scheduled in relation to the completion of portions of a construction project. Progress payments are required of buyers of many new condominium projects, whereby the they pays their down payment incrementally into escrow, with a certain amount due at the time of purchase, loan approval, completion of the building, and closing.

Construction loan funds are usually disbursed as the construction progresses and not in one lump sum at the start of the work. The owner normally retains a small percentage of each progress payment to the contractor until the owner is satisfied that the work is completed according to specifications. (*See* RETAINAGE.)

PROMISSORY NOTE - An unconditional written promise of one person (promisor) to pay a certain sum of money to another (promisee), or order, or bearer, at a future specified time. The words "or order" or "or bearer" are important to make the instrument negotiable since these words enable the instrument to be endorsed and transferred. If negotiable, the maker should be sure to execute and sign only one note and not any copies (he/she usually initials the copies).

A broker who accepts a promissory note as a deposit from a prospective purchaser must specifically disclose to the seller that the buyer's deposit is in the form of a promissory note; otherwise, his/her license might be suspended or revoked. Originally, this requirement stemmed from the agent's common law duty to inform his/her principal of all facts relating to the subject matter of the agency that would affect the principal's interest.

In real property financing, the promissory note (sometimes called the mortgage note) serves as evidence of the debt for which the mortgage or deed of trust on the property is the security. If the security is insufficient to cover the indebtedness, the holder of the note can obtain a deficiency judgment against the debtor for the balance unless the note is labeled a "nonrecourse note." (*See* HOLDER IN DUE COURSE, MORTGAGE, NEGOTIABLE INSTRUMENT, NOTE.)

PROPERTY - The rights or interests a person has in the thing he/she owns; not, in the technical sense, the thing itself. These rights include the right to possess, to use, to encumber, to transfer and to exclude, commonly called the "bundle of rights." In modern understanding, however, "property" has come to mean the thing itself to which certain ownership rights are attached. Property is either real or personal. (*See* BUNDLE OF RIGHTS, PERSONAL PROPERTY, REAL PROPERTY.)

PROPERTY LINE - The recorded boundary of a parcel of land.

PROPERTY MANAGEMENT - That aspect of real estate devoted to the leasing, managing, marketing and overall maintenance of the property of others. The property manager strives to maintain the investment and income in the property and to maintain the physical features of the building.

Most rental companies in Washington charge between six and ten percent of the gross rental income for their management services; however, the fees do vary according to the number of units in the project, the types of services offered and the geographical location of the property.

The property manager is a member of a real estate office or property management company which manages several properties for various owners. He/she performs three basic functions: (1) fiscal management of financial affairs; (2) physical management of structures and grounds; (3) administrative management of files, records, etc. The individual building manager may be employed by a property manager or directly by the owner of the building, usually on a straight salary basis, to supervise the daily operations in the building. Apartment and condominium resident managers commonly reside in one of the apartment units on the premises.

While the owner expects the greatest net return on his/her investment, the residents expect the most efficient functioning of the building. To fulfill his/her responsibilities, the property manager must possess a working knowledge of property maintenance, leasing, accounting, income tax, insurance, real estate law (especially contracts and agency principles) and human relations.

Property managers' fees are usually based on a percentage of gross income (after deducting for vacancies and other rent losses) without taking into account operating expenses.

Some of the more important provisions found in a properly drafted management agreement are the responsibilities of the management agency, the scope of the manager's authority to rent and operate the premises (e.g., can the manager grant concessions), the length of the agreement, the fee, and the identity of the parties and the property (usually not a legal description). (*See* AGENCY, CERTIFIED PROPERTY MANAGER, LICENSING LAW, MANAGEMENT, MANAGEMENT ACCOUNTING, MANAGEMENT AGREEMENT, MANAGEMENT SURVEY.)

PROPERTY REPORT - 1. A disclosure document required under the Federal Interstate Land Sales Act where applicable to the interstate sale of subdivided lots. The Property Report is in the form of questions and answers, and covers such matters as topography, accessibility of public transportation and schools, soil conditions, existence of liens and encumbrances, recreational facilities, whether special assessments will be charged, and other similar information. A prospective purchaser must be given a copy of the Property Report at least 48 hours before committing to purchase, unless the purchaser acknowledges in writing that he/she has received the report and made an inspection of the property. If a Property Report is not received at least 48 hours before the purchase, the purchaser has three business days to reconsider and cancel. Failure to provide the purchaser with a copy of the property report gives the purchaser the right to rescind the transaction at any time and have his/her money refunded plus interest. (*See* INTERSTATE LAND SALES.)

2. A disclosure document required under the Washington Land Development Act of 1973. The developer must prepare a Property Report approximately six pages in length which will cover specified areas of particular interest or risk to purchasers. Instructions on the format for the Property Report are given, but the developer is responsible for its accuracy and completeness.

The Property Report must be given to prospective purchasers, including all persons who visit the development site or who participate in a vacation or dinner program. The back page of the Property Report is a receipt form which should be filled out to include the time when the property report was delivered to a prospective purchaser. The developer is instructed to save the receipt form for three years. The receipt will serve as evidence that the Property Report was given and that the purchaser chose not to exercise revocation privileges, if that is true.

The statute provides that a purchaser may revoke a contract or agreement within 48 hours of receiving the Property Report, not counting Saturday, Sunday or a legal holiday. The notice of revocation must be in writing and delivered to the developer. No reason need be given for revoking if revocation is done within the 48-hour period. (*See* WASHINGTON LAND DEVELOPMENT ACT.)
Reference: RCW 58.19.

3. Washington State laws requires that a Real Property Transfer Disclosure Statement be used in transfers of residential real property, including multi-family dwellings up to four units; new construction; condominiums not subject to a public offering statement, and certain timeshares. (*See* REAL PROPERTY TRANSFER DISCLOSURE STATEMENT.)
Reference: RCW 64.06

PROPERTY RESIDUAL TECHNIQUE - An appraisal technique similar to the building residual technique and the land residual technique of capitalization, except that the net income is considered to be attributable to the total real property. The income is capitalized into an indicated value as a whole, based on the premise that the land and the particular improvements on the land are producing income as an economic unit. Under a different legal land use, the property could produce more or less income and thereby have a different value. (*See* BUILDING RESIDUAL TECHNIQUE, LAND RESIDUAL TECHNIQUE.)

PROPERTY TAXES - Money levied by government against property (either real or personal). There is no income tax in Washington; however, almost all real property in the state is subject to taxation. Real property has traditionally been a favorite subject of taxation due to its immobility and consequent ease to locate, evaluate and tax. The right to tax real property in the United States rests exclusively with the state and not the federal government.

In addition to the county, which is the major tax district in Washington, all of the taxing districts listed below are authorized by law to impose burdens upon property within their districts. The size of that burden (assessment) is in proportion to the value of the property (*See* ASSESSED VALUATION), and is assessed and collected for the purpose of obtaining revenue for public functions: state, county, city, town, port district, school district, road district, metropolitan park district, water district, sewer district, public hospital district, rural county library district, intercounty rural library district, and fire protection district. These districts are not uniform in size, of course, and it often happens that one property owner will find himself in five taxing districts and another property owner in twice that number. The tax statement each receives will enumerate the taxes and the amounts for each district, and the county treasurer will collect the total tax and disburse the proper amounts to the various other taxing districts. (*See* COUNTY ASSESSOR, REAL ESTATE TAX STATEMENT.)

Whenever a tax is levied, that which is taxed (the tax base) must be stipulated; and the amount of the tax per unit (the tax rate) must be stipulated as well. The tax base for property taxes is one dollar of assessed valuation, which amount is set by the County Assessor of the county in which the property is situated.

Property taxes are fixed by two processes, assessing property and levying taxes. The function of assessing property is one of evaluating or appraising property, and, in the case of homes and most businesses and industrial properties, is done by the County Assessor. Real estate is assessed at 100 percent of fair market value by state law in Washington.

It is then the responsibility of the County Assessor to calculate the millage rate to be imposed in order to raise the property tax revenue which has been budgeted by the various taxing districts interested in a particular piece of property within his/her county. These figures are the ones which subsequently appear on the tax statement mailed to the property owner before April 30 of the year. Should a property owner feel his/her assessment is unfair or inequitable, he/she may file an appeal on a form provided by the County Assessor. This appeal is considered by the Appeal Board meeting the first Monday of July. The Appeal Board is empowered to make such adjustments as it feels are warranted, and its decisions are final.

The property tax is the main source of revenue for the administration and services of these various taxing districts. However, these local governmental units may levy taxes only within the limitations of the state laws and the state constitution, unless the voters within the district vote a special levy on themselves for some special purpose. As meetings of these governing boards are open to the public, real estate brokers and salesmen certainly should participate in the budget sessions and thus come to appreciate the functions of the various taxing districts in which they intend to work.

The taxes for a condominium unit are assessed against each individual unit. It is necessary to assess and tax the common elements separately since the market value of each unit reflects not only the value of the unit itself, but also the proportionate value of ownership in the common elements (versus a co-op apartment where the entire building is assessed).

Note that real property taxes are deductible items for income tax purposes. However, the deduction does not extend to special assessment taxes for improvement districts.

The following is a quick guide to the deductibility of real property taxes in special situations:

1. Tenancy in Common — a tenant in common can deduct only his/her proportionate share of the tax even if he/she paid the entire amount of the tax bill.

2. Joint Tenancy — the one who pays the tax can take the deduction.

3. Mortgagee — a mortgagee cannot deduct property taxes paid for periods prior to acquiring title to the property. If the taxes are paid before foreclosure, they represent an additional loan on the property. If they are paid after foreclosure, they represent an additional cost of the property.

4. Back Taxes Paid by the Buyer — the buyer gets no deduction for any back taxes he/she pays. The sum paid is added to the purchase price.

When the total amount of taxes or special assessments on personal property or real property is fifty dollars or more, and one-half of such taxes are paid on or before the thirtieth day of April , the remainder shall be due and payable before the thirty-first day of October and shall be delinquent after that date.

Beginning in 1982, legislation provided for an additional penalty on top of the normal 12% per annum (computed monthly) delinquent interest rate for a delinquent payment; therefore, failure to pay property taxes will result in a total interest charge of 23% per year for the first year if paid a year late. The penalty is assessed at two stages in the year the taxes are due. A penalty of three percent of the full year amount of tax unpaid shall be assessed on June 1st of the year in which the tax is due. An additional penalty of eight percent shall be assessed on the amount due on December 1st of the year in which the tax is due. After the penalty is assessed in the first year, the interest rate for the following years is 12% per annum.

The legislation protects individuals over the age of 62. The principal residence of persons 62 years or over is now exempt from the property tax foreclosure process.

PROPRIETARY LEASE - A written lease in a cooperative apartment building, between the owner-corporation and the tenant-stockholder, in which the tenant is given the right to occupy a particular unit. The cooperative form of ownership has never been popular in Washington. The popularity of condominiums has replaced most interest in new cooperatives. (*See* COOPERATIVE.)

PROPRIETORSHIP - Ownership of a business or income property. A sole or individual proprietorship is a form of business ownership which is easy to organize and flexible to operate, and is frequently used in real estate brokerage. An individual proprietor may run his/her own brokerage company provided he/she has a valid Washington broker's license. The proprietor may use his/her own name or a fictitious name previously registered with the Real Estate Program of the Department of Licensing. It is a good idea to "trademark" the name with the State.

There is a growing tendency for sole proprietors to incorporate and thus take advantage of certain tax and fringe benefits such as those provided by pension and profit sharing plans.

PRORATE - To divide or distribute proportionately. With the exception of principal payments on a mortgage, most real estate expenses are either paid in advance (such as rent, insurance — which frequently is prepaid for several years' coverage — and the like) or in arrears (such as real property taxes, interest on a mortgage and the like). Upon closing a real estate transaction, these various expenses are prorated between the buyer and seller to assure that each is responsible for the operating expenses of the property during his/her ownership. Prorations are made because it is usually not practical to have the seller settle and pay all outstanding accounts with respect to the property. For example, a seller normally pays the fire insurance policy for a one year period and if he/she were to sell the property after the second month, he/she would be credited with a prorated amount equal to the cost of the remaining months, since the buyer is responsible for insuring the property and thus will receive the benefit of the policy for the remaining time.

In Washington, expenses are prorated as of the date of closing, which under the standard Purchase and Sale Agreement is normally the date when the final documents are recorded in the Office of the County Auditor, unless the parties specify otherwise (such as on the date of occupancy). Normally, escrow handles the proration of moneys at the time of closing, pursuant to the instructions of the parties as specified in the Purchase and Sale Agreement. (*See* CLOSING, ESCROW.)

PROSPECT - A person or corporation who may be interested in buying or selling real property. The prospect does not become a client until the parties establish a fiduciary relationship, such as upon signing a listing contract or upon executing a Purchase and Sale

Agreement. (*See* PROCURING CAUSE, REAL ESTATE BROKERAGE RELATIONSHIPS ACT.)

PROSPECTUS - A printed statement distributed to describe, advertise and give advance information on a business, venture, project or stock issue. If a real estate project is offered as a security, the prospectus must fully disclose all material aspects and investment features of the project which conceivably could affect the investor's decision whether to invest or not. The term is general limited to a publicly offered security (registered). In a private offering, the disclosure statement is called a private placement memorandum. (*See* REAL PROPERTY SECURITIES REGISTRATION, RED HERRING.)

PROXY - A person temporarily authorized to act or do business in behalf of another. Also, the document giving such person the power to act for another, e.g. a power of attorney. (*See* POWER OF ATTORNEY.)

Proxies are frequently used in voting or for quorum purposes in condominium association meetings. The proxy is not an irrevocable commitment, and the submission of a proxy merely ensures that the owner's vote will be cast in the event the owner cannot attend the meeting.

PUBLIC LANDS - Lands which are owned by the government. Public land is administered by the U.S. Department of the Interior's Bureau of Land Management. The General Services Administration participates in the sale of public land that is already fully developed.

PUBLIC OFFERING STATEMENT - Under the consumer protection provisions of the 1990 Condominium Act, the declarant/developer must provide to all prospective purchasers a Public Offering Statement.

The Public Offering Statement includes information about the background of the declarant, important information about the condominium itself, and copies of the condominium declaration, the survey map and plans, the condominium association's article of incorporation and by-laws, the association's rules and regulations, the association's budget and the association's balance sheet.

A prospective purchaser should receive the Public Offering Statement at least seven days before entering into a Purchase and Sale Agreement. If not given early, the prospective purchaser has seven days from the receipt of the Public Offering Statement to review it and cancel the purchase if he/she wishes to.

Any earnest money deposit must be placed into an escrow account while the Public Offering Statement is being reviewed. (*See* CONDOMINIUM OWNERSHIP.)
Reference: RCW 64.34.405

PUBLIC SALE - A sale at auction, made upon notice or invitation to the public so that the public can be given the opportunity to engage in competitive bidding, and held at a place to which the public has access. (*See* AUCTION, DEED OF TRUST, FORECLOSURE, MORTGAGE, TAX DEED, TAX LIEN.)

PUFFING - Exaggerated or superlative comments or opinions not made as representations of fact and thus not qualifying as grounds for misrepresentation. A statement such as the apartment has a "fantastic view" is puffing because the prospective buyer can clearly assess the view for himself, whereas a statement such as "the apartment has a fantastic view of the lake," when in fact all its windows face the street, would be misrepresentation. (*See* CAVEAT EMPTOR, MISREPRESENTATION.)

PUNCH LIST - A discrepancy list showing defects in construction which need some corrective work to bring the building up to standards set by the plans and specifications. A punch list may be filled out by the property owner and/or by the original architect in a final inspection of the building, listing discrepancies in the building plans and other construction flaws. With a punch list in hand, the building contractor may then proceed to correct the defects. (*See* CONTRACTOR.)

PUNITIVE DAMAGES - Exemplary or vindictive court-awarded damages to injured party; as opposed to compensatory damages, which are damages awarded to repay an aggrieved person for actual losses. The purpose of punitive damages is to punish the perpetrator, not to reward the injured party. The general rule is that no money damages are recoverable for purely mental suffering due to breach of contract. Also, punitive damages are not covered under errors and omission insurance and may not be awarded unless there has been some actual damage.

PURCHASE AND SALE AGREEMENT - See REAL ESTATE PURCHASE AND SALE AGREEMENT.

PURCHASE MONEY MORTGAGE OR DEED OF TRUST - A mortgage or deed of trust given as part of the buyer's consideration for the purchase of real property, and delivered at the same time that the real property is transferred as a simultaneous part of the transaction. A purchase money mortgage may be used to fill a "gap" between the buyer's down payment and a new first mortgage or a mortgage assumed, as when the buyer pays 10 percent in cash, gets an 80 percent first mortgage from a bank, and the seller takes back a purchase money second mortgage for the remaining 10 percent. Unlike states such as California, which have anti-deficiency legislation, in Washington a deficiency judgment is permitted upon default of a purchase money mortgage.

The purchase money mortgage or deed of trust given by the buyer to the seller has priority over all liens with which the purchaser might have attempted to encumber the property before he/she acquired title, or such general liens (like a judgment lien) as would have attached to the property upon delivery of the deed to him/her. The delivery of the deed and the taking back of the purchase money mortgage or deed of trust is deemed one transaction in which there is no time for any other lien to intervene.

When a seller agrees in a Purchase and Sale Agreement to take back a purchase money loan for part of the purchase price, he/she should take care to detail the terms and conditions of the loan (such as interest rate, duration); otherwise the contract might not be enforceable due to incompleteness or uncertainty. (*See* SECOND MORTGAGE OR DEED OF TRUST, SELLER FINANCING.)

Technically speaking, any loan on real property executed to secure the purchase money by a purchaser of the property contemporaneously with the acquisition of the legal title thereto is a purchase money loan. For example, the fact that a mortgage is made to a person other than the seller does not prevent its being a purchase money mortgage. The only disclosure under the federal Truth-in- Lending Law required of a first purchase money mortgagee on a dwelling is the annual percentage rate. (*See* MORTGAGE, TRUTH-IN-LENDING.)

PURCHASER'S ASSIGNMENT OF CONTRACT AND DEED - The purchaser of real property under a real estate contract may sell and convey his/her interest to another party prior to paying off the contract if the contract permits it. The instrument used to convey this interest is a purchaser's assignment of contract and deed. Excise tax must be paid on the conveyance. (*See* DUE ON SALE CLAUSE, EXCISE TAX ON REAL ESTATE SALES, PURCHASER'S POLICY, REAL ESTATE CONTRACT, STATE REVENUE STAMP.)

PURCHASER'S POLICY - A title insurance policy, usually called an **owner's policy**, generally furnished by a seller to a purchaser under a real estate contract or a purchaser's assignment of contract and deed insuring the property against defect in record title. (*See* AMERICAN LAND TITLE ASSOCIATION, TITLE INSURANCE.)

PYRAMIDING - A process of acquiring additional properties through refinancing properties already owned and then reinvesting the loan proceeds by purchasing additional properties.

QUALIFICATION - The process of reviewing a prospective borrower's credit and payment history and capacity prior to approving a loan. Brokers who assist a seller in reviewing a prospective buyer's qualification to purchase a property in which the seller is carrying back financing should be aware of the possible application of the federal Truth-in-Lending and Equal Credit Opportunity Acts and both the federal and state laws against discrimination.

QUALIFIED ACCEPTANCE - An acceptance which amounts, in law, to a rejection of an offer and is a counteroffer; an acceptance of an offer upon certain named conditions, or one that has the effect of altering or modifying the terms of the offer. The qualified acceptance does not comply with the terms of the offer, and is not an acceptance of the offer. (*See* COUNTEROFFER.)

QUALIFIED BUYER - A buyer who has demonstrated the financial capacity and creditworthiness required to afford the asking price. Before submitting an offer to buy, some buyers become pre-qualified with a lender for a loan up to a certain amount.

QUALIFIED FEE - An estate in fee which is subject to certain limitations imposed by the owner. For example, a grantor may convey his or her farm to a grantee with the stipulation that the grantee not build a liquor store on the premises. In the event that the grantee builds a liquor store on the property, the farm reverts to the grantor. A qualified fee can also be granted in a will where a testator leaves property to a spouse "so long as she (he) does not remarry." Also called a base fee, defeasible fee, or a fee determinable. (*See* POSSIBILITY OF REVERTER.)

QUANTITY SURVEY - A method of estimating construction cost or reproduction cost; a highly technical process used in arriving at the cost estimate of new construction and sometimes referred to in the building trade as the price takeoff method. A quantity survey involves a detailed estimate of the quantities of raw materials (lumber, plaster, brick, cement, and so on) used, as well as the current price of the material and the installation costs. An example of what such a survey would include would be: 10,000 concrete slabs at $2 per slab, 1,500 doorknobs at $5 each, and so on. These factors are added together to arrive at the total cost of a structure. Quantity survey is a time-consuming method and is most frequently used by contractors and experienced estimators. (*See* UNIT-IN-PLACE METHOD.)

QUANTUM - A term used in describing the amount or quantity of an estate as measured by its duration and not its quality; for example, an estate for life, or for 55 years, or forever. The quantum of an estate is generally found in the habendum clause. (*See* HABENDUM CLAUSE.)

QUANTUM MERUIT - A legal theory, also called unjust enrichment, in which a person can recover the reasonable value of services rendered in the absence of any agreement between the parties. In Washington, a real estate licensee cannot sue the seller or buyer for a real estate commission in the absence of a written agreement.

QUARTER SECTION - A land/area measure used in connection with the government (rectangular) survey of land measurement. A quarter section of land is 160 acres, 2,640 feet by 2,640 feet. Historically, it is the area of land originally granted to a homesteader.

Note that when lands throughout the country were originally surveyed, lakes, streams, and other features were sometimes encountered which resulted in fractional pieces of land less than a quarter section. These pieces were called government lots and were identified by a specific lot number which became the legal description for that parcel of land. (*See* GOVERNMENT SURVEY METHOD.)

QUASI - Latin for *as if, similar to* or *almost like.* Commonly used in real estate with such words as quasi-contract, quasi-judicial, quasi-corporation.

QUIET ENJOYMENT - The right of a new owner or a lessee legally in possession to uninterrupted use of the property without interference from the former owner, lessor or any third party claiming superior title. (*See* COVENANT.)

QUIET TITLE ACTION - A superior court action intended to establish or settle the title to a particular property, especially where there is a cloud on the title. All parties with a possible claim or interest in the property must be joined in the action. A quiet title action is frequently used by an adverse possessor to substantiate his/her title since official record title makes it easier to convey the property.

A quiet title action can be used to cure title defects; for example, to extinguish easements, remove any clouds on title, transfer title without warranties, clear tax titles, or simply release an interest when a party may have some remote claim to the property. For example, the seller who holds a forfeited Purchase and Sale Agreement, which the buyer had recorded, could bring a quiet title action to clear the cloud on title produced by the re-

corded Purchase and Sale Agreement, especially if the buyer refuses to release or quitclaim his/her interest to the Seller. (*See* ADVERSE POSSESSION, CLOUD ON TITLE, EASEMENT.)
Reference: RCW 7.28.

QUITCLAIM DEED - A deed of conveyance which operates, in effect, as a release of whatever interest the grantor has in the property; sometimes called a release deed. The grantee takes the property "as is." The quitclaim deed contains similar language to a deed, with the important exception that rather than using words of "grant and release," it contains language such as "conveys and quitclaims." The grantor, therefore, does not warrant title or possession. He/she only passes whatever interest he/she may have, "if any." In effect, he/she forever quits whatever claim he/she has in the property and the deed effectively forecloses the claim, if in fact any existed.

The quitclaim deed transfers only whatever right, title and interest the grantor had in the land at the time of the execution of the deed and does not pass to the grantee any title or interest subsequently acquired by the grantor unless an "after-acquired" title provision is included. However, it does not relieve the grantor of any obligations incurred during the ownership period, such as a debt secured by a deed of trust.

Although a quitclaim deed may not vest any title in the grantee, it is not inferior to the other types of deeds with respect to that which it actually conveys. For example, if a grantor executes and delivers a warranty deed to one person and subsequently executes and delivers a quitclaim deed for the same property to another person, the grantee under the quitclaim deed will prevail over the grantee under the warranty deed, if he/she is first to record his/her deed.

Ordinarily a warranty deed will be used to transfer a fee simple interest. A quitclaim deed is not commonly used to convey a fee, but is usually restricted to releasing or conveying minor interests in real estate for the purpose of clearing title defects (sometimes referred to as "clouds on the title").

QUORUM - The minimum legal number required to be present before a specified meeting can officially take place or authorized business be transacted. The Washington Real Estate Commission is comprised of seven members, a majority of whom (four) are required for a quorum.

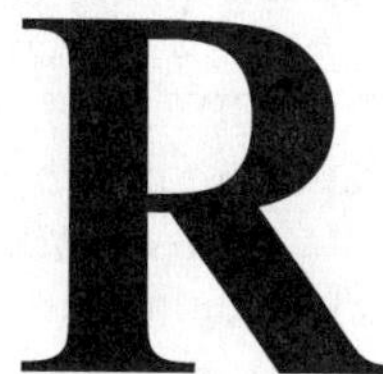

R-VALUE - A special rating or method of judging the insulating value of certain insulation products. The Federal Trade Commission requires that sellers of new homes must disclose in their sales contracts certain insulation data such as type, thickness, and R-value. (*See* INSULATION.)

RACIAL RESTRICTION - A clause in a document pertaining to real estate stating that the owner of the property shall not sell to a person who is of a particular race.

A 1969 amendment to the Washington State Law Against Discrimination holds void every provision in a written instrument which purports to forbid or restrict the conveyance, encumbrance, occupancy or lease and every condition, restriction or prohibition which directly or indirectly limits the use or occupancy of real property on the basis of race, creed, color, or national origin. Furthermore, it is an unfair practice under the Washington State Law Against Discrimination to insert in a written instrument relating to real property a provision that is void under the above restriction or to honor or attempt to honor such a provision in the chain of title. (*See* DISCRIMINATION.)
Reference: RCW 49.60

RADIANT HEAT - Heating a structure with the use of coils, pipes, or panels recessed in the ceilings, walls, or floors. The power source for the coils can be electricity, hot water, steam or hot air.

RADON - A colorless, odorless, naturally-occurring gas produced from the decay of natural radioactive minerals (uranium) in the ground. Radon's seepage into the outdoor atmosphere is not harmful but such seepage can be when built up in an enclosure such as in a basement. Brokers must disclose known radon problems, if known, with a property and advise homeowners to contact state environmental agencies for a determination if a property has an elevated level of radon.

RAFTER - One of a series of sloping beams that extend from the exterior wall to a center ridgeboard and which provides the main support for the roof.

RAM - *See* REVERSE ANNUITY MORTGAGE.

RANCHER - One who engages in one or more branches of agriculture, such as the raising of livestock, or the operation of a fruit or wheat ranch, etc. The term is often used interchangeably with the term "farmer"; as in fruit farmer, dairy farmer, sheep farmer, wheat farmer.

RANGE LINE - A measurement, used in the government survey system, consisting of a strip of land six miles wide, running in a north-south direction. (*See* GOVERNMENT SURVEY, TOWNSHIP.)

RANGE OF VALUE - The market value of a property, usually stated as a variable amount between a low and a high limit. Brokers often estimate a range of value as a first step in working with an owner to determine the listing price.

RATE OF RETURN - The relationship (expressed as a percentage) between the annual net income generated by a business and the invested capital, the appraised value, or the gross income, etc., of the business. The rate of return is the percentage of yield to the investor based on the property's production of income. (*See* CAP RATE, INCOME APPROACH, INTERNAL RATE OF RETURN.)

RATIFICATION - A confirmation of an act already performed, not an authorization of an act to be performed. The affirmance by a person, upon reaching his/her majority, of a contract made by him/her during his/her infancy. In the law of agency, a principal by his/her actions may ratify a prior act which did not bind him/her, but which was done or professed to have been done on his/her account, thus giving effect to the act as if originally authorized. (*See* AGENCY, SCOPE OF AUTHORITY.)

RAW LAND - Unimproved land; land in its unused natural state prior to the construction of improvements such as streets, lighting, sewers, and the like.

READY, WILLING AND ABLE - A phrase referring to a prospective buyer of property who is legally capable and financially able to consummate the deal. The listing agent normally earns his/her commission upon procuring a ready, willing and able buyer on the listing terms, regardless of whether the seller actually goes through with the sale. The "ready and willing" means, generally, that a real estate licensee (not necessarily the listing agent) must in fact produce a buyer who indicates that he/she is prepared to accept the terms of the seller and is willing to enter into a contract of sale with him/her. The buyer is not "ready and willing" when he/she enters into an option with the seller, but he/she is when the option is exercised. The buyer is not "ready and willing" when his/her offer is subject to any new conditions. A Purchase and Sale Agreement subject to conditions not contemplated in the listing agreement does not entitle the real estate licensee(s) to a commission until the conditions have been satisfied or waived. (*See* COUNTER OFFER, OFFER, QUALIFIED ACCEPTANCE.)

The "able" requires that the buyer be financially able to comply with the terms of the sale in both initial cash payment and any necessary financing. The real estate licensee(s) are not required to show that the purchaser has actual cash or assets to pay the purchase price. The "able" means the purchaser has the resources to produce the money when necessary, e.g., the purchaser can pay the down payment and secure financing for the balance.

When a seller accepts an offer from a buyer, he/she implicitly approves the buyer as being "able," if the buyer thereafter defaults by not coming up with the purchase price, the seller normally cannot argue that the broker had failed to produce an "able" buyer. However, there is recent case law to the effect that the broker does have the added responsibility to find out whether or not, in fact, the buyer is "able," and where the buyer turns out to be financially unable the broker is not entitled to his/her commission. A corporation not yet formed cannot be a ready, willing and able buyer. (*See* COMMISSION.)

REAL ESTATE - The physical land at, above, and below the earth's surface with all appurtenances, including any structures; any and every interest in land whether corporeal or incorporeal, freehold or nonfreehold; for all practical purposes synonymous with *real property*. (*See* LAND, REAL PROPERTY.)

REAL ESTATE ADMINISTRATOR - Formally the chief administrative officer who oversaw the operation of the Real Estate Division on a day to day basis. In Washington, the Real Estate Administrator had been under the State Civil Service System since the mid 1960's. The Administrator was responsible for hiring all division employees subject to Civil Service Rules and Regulations. He/she was charged with the responsibility of enforcing the Real Estate License Law and the Rules and Regulations adopted by the Real Estate Commission, the Escrow Agent Registration Act and the Rules and Regulations adopted by the Escrow Commission and the Washington Land Development Act. Many of the duties and responsibilities of the Director of Licensing had been delegated to him/her. (*See* LICENSING LAW, REAL ESTATE PROGRAM.)

In 1987, the Director of Licensing was reorganized along function lines of administration which resulted in the Real Estate Division being abolished.
Reference: RCW 18.85.

REAL ESTATE AUDITOR - Staff personnel of the Investigation and Enforcement Division of the Department of Licensing who inspect and audit all records of a real estate office at least once every three years. The State of Washington Investigation and Enforcement Division has the most extensive auditing program of any state. It has resulted in a substantial number of brokers having their licenses suspended or revoked. One result of the extensive audit system is that the consuming public has suffered minimum losses from the misuse of trust account funds by real estate brokers. (*See* LICENSING LAW.)
Reference: RCW 18.85, WAC 308-124.

REAL ESTATE BROKERAGE COUNCIL - A council affiliated with NAR's RealtorsÒ National Marketing Institute (RNMI), whose goal is to improve standards and professionalism in real estate brokerage management. The council awards the designation CRB (Certified Real Estate Brokerage Manager).

REAL ESTATE COMMISSION - A Washington State advisory committee to the Director of Licensing and the Real Estate Program. The primary duties of the Commission are to make Rules and Regulations to protect the general public in real estate transactions, preparation of examinations, and to oversee the conducting of educational seminars. Once the Commission has adopted a Rule and Regulation, it has the same effect and force on real estate licensees as any provision of the Real Estate License Law. Violation of a Rule and Regulation of the Commission can result in discipline of a licensee.

The Commission consists of seven (7) members, consisting of the Director of Licenses and six (6) Commissioners, appointed by the Governor. While there have been certain geographical areas represented on the Commission for a substantial period of time, e.g., Seattle, Tacoma and Spokane, the Commissioners do not represent these areas. Their interest should be on behalf of the whole State. No Commission member shall be appointed who has less than five (5) years experience in real estate sales, operation, or management in this state, or at least three (3) years experience in investigative work of a similar nature, preferably in connection with the administration of real estate licenses in this State or elsewhere.

Each member is appointed for six (6) years, with one member being appointed each year by the Governor. Appointments expire on August 14th. Members receive $50 per day compensation for each eight hours of conducting business as a Commissioner. The Commission meets on a regular basis. Meeting dates are available from the Real Estate Program of the Department of Licensing. (*See* LICENSING LAW.)
Reference: RCW 18.85.

REAL ESTATE CONTRACT - A written agreement between the seller (vendor) and buyer (vendee) for the purchase of real property. The purchase price is paid in installments (e.g., either principal and interest or interest only) over the life of the contract with the balance due at maturity. When the buyer completes his/her required payments, the seller is obligated to deliver good legal title to the buyer by way of a fulfillment deed. Under the terms of the real estate contract, the buyer is given possession of the property, and he/she is said to have equitable title to the property, while the seller retains legal title.

The real estate contract document usually contains the names of the buyer and seller, the sales price, the terms of payment, a full legal description, and a lengthy statement of the rights and obligations of the parties, including use of premises, risk of loss, maintenance of premises, payment of taxes and insurance, remedies in case of default, and others. Specific rights, such as acceleration or the right to prepay without penalty must be expressly written into the agreement. The agreement is signed by both parties (wife must sign when community property is involved), acknowledged and recorded (the excise tax must be paid prior to recording).

The real estate contract was once used quite extensively in Washington. Since the mid-1980s, the use of real estate contracts have been substantially replaced by the deed of trust. In a tight money market where it is difficult to qualify prospective buyers for a new first mortgage or deed of trust from an institutional lender, the real estate contract is frequently the best method to sell or purchase a property. A particular beneficiary of the real estate contract is the young couple who would have difficulty qualifying for a bank loan today, but whose income will increase prior to the maturity of the contract.

Some sellers prefer to sell on a real estate contract because it can create an installment sale which will enable them to defer payment of a large capital gains tax. (*See* INSTALLMENT SALE.)

The use of a real estate contract is not without some disadvantages; for instance:

FROM THE BUYER'S VIEWPOINT:

1. Since the seller need not deliver good marketable title until the final payment, the buyer must, at the risk of default, continue to make his/her payments even when he/she has doubts the seller will be able to perform when all payments are made. To protect himself, the buyer should require the seller to furnish a title insurance policy insuring the buyer's interest and record the contract promptly upon the closing of the transaction. (*See* TITLE INSURANCE.)

2. The buyer may have difficulty getting the seller to deed the property. By withholding a large enough final payment, the buyer can better persuade a seller to pay the costs of drafting the deed than if the final payment is a small one. In addition, at the time of final payment the seller might be suffering a legal disability; he/she might be missing, he/she might be bankrupt, or he/she might have died and his/her property is tied up in probate. To protect himself, the buyer may want to have set up a "true escrow" at a bank wherein the fulfillment deed is placed in escrow and upon the payment of the final installment the deed is delivered and recorded.

3. The buyer might be restricted from assigning his/her interest in the real estate contract by covenants against assignment.

4. The buyer will find it impossible to borrow against his/her equity from most institutions.

FROM THE SELLER'S VIEWPOINT:

1. In the event the buyer defaults, the process of clearing record title may be time consuming and costly, if the buyer is under a legal disability, a bankrupt or a nonresident. However, if a large enough down payment and/or a substantial number of monthly installments have been received, the seller usually will not suffer any substantial damages.

2. The seller's interest in the real estate contract may be less saleable than a beneficiary's interest would have been had the seller sold and took back a promissory note and deed of trust.

3. By its very nature the real estate contract is a contract and all contracts are subject to different interpretations and run the risk of disputes and litigation. (*See* COLLECTION ACCOUNT, EXCISE TAX ON REAL ESTATE SALES, ESCROW, REAL ESTATE CONTRACT FORFEITURE ACT.)

REAL ESTATE CONTRACT FORFEITURE ACT - In 1985 Washington passed the Real Estate Contract Forfeiture Act which establishes modern procedures governing the forfeiture of interests of purchasers under real estate contracts. There were no statutory provisions governing the forfeiture of real estate contracts prior to the enactment of the Act, although various procedures were established in court cases and through custom. The law eliminates uncertainty in forfeiting real estate contracts and limits much of the discretion previously allowed by the courts. The law retains private forfeiture as a separate remedy for real estate contracts.

The objectives of the law were clarification of the rights of the contracting parties; the avoidance of unnecessary and burdensome procedures (in particular, the necessity of obtaining the judicial blessing of a forfeiture through a quiet title judgment); reliability and usefulness of the public records when ascertaining the status of title to real property; a reasonable and equitable balance of the rights, remedies, liabilities and responsibilities among the parties to a contract and the certainty of procedure.

It provides a statutory **nonjudicial** method to forfeit real estate contracts. It provides for a 90-day period to cure the defaults; prohibits a deficiency judgment following a forfeiture; and limits the enforceability of an acceleration provision in connection with the forfeiture. The Act uses a system of "required notices" to forfeit a real estate contract: which include the "Notice of Intent to Forfeit" and the "Declaration of Forfeiture". Forfeiture must be completed by giving and recording the required notices.

It applies to all real estate contract forfeitures regardless of the date of the real estate contract. The term "contract" or "real estate contract" is defined as any written instrument for the sale of real property in which legal title to the property is retained by the seller as security for the payment of the purchase price. The act does not apply to Purchase and Sale Agreements or options to purchase.

It provides that certain conditions must be met before a real estate contract forfeiture action may be commenced. The term "forfeit" means to cancel the purchaser's rights under a real estate contract and to terminate all right, title and interest in the property of the purchaser and any persons claiming by or through the purchaser because of a breach of one or more of the purchaser's obligations under the contract. The Act provides that a purchaser's rights under a real estate contract shall not be forfeited except as provided in the Act. There are two required notices: Notice of Intent to Forfeit and Declaration of Forfeiture. A purchaser's rights under a real estate contract are forfeited by giving and recording the required notices.

Any of the persons entitled to required notices and any guarantor or surety of the purchaser may cure the default at any time during the cure period.

If the default is not cured within the 90-day period, and if the forfeiture is not stopped or delayed by court action, the seller may then complete the forfeiture by recording the Declaration of Forfeiture and providing a copy of the Declaration of Forfeiture to the purchaser.

A 1988 amendment allows a seller to choose, when the purchaser defaults, between foreclosing on the real estate contract as a mortgage, which requires court involvement, or to use the Real Estate Contract Forfeiture Act. (*See* REAL ESTATE CONTRACT.) *Reference:* RCW 61.30.

REAL ESTATE DIVISION - *See* REAL ESTATE PROGRAM

REAL ESTATE EDUCATORS ASSOCIATION (REEA) - A professional organization established by and for real estate educators, including individuals and institutional membership. REEA is international in scope and represents a broad range of real estate education from degree programs to continuing education; from sales training to GRI; from prelicense to graduate studies; from consulting to research to publishing. Members of the association come from colleges, universities, proprietary schools, state regulatory agencies, real estate organizations, boards and associations, and other delivery systems.

REAL ESTATE EXCISE TAX - *See* EXCISE TAX ON REAL ESTATE SALES.

REAL ESTATE INVESTMENT TRUSTS (REIT) - In the 1960's Congress provided a tax shelter for business trusts by exempting from corporate tax certain qualified real estate investment trusts (REITs) which hold at least 75% of assets in real estate and which distribute 95 percent or more of their ordinary income to their investors. As an alternative to the partnership or corporate methods of investing in real estate, the REIT offers the flow-through tax advantages of a partnership-syndication while retaining many of the attributes and advantages of a corporate operation. Investors purchase certificates of ownership in the trust, which, in turn, invests the money in real property and then distributes any profits to the investors free of corporate tax. The shareholder pays normal income tax on the ordinary income from the trust and receives favorable capital gains treatment for any capital gains distribution.

Some **advantages** of the REIT are: the avoidance of corporate tax (thus no double taxation), centralized management, continuity of operation, transferability of interests, diversification of investment, and benefit of skilled real estate advice. Some of the **disadvantages** are: investments are passive in nature and usually are restricted to the very large real estate transaction; losses cannot be passed through to the investor to offset his/her other income, as is the case with syndications; and usually the trust must be registered with the Securities and Exchange Commission, a burdensome and expensive process.

The Washington State Securities Commission has adopted a number of Rules and Regulations on Washington State REIT's. The use in Washington of REIT's funds has been limited, though several apartments and condominium projects have been funded.
Reference: RCW 21.20, WAC 406-36A.

In recent years, the rules for REIT's have been liberalized, making REITs a more attractive investment vehicle. The new law eases shareholder, income, and asset requirements for the first year that an entity qualifies as a REIT. Income and asset requirements are eased for the first year after a REIT receives new equity capital or certain new debt capital. In addition to these breaks, REITs will be permitted to hold assets in wholly owned subsidiaries.

Other rules have been eased for when a sale constitutes a prohibited transaction, the amount of dividends a REIT may pay, penalties on distributions of deficiency dividends, definitions of rents and interest, treatment of shared appreciation mortgage income, and distribution requirements relating to income not accompanied by the receipt of cash.

REAL ESTATE LICENSE LAW - *See* LICENSING LAW.

REAL ESTATE PROGRAM - In 1987 the Real Estate Division of the Department of Licensing was abolished.

The various functions of the former Division were assigned to newly established divisions of the Business and Profession Administration of the Department of Licensing. Real estate licensing was put under the Licensing Division. Real estate audits and investigations were placed under the Investigation and Enforcement Division. Real estate examinations were placed under the Professional Program Management Division.

The Real Estate Program was established to function as support staff for the Chairman of the Real Estate Commission and the Real Estate Commission and to handle public inquiries. (*See* ESCROW AGENT REGISTRATION ACT, LICENSING LAW, REAL ES-

TATE ADMINISTRATOR, REAL ESTATE AUDITOR, REAL ESTATE COMMISSION, WASHINGTON LAND DEVELOPMENT ACT.)

REAL ESTATE MORTGAGE INVESTMENT CONDUIT (REMIC) - *See* REAL ESTATE MORTGAGE TRUST

REAL ESTATE MORTGAGE TRUST (REMT) - REMT's operate similarly to REIT's except that the mortgage trusts buy and sell real estate mortgages (usually short-term junior instruments) rather than real property. REMT's major sources of income are mortgage interest, origination fees, and profits earned from buying and selling mortgages.

A related trust is the combination trust, which combines real estate equity investing with mortgage lending, thus earning profits from rental income and capital gains, as well as mortgage interest and placement fees.

The Tax Reform Act of 1986 creates a special tax vehicle called the Real Estate Mortgage Investment Conduit (REMIC) for entities which issue multiple classes in investor interests backed by a pool of mortgages. A REMIC is generally a conduit entity for tax purposes; the income of the REMIC is passed through to investors and reported on their individual income tax returns. Complex rules cover qualification as a REMIC, as wells as transfers to and liquidations of the entity. If the qualification requirements are met, any partnership, trust, or similar entity is granted pass-through REMIC status. The entity qualifies as a REMIC only if it meets two tests: (1) Substantially all assets at the close of the fourth month ending after the "start-up day" and each quarter ending thereafter must consist of qualified mortgages and permitted investments. (2) All interests in the REMIC must consist of one or more classes of regular interests and a single class of residual interest.

REAL ESTATE OWNED (REO) - A term used by banks, savings and loan associations and mortgage lenders to describe real property acquired by them in foreclosure and now carried on their books. Lenders often use brokers to market their REO properties.

REAL ESTATE PURCHASE AND SALE AGREEMENT - Also referred to as an earnest money and receipt agreement, this is the most frequently used term for a contract of sale and purchase of real estate in Washington. Purchase and Sale Agreements have been carefully drafted by the Washington Association of Realtors® and Multiple Listing Services. The Northwest Multiple Listing Service, for now, prevails as the most commonly used form in western Washington.

The Purchase and Sale Agreement is the blueprint for the entire real estate transaction. It is in this contract that buyer and seller come to final agreement on the essential terms of price, method of payment, proration of expenses, date of closing, and other important details which must be completed before title can pass. Great care must be given to the proper preparation of the Purchase and Sale Agreement, as it is this document which will be subject to judicial scrutiny should one of the parties want to find a way to avoid the transaction. In this sense, the Purchase and Sale Agreement is more important than the deed, and requires the utmost expertise on the part of the licensee assisting in its preparation. The importance of the Purchase and Sale Agreement is stressed by the bold face lettering at the top of the form "This contract controls the terms of sale of the property; read carefully before signing." (*See* CONTINGENCY.)

The Purchase and Sale Agreement consists of three principal parts: (1) It is a receipt for the buyer's earnest money deposit. The salesman acknowledging the form of the deposit and who will hold the deposit until the sale closes or is terminated. (2) It is the buyer's offer. (3) When accepted by the seller (and after notification of the acceptance to the buyer), it becomes the purchase contract.

The Purchase and Sale Agreement is often a five part snap-out form with NCR paper and is executed in five copies simultaneously. The usual distribution of copies is as follows: (1) buyer keeps a copy when making offer; (2) seller keeps a copy when he/she accepts or counters the offer; (3) buyer keeps a copy when he/she acknowledges receipt of the accepted offer; (4) one copy is the for the escrow closing officer; and (5) the top copy (the original) is kept in the selling broker's office. (*See* BILATERAL CONTRACT, BUYING YOUR HOME, CONTRACT, CONTRACT OF SALE.)

Since the acceptance of fax copies of contracts, the original document is often ignored, however, in the case of a dispute, the original signed Purchase and Sale Agreement with addendum can be very important (the best evidence rule), therefore, it is recommended that the selling office retain the original fully executed Purchase and Sale Agreement.

REAL ESTATE SETTLEMENT PROCEDURES ACT (RESPA) - This federal law, enacted in 1974 and since revised, ensures that the buyer and seller in a real estate transaction have knowledge of all settlement costs when the purchase of a one-to-four-family residential dwelling is financed by a federally related mortgage loan. Federally related loans include those:

1. Made by savings and loan associations or other lenders whose deposits are insured by federal agencies (FDIC or FHLB).

2. Insured by the FHA or VA.

3. Administered by the Department of Housing and Urban Development.

4. Intended to be sold by the lender to Fannie Mae or a similar federal agency.

Note that RESPA regulations apply to first mortgage loans only. RESPA requires that loans covered by the act comply with the following items:

1. **Special Information Booklet** — A lender must give every person from whom it receives or for whom it prepares a loan application a copy of the HUD published booklet, "Settlement Costs and You." The booklet provides the borrower with general information about settlement (closing) costs and explains the various RESPA provisions. It also gives a line-by-line discussion of the uniform settlement statement.

2. **Good Faith Estimate of Settlement Costs** — At the time of, or within three business days of application, the lender must provide the borrower with a good faith estimate of the settlement costs the borrower is likely to incur. This may take the form of a specific figure or a range of costs based upon comparable past transactions in the area. In addition, if the lender requires use of a particular attorney or title company to conduct the closing, the lender must state if any business relationship exists, and give an estimate of that individual's charges.

3. **Uniform Settlement Statement** — RESPA provides that loan closing information be prepared on a special HUD form (HUD-1) designed to detail all financing particulars of the transaction. The statement must itemize all charges imposed by the lender, as well as all other charges paid out of the closing proceeds. Charges incurred by the buyer and seller, contracted separately and outside the closing, do not have to be disclosed. Items paid for prior to the closing must be clearly marked as such on the statement, and are omitted from the totals. Lenders must retain these statements for two years after the date of closing unless the loan (and its servicing) is sold or otherwise disposed of. Note that the uniform settlement statement may be changed to allow for local custom; that is, certain lines may be deleted if they do not apply in the area. Upon the borrower's request, the settlement agent must permit him/her to inspect the settlement statement, to the extent that the figures are available, one business day before closing.

4. **Prohibition Against Kickbacks** — RESPA explicitly prohibits the paying of kickbacks or unearned fees, such as when an insurance agency pays a kickback to a lender for referring one of the lender's recent customers to the agency. Exempted, however, are payments made pursuant to cooperative brokerage or referral arrangements, or agreements between real estate salespeople and brokers. (*See* CLO.)

RESPA is administered by the Office of the Assistant Secretary for Consumer Affairs and Regulatory Functions at HUD. RESPA does not apply to loans secured by mortgaged property larger than 25 acres, to installment land contracts (real estate contracts); certain construction loans, home improvements loans, and loans on property where the primary purpose of purchasing is future resale.

REAL ESTATE SYNDICATE - A group of investors who pool funds for investment in real property. Normally the group is put together by a real estate broker or entrepreneur. The most common arrangement is to form a limited partnership with the real estate broker or entrepreneur acting as the general, managing partner. (*See* LIMITED PARTNERSHIP, REAL PROPERTY SECURITIES REGISTRATION.)

REAL ESTATE TAX STATEMENT - A Statement sent by the County Assessor to the property owner stating the assessed value of the real property and the amount of real property tax due.

Specifically the statement shows the name and address of the owner, legal description of the property, land value, building and improvement value, total value at 100 percent of fair market value, the taxable value which is the same as the total value, the levy rate and the general tax. The various elements which go to make up the general tax are also shown: state school support, county, port, city/road, fire, sewer/water, library, local school support and other.

If the first half of the annual tax is paid by April 30th, then the second half of the tax does not have to be paid until October 31st. (*See* ASSESSED VALUATION, EXCISE TAX ON REAL ESTATE SALES, NOTICE OF ASSESSMENT, PROPERTY TAX.)

REAL PROPERTY - All land and appurtenances to land, including buildings, structures, fixtures, fences, and improvements erected upon or affixed to the same; excluding, however, growing crops. The term "real property" refers to the interests, benefits and rights inherent in the ownership of real estate; e.g., "the bundle of rights."

That which is not real property is personal property. Because the law treats real property and personal property differently, it is important to distinguish between the two:

1. Instruments affecting **real property** must be in writing and should be recorded in the Office of the County Auditor, whereas instruments affecting personal property may be oral or written, and ordinarily they need not be recorded.

2. Tax laws make many important distinctions between real and personal property.

3. The law of the state where the real property is located governs the acquisition and transfer of title to land, including important matters such as rules of descent and probate. Personal property on the other hand is moveable, and would be governed by the laws of the jurisdiction in which it is located.

4. A leasehold, although an interest in real property, is a chattel real; it is governed by the laws and rules applicable to personal property. (*See* LAND, LEASEHOLD.)

REAL PROPERTY SECURITIES REGISTRATION - The process of disclosure and notification to the proper government agency of an issuer's intended real property security offering. A "security" for these purposes is defined as a contract, transaction or scheme whereby a person invests his/her money in a common enterprise and is led to expect profits from the efforts of a third party. The method by which some real estate is offered for sale may determine whether the offering constitutes a real property for security. Thus, for example, the offering of a limited partnership interest in a real estate venture involves the offering of a real property security.

All real property securities, unless exempt, must be registered with the federal Securities and Exchange Commission (SEC) and/or with the Washington Securities Division of the Department of Financial Institution. The two most frequently claimed exemptions are the intrastate exemption and the private offering exemption. An offering which is directed solely to residents of a state where the issuer is also a resident and doing business is exempted from registration with the SEC under the intrastate exemption. The offering must, nevertheless, be registered with the state, unless it is also exempt as a private offering. The private offering exemption rules are designed to exempt from the costly and time consuming registration process an offering which is of such a limited scope and directed to such a selected type of investor that the prospective purchasers do not need the protection afforded by the SEC disclosure requirements. The main thrust of the federal requirements for a private offering exemption is that the offering be made to investors sophisticated and knowledgeable enough to evaluate fully the risks of the investment.

If the issuer of the real property securities believes that he/she is exempt from registration, he/she may proceed to issue the securities without obtaining consent from the regulatory agency. Some issuers request a "no-action letter" from the SEC, in which the SEC, after reviewing the facts, states that it will not take any action against the issuer if the securities are issued without registration. It should be noted that if the SEC alleges that an exemption is not available, the burden of proving that the issue ought to be exempt is on the issuer. In this regard, the issuer should be careful to keep detailed records of all the transactions involved. If an issuer who is required to register a security sells a security without having it first registered, all purchasers of that security have the right to rescind the transaction and get their money back plus interest.

Even if exempt from registration, an offering is still subject to the anti-fraud provisions of the federal Securities Exchange Act of 1934, provided there is some contact with interstate commerce (such as the use of United States mails). The Act forbids fraudulent and deceptive practices in the offering. In addition, all local offerings are subject to Washington's comparable anti-fraud provisions.

The SEC also regards the offering of condominiums to be real property securities under certain circumstances, e.g., when the units are offered with emphasis placed on the economic benefits to be derived from the rental of the units or where there is a rental pool or mandatory rental arrangement. If a developer has not registered his/her condominium with the SEC, he/she should carefully instruct his/her salespeople not to make any representation as to the actual or estimated rental income that a purchaser may receive, but rather to leave the dissemination of any such information to those rental agents chosen by the purchaser. Such an offering of condominium units would be exempt from registration under the Washington Securities Act.

If the condominium is to be offered for sale in other states, the securities laws of such states (their Blue Sky laws) must be reviewed to determine whether registration in those states is necessary. (*See* ABSENTEE OWNER, ANTI-FRAUD PROVISION, INTRASTATE EXEMPTION, PRIVATE OFFERING, RED HERRING, RENTAL POOL, RESTRICTED REAL ESTATE SECURITIES, RULE 10-B5, RULE 146, RULE 147.)

REAL PROPERTY TAXES - *See* PROPERTY TAXES.

REALIZED GAIN - The profit made on the sale of a capital asset; usually the difference between the net sales price (amount realized) and the adjusted tax basis of the property. The recognized gain is that portion of the realized gain subject to tax.

REALTIST - A member of a national organization, generally composed of African American real estate brokers, known as the National Association of Real Estate Brokers. The association was formed in 1947 and has local boards in the principal cities of 40 states. In the past there was a chapter in Seattle. It is the oldest and largest of the minority trade associations serving the nation's housing industry. The Realtists subscribe to a Code of Ethics and strive to work for better housing in the communities they serve, under the theme of "Democracy in Housing."

REALTOR® - A registered word which may be used only by an active real estate broker or salesperson who is a member of the state and local real estate board affiliated with the National Association of Realtors. The designated broker of a real estate company must maintain Realtor status if he/she wishes to belong. Sales personnel have an option of holding a Realtor status or a Realtor-Associate status. In Washington the Associate status has been abolished. The term "REALTOR®" designates a professional who subscribes to the Code of Ethics promulgated by the National Association of Realtors and adopted by the Washington Association of Realtors to govern real estate practices of members of the Association.

The use of the name REALTOR® and the distinctive seal is strictly governed by the rules and regulations of the National Association. In Washington, it is further governed by the Real Estate License Law which has rules that it will not issue a real estate license to a brokerage firm with the word REALTOR® as an actual or integral part of the name. This ruling does not, however, preclude an individual or firm, if members of the National Association of Realtors, from using the designation REALTOR® in advertising, promotional materials, and letters. (*See* NATIONAL ASSOCIATION OF REALTORS, WASHINGTON ASSOCIATION OF REALTORS.)

REALTORS NATIONAL MARKETING INSTITUTE (RNMI) - A professional organization affiliated with the National Association of Realtors, dedicated to education in areas of marketing, income property investment analysis, and office management. It awards the designation of Certified Commercial and Investment Member (CCIM), Certified Residential Broker (CRB), and Certified Residential Salesperson (CRS).

REALTY - Land and everything permanently affixed thereto. (*See* LAND, PROPERTY, REAL ESTATE, REAL PROPERTY.)

REASONABLE TIME - A fair length of time that may be allowed or required for an act to be completed, considering the nature of the act and the surrounding circumstances. It is best to state a definite time for performance of a contract, otherwise the courts will imply a "reasonable time," which could vary considerably from case to case.

If the parties state in their contract a definite time for performance and add that "time is of the essence," then a court would not allow a reasonable time to perform after the expiration of the definite stated time (date).

A lender's decision to exercise a "due-on-sale" clause must be done within a reasonable time after becoming aware of the event that triggers the clause. (*See* OFFER AND ACCEPTANCE.)

REBATE - 1. A reduction or kickback of a stipulated charge. A property manager may not accept any commission, rebate or profit on expenditures made in behalf of an owner, without the owner's knowledge and consent.

2. Also, a return of an unearned finance charge where there has been a prepayment of the debt. (*See* RULE OF 78's.)

It is permissible for a broker to rebate a portion of the broker's commission to a principal (seller or buyer) in the real estate transaction. The rationale is that the payment is not for the performance of any act for which a real estate license is required since the principals are exempt. It is simply a refunded or reduced commission. However, full disclosure to the seller is required if the listing agent or seller's agent is going to rebate part of the commission to either principal.

RECAPTURE CLAUSE - A clause usually found in percentage leases, especially in shopping center leases, giving the landlord the right to terminate the lease (and thus "recapture" the premises) if the tenant does not maintain a specified minimum amount of business. A "recapture clause" may also be used to give a ground lessee the right to purchase the fee after a set period of time has elapsed.

RECAPTURE OF DEPRECIATION - All depreciation taken on depreciable real property in excess of the amount allowed under the straight-line method is subject to the recapture provisions of the Internal Revenue Code, which had the effect of taxing this excess at ordinary income rates.

Sales of depreciable realty before May 7, 1997 were subject to a variety of recapture rules depending on when the property was placed in service, its use, and the method of depreciation. These rules no longer apply to sales of depreciable realty sold after May 6, 1997.

Sales of depreciable realty after May 6, 1997, are subject to new recapture rules. Gain attributed to prior depreciation deductions may qualify for a 25% maximum tax rate. The method of allocating gain to depreciation is explained in IRS instructions to Schedule D and Form 4797.

Even though depreciation may be taxed at a higher rate than a long term capital gain rate when the property is sold, a knowledgeable investor realizes that dollars saved in taxes in the early years of investment can earn substantial income before those same dollars go to pay taxes at the time of the recapture of the depreciation. Also, if a tax deferred exchange should take place, the tax on the depreciation taken is deferred (*See* CAPITAL GAIN.)

RECAPTURE RATE - An appraisal term describing that rate at which invested capital will be returned over the period of time a prudent investor would expect to recapture his/her investment in a wasting asset. (*See* CAP RATE.)

RECASTING - The process of redesigning existing loans, especially where there is a default. The term may be extended, with the interest rate adjusted periodically to alleviate the pressure on the borrower. Care must be taken to avoid the risk of intervening liens attaining priority over the recast loan. In some cases, the lender may prefer to go along with a delinquent construction loan until the building is sold because a modification and recasting of the loan might jeopardize their lien priorities. (*See* FORBEARANCE.)

RECEIPT - A written acknowledgment of having received something. The standard Purchase and Sale Agreement serves as a receipt, in addition to being the offer to purchase and acceptance form. Thus, a real estate agent should not complete the receipt portion of the agreement unless he/she has, in fact, received the buyer's deposit. (*See* DEPOSIT, REAL ESTATE PURCHASE AND SALE AGREEMENT.)

RECEIVER - An independent party appointed by a court to impartially receive, preserve and manage property which is involved in litigation, pending final disposition of the matter before the court, as in a bankruptcy action. A receiver would not need a real estate license to sell real estate under his/her control, but the sale would require court approval.

RECIPROCITY - The practice of mutual exchanges of privileges.

Some states have reciprocal arrangements for recognizing and granting licenses to licensed salesmen from other states. Washington has limited reciprocity arrangements for real estate licenses. Washington will recognize experience as a licensee in another state for purposes of satisfying the two year experience requirement to be eligible for a broker's examination. Washington has agreements with several states which have similar licensing examinations that a portion of the out-of-state examination will be accepted. However, all prospective real estate licensees must pass an examination on Washington law prior to applying for a license.

Washington has a reciprocal agreement with the states of Oregon and Idaho which allows a real estate broker from Washington to receive a nonresident's broker's license in those states after passing the appropriate portion of their state's real estate examination. The Washington real estate broker is not required to maintain an office but must maintain a trust account in a depository in those states. After a Washington real estate broker has received a nonresident broker's license in either of the states, his/her sales people may qualify for a nonresident salesmen license by passing the appropriate part of the state licensing examination they wish to be licensed in. (*See* EXAMINATION, REAL ESTATE LICENSING.)

The Realtor's Associations in Washington, Idaho, Oregon and Nevada have signed reciprocity agreements wherein these States recognize the successful completion of GRI 100 and 200 if taken in one of the other States for the purpose of awarding the Graduate, Realtor's Institute designation. (*See* GRI.)

RECISSION OR RIGHT OF RECISSION - This regulation is part of the Truth in Lending Act, Regulation Z which applies to the refinance of real property. A three-day business period (72 hours) that allows the borrower to cancel the transaction. During the recission period, funds are withheld pending the decision of the borrower. Under certain emergency circumstances, this requirement can be waived.

RECITAL OF CONSIDERATION - A statement of what constitutes the consideration for a particular transaction. While technically a deed does not require consideration to pass title to real property, it is good practice to recite some consideration, especially to support any covenants or promises in the deed. The consideration recited in the deed need not be the actual consideration, and is frequently stated nominally as: "for $10 and other good and valuable consideration." (*See* NOMINAL CONSIDERATION.)

RECLAMATION - The process of converting wasted natural resources into productive assets, such as desert land being reclaimed through irrigation, or swamp land being filled in.

RECOGNITION - Recognition is a precise tax term meaning that the transaction is a taxable event. If a gain or loss is "recognized," the gain is taxable and the loss is deductible. Usually, recognition occurs at the time of the sale or exchange if boot is received. Some exceptions are involuntary conversion and some sales between related parties. (*See* RESIDENCES, RECAPTURE OF DEPRECIATION, TAX DEFERRED EXCHANGE.)

RECOGNITION CLAUSE - A clause included in a Real Estate Contract used to purchase a tract of land for subdivision and development; provides for the protection of the rights of the ultimate buyers of individual lots in case of default on the part of the developer/promoter. It is similar to a nondisturbance clause in a commercial office building loan.

RECONCILIATION - The final step in an appraisal process, in which the appraiser reconciles the estimates of value received from the market-data, cost, and income approaches to arrive at his/her final estimate of market value for the subject property. Also called correlation.

The balancing of entries in a double-entry accounting system.

RECONVEYANCE - A term pertaining to deed of trust financing of real estate. The trustee under a deed of trust normally receives from the beneficiary under the deed of trust a written request to reconvey stating that the obligations secured by the deed of trust have been fully satisfied. The trustee reconveys without any warranties to the grantor (borrower). A release of the security under a deed of trust. (*See* DEED OF TRUST, PARTIAL RECONVEYANCE.)
Reference: RCW 61.24.

RECORD OWNER - The owner of property as shown by an examination of public records; the one having record title; the owner of record. (See CHAIN OF TITLE, TITLE INSURANCE.)

RECORDING - The act of entering into the public record the written instruments affecting the title to real property (County Auditor's office) in the County in which the real property is located, such as deeds, mortgages, real estate contracts, options, assignments, and the like. There is also a body of public records apart from the real estate recording system that has a bearing on the quality of title. A title searcher would also check, for example, public records regarding probate, marriage, taxes, and judgments.

Under Washington's Recording Act, all instruments affecting title to real property within the state, including leases for a term of more than one year, can be recorded in the Office of the County Auditor where the property is situated. This Act was designed to encourage all persons having an interest in real property to disclose that interest in the public records, thereby protecting others dealing with the property from secret, unrecorded deeds and security liens. From a practical point of view, the recording acts give legal priority to those interests that are recorded first.

Proper recordation imparts constructive notice to all the world of the existence of the recorded document and its contents; it protects innocent purchasers for value who act in ignorance of an unrecorded instrument; and it protects the grantee in the event that the deed is altered or lost. Any conveyance **not** properly recorded is **void** as against any subsequent purchaser, lessee, mortgagee or beneficiary **in good faith and for a valuable consideration** who, without having actual notice of the unrecorded conveyance, records his/her subsequent interest in the property. The act of recordation only protects subsequent purchasers **for value** and **not** donees or beneficiaries under a will; nor does it protect against interests which arise by operation of law rather than by recordable document, such as prescriptive and implied easements and title by adverse possession. (In the case of adverse possession, however, the adverse possessor's physical possession of the property would have provided constructive notice to the subsequent purchaser of the possessor's interest in the property and thus he/she would not be in "good faith.") Further, the act of recordation raises a presumption (rebuttable) that the instrument has been validly delivered, and that it is authentic. On the other hand, failure to record a document does not impair its validity as between the parties thereto and all other parties having notice of its existence.

Property tax liens and special assessment liens need not be recorded, since they are considered to be matters of public record.

Thus, the system of recording creates a hierarchy of claims against a property with priority to be determined by the order in which the claims are recorded. Except for certain governmental liens which automatically take first priority, the order of recorded priority will not be disturbed absent a subordination or recordation of a release.

The top left-hand portion of the document should contain the name and address of the person presenting the document for recording or the name and address of the person to whom the document should be sent after recording. (*See* CHAIN OF TITLE, CONSTRUCTIVE NOTICE, EXCISE TAX ON REAL ESTATE SALES, GRANTOR-GRANTEE INDEX, NOTARY PUBLIC, PRIORITY, SUBORDINATION CLAUSE, SUBSEQUENT BONA FIDE PURCHASER.)
Reference: RCW 65.08.

For some unknown reason, the Federal Bureau of Land Management (BLM) does not file all of their surveys with the County Auditor. Rather, some of their surveys are filed in Washington D.C. Therefore, when dealing with land that borders on federal property, e.g., U.S. Forest Land, U.S. Park Department, the prudent buyer will check with the BLM to see if it has a survey that impacts the property.

RECOURSE NOTE - A debt instrument under which the lender can take action against the borrower or endorser personally rather than foreclose on the security for the note . (*See* DEED OF TRUST, DEFICIENCY JUDGMENT, MORTGAGE.)

RECTANGULAR SURVEY - Another name for the Government Survey method for determining property boundaries, which is used in about 30 states, including Washington. (*See* GOVERNMENT SURVEY.)

REDEMPTION, EQUITABLE RIGHT OF - The right of a mortgagor who has defaulted on the mortgage note to redeem the property by paying off the entire mortgage note, court costs, attorney's fees and any accrued interest from the date of foreclosure within a specified statutory redemption period.

Generally, subsequent to the public auction in a mortgage foreclosure, the borrower retains the legal title to the property. The purchaser at the auction, who may or may not be the mortgagee, does not receive title to the property but merely receives a certificate of sale authorized by the foreclosure proceedings.

The statutory period of redemption in Washington is generally one year. If the security instrument contains a nonagricultural proviso and if the right to a deficiency judgment is waived, then the period of redemption is only eight months. When nonagricultural property improved with a structure is abandoned for six months or more and no payments are made on the debt during such period, the borrower forfeits his/her rights of redemption. Ordinarily, the borrower must yield possession to the successful bidder on the date of the sale, but if the property is properly declared as the borrower's "homestead" he/she is entitled to retain possession through the entire period of redemption. (*See* DEED OF TRUST, FORECLOSURE, MORTGAGE.)

REDEVELOPMENT - The improvement of cleared or undeveloped land, usually in an urban renewal area.

RED FLAG - Something that would warn a reasonably observant person of a potential problem, thus requiring further investigation. A broker who spots uneven floors or water-stained ceilings is on notice to inquire about soil settlement and roof leakage problems. (*See* MISREPRESENTATION.)

RED HERRING - A slang term describing a prospectus for the sale of a security which is filed with the Securities and Exchange Commission but which has not yet become "effective." The term "red herring" derives from the red printing along the left-hand margin of the prospectus, which states that a registration statement has been filed but is subject to change, and that the securities covered in this prospectus may not be sold before the registration statement becomes effective. (*See* REAL PROPERTY SECURITIES REGISTRATION.)

REDISCOUNT RATE - The rate of interest charged by the Federal Reserve Bank for loans to member banks, also called the *discount rate*. The rediscount rate has an indirect effect on the interest rates charged by member banks to the public and the supply of funds for loans.

REDLINING - A practice by a lending institution to restrict the number of loans it will make or the loan-to-value ratio it will use in certain areas of a community. A redlining policy may be so severe that the lending institution has a strict prohibition against lending any money in certain areas of the community. The usual justification for redlining is that the lender wants to limit the risks in an area that is deteriorating. The lender discriminates against a range of risks rather than an individual.

A redlining policy based on the fact that a certain area of a community is racially integrated is illegal and is in violation of Title VIII of the Civil Rights Act of 1968, and the Federal Open Housing Law anti-redlining regulations. (*See* FEDERAL FAIR HOUSING LAW, HOME MORTGAGE DISCLOSURE ACT.)

Under the Home Mortgage Disclosure Act, lenders must disclose information as to how they determine their pattern of makings loans in given geographic areas. A related area of concern is insurance redlining, which may be covered under the provision in the Federal Fair Housing law prohibiting conduct which would tend to make housing unavailable.

The Federal Home Loan Bank Board has also issued a regulation prohibiting redlining. It states that refusal to lend in a particular area solely because of the age of the homes or the income level in a neighborhood may be discriminatory in effect, since minority group persons are more likely to purchase used housing and to live in low-income neighborhoods. The racial composition of the neighborhood where the loan is to be made is always an improper underwriting consideration.

REDUCTION CERTIFICATE - An instrument which shows the amount of the unpaid balance of a mortgage or deed of trust, the rate of interest and the date of maturity. A reduction certificate is normally required from a mortgagee or beneficiary when a prospective purchaser is to assume or take title subject to an existing mortgage or deed of trust; thus, the mortgagee or beneficiary cannot later claim that the mortgage or deed of trust amount or terms were different from those stated in the certificate. The reduction certificate is also useful at the time of closing because the buyer has to pay the difference between what the loan balance actually is and the purchase price. The reduction certificate is similar to an estoppel certificate, except that it is executed by the mortgagee or beneficiary. The reduction certificate is useful since only the original amount of the loan is a matter of public record; any reduction of principal is only known between the parties. The instrument is acknowledged, but need not be recorded. (*See* ESTOPPEL CERTIFICATE OR LETTER.)

RE-ENTRY - The repossession of real property in accordance with a legal right reserved when the original possession was transferred. The grantor of a fee simple subject to a condition has the right to re-entry upon the breach of that condition. In essence, it is a power of termination.

The right of re-entry should be distinguished from the right of entry that a landlord possesses to go in and inspect leased premises.

REFEREE - A disinterested, neutral party appointed by a court to arbitrate, investigate or settle some dispute or legal matter.

REFERRAL - The act of recommending or referring. A referral in real estate is a client who has been obtained through the efforts or recommendation of another person. A broker can compensate or split commissions with a person who refers a client if that person is a licensed broker in Washington or is a broker licensed in another state. If the person is a licensed salesman in Washington, the referral fee must be paid through the salesman's employing broker. While a seller can pay a referral fee to anyone, the person receiving the fee may be deemed to be acting as a real estate salesman and, if that is the case, must have a real estate license. An unlicensed individual accepting a referral fee would be guilty of a gross misdemeanor. (*See* FINDER'S FEE, LICENSING LAW.)

REFERRAL AGENCY - A licensed brokerage company in which part-time licensed salespeople agree to perform no other brokerage service but to obtain leads on prospective buyers and sellers. These leads are then assigned to other agents and the referral agency receives a fee upon a sale. Also refers to a brokerage company participating in a national or regional network of relocating services.

REFINANCE - The act of obtaining a new loan to pay off an existing loan; the process of paying off one loan with the proceeds from another. Properties are frequently refinanced when interest rates drop and/or the property has appreciated in value. Sometimes buyers purchase a property by way of a real estate contract with the expectation of either selling the property before the balance under the real estate contract becomes due or refinancing at better terms and interest rates if they should become available.

Income properties are frequently refinanced by investors seeking additional capital with which to purchase other investment properties. Large real estate holdings are often amassed in this manner, a technique known as pyramiding through refinancing.

REFORMATION - A legal action to correct or modify a contract or deed which has not accurately reflected the intentions of the parties due to some mechanical error, such as a typographical error in the legal description. If one of the parties will not execute a correction deed, the other party can seek a court order reforming such deed; also called a reformation deed. A grantor under a general warranty deed usually agrees to perform any necessary act of reformation pursuant to his/her covenant of further assurance. (*See* CORRECTION DEED.)

REGIONAL SHOPPING CENTER - A large shopping center containing from 70 to 225 stores and more than 400,000 square feet of leasable area.

REGISTERED LAND - Land registered with the County Registrar under the Torren's System of registration. (*See* TORREN'S SYSTEM.)

REGRESSION - A principle of appraisal which states that, as between dissimilar properties, the worth of the better property is adversely affected by the presence of the lesser quality property. Thus, in a neighborhood where the homes average in the $150,000 range, a better-built structure, which in another neighborhood would be worth at least

$200,000, would tend to be valued closer to $150,000. The principle of progression is the opposite; e.g., the worth of a lesser object is increased by being located among better objects. (*See* OVER-IMPROVEMENT.)

REGULATION - A rule or order prescribed for management or government, as in the rules and regulations of the Real Estate Commission.

REGULATION A - A special exemption from standard SEC registration of a security issue where the aggregate amount of the offering is less than $1,500,000. Even if the issue qualifies for exemption under Regulation A, the developer must still file a short form registration and provide prospective purchasers with an offering circular containing much of the same information contained in a formal prospectus. Thus, Regulation A is not really an exemption from registration but rather a simpler form of registration. (*See* REAL PROPERTY SECURITIES REGISTRATION.)

REGULATION T - A federal regulation, administered by the Federal Reserve Board, governing the extension of credit arrangements for the extension of credit by securities brokers and dealers. The Federal Reserve Board lists only certain securities upon which security dealers can extend credit, and then restricts the amount of credit which may be extended by means of margin requirements.

The possible application of Regulation T to condominium securities has been the subject of much controversy between developers, the Federal Reserve Board, and the SEC, because condominium securities were not approved securities upon which credit could be arranged. This continued interpretation would have had obvious adverse effects upon the financing and sales of condominium securities. However, the Federal Reserve Board effectively exempted these securities from Regulation T.

REGULATION Z - *See* TRUTH-IN-LENDING.

REHABILITATE - To restore to a former or improved condition, such as when buildings are renovated and modernized.

Rehabilitation may include additional new construction, buildings, or additions but is usually performed without changing the basic plan, form, or style of a structure. In urban renewal projects, rehabilitation is the restoration to good condition of deteriorated structures, neighborhoods, and public facilities. Neighborhood rehabilitation encompasses structural rehabilitation and in addition may extend to street improvements and a provision of such amenities as parks and playgrounds. The Internal Revenue Code provides for certain tax benefits in connection with the rehabilitation of real property.

REINSTATEMENT - To bring something back to its prior position, as in restoring a lapsed insurance policy or restoring a defaulted loan to paid-up status. A borrower in default under a deed of trust can avoid a foreclosure sale by reinstating the loan prior to foreclosure. (*See* DEED OF TRUST.)

REINVESTMENT RATE - The interest rate at which the cash flows from income-producing property, particularly the portion of the cash flows that represent a recovery of capital, are presumed to be invested. (*See* INTERNAL RATE OF RETURN.)

REIT - *See* REAL ESTATE INVESTMENT TRUSTS.

REJECTION - The refusal of an offer by the *offeree*, the person to whom the offer is made. A rejection has the legal effect of extinguishing the offer. (*See* ACCEPTANCE, OFFER.)

RELATED PARTIES - Parties standing in a certain defined relationship to each other; parties may be related because of blood or fiduciary relationship or ownership interest in a corporation, among others. Under the Internal Revenue Code, any loss on the sale of property between related parties may be nondeductible.

Installment treatment is denied if depreciable property is sold to a related party. Additionally, the taxpayer can be taxed on a second sale by the related party if it occurs within two years of the initial sale and before all payments from the first installment sale are made. Under the tax law, related parties include all entities more than 50 percent owned, directly or indirectly, by the taxpayer. For installment sales between related parties where the payments are contingent in amount, but where their fair market value can be ascertained, (1) basis is recovered ratably, and (2) the buyer cannot increase basis in the property before the seller includes the amount in income. (*See* EXCHANGE, IMPUTED INTEREST.)

RELATION BACK DOCTRINE - In a valid escrow, there is an irrevocable deposit of the executed deed, purchase money and instructions into the escrow pending performance of the escrow conditions. Under the relation back doctrine, the death of the grantor does not terminate the escrow or revoke the agent's authority to deliver an executed deed. The delivery of the deed to the grantee "relates back" to the date it was originally deposited with the escrow agent, and it is considered as if the grantor made the delivery to the grantee **before** the death of the grantor. When the escrow conditions are performed, title passes to the grantee and the deed can be formally delivered to the grantee without any probate court approval. (*See* DELIVERY, ESCROW, TRUE ESCROW.)

RELEASE - The discharge or relinquishment of a right, claim or privilege. Since a formal release is a contract relieving a person from any further legal obligation, it must contain a valuable consideration. Releases involving real property transactions should be acknowledged and recorded. A developer should make provision in a loan agreement on undeveloped land for the release of the loan lien as to land dedicated to a governmental unit or easement for utilities installation purposes. (*See* PARTIAL RECONVEYANCE, PARTIAL RELEASE, RELEASE CLAUSE.)

RELEASE CLAUSE - A provision found in many blanket mortgages or deeds of trust enabling the borrower to obtain partial releases of specific parcels from the mortgage or deed of trust upon the payment of, typically, a larger-than-pro-rata portion of the loan. Most lenders insert a clause that no partial release will be issued if the borrower is in default under the loan agreement.

Many transactions involving incremental development of land in Washington employ the use of release clauses. As the developer sells off the subdivided lots, a portion of the sales proceeds is used to partially satisfy the mortgage or deed of trust. In return, the lender executes and records a release of the particular parcels sold so that the purchasers can obtain clear title. Usually the release clause contains a formula for the release payments; for example, the payment of a sum which is in the proportion that the area of the land to be released bears to the total area of the land under the blanket loan agreement multiplied by some factor, e.g., 125 percent of the original loan amount. For example, if there were five parcels covered under the blanket mortgage or deed of trust, the lender might require the payment of one-fourth of the loan before he/she will release one parcel.

The developer could insert in the release clause a provision to the effect that all payments made on the note for which the developer did not request a release should apply to release payments. Thus, if one parcel can be released upon payment of $20,000 and the developer has already reduced the principal on the note by $8,000, then the $8,000 should be considered part of the release payment so that only an additional $12,000 is required. The description of the parcels to be released should be definite enough to avoid the argument that the provision is unenforceable for vagueness.

A release clause may also be put in a real estate contract where normally a warranty deed would be delivered to a portion of the property in partial fulfillment of the contract (often referred to as a partial fulfillment deed). This is commonly known as a deed release provision. (*See* BLANKET MORTGAGE, PARTIAL RECONVEYANCE, PARTIAL RELEASE, RELEASE.)

RELICTION - The gradual recession of water from the usual watermark and an increase of the land, as where land that once was covered by water becomes uncovered. The uncovered land is treated as alluvion and the rules of accretion apply to the ownership of this new land. This new land belongs to the riparian owner. (*See* ACCRETION.)

RELINQUISHED PROPERTY - The initial property transferred in a delayed tax-deferred exchange; sometimes called the up-leg property. The property for which the exchange is made is called the replacement property. (*See* DELAYED EXCHANGES.)

RELOCATION CLAUSE - A clause in a lease giving the landlord the right to relocate a tenant. This situation frequently occurs when an older building is renovated, or when smaller tenants are relocated to give the landlord flexibility in accommodating larger tenants' expansion requirements.

RELOCATION COMPANY - A company retained by large corporations to help their employees move from one location to another. A primary function of this service is to purchase the transferee's home so that the transferee will have the funds to locate new housing and not have to worry about the uncertainties of first selling the present home. The employee's corporation usually pays all the costs incurred by the relocation company in its buying and reselling of the employee's present home.

The relocation company's offer to purchase is usually based on two or more independent fee appraisals. Since the relocation company has purchased the property, it is concerned with marketing the property with a combination of sales price, carrying costs, closing costs, and cost of repairs and improvements as they are related to the estimated cost of services. Relocation companies frequently select a larger brokerage company in a community to handle the sales of all its properties. In addition, the relocation companies insist that their properties be listed in the multiple-listing service to get the maximum exposure.

REMAINDER ESTATE - A future interest in real estate created at the same time and by the same instrument as another estate, and limited to arise immediately upon the termination of the prior estate. For example, Joe Iberville owns a property in fee simple and conveys the property "to Barry Bienville and, upon Bienville's death, to Cora Conti and her heirs." Ms. Conti has a remainder estate, which is vested because the estate automatically passes to Ms. Conti and her heirs upon the death of Barry Bienville. Whereas a reversion is an estate which is left in the grantor by operation of law when he/she conveys a lesser estate, a remainder is a future estate created in favor of some third party.

A remainder may be either vested or contingent. It is vested if the only uncertainty is the actual date of the termination of the prior estate. It is contingent where there is some other uncertainty. For example, Hoyt wills (devises) his farm to his son as a life estate with the remainder going to his son's living children, but if there are no children, then to Hoyt's brother, Brock. Brock has a contingent remainder, which ceases if the son dies leaving a child. (*See* REMAINDERMAN, REVERSION.)

A gift of remainder interest in real property is subject to federal gift tax rules. Since it does not qualify as a "present interest," the remainder interest does not qualify for the $10,000 annual exclusion. The IRS will compute the value of the remainder interest by using tables based upon the life expectancy of the donor, and a discount factor. (*See* RULE AGAINST PERPETUITIES.)

REMAINDERMAN - One entitled to take an estate in remainder. For example, Mr. Lee, seized in fee simple of Blackacre, grants a life estate in Blackacre to Mr. Kim, remainder to Mr. Park for life, then to Mr. Yee in fee. Thus, Mr. Kim has a life estate, which upon his death remains away to Mr. Park for his life and then, upon Mr. Park's death, it passes in fee to Mr. Yee, who is also a remainderman. Although Mr. Yee has a future interest, he still has some present rights such as the right to bring action against the current possessor from committing waste. (*See* REMAINDER ESTATE)

REMISE - To give up, release, or quitclaim interest in a property (*See* QUITCLAIM.)

REMT - *See* REAL ESTATE MORTGAGE TRUST.

RENDERING - An artist's or architect's interpretation, in perspective, of a completed development, usually in color or ink.

RENEGOTIABLE-RATE MORTGAGE (R.R.M., or ROLLOVER) - A short-term loan secured by a long-term adjustable rate mortgage, with interest renegotiated at the time of established automatic renewal periods. While modeled after the Canadian Rollover Mortgage, there is a big difference: under the Canadian plan, the mortgage itself is renewed rather than short-term interest adjustments of a long-term mortgage.

Under the original plan, as approved by the Federal Home Loan Bank Board (FHLBB), a three, four, and five year renegotiable rate loan would be secured by a long-term mortgage and would be repayable in equal monthly installments. The interest rate would be adjusted at renewal periods and would be computed based on a national mortgage index representing the average interest rate of all conventional mortgages written by savings and loan associations each month. (Table 5.5.1 of the FHLBB Journal)

Since the introduction of the adjustable mortgage loan, many of the original restrictions on RRM no longer apply. (*See* ADJUSTABLE RATE LOAN, CREATIVE FINANCING.)

RENEGOTIATION OF LEASE - The review of an existing lease after a specified period of time to negotiate anew the lease terms. The most common reason for the renegotiation of a lease is to establish a new annual rent for an additional period based on changed economic conditions. Many leases provide that renegotiated rent is to be based on mutual agreement and, failing that, by an independent appraisal based upon a rate of return to the fee owner equal to some specific rate fixed when the lease is first negotiated. An alternative method sometimes used is the use of outside indicators by which the rent is increased at set intervals, e.g., U.S. Labor Department Cost of Living Indicator. In listing a leasehold, a broker should be careful to verify the renegotiation period and terms, if any. (*See* CPI, GROUND LEASE, LEASEHOLD.)

RENEWAL OPTION - A covenant in a lease which gives the lessee the right to extend the lease term for a certain period, on specified terms. Usually the landlord cannot enforce an automatic renewal against the tenant unless the landlord gives prior notice of the renewal. The covenant should state whether the option to renew is transferable in the event the lease is assigned. (*See* EXTENSION.)

RENT - Fixed periodic payment made by a tenant or occupant of property to the owner for the possession and use thereof, usually by prior agreement of the parties. The common law rule is that rent is not due until the end of the term. However, almost all leases and rental agreements state that rent is due in advance. Appreciation or depreciation of the property does not affect the amount of rent due during the time the written lease is in effect. (*See* CPI, GROUND LEASE, LEASEHOLD.)

The Landlord Tenant Act specifies that, absent any language to the contrary, rent is due in advance. The Act also provides that when the tenancy is for month-to-month, the landlord cannot increase the rent except upon 30 days prior written notice. (*See* LANDLORD TENANT ACT, STEP-UP LEASE.)

RENT CONTROL - Regulation by state or local governmental agencies restricting the amount of rent landlords can charge their tenants; such regulation is a valid exercise of the state's police power.

In 1981, the State of Washington adopted legislation which preempted the right of local municipalities or counties to pass rent control laws. Cities, towns and counties are prohibited from imposing rent controls on single-family or multiple unit residential structures or sites. They are permitted to regulate the rent charged for properties under public management and low-income rental housing made possible by joint public-private agreements. Voluntary agreements between private persons and cities, towns, or counties to regulate rent are permitted. Local ordinances that provide rent control of floating home moorage sites are also permitted.

RENT ESCALATION - Adjustment of rent by the owner to reflect changes in either the cost of maintaining the property or the cost of living index. Such escalation clauses are common in non-residential rental agreements. (*See* CPI, GRADUATED RENTAL LEASE, LEASE.)

RENT INSURANCE - Insurance for a landlord that protects his/her investment against loss due to fire or other perils which result in the space being unavailable for rent and thus the tenant not being liable for paying rent. Such insurance is normally written as a rider on the fire insurance policy carried by the landlord.

RENT ROLL - A list of tenants showing the unit occupied and the rent paid by each. Certified rent rolls are independently verified and are sometimes required by lenders. (*See* ESTOPPEL CERTIFICATE OR LETTER.)

RENT UP - (1) The process of filling a new building with tenants. (2) The requirement of a lender that the mortgagor (developer/owner) achieve the leasing of a stated amount of space in the building as a prerequisite to a permanent lender "taking out" the interim construction lender. The developer must present certified rent rolls which are usually checked by the lender's servicing agent. If the developer does not meet the rent achievement amount, a floor loan for a reduced amount will have to be disbursed and gap financing sought. (*See* FLOOR LOAN, GAP FINANCING.)

RENTABLE AREA - As standardized by the Building Owners and Managers Association International, rentable area of an office on a multiple tenancy floor is computed by measuring to the inside finish of permanent outer building walls, or to the glass line if at least 50 percent of the outer building wall is glass, to the office side of corridors and/or other permanent partitions, and to the center of partitions that separate the premises from adjoining rentable areas.

No deductions are made for columns and projections necessary to the buildings. (*See* USABLE AREA.)

RENTAL AGENCY - Any person, who for compensation or other valuable consideration, acts or attempts to act as an intermediary between a person seeking to lease, sublease, or assign a housing accommodation and a person seeking to acquire a lease, sublease, or assignment of a housing accommodation. In Washington, such a person has to obtain a real estate license. (*See* LICENSING LAW, PROPERTY MANAGEMENT.)
Reference: RCW 18.85.

RENTAL AGREEMENT - An agreement, written or oral, which establishes or modifies the terms, conditions, rules, regulations, or any other provisions concerning the use and occupancy of a dwelling unit and premises; a lease on residential property. (*See* LEASE.)

RENTAL POOL - A rental arrangement whereby participating owners of rental apartments agree to have their apartment units available for rental as determined by the rental agent, and then share in the profits and losses of all the rental apartments in the pool according to an agreed upon formula. Some rental pool plans base the payment of profits on the number of days that the unit is actually rented, and others base it on the number of days the unit was available for rental. If a condominium is offered for sale and the offer includes participation in a rental pool arrangement, the offeror must have the condominium registered with the SEC or Washington Securities Division as a security. **After** a project has been sold out to individual owners, the owners can form a rental pool without the need of SEC registration. (*See* REAL PROPERTY SECURITIES REGISTRATION, VACATION HOME.)

RENTER'S INSURANCE - An insurance policy for renters that insures the contents and personal property of the renter and provides liability coverage in case an invited guest would be injured. Since a renter does not own either the dwelling or other private structures on the property, the dwellings are not insured by the renter's insurance policy. (*See* INSURANCE.)

RENUNCIATION - The action by a person to abandon a right or interest acquired without transferring the right to someone else, e.g., a property owner could renounce his/her right to a prescriptive right to an easement across a neighboring property.

REORGANIZATION RATE - A reduced charge by a title insurance company for a new policy if a previous policy on the same property was recently issued.

REPAIRS - On going expenditures to maintain a property or to restore to as close as possible to the original condition; minor alterations made to maintain the property rather than extend the useful life of the property. The cost of repairs normally is tax deductible as a business expense if the property is income producing property. Substantial repairs, however, will be treated as capital expenditures, and will thus increase the basis of the property and will have tax consequences as a depreciable item and not an immediate write off. Capital expenditures involve changes in either the form of material of the building or the renewal of any substantial part of it; for example, a new addition or a replacement of carpeting or roof. The test as to whether or not an expenditure is a repair or a capital expenditure is whether the expenditure results in an increase in the useful life of the asset. If not, it is a deductible maintenance and repair expense. (*See* BASIS, CAPITAL EXPENDITURE, DEPRECIATION.)

There is no legal requirement that repairs be made by the lessee or lessor. The lessee must return the property in the same condition as it was leased, less reasonable wear and tear. To eliminate disputes, the lease should specify who is responsible for various types of repair. A tenant is not under a duty to make extraordinary repairs unless he/she willfully or negligently caused the damage.

Under the Washington Landlord Tenant Act, however, the landlord has a specific duty to keep the premises in a habitable condition. When repairs are needed to maintain the premises in a habitable condition, the landlord must commence repairs within a specific time period, depending on the nature of repair, or the tenant has several options, including moving out. (*See* ABATEMENT, LANDLORD TENANT ACT.)
Reference: RCW 59.18.

With respect to the sale of the property, it is strongly recommended that the parties specify in the Purchase and Sale Agreement, when applicable, the items which the seller shall fix prior to closing and who will fix the item (e.g., an individual licensed to perform the function) and the method by which the escrow agent will know that the repairs have been satisfactorily completed. For tax purposes, the seller can deduct from the selling price the cost of fix-up repairs made within 90-days of the date of sale and paid for within 30 days of closing. Such eleventh-hour expenses are treated as part of the selling cost. (*See* FIXING-UP EXPENSES.)

REPLACEMENT COST - *See* REPRODUCTION COST.

REPLACEMENT PROPERTY - In a tax-deferred exchange, the property exchanged for. The replacement property must be identified and acquired within strict time limitations from the date of sale of the relinquished property. (*See* DEFERRED OR DELAYED EXCHANGE, RELINQUISHED PROPERTY.)

REPLACEMENT RESERVE - A fund established to replace assets when they wear out. Such a reserve is particularly appropriate when an owner has property in use that has an expected short life such as the carpeting, stoves and refrigerators in an apartment building. Condominium associations maintain such a reserve to maintain the common area to minimize the need for special assessments.

REPLEVIN - Legal proceedings brought to recover possession of personal property unlawfully taken, as where a landlord has unlawfully taken the personal belongings of the tenant due to the tenant's failure to pay the rent. (*See* DISTRAINT, LANDLORD TENANT ACT.)

REPORTING REQUIREMENTS - Refers to Internal Revenue Service rules that require the escrow agent to report sales or exchanges of residences with four or fewer units. Responsibility to file the IRS Form 1099-B is with the settlement (escrow) agent, the one preparing the closing statement. If there is no settlement agent, the order of responsibility as to whom must submit the report are attorneys, title companies, mortgage lenders and real estate brokers. (*See* ESCROW.)

REPRODUCTION COST - The cost, on the basis of current prices, of reproducing a new replica property with the same or fairly similar material. Most appraisers estimate reproduction cost by the comparative cost method, in which estimates are made on the basis of the current cost to construct buildings of similar size, design and quality of construction. Other methods are the quantity-survey method and the unit-in-place method. Comparisons are usually made on a square foot or cubic foot basis.

Reproduction cost is often used synonymously with replacement cost, but the terms are different. Reproduction cost refers to exact duplication, whereas replacement cost is the current cost of replacing a building with one having the same functional ability but which can be of different size, materials, design, etc. Reproduction cost relates to the physical property whereas replacement cost relates to the functional use of the property. Reproduction costs are important for insurance claims. After arriving at the reproduction cost new, it is necessary to deduct the amount of accrued depreciation due to physical, functional and economic causes to complete the appraisal. (*See* COST APPROACH.)

REQUIRED NET YIELD - The purchasers of mortgages/deeds of trust, including lenders and investors who buy from originators, secondary market conduits buying from originators, and pension funds buying from those who loan on real estate, all have a common goal called the required net yield (RNY). Each entity has an established return (yield) it wants to make on a loan.

Conditions in secondary marketing trades dictate prices that loan originators receive for these loans at RNY requirements that can be subject to many factors, such as loan seasoning, weighted average coupon, the weighted average remaining maturity, the anticipated loan life, delivery date, and type of loan characteristics affecting the collateral. Sensitive time periods are important as to originating the loan and its sale in secondary markets since market prices do change from par to discount to premium depending upon the above qualities controlling the cash flow.

RESALE CERTIFICATE — Under the consumer protection provisions of the 1990 Condominium Act, on the resale of a condominium unit, the owner must provide a prospective purchaser with a Resale Certificate. On the initial sale of a condominium unit, a Public Offering Statement must be given to the buyer.

The Resale Certificate contains information of the condominium association's operation, its financial condition, any fee schedules and charges which the association may charge; additionally, a set of the condominium declarations, bylaws and rules and regulations must be attached.

Normally the owner will have the association or the property management company for the association prepare the Resale Certificate. A reasonable charge may be imposed and charged to the owner for the association or the property management firm preparing the Resale Certificate. (*See* CONDOMINIUM OWNERSHIP.)
Reference: RCW 64.34.425

RESCIND - To annul, cancel. (*See* RESCISSION.)

RESCISSION - The legal remedy of canceling, terminating or annulling a contract and restoring the parties to their original positions; a return to the status quo. Contracts may be rescinded due to mistake, fraud or misrepresentation. Upon rescission the contract becomes a nullity and it, and each of its terms and provisions, ceases to exist or be enforceable against the other party. Where a seller seeks to rescind a contract with a defaulting buyer, the seller must return all payments made by the buyer, minus a fair rental for the time the buyer has been in possession. Sellers often insert a forfeiture clause authorizing them to keep all payments in the event of buyer's default; however, courts are reluctant to enforce such a forfeiture clause, especially where it is in the nature of a penalty, and often will order rescission instead.

Sometimes a purchaser is given a certain "cooling off" period from the time he/she signs a contract of purchase during which he/she can rescind the contract for any reason whatsoever. For instance, the purchaser of subdivided land which is, or should be, registered with HUD is given a rescission period of three business days from the time he/she receives the public report. California gives a 14 day rescission period in connection with the sale of subdivided land; Florida gives 15 days to new condominium purchasers. In Washington, under the Land Development Act of 1973, the purchaser of registered recreational or second home site property has a two day rescission period. The Federal Truth-In-Lending Law gives a three business day right of rescission to a customer in the case of any credit transaction in which a security interest is or will be retained or acquired in any real property which is used or expected to be used as the principal residence of the customer (except a purchase money first mortgage).

Under the Washington Condominium Act, a prospective purchaser of a unit has seven days to review the Public Offering Statement on a new project; on the resale of a unit, the prospective purchaser has seven days to review a Resale Certificate, at any time during the stated review period, the purchaser can terminate the Purchase and Sale Agreement for the unit and receive a full refund of their earnest money deposit.

A first mortgage or deed of trust to finance the purchase of a residence carries no right to cancel. However, a first mortgage or deed of trust for any other purpose, e.g., refinance, and a second mortgage on the same residence may be canceled within three business days of signing the loan documents. (*See* FORFEITURE, INTERSTATE LAND SALES, TRUTH-IN-LENDING ACT, WASHINGTON LAND DEVELOPMENT ACT.)
Reference: RCW 58.19.

RESCISSION CLAUSE - A specific clause occasionally found in a real estate contract, which requires the seller to return all of the buyer's payments, minus costs and a fair rental value, in the event the buyer defaults. Obviously, such a clause overly favors the buyer and is, therefore, not found in many real estate contracts. (*See* ADHESION CONTRACT.)

RESERVATION - The creation, in behalf of the grantor, of a new right issuing out of the thing granted. Title to all the property passes to the grantee, but a use is reserved in the grantor. A reservation thus is something which did not exist as an independent right before the conveyance. For example, Sheron conveys to Burgess a 10-acre parcel "reserving to Sheron a life estate therein." A right or interest cannot be reserved in favor of a third party. (*See* EXCEPTION.)

RESERVATION MONEY - Money used as quasi-earnest money deposit to hold property being developed. A prospective buyer asks a broker to hold reservation money pending the offering of a particular condominium unit for sale after a project reaches the stage when individual units can be sold.

RESERVE FUND - Money set aside as a cushion of capital for future payment of items such as taxes, insurance, furniture replacement, deferred maintenance, etc.; sometimes referred to as an impound account. A reserve fund serves a different function than a replacement reserve. Replacement reserves should be maintained especially when the owner is installing items with a short life expectancy such as a refrigerator, furniture or carpeting in furnished apartments. (*See* REPLACEMENT RESERVE.)

RESIDENCE - One's home or place of abode. "Residence" is defined differently for tax, license, or education qualification purposes. While a person can have several residences, he/she can have only one domicile. A residence would include such things as trailers, cooperatives, condominiums, or even house boats. (*See* DOMICILE.)

RESIDENCE, SALE OF - **Prior to May 7, 1997,** the taxable gain from the sale and replacement on one's **principal** residence was recognized only to the extent that the adjusted sales price of the old residence (gross sales price less sales expenses, less fixing-up expenses) equaled or exceeded the cost of purchasing (or construction) a new residence. Gain was recognized to the extent that the purchase price of the new residence was less than the sale price of the old residence. To qualify for non-recognized status, the home must be the "principal residence" of the taxpayer. This is a question of fact based on all the facts and circumstances, including the taxpayer's good faith. The taxpayer had to replace the old principal residence and **occupy** the new home within a period beginning 24 months prior to the date of sale and ending 24 months after the date of sale. For those in active military service the replacement time was four years.

After May 6, 1997, under the Taxpayer Relief Act of 1997, the taxpayer may exclude from income up to $250,000 of gain, $500,000 if married and filing jointly, realized on a sale or exchange of a residence after May 6, 1997, if the taxpayer owned and occupied it as a principal residence for an aggregate of at least two years out of five years before the sale or exchange. Periods of use do not have to be consecutive as long as the periods of use during the five-year period total two years. In counting the period of ownership and use, the taxpayer may include periods for all residences bought under the prior law rollover rules.

The exclusion is not a one-time benefit. As often as the taxpayer meets the applicable ownership and use tests, the taxpayer may claim the exclusion on sales of principal residences.

If the taxpayer is forced to sell before two years of ownership and use because of a change in a place of employment or health or unforeseen circumstances, the gain is prorated. Unforeseen circumstances will be defined in regulations. The excludable gain is generally prorated for the time spent in the residence over the two-year period. For example, the taxpayer moves to a new job location after owning and occupying a house for one year. The taxpayer is entitled to exclude 50% of the gain.

Even though the taxpayer does not satisfy the two-year ownership and use tests and the sale was not due to a change in employment or unforeseen circumstances, you may claim a prorated gain if the following two tests are met:

1. You owned the residence on August 5, 1997, and

2. The sale or exchange occurred during the two-year period beginning August 5, 1997.

A taxpayer who becomes physically or mentally incapable of self-care is deemed to use a residence as a principal residence during the time in which the individual owns the residence and resides in a licensed care facility. For this rule to apply, the homeowner must have owned and used the residence as a principal residence for an aggregate period of at least one year during the five years preceding the sale.

A principal residence includes a mobile home, trailer, houseboat and condominium apartment used as a principal residence. An investment in a retirement community does not qualify as a principal residence unless you receive equity in the property. In case of a tenant-stockholder of a cooperative housing corporation, the residence ownership requirement applies to the ownership of the stock and the use requirement applies to the house or apartment which the stockholder occupies.

The exclusion does not apply to the extent of depreciation with respect to business or rental use of the home after May 6, 1997. That portion of the gain is taxable.

A married couple may claim a $500,000 exclusion for a sale after May 6, 1997, provided: (1) either spouse owned the residence for at least two years, and (2) both used the residence for at least two years. If only one spouse meets the two-year use and ownership test, the exclusion is limited to $250,000.

A widow or widower may count the period during which a deceased spouse owned the residence.

If a residence is transferred to a taxpayer incident to divorce, the time during which the taxpayer's spouse or former spouse owned the residence is added to the taxpayer's period of ownership. A taxpayer who owns a residence is deemed to use the residence while the taxpayer's spouse or former spouse uses the residence under the terms of a divorce or separation. (*See* BUYING YOUR HOME.)

RESIDENT MANAGER - A salaried agent of the owner employed to manage a single building. Generally, a resident manager need not be licensed under the state real estate license laws, if he/she merely acts as custodian or caretaker. (*See* PROPERTY MANAGEMENT.)

RESIDENTIAL APPRAISAL REPORT (RAR) - The residential appraisal report provides a mortgage underwriter with a complete, thoroughly analyzed valuation of the subject residential real estate by a competent appraiser who is not only price-wise, but market-wise as well. The RAR of the professional appraiser outlines the factors covering the market value of the property as it stands on the day the estimate was certified. The RAR must include the following statements: (1) the specific purpose for which the fair market value is being estimated; (2) the subject property's identification with a description of the property rights; (3) a complete explanation of the steps taken to arrive at a final conclusion of the value estimate; and (4) the date the estimate was made.

It is not intended for the appraiser to become enmeshed in aspects of the underwriting process other than those necessary to perform the appraisal.

A difficult task an appraiser must face is price vs. value. Price is the actual amount of money that the subject property was sold for, not necessarily the fair market value in the comparable sense as found in recently bought properties (indicating the same quality). A grass roots estimation of value cannot be made without access to reliable information such as the reason for the transaction in the first place.

RESIDENTIAL LANDLORD TENANT ACT - *See* LANDLORD TENANT ACT.

RESIDENTIAL RENTAL PROPERTY - Property from which 80 percent or more of the gross income is rental income from dwelling units.

RESIDENTIAL SALES COUNCIL (RS COUNCIL) - A council affiliated with the Realtors National Marketing Institute which offers advanced courses in listing, selling, managing time and career, investing and financial skills, along with publications, periodicals, audio-visual materials and sales aids. The council awards the designation CRS (Certified Residential Specialist). (*See* REALTORS NATIONAL MARKETING INSTITUTE.)

RESIDUAL - That which is left over, such as the residual value of property after its economic life is completed. Also refers to deferred commissions; e.g., commissions which are earned but payment is put off for a stated period. For example, in condominium sales, a broker earns his/her commission when the buyer signs and the seller accepts the purchase agreement, but the commission is paid in part upon the down payment and in full (the residual) upon closing which, with a new project under construction, could be as much as 18 months away. It is permissible for a salesman in certain cases to accept residuals direct from a former employing broker rather than have these pass through his/her new employing broker. (*See* DEFERRED COMMISSIONS.)

RESIDUAL PROCESS - An appraisal process used in the income approach to estimate the value of the land and/or the building, as indicated by the capitalization of the residual net income attributable to it. (*See* APPRAISAL, BUILDING RESIDUAL TECHNIQUE, CAPITALIZATION, PROPERTY RESIDUAL TECHNIQUE.)

RESORT PROPERTIES - Land devoted to the amusement, relaxation, and pleasure of the public. These include seaside, island, and lake developments, mountain cabin site developments, desert retreats, game and fish areas, properties around natural springs, waterfalls and the like. This can be due to natural resources or beauty (mountainous areas, or seaside property) or man-made improvements (tennis courts, golf courses, man-made ski hills). (*See* TIMESHARE ACT, TIME SHARING.)

RESPA - *See* REAL ESTATE SETTLEMENT PROCEDURES ACT.

RESPONDEAT SUPERIOR - A principle of agency law which states that the employer (principal) is liable in certain cases for the wrongful acts of his/her employee (agent) committed during the course of employment, including those acts of the agent performed within the scope of his/her authority. (*See* SCOPE OF AUTHORITY.)

The vicarious liability of a principal due to the act, error or omission by a real estate agent was limited with the adoption of Real Estate Brokerage Relationship Act, effective January 1, 1997.
Reference: RCW 18.86.

RESTRAINT OF TRADE - Contracts or combinations designed to, or which tend to, eliminate or stifle competition, create a monopoly, control prices, or otherwise hamper or obstruct the normal operation of business. Restraint of trade is generally illegal under federal and state antitrust laws. (*See* ANTITRUST LAWS.)

RESTRAINTS ON ALIENATION - A limitation or condition placed on the right to transfer property. Restraints can take the form of conditions and covenants in deeds or restraints on use of the property. Restrictions placed on the vesting of an estate until some remote time are regulated by the rule against perpetuities, which requires the vesting of contingent interests to take place, if at all, must occur during a time period measured by the actual life span of all the parties involved plus 21 years..

One of the "bundle of rights" in the ownership of real property is the right to convey, and the courts will not enforce any unreasonable restrictions placed by the grantor on this right. For example, a condition in a deed that the grantee may only sell to tall people would be an unreasonable restraint on alienation and hence the condition, but not the deed, is void. Restraints based on race, color, religion, sex and ancestry are void under both state and federal anti-discrimination laws. (*See* RULE AGAINST PERPETUITIES.)

RESTRICTED REAL ESTATE SECURITIES - In 1975 the Washington State Securities Act was amended to provide that a real estate licensee could be involved in the sale of registered securities which dealt with real estate in the State of Washington to Washington residents. The amendments were proposed to reduce the difficulty of registration and

to reduce associated registration costs. The legislation and Rules and Regulations adopted by the Securities Commission provide for special registration procedures and a special examination for real estate licensees on security subjects. (*See* REAL PROPERTY SECURITIES REGISTRATION.)
Reference: RCW 21.20, WAC 460- 48A.

RESTRICTIONS - Limitations on the use of property. Private restrictions are created by means of restrictive covenants written into real property instruments, such as deeds and leases. Well-drafted covenants, conditions and restrictions, (sometimes referred to as CC&Rs) have a tendency to stabilize property values, since property owners can be certain as to the permitted uses of the neighboring properties. Such covenants might restrict the number and size of structures to be placed on the land, the cost of structures, fence heights, setbacks, and the like. Restrictive covenants which discriminate by restricting the conveyance to or use by individuals of a specified race, sex, color, religion, marital status or ancestry are void. (*See* WASHINGTON STATE HUMAN RIGHTS COMMISSION.)

Public restrictions are created by means of zoning and ordinances; unlike private restrictions, they must tend to promote the public health, welfare and safety. (*See* DECLARATION OF RESTRICTIONS, RESTRICTIVE COVENANT.)

A restriction may be terminated by obtaining quitclaim deeds which releases the restrictions from all interested parties.

RESTRICTIVE COVENANT - A private agreement, usually contained in a deed or a recorded plat that contains the restriction, which restricts the use and occupancy of real property. Sometimes called "private zoning." Such a covenant is said to run with the land and binds all subsequent purchasers, their heirs and assigns; and normally covers such things as lot size, building lines, type of architecture, and uses to which the property may be put. Restrictive covenants are strictly construed against persons seeking to enforce them; thus, all ambiguities are resolved against the restriction and in favor of the free and natural use of the property.

Discriminatory racial or religious restrictive covenants imposing restrictions against the sale or transfer of real property to, or occupancy by, a person on the basis of race, creed, color, or national origin are void in Washington. Also, it is an unfair practice under the Washington State Law Against Discrimination to insert such a provision in a written instrument relating to real property. (*See* WASHINGTON STATE HUMAN RIGHTS COMMISSION.)
Reference: RCW 49.60.224.

RESUBDIVIDE - The act of taking an existing subdivision and either replatting it (e.g., changing the lots from the old grid pattern to the more modern irregular lots), or dividing it even further (e.g., taking 20-acre lots and dividing them into five-acre parcels). For purposes of county subdivision approval, and state and federal land sales registration, a resubdivision is the same as a new subdivision. (*See* SUBDIVISION.)

RESULTING TRUST - A trust which is implied by law, resulting from the acts or relationships of the parties involved. A situation, for example, in which Buck Byn supplies the money to buy a high-rise apartment building, with title taken in Sandy Edlund's name for convenience would be a resulting trust in which Edlund holds the property in trust for Byn.

RETAINAGE - A portion or a percentage of the monthly payments, made by a land owner to a contractor for construction work completed, which is withheld until the construction contract has been satisfactorily completed and the period for filing mechanics' liens has expired (or when the lien has been released by the contractor and subcontractor). The contractor also holds back some of his/her payments to his/her subcontractors until final completion of the work and waiver of any mechanics' liens has been obtained.

The amount of retainage is usually 10 percent of each progress payment, but in some situations, rather than taking it out of the progress payments, the owner will simply pay the last one or two payments into escrow for release when the lien period has expired. Also called "holdbacks."

RETAINING WALL - Any wall erected to hold back or support a bank of earth. A retaining wall is also any enclosing wall built to resist the lateral pressure of internal loads. (*See* WEEP HOLE.)

RETALIATORY EVICTION - An act whereby a landlord evicts a tenant in response to some complaint made by the tenant. The Washington Landlord Tenant Act provides that if the tenant has complained in good faith to the Department of Health of conditions which constitute a violation of a health law or regulation or if the tenant has in good faith requested repairs when authorized to do so by the Act, then the landlord cannot for these reasons alone evict the tenant or demand an increase in rent or decrease the services rendered to the tenant. If a landlord responds to a tenant's report of a code violation or the request of needed repairs by committing any of the retaliatory actions specified, it will be presumed that the landlord is retaliating against the tenant. The tenant may be entitled to damages for such actions.

However, even after a complaint is made by the tenant, a landlord can still evict a tenant for good cause, such as, when the tenant damages the premises, the landlord wants to occupy the premises himself (or his/her immediate family), or the landlord is going to take the premises off the rental market. Also, a landlord can still raise the rent if he/she can show that increased taxes and other costs have forced him/her to increase the rent. (*See* LANDLORD TENANT ACT.)
Reference: RCW 59.18.

REVENUE STAMPS - The use of revenue stamps, state or federal, on real estate documents has been abolished.

REVERSE ANNUITY MORTGAGE - A financing program which enables older homeowners to realize some of the equity growth in their homes while still occupying them. If a home is debt free or nearly so, the lender lends a sufficient amount to pay the loan off and then a monthly amount to the owner at an agreed to rate of interest and secures the gradually increasing debt by a mortgage or deed of trust on the home which the owner continues to occupy. The owner continues to occupy the home until death or some other occurrence forcing a sale of the home. The lender has no power of sale or any other method of forcing the owner to sell the home. (*See* CREATIVE FINANCING.)

REVERSE LEVERAGE - A situation that arises when financing is too costly; results when total cash yield on the investment is less than the financing constant on borrowed funds. (*See* NEGATIVE CASH FLOW.)

REVERSION - A future estate in real property created by operation of law when a grantor conveys a lesser estate than he/she has. The residue left in the grantor is called a reversion which commences in possession in the future upon the end of a particular estate granted or devised, whether it be freehold or less-than freehold. For example, Adam grants Eve a life estate. Eve in turn grants Junior a 10-year leasehold. Junior would have an estate for years, Eve would have a reversion for life which would transform into a life estate at the termination of the 10-year lease, and Adam would have a reversion in the fee, which would revert to Adam upon Eve's death. If Eve should die before expiration of the lease, Junior's leasehold estate would be terminated upon her death. (*See* COVENANTS AND CONDITIONS, REMAINDER.)

REVERSIONARY FACTOR - A mathematical factor found in present worth tables used to convert a single, lump sum future payment into present value, given the proper discount rate and time period. Frequently used to determine the value of the lessor's leased fee interest. (*See* APPRAISAL.)

REVERSIONARY VALUE - The expected worth of a property at the end of the anticipated holding period. Present worth tables are used to determine the current value of a reversion.

REVOCATION - The act of terminating, canceling, or annulling, as when a seller revokes a broker's agency by canceling the listing. The Department of Licensing can revoke the license of a real estate salesman or broker for violation of certain rules of conduct as specified in Real Estate License Law and the Commission's Rules and Regulations. An offeror can revoke his/her offer any time prior to the offeree's accepting and communicating his/her acceptance to the offeror. (*See* LICENSING LAW, OFFER.)
Reference: RCW 18.85.

RIDER - An addition, amendment or endorsement annexed to a document and incorporated into the terms of the document. Riders are frequently attached to insurance policies, usually to provide some extended coverage such as a fire liability coverage as a rider to a comprehensive personal liability policy.

On any pre-printed form (like a real estate contract) a reference should be made to a rider on the instrument to prevent it from being removed unnoticed. For example, "Additional terms and/or conditions per attached rider, which is made a part hereof by this reference." It is a good practice to have a rider addendum to a contract initialed and dated by both parties to establish its authenticity at a later time.

RIDGEBOARD - A heavy horizontal board set on edge at the apex of the roof to which the rafters are attached.

RIGHT OF CONTRIBUTION - The right of one who has discharged a common liability to recover from another who is also liable under the terms and conditions of a contract, his/her pro rata share of the liability. For instance, a right of contribution exists in favor of one co-tenant who pays taxes or other liens against the entire property. The co-tenant is entitled to an equitable lien on his/her co-tenants' shares and the co-tenant may enforce this lien by foreclosure on the shares. (*See* TENANCY IN COMMON.)

RIGHT OF FIRST REFUSAL - The right of a person to have the first opportunity either to purchase or lease real property. Unlike an option, however, the holder of a right of first refusal has no right to purchase until the owner actually offers the property for sale or entertains an offer to purchase from some third party. In a lease situation, a right of first refusal might give the tenant the right either to purchase the property, if offered for sale, or to renew the lease. This right is clearly more advantageous to the tenant than it is to the landlord. A property burdened with a right of first refusal is less marketable than one without such a right.

In an option to purchase, the tenant can decide to exercise or not to exercise the option at a fixed price during the option period. In a right of first refusal, however, the holder can exercise the right only if the owner has offered to sell the property or has entertained a bona fide offer by a third person to purchase the property. At that point, the holder can seek to purchase the property by matching the offer. If the owner first offers the property to the tenant and he/she refuses, then the owner is free to offer to any third party at that price **or higher**.

In some condominiums, the association of unit owners retains the right of first refusal on any sale of a unit. In HUD-FHA regulated condominiums and in condominiums eligible for FNMA financing, however, restrictions such as the right of first refusal are not permitted. First refusal is common in agreements between partners, shareholders, joint owners, landlords and tenants. (*See* OPTION, PREEMPTION CLAUSE.)

RIGHT OF RE-ENTRY - The future interest left in the transferor of property who transfers an estate on condition subsequent. If the condition is broken, the transferor has (at his/her option) the power to terminate the estate. Unlike a possibility of reverter, however, the transferor must take affirmative steps to terminate the estate; otherwise the condition may be discharged. For example, Joan grants Shirley the property on the condition that Shirley does not raise pigs on the property. If Shirley raises pigs, Joan must actually reenter and take the premises, that is, there is no automatic reverter. (*See* FEE SIMPLE DEFEASIBLE, POSSIBILITY OF REVERTER, REVERSION.)

RIGHT OF SURVIVORSHIP - The distinctive characteristic of a joint tenancy by which the surviving joint tenant(s) succeeds to all right, title and interest of the deceased joint tenant without the need for probate proceedings. (*See* JOINT TENANCY.)

RIGHT-OF-WAY - (1) The right or privilege, acquired through accepted usage or by contract, to pass over a designated portion of the property of another. A right-of-way may be either private, as in an access easement given a neighbor, or public, as in the right of the public to use the highways or streets, or to have safe access to public beaches. (2) Land which is either owned by a railroad or over which it maintains an easement for operating on its trackage in accordance with government safety regulations and industry standards. (*See* ACCESS.)

RIGHT, TITLE, AND INTEREST - A term often used in conveying documents to describe the transfer of all that the grantor or assignor is capable of transferring. In a quitclaim deed, the grantor transfers all right, title, and interest in a property without making any representations as to the extent of such right, title, and interest, if any.

RIGHT TO PRIVACY ACT - The Right to Financial Privacy Act of 1978. It was enacted because customers of financial institutions have a right to expect that their financial activities have a reasonable amount of privacy from federal government scrutiny.

The act establishes specific procedures for government authorities that seek information about a customer's financial records.

The act requires that the customer receive the following:

1. A written notice of the agency's intent to obtain financial records;

2. The reasons why the records are being sought; and

3. A statement describing procedures to use if the customer does not wish such information to be made available.

Before the act, customers of financial institutions could not challenge government access to their financial records, nor did they have any idea their records were being turned over to a governmental authority.

It is necessary for the financial institution to maintain a record of all instances that a customer's record is disclosed to a government authority.

RIGHT-TO-USE - The legal right to use or occupy a property. Also refers to a contractual right to occupy a time-share unit under a license, vacation lease or club membership arrangement. (*See* BUNDLE OF RIGHTS, TIMESHARING.)

RIPARIAN - Those rights and obligations which are incidental to ownership of land adjacent to or abutting on watercourses such as streams and lakes. These rights do not necessarily depend upon ownership of the land over which the water flows. Examples of such rights are the right of swimming, boating, fishing and the right to the alluvium deposited by the water. Riparian rights do not attach except where there is a water boundary on one side of the particular tract of land claimed to be riparian. Such a property right in water is a right of use or a usufructuary right. If the body of water is in movement as a stream or river, the abutting owner is called a "riparian owner." If the water is not flowing, as in the case of a pond, lake, or ocean, the abutting owner is called a "littoral owner." The word riparian literally means "river bank."

RISER - The vertical face of the step that supports the tread. As you walk upstairs, the riser is the part of the step facing you. Vertical supply pipes may also be called risers.

RISK CAPITAL - Capital invested in a speculative venture, thus being the least secure, and offering the greatest chance of loss. Risk capital, however, often yields the greatest rate of return.

RISK OF LOSS - Responsibility for damages caused to improvements. Unless the terms of the Purchase and Sale Agreement provide otherwise, the seller cannot enforce the contract and the buyer can recover all insurance proceeds paid if a material part of the real estate is destroyed or is taken by eminent domain, **provided neither legal title nor possession has passed** to the buyer. As a practical matter, most Washington agreements only transfer possession to the buyer upon closing. In other words, the risk of loss passes to the buyer when either title or possession passes, and he/she should protect himself/herself by securing proper insurance. If the buyer takes possession before closing and there is no rental agreement, then the buyer may assume the risk of loss. If, however, there is a rental agreement, the buyer would not assume the risk of loss unless the contract so provides.

ROD - A measure of length containing 5 1/2 yards or 16 1/2 feet. (Also called a "perch.")

ROLL-OVER - 1. Refers to tax provisions which enable the taxpayer to defer paying income taxes in certain situations such as involuntary conversion.

2. In a financing sense, it refers to the practice of rewriting a new loan at the termination of a prior loan, such as a three-year mortgage with a roll-over provision to grant a new loan at different terms and conditions at the end of the three years using a roll-over note. (*See* RENEGOTIABLE-RATE MORTGAGE.)

ROOF - The covering on a building.

The average life of a roof is based on the material used. Asphalt roofs will last 15 to 20 years; old growth wood shingles would last 30 to 35 years, present shingles may not last 10 to 15 years and slate should last 40 or more years.

Asphalt roofs that have granules missing in spots and shingles that are beginning to buckle will soon need replacing. Inadequate flashing around chimneys and vent pipes are indications of a roof problem. Sags in the roof can be a sign of problems with the framing structure supporting the roof.

A home with more than three layers of roofing most likely violates a housing code. Normally FHA, VA and housing codes stipulate that no more than three layers of roofing can be applied to a home.

ROOF BOARDS - Boards nailed to the top of the rafters, usually not touching each other, to tie the roof together and form a base for the roofing material. The boards, or roof sheathing, can also be constructed of sheets of plywood.

ROOF INSPECTION CLAUSE - A clause sometimes inserted in a Purchase and Sale Agreement specifying that the seller will provide the buyer with a certified report of the condition of the building's roof. If it is found faulty, the roof is usually repaired at the seller's expense.

ROOFING FELT - Sheets of felt or other close-woven, heavy material placed on top of the roof boards to insulate and waterproof the roof. Like building paper, roofing felt is treated with bitumen or some other type of tar derivative to increase its water resistance. Roofing felt is applied either with a bonding and sealing compound or with intense heat which softens the tar and causes it to adhere to the roof.

ROOFING SHINGLES - Thin, small sheets of wood, asbestos, fiberglass, metal, clay, or other material used as the outer covering for a roof. The tiles are laid in overlapping rows to completely cover the roof surface. Shingles are sometimes used as an outer covering for walls.

ROT - Deterioration of wood in a structure, such as a house, garage, or deck. There are generally two types of rot. Rot occurs when a certain combination of factors exist, such as (1) wood that lacks natural protection (such as the oils in cedar); (2) moisture in the wood reaches a certain level, often above 22%; (3) rot causing spores or fungus are present; and (4) heat and a lack of light/sunshine are type conditions. "Dry rot" is a misnomer; moisture must be present, even if it is not obvious to the observer.

ROYALTY - 1. The money paid to an owner of realty for the right of depleting the property of its natural resource, such as oil, gas, minerals, stone, builders' sand and gravel, and timber. Usually, the royalty payment is a stated part of the amount extracted, such as: one-sixth or one-eighth of the oil and gas removed, or so many cents per ton of sand and gravel taken away, or a given price per cubic yard of material extracted. The royalty payment is a combination of rent and depreciation (depletion charge).

2. Also, a franchise fee to a master franchiser.

RPAC - The Realtors' Political Action Committee of Washington; a voluntary, non-profit, unincorporated association whose membership consists of Realtors. Membership contributions are used to provide financial support for candidates campaigning for political office who have expressed views, or who have a voting record, consistent with the needs of the real estate industry. (*See* WASHINGTON ASSOCIATION OF REALTORS.)

RULE 10-B5 - The anti-fraud provisions of the Securities and Exchange Act of 1934 which make it unlawful for any person, in connection with the purchase or sale of any security, to employ any device, scheme or artifice to defraud; to make any untrue statement of a material fact, or omit to state a material fact necessary in order to make the statements made not misleading; or to engage in any act, practice or course of business which operates or would operate as a fraud or deceit on any person. The Washington Securities Law has similar anti-fraud provisions. It should be noted that even if an offering of securities is exempt from registration under the intrastate or private offering exemption, the issuer nevertheless is subject to the anti-fraud provisions of both the federal and state securities laws. In other words, if the issuer fails to state a material fact, this would give a purchaser of the security the right to rescind the transaction and recover all of his/her money plus interest from the date of purchase. (*See* PRIVATE OFFERING, REAL PROPERTY SECURITIES REGISTRATION, RESTRICTED REAL ESTATE SECURITIES.)
Reference: RCW 21.20.

RULE 146 - A rule adopted by the SEC in 1974 which permits an unlimited number of offers, provided that the issuer knows in advance that the offerees are sophisticated enough in real estate investments to evaluate the risk themselves or are represented by an independent advisor having such experience where the offeree is unsophisticated but wealthy enough to bear the risk of loss. The State of Washington has not adopted Rule 146. (*See* PRIVATE OFFERING, REAL PROPERTY SECURITIES REGISTRATION, RESTRICTED REAL ESTATE SECURITIES.)

RULE 147 - A rule adopted in 1974 by the SEC to clarify the intrastate or local offering exemption from registering a security with the SEC. The Rule sets down guidelines for determining when one is deemed a resident of a state, especially with regards to legal entities such as corporations and partnerships. The issuer must be both a resident of and doing business within the state in which all offers and sales are made. An issuer is deemed to be doing business within a state if its principal office is located within the state, at least 80 percent of its gross revenues are derived from operations within the state, 80 percent of its assets are located within the state, and it uses 80 percent of the proceeds from the sales of securities within the state. Thus a local issuer seeking to raise money for a local project might not be exempt if it has substantial assets (such as real estate holdings) in another state. The rule also sets forth restrictions on the further transfer of exempt securities to non-residents, at least for nine months from the date of the last sale by the issuer of any part of the issue. (*See* INTRASTATE EXEMPTION.)

RULE AGAINST PERPETUITIES - A rule of law designed to require the early vesting of a future contingent interest in real property and thus prevent the property from being made inalienable for long periods of time. The effect of the rule is to destroy future interests which impede the vesting of property rights for longer than the prescribed period, which is usually no later than 21 years after some life or lives-in-being at the creation of the interest. For example, in a conveyance "to George Allen for life, then to his son, Butch Allen, for life and remainder to Butch's children who reach age 24," the remainder violates the rule since it is possible that the remainder will not vest until after 21 years of some life-in-being; that is, George and Butch could die when Butch's only child is one year old. The net effect of a violation is to destroy the void interest at the outset but to leave the valid interest intact. (*See* RESTRAINTS ON ALIENATION.)

The rule applies only to contingent interests.

RULE OF FIVE - A rule of thumb used by subdividers to approximate subdivision costs. As a general rule, 1/5 (20 percent) of the final total sales price goes to land acquisition cost; 1/5 (20 percent) goes to improvement costs such as engineering, grading, roads, legal fees; 1/5 (20 percent) miscellaneous for interest and carrying charges plus unsold lots; and 2/5 (40 percent) to cover administration costs, advertising, sales commissions and the profit.

RULE OF 72 - A rule of thumb in financing which states that the interest rate at which a single sum will double can be found by dividing into the number 72 the years during which the money is growing. For example, if the money has doubled during an eight year period, a financier would figure 72 ÷ 8 = 9 percent, or 72 ÷ 9 percent = 8 years.

RULE OF 78s - A method of computing refunds of unearned finance charges on contracts which include precomputed finance charges so that the refund is proportional to the monthly unpaid balances at the time of the refund. Under this rule, on a 12-month contract, the creditor would retain 12/78 of the total finance charge for the first month, 11/78 for the second month, and so on. If the creditor held a 12-month contract for only six months, it would be entitled to 57/78 of the total finance charge (12+11+10+9+8+7=57). In turn, the consumer would be entitled to the remaining 21/78 of the finance charge.

Under the truth-in-lending laws, the creditor must identify the method of computing any unearned portion of the finance charge in the event of prepayment of the obligation.

RUNNING WITH THE LAND - Rights or covenants which bind or benefit successive owners of a property are said to run with the land, such as restrictive building covenants in a recorded deed which would affect all future owners of the property. For example, Homer sells Black Acres to George. As part of the consideration, George covenants to repair a building on other land owned by Homer; such a covenant does not run with the land and would not place a duty upon Hubert if Hubert purchases Black Acres from George. The promise does not "touch and concern" the land granted from Homer to George, but it is only a personal covenant for the benefit of Homer. (*See* APPURTENANCE.)

An easement appurtenant runs with the land and thus passes to a succeeding owner even if it is not specified in the deed. (*See* EASEMENT.)

RURAL - A land use classification pertaining to the country, as opposed to urban; land devoted to the pursuit of agriculture.

RURAL HOUSING AND COMMUNITY DEVELOPMENT (RECD) - . The Rural Economic and Community Development office was formed to replace the Farmers Home Administration. As a result of the United States Department of Agriculture Reorganization Act of 1994, the Rural Housing and Community Development Service (a division of RECD) is now charged with financing decent, affordable housing in rural areas.

These funds are divided between direct loans and loan guarantees for single-family housing, multifamily housing, low interest repair loans, grants to elderly rural residents and other special programs.

Home ownership loans are available in rural areas, including towns with a population of 10,000 or less or that are located in open country. In some cases, towns and cities between 10,000 and 20,000 qualify for these programs. These loans may be used to buy, build, improve, repair, or rehabilitate rural homes, and to provide adequate water and waste disposal systems. Home ownership loans through RECD are offered to families or persons with low and moderate income who are without safe, decent or sanitary housing, who are unable to obtain a loan from other sources, and have sufficient income to pay house payments. Loans may be made for up to 100 percent of the appraised value, and the maximum repayment period is 38 years. This programs also applies to manufactured homes, with a maximum repayment period of 30 years.

The Rural Housing and Community Development Service division of RECD also lends to qualified nonprofit organizations, public bodies, and others to construct multifamily units to house low and very low income agricultural workers. Loan rates are as low as one percent for a maximum of 33 years. Rental assistance and grants may also be available to organizations and public bodies that develop this type of housing. Community organizations may also use RECD financing for community and health care facilities in rural areas. Examples of these types of facilities include courthouses, city halls, libraries, fire stations and medical clinics.

S

SAFE HARBOR RULE - 1. In general terms, it means an area of protection. For example, the IRS has outlined certain standards for a real estate broker to meet in treating his/her salespeople as independent contractors. As long as the broker meets these criteria, the broker will be in a "safe harbor" and not subject to attack by the IRS for failing to withhold taxes from commissions disbursed to salespeople.

2. In 1991, Washington adopted legislation which created a safe harbor for the forfeiture of an earnest money deposit if the specific guidelines are followed. As a result of the legislation, most Purchase and Sale Agreement in Washington have a "liquidated damages" provision which lists the various remedies available to the seller if the buyer wrongfully breaches the contract. The parties to the contract must select the sole remedy of forfeiture of the earnest money deposit and the earnest money cannot be over five percent of the purchase price to take advantage of the safe harbor.

Subsequent case law states the earnest money can be any amount (in excess of five percent) as long as the reasonableness of liquidated damages is to be measured as the parties could foresee it at the time the contract was agreed to between the parties. However, with the exception of the commercial Purchase and Sale Agreement, the five percent selection is the normal practice.

3. IRS standards for a delayed tax-deferred 1031 exchange in which an intermediary can hold title or funds pending the identification and acquisition of the replacement property within set time limits. (*See* DEFERRED OR DELAYED EXCHANGE.)

SAFETY PROVISION IN LISTING AGREEMENT - In order to protect the real estate broker against any connivance between a principal and a prospective purchaser attempting to avoid the payment of the broker's commission, the following safety clause or one similar to it is frequently inserted in the listing agreement executed between broker and principal: "If a sale, lease or other transfer or exchange of the aforementioned property is made within (e.g., three (3) months is normal on residential property with up to a year on commercial-investment property) months after this authorization and employment contract, or any extension thereof, terminates, to parties with whom broker negotiates during the term hereof, or any extension thereof, and broker notifies me in writing of such negotiations prior to the termination, or any extension, of the listing agreement, said notice being delivered to me personally or by regular mail, then in such event I agree to pay broker the commission stipulated in this agreement." (*See* EXTENDER CLAUSE.)

SALE BY THE ACRE - The sale of land described in the Purchase and Sale Agreement and conveyance documents by stating the exact area of land, e.g., 269 acres. Under a sale by the acre contract, the buyer does not take the risk of any deficiency nor does the seller take the risk of any excess.

Sometimes large acreage is sold by stating the approximate rather than the exact acreage, such as "269 acres more or less." In such a case, neither party would receive any compensation if there were a slight variance in the exact amount of acres actually conveyed. However, if there is an unusually large excess or deficiency, a court could grant equitable relief to the injured party.

A proper legal description is necessary in the Purchase and Sale Agreement and all subsequent conveyance documents. (*See* LEGAL DESCRIPTION.)

SALE-LEASEBACK - A real estate financing technique whereby an owner sells his/her property to an investor and, at the same time, leases it back. This financing arrangement was inaugurated during the 1940s when the loan-to-value ratios for mortgages were between 50 percent and 66 2/3 percent and companies wanted to free their capital tied up in real estate for more speculative ventures. The lease utilized for this method is usually a full net lease that extends over a period of time long enough for the investor to recover his/her funds and to make a fair profit on the investment.

The sale-leaseback approach to real estate finance is generally applied to commercial properties since rents paid by businesses and professional people are fully deductible expenses in the year in which they are incurred. Using this approach, a seller/lessee enjoys many benefits: he/she retains possession of the property while obtaining the full sales price, and in some cases, keeping the right to repurchase the property at the end of the lease; he/she frees the capital which was frozen in equity; he/she maintains an appreciable interest in realty, which can be capitalized upon by subleasing or mortgaging the leasehold; and he/she gets a tax deduction for the full amount of the rent, equivalent to taking depreciation deductions for both the building and the land.

The cash secured from the sale might be utilized for plant expansion, remodeling, or investing in other opportunities. In addition, a lease appears as an indirect liability on a firm's balance sheet, whereas a mortgage shows up as a direct liability and adversely affects the firm's debt ratio in terms of obtaining future financing.

The advantages to the investor/landlord in this type of arrangement include a fair return on and of investment in the form of rent during the lease term, and ownership of a depreciable asset already occupied by a reliable tenant. In other words, the investor is buying a guaranteed income stream which can probably be sheltered through the proper use of depreciation allowances. When determining the rent to be paid on the lease, the investor can actually manage his/her risk by the amount of rent he/she requires. The rent for a quality tenant, such as Safeway Corporation, a large fully leveraged company that sells and leases back most of its stores, will be lower than the rent for a high-risk tenant.

When the lease includes an option for the tenant to repurchase the property at the end of the lease term, it is called a sale-leaseback-buyback. However, care must be taken to establish the buyback price at the fair market value at the time of sale; otherwise the arrangement is considered a long-term installment mortgage and any income tax benefits that might have been enjoyed during the term of the lease will be disallowed by the Internal Revenue Service.

SALE OF LEASED PROPERTY - An owner of property who has given a lease to one person may sell the leased property to another. The buyer, however, takes the property subject to the existing lease. The deed evidencing the sale usually states that it is "subject to existing leases and rights of present tenants," and this clause means that the seller cannot deliver actual possession of the property. The buyer does, however, have the right to collect rent due after the sale and to exercise any right of forfeiture for nonpayment of rent given under the lease. (*See* LEASE, LEASEHOLD, RIGHT OF FIRST REFUSAL.)

SALE OF PERSONAL RESIDENCE BY ELDERLY - Prior to May 7, 1997, the Tax Code provided for a once-in-a-lifetime exclusion of $125,000 that a taxpayer age 55 or over could elect for the gain from the sale of his/her personal residence. To qualify, the taxpayer had to be at least 55 years of age prior to the sale, must have owned and used the residence as her/his principal residence for a total of at least three years during the five year period prior to the date of the sale. In the case of property jointly held, a husband or wife could satisfy the age, ownership, and use requirements if one of their spouses meets the requirements and the couple files a joint return for the year of the sale. (*See* RESIDENCE, SALE OF.)

Under the Taxpayer Relief Act of 1997, the taxpayer may exclude from income up to $250,000 of gain, $500,000 if married and filing jointly, realized on a sale or exchange of a residence after May 6, 1997, if the taxpayer owned and occupied it as a principal residence for an aggregate of at least two years out of five years before the sale or exchange. Periods of use do not have to be consecutive as long as the periods of use during the five-year period total two years. In counting the period of ownership and use, the taxpayer may include periods for all residence bought under the prior law rollover rules.

The exclusion is not a one-time benefit. As often as you meet the applicable ownership and use tests, you may claim the exclusion on sales of principal residence.

A residence includes a single family residence, a condominium or the stock of a shareholder/tenant in a cooperative. (*See* RESIDENCE.)

SALES ASSOCIATE - Licensed salesperson or associate broker who works for a broker. (*See* SALESPERSON.)

SALES COMPARISON APPROACH - An appraisal method of estimating value by comparing recent sales of comparable properties to the subject property after making appropriate adjustments for any differences between the properties. (*See* MARKET DATA APPROACH.)

SALES KIT - An assortment of information about property to be sold, selected and organized to aid the salesperson in becoming familiar with the property and presenting the facts to a prospect, and to help the prospect in visualizing the property. The kit may be in the form of a small loose leaf book of typewritten pages, a large loose leaf book including maps and pictures, or an elaborate zippered briefcase with photographs, building plans, maps and other statistical data.

SALES PRICE - The actual price agreed to by the purchaser and seller.

SALESPERSON - The Washington Real Estate Licensing Law defines a real estate salesperson as: "any natural person who represents a real estate broker in any of his/her activities."

All real estate salespersons must be licensed. To obtain a license, an applicant must be at least 18 years of age, and must pass the state license examination.

A real estate salesperson is subject to the Licensing Law and to the Real Estate Commission's Rules and Regulations. A salesperson can work for only one broker and cannot accept compensation for services rendered from anyone except his/her employing broker. All sales commissions, including any referral fees, premiums, prizes, etc. must be received by the employing broker who then pays the appropriate portion according to the terms and conditions of the contract with the salesperson.

The salesperson is the agent of his/her employing broker. He/she does not enter into a direct contractual relationship with the client; only the broker does this. Although it appears that the salesperson may have the front line contracts with the buyer or seller, it is with the broker or licensed partnership or corporation with whom a listing contract exists.

A salesperson is authorized to sign the receipt portion of the Purchase and Sales Agreement, and may be authorized in writing to receive and deposit trust funds on behalf of the broker. He/she may not, however, be authorized to withdraw the funds.

A salesperson must have been an active full-time salesman for two years before he/she is eligible to sit for the state broker's examination. A part-time salesperson might require four years' work in order to qualify. The Division may grant a waiver of all or part of the two year requirement depending upon prior equivalent education or experience. (*See* BROKER, EXAMINATION, REAL ESTATE BROKERAGE RELATIONSHIP ACT, REAL ESTATE LICENSING, INDEPENDENT CONTRACTOR, LICENSING LAWS.)
Reference: RCW 18.85, WAC 308-124.

SANDWICH LEASE - A leasehold estate in which the tenant, **sandwich party,** leases the property from the fee owner and then sublets to the tenant in possession and maintains his/her middle or sandwich position. The sandwich party is the lessee of one party and the lessor of another; thus he/she is neither the fee owner nor the user of the property.

The sandwich lease presents some problems for mortgage purposes since the individual leases cannot be renegotiated until the master lease is renegotiated. (*See* LEASEHOLD.)

SATELLITE TENANT - A smaller business tenant in a shopping mall. Such tenants are dependent upon the larger and better-known tenants to attract customers to the mall. Examples of satellite tenants include cigar stores, candy stores and specialty apparel stores.

SATISFACTION - The payment of a debt or obligation such as a judgment. The time when the vendee pays in full under a real estate contract and the vendor transfers legal title is referred to as satisfaction or fulfillment.

SATISFACTION OF MORTGAGE - The certificate issued by the mortgagee when a mortgage is paid in full. It describes the mortgage, recites where it is recorded, and certifies that it has been paid and that the mortgagee consents that it be discharged of record. A satisfaction of mortgage is always an acknowledged and it should be recorded. In Washington it is sometimes called a satisfaction piece.

Even though payment in full has been made on the note and the note and mortgage may have been returned to the mortgagor, this does not change the fact that the records in the County Auditor's Office show an outstanding mortgage against the property. Clear record title is almost as important as clear actual title, and may be more important in some particular real estate transactions.

Washington State law provides that a mortgagee must acknowledge satisfaction of the mortgage in writing if requested to do so by the mortgagor. If the mortgagee fails to do so within 60 days, the mortgagor may bring action in a superior court to obtain a court order directing the auditor to cancel the mortgage. A mortgagor who is forced to bring court action may recover all costs of the legal action.
Reference: RCW 61.16.

SAVINGS AND LOAN ASSOCIATIONS (S&L) - A supplier of mortgages, lending primarily on single-family residential real estate. While savings and loan associations are not the largest financial intermediary in terms of total assets, historically they have been an important source of funds in terms of the dollars made available for financing real estate. Prior to the 1980's they were the largest supplier of single-family, owner-occupied residential permanent financing. Today savings and loan associations make home-improvement loans and loans to investors for apartments, industrial property, and commercial real estate. Deposits in federally chartered savings and loans association are insured through the *Savings Association Insurance Fund (SAIF),* a fund administered by the *Federal Deposit Insurance Corporation.* Included in the *Financial Institutions Reform, Recover, and Enforcement Act of 198,* was the creation of the *Office of Thrift Supervisors (OTS)* which replaced the Federal Home Loan Bank Board as the regulator of savings and loans associations.

SAVINGS ASSOCIATION INSURANCE FUND (SAIF) - The fund operated through the *Federal Deposit Insurance Corporation (FDIC)* which insures deposits of savings and loan associations. SAIF was created as part of the *Financial Institutions Reform, Recovery and Enforcement Act of 1989* and replaced the Federal Savings and Loan Insurance Corporation (FSLIC).

SCARCITY - In appraisal terminology, scarcity refers to increased value caused by a demand for some type of goods, the supply of which cannot be increased.

SCENIC EASEMENT - An easement created to preserve a property in a natural state. For example, the state may acquire (through condemnation proceedings) a scenic easement over certain choice property to preserve its aesthetic quality and, in effect, to prevent a developer from building on the property. A landowner might purchase a scenic easement over a neighbor's property in order to preserve the view.

Because of drastic increases in assessments and taxes, some owners of large tracts of land that possess some scenic or natural beauty attempt to make a gift of a scenic easement over part of the property to the county or state. If the gift is accepted, the landowner can possibly get a charitable deduction for tax purposes and a reduction in the real estate tax assessment. Under the federal Tax Act, a charitable deduction, for income tax purposes, may be taken for contribution of a scenic easement or other partial interest in real estate to be used for public enjoyment, historical preservation, or the preservation of wild areas. The Federal Highway Beautification Act offers incentives to states to acquire scenic or open-space easements to protect the view of historical sites or unusual scenery. (*See* CONDEMNATION, HISTORIC STRUCTURES.)

SCENIC VISTA ACT - Under the Highway Advertising Control Act of 1961, the State of Washington enacted legislation to limit the number of and the size of signs bordering the interstate highway system or scenic system highway. This legislation was adopted to

protect the public's right to the natural beauty of the State. One sign is permitted to be placed in such a location as to be seen from a highway only if the sign is on land that is for sale. The name of the owner or real estate broker offering it for sale shall be no more conspicuous than the words "for sale" or "for lease."
Reference: RCW 47.42 and WAC 252-400-040.

SCHEMATICS - Preliminary architectural drawings and sketches; basic layouts not containing the final details of design. A developer often will have an architect prepare schematics of a proposed building or development and then use those drawings either to convince the owner to sell the land or to persuade an investor or lender to finance the project. The architect will often "spec" his/her time; e.g., not charge the developer for his/her efforts in the expectation that if the project is approved he/she will be retained to perform the architectural services for the full development. If the architect does not "spec" his/her time, then it is usual to charge ten percent of the normal architect's fee, which is usually ten percent of the cost of construction. For example, a $100,000 improvement is to be built, resulting in an architect's fee of 10 percent or $10,000; thus schematics would cost $1,000.

SCOPE OF AUTHORITY - The common law on agency held that a principal was liable to third parties for all wrongful acts of his/her agent committed while transacting the principal's business. It was not necessary that the principal actually authorize the act; it is sufficient if the agent had apparent (ostensible) or implied authority to act on behalf of the principal. "Ostensible" authority is that which a principal, intentionally or by want of ordinary care, causes or allows a third person to believe the agent to possess. The principal is not liable for acts of the agent committed **outside** the scope of the agent's authority.

Under the Real Estate Brokerage Relationship Act adopted in Washington in 1996, the common law rule was substantially changed. A principal is not liable for an act, error or omission by an agent or subagent of the principal arising out of an agency relationship:

1. Unless the principal participated in or authorized the act, error or omission; or

2. Except to the extent that:

   a. The principal benefited from the act, error or omission; and

   b. the court determines that it is highly probably that the claimant would be unable to enforce a judgment against the agent or subagent.

(*See* AGENCY, REAL ESTATE BROKERAGE RELATIONSHIPS ACT - APPENDIX C, RESPONDEAT SUPERIOR.)
Reference: RCW 18.86

S CORPORATION - A corporation which for tax purposes has elected to be treated as if it were a partnership. It allows a business to operate in corporate form and yet not pay a corporate income tax, thus avoiding the double tax feature of corporate structure. Though there is no limitation on the amount of corporate income for a S corporation, each stockholder is taxable on his/her share of the corporation's income, whether or not it is distributed to him/her. Similarly, he/she can report his/her share of the corporation's ordinary losses and deduct them on his/her personal tax return.

Since S corporations pass income through to their shareholders, this makes them particularly attractive under the tax law since individual tax rates are lower than corporate rates.

The major advantages of an S corp include limited personal liability, ease of transferability of ownership shares, centralized management and comparative ease of formation. Its basic disadvantage is that aggregate losses may be passed through to the individual shareholders only equal to the amount of cash paid for the stock plus any loans made to the company. Thus, the S corporation's most efficient application for real estate investment ownership is for projects designed to be other than tax shelters.

SEAL - An embossed impression on paper used to authenticate a document or attest to a signature, as with a corporate or notary seal. The corporate seal contains the name of the corporation, the date and the state of incorporation. Sometimes the parties use the letters "L.S." after a signature which is Latin for Locus Sigilli, meaning "under seal" or "in place of seal."

In Washington a seal on instruments dealing with real estate is not necessary; however, they are sometimes encountered. Most often it is a seal of a corporation. The presence of the seal is evidence that the instrument is the action of the corporation executed by duly authorized officers or agents. A proper resolution authorizing a corporate transfer of real property would still be required.

SEASONED MORTGAGE OR DEED OF TRUST - A loan with a stable and consistent history of payments by the debtor and thus may be a good purchase risk. A real estate loan made a number of years ago in which the borrower has consistently been timely in making all payments on the debt.

SECOND HOME - A vacation home. The IRS defines a second home as a residence used by the taxpayer for personal residence purposes for at least 14 days of the year or 10% of the number of days that property is rented at fair market value, whichever is the greater. A taxpayer may deduct on his/her tax return all interest and real property tax payments.

The 1990 Housing bill prohibits FHA insurance on second homes, except in extraordinary hardship cases.

SECOND MORTGAGE OR DEED OF TRUST - A mortgage or deed of trust which is junior or subordinate to a first mortgage or deed of trust; typically, an additional loan imposed on top of the first mortgage or deed of trust which is taken out when the borrower needs more money. The risk involved to the lender is greater with a second mortgage or deed of trust and therefore the lender's conditions are usually more stringent, the term is shorter, and the interest rate is higher than on the first mortgage or deed of trust. Second mortgages or deeds of trust usually involve separate closing costs for appraisal, title report, credit check, drafting and recording documents, among others.

Sometimes second mortgages or deeds of trust contain provisions stating that they will remain subordinate to any subsequent first mortgage or deed of trust as long as the new mortgage or deed of trust is not made in an amount exceeding the present first mortgage or deed of trust. Such a "lifting clause" permits the mortgagor to lift out the first mortgage or deed of trust and refinance it with another first mortgage or deed of trust without altering the junior position of the second mortgage or deed of trust.

In the event of default under the first mortgage or deed of trust, the second mortgagee or beneficiary can elect to redeem the first mortgage or deed of trust and foreclose upon his/her own lien, or add the amount advanced to his/her junior mortgage or deed of trust whereupon it will be payable at the same rate of interest. In the event of a foreclosure sale, mortgage or deed of trust creditors shall be entitled to payment according to the priority of their liens, and not prorata. A judgment of foreclosure shall operate to extinguish the liens of subsequent mortgages or deeds of trust of the same property, without forcing prior mortgagees or beneficiaries to their right of recovery. The surplus after payment of the mortgage or deed of trust foreclosed shall be applied pro tanto ("for a much as") to the next junior mortgage or deed trust, and so on to the payment, wholly or in part, of mortgages or deeds of trust junior to the one assessed.

Banks and federal savings and loan associations are prohibited from lending on second mortgages or deeds of trust. *(See* JUNIOR DEED OF TRUST OR MORTGAGE.)

SECONDARY FINANCING - A junior mortgage or deed of trust placed on property to help finance the purchase price, such as a purchase money second mortgage taken back by the seller to assist a purchaser who has difficulty in paying a large down payment.

Governmental loan programs (FHA, VA) permit secondary financing but with restrictions. *(See* SECOND MORTGAGE OR DEED OF TRUST.)

SECONDARY MORTGAGE MARKET - A market for the purchase and sale of existing mortgages, designed to provide greater liquidity for mortgages; also called secondary money market. Secondary mortgage market lenders or investors buy mortgages as long-term investments as opposed to other types of securities, such as government and corporate bonds. The Federal National Mortgage Association (FNMA) purchases many existing mortgages, thus freeing more money for mortgagees to lend. The Government National Mortgage Association (GNMA) and the Federal Home Loan Mortgage Corporation

(FHLMC) are also active in the secondary mortgage market, especially where federally subsidized projects are involved.

Mortgage pools are created when lenders place mortgages in a package and sell securities that represent shares in these pooled mortgages. The pooled mortgages are actually removed from the balance sheets of the originators of the pools and the buyers of the securities become the joint owners. The regular mortgage payment and any prepayments may be collected by the originators (who continue to service the mortgages) and are distributed to the holders of the securities. (*See* FEDERAL HOME LOAN MORTGAGE CORPORATION, FEDERAL NATIONAL MORTGAGE ASSOCIATION, GOVERNMENT NATIONAL MORTGAGE ASSOCIATION, MAGGIE MAE.)

SECRET PROFIT - Refers to a broker making an undisclosed profit at the seller's expense; for example, the broker has an undisclosed relative buy the listed property and then resell it to a buyer whose earlier offer was never presented to the seller. (*See* AGENCY, DUAL AGENCY, LICENSING LAW.)
Reference: RCW 18.85

SECTION - As used in the Government Survey System, a section of land is an area one mile square, containing 640 acres. It is 1/36th of a township. (*See* GOVERNMENT SURVEY.)

SECTION 8 PROGRAM - A federal **rent** subsidy program for low and moderate income tenants. The Department of Housing and Urban Development (HUD) pays the subsidy to the landlord.

SECURED PARTY - The person having the security interest such as the mortgagee (mortgage), the vendee (real estate contract), or the beneficiary (deed of trust).

SECURITIES - Evidence of obligations to pay money or of rights to participate in earnings and distribution of corporate, trust or other property. A security is usually found where an investor subjects his/her money to the risks of an enterprise over which he/she exercises no managerial control.

Securities are regulated by both state and federal law. The purposes of the Washington Securities Act are to prevent fraud and to protect the public against imposition of unsubstantial schemes by regulating transactions in which promoters go to the public for risk capital. (*See* REAL PROPERTY SECURITIES REGISTRATION.)
Reference: RCW 21.20.

SECURITIES DIVISION - The Securities Division protects the public through regulation administered in two program areas: Registration and Compliance;

The primary mission of the Securities Division is to protect Washington State residents from the dishonest or fraudulent practices of people selling investments. The Division accomplishes this mission through a variety of regulatory and enforcement tools including registration, notification or exemption requirements for securities, franchise and business opportunity offerings and licensing and auditing of broker-dealers and investment advisers. It also undertakes investigations based upon complaints and undercover work. The Division works directly with the entities it regulates through supervisory activity in an effort to assure the investing public of adequate and proper services from these entities.

The Securities Division is one of the divisions of the Department of Financial Institutions. (*See* INTRASTATE EXEMPTION, PRIVATE OFFERING, REAL PROPERTY SECURITIES REGISTRATION, RENTAL POOL, RESTRICTED REAL ESTATE SECURITIES.)
Reference: RCW 21.20.

SECURITIES EXCHANGE COMMISSION (SEC) - *See* INTRASTATE EXEMPTION, PRIVATE OFFERING, REAL PROPERTY SECURITIES REGISTRATION, RENTAL POOL, RESTRICTED REAL ESTATE SECURITIES, RULE 10B5, RULE 146, RULE 147.

SECURITY AGREEMENT - A security document which creates a lien upon chattels, including chattels intended to be affixed to land as fixtures; known as a chattel mortgage prior to the adoption of the Uniform Commercial Code. Rather than record the security agreement, the Code provides for filing a notice on a short form called a "financing statement." In order to perfect a security interest, the financing statement must be filed with the Office of the Secretary of State. In a limited number of situations it is possible to perfect a security interest by filing at the County Auditor's Office. (*See* FINANCING STATEMENT, UNIFORM COMMERCIAL CODE.)
Reference: RCW 62A9.

SECURITY DEPOSIT - Money deposited by or for the tenant with the landlord, which may be held for the following purposes: (1) to remedy tenant defaults for damage to the premises (be it accidental or intentional), for failure to pay rent due, or for failure to return all keys at the end of the tenancy; (2) to clean the dwelling so as to place it in as fit a condition as when the tenant commenced possession; and (3) to compensate for damages caused by a tenant who wrongfully quits the dwelling unit. The security deposit is not regarded as liquidated damages, but rather is a fund the landlord can use to offset damages caused by the tenant. A security deposit is not taxable to the landlord until applied to remedy any tenant defaults.

If money is given to the landlord as either a security or damage deposit, the landlord must specify in the lease or rental agreement the terms and conditions under which the deposit or a portion thereof may be withheld by the landlord upon termination of the lease or rental agreement.

The rules governing the use of the moneys paid by a residential tenant to the landlord as a security deposit or damage deposit are very specific. They require that the moneys be deposited by the landlord into a trust account in a bank, savings and loan association, mutual savings bank, or a licensed escrow account located in the State of Washington. It also provides that the landlord shall provide the tenant with a written receipt for the deposit and that he/she shall provide written notice of the name and address and location of the bank where the moneys are deposited. Additionally, he/she is obligated to inform the tenant if he/she, for some reason, changes the location of that deposit.

The Landlord Tenant Act also provides that within fourteen days after the termination of the rental agreement and vacation of the premises, the landlord shall give a full and specific statement of the basis for retaining any of the deposit together with the payment of any refund due to the tenant under the terms and conditions of the rental agreement. No portion of the deposit shall be withheld on account of wear resulting from ordinary use of the premises. The notice shall be delivered to the tenants personally or by mail to their last known address.

If the landlord fails to return the deposit or any part thereof, or does not by written statement explain the reason for retaining it, the tenant may bring an action in a district or superior court. If the tenant prevails, he/she may receive an award of two times the amount of the refund due plus reasonable attorney's fees if any were incurred. The landlord may bring an action against the tenant to recover amounts in excess of the damage deposit, together with reasonable attorney's fees.

Upon the transfer of property subject to a lease, the landlord's successor in interest is bound by the Landlord-Tenant Act provisions regarding security deposits. The new purchaser should therefore be sure that he/she is credited with the security deposit at the time of closing.

The lease should clearly specify whether a payment is a security deposit or an advance rental. If it is a security deposit, the tenant is not entitled to apply it as discharge of the final month's rent. If it is an advance rental, the landlord will have to pay taxes on it when received. (*See* LANDLORD TENANT ACT.)
Reference: RCW 59.18.

SECURITY INTEREST - According to the UCC, a term designating the interest of the creditor in the property of the debtor in all types of credit transactions. It thus replaced such terms as chattel mortgage, pledge, trust receipt, chattel trust, equipment trust, conditional sale, and inventory lien. (*See* FINANCING STATEMENT, SECURITY AGREEMENT, UNIFORM COMMERCIAL CODE.)
Reference: RCW 62A-9.

SEED MONEY - Usually refers to a developer's own initial investment in starting a project. (*See* FRONT MONEY.)

SEISIN - (Also spelled "seizen") Actual possession of property by one who claims rightful ownership of a freehold interest therein. Generally considered to be synonymous with ownership. Derived from feudal times when the term ownership was not used since the sovereign was considered the owner of all lands in England. Instead a landowner was said to be seized of his/her estate. A person is seized of property when he/she is in rightful possession with the intention of claiming a freehold estate.

A general warranty deed contains the covenant of seisin in which the grantor warrants that he/she has the estate or interest which he/she purports to convey. Both title and possession at the time of the grant are necessary to satisfy the covenant. In the event of a breach, the purchaser may recover his/her expenses up to the amount paid for the property. (*See* DELIVERY, FREEHOLD.)

SELF-EMPLOYED BORROWER - A lender usually classifies a borrower as self-employed if he/she owns 25% or more of a business.

Lenders will normally consider income from a self-employed borrower if there is at least a two-year history. An applicant who has between one to two years of self-employment may be considered if there is a previous history of employment or education in a related field. A lender will usually not consider income from self-employed borrowers with a business less than one-year old.

When a borrower's income is from a business that he/she owns or is a principal owner and the income will be used for loan qualification, the amount of income considered will be either: (1) the total net profit, (2) the amount of the draw or bonus taken from the capital account, if the business is a partnerships, plus the borrower's share of the net profit, or (3) the amount of wage or salary as shown on the W-2, if the business is a corporation, plus any bonus or other compensation. Since Federal Tax returns will be used in verifying income, a lender will allow a self-employed borrower to add back to the net income: (1) all depreciation, (2) depletion, and (3) IRA/Keogh contributions. Retained earnings do not normally count as income. A self-employed borrower cannot use withdrawals from capital accounts as income.

An average monthly income is calculated for self-employed borrowers because the income is subject to fluctuations. An average figure is a better way to decide the long-term income earning ability of the borrower. A minimum of two year's income must be verified.

Self-employed or fully commissioned people will need to submit complete and signed tax returns (complete with all schedules) for the past two calendar years, plus a year-to-date income and expense statement and a current balance sheet. If the business is a corporation or partnership, copies of signed federal business income tax returns for the last two years with all application schedules attached will be required. (*See* INCOME ANALYSIS.)

SELF-HELP - The nonjudicial remedies an owner employs to regain possession of his/her property. For example, a landlord whose tenant is in default may attempt to cut off the utilities, forcibly enter the premises, or change the locks in order to force the tenant to pay the rent or move out. Washington State disapproves of self-help remedies and requires landlords to follow statutory procedures for eviction. (*See* EVICTION, LANDLORD TENANT ACT.)

SELF STORAGE LIEN - *See* ABANDONMENT.

SELLER FINANCING - An "extension of credit" made by the seller of the property to the buyer of the property to cover part or all of the sale price. The loan, like most real estate loans, will probably be a promissory note secured by a deed of trust; it could also be a mortgage or a real estate contract. While common in both residential and commercial real estate, seller financing or owner financing as it is also called, becomes more popular when interest rates are higher. Sometimes seller financing is offered when the buyer will not qualify for conventional financing, other times seller financing is offered due to the desire of the seller to earn the higher interest normally paid on a mortgage or deed of trust versus a standard bank account. Seller financing should be carefully structured to protect the desires and wishes of the seller. (*See* DEED OF TRUST, PURCHASE MONEY MORTGAGE.)

SELLERS MARKET - A real estate market condition in which the demand for a particular type of real estate is greater than the supply. The results is that owners may obtain sale prices over and above normal market prices. Often during a sellers market there will be multiple offers made on a parcel of property and the seller is able to select the offer which more closely meets the terms and conditions that the seller wants. Often in a seller's market, buyers do not take the normal safeguards to assure themselves of the condition of the property. The opposite of a buyers' market or soft market. (*See* PHYSICAL INSPECTION.)

SELLING AGENT - The real estate licensee who procures the buyer, although in an in-house sale (same office), one licensee is sometimes both the listing licensee and the selling licensee.

SEMIANNUAL - Occurring twice a year as in semiannual tax payments. (*See* BIANNUALLY.)

SENIOR DEED OF TRUST/MORTGAGE - A first deed of trust or mortgage (referred to as a deed of trust hereafter) is normally a senior deed of trust. The priority of deeds of trust can be compared to rungs on a ladder. The first deed of trust is the top rung, a second deed of trust is the second rung and continuing down the ladder for each subsequent or junior deeds of trust. If the first deed of trust matures or is refinanced and if there is an outstanding second deed of trust, it will then become the senior deed of trust unless there is a subordination agreement. (*See* SUBORDINATION AGREEMENT.)

SEPARATE PROPERTY - Property owned by a husband or wife which is not community property; acquired by either spouse prior to marriage or by gift or devise after marriage. (*See* COMMUNITY PROPERTY.)

In Washington, courts have stated the law will not convert property acquired before marriage into community property, absent a writing evidencing the mutual intent of the parties. Where there in any uncertainty in tracing an asset to a separate property source, the law resolves the uncertainty in favor of a finding of community character.

SEPTIC TANK - A sewage settling tank in which part of the sewage is converted into gas and liquids before the remaining waste is discharged by gravity into a leaching bed underground. Many local planning commissions require a developer to provide a sewage disposal system rather than use septic tanks because of the fear of pollution. Unlike cesspools, however, septic tanks are generally acceptable sanitary systems for low-density developments.

SEQUESTRATION ORDER - A writ authorizing the taking of land, rents, and/or profits owned by a defendant in a pending or concluded suit, for the purpose of forcing the defendant to comply with a court order. For example, to hold rental moneys by court order pending the outcome of litigation.

SERVICE OF PROCESS - The legal act of notifying the defendant of an impending lawsuit and the delivery to him/her of the summons and complaint in the action. Service is usually made upon the defendant by a process server delivering a certified copy of the summons and the plaintiff's complaint. In some areas of the State, the sheriff's office makes delivery. If the defendant cannot be found within the State, the court can authorize service by publication in the newspaper.

Under the Washington Landlord Tenant Act, if the landlord does not reside in the State of Washington, he/she must designate a person who resides in the county where the premises are located who is authorized to act as his/her agent for purposes of service of notices and process. If no designation is made of a person to act as the agent of the landlord, then the person to whom the rental payments are made shall be considered the agent. (*See* LANDLORD TENANT ACT.)
Reference: RCW 59.18.

SERVICING - The duties of the mortgage banker as a loan correspondent as specified in the servicing agreement for which a fee is received. The collection for an investor of payments of interest, principal, and trust items such as hazard insurance and taxes, on a note by the borrower in accordance with the terms of the note. Servicing also consists of operational procedures covering accounting, bookkeeping, insurance, tax records, loan payment follow-up, delinquency loan follow-up, and loan analysis.

A written agreement between an investor and mortgage loan correspondent stipulating the rights and obligations of each party. It is usually set up in a document called a servicing agreement. (*See* SECONDARY MORTGAGE MARKET.)

SERVICING FEE - A periodic (monthly or annual) payment made by the purchaser of a mortgage to the mortgage banker who originally made the loan for servicing the loan. The fee, which varies from one-fourth to one-half percent of the outstanding loan balance, covers the administrative costs of servicing such as collection and payment of property taxes and property insurance premiums.

SERVIENT ESTATE - Land on which an easement exists in favor of an adjacent property (called a dominant estate); also referred to as a servient tenement. If property A has a right of way across property B, property B is the servient estate.

The servient owner may not use the property in such a way as to interfere with the reasonable use of the dominant owner. (*See* EASEMENT, SERVITUDE.)

SERVITUDE - A burden or charge upon an estate. A personal servitude (such as a license) attaches to the person for whose benefit it is established and terminates (if properly renewed) with his/her life. A real servitude (such as an easement) is one which the owner of an estate enjoys on a neighboring estate for the benefit of his/her own estate and runs indefinitely with the land. (*See* EQUITABLE SERVITUDE.)

SET ASIDE LETTER - A financing term in which the lender sends the contractor of a project a letter to the effect that the lender will set aside money for him/her, and thus induces the contractor to finish a troubled project.

SETBACK REQUIREMENT - Restrictions on the amount of land that must surround improvements; the amount of space required between the lot line and the building line. These restrictions, called setbacks and sidebacks, may be contained in local zoning regulations, such as Tacoma's Comprehensive Zoning Code, or they may be established by restrictive covenants in deeds and under subdivision general plans normally noted on the recorded subdivision plat. If any of the above are inconsistent, the more restrictive will prevail.

Setback provisions are designed to keep buildings away from streets and to ensure that occupants have more light and air and less noise, smoke, dust, danger of spread of fire, and, in some cases, a better view at street intersections. It is important to clarify what is meant by a "building;" i.e., whether or not the provision includes eaves, steps, bay windows, porches, awnings, walls, or fences. (*See* ZERO LOT LINE.)

SETOFF - A claim a debtor can make against a creditor that reduces or cancels the amount the debtor owes (*See* HOLDER IN DUE COURSE.)

SETTLEMENT - 1. The act of adjusting and prorating various credits, charges and settlement costs to conclude a real estate transaction. Most Washington brokers refer to this process as the "closing" rather than the settlement. (*See* CLOSING.)

2. The act of compromising in a dispute or a lawsuit. Such an act usually does not involve an admission of liability. (*See* CONCILIATION.)

SETTLEMENT ACT - *See* REAL ESTATE SETTLEMENT PROCEDURES ACT.

SETTLEMENT STATEMENT - *See* CLOSING COSTS, CLOSING STATEMENT.

SEVERALTY - Sole ownership of real property. Most corporations hold title to real property under tenancy in severalty. In this form of ownership, the ownership of the property is in one "person," severed from anyone else. (*See* TENANCY IN SEVERALTY.)

SEVERANCE - The act of removing something attached to land or of terminating a relationship. When a fence is torn down, there is a severance of the fence from the real property. The fence thus changes from real property (fixture) to personal property.

When one joint tenant transfers his/her interest, there is a severance of the joint tenancy. The other joint tenant and the new transferee are then tenants in common in the property.

SEVERANCE DAMAGES - Where there is a partial taking of property under the state's power of eminent domain, any loss in value of remaining property caused by the partial taking of this real estate is referred to as "severance damages." Severance damages are compensable to the property owner if the partial taking lowers the highest and best use or otherwise limits the use of the remainder of the property. (*See* BEFORE AND AFTER METHOD, CONDEMNATION, SPECIAL BENEFITS.)

SHAKE SHINGLE - Shingle composed of split wood, usually cedar, most frequently used as a roofing or siding material.

SHALL - Common statutory language meaning that which is required by law.

SHARED APPRECIATION MORTGAGE - Refers to a form of participation mortgage in which the lender shares in the appreciation of a property mortgaged if and when the property is sold. For a reduction in the current market interest rate by up to 40 percent in some cases, the borrower agrees to share with the lender the appreciation in the home's (or commercial property) value in proportion to the interest reduction. The normal standard is a 10-year limit, with guaranteed long-term financing at the going rate after that, or sharing in proceeds when the house or commercial property is sold. (*See* CREATIVE FINANCING, PARTICIPATION MORTGAGE.)

SHEAR WALL - Permanent structural wall to provide lateral stability.

SHELL LEASE - A lease wherein a tenant leases the unfinished shell of a building, as in a new shopping center, and agrees to complete construction himself by installing ceilings, plumbing, heating and air conditioning systems, and electrical wiring. It is important for landlord and tenant under a shell lease to agree upon who shall pay the real property taxes against the premises. Some shell leases provide that all improvements shall remain the tenant's personal property and that the tenant must pay the taxes assessed against them.

SHERIFF'S DEED - A deed, by court order, to be delivered by the sheriff to the holder of a Certificate of Sale after the termination of the statutory period of redemption; contains no warranty, but affords good title. (*See* MORTGAGE.)

SHERIFF'S SALE - A judgment creditor in order to obtain a writ of execution on real property must file an affidavit stating that "due diligence" has been exercised in determining whether sufficient nonexempt personal property exists to execute against and whether the homestead exemption applies. The term "due diligence" as defined requires among other things a personal visit to the premises and a search of the auditor's records.

In the case of the sale of real property, the judgment creditor at least thirty days prior to the date of sale (1) must serve the judgment debtor with a notice of sale in the same manner as a summons in a civil action and (2) must also mail a copy of the notice of sale by regular and certified mail to the judgment debtor and by mail to the attorney of record for the judgment debtor. These notice requirements are in addition to the postings and publication requirements of current law.

The information to be included in the notice of sale is specified in the statute. The judgment creditor must file an affidavit of compliance with these notice requirements. Notice of the filing of the return of sale must be mailed to all parties who appeared in the action. The time period for filing any objections to the sale is increased to twenty days.

Every two months during the redemption the purchaser must mail the judgment debtor a notice of the time remaining in the redemption period and the amount needed to redeem. The sole effect of noncompliance will be to extend the redemption period two months for each missed or noncomplying notice. Real estate brokers in the county may sell the property after the redemption period expires. The sheriff's sale purchaser will receive 120% of the redemption amount, the broker his/her normal commission, and the judgment debtor the balance.

The $30,000 homestead exemption arises automatically once the property is occupied as a permanent residence. No written declaration of homestead need be filed. However, an owner of unimproved land who wishes to designate it as a homestead must file a written declaration. The owner of a mobile home is now also entitled to protection under the homestead statute. A homestead is declared abandoned if the owner is absent for more than six consecutive months. An owner may file a declaration of nonabandonment if a lengthy absence is contemplated. (*See* HOMESTEAD.)

SHOE MOLDING - A thin strip of wood placed at the junction of the baseboard and the floor boards to conceal the joint. The shoe molding improves the aesthetics of the room and helps seal out drafts

SHOPPING - The business practice of negotiating a real estate sale and then attempting to shop around for better terms from other buyers.

SHOPPING CENTER - A classification of retail stores, characterized by off-street parking and clusters of stores, subject to a uniform development plan, and usually with careful analysis given to the proper merchant mix.

The most common design for a shopping center is the strip "center," with stores built in a line and facing the street or parking area, with an anchor store at each end (such as a supermarket and super drugstore). These strip neighborhood centers have not proven to be very efficient because they lack flexibility, and many economists believe that the all purpose large discount store will replace the neighborhood shopping center in the next decade. Due to increased land costs and high taxes, it is predicted that customers may some day have to pay for shopping center parking, heretofore an important attraction of the shopping center concept.

A shopping center lease is a complicated and lengthy document (often 20 - 40 pages). It may be a net lease with the rental determined on a percentage basis. The applicable percentages vary greatly among the types and sizes of retail stores, with the large department stores paying less per- square-foot minimum rent and a lower percentage than smaller stores. Usually all tenants must belong to a merchants' association which promotes the shopping center itself through institutional advertising. The tenant usually must operate his/her store during established hours; limit his/her use to that specified in the lease; pay his/her prorata share of taxes, maintenance, insurance; and agree to keep his/her books open for audit and sometimes even to use a special type of register so that the landlord is assured that the tenant accurately records the gross sales upon which the percentage ratio is based. The landlord may go as far as employing spot buyers to make sure that sales are properly recorded on the register.

Most shopping center leases contain some form of "radius clause" which might forbid the landlord from renting the premises within a specified radius of the shopping center for a purpose that competes with the tenant, or which might forbid the tenant from opening another store within a specified radius of the center. Recently, these anti-competition clauses have been under attack by the Federal Trade Commission as unreasonable restraints upon trade which are illegal under Section 1 of the Sherman Antitrust Act.

The type of shopping center is determined by its major tenant or tenants. Neither site area nor building size determine the type. Neighborhood Center provides for the sale of convenience goods and personal service for the day-to-day living needs of the immediate neighborhood. It is built around a supermarket as the principal tenant. Community Center provides, in addition to convenience goods, a wider range of wearing apparel, hardware and appliances. It is built around a variety store or junior department store as the major tenant. Regional Center provides for a full range of general merchandise including apparel, furniture and home furnishings in full depth. It is built around one or more department stores. (*See* TRADE AREA.)

SHORELINE - The dividing line between private land and public beach on beachfront property. In it's constitution of November 11, 1889, the State of Washington asserted its rights to the beds and shores of all navigable bodies of water. Any government lot patented after that date is limited to the line of ordinary high water or ordinary high tide, in the case of tide lands. Everything beyond this line from that date belongs to the State of Washington. In 1961 the United States Supreme Court in the Hughes case, further refined the location of the "line of ordinary tide" as being "the average elevation of all high tides as observed at a location through a complete tidal cycle of 18.6 years."

The prudent seller of shoreline property will carefully describe the land area in approximate language (such as "approximately 10,000 square feet," or "10,000 square feet, more or less"); and the prudent buyer will require that the property be resurveyed to ascertain the proper land area in view of recent court cases. Sometimes a seller will insert in his/her Purchase and Sale Agreement protective language such as: "Buyer acknowledges that the property being sold is a beachfront lot and accepts the premises subject to the possibility of dispute with regard to exact location of the shoreline boundary of the property. Buyer agrees to make no claim against the seller on account of any such dispute or any decrease in the area of the property resulting from the resolution of any such dispute."

In 1971 the State of Washington passed the Shoreline Management Act in an attempt to restrict development on all shores touched by tidal water, shores of all lakes bigger than 20 acres, and all streams or rivers with a flow of more than 20 cubic feet per second. (*See* SHORELINE MANAGEMENT ACT, TIDE LANDS.)

SHORELINE MANAGEMENT ACT - The Shoreline Management Act of 1971 is based on the philosophy that the shorelines of the State are among the most valuable, and fragile, of its natural resources and that there is great concern throughout the State relating to their utilization, protection, restoration, and preservation. Therefore, coordinated planning is necessary in order to protect the public interest associated with the shorelines of the State, while at the same time, recognizing and protecting private property rights consistent with public interest. This planning is to be a rational and concerted effort, jointly performed by federal, state and local government. It is further felt that the interest of all of the people shall be paramount in the management of shorelines of statewide significance, and that the public should have the opportunity to enjoy the physical and aesthetic qualities of natural shorelines of the State.

The express purpose of the Shoreline Management Act is to provide for management of Washington's shorelines by planning for and fostering all reasonable and appropriate uses. This policy is directed at enhancement of shorelines rather than restriction of uses. The shoreline zone generally consists of bodies of water, wetlands and flood plains and shoreline 200 feet inland from the water.

The master program is to be developed by local government to provide an objective guide for regulating the use of shorelines. The master program should clearly state local policies for the development of shorelands and indicate how these policies relate to the goals of the local citizens and to specific regulations of uses affecting the physical development of land and water resources throughout the local government's jurisdiction.

The master program developed by each local government will reflect the unique shoreline conditions and the development requirements which exist and are projected in that area. As part of the process of master program development, local governments can identify problems and seek solutions which best satisfy their needs.

The act requires that, prior to approval or adoption of a master program, or a portion thereof, by the department, at least one public hearing shall be held in each county affected by the program for the purpose of obtaining the views and comments of the public.

The act not only charges the state and local government with the responsibility of making reasonable efforts to inform the people of the State about the shoreline management program, but also actively encourages participation by all persons, private groups and entities, which have an interest in shoreline management.

The act designated certain shorelines as shorelines of statewide significance. Shorelines thus designated are important to the entire state. Because these shorelines are major resources from which all people in the state derive benefit, the guidelines and master programs must give preference to uses which favor public and long-range goals.

Accordingly, the act established that local master programs shall give preference to uses which meet the principles outlined in order of preference:

1. Recognize and protect the statewide interest over local interest.

2. Preserve the natural character of the shoreline.

3. Result in long-term over short-term benefit.

4. Protect the resources and ecology of shorelines.

5. Increase public access to publicly owned areas of the shorelines.

6. Increase recreational opportunities for the public on the shorelines.

(*See* SHORELINE.)
Reference: RCW 90.58, WAC 17316.

Cities and counties planning under the Growth Management Act (GMA) must include a shoreline management master program as part of their comprehensive plan.
Reference: RCW36.70A.

SHORING - The use of timbers to prevent the sliding of earth adjoining an excavation. Shoring is also the timbers used as bracing against a wall for temporary support of loads during construction.

SHORT PLAT - In recent years short subdivisions, generally referred to as short plats, have been made subject to State law and City ordinances. A division of land into 4 or less lots is considered to be a short plat. A short plat may allow up to nine lots within incorporated cities, this is optional and must be passed by each city in their local ordinance. In these laws, standards have been set up to control the haphazard division of relatively small parcels of land. Most cities and counties in the State have adopted short plat requirements. The normal items considered before a short plat will be approved are:

1. Would the proposed subdivision be contrary to the Comprehensive Plan?

2. Would the lots proposed conform to the zoning regulations covering the property?

3. If there are existing structures on the property, would the proposed short subdivisions create any substandard side yards or front or back yards?

4. Would the lots have adequate access for vehicles, utilities, fire protection, drainage and water supply?

5. Would the proposed lots have adequate sanitary sewerage disposal?

(*See* PLAT, SUBDIVISION.)
Reference: RCW 58.17.030.

SHORT RATE - A higher periodic rate charged for a shorter term than that originally contracted. The increased premium charged by an insurance company upon early cancellation of a policy to compensate the insuror for the fact that the original rate charged was calculated on the full period of the policy. This increased charge may enter into a buyer's decision whether to assume the seller's existing homeowner's hazard insurance policy or to cancel it and obtain a new policy.

SHOULD - Common statutory language meaning that which is recommended but is not required by law.

SIDING - Boards nailed horizontally to the vertical studs, with or without intervening sheathing, to form the exposed surface of the outside walls of the building. Siding may be made of wood, metal, or masonry sheets.

SIGNATURE - Use of any name, including any trade or fictitious name, upon an instrument, or any word or mark used as and intended to be a written signature. To be valid, a signature may be handwritten, typed, printed, stamped or made in any other manner including pencil. If the party cannot write, he/she can sign by using a mark such as "John X (his mark) Brown" all but the X can be typed, the X must be affixed by the one signing in the presence of two witnesses. Normally in Washington, signatures on deeds or real estate contracts do not have to be witnessed though they must be acknowledged in order to record the document in the Office of the County Auditor.

Under the Statute of Frauds, a real estate contract must be "in writing and signed by the person to be charged therewith." This signature need not appear at the end of the document, though it customarily does. If a statute requires a document be "subscribed," however, it must be signed at the end. For example, witnesses to a will (at least two) must subscribe their names at the end of the will and in the presence of the testator who has already signed above their names in their presence.

In Washington, only the parties listed must acknowledge before the instrument may be recorded: deed — grantor; mortgage — mortgagor; deed of trust — grantor; lease — lessor; real estate contract — vendor.

In addition to the signature of an authorized corporate officer, Washington's law requires the affirmative vote or consent of two-thirds of the shareholders to sell, lease or exchange (not mortgage) all or substantially all of the property and assets of any domestic corporation. The corporation signature consists of the corporation's name, the name and title of the authorized officer or agent and usually an impression of the corporate seal.

The signature of an attorney-in-fact is not valid on a real estate contract unless his/her authority is by way of a written power of attorney (under the "equal dignities rule"). The power of attorney should also be recorded where the parties intend to record the documents. The proper form of signature is for the attorney-in-fact to sign first the name of the principal, and then sign his/her own name as attorney-in-fact; "Glenn Burgess, Principal by Shannon Burgess, Agent, his attorney-in-fact."

A listing agreement need be signed by the party to be charged therewith. Thus a broker who obtains from the husband a listing which the wife does not sign does not have an enforceable employment contract if the listing involves community property, due to the fact, that both husband and wife have equal rights when dealing with community property. When co-owner are selling property, they all must sign the necessary transfer documents though it is not necessary that they all sign one document; that is, they could convey by separate deeds.

For a written lease to be valid, it is necessary that the lessor sign since he/she is conveying possession. Though it is not necessary that the lessee sign the lease if he/she accepts the lease and takes possession of the leased premises, it is preferable that both lessor and lessee read and sign the lease document to lessen the chance of disputes arising between the parties.

When a fiduciary signs a document, he/she should indicate the capacity in which he/she is signing. For example, a guardian should sign as follows:

"Alan Brock, as legal guardian of Rae Britt, a minor."
(*See* ACKNOWLEDGMENT, COMMUNITY PROPERTY, LEGAL NAME, NAME, CHANGE OF.)

SIGNS - In Washington, it is permissible to place "FOR SALE" signs or "OPEN HOUSE" signs on private property, though it is illegal to place such signs on public property or on a public right-of-way. In some large eastern cities the use of "FOR SALE" signs is prohibited in order to prevent blockbusting, protect existing home values and eliminate the overall unattractiveness to the neighborhood of too many signs. Signs are a mode of advertising and must therefore comply with all advertising regulations such as Truth-in-Lending. If a buyer becomes interested in a parcel of real estate as a result of seeing a broker's "for sale" sign, that broker will most likely be deemed the procuring cause of the sale.

SILENT PARTNER - An inactive partner in business. Often refers to a partner who puts up money but does not appear to be involved on a day to day basis in the business activity. (*See* LIMITED PARTNER.)

SILL - The lowest horizontal member of the house frame, which rests on the top of the foundation wall and forms a base for the studs. The term can also refer to the lowest horizontal member in the frame for a window or door.

SIMPLE INTEREST - Interest computed on the principal balance only. (*See* COMPOUND INTEREST.)

SINGLE AGENCY - The action on the part of a real estate license to represent either the buyer or the seller but not both parties in the same transaction. (*See* AGENCY.)

SINGLE FAMILY RESIDENCE - A structure maintained and used as a single dwelling unit, designed for occupancy by one family, as in a private home.

The rental of single family residences is covered by the Washington Landlord Tenant Act. (*See* LANDLORD TENANT ACT.)
Reference: RCW 59.18.

A subdivider often restricts use of subdivided lots to single-family residences. It is advisable to further restrict the property to single-family **"detached"** residences, if it is intended to preclude the possibility of someone's using the property for a duplex dwelling.

SINGLE LOAD CORRIDOR - A building term used to describe a building design in which the apartment units are located on only one side of the corridor. When one gets off the elevator and walks down the corridor, there is open space on one side and apartments on the other. The alternative is a double load situation with apartments on both sides of the corridor, as in many hotels.

SINKING FUND - A fund created to gradually amass enough money to satisfy a debt or to meet a specific requirement; a fund designed to accumulate money to a predetermined amount at the end of a stated period of time. The sinking fund method of depreciation contemplates periodic investments of equal amounts of money in a compound interest bearing account wherein the investment, plus the compound interest, will replace the improvement at the end of its economic life. For example, assume a retail operator enters into a 20-year lease for a store with an option to buy it for $100,000 at the end of the lease term. In order to have $100,000 at the end of the term, the operator would have to set aside each year in a sinking fund the principal amount of $3,024, assuming a five percent return compounded annually ($100,000 ′ .03024, the factor in a sinking fund table for a 20-year 5% compound return). (*See* AMORTIZATION, INTERNAL RATE OF RETURN.)

SIOR - A profession designation denoting *Specialist in Industrial and Office Realty* earned by industrial and office-Realtorsâ who have established a creditable track record in either industrial or office real estate transactions for seven years and in addition, complete required course work. The designation is awarded by the Society of Industrial and Office Realtorsâ, a professional affiliate of the National Association of Realtorsâ. (*See* SOCIETY OF INDUSTRIAL AND OFFICE REALTORS.)

SITE - The position, situation, or location of a piece of land.

SKY LEASE - A lease of the "air rights" above a property. (*See* AIR RIGHTS.)

SKYLIGHT - An opening in a roof that is covered with glass and is designed to admit light.

SLAB - A flat, horizontal reinforced concrete area, usually the interior floor of a building but also an exterior or roof area.

SLANDER OF TITLE - A tort or civil wrong in which a person maliciously makes disparaging, untrue statements concerning another's title to property, thus causing injury. The disparaging statement may be oral or written, but must be published to some third person(s). Some statements are privileged, notably a "lis pendens" pleading filed in the appropriate court. Willful failure to remove a satisfied judgment lien may be grounds for a slander of title action.

SMALL BUSINESS ADMINISTRATION (SBA) - A federal government agency created to take over the small business functions of the Reconstruction Finance Corporation. SBA is supervised by an Administrator appointed by the President. Its function is to administer the Federal government's program for the preservation and development of small business concerns. Among other things, SBA is authorized to make loans to small businesses to finance plant construction, conversion, or expansion, including the acquisition of land. These loans may be made either directly or in participation with private lenders. Before SBA can make a direct loan, it must try to get a private lender to participate in the loan.

SMALL CLAIMS COURT - A division of the district court whose jurisdiction is limited to claims not exceeding $2,500, exclusive of interest and costs. The purpose of the small claims court is to provide an inexpensive and speedy forum for the disposition of minor controversies. Actions are commenced by the filing of a statement of claim. Neither side of the suit may be represented by an attorney. All claims based on contract, express or implied, must be verified.

If landlord and tenant disagree about the right of the landlord to claim and retain the security deposit or any portion of it, either the landlord or the tenant may commence an action in the small claims court to resolve the dispute. (*See* SECURITY DEPOSIT.)

A person who believes he/she has a valid claim for an amount in excess of $2,500 may bring a suit in small claims up to $2,500; however, they lose the right to sue for any amount over $2,500.

SOCIETY OF INDUSTRIAL AND OFFICE REALTORS (SIOR) - A professional organization affiliated with the National Association of Realtors (NAR), whose members specialize in the marketing of industrial and office properties. SIOR members subscribe to both the Code of Ethics of NAR, and a special set of professional standards. (*See* SIOR.)

SOCIETY OF REAL ESTATE APPRAISERS (SREA) - An international organization of professional real estate appraisers. There are three classifications of professional designations, each having separate qualifications and experience levels.

Senior Residential Appraiser (SRA): One who has successfully completed a program of professional training in the appraisal of single-family residential real estate, defined as one to six units.

Senior Real Property Appraiser (SRPA): One who has successfully completed the professional training and development program, and has demonstrated that he/she is competent to appraise residential and income properties.

Senior Real Estate Analyst (SREA): One who has had extensive technical training, plus long and varied experience. He/she is competent to appraise all types of real estate interests and ownerships.

SOFT MARKET - A real estate market condition in which the number of buyers are substantially fewer than the number of sellers and as a result of which sellers are not able to obtain normal market prices. Also referred to as a buyers market. (*See* BUYERS MARKET.)

SOIL BANK - A program administered by the Commodity Stabilization Service of the federal Department of Agriculture in which farmers contract to divert land from production of unneeded crops to conservation uses. Such individuals receive an annual rent from the government for this land.

SOLAR EASEMENT - An easement designed to protect an owner's access to light and the rays of the sun. There is no common law right to light and air onto one's property. Therefore, if an owner's solar heating system was rendered ineffective because of shadows cast by a neighbor's tree or a proposed nearby condominium, the owner would be left with no legal remedy except to try and negotiate a purchase of an easement to restrict blocking out the sun.

Some jurisdictions are attempting to legislate solar easements to encourage property owners to use more efficient energy systems. California has a statute declaring as a "nuisance" vegetation shading a solar collector. Other communities offer incentives to builders who protect solar access in their designs. For example, a builder might receive a density bonus of up to 20 percent for incorporating solar access into plans of streets, lots and buildings.

SOLAR HEATING - A natural system of heating using the energy of the sun. To encourage homeowners to utilize such energy-efficient systems. Passive solar heating is a system that incorporates some solar heating plus central heating as a back-up.

SOLDIERS AND SAILORS CIVIL RELIEF ACT - A federal law designed to protect persons in the military service from loss of property where the serviceman's ability to pay his/her obligations has been materially affected by reason of entering military service. If a person who has mortgaged property enters the military service and as a result of the drastic change in pay scale can no longer keep his/her loan current, the court has wide discretion to protect the defaulting serviceman. For example, the court can order the serviceman to pay only interest and taxes, and can postpone foreclosure until his/her military service ends.

After a mortgagor enters the service, the soldier can request that the mortgage bear only 6 percent interest. This is true whether the soldier enlists or is drafted into the service and regardless of whether or not he/she defaults in his/her original payments. As with the postponed principal payments, the serviceman will have to make up all deferred payments upon his/her leaving the service.

Foreclosure of a real estate loan where a serviceman is the borrower must be done by way of court proceeding, regardless of whether there is a power of sale in the security instrument (e.g. deed of trust). It is, therefore, imperative for the lender before foreclosing under a power of sale, to check whether anyone with an interest in the land has entered the military service after the loan was made. The power of sale foreclosure will be invalid if made during the period of such military service or within three months thereafter. A vendee under a real estate contract who enters the military service is likewise protected by this act.

Note that the protections of this law do not apply to career soldiers or to those servicemen who buy or encumber property after entering military service.

Members of the military, and those civilians negotiating business transactions with military personnel, are encouraged to discuss the legal ramifications of this Act as well as other military law with qualified counsel from the Staff Judge Advocate's Office of the appropriate military base. (*See* MILITARY CLAUSE.)

SOLE PROPRIETORSHIP - A business in which one person owns the entire business and reports all profits and losses directly on his/her personal income tax return, as contrasted with corporate, joint or partnership ownership.

SPACE PLAN - Preliminary drawing by an architect laying out the floor plan of a leased space to meet the tenant's requirements.

SPEC HOME - A home built on speculation. (*See* SPECULATOR.)

SPECIAL AGENT - One who is authorized by a principal to do a particular act or transaction, without contemplation of continuity of service as with a general agent. A real estate licensee is ordinarily a special agent appointed by the seller to find a ready, willing and able buyer for a particular property or by a buyer to find a piece of real estate which meets the buyer's needs. (*See* AGENCY, AGENT, GENERAL AGENT.)

SPECIAL ASSESSMENT - A tax or levy customarily imposed against only those specific parcels of realty which will benefit from a proposed public improvement, as opposed to a general tax on the entire community. Since the proposed improvement will enhance the value of the affected homes, it is only those affected owners who must pay this special lien. Common examples of special assessments are water and sewer assessments, or other special improvements such as parks and recreational facilities. Tax bills for such assessments are sent out annually from the district levying the tax.

Special assessments are usually paid in installments over several years although the owner always has the option of paying the balance in full.

For income tax purposes, real estate taxes are currently deductible. For investment properties, special assessments, however are **not** directly deductible because they increase the value of the property and thus, like any other capital expenditure, are added to the cost or basis of the property. However, the assessment is eligible for depreciation. In some cases a special assessment is deductible if the taxpayer can prove that all or part of the assessment is made for maintenance, repairs or interest charges. (*See* PROPERTY TAXES.)

SPECIAL BENEFITS - The value added to a property as a result of some governmental improvement. In determining the just compensation for a property which is partially taken by condemnation, the court considers the fair market value of the property taken plus severance damages less any special benefits. Thus, if the state takes a portion of a property for an improvement and the improvement actually increases the value of the remaining land, then the court in a condemnation proceeding will consider the value of the special benefit and reduce the just compensation accordingly. (*See* BEFORE AND AFTER METHOD, JUST COMPENSATION, SEVERANCE DAMAGES.)

SPECIAL CONDITIONS - Specific provisions inserted into a Purchase and Sale Agreement which must be satisfied before the contract is binding. In Washington, special conditions are usually referred to as "contingencies." The following are some of the most frequently encountered special conditions:

a) Financing to be obtained e.g., subject to buyer obtaining a $100,000 loan at 8 1/2 percent interest to be amortized over a 30 year period.

b) All appliances, electrical and plumbing fixtures to be in good working order on closing, to be verified by a letter of inspection from buyer to escrow.

c) Buyer shall furnish seller with a satisfactory written credit report within _____ days of acceptance of this offer. (This condition is normally used with seller financing.)

d) Seller shall furnish a certificate of clearance from a reputable termite company, showing no active, visible infestation of termites in improvements.

e) Occupancy subject to the existing lease, copy attached.

f) ______ (any repairs or additions) being completed by an appropriate licensed individual as agreed before close of escrow and approved in writing by buyer date______.

g) Subject to buyer's acceptance of written inventory (of furnishings, plants, etc.) by______date______.

h) (Seller) (Buyer) is aware that (buyer) (seller) is a licensed Real Estate (Broker) (Salesman) and is acting as a principal, for his/her own account.

i) If a work order under FHA or VA financing is required, seller will not expend more than $____________________.

(*See* CONTINGENCY.)

SPECIAL LEVY - See PROPERTY TAXES.

SPECIAL LIEN - A lien or charge against a specific parcel of property, such as a mortgage/deed of trust, attachment or mechanic's lien. A general lien, on the other hand, is a charge against all the property of the debtor. (*See* GENERAL LIEN, LIEN.)

SPECIAL PURPOSE PROPERTY - A combination of land and improvements with only one highest and best use because of some special design, such as a church, nursing home, school, post office, or hospital.

SPECIAL USE PERMIT - Permission from the local zoning authority granting a land use which is identified as a special exception in the zoning ordinance. For instance, a zoning ordinance for a residential area might authorize certain special uses such as church, hospital, or country club. A special use differs from a variance in that the latter is an authorized violation of the zoning ordinance, whereas the special use is a permitted exception. (*See* NONCONFORMING USE, VARIANCE.)

SPECIAL WARRANTY DEED - A deed in which the grantor warrants or guarantees the title only against defects arising during the period of his/her tenure and ownership of the property and not against defects existing before the time of his/her ownership. A special warranty deed is often used when a fiduciary such as an executor or trustee conveys the property of his/her principal, because the fiduciary usually has no authority to warrant against acts of his/her predecessors in title. Identified by the language "by, through, or under the grantor but not otherwise." (*See* DEED.)

SPECIFICATIONS - Written instructions to a building contractor containing all the necessary information regarding the materials, dimensions, colors, and other features of a proposed construction. Specifications supplement the plans and working drawings. (*See* PLANS AND SPECIFICATIONS.)

SPECIFIC PERFORMANCE - A legal action brought in a court of equity (Superior Court) to compel a party to carry out the terms of a contract. The basis for an equity court's jurisdiction is the fact that land is unique and mere legal damages would not adequately compensate the buyer for the seller's breach. The courts cannot, however, specifically enforce a contract to perform services, such as a broker's agreement to find a buyer.

If a seller refuses to sell to a buyer under a Purchase and Sale Agreement, the buyer can request a court specifically to enforce the contract and make the seller deed the property under threat of contempt of court. Similarly, a buyer can have a superior court judge enforce performance of a conveyance by the heirs of a deceased seller under a real estate contract.

In some jurisdictions, a seller can force a defaulting buyer to purchase the property especially if land values have declined. In most cases, however, a seller would have a difficult time showing that his/her legal remedy for money damages would not be adequate relief, and he/she must show his/her inadequacy as a condition for obtaining specific performance relief. A Washington court might not grant the seller specific performance because money damages usually will adequately compensate the seller for any loss he/she suffers.

Normally a court does not look into the adequacy of consideration in a contract. However, if the buyer had not paid an adequate consideration for the property and it is shown that he/she had superior knowledge, such as where a broker is purchasing property and does not disclose the fact he/she has a license, the court will not specifically enforce the contract against the seller. (*See* ELECTION OF REMEDIES, EQUITY, PURCHASE AND SALE AGREEMENT, REAL ESTATE CONTRACT.)

SPECULATOR - 1. One who analyzes a real property market and acquires properties with the expectation that prices will greatly increase, at which time he/she can sell at a large profit. Many states have enacted legislation against certain land speculation. Some states impose a land gains tax on the gain derived from the sale or exchange of land held less than a set period of time. The greater the gain and the shorter the time the land is held before the sale, the greater the tax. Similar legislation has been considered, but not enacted, in Washington.

2. An owner/builder who constructs homes ("spec homes") in the expectation that he/she will find willing buyers when the homes are completed (rather than have a specific buyer ready at the time construction begins). This practice is often called building on spec.

SPENDTHRIFT TRUST - A trust created to provide a source of money for the maintenance and support of a designated beneficiary and, at the same time, to secure the property from being wasted or depleted by the beneficiary's improvidence or irresponsibility. Income producing real property is sometimes the subject of a spendthrift trust containing provisions against alienation of the trust fund by the voluntary or involuntary act of the beneficiary.

SPIN-OFF - The transfer of a company's assets to a recently formed subsidiary, as where a corporation trades part of its assets to a new corporation in exchange for stock in the new corporation, which stock is then distributed to the stockholders of the parent company.

SPITE FENCE - A fence of such a height or type that is erected to annoy one's neighbor. Some states have spite fence statutes which limit the height of fences to, say, ten feet. There is some dispute as to whether a maliciously erected fence under the statutory height can be abated.

SPLIT FEE FINANCING - Type of equity participation in which the lender purchases the land, leases it to the developer, and finances the leasehold improvements, in return for a basic rental plus a percentage of the profits.

SPLIT-LEVEL - A house in which two or more floors are usually located directly above one another, and one or more additional floors, adjacent to them, are placed at a different level.

SPLIT-RATE - Capitalization rates applied separately to land and improvements, to determine the value of each.

SPLITTING FEES - The act of sharing compensation. A broker can split his/her commission only with another Washington licensee licensed under said broker, another Washington broker, or with a broker from another state. Paying any remuneration to an unlicensed person for referring a client is illegal and could result in the suspension or revocation of the broker's license. If the broker wishes to split fees with a licensed salesman with another company, the money must pass through the salesman's employing broker. (*See* FINDER'S FEE, LICENSING LAW.)
Reference: RCW 18.85.

SPOT LOAN - A loan on a particular property, usually a condominium unit, by a lender who has not previously financed that particular condominium building. Because of the great amount of background work and investigation required to investigate the entire condominium project and to inspect all relevant documents, some lenders are unwilling to lend money for a single unit in a large condominium development. Other lenders will make "spot loans" if they are reimbursed for their legal and other service fees in analyzing the loan.

SPOT SURVEY - A survey which shows the locations, sizes and shapes of buildings, improvements and easements located on a property and those on any neighboring property which may encroach on the surveyed property. This survey, together with a legal description of the land, is frequently required by a lender as a prerequisite to his/her committing to provide the financing, especially on large developments.

SPOT ZONING - A change in the local zoning ordinance permitting a particular use inconsistent with the zoning classification of the area; the reclassification of a small area of land in such a manner as to disturb the tenor of the surrounding neighborhood, such as a change to permit one multi-unit structure in an area zoned for single-family residential use. Spot zoning is not favored in the law. If the change affects only a small area and is not in harmony with the comprehensive general plan for that area, such as a factory in a residential neighborhood, spot zoning will not be permitted by the courts. (*See* VARIANCE, ZONING.)

SPREAD - (1) The difference between the cost of money to a lender or bank and the average rate it can be loaned. (2) The profit made in the difference of interest rates, such as in a wraparound mortgage. (3) The difference between bid price and asking price. (4) The extension of a lien or an existing mortgage with additional real estate servicing as collateral. (*See* ARBITRAGE, BLANKET MORTGAGE, WRAPAROUND MORTGAGE.)

SPUR TRACK - That segment of rail track, usually privately-owned by the industry using it, which leads off a drill track or main line and services an industrial plant or site.

SQUARE - In the government (rectangular) survey of land description, an area measuring 24 miles by 24 miles; sometimes referred to as a check.

SQUARE-FOOT METHOD - An area measured in square feet. A method of estimating a building's construction, reproduction, or replacement costs whereby the structure's square-foot floor area is multiplied by an appropriate square-foot construction cost figure.

SQUATTER'S RIGHT - The right of a person in adverse possession of real property. A squatter's possession must generally be actual, open, notorious, exclusive, and continuous for a statutory prescribed period of time. The term is not normally used in Washington. (*See* ADVERSE POSSESSION.)

STAGING - A temporary scaffolding to support workers and materials during construction.

STAGING AREA - An area, either outside at a construction site or inside a building, usually close to its loading doors, where material, apparatus, equipment, or merchandise is collected or assembled before it is moved to where it will finally be used or stored.

STAKING - A method of identifying the boundaries of a parcel of land by placing stakes or pins in the ground or painting marks on stone walls or rocks. It is customary in Washington for the parties to a Purchase and Sale Agreement to negotiate who will be responsible to pay for a survey if one is necessary. Normally the buyer pays for the survey; however, a Purchase and Sale Agreement could provide if a survey should show that the legal description provided by the seller was inaccurate, then the seller will be responsible for survey costs. (*See* CONTINGENCY, SPECIAL CONDITIONS, SURVEY.)

STANDARD PARALLEL - In the government (rectangular) survey system of land description, one of a series of lines running east and west, generally spaced 24 miles apart and located north and south of, and parallel to, the base lines. Such parallels establish township boundaries at 24-mile intervals and correct inaccuracies due to the curvature of the earth; also called correction lines.

STANDARDS OF PRACTICE - A set of ethical criteria formulated by the Professional standards Committee of the National Association of Realtors. Such standards of practice are interpretations of certain articles of the Realtorsâ Code of Ethics In filing a charge of an alleged violation of the Code of Ethics by a Realtorâ, the charge should read as an alleged violation of one or more articles of the code. A standards of practice may be cited only in support of the charge. (*See* APPENDIX B, UNIFORM STANDARDS OF PROFESSIONAL APPRAISAL PRACTICE.)

STANDBY COMMITMENT OR LOAN - An arrangement whereby the lender agrees to keep a certain amount of money available to the borrower, usually a developer, for a specified period of time. Thus a standby loan is like an option on a loan since the developer has the right to borrow the money but he/she is not obligated to take it. In fact, the terms of the standby commitment may be so onerous as to discourage the developer from exercising the loan, and it is thus a commitment to make a loan in the future, in the event the borrower cannot get better financing elsewhere. Standby loans are usually made by noninstitutional lenders, and the commitments are usually short-term, from 18 to 24 months. The standby fee is typically 2 to 3 percent of the loan per year. The developer should be careful to specify those conditions which will excuse his/her performance of the standby loan agreement such as condemnation of a building site or refusal of a building permit.

STANDBY FEE - A fee paid by a borrower at the time of issuance of a standby commitment letter, as a charge for the lender's risk and responsibility in committing to the loan. The standby fee is forfeited if the loan is not closed within a specified time. Most courts uphold the forfeiture of the standby fee as a lawful damage provision and not as an unlawful penalty. (*See* STANDBY LOAN.)

STANDING LOAN - A commitment by the interim or construction lender to keep the money he/she has already funded in the project for a specified period of time after the expiration of the interim loan, usually until permanent takeout financing is secured. For instance, a lender might agree to provide an interim construction loan for one year and a standing loan for two years from the date of termination of the one-year loan. This usually enables the borrower to build and rent his/her shopping center or office building before obtaining permanent financing, thus giving him/her a better chance of obtaining favorable permanent financing.

A standing loan also refers to a straight mortgage, i.e., one that calls for payments of interest only with no amortization during its term and the entire principal becoming due at maturity; i.e., the entire principal "stands" until satisfaction. (*See* STRAIGHT NOTE.)

STARKER EXCHANGE - *See* DEFERRED OR DELAYED EXCHANGE.

START RATE - The rate of interest for the initial period on an Adjustable Rate Mortgage. (*See* ADJUSTABLE RATE MORTGAGE.)

STARTER HOME - The first home purchaser by someone.

STARTS - A terms commonly used to indicate the number of residential units begun within a stated period of time in a specific area.

STATEMENT OF RECORD - A document that must be filed with a HUD registration of subdivided land intended to be sold using any means of interstate commerce. The lengthy and detailed statement of record requires information dealing with the property, the site, and the developer, including such information as the name and address of each person having an interest in the property, a legal description of the property, general terms and conditions of contracts, including prices, descriptions of access to the property and public utilities, and all encumbrances. In addition, copies of the corporation or partnership documents of the developer and other instruments relating to the property are required. In support of the statement of record the developer must also provide financial statements (certified in certain cases). (*See* INTERSTATE LAND SALES.)

STATE ENVIRONMENTAL POLICY ACT (SEPA) - SEPA enacted in Washington State in 1971, requires all subdivisions of the state to interpret and administer all policies, regulations and laws with concern for the preservation of the environment. The purposes of this legislation are: (1) To declare a state policy which will encourage productive and enjoyable harmony between man and his/her environment; (2) to promote efforts which will prevent or eliminate damage to the environment and biosphere; (3) to stimulate the health and welfare of man; and (4) to enrich the understanding of the ecological systems and natural resources important to the state and nation.

SEPA regulates governmental action such as permits, funding of a project, rezones or a plan. SEPA is considered to "overlay," that is it supplements other laws.

In 1974, the legislature amended SEPA to require all State subdivisions to adopt rules, ordinances, or resolutions pertaining to the integration of the policies and procedures of

the State Environmental Policy Act of 1971 into the various programs under their jurisdiction for implementation.
Reference: RCW 43.21C.

Accordingly, the Washington State Department of Ecology (DOE) has adopted uniform statewide rules. The statewide rules are commonly referred to as the "Green Book." Under the Act, each unit of government is required to adopt SEPA policies and procedures that are specific to that agency's operations.
Reference: RCW 43.21C.095; WAC 197-11.

The State Guidelines establish a detailed process for conducting environmental review, and for the most part, the process is mandatory for local jurisdictions. However, there are significant issues concerning environmental review which are not resolved by the State Guidelines. The resolution of these issues is left to the discretion of local jurisdictions.

In 1995, SEPA was substantially amended in light of the development of the Growth Management Act (GMA) which was first adopted in 1990. The 1995 Amendments are proposed to shift SEPA from project level to planning level environmental review. Local governments must undertake SEPA review in the development of their GMA plans and development regulations. (*See* GROWTH MANAGEMENT ACT.)

STATUTE - A law enacted by congress (federal law) or by the state legislature (state law).

STATUTE OF FRAUDS - That law which requires certain contracts to be in writing and signed by the party to be charged therewith in order to be legally **enforceable**. The Statute of Frauds requires that all contracts for the sale of land or any interest therein and all listings must be written. Oral leases for a period not exceeding one year, however, are valid and enforceable. The law does not require a single, formal contract; the writing could consist of a memorandum of the contract or several items of correspondence as long as the material terms agreed upon are stated and signed by the necessary parties.

The parties to an oral real estate contract may have a valid contract but the contract is not **enforceable** if it is not in writing. The Statute of Frauds relates to the remedy only and not to the inherent validity of the contract. Thus, the parties to a fully executed or performed oral agreement cannot thereafter assert the Statute of Frauds to seek rescission of the contract.

The purpose of the Statute of Frauds is to prevent the perpetration of fraud by one seeking enforcement of a contract that was never in fact made; it is not designed to prevent the performance of oral contracts. There are thus exceptions to the Statute of Frauds mostly where the assertion of the Statute of Frauds as a defense to an oral contract would, in itself, amount to a fraud. Thus there are cases where part performance of an oral agreement takes the case out of the Statute of Frauds. For example, a contract will be taken out of the "Statute of Frauds" if the buyer, in reliance on a seller's oral promise to sell the property, pays part or all of the purchase price, enters into possession and makes substantial improvements on the property. In such a case of part performance, some courts refuse to allow the seller to assert the Statute of Frauds as a defense against the buyer's action to force the seller to fulfill the terms of the oral agreement to sell.

Another purpose is to protect the unsophisticated from assuming significant obligations without being aware of the legal consequences, to impress upon the parties the consequence of such contracts, as well as to provide a record of the agreement.

Because the statute is inconsistent with public policy favoring freedom of contract it is strictly construed by the courts. (*See* ESTOPPEL, UNENFORCEABLE CONTRACT.)
Reference: RCW 19.36, RCW 64.04.

STATUTE OF LIMITATIONS - That law pertaining to the period of time within which certain actions must be brought to court. The law is intended to protect the vigilant by requiring the prompt assertion of claims to prevent stale claims; thus actions must be brought within a specified time of the occurrence of the cause of action. Some relevant general statutes of limitations in Washington are:

1. Any action for the recovery of real property or for the recovery of the possession of real property — 10 years.

2. Adverse possession — Recovery of real property with color of title and payment of taxes — 7 years.

3. Prescriptive rights — 10 years.

4. Action to collect a special assessment for local improvements or to enforce a lien for a special assessment for local improvements — within 10 years from the time when the assessment became delinquent.

5. Judgment lien or decree of a court of the State of Washington — 6 years.

6. Any action upon a contract in writing or upon a liability rising out of a written instrument — 6 years.

7. Any action for waste or trespass upon real property — 3 years.

8. Any action for rent — 6 years.

9. Any action for the taking, detaining or injury of personal property including any action for the specific recovery of personal property — 3 years.

10. Any action for relief upon the grounds of fraud — within 3 years of the discovery of the facts which constitute the fraud.

STATUTORY LAW - Law created by the enactment of legislation, as opposed to case law created by a judicial decision of a court of law.

STEERING - The illegal practice of channeling homeseekers to particular areas, either to maintain the homogeneity of an area or to change the character of an area in order to create a speculative situation. This practice makes certain homes unavailable to homeseekers on the basis of race or national origin, and on these grounds it is prohibited by the provisions of the federal Fair Housing Act. Steering is often difficult to detect, however, because the steering tactics can be so subtle that the homeseeker is unaware that his/her choice has been limited. (*See* FEDERAL FAIR HOUSING LAW.)

Steering could be the use of a word, phrase, or act by a real estate licensee which is intended to influence the choice of a prospective property buyer on a discriminatory basis. (*See* WASHINGTON STATE HUMAN RIGHTS COMMISSION.)
Reference: RCW 49.60.

STEPPED UP BASIS - The basis of property acquired from a decedent is equal to the fair market value of the property as of the date of death of the decedent or six months later. Assume Veronica Mathy purchased an apartment complex January 1, 1970 for $200,000. When she died January 1, 1990, the fair market value of the property was determined to be $400,000 with an adjusted cost basis of $80,000 (original cost less depreciation, plus improvements). Six months later on June 30, 1990, it was determined that the fair market value was $405,000. Her heirs could elect a stepped up basis, "fresh start" in the property to the fair market value of January 1 or June 30, 1990. When the heirs dispose of the property, the gain over the **elected** fair market value will be taxed. (*See* BASIS, ESTATE TAX.)

STEP-UP LEASE - A lease with fixed rent for an initial term and provision for predetermined rent increases at specified intervals and/or increases based upon periodic appraisals or some other factor (e.g., federal cost of living indexes); sometimes called a graduated lease. (*See* CPI, LEASE.)

STRAIGHT NOTE - A promissory note evidencing a loan in which "interest only" payments are made periodically during the term of the note, with the principal payment due in one lump sum upon maturity. A straight note is usually a nonamortized note made for a short term, such as three to five years, and is renewable at the end of the term. A mortgage which secures a straight note is a term mortgage or straight term mortgage.

STRAW MAN - One who purchases property for another, to conceal the identity of the real purchaser; a dummy purchaser; a nominee.

A real estate licensee may not use a straw man to purchase real property for his/her own account. There must be full disclosure as required under the License Law.
Reference: RCW 18.85.

In Washington, the joint tenancy Initiative 208 stated that a joint tenancy must be "declared in its creation to be a joint tenancy." Because of the statutory language, it was thought necessary to use a straw man when an individual who had an interest in real property wanted to create a joint tenancy between himself/herself and another party. The adoption of legislation eliminates the need for a straw man conveyance. (*See* JOINT TENANCY.)

Where several tracts of land are being assembled for development, confidentiality may be very important — hence the desirability of nominees and straw men. However, a federal court has held that if the nominee misrepresents the identity of his/her principal, with knowledge that the seller would not have negotiated if he/she were in possession of the true facts, the seller may set aside the transaction. In addition, if the nominee or straw man exercises any managerial control over the property, he/she may be held to the real owner for tax purposes.

If a strawman/nominee is being used to purchase real property, the name of the true name of the actual eventual owner must be disclosed on an affidavit attached to the excise tax affidavit when the real estate contract or deed is recorded or a double tax may be incurred when the strawman transfers to the true owner.

In a pre-sale of a condominium, a developer normally must attain a certain percentage of purchases before a lender will commit to lend money; straw men are sometimes used to meet this minimum requirement, though this practice is clearly against the lender's policy and would be illegal in connection with VA and FHA loans.

STRINGER - One of the sloping enclosed sides of a staircase that supports the treads and risers. The term can also refer to a horizontal beam which connects the uprights in a frame.

STRUCTURAL ALTERATIONS - Any change in the supporting members of a building, such as bearing walls or partitions, columns, beams, or girders; or any structural change in the roof, but not normally including extension or enlargement of the building. (*See* NONCONFORMING USE.)

STRUCTURAL DEFECTS - In residential homes, actual damage to the load-bearing portion of a home, which affects it load-bearing function and vitally affects the use of the home for residential purposes. This includes damage from shifting soil from causes other than earthquake or flood.

STRUCTURAL DENSITY - The ratio of the total ground floor area of a building to the total land area. The average density for a general purpose industrial building is about one-third.

STRUCTURE - Something built or constructed; an improvement. A structure is often defined in local building codes, usually as "anything that is more than 18 inches off the ground and cannot be lifted by a person without mechanical aid." As a rule, a structure can be built only after obtaining a building permit.

STUCCO - A cement or plaster wallcovering that is installed wet and dries into a hard surface coating.

STUD - In wall framing, the vertical members to which horizontal pieces are attached. Studs are placed between 16 and 24 inches apart and serve as the main support for the roof and/or the second floor.

STUDIO - An efficiency apartment; a dwelling that consists of a combination living room and bedroom, plus a bathroom and kitchen.

SUBAGENT - An agent of a person who is already acting as an agent for a principal. The original agency can delegate authority to a subagent where such delegation is either expressly authorized or customary in the trade. For example, it is customary for listing brokers to delegate certain functions of a ministerial nature to subagents, such as to show property and solicit buyers.

Many multiple listing services are based on the theory that a listing is an offer of sub-agency to members and that members who work on such listings do so as subagents of the listing broker.

Where it is clear that the principal has authorized the agent to appoint subagents, the relation of principal and agent exists between the principal and subagent. Some courts hold that a subagent who is lawfully appointed represents the principal in like manner with the prime agent; and the prime agent is not responsible to third persons for acts of the sub-agent. (*See* AGENCY.)

SUBCHAPTER S CORPORATION - *See* S CORPORATION.

SUBCONTRACTOR - A builder or contractor who enters into an agreement with a developer or the prime contractor to perform a special portion of the construction work, such as electrical, plumbing, air conditioning, and the like. The subcontractor does not deal directly with the owner; however, if not paid by the prime contractor, he/she can assert a mechanic's lien against the property any time prior to the elapse of 90 days from the date of notice of completion is published. (*See* CONTRACTOR, MECHANIC'S LIEN.)
Reference: RCW 60.04.

SUBDIVIDER - An owner whose land is divided into two or more lots and offered for disposition. Under the Uniform Land Sales Practices Act, a "subdivider" may also be the principal agent of an inactive owner. If the subdivider later puts improvements on the property, he/she becomes a developer.

SUBDIVISION - Any land which is divided or is proposed to be divided for the purpose of disposition into two or more lots, parcels, units or interests. "Subdivision" refers to any land, whether contiguous or not, if two or more lots, parcels, units or interests are offered as part of a common promotional plan of advertising or sale. The law would thus apply to the sale of 1/125th undivided interests in a large parcel of land. The word "subdivision" has been redefined to allow short platting of previously platted land without vacating the original plat or lot.

A developer of a subdivision must first comply with the subdivision regulations of the county or city in which the property is located. These regulations differ significantly from county to county and city to city. The various subdivision regulations have become land-use controls.

A "preliminary plat" of proposed subdivisions and dedications of land must be submitted for approval to the legislative body of the city, town or county within which the plat is situated. If the proposed subdivision is within one mile of the municipal boundaries of a city or town, or will use the utilities of any city or town, then notice of the filing of the preliminary plat must be given to the appropriate city or town authorities. If the proposed subdivision is located in a city or town adjoining the municipal boundaries thereof, then notice of filing must be given to the appropriate county officials. If the land is adjacent to a right-of-way of a state highway, the State Department of Highways is similarly given notice.

Washington law provides, "The city, town, or county legislative body shall inquire into the public use and interest proposed to be served by the establishment of the subdivision and dedication. It shall determine if appropriate provisions are made in the subdivision for, but not limited to, drainage ways, streets, alleys, other public ways, water supplies, sanitary wastes, parks, playgrounds, sites for schools and school grounds, and shall consider all other relevant facts and determine whether the public interest will be served by the subdivision and dedication."

Recently a number of significant changes were made in the requirements for subdivision, among the changes were:

—Boundary line adjustments are exempted entirely from platting requirements so long as the adjusted lots are not reduced below minimum zoning or health requirements.

—Divisions of land made because a portion of the site was filed as a condominium are also exempt provided a binding site plan was approved by the jurisdiction for the entire property.

—Plats and other applications such as rezones, variances, PUD's, etc., must be processed simultaneously as much as possible.

—Public hearing notices for plats will be required to be sent to property owners within 300 feet of the plat. Also the notice must be published in a newspaper in the area of the plat as well as in a paper of general circulation.

—The bill clarifies that the Planning Commission reviews only preliminary plats. Also requires all decision on plats to include written findings and conclusions.

—The provisions regarding the expiration of approval on preliminary plats are modified. It is now required that all preliminary plats be valid for three years with an additional one-year period if requested by the applicant, upon showing good faith toward completion.

—The bill requires that when the government agency recommends approval of the method of sewage disposal and water supply in the preliminary plat stage, those terms and conditions shall not be modified, unless agreed to by the applicant.

—A dedication is allowed to be in a separate written instrument provided it is recorded with the final plat.

—Further consideration of "public use and interest" at the time of final plat approval is removed as it would have been fully considered at the preliminary plat stage. If a plat meets conditions of preliminary approval and the local ordinances, then it shall be approved. Health and engineering approval is guaranteed for five years unless a serious health problem is found to exist.

—Any offer to sell lots prior to final plat recording is legal. The offer to sell can only be made after preliminary approval and must be subject to recording of the final plat with all earnest moneys placed in a regulated trust account or escrow.

—Cities and counties will not be required to establish better procedures to provide reasonable advance notice when local subdivision laws are adopted or amended. Advance notice must be sent to individuals or organizations who request notice.

Every final plat or short plat filed for record must contain:

1. Certificate giving full and correct description of the lands divided;

2. Statement of free consent to subdivide by the owners; and

3. If a dedication is included:

a. the dedication and to whom;

b. waiver of damage claims against government for damages which may be occasioned to the adjacent land by the established construction, drainage and main tenance of said road;

c. title report confirming title is in the signing "owners" names, and

d. (optional) waiver of right of direct access to any street from any property.

The written approval of the city, town, or county authority is inscribed on the face of the plat and must be obtained before filing it with the county auditor. The original of the final plat is filed for record with the county auditor. Copies are furnished to the city, town, or county engineer and filed with the county assessor. In addition the subdivider must register his/her subdivision with the Land Registration Section of the Real Estate Management Program if the subdivision is of recreational nature and has over 25 lots. (*See* PLAT BOOK, SHORT PLAT, WASHINGTON LAND DEVELOPMENT ACT.)
Reference: RCW 58.17.

Commercial and industrial divisions of land are exempted completely from the platting and subdivision law as long as the local jurisdiction has approved a binding site plan for the property.

SUBDIVISION REGISTRATION LAW - The main thrust of a subdivision registration law is to protect prospective purchasers from the deceptive practices and abuses once common in the unregulated sale of unimproved recreational lots.

Federal legislation protecting the purchaser of unimproved recreational lots was adopted in 1968 and similar legislation was passed in Washington in 1973. (*See* INTERSTATE LAND SALES, WASHINGTON LAND DEVELOPMENT ACT.)

SUBFLOORING - Boards or plywood sheets nailed directly to the floor joists serving as a base for the finish flooring. Subflooring is usually made of rough boards, although some houses have concrete subflooring.

SUBJACENT SUPPORT - The support which the surface of the earth receives from its underlying strata. (*See* LATERAL AND SUBJACENT SUPPORT.)

SUBJECT PROPERTY - The property that is the subject of an appraisal, sale, lease, option, or loan. The property in question. The term is most often used in real estate agreements as a shorthand reference to property fully described earlier in the document.

SUBJECT TO CLAUSE - The clause in a Purchase and Sale Agreement (E/M) setting forth any contingencies or special conditions of purchase and sale, such as an offer made and accepted "subject to" obtaining financing, approving leases, securing certain zoning, etc. The seller might sell the property "subject to" existing leases, certain liens, specific restrictions, etc. If exceptions are not noted in the subject to clause, any encumbrances will render the title unmarketable. (*See* CONTINGENCY, SPECIAL CONDITIONS.)

SUBJECT TO MORTGAGE OR DEED OF TRUST - A grantee taking title to real property "subject to deed of trust or mortgage" is not personally liable to the lender for payment of the note. In the event his/her grantor defaults in paying the note, the grantee could, however, lose the property, and thus his/her equity. The purchaser could request an estoppel certificate from the lender so that the purchaser is aware that no defaults have occurred, all installments of the loan and interest have been paid; and that the interest rates, terms and unpaid balance of the loan are as represented by the seller.

For example, if Ms. Adair owned a farm valued at $175,000 and had an existing $150,000 mortgage with the Bank of Olga, Adair could sell the property to Mr. Greer for $175,000 subject to the mortgage. Greer's payments would be used to meet the mortgage payments. If Greer were to default, however, Greer would merely lose the property; the bank would not be able to sue Greer for any mortgage deficiency. In response to this, most mortgages now contain acceleration clauses giving the mortgagee the options of whether to declare the debt due when the property is sold, to allow assumption (usually with an assumption fee) or to permit the mortgagor to sell subject to the mortgage.

Real estate brokers sometimes buy property "subject to" existing mortgages or deeds of trust where they expect to resell the property shortly and don't want to be named parties on too many mortgages or deeds of trust. In such cases, brokers must be especially careful to disclose to the sellers all the ramifications of selling "subject to the mortgage or deed of trust," as well as the fact that they have a real estate license. (*See* ACCELERATION CLAUSE, ASSUMPTION OF MORTGAGE, DUE ON SALE CLAUSE.)

SUBJECTIVE VALUE - Also called personal value, it is the amount a specific person might pay to possess a property. As opposed to objective value, or what a reasonable person might be expected to pay for the same property.

SUBLEASE - A lease given by a lessee for a **portion** of the leasehold interest but retaining some reversionary interest in the lessee. The sublease may be for all or part of the premises, for the whole term, or for part of it, as long as the original lessee retains some interest. Leases normally contain a clause prohibiting subletting without prior consent of the lessor. The original lessee remains directly liable to the lessor for the rent, which is usually paid by the sublessee to the lessee and then from the lessee to the lessor. The sublessee does not have a contractual obligation to pay rent to the original lessor.

If the lessee transfers his/her entire interest in the lease, however, this is called an assignment of lease. In an assignment the transferee comes into privity of estate with the lessor, which means that each is liable to the other on the covenants in the original lease that run with the land. (*See* ASSIGNMENT OF LEASE, LEASE, SANDWICH LEASE.)

SUBMITTAL NOTICE - Written notice by a broker to a seller with whom he/she has a listing agreement, stating that the broker has shown the seller's property and indicating the prospect's name, address, and the selling price quoted.

SUBORDINATION AGREEMENT - An agreement whereby a prior mortgagee/beneficiary agrees to subordinate or give up his/her priority to an existing or anticipated future lien. Subordination means "coming after." Also, an agreement of a fee owner to allow his/her land to become subject to a mortgage or deed of trust as a condition of a sale or lease transaction. Subordination agreements are frequently used in development projects where the seller of property takes back a purchase money mortgage or deed of trust and agrees to subordinate or become subject to a construction loan, thereby enabling the developer-purchaser to improve the property. The subordination agreement thus deviates from the normal rule of giving priority to the mortgage or deed of trust which is recorded first. As a result, the construction loan, even though recorded after the existing purchase money mortgage or deed of trust becomes first. A seller/lender should exercise caution before subordinating her/his priority position.

A subordination is either (1) specific, or (2) future, or a future automatic subordination clause. Great care should be exercised in making a future clause certain; e.g., it is sometimes held to be uncertain and therefore void, if it does not state the amount, terms, due date, interest rate, etc., of the construction loan which would be placed on the property. Any subordination must be carefully drafted so as to avoid argument that it is vague, uncertain and/or implies further negotiations were contemplated.

Many interim lenders refuse to lend any money in the absence of a subordination clause. Thus, most purchase contracts for proposed condominium units have a clause subordinating the apartment purchaser's equitable lien to any future interim construction loan given by the developer; also the developer of leasehold property will often try to get the fee owner to subordinate his/her fee to any construction loan. In this connection, subordinating the fee is really a misnomer since one cannot subordinate the fee to a leasehold mortgage or deed of trust. What the fee owner is really doing is encumbering his/her fee. Sometimes a fee owner will partially subordinate the fee, in which case the landlord-owner is saying to the lender that in the event of foreclosure, no ground rent will be due; the owner is not risking his/her fee, just his/her ground rent. (*See* SECOND MORTGAGE OR DEED OF TRUST, SUBORDINATION CLAUSE.)

SUBORDINATION CLAUSE - A clause in which the mortgagee permits a subsequent mortgage or deed of trust to take priority. This clause sometimes provides that if a prior debt is paid off or renewed, the junior debt will continue in its subordinate position and will not automatically become a higher or first mortgage or deed of trust. A subordination clause is not unusual in a junior debt since the junior debtor often gets a higher interest rate and is often not concerned about his/her inferior position. A sample subordination clause might read: "This mortgage shall be and remain subordinate to the present first mortgage or any renewal thereof, or in event of its payment, to any new mortgage provided the excess, if any, of said mortgage over the amount of the present first mortgage be applied in reduction of the principal of this mortgage."

A broker should take care to point out to his/her client the implications to all parties of any subordination clauses contained in the mortgage/deed of trust documents. (*See* SECOND MORTGAGE OR DEED OF TRUST. SUBORDINATION AGREEMENT.)

SUBPOENA - A legal process ordering a witness to appear and give testimony under penalty of law. Under the Real Estate Licensing Act, the Department of Licensing has the authority to subpoena witnesses and compel testimony. If a person does not honor a subpoena, the Director can go to the appropriate superior court and request an order compelling compliance with the subpoena. Anyone refusing to obey the court order can be jailed until he/she complies. (*See* REAL ESTATE PROGRAM.)
Reference: RCW 18.85, RCW 18.44, RCW 58.19.

SUBPOENA DUCES TECUM - A court order to produce books, records and other documents. The Department of Licensing has authority to compel the production of documentary evidence in all proceedings before it for violation of the licensing laws. Similarly, the Department has the power to subpoena the production of books and records of a licensee in any investigation regarding violation of the discrimination or subdivision registration laws.

SUBROGATION - The substitution of a third person in place of a creditor to whose rights the third person succeeds in relation to the debt. Insurance policies typically contain subrogation clauses. A title company that pays a loss within the scope of its policy is subrogated to any claim which the buyer had against the seller by reason of the loss.

SUBSCRIBE - To place one's signature at the end of a document. Most documents do not need to be subscribed. For example, in a promissory note it is sufficient to write, "I, Norbert Cletus, hereby promise to pay Vicky Rae $100,000." Some statutes, however, require subscribing witnesses, e.g., witnesses who sign at the end of the document after the principal's signature. For example, it is essential to the validity of a will in Washington that there be two disinterested subscribing witnesses. (*See* SIGNATURE.)

SUBSEQUENT BONA FIDE PURCHASER - One who purchases an interest in real property without notice, actual or constructive, of any other superior rights in the property. The recording laws are designed to protect subsequent purchasers for value who deal with the property without notice of prior unrecorded interests. Thus, a conveyance which is not recorded is void as against any subsequent purchaser who, without having actual notice of the unrecorded conveyance, records first. Possession of property under an unrecorded deed imparts constructive notice to a subsequent purchaser who records his/her deed. Thus, the subsequent purchaser would not then be "bona fide" and is not protected by the recording act. Also unprotected would be a subsequent donee or a devisee under a will since neither is a "purchaser." (*See* CONSTRUCTIVE NOTICE, RECORDING.)

SUBSIDIZED HOUSING - Residential developments for low-income families that are insured or financed in part by a governmental agency. (*See* SECTION 8.)

SUBSIDY - Monetary grants by the government or other entity made to reduce the cost of one or more of the housing components — land, labor, management, materials — to lower the cost of housing to the occupant. (*See* SUBSIDY RENT.)

SUBSIDY RENT - The difference between the developer's cash out-of-pocket annual costs allocable to a particular tenant's space and the tenant's minimum rental. Some shopping center developers subsidize the rent of certain specialized tenants, such as banks or post offices, in the hopes of attracting more customers to the center complex. In reality, both the developer and the other tenants are subsidizing the rent since the cash deficit on that tenant must be made up from other tenants before the developer can make any profit at all. (*See* SHOPPING CENTER.)

Since the mid-1960s, a number of federal subsidized rent programs have been administered by the FHA. The Housing and Urban Development Act of 1968 and subsequent amendments, the 1969 Housing Act, and The Emergency Home Finance Act of 1970 contained a number of programs enabling lower income families to either rent or purchase shelter under subsidized programs. These laws reflect Congressional concern with meeting a growing population's needs for housing, setting up an urban policy, and encouraging and supporting sound real estate development, including new community and intercity development.

SUBSTANTIAL IMPROVEMENT - As defined by the Internal Revenue Code, it is any improvement made to a building at least three years after the building was placed in service and, over a two-year period, the amounts added to the capital account of the building (not repairs) must be at least 25 percent of the adjusted basis of the building as of the first day of that period.

SUBSTITUTION - An appraisal principle which states that the maximum value of a property tends to be set by the cost of acquiring, through purchase or construction, an equally desirable and valuable substitute property, assuming that no costly delay is encountered in making the substitution.

SUBSTITUTION OF COLLATERAL - Provision in a mortgage which permits the mortgagor or the grantor in a deed of trust to obtain a release of the original collateral by replacement with other collateral acceptable to the mortgagee.

SUBSTITUTION OF ELIGIBILITY - *See* CERTIFICATE OF ELIGIBILITY.

SUBSTITUTION OF LIABILITY - The assumption of liability by another on a mortgage or deed of trust note, with the concurrent release of the original maker by the mortgagee.

SUBSURFACE EASEMENT - An easement permitting the use of below ground space for such purposes as power lines, sewers, tunnels; also called a subsurface right.

SUBURB - A town or community located near, and economically linked to, a central city.

SUCCESSORS AND ASSIGNS - Words of limitation used in deeds to corporations, referring to those who succeed to or to whom are transferred the corporation's rights in the property. (*See* HEIRS AND ASSIGNS.)

SUFFERANCE - *See* TENANCY AT SUFFERANCE.

SUMMARY POSSESSION - A legal process, also called actual eviction, used by a landlord to regain possession of the leased premises if the tenant has breached the lease or is holding over after the termination of tenancy. Summary possession proceedings are based on the theory that a landlord-tenant relationship existed and that the tenant is wrongfully holding possession of the demised premises after termination of tenancy by reason of forfeiture or termination under conditions or covenants of lease, including proper notice.

In many states, summary possession can occur in 3 to 4 days. Since the comprehensive revision of the Landlord Tenant Act in 1973, true summary possession does not exist in Washington. If the attorney representing the landlord aggressively pushes the legal action, the period of time necessary to evict will be from 20 to 30 days. Under the Act, all eviction proceedings require at least one hearing and the tenant has the right to raise defenses against the eviction. The defenses may be of a statutory nature (*See* LANDLORD TENANT ACT) or disputes of fact (*See* EVICTION).

SUM-OF-THE-YEARS' DIGITS METHOD - Under the Economic Recovery Act of 1981 this method of depreciation was abolished for property acquired in 1981 or later. A method of depreciation designed to provide the greatest depreciation in the early years of ownership, gradually lessening in the later years. This method could be used only with new residential property, and only by the first owner.

SUMMATION APPROACH - The value derived at by adding the estimated value of improvements to the estimated value of the site as of the date of the appraisal. (*See* COST APPROACH.)

SUMMONS - A legal notice that a lawsuit has been started against a defendant and that unless the defendant answers the complaint within the specified time (usually 20 days) then a default judgment will be entered against the defendant.

SUPERFUND - *See* TOXICS CONTROL ACT.

SUMP PUMP - A pit or reservoir used for collecting and holding water (or some other liquid) which is subsequently disposed of, usually by a pump.

SUPPLY AND DEMAND - An economic valuation principle which states that market value is determined by the interaction of the forces of supply and demand in the appropriate market as of the date of the appraisal.

SUPPORT DEED - A deed used to convey property which specifies that, as consideration, the buyer will support the grantor for the rest of his/her life. If proper support ceases, the courts will disallow the deed.

SURCHARGE - **Additional** rent charged to tenants who consume utility services (gas, water, electric) in excess of the amounts allowed in the terms of the lease. Also, an additional charged imposed by the Federal Reserve Bank on member banks who borrow money too frequently.

SURETY - One who becomes a guarantor for another. Surety companies typically execute surety agreements in the form of completion and performance bonds on contractors. If the bonded contractor fails to complete the job, the surety of a completion bond will step in and guaranty its satisfactory completion. If, however, the owner defaults, the surety under a performance bond would have the same defenses as the contractor and might not be compelled to complete the contract.

The surety does not insure against loss, but rather provides an assurance to the owner that the contractor is financially sound and professionally capable, efficient reliable; otherwise the surety company would not bond him/her. Under the bond, the contractor is the principal, the owner is the obligee and the bonding company is the surety. The bond premium is more of a service charge than a buildup fund against loss.

In an assumption of mortgage, the grantee of the mortgagor becomes personally and primarily liable to the mortgagee for any deficiency judgment after a foreclosure sale, with the mortgagor standing in the position of a surety. The lessee under an assigned lease is, in essence, a surety. (*See* PERFORMANCE BOND, SUBROGATION.)

SURFACE WATERS - Diffused storm waters as contrasted to a concentrated flow within a stream. Washington case law supports the "sheet flow" theory; e.g., a person has the right to let waters flow through his/her yard and on to the lot below as long as it is in sheet form and not artificially concentrated by him/her onto the party below. Under the common law, the landowner could take any steps (regrading, paving, etc.) to protect his/her land even if this construction had an adverse effect on his/her neighbor's land.

SURRENDER - A premature conveyance of a possessory estate to a person having a future interest, as when a lessee surrenders his/her leasehold interest to the owner of the reversion interest, the lessor **before** the normal expiration of the lease. Surrender requires that the tenant vacate the premises.

If the surrender is accepted by the lessor, then the lessee is no longer liable for rent. However, if the tenant abandons the premises without a formal surrender, the landlord can collect the lesser of (1) the rent due for the entire period of the rental agreement, or (2) the rent for the time it takes to re-rent the dwelling unit at a fair rental **plus** the difference between the fair rental and the rent the tenant had been paying, **plus** a fee for re-renting.

If the parties had recorded the lease, they should execute and record a written surrender agreement to clear the title in the event the lease is terminated prior to its normal expiration. (*See* ABANDONMENT.)

SURVEY - The process by which boundaries are measured and land areas are determined; the on-site measurement of lot lines, dimensions, and position of houses in a lot including the determination of any existing encroachments or easements. In Washington, the most common type of survey is a metes and bounds survey.

When dealing with raw land, a broker should check the property at the time of the listing to see if survey stakes are visible. If not visible, the broker should inform the seller that a survey may have to be ordered at seller's expense. (Occasionally, a buyer will elect to have the property resurveyed at his/her own expense.) The survey should reveal easements and encroachments that the public records do not reveal.

If there is any discrepancy between the new survey and the original survey, the seller would be required to remedy the discrepancy as well as pay for the cost of the survey. As a result of recent court decisions affecting the location of shoreline boundaries, purchasers of beachfront land should have the property resurveyed prior to actual acquisition.

A lender may require an accurate survey before lending money to finance the acquisition of or construction on certain properties. A large construction loan may require a "date-down" survey as the construction progresses to insure that the new building does not encroach beyond the building or lot lines. (*See* METES AND BOUNDS, SHORELINE.)

SURVEY MAP - The detailed site plan containing the layout, location, unit numbers and dimensions of the condominium units in a condominium development, which is filed for record at the office of the County Auditor when the Declaration is recorded. The survey map is generally certified by a Registered Architect, Registered Land Surveyor, or Professional Engineer. (*See* CONDOMINIUM OWNERSHIP, CONDOMINIUM ASSOCIATION.) *Reference:* RCW 64.32.

SURVIVORSHIP - The right of survivorship is that special feature of a joint tenancy whereby all title, right and interest of a decedent joint tenant in certain property passes to the surviving joint tenants by operation of law, free from claims of heirs and creditors of the decedent. Upon the death of a joint tenant, it is said that the property is released of his/her interest and the remaining joint tenants share equally in the entire property. (*See* JOINT TENANCY, PARTNERSHIP.)

SUSPENSION - A period of enforced inactivity. The Director of Licensing has the power, after a hearing, to suspend a real estate license for a violation of the licensing law. During the period of suspension, the licensee is prohibited from engaging in real estate activities for the purpose of earning a commission or fee. A suspended broker may not employ any salespeople during the period of suspension; the salespeople must switch their licenses to other firms if they wish to continue to practice. (*See* LICENSING LAW.)

SWEAT EQUITY - Equity created in a property by the performance of work or labor by the purchaser or borrower. It directly increases the value of the property.

SWING LOAN - A short-term loan used to enable the purchaser of a new property to purchase that property on the strength of the equity from the property the purchaser is now selling. Thus the loan swings on the equity the borrower has in the existing home. (*See* BRIDGE LOAN.)

SYNDICATION - A descriptive term for a group of two or more people united for the purpose of making and operating an investment. A syndication may operate in the form of a corporation, general partnership, or limited partnership. Some of the parties take an active role in the creation and management of the investment, while others assume a passive role, usually limited to supplying capital. A syndication is not a form of legal ownership, but is rather a term used to describe multiple ownership of an investment. Most real estate syndications are organized as limited partnerships with the syndicator acting as general partner and the investors being limited partners. This enable the partnership to act as a conduit to pass through high depreciation deductions directly to the individual investors and thus avoid the double taxation aspects of corporate ownership. Syndication frequently offers the small investor a chance to participate in a real estate investment that will be managed by experienced persons. The 1976 Tax Reform Act provides that amounts paid to organize a partnership or promote the sale of interests are not deductible. (*See* HUI, LIMITED PARTNERSHIP, ORGANIZATIONAL EXPENSES, PARTNERSHIP, REAL PROPERTY SECURITIES REGISTRATION.)

T

TACKING - Adding or combining successive periods of continuous occupation of real property by adverse possessors, thus enabling one not in possession for the entire required statutory periods to establish a claim of adverse possession. In order to tack one person's possession to that of another, each of the possessions must be continuous and uninterrupted, and the parties must have been successors in interest, such as ancestor and heirs, landlord and tenant, or seller and buyer. (*See* ADVERSE POSSESSION.)
Reference: RCW 4.16, RCW 7.28.

TAKE DOWN - To borrow or draw against funds which were committed by a lender earlier, as in a construction loan. (*See* PROGRESS PAYMENTS.)

TAKEOUT FINANCING - Long-term permanent financing. Often on a large construction project, the developer obtains financing from two main sources. The first is the interim lender who specializes in short-term loans to cover construction financing. Before lending any money, however, the interim lender normally requires a commitment by a permanent lender to agree to "take out" the interim lender by taking over the mortgage as a permanent (in the sense of being long-term) investment when the building has been completed. Such a commitment, called a takeout commitment or a takeout letter, typically is the second phase of financing a development. (*See* END LOAN, INTERIM FINANCING, PERMANENT FINANCING, STANDBY LOAN.)

TAKING - Reference to the "takings clause" of the First Amendment that states "...nor shall private property be taken for public use, without just compensation." (*See* CONDEMNATION, EMINENT DOMAIN, POLICE POWER.)

TAX APPEAL BOARD - *See* BOARD OF TAX APPEALS.

TAX AND LIEN SEARCH - A title search issued to cover Torrens property. Since the Torrens Certificate of Title does not reflect certain encumbrances such as real property taxes, city and county assessments, and federal tax liens or bankruptcies, the tax and lien search is used to provide this information for a specific Torrens registered property by the registrar of titles. The report issued is sometimes called a lien letter. (*See* TORRENS SYSTEM.)

TAX BASE - 1. Refers to the assessed valuation of all real property within an area subject to taxes. This would exclude exempt church or government owned property. 2. For income tax purposes, the tax base is the net taxable income.

TAX BRACKET - The rate at which a taxpayer pays tax on income. Individual tax rates are structured on a graduated basis.

TAX CERTIFICATE - The document issued to a person as a receipt for paying the delinquent taxes on real property owned by another. (*See* TAX DEED.)

TAX CREDIT - An offset against federal income taxes usually on a dollar-for-dollar basis. At times, the government uses tax credits as incentives to develop low-income housing, historic properties or elderly housing, or to encourage businesses to make alterations in compliance with the ADA accessibility rules.

TAX DEED - The instrument used to convey legal title to property which is sold by the government for nonpayment of taxes.

After real property taxes have been delinquent for three years, two things occur under Washington law:

1. The county treasurer issues a Certificate of Delinquency in the amount of the unpaid taxes, plus interest and administrative costs. The treasurer then files the Certificate with the Clerk of the Superior Court.

2. The treasurer then brings an action to foreclose on the property. A notice of foreclosure must be served on the property owner, who has the right to redeem the property by paying the taxes, plus any accrued interest and all costs. If the property is not redeemed, the property is sold to the highest bidder. From the proceeds of sale, an amount sufficient to the taxes and interest and an amount to reimburse the county for the cost of the foreclosure act and sale is deducted from the bid amount, any surplus is paid to the record title holder.

The purchaser of the property at the foreclosure sale receives a tax deed executed by the county treasurer. Once the tax deed is issued, the property cannot be redeemed. (*See* TAX LIEN, TAX SALE.)
Reference: RCW 84.64

TAX-DEFERRED EXCHANGE - Under Section 1031 of the Internal Revenue Code, some or all of the realized gain from the exchange of one property for another may not have to be immediately recognized for tax purposes. It is not, however a tax free transaction; the payment of taxes is simply deferred to a later transfer.

Both the property received and the property given in exchange must be held for productive use in trade or business or for investment (not a principal residence) and both properties must be "of a like kind". (*See* EXCHANGE, LIKE-KIND PROPERTY.)

A sale of property which generates cash may be structured as a delayed exchange as long as the procedural process is strictly followed. (*See* DELAYED EXCHANGE.)

TAX FREE EXCHANGE - A misnomer. There is really no such item under the Internal Revenue Code as a tax-free exchange. There is a tax deferred exchange under IRC Section 1031. (*See* DELAYED EXCHANGE.)

TAX LIEN - A general statutory lien imposed against real property for payment of taxes. Note that a tax lien remains on the property until the taxes are paid, even if the real estate is conveyed to another person. There are federal tax liens and state tax liens. A federal tax lien results from a failure to pay any Internal Revenue tax, including income tax, estate tax and payroll tax. A federal tax lien is a general lien on all property and rights to property of the person liable, but its priority depends upon the number of liens previously recorded when notice is recorded.

The state tax lien for unpaid real property taxes generally has priority over all other liens on the property, regardless of whether such liens were recorded prior to the recording of the state tax lien. (*See* FEDERAL TAX LIEN, INHERITANCE TAX, LIEN, TAX CERTIFICATE, TAX DEED, TAX SALE.)
Reference: RCW 84.60

TAX PARTICIPATION CLAUSE - A clause in a commercial lease that requires the tenant to pay a pro rata share of any increases in taxes or assessments above an established base year.

TAX RATE - The rate, set by the counties, which is applied to the assessed value (as determined by the county) to arrive at the amount of annual property tax. (*See* ASSESSED VALUATION.)

TAX REGISTRATION - A service provided by title companies for real estate lenders whereby they annually search the public records for unpaid property tax liens.

TAX ROLL - Public records maintained by the County Treasurer's office showing all taxable property, tax amounts, assessed valuations and millage rates.

TAX SALE - The sale of real property by a governmental unit to satisfy unpaid real property tax liens. The property can be redeemed up to the date of the tax sale by the payment of the delinquent amount, interest and costs. (*See* TAX CERTIFICATE, TAX DEED, TAX LIEN.)

TAX SEARCH - A specific part of a title search which determines if there are any unpaid taxes or special assessments that may be a lien against the property under search.

TAX SERVICE FEE - A fee paid by a borrower at closing in escrow either upon the purchase of real property or upon the refinance of a loan on real property. The fee is really paid for the benefit of the lender. The fee is disburse to the lender, who then pays it to a local title insurance company which on a semi-annual or annual basis checks to see if the property tax on the property has been paid. If not, the title company informs the lender and the lender sends a notice to the borrower informing the borrower to pay it or the lender will start foreclosing on its loan. Property taxes have first lien priority, and if the taxes are not paid, the home could be sold at a foreclosure action, in theory wiping out the lender's entire collateral for the loan.

TAX SHELTER - A term often used to describe some of the tax advantages of real estate investment, such as deductions for depreciation, interest, taxes, etc., which may offset the investor's other ordinary income to reduce his/her overall tax liability.

It should be noted that because of changes in the tax laws in the 1980s many of the tax benefits gained through accelerated depreciation were offset by the recapture of the depreciation. Thus the primary concern in investing in real estate should be the economic soundness of the property and not just the tax shelter aspects.

The Tax Reform Act of 1986 significantly limits the use of tax shelter losses to reduce taxable income from other sources, such as salary, interest, and dividends. The passive loss rule disallows the deduction of passive activity losses against other active sources of income. Profits and losses from passive activities, including rental activities, are first netted against each other. Passive investments are defined as any trade or business in which the taxpayer does not materially participate and any rental activity, whether or not the taxpayer materially participates. Limited partnerships are passive activities under the new law. (*See* INTEREST, LEVERAGE, PASSIVE LOSS, RECAPTURE OF DEPRECIATION, TAX PREFERENCE.)

TAX STOP CLAUSE - A clause in a commercial lease providing that the lessee will pay any increases in taxes over the base or initial year's taxes; also referred to as a tax escalation clause. The lease often states that this added amount will be deemed to be **additional rent.** (*See* LEASE.)

TAXING AUTHORITY - A statutory authority given to a governmental body to levy and collect taxes for public purposes. In Washington, the county is the major taxing authority. However, many lesser taxing districts are authorized by law to levy a tax upon real estate within their district. (*See* PROPERTY TAXES.)

TEASER RATE - An adjustable rate mortgage with an interest rate initially set below the market rate.

TEMPORARY BROKER'S PERMIT - A license issued in the discretion of the Director of Licensing to a qualified representative of a deceased real estate broker permitting the representative to engage in business for a limited time period as an acting broker in place of the one who is deceased. (*See* LICENSING LAW.)
Reference: RCW 18.85.150

TEMPORARY SALESMAN'S PERMIT - Prior to 1977 an individual was able to obtain a temporary salesman permit which allowed the individual to act as a real estate salesperson for a period of time prior to taking the state's salesman examination. In 1977 this permit system was abolished and nothing of a comparable nature exists in Washington.

TENANCY AT SUFFERANCE - A tenancy or estate which exists when a tenant wrongfully holds over after the expiration of a lease, without the landlord's consent, as where the tenant fails to surrender possession after termination of the lease. A tenancy at sufferance is the lowest estate in real estate, and no notice of termination is required for the landlord to evict the tenant.

A tenancy at sufferance differs from a tenancy at will in that under the former, the landlord has not indicated his/her consent to the continuation of the tenant's possession. It cannot arise by agreement which distinguishes it from a tenancy at will. A tenant at sufferance cannot grant such an estate to a third party. Even though the tenant at sufferance may be acting wrongfully, he/she is not considered to be a trespasser because he/she originally entered upon the property with the landlord's consent. A tenancy at sufferance can be converted into a tenancy at will or periodic tenancy upon the consent of the landlord. (*See* HOLDOVER TENANT, SUMMARY POSSESSION.)

TENANCY AT WILL - A tenancy or estate in which a person is in possession of real estate with the permission of the owner, for a term of unspecified or uncertain duration, as when an owner permits a tenant to occupy a property until it is sold. The main features of the tenancy are its uncertainty of duration and its continuing permissive status. The tenancy is not assignable though it is usually permissible for the tenant to sublet the premises. Unlike a tenancy at sufferance, all the duties and obligations of a landlord-tenant relationship exist in a tenancy at will, and notice of termination is required. A tenancy at will is also terminated by death of either landlord or tenant, or by a sale of the property (since the sale results in a conveyance of the reversion).

TENANCY FOR LIFE - A freehold estate of uncertain duration, which is not an estate of inheritance; a life estate. (*See* LIFE ESTATE.)

TENANCY FOR YEARS - A less-than-freehold estate or tenancy in which the property is leased for a definite, fixed period of time, be it for 30 days or any fraction of a year, a year, ten years, etc. Such a tenancy can be created only by express agreement, which should be written if the tenancy is longer than one year in duration. The tenancy for years must have a definite term, beginning and ending on dates specified in the lease. Unless the lease provides otherwise, the tenancy is considered personal property and passes to the tenant's heirs at death with all the rights and obligations contained in the lease. The tenancy ends on the last day of the term of the lease without the necessity of the parties giving notice of termination. If the tenant continues in possession, he/she is a holdover tenant or a tenant at sufferance. Most ground leases and commercial leases are tenancies for years. (*See* LEASEHOLD.)

TENANCY IN COMMON - A form of concurrent ownership of property between two or more persons, in which each has an undivided interest in the whole property; frequently found when the parties acquire title by descent or by will. Each co-tenant is entitled to the undivided possession of the property, according to his/her proportionate share and subject to the rights of possession of the other tenants. No co-tenant can exclude another co-tenant, or claim ownership of a specific portion of the property; each holds an estate in land by separate and distinct titles, but with unity of possession. Their interests may be equal (as in a joint tenancy) or unequal. Where the conveyance document does not specify the extent of interest of each co-tenant, there is a rebuttable presumption that the shares are equal. Unlike joint tenancy, there is no right of survivorship in a tenancy in common. Therefore when one of the co-tenants dies, his/her interest passes to his/her heirs or beneficiaries and not to the surviving tenants in common. The property is thus subject to probate. The law has favored tenancy in common since the right of survivorship has often been used to defeat the justifiable expectations of creditors and sometimes results in property passing to other than those intended.

Any tenant in common can sell his/her interest in property without the consent of his/her co-tenants, but no co-tenant can attempt to transfer the entire property without the consent of all the co-tenants. If one of the common owners wishes to sell the entire property and the other co-tenants do not, he/she can bring an action for partition and seek to have the property divided up or sold at auction and each owner paid his/her share of the proceeds. If the property is sold pursuant to a partition action, a tenant in common who advanced money to preserve the property (taxes, insurance, mortgage, etc.) is entitled to be reimbursed his/her entire advancement before the balance of the sale proceeds are equally divided.

There is a legally imposed relationship of trust and confidence among co-tenants. Each co-tenant has the right to possess all portions of the property and to retain profits from his/

her own use of the property, though he/she must share net rents received from third parties. No tenant in common can be charged for his/her use of the land or may charge rent for other co-tenants' use of the land. If one of the co-tenants pays taxes or assessments due, then he/she has a lien on the interest of each co-tenant for their prorata share. However, there is no way of enforcing the lien except through a partition action.

A potential problem in a long-term real estate contract where the buyers take equitable title as tenants in common is the confusion which arises when one of the co-tenants dies before the property has been finally conveyed. If one of the co-tenants has died during the term of the real estate contract, the seller/vendor when requested to give a fulfillment deed should be cautious and check with the court to determine the rightful heirs of the deceased co-tenant to whom the property should be deeded. There is less of a problem in the situation where the sellers hold title as tenants in common and one dies, since a Washington court can specifically enforce the contract against the seller's heirs. The problem with tenancy in common is the element of uncertainty. Suppose three individuals who are unrelated hold a piece of investment property as tenants in common. If one of the individuals should die, it would be necessary to obtain all the signatures of all the heirs or devise of the deceased in order to sell the property.

Unless the intention to create a different form of tenancy is manifestly clear, a conveyance to two or more persons is deemed to create a tenancy in common. If a married couple should take title to real property in Washington as tenants in common, it will be presumed community property.

While a broker may advise his/her principal of the features of a tenancy in common as compared to a joint tenancy, he/she should not presume to advise as to which is the best form of ownership.

Sample language in a deed creating a tenancy in common would be "... to Mollie Erickson, single, an undivided 1/4 interest and to Cene Hansen, unmarried, an undivided 3/4 interest as tenants in common in the following described property..." (*See* COMMUNITY PROPERTY; CONTRIBUTION, RIGHT OF; COTENANCY; GRANTEE; JOINT TENANCY; PARTITION; PROPERTY TAXES; TAX LIEN; UNDIVIDED INTEREST.)

TENANCY IN PARTNERSHIP - A partnership is an association of two or more persons to carry on a business as co-owners and to share in the profits and losses. In the common law a partnership was not a legal entity and from a technical standpoint could not own real estate. Washington has enacted the Uniform Partnership Act which permits a partnership to own real estate. The main features of such tenancy as it affects each partner are:

1. A partner has an equal right of possession of the property, but only for partnership purposes.

2. A partner's right is not assignable, except in connection with the assignment of the rights of all partners. Thus a purchaser can only acquire the whole title.

3. A partner's right is not subject to attachment or execution except on a claim against the partnership itself, and there can be no homestead exemption claim with respect thereto. The entire property, however, can be sold on execution sale to satisfy a partnership creditor. The partner's interest cannot be seized or sold separately by his/her personal creditor, but a partner's share of the profits may be obtained by a personal creditor.

4. Upon the death of a partner, his/her rights vest in the surviving partner(s), though the decedent's estate is reimbursed for the value of his/her interest. The partner's interest in the partnership firm, a personal "chose in action," is all that passes to his/her administrator as personal property on his/her death intestate. If there are no surviving partners, his/her rights in the property vest in his/her legal representative. The vesting in the surviving partner or partners and in the legal represen tative of the last surviving partner conveys no greater right on them than to possess the partnership property for a partnership purpose. (*See* PARTNERSHIP.)

Reference: RCW: 25.04.

TENANCY IN SEVERALTY - Ownership of property vested in one person alone, and not held jointly with another; also called Several Tenancy or Sole Tenancy. The owner's title is thus severed from anyone else. When the sole owner dies, the property is probated and passes to his/her heirs or devisees. A corporation, state, or county often holds title and property in severalty.

TENANT - In general, one who exclusively holds or possesses property, such as a life tenant or a tenant for years; commonly used to refer to a lessee under a lease. A tenant's occupancy, although exclusive, is always subordinate to the rights of the owner. Tenant refers to an occupant, not necessarily a renter. (*See* LANDLORD TENANT ACT.)

TENANT CONTRIBUTIONS - All costs that are a pro rata responsibility of the tenant over and above the rent specified in the lease, such as common area maintenance (CAM). Usually referred to as additional rent. (*See* LEASE.)

TENANT IMPROVEMENT COSTS (T.I.s) - The cost of construction and remodeling needed to make the premises usable by a particular tenant. These costs may be paid by the owner, the tenant, or shared by both as a result of negotiations. (*See* LEASE.)

TENANT MIX - The selection and location of retail tenants so as to maximize the income to the lessor and stimulate business in general. Stores in a shopping center complex should be situated so that pedestrian traffic stimulated by one business benefits the others, and yet competition does not become a detriment.

TENANT'S RIGHT OF FIRST REFUSAL - The right of a tenant to purchase property from the owner in the event the owner decides to sell the property. Such a right is normally included in the lease agreement and, thus, allows the tenant to match any offer the owner may have from an interested third party. By having such a provision in the lease, the tenant is assured that he/she will at least be able to purchase the property rather than having someone else purchase it from the owner.

TENANT UNION - A local organization of residential tenants working for their common interests and rights.

TENDER - An unconditional offer by one of the parties to a contract to perform his/her part of the bargain. When a seller brings an action seeking enforcement of the buyer's obligation to pay the purchase price, the seller must first make a tender of the deed, usually by placing it into escrow. This is so because the buyer's duty to pay is a concurrent condition of the seller's duty to tender the deed. Likewise, a tender of performance by the buyer, usually by depositing the purchase money into escrow, places the seller in default if he/she refuses to accept it. Where money is due on an indebtedness, a tender discharges any lien which is security for the debts, releases sureties, and stops debts from accruing interest. (*See* ELECTION OF REMEDIES.)

When the parties to a contract clearly show an intent not to perform; e.g., where there is an anticipatory repudiation or where the vendor has already sold the property to a third party, then no tender is necessary since it would be a useless act. The parties then follow the remedies as provided in the contract to recover appropriate damages for breach of performance. The seller should not try to resell the property until he/she can establish he/she has made a valid tender or that the other party has repudiated the contract. (*See* BILATERAL CONTRACT.)

TENEMENT - A common law real estate term describing those real property rights of a permanent nature which related to the land and passed with a conveyance of the land, such as buildings and improvements. Tenements includes corporeal (e.g., land) and incorporeal (e.g., easements) rights in real property. (*See* CORPOREAL PROPERTY.)

TENURE - A common law term indicating the manner in which land is held. The tenure of most land held in Washington is fee simple. The condominium and the cooperative are modern forms of tenure.

TERM - A provision or condition in a contract. A length of time. For example: a mortgage term is the length of time (as set forth in the mortgage) in which the mortgage loan must be paid off; a lease term is the length of time (as set forth in the lease) in which the tenant can rightfully occupy the premises (e.g., 60 days; 10 years; life); an option term is the time stipulated in the option agreement for the optionee to exercise his/her rights under the agreement.

TERM MORTGAGE - A short-term mortgage securing a loan that requires interest-only payments until the maturity date at which time the entire principal is due and payable. (*See* STRAIGHT NOTE.)

TERMINATION OF AGENCY RELATIONSHIP - The cancellation of a broker-principal employment contract. If a listing contains no specific termination date, it is terminated after a reasonable time. The seller can revoke this type of listing at any time prior to the broker's producing a ready, willing and able buyer at the listing terms. If, however, the listing does contain a specific termination date (required of all exclusive listings), the seller cannot revoke the listing prior to said date without liability for the broker's commission. Courts do not look favorably upon provisions for automatic extension of the listing period; (e.g., "thirty days and continuing thereafter indefinitely until written cancellation is given.")

A listing is basically an agency contract and can be terminated under general agency and contract principles as follows:

1. Death or insanity of principal or agent.

2. Expiration of listing period.

3. Mutual agreement.

4. Sufficient written notice.

5. Completion of performance under the agreement; thus under an open listing the sale by one broker would terminate the agency for all brokers.

6. Condemnation or destruction of the subject property.

7. Bankruptcy of either party.

8. Abandonment of the agency by the broker (broker might be liable for damages).

9. Revocation by the principal (the principal always has the power to terminate, but may or may not have the right to terminate without being liable for damages to the broker).

10. A change in a law which prohibits the current or intended use of the property.

(*See* BUYER BROKER AGREEMENT, EXTENDER CLAUSE, LISTING).

TERMINATION OF OFFER - An offer which specifies a period of time for its duration and terminates upon the lapse of the time specified. An offer may be terminated by revocation, death of a party, or rejection. An acceptance in terms different from those contained in the offer is a rejection of the offer. (*See* COUNTEROFFER, OFFER.)

TERMITE INSPECTION - A visible check of the premises for the presence of termites, usually performed by a licensed exterminator. Sometimes a buyer inserts a condition in the Purchase and Sale Agreement requiring the seller to furnish a satisfactory termite inspection report (also called a pest control report) from a reputable firm chosen by or approved by the buyer, showing the improvements to be free and clear of any live, visible infestation.

If the seller were required to warrant the "premises" (rather than just the improvements) to be free and clear, he/she could run into the potential problem of having to go to enormous expense to correct infestation in items on the property such as the grounds and trees.

TERRE TENANT - One who has actual possession of the land.

TESTATE - The estate or condition of leaving a will at death. (*See* TESTATOR.)

TESTATOR - A person who makes a last will and testament; one who dies leaving a will and is said to have died testate. If the testator (female counterpart testatrix) leaves real property to certain people (devisees), they take title to the property **subject to** any liens in favor of the creditors of the estate. Thus, if the testator dies leaving behind many debts, it is possible that, after exhausting all the personal property in the estate, it might be necessary to sell the real property and give the devisees the balance of the proceeds, if any, after satisfying the debts. (*See* PROBATE, WILL.)

TESTIMONIUM CLAUSE - A clause found in legal documents beginning "In Witness Whereof..." and then citing the act and date of execution.

THIN CAPITALIZATION - Excessively high ratio of debt to equity in corporation's capital structure resulting in IRS's treatment of at least some of the debt capitalization as equity and the consequent loss of the tax benefits of debt.

THIN MARKET - A real estate market in which there are few buyers and sellers and a slow turnover of properties. This makes it difficult to obtain reliable comparable sales information.

THIRD PARTY - A person who is not party to a contract but who may be affected by it. One who is not a principal to the transaction such as the broker or escrow agent.

TIDE LANDS - The lands over which the tide ebbs and flows. In recent years the question of whether or not tide lands could be developed or had to be left in their natural state has been in front of the Washington Supreme Court several times. Tide lands may be developed when it does not conflict with the rights of the public.

Since 1971, the State has been prohibited from selling any more of its tide lands to other than public entities.

The freedom to develop tide lands is now regulated by the Shoreline Management Act of 1971.
Reference: RCW 79.01, RCW 90.58.

TIDEWATER LAND - Land beneath the ocean from low tide mark to a state's outer territorial limits.

TIE-IN CONTRACT - A contract in which one transaction is dependent on another. For example, a developer might agree to sell a choice lot only if the buyer (a builder) also agrees to buy a less desirable lot from the developer or agrees to list the improved property for sale with the developer's brokerage company. A tie-in arrangement may violate laws and state and federal anti-trust regulations. (*See* ANTITRUST.)

TIER - A row of townships extending east and west for six miles within a range. (*See* GOVERNMENT SURVEY.)

TIGHT MONEY MARKET - An economic situation in which the supply of money is limited and the demand for money is high, as evidenced by high interest rates.

TIMBER TRESPASS - In Washington a person who acts without lawful authority and cuts down trees or timber belonging to another is subject in a civil lawsuit to up to triple damages. Where the cutting is casual or involuntary and the party cutting had probable cause to believe that the land on which the trespass was committed was his/her own, the defendant will only be liable for single damages. However, once the trespass is established, the burden shifts to the party cutting the trees or timber to show that the action was casual or involuntary.

Liability for damages, including triple damages, extends to the one who authorized or directs the trespass as well as those who actually perform the trespass. (*See* TRESPASS.)
Reference: RCW 64.12

TIME IS OF THE ESSENCE - A clause in a contract which emphasizes that punctual performance is an essential requirement of the contract. Thus, if any party to the instrument does not perform within the specified time period (the "drop-dead" date), that party is in default, provided the nondefaulting party has made a valid tender of performance. If a party is late in his/her performance but no tender is made by the non-defaulting party, then a "time is of the essence" clause is waived. The one in default is not in breach of contract merely because of his/her delayed performance. For example, time is of the essence in option contracts; e.g., the option must be exercised by the option date or it terminates.

TIME PRICE DIFFERENTIAL - The difference between the purchase price for a property in a cash transaction and the higher price for the same property purchased on an installment basis. Under Truth-in-Lending the lender must disclose the time price differential in the Finance Charge. (*See* TRUTH-IN-LENDING.)

TIMESHARE ACT - The State of Washington's Timeshare Act took effect in 1983. The Act covers any sale of a right to the periodic occupancy or use of property, real or personal, that extends for a term of at least three years, including renewal options. Promoters of timeshare projects containing in excess of four time-shares use periods must first register the timeshare offering with the Department of Licensing. The Act has as its principal purpose the disclosure in a standardized written format of pertinent project information and potential risks to prospective purchasers.

Resale of timeshares is also covered under the Act. The Director of the Department of Licensing has the authority, by rule or order, to exempt the casual resale of timeshare from the registration requirements of the Act. Those advertising or marketing timeshares must provide prospective purchasers with a disclosure document known as a **public offering statement**.

Purchasers have seven days after receiving the public offering statement or signing a commitment to purchase to cancel the contract and receive a refund of any payment made. In order to assure product delivery and future quiet enjoyment of the time-shares property, the Department of Licensing may require impounds, escrows, trusts and other protective arrangements.

The Act also requires that those offering timeshares for sale be registered with the Department as timeshare salespersons. A broker licensed under Chapter 18.85 RCW is not required to be licensed under the Timeshare Act as well. However, such a broker is liable for violations of the Timeshare Act in the same way as a person licensed under the Timeshare Act.

A promoter may not offer an award, prize or other item of value for attending a sales presentation for a timeshare or for touring a timeshare facility unless the promoter provides the Director of the Department of Licensing with a security agreement which will assure performance of the promise. A promoter who fails to fulfill a promise may be liable for triple the stated value of the gift, plus reasonable attorney fees. An individual who owns ten percent or more of a corporation or a general partnership may be held personally liable for violations of the Timeshare Act. (*See* TIME SHARING.)
Reference: RCW 64.36, WAC 308-127.

TIME SHARING - Communal ownership and use of real estate which permits multiple purchasers to buy undivided interests in real property (usually a resort condominium or hotel) with a right to use the facility for a fixed or variable time period. The general concept has a number of different labels in the promotion literature including: "*interval ownership*", "*vacation license*" and "*resort sharing*". Under the time sharing forms of ownership, potential purchasers of property buy specific or floating time periods for use of specific property within a project or of the project itself. The cost of common expense is prorated among the owners. For example, under one approach, twelve individuals could own equal, undivided interests in one condominium unit and agree that each individual would be entitled to use the premises for one month (fixed or floating) out of each year. Sometimes, time sharing programs have a reservation system or a rotation of unit system in which the tenant in common can occupy his/her unit at different times of the year. Other time sharing programs strictly sell specific months of the year. Some time sharing programs are based on the purchase or lease of the property; others are based on mere licenses to use the property for a period of time. (*See* ABSENTEE OWNER, REAL PROPERTY SECURITIES REGISTRATION, RENTAL POOL.)

Because of the opportunity for fraud and financial loss to innocent buyers inherent in some of the timeshare offerings, the Director of Licensing has assumed jurisdiction over those which offer any interest in real property, either individually or through a club membership.

The Office of Thrift Supervision has granted authority to federally chartered savings and loan associations and mutual savings banks to provide financing to time-sharing purchasers, including both ownership and right-to-use time-sharing arrangements.

Time share programs which convey fee title or leasehold interests in property may be offered in Washington through licensed real estate brokers. (*See* TIMESHARE ACT.) *Reference:* RCW 18.85, RCW 58.19.

TIME VALUE OF MONEY - An economic principle that the worth of a dollar received today is greater than the worth of a dollar received at some date in the future. (*See* INTERNAL RATE OF RETURN.)

TITLE - The right to or ownership of land. Also, the evidence of ownership. Title to property encompasses all that bundle of rights an owner possesses; the totality of rights and property possessed by a person. Title may be held individually, jointly, in trust, or in corporate or partnership form. Title is a common term used to denote the facts which, if proved, would enable a person to recover or retain possession of something.

If one owns real property outright, he/she is said to have title to it. Titles are either original or derivative. Original title can be vested only in the state. This means a title gained through discovery, occupancy, conquest, or cession to the state. All other titles are derivative and these are vested in individuals. Such titles may be divided into titles by descent (no will) and titles by purchase (deed, land contract, will).

TITLE INSURANCE - A comprehensive indemnity contract under which a title insurance company agrees to make good a loss arising through defects in title to real estate or any liens or encumbrances thereon not excluded from or the subject of exceptions to coverage. Unlike other types of insurance which protect a policy holder against loss from some future occurrence (such as a fire or auto accident), title insurance, in effect, protects a policy holder against loss from some occurrence that has already happened, such as a forged deed somewhere in the chain of title.

Needless to say, a title company will not insure a bad title any more than a fire insurance company would insure a burning building. However, if upon investigation of the public records and all other material facts, the title company feels that it has an insurable title, it will issue a policy. Generally, a title insurance policy will protect the insured against losses arising from such title defects as:

1. forged documents;

2. undisclosed heirs;

3. mistaken legal interpretation of wills;

4. misfiled documents;

5. confusion arising from similarity of names;

6. incorrectly given marital status.

In addition, and most importantly, the title company will also agree to defend the policy holder's title in court against any and all lawsuits which may arise from defects covered in the policy.

A title insurance policy generally consists of four sections:

1. the agreement to insure the title and indemnify against loss (the insuring provisions);

2. a list of general conditions (conditions and stipulations) of and exclusions from coverage (Exclusions);

3. a description of the estate and property being insured, e.g., legal description (Sched ule A);

4. a list of specific exceptions to coverage (Schedule B).

The exceptions to coverage include:

1. rights of parties in possession, not shown in the public records, including unrecorded easements;

2. any state of facts that an accurate survey would reveal;

3. taxes and assessments not yet due or payable;

4. unpatented mining claims;

5. certain water rights.

Title indemnity (insurance) is made as of a specific date, a one time premium is paid, and coverage continues until the property is conveyed to a new owner and thereafter so long as the insured is liable for any covenants of warranty made in the conveyance to the new owner.

There are two major types of title insurance policies, the owner's policy and the mortgagee's or lender's policy. An owner's policy is issued for the benefit of the owner, his/her heirs and devisees, or, in the case of a corporation, its successors by dissolution, merger, or consolidation. For an added charge, title companies will issue an extended coverage owner's policy for certain properties to cover possible additional title defects not covered under standard coverage. An extended coverage policy. usually referred to as an ALTA extended coverage policy, usually protects the policy holder against such title defects as rights of parties in possession, questions of survey, and unrecorded liens. The protection afforded in an owner's policy continues until the owner's interest in the property is transferred or conveyed, it does not run with the land.

A lender's policy is issued for the benefit of a mortgage lender and any future assignees of the loan. It protects the lender against the same defects as an owner under an owner's policy, **plus** some additional defects related to the lender's security, but is good for only the amount of the mortgage loan balance outstanding as of the date of a possible claim. In other words, liability under a lender's policy is reduced with each mortgage payment, and is voided when the loan is completely paid off and released. Because of this reduced liability, a lender's policy usually costs less than an owner's policy. Under a mortgagee policy, the loss payable is automatically transferred to the assignee of the debt and security. Upon foreclosure and purchase by the mortgagee, the policy coverage continues, insuring him/her, as owner of the fee, against loss or damage arising out of matters existing prior to the effective date of the policy. In addition to these policies, title companies also issue policies to cover the leasehold interests of a lessee under a lease or a lender under a leasehold mortgage.

Local practice and custom usually dictate which party to a transaction buys what policy. It is an established practice in Washington that the seller is required to pay for the owner's policy, insuring the title while the buyer pays for a lender's policy, protecting his/her mortgagee's interest in the real estate. Title insurance may be required by custom, even where title is registered in Torrens, to protect against unrecorded liens, such as federal tax liens.

Note that, if an insured property appreciates a great deal (such as when many expensive improvements are made), it is generally good practice to obtain a new title insurance policy with increased limits to cover such possible increased losses.

Many (nearly 2,000) title companies belong to the American Land Title Association (ALTA), and use standardized ALTA title insurance policies. (*See* AMERICAN LAND TITLE ASSOCIATION, CERTIFICATE OF TITLE, EXTENDED COVERAGE, HIDDEN RISK, LEASEHOLD MORTGAGE, TORRENS SYSTEM.)

TITLE PARAMOUNT - A superior title.

TITLE PLANT - It is a requirement under Washington Insurance Law that a title insurance company maintain a complete title plant in each county in which it operates. The records maintained in a title plant consist of copies of all instruments recorded or filed in the county and all material of public record affecting real estate in the county. (*See* TITLE INSURANCE.)

TITLE REPORT - A preliminary report of the condition of title issued by a title insurance company. A title report shows the current state of the title along with the recorded objections to clear title such as unpaid mortgages and easements. The title insurance policy is issued based on the title report. The title company incurs **no liability** under a preliminary report. (*See* TITLE INSURANCE.)

TITLE SEARCH - An examination of the public records to determine what, if any, defects there are in the chain of title. In Washington, the title search is performed by a title company. Before a lender will loan money secured by real estate, it will order a title search, at the expense of the borrower, to assure itself that there are no liens on the property.

The title searcher checks back to the original source of title, which dates from a patent granted by the United States of America or the State of Washington. As a practical matter, the title insurance company searches forward from the last policy (called a "prior") they wrote on the parcel being searched. (*See* CHAIN OF TITLE.)

After conducting an exhaustive search, the title company will issue a Preliminary Report and then a Title Insurance Policy. (*See* FEDERAL TAX LIEN, GRANTOR/GRANTEE INDEX, TITLE INSURANCE.)

TITLE THEORY STATES - States in which the law considers the lender on real estate to have legal title to the property and the borrower to have equitable title. Title theory states follow the common law approach that a mortgage is a conveyance defeasible upon a condition subsequent, the condition being the payment of the mortgage debt when it becomes due. Title to the property passes to the creditor, the debtor regaining ownership when he/she pays the debt. Washington is a **lien theory state**, where legal title remains in the borrower and the lender possesses a security interest in the property. (*See* LIEN THEORY STATES.)

TOLLING - Refers to the suspension or interruption of the running of the statute of limitations period. For example, the running of the statute of limitations regarding adverse possession may be suspended during the time the record owner is mentally incompetent. (*See* STATUTE OF LIMITATIONS.)

TONGUE AND GROOVE - A method of joining two pieces of material wherein one has a tongue cut in the edge and the other board has a groove cut to receive the corresponding tongue. The method is used to modify any material prepared for joining in this fashion, as tongue and groove lumber.

TOPOGRAPHIC MAP - A map of a parcel of land showing the changes in elevation of a surface area through the use of contour lines.

TORRENS SYSTEM - A legal system for the registration of land, used to verify the ownership of the land and establish the status of the title, including ownership and encumbrances, without the necessity of an additional search of the public records.

The purpose of the Torrens Act pertaining to registration of title to land is to establish an indefeasible title free from all rights or claims not registered with the registrar of title to the end that anyone may deal with such property with the assurance that the only rights or claims of which he/she need take notice are those so registered.

The Torrens System provides for registration after a court decree, in an action similar to a quiet title suit. The system was developed in 1857 by an Australian seaman, Sir Robert Torrens, who took the idea from the system of registering title to shipping vessels. Washington and approximately nine (9) other states have adopted the Torrens System. It is rarely used in Washington.
Reference: RCW 65.12.

TORT - A negligent or intentional wrongful act arising from breach of duty created by law and not contract; violation of a legal right; a civil wrong such as negligence, libel, trespass, slander of title, false imprisonment. For example, an escrow agent who negligently or intentionally fails to comply with the escrow instructions may be liable in a tort action for the damages caused by its negligence. The escrow agent may also be liable for breach of its contract for failure to perform according to its agency.

TOWNHOUSE - A type of dwelling unit normally having two floors, with the living area and kitchen on the base floor and the bedrooms located on the second floor. A residential unit on a small lot which has coincidental exterior limits with other similar units. Title to the unit and its lot is vested in the individual buyer with a fractional interest in common areas, if any. Townhouse developments are usually planned-unit-developments, with each individual owner possessing fee title to the structure and the land underlying the structure; many are in condominium form of ownership. The surrounding land, including sidewalks, open spaces and recreational facilities, is normally owned in common with others. The townhouse concept is a hybrid of the single family home and the apartment, and is sometimes used in areas which have height restrictions preventing high-rise. (*See* PLANNED UNIT DEVELOPMENT.)

Due to the confusing use of the term "townhouse" in the advertising media, the exact definition of the word has become blurred in Washington State. It may now mean the type of dwelling combined with an ownership interest or it may only describe the type of dwelling units which may share common walls such as in an apartment complex.

TOWNSHIP - A parcel of real property, used in the government survey system of land description, which is 6 miles square, and contains 36 sections, each 1 mile square; and consists of 23,040 acres. (*See* GOVERNMENT SURVEY.)

TOXIC CONTROL ACT - In 1987, Washington adopted the "Toxic Control Act" or Washington's Super Fund. The Act is intended to encourage private parties to clean up hazardous waste sites for which they are responsible and to make them pay if they do not.

The Act makes certain specific categories of "persons" liable for the costs of cleaning up contaminated real property, i.e., removing hazardous substances from the property and either treating the substances on site or disposing of the removed material in an approved site. "Potentially liable persons" are those the Department of Ecology finds liable, based on credible evidence. In the real estate context, "Owners and operators" are the primary category, but lenders can become liable, sellers have specific duties imposed, and purchasers may have new damage claims.

"Owners" and "operators," both past and present, include any person who owned or operated the facility at the time of a disposal or release of a hazardous substance. The definitions of "disposal" and "release" are especially important because they can mean that a person who owns contaminated property, even though performing no affirmative or overt act of contamination, can nevertheless be liable simply because unintentional leaking, leaching, or seepage occurred during ownership.

Liability attaches to: (a) "facility"; any building, structure, installation, equipment, pipe or pipeline (including any pipe into a sewer or publicly owned treatment works), well, pit, pond, lagoon, impoundment, ditch, landfill, storage container, motor vehicle, rolling stock, vessel, or aircraft, or (b) any site or area where a hazardous substance, (other than a consumer product in consumer use), has been disposed of, or placed, or otherwise come to be located.

Thus, nearly anyone who has had any interest in a parcel of real property that contains any hazardous substance is potentially within coverage of the Act. Indeed, the only exclusion is a "consumer product in consumer use." Anyone buying, selling, leasing, or lending on real estate will want to be sure of his/her rights and liabilities. (*See* HAZARDOUS SUBSTANCE OR WASTE.)

The Act also imposes a disclosure obligation upon the "owner" of public or private nonresidential real property. Where there has been a release of a "significant quantity" of hazardous substance, the owner must place a notice in the records of real property kept by the auditor of the county in which the property is located. That notice must identify the property, the owner, and the person causing the notice to appear.

In addition to the owner's liability for cleanup and public disclosure, a seller has an additional disclosure obligation. A seller of real property - or of any right, title or interest in real property, whether public or private, must provide a written statement to the purchaser describing any release of a significant quantity of hazardous substance that the seller knows to have occurred during the prior 20 years on the property to be sold.

Lenders are not liable for cleanup so long as they hold only a security interest and do not participate in management or operation. If, however, they purchase at a foreclosure sale, accept a deed in lieu, or otherwise acquire title, they then become an owner and therefore liable.

Washington's "Superfund" has made substantial changes in the substance and form of real estate transactions.
Reference: RCW 70.105B

TRACK RECORD - The operating history of a sponsor (or developer) of a real estate project. In a credit check, the creditor looks at the debtor's track record or past history of paying other creditors. Also refers to the past history of a condominium developer and is required to be disclosed in a public placement offering.

TRACT - A lot or parcel of land; a certain development. Generally refers to a large area of land.

TRACT HOUSE - A house mass-produced according to the plans of the builder, as one of many residences in a subdivision, which are very similar in style, materials, and price. It is distinguished from a custom home, which is built to the specifications of the homeowners.

TRACT INDEX - An index of records of title according to the description of the property conveyed, mortgaged, or otherwise encumbered, or disposed of. (*See* CHAIN OF TITLE.)

TRADE AREA - The geographic area from which a particular business or project will attract the majority of its customers. The potential trade area of a certain location is of importance to a real estate developer/lessor who is attempting to put together a particular type of shopping or retail outlet and needs to know the boundaries of the area from where future customers will be attracted.

TRADE FIXTURES - Articles of personal property annexed to leased premises by the tenant, as a necessary part of his/her trade or business. Trade fixtures are removable by the tenant before expiration of the lease, and the tenant is responsible for any damages caused by their removal. If the tenant fails to remove trade fixtures within a reasonable time of the expiration of the lease, the fixtures will be deemed to have been abandoned and will become the property of the landlord. A tenant usually may not remove a "replacement" fixture; e.g., tenant installs a new bar to replace the old bar in the tavern he/she leases. (*See* FIXTURE.)

TRADE-IN - An agreement by a developer or broker to receive a designated piece of real property as a part of the purchase price of another property. The usual scenario is: a homeowner agrees to purchase another home and the builder of the other home or the selling broker agrees to purchase the owner's present home at a specified price if it has not sold for that price or more within a certain time. This arrangement guarantees that the owner will have the necessary financial resources to purchase the new home. (*See* GUARANTEED SALES PROGRAM.)

TRADE USAGE - A uniform course of conduct followed in a particular trade, calling, occupation or business. Any practice or method of dealing having such regularity of observance in a place, vocation or trade as to justify an expectation that it will be observed with respect to the transaction in question.

TRADING UP - Selling an improved parcel of real estate and buying another parcel which is more expensive or has better improvements on it than what is currently owned. (*See* RESIDENCE.)

TRAILER PARK - A developed site having facilities for permanent and/or semipermanent mobile homes. The trailer park contains all utilities, streets, parking and amenities. (*See* MOBILE HOME.)

TRANSFER OF DEVELOPMENT RIGHTS (TDR) - A concept of land use planning which looks at land development rights as being a part of the "bundle of individual rights" of land ownership, any one of which may be separated from the rest and transferred to someone else, leaving the original owner with all other rights of ownership. By viewing development rights as a separable economic entity, communities gain considerable strength in their battle to direct growth, preserve landmarks or unique environmental features, and maintain adequate amounts of open space, all without placing undue financial burden on the community, or on the owners of the lands which will remain "undevelopable" in the community interest. TDR may be implemented in a variety of ways, but the end result is that the owner of the development rights will be reimbursed for the rights which he/she is giving up by the person acquiring the rights for use on another property.

Although still in its infancy, TDR has been proposed or adopted in some fashion to promote the following community values: New York and Chicago have used it to preserve landmarks; it was proposed to preserve the ecologically fragile Phosphorescent Bay in Puerto Rico; Southampton, New York has adopted TDR to encourage construction of moderate and low income housing; and the state of New Jersey and counties in Virginia and California are developing proposals to use TDR as a primary system of land use regulation and preservation of open space.

TRANSFER TAX - Washington has enacted a real estate transfer tax. The transfer tax is paid by the seller. (*See* EXCISE TAX ON REAL ESTATE SALES.)

TREAD - The horizontal surface of a stair step resting on the riser. The tread is the part you step on.

TREBLE DAMAGES - Damages given by Washington statute in certain cases, whereby the jury determines the amount of damages and the court trebles/triples that amount. For example, the court has this power when a residential landlord wrongfully seizes a tenant's property as security against rent due.

In Washington, a person who without lawful authority cuts down the trees or timber belonging to another is subject to an action for triple damages. (*See* TIMBER TRESPASS, TRESPASS.)

TRESPASS - Any wrongful, unauthorized invasion of land ownership by a person having no lawful right or title to enter on the property. Trespass can occur on the land, below the surface, or even in the air space. Certain trespasses are privileged, such as trespasses to prevent waste, to serve legal process, and to use reasonable airspace for flights by aircraft.

The unauthorized possession of real property is a mere trespass and cannot ripen into ownership, unless all the elements of adverse possession are present. Since a tenant is entitled to the exclusive possession of the leased premises, not only against third parties but the landlord as well, any unauthorized entry by either the landlord or a third party would constitute trespass.

Generally, a landowner is not liable for injuries to a trespasser whose presence is not known. When the landowner knows of the trespass, however, he/she must not create conditions or do anything which may imperil the trespasser. Washington's statute of limitations for trespass is 3 years. (*See* ADVERSE POSSESSION, ATTRACTIVE NUISANCE.)

One who intentionally enters on to the land of another or causes a tangible object to enter the land of another is liable for any damages caused thereby. Intentional entry may occur when the actor causes something to enter the land of another even if the actor did not desire the trespass so long as it can be determined there was substantial certainty that such an entry would occur. In a civil suit there must be actual damages for there to be a recovery by the property owner.

TRIM - Wood or metal interior finishing pieces such as door and window casings, moldings and hardware.

TRIPLE "A" TENANT - A commercial tenant with a top credit rating, especially desirable as an anchor tenant in a shopping center. (*See* AAA TENANT, ANCHOR TENANT.)

TRIPLE NET LEASE - A net-net-net lease, where in addition to the stipulated rent, the lessee assumes payment of all expenses associated with the operation of the property. This includes both fixed expenses, such as taxes and insurance, plus all operating expenses, including costs of maintenance and repair. In some cases the triple net tenant even pays the interest payments on the lessor's mortgage or deed of trust on the property.

Strictly speaking, a triple net lease is a redundant term since a net lease is enough to describe the situation. Rather than relying on labels, however, it is important to examine the provisions of the lease to discover the extent of the tenant's responsibilities.

TRIPLEX - A building comprised of three dwelling units, each having a front and rear (or side) door and yard.

TRUCK WELL - A depressed area abutting a loading dock (either inside or outside a building) sufficient in depth to permit direct loading from the floor of the building onto the bed of a truck which has backed into the well.

TRUE ESCROW - An arrangement whereby an escrow agent, usually a bank, holds the final title documents to a real estate contract or the promissory note and deed of trust pending payment in full. True escrows are often suggested as the solution for the nagging problems that arise where the buyer is ready to pay off the balance owing on the real estate contract or promissory note but the seller either cannot be found or is not cooperative about executing the required satisfaction document. Under a true escrow, the seller, at the time the real estate transaction is closed, puts into escrow executed copies of the required document(s), e.g., a fulfillment deed under a real estate contract, a request for full reconveyance under a deed of trust, a satisfaction of mortgage under a mortgage, and instructs escrow to deliver same when full payment is made. Many escrow companies are reluctant to handle true escrows even when they are indemnified against loss. They raise these objections:

1. It is difficult for escrow to ascertain whether there has been a full payoff, or whether the amount deposited in escrow is the correct amount, or whether the buyer is in default under any other terms of the real estate contract.

2. What happens if the seller has died? Who determines the rights of the heirs? What if the seller has remarried and there are new community property rights?

3. What if the buyer has resold the property and used a different escrow agent and the seller is requested to draft new documents conveying title directly to the new buyer; thereby resulting in additional costs which should not be the responsibility of the original seller.

While the true escrow practice is good in theory, these practical problems often prevent its effective use, except in special situations. The best alternative is to set up a collection account with the lending institution where the seller has his/her existing mortgage or deed of trust. At least then the collecting agent will know the whereabouts of the seller. Also, the buyer will be protected in that he/she is assured the seller's mortgage payment is being made as long as he/she makes his/her real estate contract or deed of trust payment, and, vice versa, the seller will be notified if the buyer is in default in making his/her payments. (*See* COLLECTION ACCOUNT, REAL ESTATE CONTRACT, RELATION BACK DOCTRINE.)

TRUSS - A type of roof construction, employing a rigid framework of beams or members, which supports the roof load and usually achieves relatively wide spans between its supports.

TRUST - An arrangement whereby legal title to property is transferred by the grantor (or trustor) to a third person called a trustee, to be held and managed by that person for the benefit of another, called a beneficiary. The beneficiary holds equitable title. The grantor and trustee may be the same person as in a trust agreement (i.e., a "declaration of trust"). Trusts may be created by express agreement or by operation of law, and may be actual or constructive. For purposes of estate planning, there are inter vivos (or living) trusts and testamentary trusts. (*See* INTER VIVOS TRUST.)

TRUST ACCOUNT - Any real estate broker, escrow agent, or licensed escrow officer who receives funds or money from any principal or party to a real estate or escrow transaction, property management agreement, or collection account must hold the funds in trust for the purposes of the transaction or agreement, and may not utilize them for the benefit of the licensee or any person not entitled to that benefit. Funds received in trust must be deposited in a Washington State banking institution approved by the Banking Division, Department of General Administration, of the State of Washington and must be designed as trust accounts in the firm name of the real estate broker or escrow agent. Broker accounts must be demand deposit accounts. Every real estate broker who has a trust account, must maintain it as a pooled interest bearing escrow account for deposit of clients funds which are nominal ($5,000 or less). A nominal or short term deposit is one which, if placed in a separate account, would not produce positive net interest income after payment of bank fees or other institution fees, and other administrative expenses.

The interest accruing on this account, minus reasonable transaction costs, is paid to the Washington State Treasurer who places twenty-five percent of the remittances into the Washington State real estate commission account and seventy-five percent into the Washington State housing trust fund.

Funds not deposited as indicated above shall be deposited in interest bearing accounts with the interest accruing to one of the principals.

Interest-bearing trust bank accounts that contain only damage deposits or security deposits received from tenants of residential rent income properties managed by a broker for an individual owner may be established by the broker as **directed** by a written management agreement.

A real estate broker shall be responsible for keeping trust account records as follows:

1. The trust bank account shall be a demand deposit account designated as a trust account in the name (firm name) of the real estate broker as licensed. Rents collected in performing property management services may at the option of a licensed real estate broker be deposited in an identified trust account separate from other trust accounts maintained by the broker.

2. The real estate broker shall sign all real estate trust account checks or assume all responsibility for any person or persons authorized by the broker to sign such checks.

3. All funds or moneys received for any reason pertaining to the sale, renting, leasing or option of real estate or business opportunities or contract or mortgage collections shall be deposited in the broker's real estate trust bank account not later than the first banking day following receipt thereof, except:

    a. Checks received as earnest money deposits when the Purchase and Sale Agreement states that a check is to be held for a specified length of time, or

b. Funds or moneys received as rent, contract payments or mortgage payments on real estate or business opportunities or mortgages owned by the real estate broker or the broker's real estate firm.

4. Each deposit made to the real estate trust bank account shall be identified on the duplicate deposit slip to the specific transaction to which it applies.

5. The real estate trust bank account must be in agreement at all times with the outstanding trust liability. The balance shown in the checkbook must equal the total of the outstanding liability as shown in the clients' ledger.

6. The broker shall prepare a monthly trial balance of the clients' ledger, reconciling the ledger with the trust account bank statement and the trust account check book.

7. The debit entries made to a client's ledger sheet must show the date of the check, check number, the amount of the check, the name of payee and the item covered.

8. The credit entries made to a client's ledger sheet must show the date of deposit, amount of deposit, item covered to include but not limited to earnest money deposit, down payment, rent, damage deposit, rent or lease deposit.

9. All disbursements of trust funds shall be made by check, drawn on the real estate trust bank account, identified thereon to a specific real estate or business opportunity transaction. The number of each check, amount, date, payee, items covered and the specific transaction, rental, contract, mortgage or collection account must be shown on all check stubs or check register and agree exactly with the check written.

10. Voided checks written on the real estate trust bank account shall have the "signature line" removed, be marked void, and be retained.

11. A separate check shall be drawn on the real estate trust bank account, payable to the real estate broker as licensed, for each commission earned upon the final closing of the real estate or business opportunity transaction. Each commission check shall be identified to the specific transaction to which it applies.

12. Commissions due another real estate broker or real estate firm may be paid from the real estate trust bank account. Such commissions shall be paid upon receipt of the funds. Commissions shared with another broker shall constitute a reduction of the gross commission.

13. No deposits to the real estate trust bank account shall be made of funds received:

a. Of any kind that belong to the real estate broker or the real estate firm, including funds to "open" the bank account or to keep the account from being "closed" or

b. That do not pertain to a client's real estate or business opportunity sales trans action or received in connection with a client's rental, contract or mortgage collection account.

14. No disbursements from the real estate trust bank account shall be made:

a. For items not pertaining to a specific real estate or business opportunity trans action or rental, contract or mortgage collection account.

b. In advance of the closing of a real estate or business opportunity transaction, or before the happening of a condition set forth in the earnest money receipt and agreement, to the seller or to an escrow agent or to any person or for any reason without a written release from both the purchaser and the seller.

c. Pertaining to a specific real estate or business opportunity transaction or rental, contract or mortgage collection account in excess of the actual amount held in the real estate trust bank account in connection with such account.

d. In payment of a commission due any person licensed to the real estate broker or in payment of any "overhead expense" of the office. All expenditures for commission and other office expense must be paid from the regular business bank account.

e. For bank charges of any nature to include the cost of printing checks. Such charges are "overhead expense." Arrangements must be made with the bank to have any charges that may be applicable to the real estate trust bank account charged to the regular business bank account or to have the bank submit a separate monthly statement of such charges in order that they may be paid from the regular business bank account.

f. Of funds received as damage deposit on a lease or rental to the landlord (lessor-owner) or to any person or persons without the specific written authority of the tenant (lessee). Such deposits belong to the (lessee) tenant and are to remain in the real estate trust bank account until the end of the tenancy when they are to be disbursed to the person or persons (tenant or landlord) entitled to the deposit.

An escrow agent should handle all trust funds in the same manner that a real estate broker does. (*See* ESCROW AGENT REGISTRATION ACT, LICENSING LAW.)
Reference: RCW 18.44, RCW 18.85, RCW 43.185, RCW 59.18.270, WAC 308-124E.

TRUST BENEFICIARY - The person for whom a trust is created. The beneficiary is the party who receives the benefits or proceeds of the trust and it may be the same person as the grantor.

TRUST DEED - Security for a loan. (*See* DEED OF TRUST.)

TRUSTEE - 1. One who holds property in trust for another as a fiduciary, and is charged with the duty to protect, to preserve, and to enhance the value and the highest and best use of the trust property. Great care should be taken to set forth in the trust agreement the powers and responsibilities of the trustee.

2. One who holds property in trust for another to secure the performance of an obligation.

3. In Washington under a deed of trust, the trustee holds a bare legal power to sell the real estate secured by the deed of trust if the grantor (owner/borrower) is in default under one or more of the terms of the promissory note or deed of trust.

The trustee stands in a fiduciary relationship to both the beneficiary and the grantor. For example, the trustee cannot be the agent, employee or subsidiary of beneficiary, nor can the trustee bid at a sale which he/she is conducting. Under the Washington law, authority to act as trustee is limited to: (1) any corporation or association authorized to engage in a trust business in the State of Washington, (2) any title insurance company authorized to insure title to real property located in the state, and (3) any attorney who is an active member of the Washington State Bar Association at the time he/she is named trustee. (*See* DEED OF TRUST.)

TRUSTEE IN BANKRUPTCY - An agent of the court authorized to liquidate the assets of the bankrupt, protect them, and bring them to the court for final distribution for the benefit of the bankrupt and all the creditors. (*See* BANKRUPTCY.)

TRUTH-IN-LENDING LAWS - Regulation that requires full disclosure in writing of all costs connected with the credit portion of a real estate purchase, including the APR. A federal law effective in 1969 as part of the Consumer Credit Protection Act. It is implemented by the Federal Reserve Board's **Regulation Z**. The main purpose of this law is to assure that borrowers and customers in need of consumer credit are given meaningful information with respect to the cost of credit. In this way consumers can more readily compare the various credit terms available to them and thus avoid the uninformed use of credit. This law creates a disclosure device only, and does not establish any set maximum or minimum interest rates or require any charges for credit.

The Federal Trade Commission is responsible for enforcement of Regulation Z.

All real estate credit is covered by Regulation Z when it is to a natural person (the customer) and is not for business, commercial or agricultural purposes. Both personal property and agricultural credit transactions over $25,000 are exempt from Regulation Z, as is the extension of credit to the owner of a dwelling containing more than four family housing units (this is considered to be a business purpose).

The credit offered must either involve a finance charge or, by agreement, be payable in more than four installments. Any advertisement to aid, promote or assist directly or indirectly the extension of consumer credit repayable in more than four installments must (unless a finance charge is imposed) clearly and conspicuously state: "The cost of credit is included in the price quoted for the goods and services."

Finance Charge: The finance charge and the annual percentage rate are the two most important disclosures required. These disclosures provide a quick reference for customers, informing them how much they are paying for credit and its relative cost in percentage terms. The finance charge is the total of all costs which the customer must pay, directly or indirectly, for obtaining credit, and includes such costs as interest, loan fee, loan finder's fee, time-price differential, discount points, service fee, and premium for credit life insurance if it is made a condition for granting credit. Real estate purchase costs which would be paid regardless of whether or not credit is extended such as legal fees, taxes not included in the cash price, recording fees, title insurance premiums, investigation or credit report fees, and the like are not included in the finance charge, provided these fees are bona fide, reasonable in amount, and are not excluded for the purpose of circumvention or evasion of the law. Such fees must, nevertheless, be itemized and disclosed to the customer. In the case of first mortgages to purchase residential dwellings, the total dollar finance charge need not be stated, although the annual percentage rate must be disclosed.

Annual Percentage Rate: The annual percentage rate as it is used in Regulation Z is not interest, though interest is figured in along with the other finance charges in computing the annual percentage rate. This rate is the relationship of the total finance charge to the total amount to be financed and must be computed to the nearest 1/8th of one percent. Note, however, that many real estate mortgages call for interest based on a simple annual rate, which is lower than the annual percentage rate because certain elements in addition to interest (for example, points or other fees) which must be included in the total finance charge are not included in the calculation of the simple annual interest rate.

Disclosure Statement: The disclosure statement for real estate transactions must contain the following information.

1. The total dollar amount of the **finance charge** using that term, and a brief description such as the "dollar amount the credit will cost you."

2. the date on which the finance charge begins to apply, if it is different from the date of consummation of the transaction.

3. the **annual percentage rate** using that term and a brief description such as "the cost of your credit as a yearly rate."

4. the number, amounts, and due dates of payments. If any payment is more than twice the amount of an otherwise regularly scheduled equal payment, the creditor must identify the amount of such payment as a balloon payment and state the conditions, if any, under which that payment may be refinanced if not paid when due.

5. the number, amounts, and timing of payments.

6. the **total of payments** using that term, and a descriptive explanation such as "the amount you will have paid when you have made all scheduled payments."

7. the amount charged or method of computation for any default, delinquency, or late payment.

8. a description of any security interest to be retained by the lender and a clear identification of the property to which the security interest relates.

9. a description of any penalty charge for prepayment of principal and whether the debtor will be entitled to a refund of part of the finance charge.

10. an identification of the method used to compute any finance charge rebate which might arise in the case of prepayment of contracts involving precomputed finance charges.

11. the total amount of credit which will be made available to the borrower, including all charges (individually itemized) which are included in the **amount financed.**

12. amounts that are deducted as prepaid finance charges (for example, points) and required deposit balances, such as tax reserves.

13. in the case of a real estate contract, the cash price (purchase price), total down payment, the unpaid balance of the cash price, and the deferred payment price (which is the total of the cash price, finance and all other charges). The deferred payment price, however, does not apply to the sale of a residential dwelling.

Right to Rescind: The customer has a limited right to rescind or cancel a credit transaction. This rescission is intended to protect the homeowner from losing his/her home to unscrupulous sellers of home improvements, appliances, furniture, and so on, who secure the credit advance by taking a second mortgage on the purchaser's home. If a creditor extends credit and receives a security interest (mortgage, contract for deed, mechanic's lien) in any real property which is used or expected to be used as the principal residence of the borrower, the creditor must give the borrower the prescribed notice of right of rescission. The borrower then has the right to cancel the transaction (in writing) by midnight of the third business day (including Saturdays) following the date of consummation of the transaction or delivery of all material disclosures, whichever is later. A transaction is considered to be consummated at the time a contractual relationship is created between a creditor and a customer, irrespective of the time of performance of either party. Further, the disclosures are now required to be made before the transaction has been consummated. Disclosures involving real property must be made at the time the creditor makes a firm loan commitment with respect to the transaction.

Transactions involving the creation, retention, or assumption of a first lien or equivalent security interest to finance the acquisition of a dwelling in which the customer resides or expects to reside are exempt from the requirements of showing the "total of payments" (sum of all monthly payments), the finance charge, and the provision giving the customer three business days in which to cancel the transaction. But all loans, secured or otherwise, to finance the acquisition of building lots or raw acreage where the buyer expects to use the lot as a principal residence must disclose the total of payments and the finance charge, and give notice of the three-day right of rescission. In this regard, a purchaser of unimproved land may have a basis to rescind his/her real estate purchase since many subdividers who sell under a contract for deed do not give the purchaser a notice of the right of rescission. The prudent developer might have the prospective purchaser execute a statement to the effect that he/she purchased the lot for investment and resale and does not intend ever to use the lot to build his/her principal residence.

Without such a written declaration or other exemption, the developer must give the purchaser notice of the right to cancel by giving him/her two copies of a notice of rescission in the form prescribed by Regulation Z. One of these may be used to cancel the transaction. The customer may waive his/her right to cancel a credit agreement only if the credit is needed to meet a bona fide personal financial emergency, such as emergency repair work (for example, a flooded basement). The use of printed waiver forms for this purpose is prohibited.

If the required disclosures were not made or a notice of rescission was not given to a borrower, the borrower's right to rescind continues for a period of three years after the date of consummation of the transaction or upon sale of the property, whichever occurs earlier. When a customer exercises the right to rescind under the federal Truth-in-Lending law, he/she must tender any property received to the creditor. The tender must be made at the location of the property or at the residence of a customer, at the customer's option. If the creditor does not take possession of the property within ten days after tender by the customer, ownership of the property rests in the customer without obligation on his/her part to pay for it. Upon rescission, the borrower is not liable for any charges. Also, the creditor must return all money within 10 days.

A first mortgage on a home, given to a contractor for home improvements, would be subject to both the finance charge and the notice of rescission requirements. In such a case, the contractor should not commence work until the expiration of the cancellation period, i.e., three business days. Many contractors are unaware that they are deemed to be creditors and subject to the law where they permit payment in more than four installments.

Creditors: This law requires compliance by all creditors who regularly extend credit. Thus, the owner/occupant of a single family home ordinarily does not have to comply with the disclosure requirements of Regulation Z even when selling under a contract for deed payable in more than four installments. However, if such owner/occupant were to prearrange to discount the contract for deed immediately to a lender, he/she may be deemed to be a mere straw man and thus lose the exemption. A broker who assists a buyer in preparing a credit application is normally not an arranger of credit and thus is not subject to the law, except where he/she charges a fee for such services. But a broker who is an operative builder, a subdivider, a broker selling property on his/her own account (except for the sale of his/her own permanent dwelling), or a broker taking a second mortgage as a commission, may be deemed to be a creditor and thus must comply with the law. According to one U.S. court of appeals decision, a broker "regularly extended credit" when he/she sold three properties within a 19 month period by way of contracts for deed.

Advertising: Regulation Z also affects all advertising to aid or promote any extension of consumer credit, regardless of who the advertiser may be. All types of advertising are covered, including window displays, fliers, billboards, multiple listing cards if shown to the public, and direct mail literature. The ad is subject to the full disclosure requirements if it includes:

1. the amount of down payment or the fact that none is required (for example, "no closing costs until your first monthly payment")

2. the amount of any installment payment

3. the dollar amount of any finance charge

4. the number of installments or the period of repayment, or that there is no charge for credit.

If any of these items were included, the ad would be required to disclose the cash price, the required down payment, the number, amount and due dates of all payments, and the annual percentage rate. In addition, the total of all payments over the term of the mortgage must be set forth unless the credit advertised refers to a first mortgage to purchase a dwelling. General terms such as "small down payment ok," "FHA financing available," or "compare our reasonable rates," are not within the scope of Regulation Z. When advertising an assumption of mortgage, the ad can state the rate of finance charge without any other disclosure. The finance charge, however, must be stated as an annual percentage rate, using that term. For example, "assume 8 percent mortgage" is improper, whereas "assume 8 1/2 percent annual percentage rate mortgage" is permissible. The interest rate can be stated in advertisements in conjunction with, but not more conspicuously than, the annual percentage rate.

Also, the annual percentage rate should be spelled out, however, it is permissible to abbreviated it to APR. Bait advertising is prohibited; thus, an advertisement offering new homes at "$1,000 down" is improper if the seller normally does not accept this amount as a down payment, even if all the other required credit terms are disclosed in the ad.

Certain credit terms, when mentioned in an ad, trigger the required disclosure of other items. The purpose of this requirement is to give the prospective purchaser a complete and accurate picture of the transactions being offered. The trigger terms and required disclosures are:

Column A Trigger Terms	Column B Required Disclosures
Appearance of any of these items in Column A requires inclusion of everything in Column B	
***the down payment or no down payment**	***The amount of percentage of down payment**
***the amount of any installment**	***The terms of repayment**
***the finance charge in dollars or that there is no charge for credit**	***The annual percentage rate and whether an increase is possible**
***the number of installments**	
***the period of repayment**	

Any advertisement that mentions an interest rate, but omits the annual percentage rate or omits the words "annual percentage rate" is in violation. Any advertisement which includes any trigger term (Column A) without all of the required disclosures (everything in Column B) is in violation.

Creditors should keep records of all compliance with the disclosure requirements of the federal Truth-in-Lending Law for at least two years after the transaction. Truth-in-lending requires advance disclosure of any variable rate clause in a credit contract that may result in an increase in the cost of credit to the customer.

Where joint ownership is involved, the right to receive disclosures and notice of the right of rescission, the right to rescind, and the need to sign a waiver of such right, applies to each joint owner who is a party to the transaction.

Penalties: The penalty for violation of Regulation Z is twice the amount of the finance charge for a minimum of $100, up to a maximum of $1,000, plus court costs, attorney's fees and any actual damages. Willful violation is a misdemeanor punishable by a fine up to $5,000 or one year imprisonment, or both. (*See* ANNUAL PERCENTAGE RATE, FINANCE CHARGE, RULE OF 78s, SETTLEMENT ACT.)

TURNKEY HOUSING - Turnkey Housing is a federal program to provide housing to lower income groups, including those on welfare, on relief, the ill, the indigent and the retired whose incomes are low enough to make them eligible for public housing. Under the program, HUD makes a financial commitment to a Local Housing Authority (LHA), which then contracts with a private developer, who turns over the completely finished project to the LHA. It then has nothing to do but turn the key. Prior to 1974 it was customary for the LHA to actually purchase the project; now it is more customary for the LHA to lease it. If the LHA fails to meet its obligations either under a purchase or a lease, HUD takes over the project. Often property management is provided by the developer or a local real estate company.

TURNKEY PROJECT - A development term meaning the complete construction package from ground breaking to the completion of the building. All that is left undone is to turn over the keys to the buyer. Some governmental housing projects are turnkey projects with a private developer completing a housing development which is then totally purchased by a governmental agency for use as low-income family housing. A turnkey job is different from a "package deal" which typically includes the financing as well.

A turn-key lease is one in which the landlord agrees to give the leased premises to the tenant in a ready-to-occupy condition. (*See* BUILD TO SUIT.)

TURNOVER - Refers to the frequency with which units in a specific project are vacated and rerented or how often real property in a given area is sold and resold.

U

ULTRA VIRES - Acts of a corporation that are beyond its legal powers as provided in its articles of incorporation.

UNAUTHORIZED PRACTICE OF LAW - *See* PRACTICE OF LAW.

UNBALANCED IMPROVEMENT - An appraisal term describing an improvement which is not the highest and best use for the site. It may be either an overimprovement or an underimprovement. (*See* UNDERIMPROVED LAND.)

UNCONSCIONABILITY - A legal doctrine whereby a court will refuse to enforce a contract which was grossly unfair or unscrupulous at the time it was made; a contract offensive to the public conscience. In the absence of any mistake, fraud, or oppression, the courts are not interested in the wisdom of contracts and agreements voluntarily entered into between parties. If what the parties agree upon is ordinarily valid, they are bound by the agreements they have made, and the fact that a bargain is a hard one does not entitle a party to be relieved therefrom if he/she assumed it fairly and voluntarily. But a contract may be held invalid, or will not be enforced, if it is so improvident and unreasonable that, for the protection of the public, it should not be enforced. Under the Uniform Commercial Code unconscionable contracts are specifically rendered unenforceable.
Reference: RCW 62A.

UNDERFLOOR DUCTS - Floor channels which provide for the placement of telephone and electrical lines. This placement should allow flexibility in space planning and furniture arrangement in commercial office buildings.

UNDERIMPROVED LAND - A particular land use that, due to the fact the land is not being used to *its highest and best use*, does not generate the maximum level of income that could be generated from the land. The land may be underimproved due to economic, political, physical, and social changes that affect land use. (*See* HIGHEST AND BEST USE, OVER-IMPROVEMENT.)

UNDERINSURANCE - Insurance coverage for an amount less than the value of the property being insured. (*See* COINSURANCE, INSURANCE.)

UNDERLYING FINANCING - A mortgage or deed of trust which takes precedence over subsequent liens, such as real estate contracts or mortgages on the same property. When taking a listing, a broker should check the terms of any underlying financing documents affecting the property.

UNDERSIGNED - The person whose name is signed at the end of a document, the subscriber.

UNDERTENANT - One who holds property under one who is already a tenant, as in a sublease; a subtenant.

UNDERWRITER - As an insurance term, it refers to a person who selects risks to be solicited and then rates the acceptability of the risks solicited.

As the terms applies to real property securities, an underwriter is a person who has purchased securities from the issuer with the intention to offer or who actually does sell or distribute the securities for the issuer. For example, if a syndicator retains a securities firm to sell its limited partnership units, that firm is an underwriter. If the entire issue is sold within the State of Washington, the underwriter need only be licensed as a securities dealer in Washington. If, however, any of the security interests are to be sold outside of Washington, then the underwriter would have to be registered as a broker/dealer with the Securities and Exchange Commission.

In real estate financing, the term commonly indicates the employee who evaluates the "loan package." Underwriting a loan is the analysis of the extent of risk assumed in connection with a loan. It includes the entire process of preparing the conditions of the loan, determining the borrower's ability to repay, and the subsequent decision whether to give loan approval.

UNDISCLOSED AGENCY - The situation where an agent deals with a third person without notifying that person of the agency relationship the licensee has with another person. In some cases, the broker is instructed not to reveal the name of his/her client. When the agent signs his/her own name to any contract without disclosing the agency, he/she becomes fully liable for any breach or failure to perform on the contract. In order to avoid liability, the broker must insert the name of his/her principal on the contract so it is clear that all parties intended to bind the principal and not the agent. (*See* AGENCY, AGENCY DISCLOSURE.)

A seller does not have the right to know the identity of the purchaser. A buyer may purchasing using a nominee or a strawman. However, if the seller's agent knows the name of the buyer and the seller asks his/her agent who the buyer is, his/her agent must disclose everything he/she knows.

UNDISTRIBUTED TAXABLE INCOME - Income received by a S corporation which has not been distributed to the shareholders but is taxed as part of the shareholders' income. (*See* S CORPORATION.)

UNDIVIDED INTEREST - That interest a co-owner has in property which gives him/her a right to possession of the whole property along with the other co-owners. The undivided interests may be equal, as in a joint tenancy, or unequal, as it sometimes is in a tenancy in common. No owner has the right to any specific part of the whole. To acquire such a right, a single owner must petition the court for a partition or division of the property. For example, if Hoyt John owned 9/10 of a ten acre parcel of land, he would not own nine acres; all owners with undivided interests have the right of complete possession. In other words, there is no physical division of the land between the co-owners. Thus, one co-tenant cannot convey or encumber a specific part of the property. There is no limit to the number of persons who may own an undivided interest in real property.

Each of the co-owners has a separate economic right in a property. Thus, if part of the parcel is arid and part is fertile, it would be unlikely, in a partition action, for a court to partition the property into equal geographic areas. (*See* OWELTY.)

Condominium owners have a specified undivided interest in the common areas according to their percentage of common interest.

UNDUE INFLUENCE - Strong enough persuasion to completely overpower the free will of another and prevent him/her from acting intelligently and voluntarily, such as where a broker guilty of "blockbusting" has induced someone to sell in fear of a change in the racial character of the community. Undue influence usually requires a close or confidential relationship such as parent-child, broker-seller, attorney-client, or trustee-beneficiary. Where a person has been unduly influenced to sign a contract, he/she can void the contract.

UNEARNED INCOME - Any income that is not earned from personal services, e.g., income from rents, dividends and royalties.

UNEARNED INCREMENT - An increase in value to real property which comes about from forces outside the influence and control of the property owner, such as favorable rezoning or a favorable shift of population in the neighborhood.

UNEARNED INTEREST - Interest on a loan that has been collected but that has not yet been earned because the principal has not been outstanding long enough to earn it.

UNENCUMBERED PROPERTY - A property that is free and clear of liens and other encumbrances.

UNENFORCEABLE CONTRACT - A contract which was valid when made but either cannot be proved or will not be enforced by a court. An unenforceable contract is not merely one which is void or illegal. A contract may be unenforceable because it is not in writing, as may be required under the state statutes of fraud, or because the statute of limitations period has elapsed. The contract is nevertheless valid for certain purposes, such as evidence of a pre-existing debt. (*See* CONTRACT, STATUTE OF FRAUDS.)

UNETHICAL - Lacking in moral principles; failing to conform to an accepted code of behavior.

UNFAIR AND DECEPTIVE PRACTICES - Sales practices which do not necessarily involve deception but are still illegal under the regulations of the Federal Trade Commission. A sales practice is unfair if: 1. the practice offends public policy; 2. it is immoral, unethical, oppressive, or unscrupulous; or 3. it causes injury to consumers. This concept applies to practices such as inducing purchases by intimidation and scare tactics; substitution of products; wrongful refusal to return deposits or refunds. (*See* LICENSING LAW.)

Under the Federal Trade Commission regulations, the Commission can enjoin unfair and deceptive practices, issue complaints and prosecute, issue cease-and-desist orders, and impose fines.

UNFINISHED OFFICE SPACE - Space in a shell condition excluding dividing walls, ceiling, lighting, air-conditioning, floor covering, and the like. Sometimes called a "vanilla" stage of use. In leasing unfinished office space, the landlord often provides the tenant with standard items and/or a construction allowance. (*See* TENANT IMPROVEMENT COSTS (TIs).)

UNIFORM BUILDING CODE - A national code published by the International Conference of Building Officials and used mostly in the western states. It has been adopted in part by over 1,000 municipalities throughout the United States. It is anticipated the Code will be adopted nationally in the future.

UNIFORM COMMERCIAL CODE (UCC) - A body of law which attempts to codify and make uniform throughout the country all law relating to commercial transactions, such as conditional sales contracts, pledges, and chattel mortgages. The UCC covers personal property transactions, including stocks and commercial paper. The main relevance of the UCC to real property is in the area of fixtures, as covered in Section 9 of the Code. Where a chattel is purchased on credit or is pledged as security, a security interest is created in the chattel by the execution of a security agreement. Rather than recording the agreement, the creditor would file a financing statement in the recorder's office. If the

financing statement has been properly filed, the creditor, upon default, could repossess the chattel and remove it from the property. (*See* FINANCING STATEMENT, SECURITY AGREEMENT.)
Reference: RCW 62A.

UNIFORM FEDERAL LIEN REGISTRATION ACT - In 1988, Washington replaced the Internal Revenue lien statues with the Uniform Federal Lien Registration Act. Notices of liens, certificates, and other notices affecting federal tax liens or other federal liens are covered by this act.

All such liens affecting real property must be recorded in the county where the property is located.
Reference: RCW 60.68

UNIFORM LAND SALES PRACTICES ACT - *See* INTERSTATE LAND SALES.

UNIFORM LIMITED PARTNERSHIP ACT - A model act, adopted in part by Washington State, which establishes the legality of the limited partnership form of ownership and provides that realty may be held in the name of the limited partnership. (*See* LIMITED PARTNERSHIP.)

UNIFORM PARTNERSHIP ACT - A model act, adopted in part by Washington State, which establishes the legality of the partnership form of ownership and provides that real estate may be held in the partnership's name. (*See* PARTNERSHIP.)

UNIFORM SETTLEMENT STATEMENT - The standard HUD Form 1 is required to be given to the borrower and the seller at or prior to settlement by the settlement agent in a transaction covered under the Real Estate Settlement Procedures Act. The form is a summary of all funding into the closing and the disbursement of same

UNIFORM STANDARDS OF PROFESSIONAL APPRAISAL PRACTICE - A set of ten standards developed in 1987 by an ad hoc committee composed of representatives of several appraisal associations in response to congressional criticism that the appraisal industry lacked uniform standards. The standards, which deal with the development and communicating of appraisals and analyses, have been adopted by several of the leading appraisal associations. These associations have recommended that all associations adopt the standards, and that all lenders require that appraisals be prepared in accordance with their requirements.

UNIFORMITY - An appraisal term used in tax assessment practice to describe assessed values that have the same relationship to market value and thus imply the equalization of the tax burden.

UNILATERAL CONTRACT - A contract in which one party makes an obligation to perform without receiving in return any express promise of performance from the other party. One party gives a promise in exchange for an act; that party is not obligated to perform on that promise unless the other party acts. An example would be an open listing contract, where the seller agrees to pay a commission to the first broker who brings a ready, willing, and able buyer. The contract actually is created by the **performance** of the act requested of the promisee, not by the mere **promise** to perform. Note that a unilateral contract contains a promise on one side, whereas a bilateral contract contains promises on two sides.

Before the act is performed, the promise of the promisor is a mere unilateral offer. When the act is performed, this unilateral offer and the performed act give rise to a unilateral contract. The broker makes no promise to perform or to do any acts such as advertising. He/she can accept the contract and thus bind the seller only by actual performance, that is, by producing such a buyer. (The standard listing used in Washington is a bilateral contract wherein the broker agrees to use reasonable efforts to locate a buyer and the seller agrees to pay a commission if the property is sold by the broker, the seller or anyone else.) (*See* REAL ESTATE BROKERAGE RELATIONSHIP ACT, APPENDIX C.)
Reference: RCW 18.86

The classic example of a unilateral contract is a newspaper notice offering a reward for the return of a lost dog. The offeree is under no obligation to look for the dog, but if he/she does in fact find and returns the dog, then the offeror owes him/her the reward money. If a deed is signed by the grantor only, this would be an executed unilateral contract. Another example would be where a brokerage company promises to pay a $1000 bonus to the salesperson who sells the most units in a specific condominium project. An option in which the seller agrees to sell for a certain period of time at set terms provided the buyer performs by paying the specified option price is also a unilateral contract. (*See* BILATERAL CONTRACT, LISTING.)

UNILATERAL MISTAKE - A misunderstanding or mistake of a material fact made by just one of the parties to a contract.

UNIMPROVED PROPERTY - Land without buildings, improvements, streets, etc. The fact that property is unimproved must be clearly stated in all disclosure statements in promoting subdivided land. (*See* RAW LAND, SUBDIVISION.)

UNINCORPORATED ASSOCIATION - An assembly of people associated for some religious, scientific, fraternal, or recreational purpose. The association itself normally does not hold title to property. Any title is held through a trustee. It is, therefore, important when dealing with unincorporated associations, such as churches, that the broker check to see whether the person representing the association has actual authority to convey title to the property. Most condominium associations in Washington are incorporated.

The Internal Revenue Code allows two types of housing associations, condominium management associations and residential real estate management associations, to elect to be treated as tax-exempt organizations. But this tax-exempt status will protect the association from tax only on its exempt function income, such as membership dues, fees, and assessments received from member-owners of residential units in the particular condominium or subdivision involved. On any net income that is not exempt function income, the association is taxed at corporate rates but is not permitted the corporate surtax exemption granted to regular domestic corporations. (*See* CONDOMINIUM ASSOCIATION, COOPERATIVE.)

UNINSURABLE TITLE - Title to real estate that is not marketable and that a title insurance company refuses to insure due to some existing claim or encumbrance against the property. (*See* MARKETABLE TITLE, TITLE.)

UNIT - A part of the property intended for any type of independent use and with an exit to a public street or corridor. **Unit** commonly refers to the individual apartment units in a condominium, exclusive of the common areas. A unit normally consists of the walls and partitions which are not loadbearing within its perimeter walls, the inner decorated or furnished surfaces of all walls, floors and ceilings, any doors, windows or panels along the perimeters, all original fixtures and usually the unit's deck. The particular condominium declaration should be consulted for the exact definition of the unit. (*See* CONDOMINIUM OWNERSHIP.)

UNIT-IN-PLACE METHOD - An appraisal method of computing replacement cost, also called the segregated cost method, which uses prices for various building components, as installed, based on specific units of use such as square footage, or cubic footage. These cost figures include the cost of labor, overhead, and profit. For example, insulation may cost so much per square foot, dry wall so much per square yard, painting so much per square foot, and so on. The total in place cost of each unit (unit value) is multiplied by the number of such units in the building to determine the total replacement cost for the entire building. (*See* QUANTITY SURVEY.)

UNIT VALUE - Value or price related to a unit of measurements, for example, $20 per square foot, $200 per front foot, and so on.

UNITY (JOINT TENANCY) - A concurrence of certain requirements. Under common law rules, there are four unities essential to the creation of a joint tenancy: unity of interest, title, time, and possession. In Washington, however, an owner of property can convey to him/herself and another as joint tenants, thus altering the common law rule requiring unity of title. In a tenancy in common, the only unity is that of possession. (*See* JOINT TENANCY.)

UNJUST ENRICHMENT - The circumstances in which a person has received and retains money or goods which in fairness and justice belong to another. A lawsuit may be necessary to recover such money or goods.

UNLAWFUL DETAINER ACTION - A legal action which provides a method of evicting a tenant who is in default under the terms of the lease or rental agreement. A summary proceeding to recover possession of property or the right of possession as between landlord and tenant. The action is a narrow one limited to the one of possession and related issues such as restitution of the premises and rent. (*See* EVICTION, LANDLORD TENANT ACT, SUMMARY POSSESSION.)
Reference RCW 59.12.030

UNMARKETABLE TITLE - A title to property which contains substantial defects such as undisclosed encroachments, building code violations, easements, and so on. A title acquired by adverse possession is usually not marketable until a quiet title suit is won. (*See* MARKETABLE TITLE, UNINSURABLE TITLE.)

UNREASONABLY WITHHELD CONSENT - Many legal documents, such as leases and real estate contracts, contain a transfer clause which states, in effect, that the property may be transferred only with the owner's consent, "which consent shall not be unreasonably withheld." There is no single definition of what is unreasonable. For example, it would be reasonable for a lessor to refuse to transfer a lease to a new tenant whose business would directly compete with another tenant in the same shopping center complex (i.e, poor tenant mix). In a real estate contract situation, it would generally be unreasonable for the vendor to refuse an assignment or to demand a share in the profits where the assignee is as good a credit risk, if not better, as the assignor-vendee. (*See* ASSIGNMENT.)

UNRECORDED DEED - A deed which has not been recorded. An unrecorded deed is valid only between grantor and grantee, and anyone with actual notice of the ownership of the property. (*See* WILD DEED.)

UNSECURED - A debt instrument, such as a promissory note or debenture, which is backed only by the debtor's promise to pay. (*See* DEBENTURE, NONRECOURSE.)

UPGRADES - Changes in design or improvements made to a property after the Purchase and Sale Agreement has been mutually executed but before closing, such as added appliances, carpeting, reconstructed roof, and so on. Usually, the purchaser would pay for such improvements.

UP-RAMP - An inclined or sloping roadway or walk leading from one level to another often employed to gain access from ground level to the floor level of a dock-high building for either personnel or vehicles.

UPSET DATE - A date stipulated in a contract which specified when a building must be ready for occupancy or when the buyer has the option to rescind the agreement.

UPSET PRICE - A minimum price set by a court in a judicial foreclosure, below which the property may not be sold by a court appointed commissioner at public auction; the minimum price which can be accepted for the property after the court has had the property appraised. (The mortgagee may bid on the property and obtain title to the property.) The upset price should not exceed the reasonable market value of the property at the time of foreclosure. It sometimes happens that the upset price is so high that there are no bidders, the entire process leading up to the public auction must be repeated. (*See* FORECLOSURE.)

UPZONING - A change in zoning classification from a lower to a higher more intensive use. (*See* DOWNZONING.)

URBAN LAND INSTITUTE (ULI) - The Urban Land Institute based in Washington D.C. is an independent, nonprofit research and educational organization incorporated in 1936 to improve the quality and standards of land use and development. It conducts practical research in the various fields of real estate knowledge, identifies and interprets land use trends in relation to changing needs, and disseminates information to promote orderly and efficient land use.

URBAN RENEWAL - Process through which deteriorated neighborhoods are upgraded through clearance and redevelopment, or through rehabilitation. It may include the installation of new or the modernization of existing public improvements. Urban renewal activities may be financed with a combination of federal and local funds or strictly with private funds.

USABLE AREA - On a multi-tenancy floor, usable area is the gross area minus core space. Core space includes the square footage used for public corridors, stairwells, washrooms, elevators, electrical and janitorial closets, and fan rooms. On a single tenant floor, the usable area is the gross square footage excluding building lobby and all penetrating shafts (that is, ducts, stairwells and elevators.)

USEFUL LIFE - That period of time over which an asset, such as a building, is expected to remain economically feasible to the owner.

U.S. GEOLOGICAL SURVEY - An agency within the U.S. Department of the Interior with responsibility for conservation, geological surveys, and mapping of lands within U.S. boundaries. (*See* BENCHMARK.)

USUFRUCTUARY RIGHT - It is the right to the use, enjoyment, and profits of property belonging to another, such as an easement or profit a prendre. (*See* EASEMENT.)

USURY - Charging a rate of interest in excess of that permitted by law. The statutory usury rate in Washington is the higher of 12 percent, or four percentage points above the first 26-week treasure bill auction of the prior month. (e.g., The "T" bill rate for the first week of January 1998 was 5.09% so an interest rate in excess of 12% for a loan entered into January 2, 1998 would have been usurious.)

Loans to the following are exempt from State usury laws **regardless of purpose or amount**: corporations, Massachusetts Trusts, associations, trusts, partnerships (general and limited), joint ventures and governments.

Loans to individuals, **primarily for the following purposes**, are exempt regardless of amount: business, agricultural, commercial, and investments.

Due to the exclusions under the Act, only consumer loans and residential loans are covered by the usury statute. Residential loans (owner-occupied) are covered whether the financing is by real estate contract, deed of trust, purchase money mortgage or second mortgage.

In the event the contract does provide for a usurious rate of interest, the contract itself is still valid. However, in any action on such contract, if proof be made that a greater rate of interest has been directly or indirectly contracted for or taken or reserved, the creditor shall only be entitled to the principal, less the amount of interest accruing thereon at the rate contracted for; and if interest shall have been paid, the creditor shall only be entitled to the principal less twice the amount of the interest paid, and less the amount of all accrued and unpaid interest; and the debtor shall be entitled to costs and reasonable attorney's fees plus the amount by which the amount he/she has paid under the contract exceeds the amount to which the creditor is entitled. (*See* FLOAT, INTEREST.)
Reference: RCW 19.52.

UTILITIES - The basic service systems required by a developed area such as telephone, electricity, water, gas, etc. Utility easements are usually gross easements running on, over, or under the property.

UTILITY ROOM - A room, often located on the ground floor, that is designed for use as a laundry or service room.

UTILITY VALUE - The value in use to an owner-user, which includes a value of amenities attaching to a property; also known as subjective value.

VA GUARANTEED LOAN (GI LOAN) - SEE VETERANS AFFAIRS (VA) LOANS.

VACANCY ALLOWANCE OR RATE - An allowance or discount for estimated vacancies (unrented units) in a rental project. The vacancy factor is important in assembling an investment income analysis of a property. Rent loss can result for any number of reasons, e.g., periods of remodeling or rehabilitation, low occupancy rates or rent loss because of the tenant's inability to pay. The vacancy rate could be the ratio between the number of vacant units and the total number of units in a specified project or area, or the difference between the unleased square footage of a project and the total square footage of a project.

The vacancy allowance or rate, usually indicated as a percentage factor, when subtracted from potential or gross income, equals effective gross income, the amount of income actually collected.

Current statistics on vacancy factors can be obtained from the U.S. Census Bureau, regional housing reports published by the Department of Commerce, and local utility companies.

VACANT LAND - *See* UNIMPROVED LAND.

VACATE - To give up occupancy or surrender possession.

VACATION HOME - A dwelling unit including a house, apartment, condominium, house trailer, boat or similar property used for recreational purposes. It also includes any environs and outbuildings, such as a garage, which relate to the use of the dwelling unit for living accommodations.

If the only use of the vacation home is personal, you are allowed to deduct 100% of your real estate taxes and interest portion of your mortgage payments. However, many owners of vacation type property try to rent it to help pay the carrying costs of ownership.

The Tax Reform Act of 1976 placed limitations on the deductibility of certain business expenses taken by a taxpayer who rents out his/her/her vacation home. Effective January 1, 1976, if a taxpayer uses a vacation home for more than fourteen days a year or more than 10% of the annual rental time, deductions for depreciation, maintenance, utilities and the like won't be allowed to exceed rental income. But if the vacation home is rented out for less than 15 days a year, the taxpayer won't have to report the income and won't be allowed any business deductions on his/her/her tax return (*See* ABSENTEE OWNER, DEPRECIATION (TAX), RENTAL POOL.)

The 1976 Act eases the deduction limitation rule for rented vacation homes that are converted to a taxpayer's principal residence or where a taxpayer converts his/her/her principal residence to a vacation home that he/she then rents out. It provides that the number of days a taxpayer uses a home as his/her/her principal residence is not treated as personal use for the purposes of determining whether the deductions attributable to "a qualified rental period" are subject to the 14-day or 10% rule. For this purpose, "a qualified rental period" will be a consecutive period of 12 months or more, beginning or ending during the taxable year, during which the unit is rented (other than to a brother, sister, spouse, ancestor or lineal descendant of the taxpayer), or held for rental, at its fair market rental.

VALID - Legally sufficient or effective, such as a valid contract. A contract which must in all respects comply with the provisions of the law appertaining thereto. A valid contract should be executed with proper formalities, satisfy legal requirements, and have sufficient legal force to stand against attack; it must be legally efficacious for the purpose designed. (*See* CONTRACT.)

VALUABLE CONSIDERATION - The granting of some beneficial right, interest, profit or the suffering of some legal detriment or default by one party in return for the performance of another, usually as an inducement for a contract; different from "good consideration," which is love and affection with no pecuniary measure of value, such as a father might use as consideration to grant an estate to his/her son.

Valuable consideration is always sufficient to support a contract, whereas good consideration may in some cases be insufficient. For example, a father might agree to transfer his/her title to real property to his/her son in consideration for the son's forbearing from smoking, drinking and going out with loose women until he reaches the age of 21. If the son does so forbear, at the age of 21 the son can enforce the contract because he has provided valuable consideration. If, however, the father had promised to convey title to the property in consideration of the love and affection that he has for the son, this is not sufficient consideration to support the contract and thus the son would not be able to force the father to transfer (deed) the property to him. (*See* CONSIDERATION, LOVE AND AFFECTION.)

VALUE - The power of goods or services to command other goods in exchange for the present worth of future rights to income or amenities; the present worth to typical users and investors of future benefits arising out of ownership of a property; the amount of money deemed to be the equivalent in worth of the subject property. The four essential elements of value are utility, scarcity, demand and transferability. Cost does not equal value, nor does equity. There are various types of value, such as market value, tax assessed value, book value, par value, rental value, reproduction value, etc.

There are many factors which influence the value of a particular property. It is generally agreed that of them all, "location" is the most important. Other factors are size and shape, utility, access and exposure. For example, the south and west sides of business streets in eastern Washington are usually more valuable because pedestrians seek the shady side of the street and display merchandise is not damaged by the sun in the summer. (*See* APPRAISAL.)

VARIABLE INTEREST RATE - A modern approach to financing in which the lender is permitted to alter the interest rate at preagreed to intervals based on an agreed basic index. The monthly payments can then be increased or decreased, or the maturity extended, depending on how the base index varies. For example: "The sum of $50,000 payable in monthly installments of $400 each, including interest on the unpaid balance at the rate of 8.5 percent per year or two percent higher than the prime interest rate in effect at the Bank of Lacey, whichever is greater (such rate to be established once each year on the first banking day of each calendar year), provided that the interest rate shall not exceed the maximum rate permitted by law."

VARIABLE PAYMENT PLAN - A mortgage repayment plan which allows a person to make small payments early in the loan term, increasing in future years, presumably as the mortgagor's income increases. This is also called the *flexible rate mortgage*, the design of which is to help borrowers qualify for loans by basing repayment schedules on salary expectations.

VARIABLE-RATE MORTGAGE (VRM) - A mortgage in which the interest rate will vary in accordance with an agreed upon base index, thus resulting in a change in the dollar amount of the borrower's monthly installment payments. Some lending institutions use the cost-of-funds index of the Federal Home Loan Board (FHLBB) as the base index.

In some instances, if the interest rate is increased, the borrower has the option of increasing the monthly payment, keeping the payment constant but extending the term of the loan, or refinancing without penalty. (*See* ADJUSTABLE RATE MORTGAGE, CREATIVE FINANCING, VARIABLE INTEREST RATE.)

VARIANCE - Permission obtained from governmental zoning authorities to build a structure or conduct a use which is expressly prohibited by the current zoning laws; an exception from the zoning laws.

An example of a use variance is where the owner attempts to get a new use permitted on the premises such as duplex use for a single family residential area. There is also an area or building variance where the owner attempts to get permission to build a structure larger than permitted.

For a variance to be granted, the owner must be able to show a hardship. However, the hardship must be special and peculiar to the subject property, it must not be self-created, and the proposed new use must not change the essential character of the neighborhood, e.g., it must be consistent with the general plan for the area.

Several examples of requests for variances which have been denied are: (1) An owner of a parcel of land which was zoned general commercial for the front 280 feet and the rear portion zoned residential, requested a variance to use the rear portion for commercial purposes as well. On appeal the court denied the variance because it could not find an undue hardship. (2) The owner of a home sought a variance to operate a beauty parlor in the basement. The court found that the plaintiff failed to carry an affirmative burden of proving "unnecessary hardship, unique or peculiar to the property itself, and that the proposed use will not adversely affect the public." (*See* NONCONFORMING USE.)

VENDEE - The purchaser of realty; the buyer. The buyer under a real estate contract.

VENDOR - The seller of realty. The seller under a real estate contract. In an unusual case, such as a the vendor who simply holds an option on the property.

VENEER - A layer of material covering a base of another substance, such as a mahogany veneer over less valuable wood, or brick exterior finish over wood framing.

VENT - A small opening to allow the passage of air through any space in a building, as for ventilation of an attic or the unexcavated area under a first floor construction.

VENT STACK - A small chimney-like stack allowing ventilation through a roof. An integral part of a residence's drain-waste-vent (DWV) system which both carries off waste and allows air into the system for proper drainage. Sewer gases can also escape through the stack.

VENTURE CAPITAL - Unsecured money directed toward an investment. Because of the risks involved, it usually commands the highest rate of return for its investment.

VENUE - From the Latin word meaning **to come**, it refers to the place where the cause of action arose, or the place where the jury is selected and the trial is brought.

Even though the court has jurisdiction to hear a particular matter, the action must still be commenced in the proper place. Thus, a Pierce County Superior Court has **jurisdiction** or power to hear a $20,000 breach of purchase contract action on a King County property, but the proper **venue** is the King County Superior Court.

VERIFY - To confirm or substantiate by oath. Claims made to small claims court must be verified. (*See* AFFIRMATION.)

VESTED INTEREST - A present right, interest or title to realty, which carries with it the existing right to convey, even though use or possession is postponed to some uncertain time in the future. For example, when Mr. Tripp grants Ms. Balon a life estate in his/her ranch, the property reverts to Mr. Tripp upon the death of Ms. Balon; the reversion is a vested interest.

VESTIBULE - A small entrance hall to a building or to a room.

VETERANS AFFAIR (V.A.) LOAN - Under the Serviceman's Readjustment Act of 1944, as amended in 1952, 1970, 1974, and 1987, eligible veterans who were honorably discharged (generally applies to all veterans having served 181 days on active service between 1944 and 1981) and unremarried widows or widowers of veterans who died in service or from service connected causes may obtain **guaranteed** loans for the purchase or construction of a home.

Any enlisted member of the Armed Forces who began service after September 7, 1981 or any commissioned officer who began active service after October 16, 1981, must complete a total of two years active service to be eligible for a VA-guaranteed home loan. There is a special provision allowing active duty personnel with less than two years service to obtain a VA-guaranteed home loan after 181 days so long as they are still on active duty. Eligibility can be determined by contacting any Veterans Affairs Regional Office or through most VA-approved lending institutions.

The main purpose of the "G.I Loan" as it often called, is to assist veterans in financing the purchase of reasonably priced homes, including condominium units and mobile homes, with little or no down payments, at the prevailing market interest rate. The VA program encourages private lending institutions to make larger loans than the veteran would normally qualify for by guaranteeing part of the loan. There is no VA limit on the amount of the loan the veteran can obtain; there is just a limit on the amount of the guarantee the VA will extend.

Low Risk Loan: Only in certain rural areas where financing is not reasonably available does the VA lend the money itself. Usually the veteran makes his/her or her own application with a lending institution. Assuming the lender is VA-approved, the VA will then guarantee the lender against loss up to 60 percent of the loan. Under the 1987 amendments, the maximum guarantee on loans of $45,000 and under is 50 percent. On mortgages over $56,250, the VA guarantee covers 40 percent of the loan amount. The VA pays up to $46,000 on a guaranteed loan claim but no less than $22,500. While the figures may sound low, remember that it is simply the maximum amount the VA will pay the lender after foreclosure, in case there is a deficiency upon the sale of the property. Most lenders feel a VA loan is a low-risk loan.

Loan Requirements: The VA loan to purchase, construct, alter, improve, or repair a home cannot be approved by Veterans Affairs unless the veteran certifies that he/she or she occupies or intends to occupy the property as his/her or her home. This certification must be given at the time of loan application, and again at closing. The veteran is subject to criminal prosecution for making a false certification. At a later time, the veteran owner/occupant would be allowed to rent the home.

Provided the veteran meets the VA requirements with respect to income and credit, the VA will guarantee any loan from an approved lender as long as it does not exceed the reasonable value of the property. The VA has an approved appraiser use prescribed appraisal procedures to determine the value in the housing market prevailing at the time the appraisal is made. The VA issues a certificate of reasonable value (CRV) which, in effect, sets an upper limit on the loan. If the purchase price exceeds the CRV value, the veteran must pay this amount in cash, out of his/her or her own resources, and sign a statement acknowledging he/she understands that the purchase price is higher than the appraised value.

Unlike the FHA loan, the VA borrower is permitted to use secondary financing to obtain additional money for the purchase of the dwelling. However, the interest rate cannot exceed the rate of the first mortgage, and the second mortgage term must be at least as long as that of the first mortgage. Because of these and other restrictions, secondary financing is rarely used in VA loans. (After closing, however, the veteran can place a second mortgage on the property.) In addition, co-mortgagors are not accepted by the VA without a pro rata reduction in the loan amount of the guaranty.

Closing Costs and Other Costs: The broker should make the buyer aware that he/she must have sufficient cash to pay any down payment required, plus closing costs. Closing costs may not be included in the loan. While the distribution of closing cost items may be agreed to in the purchase agreement, all or a significant part of the closing costs are often paid by the buyer. Since the loan cannot cover these costs, they must be paid in cash. In addition, the monthly amortized payments include 1/12 of the annual taxes and lease rent, if applicable, and one month's hazard insurance premium, as in a FHA loan. Note that the VA limits loan fees to one percent of the face value of the loan.

Anti-Discrimination: Pursuant to the late President Kennedy's Executive Order 11063, entitled "Equal Opportunity in Housing," (1963) the VA has set up strict regulations to prevent discrimination in the sale of housing because of race, color, religion, or national origin.

VA Assumption: A veteran may sell a home purchased with a VA guaranteed loan to anyone, even to a non-veteran, without first obtaining VA approval and without paying off the loan. The new buyer may take subject to, or assume, the mortgage obligation. If the buyer takes subject to the mortgage, he/she is not personally liable on the debt and the veteran remains liable. If the purchaser assumes the mortgage, he/she becomes personally liable. The veteran also remains personally liable, unless the lender, with the prior approval of the VA, consents to the release from liability. The recommended procedure for a VA assumption is to make the purchase agreement contingent on VA approval of the income and credit of the purchaser. If the sale were consummated without the prior submission of a release application to VA, and without the purchaser's even assuming the payment of the loan, it would be almost impossible for the veteran to obtain a release from the VA at a later date. In addition, the veteran will lose VA (entitlement) status for another loan until the original loan is completely satisfied or his/her or her VA liability is released. Anyone assuming the loan must pay a one-half percent user fee. Buyers assuming a VA guaranteed loan must also undergo a creditworthiness check. If a purchaser does not meet these standards, the veteran can request that the VA approve the assumption, so long as the veteran agreed to be secondarily liable for the loan.

Interest: The maximum interest rate on VA loans is set by the VA Administrator according to the governing law, and may vary from time to time. The rate is usually the same as under the FHA loan program and has more than doubled since the original four percent rate set in 1944. Once a loan has been made, the interest rate set forth in the loan will remain constant for the life of the loan. As with an FHA loan, the borrower can prepay the loan at any time without penalty. Also, just as with the FHA loans, the veteran is not allowed to pay more than a one percent loan fee. Since 1992, discount points may be paid in cash by the veteran and cannot be added to the loan amount. The seller must pay whatever discounts or points are charged by the lender, with a limitation established by the agreement in the Purchase and Sale Agreement.

Foreclosure: If the veteran defaults, the VA must pay the lender up to the amount of the guaranty. The veteran is liable to repay the guaranteed amounts to the VA. The VA may appraise the property prior to the foreclosure sale and set the minimum upset price acceptable to the VA. The VA must be notified by the trustee conducting the foreclosure not less than 10 days prior to the date of sale. The VA is more liberal than FHA in reimbursing the mortgagee for the costs and expenses of foreclosure.

Veterans Housing Act of 1974: This Act authorized the complete restoration of a veteran's entitlement to a loan guarantee if any prior VA loan has been paid in full and the property has been disposed of by the veteran. The act eliminated the requirement that the FHA must have insured at least one loan in a condominium project before VA would guarantee a condominium loan in that project, and, finally, the act provided for increasing loan guarantee limits for mobile homes, lots on which to place them, and specially adapted housing for disabled veterans. Projects converted or proposed to be converted to condominium ownership are not, however, eligible for VA loan financing.

On new homes appraised by the VA, builders are required to give the veteran purchasers a one year warranty that the home has been constructed in substantial conformity with VA-approved plans and specifications. (*See* CERTIFICATE OF ELIGIBILITY, CERTIFICATE OF REASONABLE VALUE, FEDERAL HOUSING ADMINISTRATION.)

COMPARISON OF FHA AND VA LOAN PROGRAMS

Veterans Administration

1. Financing available only to veterans and certain unremarried widows and widowers.

2. VA financing limited to owner/occupied residential (one to four family) dwellings — must sign occupancy certificate on two separate occasions.

3. Does not require down payment, though lender may request small down payment.

4. Methods of valuation differ — VA issues a "certificate of reasonable value."

5. With regard to a home loans, the law requires that the VA loan may not exceed the reasonable value of the home.

6. No prepayment penalty.

7. Following default, foreclosure and claim, the lender usually receives cash.

8. Guarantees the loan up to 50 percent of $45,000, whichever is lower.

9. Secondary financing permitted in exceptional cases.

10. Buyer can pay discount points in cash; he/she can pay a one percent origination fee.

11. VA loan can be assumed by non-veteran without VA approval.

Federal Housing Administration

1. Financing is available to both veterans and non-veterans alike.

2. Financing programs for owner-occupied, rental and other types of construction; owner-occupied has greater loan-to-value ratio.

3. Requires a larger down payment than VA.

4. Different evaluation methods; as with VA financing there are prescribed valuation procedures for the approved appraisers to follow.

5. FHA valuation sets the maximum loan FHA will insure but does not limit the sales price

6. No prepayment penalty.

7. Insures the loan by way of mutual mortgage insurance; premiums paid by buyer in amount of 1/2 of one percent of unpaid balance of loan.

8. No secondary financing permitted until after closing.

9. Buyer prohibited from paying discount points; he/she can pay a one percent origination fee.

10. FHA loan can be assumed with FHA approval

(*See* CLOSING COSTS.)

VETO CLAUSE - A provision in a contract which gives one party to the contract the authority to allow or disallow certain action. For example, a clause in a shopping center lease, which gives the tenant, usually an anchor tenant, the right to bar any lease between the landlord and another tenant. Such a clause may be held invalid under modern antitrust interpretation. (*See* ANCHOR TENANT, LEASE.)

VIOLATION - An act, deed or condition contrary to law or permissible use of real property.

VISUAL RIGHTS - The right to prevent a structure (e.g., billboards) from being erected where it would obstruct a scenic view or interfere with clear vision at a traffic intersection.

VOCATION - One's regular calling or business. The work in which a person is regularly employed. In Washington, one can be a real estate broker or salesman as a part-time vocation.

VOID - Having no legal force or binding effect; a nullity; not enforceable. A contract for an illegal purpose (e.g., gambling) is void. A void agreement is no contract at all. Under Washington's discrimination laws, any restrictive covenant which discriminates on the basis of race, sex, color, religion, marital status or ancestry is void, although the nondiscriminating portions of the document in which it appears will remain valid. (*See* UNENFORCEABLE CONTRACT, VOIDABLE.)

VOIDABLE - A contract which appears valid and enforceable on its face, but is subject to rescission, e.g., by a party who acted under a disability, such as being a minor or being under duress or undue influence; that which may be avoided or adjudged void but which is not, in itself, void. "Voidable" implies a valid act which may be rejected by an act of disaffirmance, rather than an invalid act which may be confirmed. For example, assume that a minor contracts to buy a diamond ring; the contract can be avoided by the minor because of his/her lack of age. If, however, the minor elects to enforce the contract, the contract is valid and the other party cannot assert the minor's lack of age as a defense.

In cases of fraud against the buyer of real estate, the buyer may affirm or disaffirm the contract within a reasonable time after the truth is discovered. For the duration of a license suspension, an individual broker's listings are voidable because of his/her or her inability to perform contractual obligations. (*See* INFANT, MINOR, VOID.)

VOLUNTARY LIEN - A lien placed on a property by the owner, such as a mortgage, a deed of trust, etc.

VOUCHER SYSTEM - In construction lending, a process of giving subcontractors a voucher in lieu of cash that they may redeem with the construction lender. The voucher system is the opposite of a fixed disbursement schedule under which the lender forwards certain amounts of capital under a fixed schedule to the subcontractors.

WAINSCOTING - Wood lining of an interior wall. Wainscoting is also the lower part of a wall when finished differently from the wall above.

WAIVER - To voluntarily give up or surrender a right. In some cases, the law prohibits a person from waiving certain rights granted by statute. For example, a provision in a contract purporting to bind any prospective purchaser of subdivided lands to waive compliance with the protections afforded under the subdivision registration law is void. Also void are agreements to waive rights provided under the Landlord Tenant Act.

In building construction situations, the general contractor usually retains a portion of the final payment to his/her subcontractors until they present waivers of their mechanic's lien rights. This is called a waiver of lien.

The general rule is that a contingency placed in a contract for one person's benefit can be waived by that person for any reason. For example, a buyer who agrees to buy a farm contingent on favorable soil tests can decide to waive the contingency and purchase the farm even if the soil tests are negative.

Waiver is the most frequently raised defense in a breach of contract lawsuit. Therefore; legal counsel should provide in all agreements that no waiver, modification, amendment, etc., of any provision of the contract will be valid unless reduced to writing and signed by the party against whom enforcement is sought.

WALK-THROUGH - A final inspection of a property just prior to closing. This assures the buyer that the property has been vacated, that no damage has occurred and/or that the seller has not taken or substituted any property contrary to the terms of the sales agreement. If damage has occurred, the buyer could ask that funds be withheld at the closing to pay for the repairs.

WALLBOARD - A board used as the finishing covering for an interior wall or ceiling. Wallboard can be made of plastic laminated plywood, cement sheeting, plywood, molded gypsum, plasterboard, or other materials. Wallboard is applied in thin sheets over the insulation. It is often used today as a substitute for plaster walls but can also serve as a base for plaster.

WALL SHEATHING - Sheets of plywood, gypsum board, or other material nailed to the outside face of the wall studs to form a base for the exterior siding.

WALL STUD - *See* STUD.

WALL-TO-WALL CARPETING - Carpeting which fully covers the floor area in a room. When a seller lists property to include wall-to-wall carpeting, the listing agent should take care to verify that there is, in fact, wall-to-wall carpeting, avoiding the not too uncommon problem which occurs when the seller removes his/her furniture and the buyer discovers that there are gaps in the carpeting. In most cases, wall-to-wall carpeting is treated as a fixture, but to avoid disputes the buyer and seller should specify in their Purchase and Sale Agreement whether or not the wall-to-wall carpeting will pass to the buyer.

Wall-to-wall carpeting meeting minimum FHA standards, which isn't very high, is now accepted as finished flooring in proposed or existing homes and multifamily properties, and as such is considered to be part of the real property.

WAREHOUSE - A building used to store merchandise and other materials or equipment. As an investment, a warehouse is considered low risk, has a relatively low rate of return and is usually operated under a net lease. Such properties are usually classified as industrial.

WAREHOUSING - A term used in financing to describe the process employed by loan correspondents to assemble into one package a number of mortgage loans, which the correspondent has originated and which he/she sells in the secondary mortgage market. The sale of these mortgages provides added capital with which to make more loans, which can then be packaged and sold, thus repeating the cycle. Lenders frequently accumulate FHA loans to process in a group package.

A mortgage banker will often borrow short-term money to initially fund mortgage loans. The banker will then warehouse a number of such loans (much as a wholesaler will warehouse clothing or furniture) to be sold at a later date to a large financial institution. When the loans are sold, the mortgage banker will generally receive the value of the warehoused mortgage loans, plus a 1 percent origination charge and a commitment for approximately 1/2 of 1 percent servicing fee over the life of the loan.

WARRANTY - A promise that certain stipulated facts are true as stated. A guaranty by the seller, covering the title as well as the physical condition of the property. A warranty is different from a representation in that a representation is a statement made in the course of negotiations leading up to the sale, but not incorporated into the contract. A warranty, on the other hand, would be a statement in the contract asserting the truth of certain things about the property. In order to prove a breach of warranty, a buyer must prove that the situation in violation of the warranty was in effect as of the date of closing (such as when the seller asserts that there is adequate water available for drinking purposes when, in fact, there is not). A breach of warranty action can only result in damages being awarded by the court, not rescission of contract as with a misrepresentation.

In contract law, a warranty is basically a written or oral undertaking or stipulation that a certain fact in relation to the subject matter of the contract is or will be as it is stated or promised to be. A warranty differs from a representation in that a warranty must always be given contemporaneously with, and as a part of, the contract, while a representation precedes and induces the contract. While that is their difference in nature, their difference in consequence or effect is this: upon the breach of a warranty, the contract remains binding, and only damages are recoverable for the breach. Upon a false representation by the seller, the purchaser may elect to void the contract and recover the entire price paid. There is a current trend in the courts to enforce an implied warranty of fitness and merchantability against builders and sellers of new homes, including condominium units. This rejection of the common law caveat emptor doctrine has not yet been applied to the resale of older homes. (*See* CAVEAT EMPTOR, IMPLIED WARRANTY OF HABITABILITY.)

The Magnusen-Moss Warranty Act is a federal law requiring the full and fair disclosures of any warranty on any consumer product in the home, whether the manufacturer's or the seller's. The law covers separate items of equipment attached to real property, such as air-conditioners, furnaces, and water heaters. The Act is administered by the Federal Trade Commission.

WARRANTY DEED - A deed in which the grantor fully warrants good clear title to the premises. Also called a general warranty deed. The usual covenants of title are: covenant of seisin, covenant of quiet enjoyment, covenant against encumbrances, covenant of right to convey, and covenant of further assurance. A warranty deed is used in most Washington real estate sales.

A warranty deed, when properly executed and delivered, is a conveyance in fee simple to the grantee, his/her heirs and assigns, with covenants on the part of the grantor that: (1) At the time of the making and delivery of the deed, the grantor was lawfully seized of an indefeasible estate in fee simple in and to the premises therein described, and had the right and power to convey the same; and (2) the property was then free of all encumbrances; and (3) the grantee, his/her heirs and assigns, shall have quiet and peaceable possession of the premises, and the grantor will defend title thereto against all persons who may lawfully claim them. (*See* DEED.)

WASHINGTON ASSOCIATION OF REALTORS® (WAR) - A statewide chapter of the National Association of Realtors comprised of members designated as Realtors. WAR focuses its attention on the protection of private property rights, education and legislation pertaining to real estate, and special events such as state and national conventions. (*See* LOCAL REALTORS® ASSOCIATION OR BOARD, NATIONAL ASSOCIATION OF REALTORS®.)

WASHINGTON ENVIRONMENTAL PROTECTION AGENCY - *See* ENVIRONMENTAL PROTECTION AGENCY.

WASHINGTON ESCROW AGENT REGISTRATION ACT - *See* ESCROW AGENT REGISTRATION ACT.

WASHINGTON HORIZONTAL PROPERTY REGIMES ACT - *See* HORIZONTAL PROPERTY REGIMES ACT.

WASHINGTON HOUSING TRUST FUND - In 1988, the real estate license law was amended to clarify that a broker shall maintain a pooled interest-bearing escrow account for deposit of client funds **not in excess of five thousand dollars**, with the exception of property management trust accounts. This account is to be identified as the "**Housing Trust Fund Account.**"

In addition, the legislation provides that all client deposits greater than five thousand dollars **may be** deposited in a separate interest-bearing trust account with the interest paid to one of the principals, as agreed to in the Purchase and Sale Agreement.

Transaction costs of the financial institutions, which can be deducted from the interest earned on the deposits, are also clarified as any reasonable and appropriate financial institution service charges or fees. Appropriate service charges or fees are those charges made by financial institutions on other demand deposit or "now" accounts. Some brokers are requiring the party who is entitled to the interest on deposits in excess of $5,000 to be responsible for all costs, due to the fact that the interest on some client's interest bearing accounts will not cover the cost of setting up such an account.

WASHINGTON INFORMATION NETWORK (WIN) - WIN is a nonprofit association of multiple listing services; it currently encompasses ten Western Washington counties and Alaska. WIN was formed to facilitate the sharing of data and services among members of different multiples. The members of WIN may access, at no charge, the online and keybox systems of the affiliated multiples, as well as other selected services.

WASHINGTON LAND DEVELOPMENT ACT - The Land Development Act of 1973 is consumer legislation intended to put complete, truthful information about lots in a development in the hands of purchasers before sale or at the time of sale. After receiving the information in the form of a Public Offering Statement prepared by the developer, the purchaser has a period of two (2) business days in which to change his/her mind about buying. If no Public Offering Statement is given, the purchaser has an indefinite time in which to rescind the sale. If the sale closes without a Public Offering Statement, the purchaser is entitled to actual damages suffered as a result of nondelivery.

What Land is Included: If **twenty-six** or **more lots** are offered for sale in a twelve month period, a current Public Offering Statement must be provided under the Land Development Act unless it qualifies for an exemption. Developments located outside of Washington are subject to the same regulation if the land is offered to Washington residents by advertising inside Washington or if any part of the agreement is made in Washington.

Several exemptions are available if the method of disposition is not for the purpose of evading the Act. The principal exemptions are:

1. The entire inventory of lots is sold in a single sale to a purchaser.

2. Each lot in a development is five acres in size or larger. Note that this exemption is lost if any lot is smaller than five acres.

3. There is a residential or recreational building on each lot in the development.

4. Either the developer will build on each lot or the developer will sell lots only to contractors who will build on each lot within two years of the sale.

5. The development is located entirely inside city limits as they were established on January 1, 1974.

6. Ten or fewer separate lots, parcels, units, or interests in developed lands are offered for sale in a period of twelve months. If the developer owns ten or more lots, a special application for this exemption should be made so that no confusion about right to the exemptions can arise later.

Waiver: A waiver of the Land Development Act involving a short form registration is available for developers not otherwise exempt who are offering 25 or less lots. This waiver is limited to those developments which appear to present little problem to purchasers. The ownership of 25 lots is computed from March 1, 1974, or the time of purchase, whichever is later. If other lots or undeveloped land are owned nearby, the owner may own more than 25 lots. Waiver is not granted unless the land is (1) owned free and clear or unconditional deed releases will be given purchasers; (2) all promised improvements have been completed or are assured of completion; (3) advertising is directed to the local community, which is interpreted to permit advertising in the nearest daily newspaper; (4) the development is not in a flood zone or subject to landslides or avalanches; (5) sewage disposal and water can be promised; and (6) any real estate contract used is a fair agreement.

Registration with the Office of Interstate Land Sales Registration (OILSR): Developments which are required to register with the Office of Interstate Land Sales Registration, a federal agency, are covered by the Land Development Act. Those developers who offer over 50 lots and who use the mails or telephones to do business are wise to contact OILSR to ask for exemption or to begin registration. OILSR may require that all those purchasers who buy before exemption is determined or registration is granted be given a right to rescind their contract. If the developer is found to be exempt from OILSR, compliance with the Land Development Act will be required unless a Washington exemption is applicable.

Escrow Requirements: For a development platted after January 1, 1974, the statute requires that purchase money be escrowed or otherwise safeguarded to pay off any mortgage or other indebtedness which is a lien against the land. Where no provision is made for deed release, money collected from a purchaser from the time of purchase must be applied against the developer's debt.

Where a deed on a lot will be released upon payment of a specific sum, money collected from a purchaser must be applied towards the release. The escrow or other safeguarding arrangement should usually be set up at the time a contract is made. The safeguarding agency selected must be independent of the developer.

Where an unconditional deed release is provided, no escrow or other safeguarding arrangements need be made. A deed release becomes unconditional when the developer's lender agrees that, even if an action of foreclosure is brought against the developer, no action of foreclosure will be brought against a person who purchases from the developer so long as the purchaser's payments are kept current.

Contract Requirements: Those developers not registered with the Office of Interstate Land Sales Registration may need to make changes in contracts or agreements of sale.

1. The following provision must appear in the contract somewhere before the signature line: "If, at the time the developer has contracted to deliver good title, good title cannot be provided because of actions by the developer, the purchaser must have a right of rescission."

2. The document of sale must be in a form which can be recorded in the state where the land is located.

3. The document must contain on its face in type four points larger than the print in the body of the document the notice: YOU MAY REVOKE ANY CONTRACT OR AGREEMENT WITHIN 48 HOURS, IF YOU RECEIVED THE PROPERTY REPORT LESS THAN 48 HOURS BEFORE YOU SIGNED THE CONTRACT OR AGREEMENT. NOTICE OF REVOCATION MUST BE BY WRITTEN NOTICE DELIVERED TO THE

DEVELOPER OR HIS/HER AGENT. THE TIME PERIOD OF 48 HOURS DOES NOT INCLUDE A SATURDAY, SUNDAY OR LEGAL HOLIDAY.

In 1992, an extensive registration system with the Department of Licensing was eliminated due to the decrease in the number of consumer complaints.
Reference: RCW 58.19

WASHINGTON LANDLORD TENANT ACT - *See* LANDLORD TENANT ACT.

WASHINGTON REAL ESTATE COMMISSION - *See* REAL ESTATE COMMISSION.

WASHINGTON REAL ESTATE DIVISION - *See* REAL ESTATE PROGRAM.

WASHINGTON REAL ESTATE EDUCATIONAL FOUNDATION (WREEF) - A Washington nonprofit corporation incorporated January 1, 1966, through a combined effort of the Washington Real Estate Commission and Division and Washington Association of Realtors. The charge imposed on the Foundation was to develop a well-balanced and effective educational program concerning real estate in the State of Washington, aimed at conducting research in, and informing the general public, consumers, educators and students at institutions of higher learning in the State, and the members of the real estate profession about all aspects of the nature, role and value of real estate in our economy, including the most efficient and socially useful means of conducting transactions in real estate.

Directly or indirectly, through the joint efforts of WREEF, the Real Estate Commission, the Department of Licensing and the Washington Association of Realtor, real estate education in the State of Washington has become a prototype for other states to copy.

In the mid 1980s, the educational efforts of WREEF were integrated in the activities of the Washington Association of Realtors and WREEF ceased operations.

WASHINGTON REAL ESTATE LICENSING LAWS - *See* LICENSING LAW.

WASHINGTON SCENIC VISTA ACT - *See* SCENIC VISTA ACT.

WASHINGTON SECURITIES LAW - *See* REAL PROPERTY SECURITIES REGISTRATION.

WASHINGTON SHORELINE MANAGEMENT ACT - *See* SHORELINE MANAGEMENT ACT.

WASHINGTON STATE ENVIRONMENTAL POLICY ACT - *See* STATE ENVIRONMENTAL POLICY ACT.

WASHINGTON STATE HUMAN RIGHTS COMMISSION - The Commission was called the Washington State Board Against Discrimination prior to August 7, 1971. The Commission is composed of five members appointed by the governor, one of whom is designated as chairman by the governor. It is a state agency created with powers with respect to the elimination and the prevention of discrimination in employment, in credit and insurance transactions, in places of public resort, accommodations, or amusement, and in real property transactions because of race, creed, color, national origin, sex, marital status, age, or the presence of any sensory, mental, or physical handicap. The Commission has the authority to receive, investigate, and pass upon complaints alleging unfair practices in real estate transactions because of discrimination. A real estate transaction under the law includes the sale, exchange, purchase, rental or lease of real property. Real property under the law includes buildings, structures, real estate, lands, tenements, leaseholds, interest in real estate cooperatives and condominiums. If the Commission should determine an individual has committed an unfair practice, it may award up to $1,000 to the aggrieved party and order other corrective measures. In addition, if the individual has a real estate license, the Real Estate Program of the Department of Licensing may suspend or revoke the individual's license. (*See* AIDS, LICENSING LAW.)
References: RCW 18.85, RCW 49.60 and WAC 162-36.

WASHINGTON STATE LAW AGAINST DISCRIMINATION - *See* DISCRIMINATION, WASHINGTON STATE HUMAN RIGHTS COMMISSION.

WASHINGTON STATE POLLUTION LIABILITY INSURANCE AGENCY (PLIA) - PLIA was created by the Washington State Legislature in 1989.

The Legislature found that many owners and operators of underground petroleum storage tanks (USTs) could not purchase pollution liability insurance either because private insurance was unavailable, at any cost, or because owners and operators could not meet the rigid underwriting standards of existing insurers.

PLIA was established to provide a temporary program to provide pollution liability insurance that is available and affordable, thereby allowing owners and operators to comply with the financial responsibility regulations of the Federal Environmental Protection Agency (EPA) and the Washington State Department of Ecology (DOE).

PLIA has entered into contracts with two private insurers to market pollution liability insurance to the owners and operators of USTs located in Washington State. PLIA acts as the reinsurer for those private insurance companies.

Insurance policies are available to any owner or operator whose tanks meet the minimum EPA technical requirements, are properly registered with DOE and meet minimum leak detection standards. Coverage can be provided for UST sites where petroleum contamination or a pre-existing leak is known to exist. Such sites may be insured under the program

only if the owner or operator has a plan for proceeding with corrective action. Where pre-existing contamination has been identified, the owner or operator at the time of filing a claim would have the burden of proof that the claim is not related to that pre-existing release.
Reference: WAC 374.

WASHINGTON SUPERFUND - *See* TOXICS CONTROL ACT

WASTE - An improper use or abuse of property by one in possession of land who holds less than the fee ownership, such as a tenant, life tenant, or vendee. Such waste thus impairs the value of the land or the interest of the one holding title or the reversion (e.g., lessor). The term "waste" includes **ameliorating waste**, which is the unauthorized alteration by the occupant of improvements on the land, even though such changes in fact increase the value of the property. While the tenant is usually not liable for ameliorating waste (since it increases the worth of the future interest), the owner of the future interest does not have to pay for the improvement.

Waste could occur through failure to pay property taxes, insurance, or mortgage payments, as well as by making material changes to the original use of the property, such as converting from residential to heavy industrial. In essence, any act on the land which substantially impairs the security value of the real estate is considered waste. Other examples of affirmative or voluntary waste would be cutting timber, removing minerals, or destroying buildings.

WASTE LINE - A pipe that carries waste from a bathtub, shower, lavatory, or any fixture or appliance.

WASTING ASSET - Property such as timber, an oil well, a quarry, or a mine, the substance of which is depleted through drilling and exploitation. Also refers to rights such as patent rights and franchises for a fixed term. (*See* DEPLETION.)

WATER - In its natural state, water is real property. When it is severed from the realty and reduced to possession by putting it in containers, it becomes personal property. (*See* RIPARIAN.)

There are three classifications of water. *Surface water* is water diffused over the land surface, or contained in depressions therein, resulting from rain, snow, or that which rises to the surface from springs. It is thus distinguishable from water flowing in a fixed channel, so as to constitute a *watercourse*, or water collected in an identifiable body, such as a river or lake. The extraordinary overflow of rivers and streams is known as *flood water*.

WATER TABLE - The distance from surface of ground to a depth at which natural ground water is found.

WATERCOURSE - A running stream of water following a regular course or channel and possessing a bed and banks.

WATERFRONT PROPERTY - A real estate (improved or unimproved) abutting a body of water such as a stream, river, lake, or ocean.

WATERSHED - The drainage area contributing to the water found in the abutting stream; the drainage basin. Many municipalities restrict owners from filling in or otherwise disrupting water flow in a watershed area.

WAY - A street, alley, or other thoroughfare of easement permanently established for passage of persons or vehicles.

WEAR AND TEAR - The gradual physical deterioration of the improvements of investment property, resulting from ordinary and normal use, passage of time and weather. Only property subject to wear and tear is subject to cost recovery (depreciable). Generally, a tenant must return the leased premises to the landlord in good condition, ordinary wear and tear excepted. (*See* NORMAL WEAR AND TEAR.)

WEEP HOLE - One of several small holes left in a wall to permit surplus water to drain; as used in a retaining wall or foundation.

WET COLUMN - A column in a wall containing plumbing lines facilitating the installation of sinks, drinking fountains, and like things.

WET WALL - Typically a wall between two bathrooms or a bathroom and kitchen where much of the plumbing for these rooms is concentrated. Wet walls are often several inches thicker than most walls to accommodate the plumbing.

WETLANDS - Land areas where ground water is at or near the surface of the ground for a portion of each year so as to produce a wetland plant community, such as swamps, flood plains, and marshes. Since these areas are so susceptible to flooding, they are subject to many federal, state, and local controls, including environmental protection and zoning for special preservation and conservation. (*See* ENVIRONMENTAL IMPACT STATEMENT.)

WILD DEED - A deed appearing in the chain of title in which the first party (grantor) has no recorded interest in the subject property. The grantor is a stranger to the chain of title and the deed does not give constructive notice of its existence. However, actual knowledge of its existence puts one on notice that any such first party may have had a legitimate interest in the subject property under an unrecorded instrument. (*See* CHAIN OF TITLE; NAME, CHANGE OF.)

WILL - A written instrument disposing of property upon the death of the maker (male/testator - female/testatrix) A will takes effect only upon the decease's death, not during his/her life, and thus can be revoked or amended at anytime during the testator's life. In Washington, the testator must be of sound mind, of age (18 or over), and must declare the writing to be his/her last will and testament in the presence of two or more credible persons who subscribe their names as witnesses to the will. A witness should be a person other than a beneficiary under the will. The testator often designates an executor and where there are minor children, he/she usually nominates a guardian. No one should attempt to write a will without first consulting an attorney. When a person dies either without a will or with a defectively executed will, his/her property passes to his/her heirs according to the laws of intestacy. (*See* COMMUNITY PROPERTY, DESCENT, HOLOGRAPHIC WILL, INTESTATE, PROBATE, TESTATOR.)

WINDOW JAMB TRIM - A thin vertical strip of molding covering the junction of the vertical members of the window frame and the jamb.

WINDOW SASH - The moveable frame that holds the window glass. Sash windows move vertically and may be a single in which only the lower half of the window opens or a double in which both the upper and lower portions are moveable.

WITHOUT RECOURSE - A form of qualified endorsement relieving the maker of personal liability. In a promissory note secured by a mortgage or deed of trust on real property, a without recourse note means that the lender can only satisfy the claim against the property; that is, he/she is not entitled to a deficiency judgment against the defaulting borrower.

WITNESS - To subscribe one's name to a contract, deed, will, or other document for the purpose of attesting to its authenticity and proving its execution by testifying, if required.

As a general rule, witnesses are not necessary to the validity of a real estate contract. A will, however, must usually be witnessed by at least two disinterested third persons. (*See* SUBSCRIBE.)

WOMEN'S COUNCIL OF REALTORS® - An organization within the National Association of REALTORS® whose purpose is to expand its members' knowledge of the real estate business and provide an opportunity for sharing experiences and exchanging information.

WORKERS' COMPENSATION LAW - Washington law requires all employers to provide industrial insurance coverage for their employees. This law applies to real estate brokers, regardless of whether or not the broker considers his/her salespeople to be employees or independent contractors. If a salesperson is thus injured on the job, he/she will be covered for specified medical expenses and lost wages. If a broker does not carry the requisite insurance, the broker may be subject to civil penalties, including suspension or revocation of the broker's real estate license. (*See* INDEPENDENT CONTRACTOR.)

WORK LETTER - A detailed addition to a lease defining all improvement work to be done by the landlord for the tenant and specifying what work the tenant will perform at his/her own expense.

WORKING CAPITAL - Liquid assets available for conducting daily business.

WORKING DRAWINGS - Drawings by an architect showing lighting layout, electrical plugs, telephone outlets, and similar items, as well as details of the precise method of construction. (*See* BLUEPRINT, PLANS AND SPECIFICATIONS.)

WORKOUT PLAN - An attempt by a mortgagee to assist a mortgagor in default to workout a payment plan rather than proceed directly with a foreclosure. Some possible work-out plans could include extending the loan term, accruing interest, or reducing the interest rate. (*See* FORBEARANCE.)

WORTHIER TITLE DOCTRINE - A common law doctrine which held that where a testator devised to an heir exactly the same interest in land, as such, that the heir would take by the laws of descent, then the latter was regarded as worthier and the heir took his/her title by descent rather than by devise. (*See* DESCENT.)

WRAPAROUND - A mortgage or deed of trust which secures a debt which includes the balance due on an existing senior mortgage or deed of trust and an additional amount advanced by the wraparound mortgagee/beneficiary. The wraparound borrower thereafter makes the amortizing payments on the senior loan. In essence, it is an additional loan in which another lender refinances a borrower by lending an amount over the existing first loan amount, without cashing out or disturbing the existence of the loan. The entire loan combines two or more debts and is treated as a single obligation. In some cases, a single payment is made to the secondary lender who makes the debt payment on the first loan. The difference between the interest of the two loan notes is called the arbitrage. The wrap lender utilizes financial leverage to increase his/her yield over the nominal rate of the new loan.

For example, assume a businessman owns a property worth $300,000 and there is an existing first mortgage against the property with a balance of $100,000 at 6.5 percent interest with 15 years remaining on the term. The owner wishes to raise $100,000 in capital for business purposes. Under conventional financing, he/she would refinance the building for $200,000, probably at a higher interest rate, say 9.75 percent, and use $100,000 of the fresh money to pay off the existing first mortgage and then use the balance for his business purposes. By using a wraparound he could obtain a lower interest rate, say 8.5 percent. Actually the lender on the wrap would be receiving a 10.5 percent yield. The owner could afford to pay 10.5 percent for the $100,000 of fresh money and save money. A basic assumption is that the loan at 9.75 percent and that of 8.5 percent are for 25 years. On the $200,000 of fresh money he would pay $21,387.84 annually. On the wrap at 8.5 percent he would pay $19,326.24, thereby, realizing a savings of $2,061.60 per year. At the same time the lender by making a wrap would realize a higher yield, 10.5 percent versus 9.75 percent. The actual amount advanced to the borrower under the wraparound mortgage is $100,000 and the new lender makes the payments on the previously existing $100,000 first mortgage at 6.5 percent and receives payments from the owner on the newly negotiated 8.5 percent $200,000 wraparound mortgage.

It is essential that the first mortgage or deed of trust not contain an acceleration clause, **due on encumbrance**, since this could effectively preclude the use of the wraparound mortgage. (*See* ALL-INCLUSIVE DEED OF TRUST, ARBITRAGE, PREPAID INTEREST.)

WRIT OF EXECUTION - A court order authorizing and directing an officer of the court to levy upon and sell property of the defendant to satisfy a judgment. (*See* SHERIFF'S SALE.)

WRITE-OFF - 1. To clear an asset off the accounting books, as with an uncollectible debt. 2. A tax deduction. (*See* TAX SHELTER.)

WYTHE - A partition in a chimney which contains more than one flue, separating the flues.

"X" - When an individual cannot write his/her name, he/she can indicate his/her intention to sign by marking an "X" in the place for signature. A witness would then write the name of the signatory along side the "X". When a person appearing before a notary cannot sign his/her name, the notary must first be satisfied as to the identity of the person by requiring some proof of identification. The notary would then have the person sign an "X" on the document, after which the notary would indicate that it is the mark of the person. For example, "X" (mark of Charlie Wilhelm). An instrument signed with a mark and notarized, would be recordable, but in the absence of two witnesses may not be insurable by a title insurance company. (*See* SIGNATURE.)

X-BRACING - Cross bracing in a partition.

YARD - 1. A unit of measurement equaling three feet.

2. The open, unoccupied space on the plot between the property line and the front, rear or side wall of the building. There are three main types of yard:

Front Yard: The yard across the full width of the plot facing the street, extending from the front line of the building to the front property line. On a corner lot, both yards facing a street are considered front yards.

Rear Yard: The yard across the full width of the plot opposite the front yard, extending from the rear line of the building to the rear property line.

Side Yard: The yard between the side line of building and the adjacent side property line, extending from the front yard to the rear yard. (*See* SETBACK.)

YEAR - A determinate period, consisting for all practical purposes of 365 days, except as 366 days appear in a leap year. A calendar year in the absence of qualification. A season, particularly a farming season, in which crops are planted, cultivated and harvested, or a season as known to proprietors of vacation resorts.

YEAR-TO-YEAR TENANCY - A periodic tenancy in which the rent is reserved from year to year. Sufficient notice (if not specified in the contract, then a reasonable time) must be given to terminate this tenancy. Where the tenant holds over after the first year, he/she normally creates another year-to-year tenancy if he/she holds over with the consent of the landlord; if he/she holds over without the consent of the landlord this action creates a tenancy at sufferance. (*See* PERIODIC TENANCY.)

YIELD - The return on an investment or the amount of profit, stated as a percentage of the amount invested; the rate of return. In real estate, yield refers to the effective annual amount of income which is being accrued on an investment. The yield on income property is the ratio of the annual net income from the property to the cost or market value of the property. The yield, or profit, to a lender is the spread or differential between the cost of acquiring the funds lent and the interest rate charged. (*See* CAP RATE, INTERNAL RATE OF RETURN.)

YIELD TO MATURITY - A method of financing repayment in which a borrower pays a certain percentage of actual funds borrowed each year (such as interest only) and pays the loan off in full at the end of its maturity.

ZERO LOT LINE - A term generally used to describe the positioning of a structure on a lot so that one side rests directly on the lot's boundary line. Such a construction is usually prohibited by setback ordinances, unless it is a part of a special space-conserving project. (*See* CLUSTER DEVELOPMENT, PARTY WALL, PLANNED UNIT DEVELOPMENT.)

ZONE - An area set off by proper authorities for specific use, subject to certain restrictions or restraints.

ZONING - The regulation of structures and uses of property within designated districts or zones. Zoning regulates and affects such things as use of the land, types of structure permitted, building heights, setbacks and density (the ratio of land area to improvement area). It is concerned with controls on the use of property rather than governmental taking of property as in eminent domain.

The responsibility for zoning rests with municipalities. This power is granted by the State government. States confer zoning authority to cities from "police powers" granted to states by the Constitution. These powers seek to prevent violations of the public interest. This right of local governments has today been upheld as constitutional in every state; the U.S. Supreme Court has upheld zoning as an appropriate function of local government. Zoning is a legislative function. The legislature, not the judiciary, is charged with determining the soundness of zoning regulations. Unless there is a clear abuse of power, a court has no power to interfere.

Zoning is guided by a long-range plan called a Comprehensive Plan. The Comprehensive Plan has many elements, such as land use, major street locations and public facilities.

A request for rezoning can only be granted if the change implements the General Plan. If it varies from the General Plan, then the General Plan must be amended. The City Council must approve all rezoning since the change can be accomplished only by passage of a city ordinance.

Purchasers of property must be aware of the zoning requirements; e.g., a zoning ordinance is not an encumbrance on real property, and it does not render title unmarketable.

Consequently, the broker has an obligation to ascertain whether the contemplated use of the property conforms to existing zoning. However, **violations** of zoning regulations **do** render the title unmarketable; e.g., where the zoning permits single family dwellings only and the seller has a duplex, the title is therefore rendered unmarketable unless the buyer agrees to accept title under those conditions. A change in zoning restrictions between the time of the Purchase and Sale Agreement and the time of the closing has been held not to justify the buyer rejecting title in the absence of a specific condition to that effect in the Purchase and Sale Agreement. The best procedure for a buyer is to have the Purchase and Sale Agreement contain a representation by the seller that the property may be used for a specifically identified purpose. This representation should survive the delivery of the deed. Also, where either the seller or broker misrepresents the actual permitted zoning use, the buyer can rescind the transaction on the basis of misrepresentation.

Where the "down zoning" (e.g., from high rise to low rise) of an area results in the lessening of property values, the state is not responsible to make "just compensation" payments to the owners (as it is when property is condemned under the power of eminent domain). (*See* BUFFER ZONE, DOWN ZONING, SPOT ZONING, VARIANCE, WARRANTY.)

Previous to the adoption of the State Growth Management Act (GMA), a comprehensive plan was just a general blue print for possible future growth. In and of itself, the comprehensive plan was not a regulatory control. Since the adoption of GMA in 1990 and amendments to the Act thereafter, the development controls of a city or county that does not plan under the GMA cannot be inconsistent with the comprehensive plan. (*See* GROWTH MANAGEMENT ACT.)
Reference: 36.63

Some special types of zoning are:

Bulk Zoning: The primary purpose of this kind of zoning is to control density and avoid overcrowding, such as restrictions on setback, building height and percentage of open area.

Aesthetic Zoning: Requirement that new buildings conform to specific types of architecture.

Incentive Zoning: Require the street level of office buildings be used for retail establishments.

Directive Zoning: The use of zoning as a planning tool to encourage use of land for its highest and best use.

Zoning laws are generally enforced through the requirement that a building permit must first be obtained in order for one to build on his/her land. A permit will not be issued, among other things, unless the proposed structure conforms to the permitted zoning.

Often the purpose of zoning is to implement the comprehensive plan. Zoning codes determine such things as the type and intensity of use, the density of living or business population, height regulations, accessory buildings and essential facilities such as recreation and parking standards, including off-street parking and loading. Where zoning and private restrictions conflict, whichever is the most restrictive must be followed. (*See* BUFFER ZONE, COMMINGLING, GENERAL PLAN, NONCONFORMING USE, SPOT ZONING, VARIANCE, ZONING SYMBOLS.)

ZONING ESTOPPEL - A rule which bars the government from enforcing a new down-zoning ordinance against a landowner who had incurred substantial costs in reliance on the government's assurances that the landowner had met all the zoning requirements before the new down-zoning took place.

ZONING SYMBOLS - The basic kinds of uses under a zoning ordinance are: (1) Residential uses such as single family residences, duplexes, apartments, schools, churches and libraries. (2) Business uses such as groceries, drug stores, meat markets, bakeries and small retail stores. (3) Commercial uses such as large retail and wholesale businesses, warehouses, outdoor sales and activities (such as boats or cars). (4) Manufacturing and industrial uses such as machine shops, boat buildings, railroad or port terminals, and blast furnaces.

The zoning codes are very specific about the requirements of each zone. These requirements include: (1) The uses that are allowed. (2) The minimum lot area required for each zone. (3) The maximum percentage of space that a building may cover on a lot. (4) The minimum number of feet that must be provided for the front, side, and rear yards. (5) The maximum height of a building.

Zoning symbols for each of these diverse uses are easy to identify. They are R for residential uses, B for business uses, C for commercial uses, M for manufacturing uses and I for industrial uses.

Each zoning symbol also contains references to the type of development within, say a residential or business use. For example:

Abbreviation	Means
SF	Single Family Residence
RSL	Residential Small Lot - one house per lot
RSL/T	Residential Small Lot - allows Tandem Housing
RLS/C	Residential Small Lot - allows Cottage Housing
LDT	Lowrise Duplex/Triplex
L1	Lowrise 1
L2	Lowrise 2
L3	Lowrise 3
L4	Lowrise 4
MR	Midrise
HR	Highrise
NC1	Neighbor Commercial 1
NC2	Neighbor Commercial 2
NC3	Neighbor Commercial 3
NC/R	Neighbor Commercial Residential
C1	Commercial 1
C2	Commercial 2
P1, P2	Pedestrian Designated Zones 1 and 2
IG1	General Industrial 1
IG2	General Industrial 2
IB	Industrial Buffer
IC	Industrial Commercial

These abbreviations may be accompanied by numbers (SF 5000 for example); the numbers indicate the basic lot size for determining density in the zone classification.

For illustration purposes, a summary of some of the basic provisions of the City of Seattle zoning code as of 1998 are provided:

Zone	Characteristic Zone Uses	Minimum Lot Area	Maximum Lot Cover
Single Family Residential Zones			
SF5000	Single Family	5,000 sq. ft.	35%
SF 7200	Single Family	7,200 sq. ft.	35%

ZONING SYMBOLS

Zone	Characteristic Zone Uses	Minimum Lot Area	Maximum Lot Cover
RS 9600	Single Family	9,600 sq. ft.	35%
	Urban Village with Neighbor Plan Classification*		
RSL*	Single Family with one accessory unit	2,500 sf. ft.	No limit
RSL/T*	Two detached single family houses on one lot	5,000 sf. ft.	50%
RSL/C*	Four to twelve detached single family houses on one lot	6,400 sf. ft	40%
Multi-family Residential Zones			
LDT	Duplex and Triplex house - one unit per	2,000 sq. ft.	35%
L1	Townhouse - one unit per	1,600 sq. ft.	40%
L2	Variety of multi-family housing types - two to three story - one unit per	1,200 sq. ft.	40%
L3	Multi-family - three story - one unit per	800 sq. ft	45%
L4	Moderate density multi-family - four story lowrise - one unit per	600 sq. ft.	50%
MR	Midrise Apartment Building	No limit	No limit
Commercial Zones			
HR	High Density Apartment Building	No limit	No limit

Zone	Characteristic Zone Uses	Minimum Lot Area	Maximum Lot Cover
NC1	Pedestrian - oriented shopping area	4,000 sq. ft. for most uses	No limit
		10,000 sq. ft. for multi-purpose stores/ medical offices	No limit
NC2	Pedestrian - oriented small to medium size businesses	15,000 sq. ft. for most uses	No limit
		50,000 sq. ft. multi-purposes convenience stores	
NC3	Pedestrian - oriented shopping district	No limit	No limit
NCR	Adopted of a neighbor-hood Plan - moderate density residential development in multi-story - can have street front commercial	Commercial space limited	No limit
C1	Auto-oriented, primarily retail service commercial area - stores	No limit	No limit
C2	Auto-oriented, primarily non-retail, commercial area - office building, wholesale warehouses, biotech research and manufacturing	No limit	No limit
P1, P2	Designations applied to NC zones along pedestrian - oriented commercial streets - preserves and encourages	No limit	No limit

Zone	Characteristic Zone Uses	Minimum Lot Area	Maximum Lot Cover
	pedestrian-oriented shopping - preserves and encourages pedestrian-oriented shopping		
Industrial Zones			
IG1	Marine and retail related industrial areas - general and heavy manufacturing and commercial uses	No limit	No limit
IG2	Broad range of uses where industrial function is less established that in IGI zones	No limit	No limit
IB	A transition area between industrial areas and adjacent residential zones or commercial zones	No limit	No limit
IC	Industrial Commercial - promote development of business which incorporate a mix of industrial and commercial, including light manufacturing	No limit	No limit

ZONING VARIANCE - *See* VARIANCE.

appendix a: abbreviations

A

ABR	Accredited Buyers Representative
a/c	Air conditioning
AC	Acre
ACM	Asbestos containing material
ACR	Accredited Resident Manager
ACRS	Accelerated Cost Recovery System
ADA	Americans with Disabilities Act
ADR	Asset Depreciation Range System
ADS	Alternative Depreciation System
ADT	Average daily traffic
AFIDA	Agricultural Foreign Investment Disclosure Act
AFLM	Accredited Farm and Land Member
AFM	Accredited Farm Manager
AGC	Associated General Contractors
AI	All-inclusive
AIA	American Institute of Architects
AIDS	Acquired Immune Deficiency Syndrome
AIP	American Institute of Planners
AIR	American Industrial Real Estate Association
AIREA	American Institute of Real Estate Appraisers
aka	Also known as
A/L	Assignment of lease
ALTA	American Land Title Association
ALC	Accredited Land Consultant
ALDA	American Land Development Association
A/M	Assignment of mortgage
AMA	Affirmative marketing agreement
AMO	Accredited Management Organization
ANSI	American National Standards Institute
AOMA	American Owners and Managers
APA	American Planning Association
APOD	Annual Property Operating Data Form
APR	Annual percentage rate
APR 12	Admission to Practice Rule
AREUEA	American Real Estate and Urban Economics Association
ARM	Accredited Resident Manager

ARM	Adjustable Rate Mortgage
ARRELLO	Association of Real Estate License Law Officials
ARWA	American Right of Way Association
ASA	American Society of Appraisers
ASAE	American Society of Association Executives
ASHI	American Society of Home Inspectors
ASLA	American Society of Landscape Architects
ASREC	American Society of Real Estate Counselors

B

BAB	Build America Better Program
BBB	Better Business Bureau
BFP	Bona fide purchaser
BLM	Bureau of Land Management
BLS	Bureau of Labor Statistics
B&O	Business and Occupation Tax
BOCA	Building Officials Conference of America
BOMA	Building Owners and Managers Association
BOMI	Building Owners and Managers Institute
BTU	British thermal unit

C

CAE	Certified Association Executive
CAI	Community Associations Institute
CAM	Certified Apartment Manager
CAM	Common Area Maintenance
CAO	Certified Appraisal Organization (NAMA)
CBA	Commercial Brokers Association (MLS)
CBD	Central Business District
CBS	Concrete, block, and stucco
CCIM	Certified Commercial Investment Member
CCRE	Certified Commercial Real Estate
CC&Rs	Covenants, Conditions, and Restrictions
CD	Certificate of deposit
CEP	Council on Environmental Policy (Wm.)
CERCLA	Comprehensive Environmental Response Compensation and Liability Act
CID	Commercial Investment Division
CIPS	Certified International Property Specialist
CIREI	Commercial Investment Real Estate Institute
CLIC	Commercial Leasehold Insurance Corporation
CLO	Computerized loan origination

CMB	Certified Mortgage Banker
Co.	Company
CO	Certificate of occupancy
COB	Close of business
CON	Connected (sewer)
CPA	Certified Public Accountant
CPE	Certified Personalty Evaluation
CPI	Consumer Price Index
CPM	Certified Property Manager
CPP	Certified Protection Professional
CRA	Certified Review Appraiser
CRB	Certified Residential Broker
CRE	Counselor of Real Estate
CRE	Certificate in Real Estate
CREA	Certified Real Estate Appraiser
CREA	Canadian Real Estate Association
CRS	Certified Residential Specialist
CRV	Certificate of Reasonable Value
CTF	Customer Trust Fund
CZC	Comprehensive Zoning Code

D

DB	Designated Broker
dba	"Doing business as"
DCR	Debt Coverage Ratio
DIA	Downtown Improvement Association
DLUM	Detailed land-use map
DOL	Department of Licensing
DOT	Deed of Trust
DP	Down payment
DPC	Debt previously contracted
DREI	Designated Real Estate Instructor
DT	Depth table
DWV	Drain-waste-vent

E

ECOA	Equal Credit Opportunity Act
EIS	Environmental Impact Statement
E/M	Earnest Money Agreement (Purchase and Sale Agreement)
E&O	Errors and Omission Insurance
EPA	Environmental Protection Agency (U.S.)

F

FAR	Floor area ratio
FASA	Fellow American Society of Appraisers
FASB	Financial Accounting Standards Board
FCRA	Fair Credit Report Act
FDIC	Federal Deposit Insurance Corporation
FEA	Federal Energy Administration
FH	Flood hazard
FHA	Federal Housing Administration
FHLB	Federal Home Loan Bank
FHLMC	Federal Home Loan Mortgage Corporation (Freddie Mac)
FIABCI	International Real Estate Federation
FICA	Federal Income Contributions Act
FICB	Federal intermediate credit banks
FIDA	Federal Institution Deregulation Act
FIFO	First in, first out (accounting)
FIRPTA	Foreign Investment in Real Property Tax Act
FIRREA	Financial Institutions Reform and Recovery Act
FLB	Federal Loan Bank
FLI	Farmers and Land Institute
FLIP	Flexible Loan Insurance Program
FmHA	Farmers Home Administration
FMRR	Financial Management Rate of Return
FMV	Fair market value
FNMA	Federal National Mortgage Association (Fannie Mae)
FPM	Flexible Payment Mortgage
FRS	Federal Reserve System
FS	Fee simple
FSBO	For Sale by Owner
FSLIC	Federal Savings and Loan Insurance Corporation
FTC	Federal Trade Commission
FY	Fiscal Year

G

GBA	Gross buildable area
GCR	Guest-car ratio
GIT	Gross income tax
GLA	Gross leasable area
GMA	Growth Management Act
GMC	Guaranteed Mortgage Certificate
GNMA	Government National Mortgage Association (Ginnie Mae)

GP	General plan
GRI	Graduate, RealtorsÒ Institute
GRM	Gross rent multiplier
GSA	General Services Administration

H

HLBB	Home Loans Bank Board
HOA	Homeowners' association
HOW	HomeOwners Warranty Program
HUD	U.S. Department of Housing Urban Development
HVAC	Heating, ventilation and air conditioning

I

IAAO	International Association of Assessing Officers
ICSC	International Council of Shopping Centers
IFA	Independent Fee Appraiser
IFFA	Agricultural Member, National Association of Independent Fee Appraisers
IRA	Individual Retirement Account
Inc.	Incorporated
IRC	Internal revenue code
IREM	Institute of Real Estate Management
IRR	Internal Rate of Return
IRS	Internal Revenue Service
IRWA	International Right-of-way Association

J

J/T	Joint tenant

K

KCA	King County Auditor
KCR	King County Recorder

L

L	Leasehold
L#	Liber number (book number)
LAL	Limit on artificial accounting losses
LH	Leasehold
LHA	Local Housing Authority
LIFO	Last in, first out
LIR	Land use intensity rating

Lis/P	Lis pendens
LLC	Limited Liability Company
L.P.	Land patent
LPO	Limited Practice Officer
LS	Locus sigilli (Latin "place of seal")
LSR	Livability space ratio
Ltd.	Limited
LUI	Land use intensity
LUL	Land use law
LUMS	Land utilization and marketing study
LUST	Leaking underground storage tank
L/V	Loan-to-value ratio

M

MACRS	Modified Accelerated Cost Recovery System
MAGIC	Mortgage Guaranty Insurance program (MGIC)
MAI	Member, Appraisal Institute (AIREA)
MBA	Mortgage Bankers Association of America
MBS	Mortgage backed security
MC	Model Cities Program
MF	Multifamily
MFLA	Master Farm and Land Appraiser (NAMA)
MGIC	Mortgage Guaranty Insurance Corporation
MGRM	Monthly gross rent multiplier
MICA	Mortgage Insurance Companies of America
MIP	Mortgage insurance premium
MLP	Master Limited Partnership
MLS	Multiple listing service
MPR	Minimum property requirement
MRA	Master Residential Appraiser
MSA	Master Senior Appraiser

N

n/a	Not available, or not applicable
NAA	National Apartment Association
NAAO	National Association of Assessing Officers
NACORE	National Association of Corporate Real Estate Executives
NAHB	National Association of Home Builders
NAHC	National Association of Housing Cooperatives
NAIFA	National Association of Independent Fee Appraisers
NAIOP	National Association of Industrial and Office Parks
NAMA	National Association of Master Appraisers

NAMSB	National Association of Mutual Savings Banks
NAPRM	National Association of Professional Resident Mangers
NAR	National Association of Realtors
NARA/MU	National Association of Review Appraisers and Mortgage Underwriters
NAREA	National Association of Real Estate Appraisers
NAREB	National Association of Real Estate Boards (now NAR)
NAREB	National Association of Real Estate Brokers
NAREE	National Association of Real Estate Editors
NARELLO	National Association of Real Estate Licensing Law Officials (now ARELLO)
NASD	National Association of Securities Dealers
NC	Not connected (sewer)
NCHP	National Corporation for Housing Partnerships
NEPA	National Environmental Policy Act
NFCA	National Federation of Condominium Associations
NHP	National Housing Partnerships
NIFLB	National Institute of Farm and Land Brokers (now RLI)
NIREB	National Institute of Real Estate Brokers (now RNMI)
NOI	Net operating income
NPR	Net Present Value
NRV	Net realizable value
NSF	Not sufficient funds
NTC	National Timesharing Council
NTO	National Tenants Organization
NWMLS	Northwest Multiple Listing Service

O

OAR	Overall rate of Capitalization
OCC	Office of the Comptroller of the Currency
OEO	Office of Equal Opportunity
OEO	Office of Economic Opportunity
OEQC	Office of Environmental Quality Control
OE&T	Operating expenses and taxes
OILSR	Office of Interstate Land Sales Registration
OIR	Official interpretation rulings
O.L.&T.	Owner's, landlord's, and tenant's public liability insurance
ORE	Owned real estate
OTC	Over the counter

P

PAM	Pledged Account Mortgage
PCB	Polychlorinated biphenyls
PDH	Planned development housing
PE	Professional engineer
PHA	Public Housing Administration
P&I	Principal and interest (payment)
P&L	Profit and Loss Statement
PITI	Principal, interest, taxes, and insurance (monthly payments)
PMI	Private mortgage insurance
POB	Point of beginning
POC	Paid outside of closing
PRM	Permanent Reference Mark
P&SA	Purchase and Sale Agreement
PSC	Participation sale certificate
PUD	Planned Unit Development

R

R	Realtor® (NAR)
RAM	Reverse Annuity Mortgage
REBAC	Real Estate Buyer's Agent Council
REC	Real Estate Commission
REEA	Real Estate Educators Association
REG.	Regular system (recording)
Reg A	Regulation A (SEC)
REIT	Real Estate Investment Trust
RELO	Real Estate Relocation Service
REMT	Real Estate Mortgage Trust
REO	Real Estate Owned
RESPA	Real Estate Settlement Procedures Act
REPSA	Real Estate Purchase and Sale Agreement
RLI	Realtors® Land Institute (NAR)
RLS	Registered Land Surveyor
RM	Residential Member (AIREA)
RMU	Register Mortgage Underwriter (NARA/MU)
RNMI	Realtors® National Marketing Institute (NAR)
ROI	Return on investment
RPA	Real property administrator
RPAC	Realtors' Political Action Committee (NAR)
RRA	Registered Review Appraiser
RRM	Renegotiable Rate Mortgage

RS	Revenue stamp
RTC	Resolution trust corporation
R/W	Right of way

S

S	Salesperson
S	Section
SAIF	Savings Association Insurance Fund
SAM	Shared Appreciation Mortgage
SARA	Society of American Registered Architects
SARA	Superfund Amendment and Reauthorization Act
SBA	Small Business Administration
SBLN	Setback line
SBS	Sick building syndrome
SEC	Securities and Exchange Commission
SEPA	State Environmental Policy Act
SIOR	Society of Industrial and Office Realtors (NAR)
SL	Savings and loan association
SMSA	Standard metropolitan statistical area
SOYD	Sum of the years' digits
SRA	Senior Residential Appraiser (SREA)
SREA	Society of Real Estate Appraisers
SRPA	Senior Real Property Appraiser (SREA)
SS	Scilicet (Latin "namely")
SSCRA	Soldiers and Sailors Civil Relief Act

T

T/C	Tenant in Common
TCT	Transfer certificate of title
TDD	Telecommunication devices for deaf
TDI	Temporary disability insurance
TDR	Transfer of development rights
T/E	Tenancy by entirety
TIL	Truth-in-Lending Law
TIs	Tenant Improvements
TSO	Time Share Ownership

U

UBC	Uniform Building Code
UCC	Uniform Commercial Code

UFFI	Urea-formaldehyde foam installation
ULI	Urban Land Institute
ULSPA	Uniform Land Sales Practices Act
UPA	Uniform Partnership Act
URETSA	Uniform Real Estate Timeshare Act
USGA	United States Geological Survey
UST	Underground storage tank

V

VA	Veterans Affairs
VRM	Variable Rate Mortgage
Vs	Versus

W

WAR	Washington Association of Realtors®
WCR	Women's Council of Realtors® (NAR)
WREEF	Washington Real Estate Educational Foundation
WROS	With Right of Survivorship
W/W	Wall to Wall

Z

Z	Zone

appendix b:

Code of Ethics and **Standards of Practice**

of the
National Association of Realtors®
Effective January 1, 1998

Where the word REALTORS® is used in this Code and Preamble, it shall be deemed to include REALTOR-ASSOCIATE®S

While the Code of Ethics establishes obligations that may be higher than those mandated by law, in any instance where the Code of Ethics and the law conflict, the obligations of the law must take precedence.

Preamble...
Under all is the land. Upon its wise utilization and widely allocated ownership depend the survival and growth of free institutions and of our civilization. REALTORS® should recognize that the interests of the nation and its citizens require the highest and best use of the land and the widest distribution of land ownership. They require the creation of adequate housing, the building of functioning cities, the development of productive industries and farms, and the preservation of a healthful environment.

Such interests impose obligations beyond those of ordinary commerce. They impose grave social responsibility and a patriotic duty to which REALTORS® should dedicate themselves, and for which they should be diligent in preparing themselves. REALTORS®, therefore, are zealous to maintain and improve the standards of their calling and share with their fellow REALTORS® a common responsibility for its integrity and honor.

In recognition and appreciation of their obligations to clients, customers, the public, and each other, REALTORS® continuously strive to become and remain informed on issues affecting real estate and, as knowledgeable professionals, they willingly share the fruit of their experience and study with others. They identify and take steps, through enforcement of this Code of Ethics and by assisting appropriate regulatory bodies, to eliminate practices which may damage the public or which might discredit or bring dishonor to the real estate profession.

Realizing that cooperation with other real estate professionals promotes the best interests of those who utilize their services, REALTORS® urge exclusive representation of clients; do not attempt to gain any unfair advantage over their competitors; and they refrain from making unsolicited comments about other practitioners. In instances where their opinion is sought, or where REALTORS® believe that comment is necessary, their opinion is offered in an objective, professional manner, uninfluenced by any personal motivation or potential advantage or gain.

The term REALTOR® has come to connote competency, fairness, and high integrity resulting from adherence to a lofty ideal of moral conduct in business relations. No inducement of profit and no instruction from clients ever can justify departure from this ideal.

In the interpretation of this obligation, REALTORS® can take no safer guide than that which has been handed down through the centuries, embodied in the Golden Rule, "Whatsoever ye would that others should do to you, do ye even so to them."

Accepting this standard as their own, REALTORS® pledge to observe its spirit in all of their activities and to conduct their business in accordance with the tenets set forth below.

DUTIES TO CLIENTS AND CUSTOMERS

ARTICLE 1

When representing a buyer, seller, landlord, tenant, or other client as an agent, REALTORS® pledge themselves to protect and promote the interests of their client. This obligation of absolute fidelity to the client's interests is primary, but it does not relieve REALTORS® of their obligation to treat all parties honestly. When serving a buyer, seller, landlord, tenant or other party in a non-agency capacity, REALTORS® remain obligated to treat all parties honestly. (Amended 1/93)

- **Standard of Practice 1-1**

REALTORS®, when acting as principals in a real estate transaction, remain obligated by the duties imposed by the Code of Ethics. (Amended 1/93)

- **Standard of Practice 1-2**

The duties the Code of Ethics imposes are applicable whether REALTORS® are acting as agents or in legally recognized non-agency capacities except that any duty imposed exclusively on agents by law or regulation shall not be imposed by this Code of Ethics on REALTORS® acting in non-agency capacities.

As used in this Code of Ethics, "client" means the person(s) or entity(ies) with whom a REALTOR® or a REALTORS®'s firm has an agency or legally recognized non-agency relationship; "customer" means a party to a real estate transaction who receives information, services, or benefits but has no contractual relationship with the REALTOR® or the

REALTORS®'s firm; and "agent" means a real estate licensee acting in an agency relationship as defined by state law or regulation. (Adopted 1/95, Amended 1/98)

· **Standard of Practice 1-3**

REALTORS®, in attempting to secure a listing, shall not deliberately mislead the owner as to market value.

· **Standard of Practice 1-4**

REALTORS®, when seeking to become a buyer/tenant representative, shall not mislead buyers or tenants as to savings or other benefits that might be realized through use of the REALTOR®'s services. (Amended 1/93)

· **Standard of Practice 1-5**

REALTORS® may represent the seller/landlord and buyer/tenant in the same transaction only after full disclosure to and with informed consent of both parties. (Adopted 1/93)

· **Standard of Practice 1-6**

REALTORS® shall submit offers and counter-offers objectively and as quickly as possible. (Adopted 1/93, Amended 1/95)

· **Standard of Practice 1-7**

When acting as listing brokers, REALTORS® shall continue to submit to the seller/landlord all offers and counter-offers until closing or execution of a lease unless the seller/landlord has waived this obligation in writing. REALTORS® shall not be obligated to continue to market the property after an offer has been accepted by the seller/landlord. REALTORS® shall recommend that sellers/landlords obtain the advice of legal counsel prior to acceptance of a subsequent offer except where the acceptance is contingent on the termination of the pre-existing purchase contract or lease. (Amended 1/93)

· **Standard of Practice 1-8**

REALTORS® acting as agents of buyers/tenants shall submit to buyers/tenants all offers and counter-offers until acceptance but have no obligation to continue to show properties to their clients after an offer has been accepted unless otherwise agreed in writing. REALTORS® acting as agents of buyers/tenants shall recommend that buyers/tenants obtain the advice of legal counsel if there is a question as to whether a pre-existing contract has been terminated. (Adopted 1/93)

· **Standard of Practice 1-9**

The obligation of REALTORS® to preserve confidential information provided by their clients continues after the termination of the agency relationship. REALTORS® shall not knowingly, during or following the termination of a professional relationship with their client:

1) reveal confidential information of the client; or

2) use confidential information of the client to the disadvantage of the client; or

3) use confidential information of the client for the REALTOR®'s advantage or the advantage of a third party unless:

a) the client consents after full disclosure; or

b) the REALTOR® is required by court order; or

c) it is the intention of the client to commit a crime and the information is necessary to prevent the crime; or

d) it is necessary to defend the REALTOR® or the REALTOR®'s employees or associates against an accusation of wrongful conduct. (Adopted 1/93, Amended 1/95)

• **Standard of Practice 1-10**

REALTORS® shall, consistent with the terms and conditions of their property management agreement, competently manage the property of clients with due regard for the rights, responsibilities, benefits, safety and health of tenants and others lawfully on the premises. (Adopted 1/95)

• **Standard of Practice 1-11**

REALTORS® who are employed to maintain or manage a client's property shall exercise due diligence and make reasonable efforts to protect it against reasonably foreseeable contingencies and losses. (Adopted 1/95)

• **Standard of Practice 1-12**

When entering into listing contracts, REALTORSÒ must advise sellers/landlords of:

1) the REALTORÒ's general company policies regarding cooperation with subagents, buyer/tenant agents, or both;

2) the fact that buyer/tenant agents, even if compensated by the listing broker, or by the seller/landlord will represent the interests of buyers/tenants; and

3) any potential for the listing broker to act as a disclosed dual agent, e.g. buyer/tenant agent. (Adopted 1/93, Renumbered 1/98)

• **Standard of Practice 1-13**

When entering into contracts to represent buyers/tenants, REALTORÒ's must advise potential clients of:

1) the REALTORÒ's general company policies regarding cooperation with other firms; and

2) any potential for the buyer/tenant representative to act as a disclosed dual agent, e.g. listing broker, subagent, landlord's agent, etc. (Adopted 1/93, Renumbered 1/98)

ARTICLE 2

REALTORS® shall avoid exaggeration, misrepresentation, or concealment of pertinent facts relating to the property or the transaction. REALTORS® shall not, however, be obligated to discover latent defects in the property, to advise on matters outside the scope of their real estate license, or to disclose facts which are confidential under the scope of agency duties owed to their clients. (Amended 1/93)

· **Standard of Practice 2-1**

REALTORS® shall only be obligated to discover and disclose adverse factors reasonably apparent to someone with expertise in those areas required by their real estate licensing authority. Article 2 does not impose upon the REALTOR® the obligation of expertise in other professional or technical disciplines. (Amended 1/96)

· **Standard of Practice 2-2**

(Renumbered as Standard of Practice 1-12 1/98)

· **Standard of Practice 2-3**

(Renumbered as Standard of Practice 1-13 1/98)

· **Standard of Practice 2-4**

REALTORS® shall not be parties to the naming of a false consideration in any document, unless it be the naming of an obviously nominal consideration.

· **Standard of Practice 2-5**

Factors defined as "non-material" by law or regulation or which are expressly referenced in law or regulation as not being subject to disclosure are considered not "pertinent" for purposes of Article 2. (Adopted 1/93)

ARTICLE 3

REALTORS® shall cooperate with other brokers except when cooperation is not in the client's best interest. The obligation to cooperate does not include the obligation to share commissions, fees, or to otherwise compensate another broker. (Amended 1/95)

· **Standard of Practice 3-1**

REALTORS®, acting as exclusive agents of sellers/landlords, establish the terms and conditions of offers to cooperate. Unless expressly indicated in offers to cooperate, cooperating brokers may not assume that the offer of cooperation includes an offer of compensation. Terms of compensation, if any, shall be ascertained by cooperating brokers before beginning efforts to accept the offer of cooperation. (Amended 1/94)

· **Standard of Practice 3-2**

REALTORS® shall, with respect to offers of compensation to another REALTOR®, timely communicate any change of compensation for cooperative services to the other REALTOR® prior to the time such REALTOR® produces an offer to purchase/lease the property. (Amended 1/94)

· **Standard of Practice 3-3**
Standard of Practice 3-2 does not preclude the listing broker and cooperating broker from entering into an agreement to change cooperative compensation. (Adopted 1/94)

· **Standard of Practice 3-4**
REALTORS®, acting as listing brokers, have an affirmative obligation to disclose the existence of dual or variable rate commission arrangements (i.e., listing where one amount of commission is payable if the listing broker's firm is the procuring cause of sale/lease and a different amount of commission is payable if the sale/lease results through the efforts of the seller/landlord or a cooperating broker). The listing broker shall, as soon as practical, disclose the existence of such arrangements to potential cooperating brokers and shall, in response to inquiries from cooperating brokers, disclose the differential that would result in a cooperative transaction or in a sale/lease that results through the efforts of the seller/landlord. If the cooperating broker is a buyer/tenant representative, the buyer/tenant representative must disclose such information to their client. (Amended 1/94)

· **Standard of Practice 3-5**
It is the obligation of subagents to promptly disclose all pertinent facts to the principal's agent prior to as well as after a purchase or lease agreement is executed. (Amended 1/93)

· **Standard of Practice 3-6**
REALTORS® shall disclose the existence of an accepted offer to any broker seeking cooperation. (Adopted 5/86)

· **Standard of Practice 3-7**
When seeking information from another REALTOR® concerning property under a management or listing agreement, REALTORS® shall disclose their REALTOR® status and whether their interest is personal or on behalf of a client and if, on behalf of a client, their representational status. (Amended 1/95)

· **Standard of Practice 3-8**
REALTORS® shall not misrepresent the availability of access to show or inspect a listed property. (Amended 11/87)

ARTICLE 4
REALTORS® shall not acquire an interest in or buy or present offers from themselves, any member of their immediate families, their firms or any member thereof, or any entities in which they have any ownership interest, any real property without making their true position known to the owner or the owner's agent. In selling property they own, or in which they have any interest, REALTORS® shall reveal their ownership or interest in writing to the purchaser or the purchaser's representative. (Amended 1/91)

· **Standard of Practice 4-1**

For the protection of all parties, the disclosures required by Article 4 shall be in writing and provided by REALTORS® prior to the signing of any contract. (Adopted 2/86)

ARTICLE 5

REALTORS shall not undertake to provide professional services concerning a property or its value where they have a present or contemplated interest unless such interest is specifically disclosed to all affected parties.

ARTICLE 6

When acting as agents, REALTORS® shall not accept any commission, rebate, or profit on expenditures made for their principal, without the principal's knowledge and consent. (Amended 1/92)

· **Standard of Practice 6-1**

REALTORS® shall not recommend or suggest to a client or a customer the use of services of another organization or business entity in which they have a direct interest without disclosing such interest at the time of the recommendation or suggestion. (Amended 5/88)

· **Standard of Practice 6-2**

When acting as agents or subagents, REALTORS® shall disclose to a client or customer if there is any financial benefit or fee the REALTOR® or the REALTOR®'s firm may receive as a direct result of having recommended real estate products or services (e.g., homeowner's insurance, warranty programs, mortgage financing, title insurance, etc.) other than real estate referral fees. (Adopted 5/88)

ARTICLE 7

In a transaction, REALTORS® shall not accept compensation from more than one party, even if permitted by law, without disclosure to all parties and the informed consent of the REALTOR®'s client or clients. (Amended 1/93)

ARTICLE 8

REALTORS® shall keep in a special account in an appropriate financial institution, separated from their own funds, monies coming into their possession in trust for other persons, such as escrows, trust funds, clients' monies, and other like items.

ARTICLE 9

REALTORS®, for the protection of all parties, shall assure whenever possible that agreements shall be in writing, and shall be in clear and understandable language expressing the specific terms, conditions, obligations and commitments of the parties. A copy of each agreement shall be furnished to each party upon their signing or initialing. (Amended 1/95)

· **Standard of Practice 9-1**

For the protection of all parties, REALTORS® shall use reasonable care to ensure that documents pertaining to the purchase, sale, or lease of real estate are kept current through the use of written extensions or amendments. (Amended 1/93)

DUTIES TO THE PUBLIC

ARTICLE 10

REALTORS® shall not deny equal professional services to any person for reasons of race, color, religion, sex, handicap, familial status, or national origin. REALTORS® shall not be parties to any plan or agreement to discriminate against a person or persons on the basis of race, color, religion, sex, handicap, familial status, or national origin. (Amended 1/90)

· **Standard of Practice 10-1**

REALTORS® shall not volunteer information regarding the racial, religious or ethnic composition of any neighborhood and shall not engage in any activity which may result in panic selling. REALTORS® shall not print, display or circulate any statement or advertisement with respect to the selling or renting of a property that indicates any preference, limitations or discrimination based on race, color, religion, sex, handicap, familial status or national origin. (Adopted 1/94)

ARTICLE 11

The services which REALTORS® provide to their clients and customers shall conform to the standards of practice and competence which are reasonably expected in the specific real estate disciplines in which they engage; specifically, residential real estate brokerage, real property management, commercial and industrial real estate brokerage, real estate appraisal, real estate counseling, real estate syndication, real estate auction, and international real estate.

REALTORS® shall not undertake to provide specialized professional services concerning a type of property or service that is outside their field of competence unless they engage the assistance of one who is competent on such types of property or service, or unless the facts are fully disclosed to the client. Any persons engaged to provide such assistance shall be so identified to the client and their contribution to the assignment should be set forth. (Amended 1/95)

· **Standard of Practice 11-1**

The obligations of the Code of Ethics shall be supplemented by and construed in a manner consistent with the Uniform Standards of Professional Appraisal Practice (USPAP) promulgated by the Appraisal Standards Board of the Appraisal Foundation.

The obligations of the Code of Ethics shall not be supplemented by the USPAP where an opinion or recommendation of price or pricing is provided in pursuit of a listing, to assist a potential purchaser in formulating a purchase offer, or to provide a broker's price opinion, whether for a fee or not. (Amended 1/96)

· **Standard of Practice 11-2**

The obligations of the Code of Ethics in respect of real estate disciplines other than appraisal shall be interpreted and applied in accordance with the standards of competence and practice which clients and the public reasonably require to protect their rights and interests considering the complexity of the transaction, the availability of expert assistance, and, where the REALTOR® is an agent or subagent, the obligations of a fiduciary. (Adopted 1/95)

· **Standard of Practice 11-3**

When REALTORS® provide consultive services to clients which involve advice or counsel for a fee (not a commission), such advice shall be rendered in an objective manner and the fee shall not be contingent on the substance of the advice or counsel given. If brokerage or transaction services are to be provided in addition to consultive services, a separate compensation may be paid with prior agreement between the client and REALTOR®. (Adopted 1/96)

Article 12

REALTORS® shall be careful at all times to present a true picture in their advertising and representations to the public. REALTORS® shall also ensure that their professional status (e.g., broker, appraiser, property manager, etc.) or status as REALTORS® is clearly identifiable in any such advertising. (Amended 1/93)

· **Standard of Practice 12-1**

REALTORS® may use the term "free" and similar terms in their advertising and in other representations provided that all terms governing availability of the offered product or service are clearly disclosed at the same time. (Amended 1/97)

· **Standard of Practice 12-2**

REALTORS® may represent their services as "free" or without cost even if they expect to receive compensation from a source other than their client provided that the potential for the REALTOR® to obtain a benefit from a third party is clearly disclosed at the same time. (Amended 1/97)

· **Standard of Practice 12-3**

The offering of premiums, prizes, merchandise discounts or other inducements to list, sell, purchase, or lease is not, in itself, unethical even if receipt of the benefit is contingent on listing, selling, purchasing, or leasing through the REALTOR® making the offer. However, REALTORS® must exercise care and candor in any such advertising or other public or private representations so that any party interested in receiving or otherwise benefiting from the REALTOR®'s offer will have clear, thorough, advance understanding of all the terms and conditions of the offer. The offering of any inducements to do business is subject to the limitations and restrictions of state law and the ethical obligations established by any applicable Standard of Practice. (Amended 1/95)

- **Standard of Practice 12-4**

REALTORS® shall not offer for sale/lease or advertise property without authority. When acting as listing brokers or as subagents, REALTORS® shall not quote a price different from that agreed upon with the seller/landlord. (Amended 1/93)

- **Standard of Practice 12-5**

REALTORS® shall not advertise nor permit any person employed by or affiliated with them to advertise listed property without disclosing the name of the firm. (Adopted 11/86)

- **Standard of Practice 12-6**

REALTORS®, when advertising unlisted real property for sale/lease in which they have an ownership interest, shall disclose their status as both owners/landlords and as REALTORS® or real estate licensees. (Amended 1/93)

- **Standard of Practice 12-7**

Only REALTORS® who participated in the transaction as the listing broker or cooperating broker (selling broker) may claim to have "sold" the property. Prior to closing, a cooperating broker may post a "sold" sign only with the consent of the listing broker. (Amended 1/96)

ARTICLE 13

REALTORS® shall not engage in activities that constitute the unauthorized practice of law and shall recommend that legal counsel be obtained when the interest of any party to the transaction requires it.

ARTICLE 14

If charged with unethical practice or asked to present evidence or to cooperate in any other way, in any disciplinary proceeding or investigation, REALTORS® shall place all pertinent facts before the proper tribunals of the Member Board or affiliated institute, society, or council in which membership is held and shall take no action to disrupt or obstruct such processes. (Amended 1/90)

- **Standard of Practice 14-1**

REALTORS® shall not be subject to disciplinary proceedings in more than one Board of REALTORS® or affiliated institute, society or council in which they hold membership with respect to alleged violations of the Code of Ethics relating to the same transaction or event. (Amended 1/95)

· **Standard of Practice 14-2**

REALTORS® shall not make any unauthorized disclosure or dissemination of the allegations, findings, or decision developed in connection with an ethics hearing or appeal or in connection with an arbitration hearing or procedural review. (Amended 1/92)

· **Standard of Practice 14-3**

REALTORS® shall not obstruct the Board's investigative or disciplinary proceedings by instituting or threatening to institute actions for libel, slander or defamation against any party to a professional standards proceeding or their witnesses. (Adopted 11/87)

· **Standard of Practice 14-4**

REALTORS® shall not intentionally impede the Board's investigative or disciplinary proceedings by filing multiple ethics complaints based on the same event or transaction. (Adopted 11/88)

DUTIES TO REALTORS®

ARTICLE 15

REALTORS® shall not knowingly or recklessly make false or misleading statements about competitors, their businesses, or their business practices. (Amended 1/92)

ARTICLE 16

REALTORS® shall not engage in any practice or take any action inconsistent with the agency or other exclusive relationship recognized by law that other REALTORS® have with clients. (Amended 1/98)

· **Standard of Practice 16-1**

Article 16 is not intended to prohibit aggressive or innovative business practices which are otherwise ethical and does not prohibit disagreements with other REALTORS® involving commission, fees, compensation or other forms of payment or expenses. (Adopted 1/93, Amended 1/95)

· **Standard of Practice 16-2**

Article 16 does not preclude REALTORS® from making general announcements to prospective clients describing their services and the terms of their availability even though some recipients may have entered into agency agreements or other exclusive relationships with another REALTOR®. A general telephone canvass, general mailing or distribution addressed to all prospective clients in a given geographical area or in a given profession, business, club, or organization, or other classification or group is deemed "general" for purposes of this standard. (Amended 1/98)

Article 16 is intended to recognize as unethical two basic types of solicitations:

First, telephone or personal solicitations of property owners who have been identified by a real estate sign, multiple listing compilation, or other information service as having exclusively listed their property with another REALTOR®; and

Second, mail or other forms of written solicitations of prospective clients whose properties are exclusively listed with another REALTOR® when such solicitations are not part of a general mailing but are directed specifically to property owners identified through compilations of current listings, "for sale" or "for rent" signs, or other sources of information required by Article 3 and Multiple Listing Service rules to be made available to other REALTORS® under offers of subagency or cooperation. (Amended 1/93)

- **Standard of Practice 16-3**

Article 16 does not preclude REALTORS® from contacting the client of another broker for the purpose of offering to provide, or entering into a contract to provide, a different type of real estate service unrelated to the type of service currently being provided (e.g., property management as opposed to brokerage). However, information received through a Multiple Listing Service or any other offer of cooperation may not be used to target clients of other REALTORS® to whom such offers to provide services may be made. (Amended 1/93)

- **Standard of Practice 16-4**

REALTORS® shall not solicit a listing which is currently listed exclusively with another broker. However, if the listing broker, when asked by the REALTOR®, refuses to disclose the expiration date and nature of such listing; i.e., an exclusive right to sell, an exclusive agency, open listing, or other form of contractual agreement between the listing broker and the client, the REALTOR® may contact the owner to secure such information and may discuss the terms upon which the REALTOR® might take a future listing or, alternatively, may take a listing to become effective upon expiration of any existing exclusive listing. (Amended 1/94)

- **Standard of Practice 16-5**

REALTORS® shall not solicit buyer/tenant agreements from buyers/tenants who are subject to exclusive buyer/tenant agreements. However, if asked by a REALTOR®, the broker refuses to disclose the expiration date of the exclusive buyer/tenant agency agreement, the REALTOR® may contact the buyer/tenant to secure such information and may discuss the terms upon which the REALTOR® might enter into a future buyer/tenant agreement or, alternatively, may enter into a buyer/tenant agreement to become effective upon the expiration of any existing exclusive buyer/tenant agreement. (Adopted 1/94, Amended 1/98)

- **Standard of Practice 16-6**

When REALTORS® are contacted by the client of another REALTOR® regarding the creation of an exclusive relationship to provide the same type of service, and REAL-

TORS® have not directly or indirectly initiated such discussions, they may discuss the terms upon which they might enter into a future agreement or, alternatively, may enter into an agreement which becomes effective upon expiration of any existing exclusive agreement. (Amended 1/98)

- **Standard of Practice 16-7**

The fact that a client has retained a REALTORâ as an agent or in another exclusive relationship in one or more past transactions does not preclude other REALTORS® from seeking such former client's future business. (Amended 1/98)

- **Standard of Practice 16-8**

The fact that an exclusive agreement has been entered into with a REALTOR® shall not preclude or inhibit any other REALTOR® from entering into a similar agreement after the expiration of the prior agreement. (Amended 1/98)

- **Standard of Practice 16-9**

REALTORS®, prior to entering into an agreement or other exclusive relationship, have an affirmative obligation to make reasonable efforts to determine whether the client is subject to a current, valid exclusive agreement to provide the same type of real estate service. (Amended 1/98)

- **Standard of Practice 16-10**

REALTORS®, acting as agents of, or in another relationship with, buyers or tenants shall disclose that relationship to the seller/landlord's agent or broker at first contact and shall provide written confirmation of that disclosure to the seller/landlord's agent or broker not later than execution of a purchase agreement or lease. (Amended 1/98)

- **Standard of Practice 16-11**

On unlisted property, REALTORS® acting as buyer/tenant agents or brokers shall disclose that relationship to the seller/landlord at first contact for that client and shall provide written confirmation of such disclosure to the seller/landlord not later than execution of any purchase or lease agreement.

REALTORS® shall make any request for anticipated compensation from the seller/landlord at first contact. (Amended 1/98)

- **Standard of Practice 16-12**

REALTORS®, acting as agents or brokers of sellers/landlords or as subagents of listing brokers, shall disclose that relationship to buyers/tenants as soon as practicable and shall provide written confirmation of such disclosure to buyers/tenants not later than execution of any purchase or lease agreement. (Amended 1/98)

· **Standard of Practice 16-13**

All dealings concerning property exclusively listed, or with buyer/tenants who are subject to an exclusive agreement shall be carried on with the client's agent or broker, and not with the client, except with the consent of the client's agent or broker or except where such dealings are initiated by the client. (Adopted 1/93, Amended 1/98)

· **Standard of Practice 16-14**

REALTORS® are free to enter into contractual relationships or to negotiate with sellers/ landlords, buyers/tenants or others who are not subject to an exclusive agent but shall not knowingly obligate them to pay more than one commission except with their informed consent. (Amended 1/98)

· **Standard of Practice 16-15**

In cooperative transactions REALTORS® shall compensate cooperating REALTORS® (principal brokers) and shall not compensate nor offer to compensate, directly or indirectly, any of the sales licensees employed by or affiliated with other REALTORS® without the prior express knowledge and consent of the cooperating broker.

· **Standard of Practice 16-16**

REALTORS®, acting as subagents or buyer/tenant agents or brokers, shall not use the terms of an offer to purchase/lease to attempt to modify the listing broker's offer of compensation to subagents or buyer's agents or brokers nor make the submission of an executed offer to purchase/lease contingent on the listing broker's agreement to modify the offer of compensation. (Amended 1/98)

· **Standard of Practice 16-17**

REALTORS® acting as subagents or as buyer/tenant agents or brokers, shall not attempt to extend a listing broker's offer of cooperation and/or compensation to other brokers without the consent of the listing broker. (Amended 1/98)

· **Standard of Practice 16-18**

REALTORS® shall not use information obtained by them from the listing broker, through offers to cooperate received through Multiple Listing Services or other sources authorized by the listing broker, for the purpose of creating a referral prospect to a third broker, or for creating a buyer/tenant prospect unless such use is authorized by the listing broker. (Amended 1/93)

· **Standard of Practice 16-19**

Signs giving notice of property for sale, rent, lease, or exchange shall not be placed on property without consent of the seller/landlord. (Amended 1/93)

· **Standard of Practice 16-20**

REALTORS®, prior to or after terminating their relationship with their current firm, shall not induce clients of their current firm to cancel exclusive contractual agreements between the client and that firm. This does not preclude REALTORS® (principals) from establishing agreements with their associated licensees governing assignability of exclusive agreements. (Adopted 1/98)

ARTICLE 17

In the event of contractual disputes or specific non-contractual disputes as defined in Standard of Practice 17-4 between REALTORS® associated with different firms, arising out of their relationship as REALTORS®, the REALTORS® shall submit the dispute to arbitration in accordance with the regulations of their Board or Boards rather than litigate the matter.

In the event clients of REALTORS® wish to arbitrate contractual disputes arising out of real estate transactions, REALTORS® shall arbitrate those disputes in accordance with the regulations of their Board, provided the clients agree to be bound by the decision. (Amended 1/97)

- **Standard of Practice 17-1**

The filing of litigation and refusal to withdraw from it by REALTORS® in an arbitrable matter constitutes a refusal to arbitrate. (Adopted 2/86)

- **Standard of Practice 17-2**

Article 17 does not require REALTORS® to arbitrate in those circumstances when all parties to the dispute advise the Board in writing that they choose not to arbitrate before the Board. (Amended 1/93)

- **Standard of Practice 17-3**

REALTORS®, when acting solely as principles in a real estate transaction, are not obligated to arbitrate disputes with other REALTORS® absent a specific written agreement to the contrary. (Adopted 1/96)

- **Standard of Practice 17-4**

Specific non-contractual disputes that are subject to arbitration pursuant to Article 17 are:

1) Where a listing broker has compensated a cooperating broker and another cooperating broker subsequently claims to be the procuring cause of the sale or lease. In such cases the complainant may name the first cooperating broker as respondent and arbitration may proceed without the listing broker being named as a respondent. Alternatively, if the complaint is brought against the listing broker, the listing broker may name the first cooperating broker as a third-party respondent. In either instance the decision of the hearing panel as to procuring cause shall be conclusive with respect to all current or subsequent claims of the parties for compensation arising out of the underlying cooperative transaction. (Adopted 1/97)

2) Where a buyer or tenant representative is compensated by the seller or landlord, and not by the listing broker, and the listing broker, as a result, reduces the commission owed by the seller or landlord and, subsequent to such actions, another cooperating broker claims to be the procuring cause of sale or lease. In such cases the complainant may name the first cooperating broker as respondent and arbitration may proceed without the listing broker being named as a respondent. Alternatively, if the complaint is brought against the listing broker, the listing broker may name the first cooperating broker as a third-party respondent. In either instance the decision of the hearing panel as procuring cause shall be conclusive with respect to all current or subsequent claims of the parties for compensation arising out of the underlying cooperative transaction. (Adopted 1/97)

3) Where a buyer or tenant representative is compensated by the buyer or tenant and, as a result, the listing broker reduces the commission owed by the seller or landlord and, subsequent to such actions, another cooperating broker claims to be the procuring cause of sale or lease. In such cases the complainant may name the first cooperating broker as respondent and arbitration any proceed without the listing broker being named as a respondent. Alternatively, if the complaint is brought against the listing broker, the listing broker may name the first cooperating broker as third-party respondent. In either instance the decision of the hearing panel as to procuring cause shall be conclusive with respect to all current or subsequent claims of the parties for compensation arising out of the underlying cooperative transaction. (Adopted 1/97)

4) Where two or more listing brokers claim entitlement to compensation pursuant to open listing with a seller or landlord who agrees to participate in arbitration (or who requests arbitration) and who agrees to be bound by the decision. In cases where one of the listing brokers has been compensated by the seller or landlord, the other listing broker, as complainant, may name the first listing broker as respondent and arbitration may proceed between the brokers. (Adopted 1/97)

The Code of Ethics was adopted in 1913.
Amended at the Annual Convention in 1924, 1928, 1950, 1951, 1952, 1955, 1956, 1961, 1962, 1974, 1982, 1986, 1987, 1989, 1990, 1991, 1992, 1993, 1994, 1995, 1996 and 1997.

EXPLANATORY NOTES

The reader should be aware of the following policies which have been approved by the Board of Directors of the National Association:

In filing a charge of an alleged violation of the Code of Ethics by a REALTOR®, the charge must read as an alleged violation of one or more Articles of the Code. Standards of Practice may be cited in support of the charge.

The Standards of Practice serve to clarify the ethical obligations imposed by the various Articles and supplement, and do not substitute for, the Case Interpretations in Interpretations of the Code of Ethics.

Modifications to existing Standards of Practice and additional new Standards of Practice are approved from time to time. Readers are cautioned to ensure that the most recent publications are utilized.

Form No. 166-288 (12/97)

National Association of Realtors®
430 North Michigan Avenue
Chicago, Illinois 60611

appendix c: the real estate brokerage relationship act

SAMPLE OF PAMPHLET
1998

The LAW of REAL ESTATE AGENCY
This pamphlet describes your legal rights in dealing with a real estate broker or salesperson. Please read it carefully before signing any documents.

The following is only a brief summary of the attached law.

SECTION 1. **Definitions.** Defines the specific terms used in the law.

SECTION 2. **Relationships between Licensees and the Public.** States that a licensee who works with a buyer or tenant represents that buyer or tenant — unless the licensee is the listing agent, a seller's subagent, a dual agent, the seller personally or the parties agree otherwise. Also states that in a transaction involving two different licensees affiliated with the same broker, the broker is a dual agent and each licensee solely represents his or her client — unless the parties agree in writing that both licensees are dual agents.

SECTION 3. **Duties of a Licensee Generally.** Prescribes the duties that are owed by all licensee, regardless of who the licensee represents. Requires disclosure of the license's agency relationship in a specific transaction.

SECTION 4. **Duties of a Seller's Agent.** Prescribes the additional duties of a licensee representing the seller or landlord only.

SECTION 5. **Duties of a Buyer's Agent.** Prescribes the additional duties of a licensee representing the buyer or tenant only.

SECTION 6. **Duties of a Dual Agent.** Prescribes the additional duties of a licensee representing both parties in the same transaction, and requires the written consent of both parties to the licensee acting as dual agent.

SECTION 7. **Duration of Agency Relationship.** Describes when an agency relationship begins and ends. Provides that the duties of accounting and confidentiality continue after the termination of an agency relationship.

SECTION 8. **Compensation.** Allows brokers to share compensation with cooperating brokers. States that payment of compensation does not necessarily establish an agency relationship. Allows brokers to receive compensation from more than one party in a transaction with the parties' consent.

SECTION 9. **Vicarious Liability.** Eliminates the common law liability of a party for the conduct of the party's agent or subagent, unless the agent or subagent is insolvent. Also limits the liability of a broker for the conduct of a subagent associated with a different broker.

SECTION 10. **Imputed Knowledge and Notice.** Eliminates the common law rule that notice to or knowledge of an agent constitutes notice to or knowledge of the principal.

SECTION 11. **Interpretation.** This law replaces the fiduciary duties owed by an agent to a principal under the common law, to the extent that it conflicts with the common law.

RCW 18.86

SECTION 1
Definitions.

Unless the context clearly requires otherwise, the definitions in this section apply throughout this chapter.

(1) "Agency relationship" means the agency relationship created under this chapter or by written agreement between a licensee and a buyer and/or seller relating to the performance of real estate brokerage services by the licensee.

(2) "Agent" means a licensee who has entered into an agency relationship with a buyer or seller.

(3) "Business opportunity" means and includes a business, business opportunity, and goodwill of an existing business, or any one or combination thereof.

(4) "Buyer" means an actual or prospective purchaser in a real estate transaction, or an actual or prospective tenant in a real estate rental or lease transaction, as applicable.

(5) "Buyer's agent" means a licensee who has entered into an agency relationship with only the buyer in a real estate transaction, and includes subagents engaged by a buyer's agent.

(6) "Confidential information" means information from or concerning a principal of a licensee that:

(a) Was acquired by the licensee during the course of an agency relationship with the principal;

(b) The principal reasonably expects to be kept confidential;

(c) The principal has not disclosed or authorized to be disclosed to third parties;

(d) Would, if disclosed, operate to the detriment of the principal; and

(e) The principal personally would not be obligated to disclose to the other party.

(7) "Dual agent" means a licensee who has entered into an agency relationship with both the buyer and seller in the same transaction.

(8) "Licensee" means a real estate broker, associate real estate broker, or real estate salesperson, as those terms are defined in chapter RCW 18.85.

(9) "Material fact" means information that substantially adversely affects the value of the property or a party's ability to perform its obligations in a real estate transaction, or operates to materially impair or defeat the purpose of the transaction. The fact or suspicion that the property, or any neighboring property, is or was the site of a murder, suicide, or other death, rape or other sex crime, assault or other violent crime, robbery or burglary, illegal drug activity, gang-related activity, political or religious activity, or other act, occurrence, or use not adversely affecting the physical condition of or title to the property is not a material fact.

(10) "Principal" means a buyer or a seller who has entered into an agency relationship with a licensee.

(11) "Real estate brokerage services" means the rendering of services for which a real estate license is required under chapter RCW 18.85.

(12) "Real estate transaction" or "transaction" means an actual or prospective transaction involving a purchase, sale, option, or exchange of any interest in real property or a business opportunity, or a lease or rental of real property. For purposes of this chapter, a prospective transaction does not exist until a written offer has been signed by at least one of the parties.

(13) "Seller" means an actual or prospective seller in a real estate transaction, or an actual or prospective landlord in a real estate rental or lease transaction, as applicable.

(14) "Seller's agent" means a licensee who has entered into an agency relationship with only the seller in a real estate transaction, and includes subagents engaged by a seller's

agent.

(15) "Subagent" means a licensee who is engaged to act on behalf of a principal by the principal's agent where the principal has authorized the agent in writing to appoint subagents.

SECTION 2
Relationships between Licensees and the Public.

(1) A licensee who performs real estate brokerage services for a buyer is a buyer's agent unless the:

(a) Licensee has entered into a written agency agreement with the seller, in which case the licensee is a seller's agent;

(b) Licensee has entered into a subagency agreement with the seller's agent, in which case the licensee is a seller's agent;

(c) Licensee has entered into a written agency agreement with both parties, in which case the licensee is a dual agent;

(d) Licensee is the seller or one of the sellers; or

(e) Parties agree otherwise in writing after the licensee has complied with section 3(1)(f) of this act.

(2) In a transaction in which different licensee affiliated with the same broker represent different parties, the broker is a dual agent, and must obtain the written consent of both parties as required under section 6 of this act. In such a case, each licensee shall solely represent the party with whom the licensee has an agency relationship, unless all parties agree in writing that both licensees are dual agents.

(3) A licensee may work with a party in separate transactions pursuant to different relationships, including, but not limited to, representing a party in one transaction and at the same time not representing that party in a different transaction involving that party, if the licensee complies with this chapter in establishing the relationships for each transaction.

SECTION 3
Duties of a Licensee Generally.

(1) Regardless of whether the licensee is an agent, a licensee owes to all parties to whom the licensee renders real estate brokerage services the following duties, which may not be waived:

(a) To exercise reasonable skill and care;

(b) To deal honestly and in good faith;

(c) To present all written offers written notices and other written communications to and from either party in a timely manner, regardless of whether the property is subject to an existing contract for sale or the buyer is already a party to an existing contract to purchase;

(d) To disclose all existing material facts known by the licensee and not apparent or readily ascertainable to a party; provided that this subsection shall not be construed to imply any duty to investigate matters that the licensee has not agreed to investigate;

(e) To account in a timely manner for all money and property received from or on behalf of either party;

(f) To provide a pamphlet on the law of real estate agency in the form prescribed in section 13 of this act to all parties to whom the licensee renders real estate brokerage services, before the party signs an agency agreement with the licensee, signs an offer in a real estate transaction handled by the licensee, consents to dual agency, or waives any rights, under section 2(1)(e), 4(1)(e), 5(1)(e), or 6(2)(e) or (f) of this act, whichever occurs earliest; and

(g) To disclose in writing to all parties to whom the licensee renders real estate brokerage services, before the party signs an offer in a real estate transaction handled by the licensee, whether the licensee represents the buyer, the seller, both parties, or neither party. The disclosure shall be set forth in a separate paragraph entitled "Agency Disclosure" in the agreement between the buyer and seller or in a separate writing entitled "Agency Disclosure."

(2) Unless otherwise agreed, a licensee owes no duty to conduct an independent inspection of the property or to conduct an independent investigation of either party's financial condition, and owes no duty to independently verify the accuracy or completeness of any statement made by either party or by any source reasonably believed by the licensee to be reliable.

SECTION 4
Duties of a Seller's Agent.

(1) Unless additional duties are agreed to in writing signed by a seller's agent, the duties of a seller's agent are limited to those set forth in section 3 of this act and the following, which may not be waived except as expressly set forth in (e) of this subsection:

(a) To be loyal to the seller by taking no action that is adverse or detrimental to the seller's interest in a transaction;

(b) To timely disclose to the seller any conflicts of interest;

(c) To advise the seller to seek expert advice on matter relating to the transaction that are beyond the agent's expertise;

(d) Not to disclose any confidential information from or about the seller, except under subpoena or court order, even after termination of the agency relationship; and

(e) Unless otherwise agreed to in writing after the seller's agent has complied with section 3(1)(f) of this act, to make a good faith and continuous effort to find a buyer for the property; except that a seller's agent is not obligated to seek additional offers to purchase the property while the property is subject to an existing contract for sale.

(2) (a) The showing of properties not owned by the seller to prospective buyers or the listing of competing properties for sale by a seller's agent does not in and of itself breach the duty of loyalty to the seller or create a conflict of interest.

(b) The representation of more than one seller by different licensees affiliated with the same broker in competing transactions involving the same buyer does not in and itself breach the duty of loyalty to the sellers or create a conflict of interest.

SECTION 5
Duties of a Buyer's Agent.

(1) Unless additional duties are agreed to in writing signed by a buyer's agent, the duties of a buyer's agent are limited to those set forth in section 3 of this act and the following, which may not be waived except as expressly set forth in (e) of this subsection:

(a) To be loyal to the buyer by taking no action that is adverse or detrimental to the buyer's interest in a transaction;

(b) To timely disclose to the buyer any conflicts of interest;

(c) To advise the buyer to seek expert advice on matters relating to the transaction that are beyond the agent's expertise;

(d) Not to disclose any confidential information from or about the buyer, except under subpoena or court order, even after termination of the agency relationship; and

(d) Unless otherwise agreed to in writing after the buyer's agent has complied with section 3(1)(f) of this act, to make a good faith and continuous effort to find a property for the buyer; except that a buyer's agent is not obligated to:

(i) seek additional properties to purchase while the buyer is a party to an existing contract to purchase; or

(ii) show properties as to which there is not written agreement to pay compensation to the buyer's agent.

(2) (a) The showing of property in which a buyer is interested to other prospective buyers by a buyer's agent does not in and of itself breach the duty of loyalty to the buyer or create a conflict of interest.

(b) The representation of more than one buyer by different licensee affiliated with the same broker in competing transactions involving the same property does not in and itself breach the duty of loyalty to the buyers or create a conflict of interest.

SECTION 6
Duties of a Dual Agent.

(1) Notwithstanding any other provision of this chapter, a licensee may act as a dual agent only with the written consent of both parties to the transaction after the dual agent has complied with section 3(1)(f) of this act, which consent must include a statement of the terms of compensation.

(2) Unless additional duties are agreed to in writing signed by a dual agent, the duties of a dual agent are limited to those set forth in section 3 of this act and the following, which may not be waived except as expressly set forth in (e) and (f) of this subsection:

(a) To take no action that is adverse or detrimental to either party's interest in a transaction;

(b) To timely disclose to both parties any conflicts of interest;

(c) To advise both parties to seek expert advice on matters relating to the transaction that are beyond the dual agent's expertise;

(d) Not to disclose any confidential information from or about either party, except under subpoena or court order, even after termination of the agency relationship;

(e) Unless otherwise agreed to in writing after the dual agent has complied with section 3(1)(f) of this act, to make a good faith and continuous effort to find a property for the buyer; except that a dual agent is not obligated to seek additional offers to purchase the property while the property is subject to an existing contract for sale; and

(f) Unless otherwise agreed to in writing after the dual agent has complied with section 3(1)(f) of this act, to make a good faith and continuous effort to find a property for the buyer; except that a dual agent is not obligated:

(i) Seek additional properties to purchase while the buyer is a party to an existing contract to purchase; or

(ii) show properties as to which there is no written agreement to pay compensation to the dual agent.

(3) (a) The showing of properties not owned by the seller to prospective buyers or the listing of competing properties for sale by a dual agent does not in and of itself constitute action that is adverse or detrimental to the seller or create a conflict of interest.

(b) The representation of more than one seller by different licensees affiliated with the same broker in competing transactions involving the same buyer does not in and of itself constitute action that is adverse or detrimental to the sellers or create a conflict of interest.

(4) (a) The showing of property in which a buyer is interested to other prospective buyers or the presentation of additional offers to purchase property while the property is subject to a transaction by a dual agent does not in and of itself constitute action that is adverse or detrimental to the buyer or create a conflict of interest.

(b) The representation of more than one buyer by different licensees affiliated with the same broker in competing transactions involving the same property does not in and of itself constitute action that is adverse or detrimental to the buyer or create a conflict of interest.

SECTION 7
Duration of Agency Relationship.

(1) The agency relationship set forth in this chapter commence at the time that the licensee undertakes to provide real estate brokerage services to a principal and continue until the earliest of the following:

(a) Completion of performance by the licensee;

(b) Expiration of the term agreed upon by the parties;

(c) Termination of the relationship by mutual agreement of the parties; or

(d) Termination of the relationship by notice from either party to the other. However, such a termination does not affect the contractual rights of either party.

(2) Except as otherwise agreed to in writing, a licensee owes no further duty after termination of the agency relationship, other than the duties of:

(a) Accounting for all moneys and property received during the relationship; and

(b) Not disclosing confidential information.

SECTION 8
Compensation.

(1) In any real estate transaction, the broker's compensation may be paid by the seller, the buyer, a third party, or by sharing the compensation between brokers.

(2) An agreement to pay or payment of compensation does not establish an agency relationship between the party who paid the compensation and the licensee.

(3) A seller may agree that a seller's agent may share with another broker the compensation paid by the seller.

(4) A buyer may agree that a buyer's agent may share with another broker the compensation paid by the buyer.

(5) A broker may be compensated by more than one party for real estate brokerage services in a real estate transaction, if those parties consent in writing at or before the time of signing an offer in the transaction.

(6) A buyer's agent or dual agent may receive compensation based on the purchase price without breaching any duty to the buyer.

(7) Nothing contained in this chapter negates the requirement that an agreement authorizing or employing a licensee to sell or purchase real estate for compensation or a commission be in writing and signed by the seller or buyer.

SECTION 9
Vicarious Liability.

(1) A principal is not liable for an act, error, or omission by an agent or subagent of the principal arising out of an agency relationship:

(a) Unless the principal participated in or authorized the act, error, or omission; or

(b) Except to the extent that:

(i) The principal benefited form the act, error, or omission; and

(ii) the court determines that it is highly probably that the claimant would be unable to enforce a judgment against the agent or subagent.

(2) A licensee is not liable for an act, error, or omission of a subagent under this chapter, unless the licensee participated in or authorized the act, error, or omission. This subsection does not limit the liability of a real estate broker for an act, error, or omission by an associate real estate broker or real estate salesperson licensed to that broker.

SECTION 10
Imputed Knowledge and Notice.

(1) Unless otherwise agreed to in writing, a principal does not have knowledge or notice of any facts known by an agent or subagent of the principal that are not actually known by the principal.

(2) Unless otherwise agreed to in writing, a licensee does not have knowledge or notice of any facts known by a subagent that are not actually known by the licensee. This subsection does not limit the knowledge imputed to a real estate broker of any facts known by an associate real estate broker or real estate salesperson licensed to such broker.

SECTION 11
Interpretation.

This chapter supersedes only the duties of the parties under the common law, including fiduciary duties of an agent to a principal, to the extent inconsistent with this chapter. The common law continues to apply to the parties in all other respects. This chapter does not affect the duties of a licensee while engaging in the authorized or unauthorized practice of law as determined by the courts of this state. This chapter shall be construed broadly.